STRATEGIC MARKETING
MANAGEMENT CASES

THE IRWIN/McGRAW-HILL SERIES IN MARKETING

Perreault & McCarthy
ESSENTIALS OF MARKETING: A GLOBAL MANAGERIAL APPROACH, 7/E

Peter & Donnelly
A PREFACE TO MARKETING MANAGEMENT, 7/E

Peter & Donnelly
MARKETING MANAGEMENT: KNOWLEDGE AND SKILLS, 5/E

Peter & Olson
CONSUMER BEHAVIOR AND MARKETING STRATEGY, 5/E

Peter & Olson
UNDERSTANDING CONSUMER BEHAVIOR, 1/E

Quelch
CASES IN PRODUCT MANAGEMENT, 1/E

Quelch, Dolan & Kosnik
MARKETING MANAGEMENT: TEXT & CASES, 1/E

Quelch & Farris
CASES IN ADVERTISING AND PROMOTION MANAGEMENT, 4/E

Quelch, Kashani & Vandermerwe
EUROPEAN CASES IN MARKETING MANAGEMENT, 1/E

Rangan
BUSINESS MARKETING STRATEGY: CASES, CONCEPTS & APPLICATIONS, 1/E

Rangan, Shapiro & Moriarty
BUSINESS MARKETING STRATEGY: CONCEPTS & APPLICATIONS, 1/E

Rossiter & Percy
ADVERTISING COMMUNICATIONS AND PROMOTION MANAGEMENT, 2/E

Stanton, Spiro, & Buskirk
MANAGEMENT OF A SALES FORCE, 10/E

Sudman & Blair
MARKETING RESEARCH: A PROBLEM-SOLVING APPROACH, 1/E

Thompson & Stappenbeck
THE MARKETING STRATEGY GAME, 1/E

Ulrich & Eppinger
PRODUCT DESIGN AND DEVELOPMENT, 1/E

Walker, Boyd & Larreche
MARKETING STRATEGY: PLANNING AND IMPLEMENTATION, 3/E

Weitz, Castleberry & Tanner
SELLING: BUILDING PARTNERSHIPS, 3/E

Zeithaml & Bitner
SERVICES MARKETING, 1/E

SIXTH EDITION

STRATEGIC MARKETING MANAGEMENT CASES

David W. Cravens
Charles W. Lamb, Jr.
M. J. Neeley School of Business
Texas Christian University

Victoria L. Crittenden
The Wallace E. Carroll School of Management
Boston College

Boston   Burr Ridge, IL   Dubuque, IA   Madison, WI   New York   San Francisco   St. Louis
Bangkok   Bogotá   Caracas   Lisbon   London   Madrid
Mexico City   Milan   New Delhi   Seoul   Singapore   Sydney   Taipei   Toronto

Irwin/McGraw-Hill

A Division of The McGraw·Hill Companies

STRATEGIC MARKETING MANAGEMENT CASES
International Editions 2000

Exclusive rights by McGraw-Hill Book Co – Singapore, for manufacture and export. This book cannot be re-exported from the country to which it is consigned by McGraw-Hill.

10 9 8 7 6 5 4 3 2
20 9 8 7 6 5 4 3 2 1 0
PMP   SLP

Cover image: Robert Hudson, *After Wood*, 1990, National Museum of American Art, Washington DC/Art Resource, NY

Vice president and editorial director: *Michael W. Junior*
Publisher: *Gary Burke*
Executive editor: *Stephen M Patterson*
Editorial coordinator (and photo research): *Andrea Hlavacek-Rhoads*
Senior marketing manager: *Colleen J. Suljic*
Project manager: *Carrie Sestak*
Production supervisor: *Heather D. Burbridge*
Designer: *Jennifer McQueen Hollingsworth*
Compositor: *ElectraGraphics, Inc.*
Typeface: *10/12 Times Roman*

Library of Congress Cataloging-In-Publication Data

Cravens, David W.
    Strategic marketing management cases / David W. Cravens,
 Charles W. Lamb, Jr., Victoria L. Criitenden. – 6th ed.
       p.   cm. – (The Irwin/McGraw-Hill series in marketing)
    ISBN 0-256-26125-3
    Includes bibliographical references and index.
  1. Marketing – Case studies.   I. Lamb. Charles W.   II. Crittenden,
Victoria Lynn.   III. Title   IV. Series.
HF5415.C6944 1998
658.8'02--dc21   98-3555
                                                                             CIP

www.mhhe.com

When ordering this title, use ISBN 0-07-116175-9

Printed in Singapore

To Our Children:

Karen Cravens
Christine Stock and Jennifer Lamb
Carl, Drew, and John Crittenden

PREFACE

The sixth edition of *Strategic Marketing Management Cases* focuses on the changing role of marketing in the organization as we enter the 21st century. This edition has been substantially revised to reflect marketing management priorities in the decade ahead. The section headings, reflecting these priorities, are as follows:

- Market-Driven Strategy
- Market Orientation and Organizational Learning
- Growth Strategies
- Market Target Strategies
- Marketing Relationship Strategies
- Marketing Program Development
- Planning, Organizing, and Implementing Marketing Plans and Assessing Performance

This edition incorporates several new cases that address marketing management issues that promise to be important in the rapidly changing business environment. At the center of these changes is the substantial adoption of market-driven, customer-oriented strategies by many organizations. Importantly, there is mounting evidence from business practice and academic research that market-oriented companies perform better than those that are not market-oriented.

Several major features are included in the sixth edition:

- We continue the versatile, flexible paperback format to meet the rapid changes in curricula at both the undergraduate and graduate levels.
- Two-thirds of the cases in this edition are new or revised.
- Cases reflect the workplace of the late 1990s by featuring women as case protagonists in over 25 percent of the situations. The goal is to influence the marketing curriculum at the core of the learning process by portraying women in top management positions.
- Over 40 of the 45 situations described in the cases in this edition took place in the 1990s, some as recently as 1997.
- Twelve video cases are included in this edition, responding to the high interest

generated by the videos included in the last edition. Another video available in libraries is noted in the *Instructor's Manual*.

- Substantial emphasis continues on international marketing decisions facing managers. Cases in this edition focus on situations in Canada, India, Ireland, Japan, Mexico, the Philippines, Trinidad, Western and Eastern Europe, and Zimbabwe.

- Instructors are provided data files that contain numerical exhibits from cases in this edition. Data files are available on Excel spreadsheet format.

- Transparency masters have been included in the *Instructor's Manual* to assist in the development of lectures regarding the case method and to introduce the various sections of the book. These masters are also available as PowerPoint slides.

Many instructors prefer that students focus their case analyses on the time frame and situation described in the case. However, Web information may be useful as a follow-up to the class discussion of the case. The *Instructor's Manual* lists Web addresses for 25 of the cases.

We have also retained key features from previous editions.

- The cases illustrate marketing problems and decisions faced by large, medium-sized, and small organizations, goods and services marketers, manufacturers and channel intermediaries, business and consumer products firms, profit and nonprofit organizations, and domestic, foreign, and multinational companies.

- The selection of cases includes a balance of short, medium-length, and long cases.

- Over half of all cases include some form of quantitative data, most frequently financial information.

- Situations described in this edition do not fall neatly into individual marketing mix categories. Rather than organize the book around the four P's (product, place, price, and promotion), we have chosen section classifications that more realistically reflect the types of decisions frequently encountered by marketing managers in the late 1990s.

- The *Instructor's Manual* continues to provide detailed, comprehensive analyses and supporting materials for each case. Several teaching notes include epilogues describing actions taken by the organization and/or how it has fared since the case was prepared. Suggestions for course design are also included in the *Instructor's Manual*.

- To meet the teaching/learning preference of instructors who wish to use the case analysis process described in detail in the Appendix, a substantial portion of the teaching notes follow this format. The discussion questions are not listed at the end of the cases so instructors can assign questions in advance or raise them during case discussions.

Acknowledgments

We appreciate the opportunity to include cases in this edition prepared by the following colleagues:

Lisa Robie Adam
Boston College

David Angus
Boston College

Reinhard Anglemar
INSEAD

Gary Armstrong
University of North Carolina at Chapel Hill

Michael D. Atchison
University of Virginia

John E. Bargetto
University of Notre Dame

Karen Bickmore
Northeastern University

Gyula Bosnyak
Taurus Hungarian Rubber Works

Lew G. Brown
University of North Carolina at Greensboro

Marnie L. Cameron
Boston College

Janet L. Caswell
University of Virginia

Victoria L. Crittenden
Boston College

William F. Crittenden
Northeastern University

Robert P. Crowner
Eastern Michigan University

Lee Dahringer
Butler University

Niraj Dawar
INSEAD

John Devoy
Boston College

Sharon M. Doherty
Northeastern University

James J. Dowd
University of Virginia

Neil M. Ford
University of Wisconsin at Madison

Jennifer Fraser
Boston College

Laura Gow
Boston College

Robert W. Haas
San Diego State University

Timothy J. Halloran
Washington and Lee University

Paula J. Haynes
University of Tennessee at Chattanooga

Marilyn M. Helms
University of Tennessee at Chattanooga

Stephanie Hillstrom
Boston College

Charles Hoffheiser
University of Tulsa

Cynthia Jaffe
Boston College

Raymond Keyes
Boston College

Philip Kotler
Northwestern University

Lawrence M. Lamont
Washington and Lee University

Frederick W. Langrehr
Valparaiso University

John H. Lindgren, Jr.
University of Virginia

Thomas D. Lowell
Washington and Lee University

Ken Manning
Gonzaga University

Jakki Mohr
University of Colorado, Boulder

Donna Moore
Boston College

Patrick E. Murphy
University of Notre Dame

Lester A. Neidell
University of Tulsa

James E. Nelson
University of Montana

Eric Nyman
Boston College

Don O'Sullivan
University College–Cork, Ireland

Marie Pribova
Czechoslovak Management Center

Erin L. Quinn
Boston College

Patrick M. Quinn
Boston College

Richard Sharpe
University of Tennessee at Knoxville

Piyush K. Sinha
Xavier Institute of Management

Neil H. Snyder
University of Virginia

Anne Stöcker
Nijenrode University, Netherlands

Elizabeth W. Storey
Washington and Lee University

Tammy L. Swenson
University of Tennessee at Chattanooga

George Tesar
University of Wisconsin–Whitewater

Janos Vecsenyi
International Management Center, Budapest

Joseph Wolfe
University of Tulsa

William R. Woolridge
University of Colorado at Boulder

Thomas R. Wotruba
San Diego State University

In addition to the important contributions made to the book by case authors, we would like to acknowledge several others who have contributed to the development of this project. We appreciate the assistance that Andrea Hlavacek-Rhoads and the guidance that Steve Patterson, our sponsoring editor, have provided during the development of this edition and previous editions of the book.

We were fortunate to have the input of the following colleagues in developing this edition and previous editions of *Strategic Marketing Management Cases:*

C. L. Abercrombie
University of Memphis

Seymour T. R. Abt
McGill University

Scott Alden
Purdue University

Robert P. Allerheiligen
Colorado State University

Robert M. Ballinger
Sienna College

Benny Barak
Hofstra University

Joseph L. Bonnici
Bryant College

Betty Bose
University of Alaska at Anchorage

E. Wayne Chandler
Eastern Illinois University

John I. Coppett
University of Houston at Clear Lake

Jack R. Dauner
Fayetteville State University

M. Wayne DeLozier
Nicholls State University

Laurence P. Feldman
University of Illinois at Chicago

Troy A. Festervand
Middle Tennessee State University

Charles W. Fojtik
Pepperdine University

Jack E. Forrest
Middle Tennessee State University

Frank J. Franzak
Virginia Commonwealth University

Betsy D. Gelb
University of Houston

Ralph W. Giacobbe
Southern Illinois University at Edwardsville

Myron Glassman
Old Dominion University

Kenneth Grant
Monash University

Michael T. Greenwood
Suffolk University

David E. Hansen
Ohio University

Ray Hehman
San Francisco State University

Mary A. Higby
University of Detroit at Mercy

Foo Nin Ho
San Francisco State University

William M. Kawashima
University of North Carolina at Greensboro

D. M. King
Avila College

Max E. Lupul
California State University at Northridge

Richard Mahan
Anna Maria College

Oswald A. Mascharenhas
University of Detroit at Mercy

Joseph McAloo
Fitchburg State College

Dennis McDermott
Virginia Commonwealth University

Rob M. Morgan
University of Alabama at Tuscaloosa

Cliff Olson
Southern College

Peter W. Olson
Hartford Graduate Center

Thomas J. Page, Jr.
Michigan State University

Charles R. Patton
University of Texas at Brownsville

Gordon L. Patzer
University of Northern Iowa

A. M. Pelham
University of Northern Iowa

Linda Rochford
University of Minnesota at Duluth

William N. Rodgers
University of San Francisco

Mary Rousseau
Delta College

Nancy Panos Schmitt
Westminster College

Gary R. Schornack
University of Colorado at Denver

Patrick L. Schul
University of Memphis

Carol A. Scott
University of California at Los Angeles

Harold S. Sekiguchi
University of Nevada

Richard J. Shenkus
Central Michigan University and Highland Park College

Kirk Smith
Boise State University

Theodore F. Smith
Old Dominion University

Ravi Sohi
University of Nebraska

Sudhir Tandon
Prairie View A&M University

Jennifer Tarbell
Davenport College

Peter K. Tat
University of Memphis

James W. Taylor
California State University at Fullerton

R. Viswanathan
University of Northern Colorado

Several of our research assistants have made essential contributions to this edition of the book, especially Peter Tsvetkov at Texas Christian University and David Angus at Boston College. Special thanks to Fran Eller and Lisa Wills at TCU and Elizabeth Shanley at Boston College for typing the manuscript and for their assistance in other aspects of the project. We appreciate the support and encouragement of our deans, H. Kirk Downey and John J. Neuhauser, and our colleagues in the marketing departments at TCU and Boston College.

Finally, we would like to acknowledge the support and suggestions that we have received from adopters of the previous five editions of this book. Many features of this edition were implemented in response to advice and counsel from colleagues around the world.

David W. Cravens
Charles W. Lamb, Jr.
Victoria L. Crittenden

CONTENTS

MARKET-DRIVEN STRATEGY

Gaining competitive advantage in marketing is a continuing process. An important part of this challenge is analyzing and strategically responding to changing environmental opportunities and threats. To do this, managers need to develop effective strategic analysis, planning, implementation, and control skills.

Analysis of successful business strategies points to the central importance of market-based strategies. These strategies start with a clear understanding of the market and how it is likely to change. A market-driven orientation becomes the basis for deciding how, when, and where to compete.

Southwest Airlines is an interesting example of a company that has performed very well using a market-driven strategy. The regional, point-to-point carrier has a major advantage over many competing U.S. domestic airlines. Southwest's distinctive competencies center on performing air carrier activities more efficiently than competing airlines. The entire Southwest work force is market-driven, being guided by a culture committed to customer satisfaction. A key advantage is the airline's high aircraft utilization, which is achieved by minimizing the time between landing and take-off. Southwest does not serve meals or provide seat reservations so it does not meet the needs of passengers who want these amenities. Nonetheless, the economy airline has developed a substantial customer base which consistently reports high levels of customer satisfaction.

Market-Driven Strategy and Performance

The market-driven era of business practice offers several different opportunities and challenges compared to previous periods. Market-driven organizations are customer-oriented, understand the relationships between strategy and performance, and stress ethical marketing behavior.

Customer Orientation

Market-driven strategy places the customer at the center of attention for everyone in the organization. This means that all business strategy decisions start with the market and the objective of matching company capabilities with customers who perceive value in what the company offers. Southwest's avenue to value is low operating costs in providing point-to-point airline services. Its market segments consist of business and pleasure travelers who want reliable service at economy prices.

Our traditional view of competition is changing. Increasingly, market-driven companies are partnering with other companies in seeking to deliver superior customer value by combining the capabilities of two or more organizations. For example, Dell Computer's remarkable success in the personal computer market is due in part to its partnering with other companies in the design, production, distribution, and servicing of its products.

Industry and market structures are becoming increasingly complex and interrelated, creating new opportunities and challenges for companies developing market-driven strategies. Moreover, these interlinked product markets are experiencing rapid, often turbulent, change. For example, markets for computers, telecommunications, software, and home electronics are interlinked by digital technology.

Strong organizational performance is essential to survival. Weak performers will be acquired by their competition or pursue other avenues to exit from the marketplace. Western Union's failure to recognize changes in telecommunications had a drastic impact on this century-old company. Encyclopedia Britannica experienced similar problems by discounting the potential impact of CD-ROM technology on the reference book market.

Strategy and Performance

There is persuasive evidence from business practice and academic studies that superior strategies lead to superior performance, regardless of the attractiveness of the business environment.[1] High performance is more difficult to achieve in a demanding environment but the evidence suggests that organizations with sound strategies outperform their competition.

Environmental factors clearly impact performance, both negatively and positively, but companies with effective strategies sustain their competitiveness and perform better than their competitors.[2] For example, Singapore Airlines has an impressive record of performance even though many international airlines report major losses.

Strategy for Competitive Advantage

Competitive advantage results from offering superior value to customers through (1) lower prices than competitors charge for equivalent benefits and/or (2) unique benefits that more than offset a higher price.[3] Competitive advantage often occurs within specific segments rather than spanning an entire product market. For example, Dell Computer quickly obtained a position in the personal computer market by targeting selected organizational buyers. Founded in 1984, Dell's sales in 1997 exceeded $10 billion. Dell's targeting strategy is to sell PCs by mail at competitive prices. The company offers a 30-day money-back guarantee, a one-year warranty, and guaranteed 24-hour on-site service.[4] These service features give Dell an important competitive advantage with small and medium-size business buyers. Other mail order PC marketers do not offer comparable services.

Compressing the length of time necessary to develop new products, enter new markets, keep products in inventory, and move products through distribution channels offers a potentially powerful competitive advantage. Speed as an element of strategy is important because[5]

- Shorter life cycles impose pressures to move products quickly into the marketplace.
- Speed allows companies to more quickly obtain profits from new products.
- Competitive threats can be avoided or reduced by doing things faster.

Time compression requires analysis of the activities that make up a process like new product development. The objective is to eliminate unnecessary activities and to reduce the time required to perform essential activities. Boeing, for example, substantially cut development time for the Boeing 777 by eliminating paper drawings and testing by use of a computerized design process. Caylx and Corolla (C&C), a fresh flower retailer, moves flowers from growers to consumers in less than three days compared to nine or more days via conventional flower distribution. C&C receives orders by phone from catalog displays and the order is transmitted to the grower and picked up the next day for delivery by Federal Express.

Ethics in Marketing

Ethical responsibilities of managers and professionals include (1) identifying ethical issues, (2) determining guidelines for ethical behavior, and (3) encouraging employees to practice ethical behavior. The typical ethical appeal is based on moral philosophy—doing good because it is right. The reality is that "Back in the real world, however, no businessman is going to sacrifice his company on the altar of such altruistic extremism."[6] The marketing manager wants (and needs) guidelines for coping with the pressures of self-interest and encouraging altruism. The challenge is to show that practicing good ethics leads to long-term favorable business performance.

The situations that are most difficult and perhaps encountered most frequently are those described as amoral management.[7] Amoral judgments may be intentional (managers do not include ethical considerations in their decisions) or unintentional (managers do not recognize the ethical impact of their decisions). Both situations should be avoided.

Ethical guidelines that are too general provide limited direction for employees who want to practice ethical behavior. Such guidelines also give those people who lack a strong commitment to ethics a basis for pursuing unethical behavior. The following checklist offers a useful basis for evaluating a situation that may require ethical decision making:[8]

- Does my decision presume that I or my company is an exception to a common practice or convention? In other words, do I think I have the authority to break a rule?
- Would I offend customers by telling them about my decision?
- Would I offend qualified job applicants by telling them about my decision?
- Have I made this decision without input from others, so that important issues might be overlooked?
- Does my decision benefit one person or group but hurt or not benefit other individuals or groups?
- Will my decision create conflict between people or groups in the company?
- Will I have to pull rank and use coercion to enact my decision?
- Would I prefer to avoid the consequences of this decision?
- Did I avoid truthfully answering any of the above questions by telling myself that I could get away with it?

Pragmatic, easily understood guidelines like these should enhance the possibilities of making ethical decisions. Evaluating ethical implications of decision situations is a continuing challenge for managers.

Corporations are placing unprecedented emphasis on the ethical behavior they expect of their personnel. One estimate indicates that over three-quarters of major U.S. companies are actively trying to encourage ethical behavior in their organizations.[9] Companies employ several methods to encourage managers to recognize the ethical content of their decisions. Such methods include workshops, drawing up corporate and industry codes of ethics, and establishment of leadership role models.

Marketing Strategy

Exhibit 1 shows the four-step process of designing and managing a marketing strategy (analysis, planning, implementation, and, finally, management) that we follow in this book.[10] First, a situation analysis considers market and competitor analysis, market segmentation, and continuous learning about markets. Second, designing a marketing strategy entails customer targeting and positioning strategies, marketing relationship strategies, and planning for new products. Third, marketing program development consists of product/service, distribution, price, and promotion strategies designed and implemented to meet the needs of targeted buyers. Fourth, strategy implementation and management look at organizational design and marketing strategy implementation and control. A brief overview of each stage in the marketing strategy process follows.

Marketing Situation Analysis

Marketing management needs the marketing situation analysis to guide the design of a new strategy or to change an existing strategy. The situation analysis is conducted on a regular basis to guide strategy changes.

Analyzing Markets and Competition.   Markets need to be defined so that the buyers and competition can be analyzed. For a market to exist, there must be people with particular needs and wants and one or more products that can satisfy these needs. Also,

EXHIBIT 1

Designing and Managing a Marketing Strategy

the buyers must be both willing and able to purchase a product that satisfies their needs and wants.

A product market consists of a specific product (or line of related products) that can satisfy a set of needs and wants for the people (or organizations) willing and able to purchase the product. The term *product* refers to either a physical good or an intangible service. Analyzing product markets and forecasting how they will change in the future will supply vital information for business and marketing planning. Decisions to enter new product markets are critical strategic marketing choices. The objective is to identify and describe the buyers, understand their preferences for products, estimate the size and rate of growth of the market, and find out which companies and products are competing in the market.

Evaluation of competitors' strategies, strengths, limitations, and plans is also a key aspect of the situation analysis. It is important to identify both existing and potential competitors. A few of the firms in an industry are often a company's key competitors. Analysis includes evaluating each key competitor. The analyses highlight the competition's important strengths and weaknesses. A key issue is trying to figure out what the competition is likely to do in the future.

Market Segmentation.   Segmentation considers the nature and diversity of buyers' needs and wants in a market. It offers an opportunity for an organization to focus its business competencies on the requirements of one or more specific groups of buyers. The intent of segmentation is to consider differences in needs and wants and to identify segments within the product market of interest. Each segment includes buyers with similar needs and wants for the product category of interest to management. The segments are described using the various characteristics of people, the reasons that they buy or use certain products, and their preferences for certain brands of products. Segments for business product markets may be formed according to the type of industry, the uses for the product, frequency of product purchase, and various other factors.

Designing Marketing Strategy

The situation analysis identifies market opportunities, defines market segments, evaluates competition, and assesses the organization's strengths and weaknesses. This information plays a key role in designing marketing strategy, which includes market targeting and positioning analysis, building marketing relationships, and developing and introducing new products.

Market Targeting and Positioning Strategy.   Market targeting determines the people (or organizations) that management decides to pursue with the marketing program. The target(s) typically consist of one or more market segments. The targeting decision sets the stage for setting objectives and developing the positioning strategy.

The options range from targeting most of the segments to targeting one or a few segments in a product market. The targeting strategy may be influenced by the market's maturity, the diversity of buyers' needs and preferences, the firm's size compared to the competition, corporate resources and priorities, sales potential, and financial projections.

Positioning seeks to position the product in the eyes and mind of the buyer and distinguish the company, product, or brand from the competition. The positioning strategy is the combination of product, channel of distribution, price, and promotion strategies a firm uses to position itself against its key competitors in meeting the needs and wants of the market target. This strategy is also called the *marketing mix* or the *marketing program*.

Marketing Relationship Strategies.   Marketing relationship strategies are intended to create high levels of customer satisfaction through collaboration of the parties involved. Marketing relationship partners may include end user customers, marketing channel members, suppliers, competitor alliances, and internal teams. The intent is that a company may enhance its ability to satisfy customers and cope with a rapidly changing business environment through partnering.

Building long-term relationships with customers offers companies a way to gain competitive advantage. Similarly, forging relationships with suppliers, channel of distribution members, and sometimes competitors helps to provide superior customer value.

New Product Strategies.   New products are needed to replace old products because of declining sales and profits. Strategies for developing and positioning new market entries involve all functions of the business. Closely coordinated new product planning is essential to satisfy customer requirements and produce high-quality products at competitive prices. New product decisions include finding and evaluating ideas, selecting the most promising for development, designing marketing programs, market testing the products, and introducing them to the market. New product planning includes both goods and services.

Marketing Program Development

Market targeting and positioning strategies for new and existing products set guidelines for the choice of strategies for the marketing mix components. Product, distribution, price, and promotion strategies are combined to form the positioning strategy selected for each market target.

The marketing mix decisions help implement the positioning strategy.[11] The objective is to achieve favorable positioning while allocating financial, human, and production resources to markets, customers, and products as effectively and efficiently as possible.

Product/Service Strategy.   Marketing management needs the following information on current and anticipated performance of the products (services) to guide product strategy decisions:

1. Consumer evaluation of the company's products, particularly their strengths and weaknesses vis-à-vis competition (i.e., product positioning by market segment information).
2. Objective information on actual and anticipated product performance on relevant criteria such as sales, profits, and market share.[12]

Product strategy includes (1) developing plans for new products, (2) managing existing products, and (3) deciding what actions to take on problem products (e.g., improve product performance, lower cost, reposition).

Distribution Strategy.   Market target buyers may be contacted on a direct basis using the firm's sales force or, instead, through a distribution channel of marketing intermediaries (e.g., wholesalers, retailers, or dealers). Distribution channels are often used in linking producers with end user household and business markets. Decisions include (1) type of channel organizations to use and (2) the intensity of distribution appropriate for the product of service.

Price Strategy.   Price plays an important role in positioning a product or service. Customer reaction to alternative prices, the cost of the product, the prices of the competition, and various legal and ethical factors establish management flexibility in setting prices. Price strategy involves choosing the role of price in the positioning strategy, including the desired positioning of the product or brand as well as the margins necessary to satisfy and motivate distribution channel participants.

Promotion Strategy.   Advertising, sales promotion, sales force, direct marketing, and public relations help the organization to communicate with its customers, cooperating organizations, the public, and other target audiences. These activities make up the promotion strategy, which performs an essential role in positioning products in the eyes and minds of buyers. Promotion informs, reminds, and persuades buyers and others who influence the purchasing process.

Implementing and Managing a Marketing Strategy

Selecting the customers to target and the positioning strategy for each target moves marketing strategy development to the final stage, implementation, shown in Exhibit 1. Here we consider the design (or modification) of the marketing organization and implementation and control of the strategy.

The Marketing Organization.   A good organization design matches people and work responsibilities in a way that is best for accomplishing the firm's marketing strategy. Deciding how to assemble people into organizational units and assigning responsibility to the various mix components that make up marketing strategy are important influences on marketing performance. Organizational structures and processes must be matched to the business and marketing strategies that are developed and implemented. Restructuring and reengineering of many organizations in the 1990s led to numerous changes in the structure of marketing units.

Implementing and Assessing Marketing Strategy.   Marketing strategy implementation and assessment consists of (1) preparing the marketing plan and budget, (2) implementing the plan, and (3) managing and assessing the strategy on an ongoing basis.

The typical marketing plan includes details concerning targeting, positioning, and marketing mix activities. The plan indicates what is going to happen during the planning period, who is responsible, how much it will cost, and expected results (e.g., sales forecasts).

The marketing plan includes action guidelines for activities to be implemented, who does what, the dates and location of implementation, and how implementation will be accomplished. Several factors contribute to implementation effectiveness, including the skills of the people involved, organizational design, incentives, and the effectiveness of communication within the organization and externally.

Marketing strategy is an ongoing process of making decisions, implementing them, and gauging their effectiveness over time. In terms of its time requirements, evaluation is far more demanding than planning. Evaluation and control are concerned with tracking performance and, when necessary, altering plans to keep performance on track. Evaluation also includes looking for new opportunities and potential threats in the future. It is the connecting link in the strategic marketing planning process of Exhibit 1.

Preparing the Marketing Plan

The marketing plan spells out the marketing strategy. Plans vary widely in scope and detail. Nevertheless, all plans need to be based on analyses of the product market and segments, industry and competitive structure, and the organization's competitive advantage.

An outline for a typical marketing plan is shown in Exhibit 2. We briefly discuss the major parts of the outline, highlighting the nature and scope of the planning process. The market target serves as the planning unit.

The Situation Summary.   This part of the plan describes the market and its important characteristics, size estimates, and growth projections. Market segmentation analysis indicates the segments to be targeted and their relative importance. The com-

---

EXHIBIT 2   Outline for Preparing an Annual Marketing Plan

Strategic Situation Summary
   A summary of the strategic situation for the planning unit (business unit, market segment, product line, etc.).

Market Target(s) Description
   Define and describe each market target, including customer profiles, customer preferences and buying habits, size and growth estimates, distribution channels, analysis of key competitors, and guidelines for positioning strategy.

Objectives for the Market Target(s)
   Set objectives for the market target (such as market position, sales, and profits). Also state objectives for each component of the marketing program. Indicate how each objective will be measured.

Marketing Program Positioning Strategy
   State how management wants the firm to be positioned relative to competition in the eyes and mind of the buyer.
   A. *Product Strategy*
      Set strategy for new products, product improvements, and product deletions.
   B. *Distribution Strategy*
      Indicate the strategy to be used for each distribution channel, including role of middlemen, assistance and support provided, and specific activities planned.
   C. *Price Strategy*
      Specify the role of price in the marketing strategy and the planned actions regarding price.
   D. *Promotion Strategy*
      Indicate the planned strategy and actions for advertising, publicity, personal selling, and sales promotion.
   E. *Marketing Research*
      Identify information needs and planned projects, objectives, estimated costs, and timetable.
   F. *Coordination with Other Business Functions*
      Specify the responsibilities and activities of other departments that have an important influence upon the planned marketing strategy.

Forecasts and Budgets
   Forecast sales and profit for the marketing plan and set the budget for accomplishing the forecast.

Contingency Plans
   Indicate planned actions if events differ from those assumed in the plan.

petitor analysis indicates the key competitors (actual and potential), their strengths and weaknesses, probable future actions, and the organization's competitive advantage(s) in each segment of interest. The situation summary should be brief. Supporting information for the summary is sometimes placed in an appendix or separate analysis.

Description of the Market Target.   A description of each market target—including size, growth rate, end users' characteristics, positioning strategy guidelines, and other available information useful in planning and implementation—is an essential part of the plan. When two or more targets are involved, it is important to assign priorities to aid in resource allocation.

Objectives for the Market Target(s).   In this part of the plan we discuss what the marketing strategy is expected to accomplish during the planning period. Objectives are needed for each market target, and they may be financial, market position, and customer satisfaction targets. Objectives are also usually included for each marketing mix component.

Marketing Program Positioning Strategy.   The positioning statement indicates how management wants the targeted customers and prospects to perceive the brand. Specific strategies for product, distribution, price, and promotion are explained in this part of the plan. Actions to be taken, responsibilities, time schedules, and other implementation information are indicated.

Planning and implementation responsibilities often involve more than one person or department. A planning team may be assigned the responsibility for each market target and each marketing mix component. The planning process should encourage participation from all the areas responsible for implementing the plan.

Contingency plans may be included in the plan. These plans consider possible actions if the anticipated planning environment is different from what actually occurs. The contingency plan considers how the marketing strategy will be changed if the future is different than anticipated.

Forecasting and Budgeting.   Financial planning includes (1) forecasting revenues and profits and (2) gives estimating the costs necessary to carry out the marketing plan. The people responsible for market target, product, geographic area, or other units may prepare the forecast. Comparative data on sales, profits, and expenses for prior years are useful to link the plan to previous results.

Exhibit 3 shows the marketing plan outline for Sonesta Hotels. The activities include making the situation assessment, setting objectives, developing targeting and positioning strategies, deciding action programs for the marketing mix components, and preparing supporting financial statements (budgets and profit-and-loss projections).

EXHIBIT 3   Sonesta Hotels: Marketing Plan Outline

Note: Please keep the plan concise—maximum of 20 pages plus summary pages. Include title page and table of contents. Number all pages.

   I. *Introduction.* Set the stage for the plan. Specifically identify marketing objectives such as "increase average rate," "more group business," "greater occupancy," or "penetrate new markets." Identify particular problems.

  II. *Marketing Position.* Begin with a single statement that presents a consumer benefit in a way that distinguishes us from the competition.

 III. *The Product.* Identify all facility and service changes that occurred this year and are planned for next year.

  IV. *Marketplace Overview.* Briefly describe what is occurring in your marketplace that might impact on your business or marketing strategy, such as the economy or the competitive situation.

   V. *The Competition.* Briefly identify your primary competition (three or fewer), specifying number of rooms, what is new in their facilities, and marketing and pricing strategies.

  VI. *Marketing Data*
     A. Identify top five geographic areas for transient business, with percentages of total room nights compared to the previous year.
     B. Briefly describe the guests at your hotel, considering age, sex, occupation, what they want, why the come, etc.
     C. Identify market segments with percentage of business achieved in each segment in current year (actual and projected) and projected for next year.

 VII. *Strategy by Market Segment*
     A. Group
        1. *Objectives:* Identify what you specifically wish to achieve in this segment (for example, more high-rated business, more weekend business, larger groups).
        2. *Strategy:* Identify how sales, advertising, and public relations will work together to reach the objectives.
        3. *Sales Activities:* Divide by specific market segments:
           a. Corporate
           b. Association
           c. Incentives
           d. Travel agent
           e. Tours
           f. Other

           Under each category include a narrative description of specific sales activities geared toward each market segment, including geographically targeted areas, travel plans, group site inspections, correspondence, telephone solicitation, and trade shows. Be specific on action plans, and designate responsibility and target months.
        4. *Sales Materials:* Identify all items, so they will be budgeted.
        5. *Direct Mail:* Briefly describe the direct mail program planned, including objectives, message, and content. Identify whether we will use existing material or create a new piece.
        6. *Research:* Indicate any research projects you plan to conduct, identifying what you wish to learn.
     B. Transient (The format here should be the same as it was under "Group" throughout.)
        1. *Objectives*
        2. *Strategy*

EXHIBIT **3**   (concluded)

3. *Sales Activities:* Divide by specific market segments:
   a. Consumer (rack rate)
   b. Corporate (prime and other)
   c. Travel agent: business, leisure, consortia
   d. Wholesale/Airline/Tour (foreign and domestic)
   e. Packages (specify names of packages)
   f. Government/Military/Education
   g. Special interest/Other
4. *Sales Materials*
5. *Direct Mail*
6. *Research*

C. Other Sonesta Hotels
D. Local/Food and Beverage
1. *Objectives*
2. *Strategy*
3. *Sales Activities:* Divide by specific market segments:
   a. Restaurant and Lounge, external promotion
   b. Restaurant and Lounge, internal promotion
   c. Catering
   d. Community Relation/Other
4. *Sales Materials* (e.g., banquet menus, signage)
5. *Direct Mail*
6. *Research*

VIII. *Advertising*
A. Subdivide advertising by market segment and campaign, paralleling the sales activities (group, transient, F&B).
B. Describe objectives of each advertising campaign, identifying whether it should be promotional (immediate bookings) or image (longer-term awareness).
C. Briefly describe contents of advertising, identifying key benefit to promote.
D. Identify target media by location and type (newspaper, magazine, radio, etc.).
E. Indicate percentage of the advertising budget to be allocated to each market segment.

IX. *Public Relations*
A. Describe objectives of public relations as it supports the sales and marketing priorities.
B. Write a brief statement on overall goals by market segment paralleling the sales activities. dentify what proportion of your effort will be spent on each segment.

X. *Summary:* Close the plan with general statement concerning the major challenges you will face in the upcoming year and how you will overcome these challenges.

Source: Adapted from Howard Sutton, *The Marketing Plan in the 1990s* (New York: The Conference Board, Inc., 1990), pp. 34-35.

End Notes

1. Shelby D. Hunt and Robert M. Morgan, "The Comparative Advantage Theory of Competition," *Journal of Marketing,* August 1995, 1–15; Richard P. Rumelt, "How Much Does Industry Matter?" *Strategic Management Journal* 12, 1991, 167–85.

2. David W. Cravens, Gordon Greenley, Nigel F. Piercy, and Stanley Slater, "Integrating Contemporary Strategic Management Perspectives," *Long Range Planning,* August 1997, 493–506.

3. Michael E. Porter, *Competitive Advantage* (New York: Free Press, 1985), 3.

4. Andy Zipser, "Can Dell, CompuAdd Broaden Niches?" *The Wall Street Journal,* January 5, 1990, B1, B6.

5. For an extensive discussion of speed as a competitive advantage, see Steven P. Schnaars, *Marketing Strategy* (New York: Free Press, 1991), Chapter 13.

6. *The Economist,* "How to Be Ethical and Still Come Out on Top," June 5, 1993, 71. See also Andrew Stark, "What's the Matter with Business Ethics," *Harvard Business Review,* May-June 1993, 38–48.

7. Archie B. Carroll, "In Search of the Moral Manager," *Business Horizons,* March-April 1987, 7–15.

8. Stark, "What's the Matter with Business Ethics," 38.

9. Adapted from Michael R. Hyman, Robert Shipper, and Richard Tansey, "Ethic Codes Are Not Enough," *Business Horizons,* March-April 1990, 15–22.

10. This section is adapted from David W. Cravens, *Strategic Marketing,* 5th ed. (Chicago: Richard D. Irwin, 1997), Chapter 1.

11. Frederick E. Webster, Jr., "The Changing Role of Marketing in the Organization," *Journal of Marketing,* October 1992, 11.

12. Yoram Wind and Henry J. Claycamp, "Planning Product Line Strategy: A Matrix Approach," *Journal of Marketing,* January 1976, 2.

CASES FOR PART I

The six cases in Part 1 consider a broad range of marketing issues in various types of companies. Four cases involve companies with goods and services such as canned ice tea, rental cars, industrial components, and art museum gift items. Two cases (one regarding human rights and the other concerning consumers of fortified wine), have strong social responsibility implications in their growth efforts. Nonprofit organizations are featured in two cases; however, their services and markets are quite different from each other.

The video case, **Enterprise Rent-A-Car (Case 1–1),** looks at an interesting strategy for competing in a mature, highly competitive industry. Developing successful strategies in this industry is a major management challenge. Enterprise offers career opportunities for college graduates.

The video case, **Coca-Cola (Japan) Company (Case 1–2),** focuses on deciding whether to enter the Japanese canned tea market. Tea is a "drink of tradition" in Japan, and there is concern about the long-term acceptance of a canned tea. The stakes are high, not just for Coca-Cola (Japan) Company but for the brand manager making the "go/no-go" recommendation.

Case 1–3, Battered Women Fighting Back! (video) is about a nonprofit human rights organization. The executive director thinks that marketing can benefit BWFB! However, she is not quite sure where to start and what to do regarding BWFB!'s marketing challenges.

Case 1–4, Wind Technology, presents a situation requiring evaluation and marketing planning for a possible new industrial product. The company needs to generate revenues because of the cash flow problems created by the wind profiling project.

Decreasing government support, changing tax laws regarding charitable giving, and rising expenditures are forcing management of the **Metropolitan Museum of Art (Case 1–5)** to become more self-sufficient. Management must find creative ways to sustain financial stability by generating additional revenue. The museum's merchandising activities may be key to generating additional internal sources of funds.

Case 1–6, California Valley Wine Company, looks at the decision of introducing one of two potential new products. Both options present serious problems. The challenge is to evaluate the merits of the options and make a recommendation. Whatever the recommendation, presentations must be made to a new product evaluation committee and a social responsibility committee. This strongly implies that the accompanying marketing strategy will be critiqued based on more than just sales volume and market share projections.

CASE 1–1
ENTERPRISE RENT-A-CAR: SELLING THE DREAM

On a bright January 1997 morning, Dean Pittman, Enterprise Rent-A-Car's area rental manager for Durham/Chapel Hill, North Carolina, got out of his car at Enterprise's new office on Hillsborough Road in Durham. He reached back in to retrieve his cellular phone and locked the new Dodge Intrepid, his latest company car. Then, leaning against the car, he admired the line of clean cars and the new office with its green and white Enterprise sign. To Dean, it seemed that dreams really did come true.

In the Fast Lane

A little over six years ago, Dean had graduated with a degree in Industrial Relations from The University of North Carolina at Chapel Hill. In the job-search process, he had scheduled an interview with Enterprise Rent-A-Car, even though he'd known little about the firm. During the first part of the interview, Dean had been skeptical. He wasn't certain that he liked the idea of renting cars for a living or of working at a retail job that included doing work like washing cars. But he'd seen the potential to advance quickly, to develop strong management skills, and to learn about running a business. Enterprise had hired Dean and assigned him to Durham's University Drive office. He was promoted quickly to management assistant, then to branch manager at Enterprise's new office in Rocky Mount, North Carolina. Dean performed well, and a year ago the company made him an area manager, giving him responsibility for the Durham/Chapel Hill area. He now supervised three branch offices with 22 employees, 495 cars, and annual revenues of more than $3 million. Even though he worked for a big company, he felt as though he was running his own business. Enterprise gave its managers considerable autonomy and paid them based on a percentage of their branches' profits. Dean's starting salary was in line with those of his classmates, but within three years his pay had doubled, and now it had tripled. There couldn't be many other companies, Dean thought, where a person his age could have so much responsibility, so much fun, and such high earnings. He still had to work long hours and do his share of grunt work, but the rewards were there.

Dean's good fortune mirrored that of Enterprise itself. Starting its rental operation in 1962 with a single location and 17 cars in St. Louis, Missouri, Enterprise had grown dramatically to become the nation's largest rent-a-car company in terms of fleet size and number of rental locations. By 1997, the company had more than 3,000 locations, 325,000 cars, $3.1 billion in sales, $5 billion in assets, and 30,000 employees (see Exhibit 1). In 1996, *Fortune* ranked Enterprise 37th on its list of the top 50 privately held U.S. firms. If it were public, Enterprise would have ranked about 390th among the Fortune 500.

The company's success resulted from its single-minded focus on one segment of the rent-a-car market. Instead of following Hertz, Avis, and other rent-a-car companies

This case was prepared by Dr. Lew Brown, Joseph M. Bryan School of Business and Economics, University of North Carolina at Greensboro, Dr. Gary Armstrong, Kenan-Flagler Business School, University of North Carolina at Chapel Hill, and Dr. Philip Kotler, Kellogg Graduate School of Management, Northwestern University. The authors wish to thank officials at Enterprise Rent-A-Car and *Auto Rental News* for their support in development of this case. The case is for classroom discussion purposes only. Copyright © 1997 Lew Brown, Gary Armstrong, Philip Kotler. All rights reserved.

EXHIBIT 1   **Enterprise Rent-A-Car Growth in Units, Locations, and Employees**

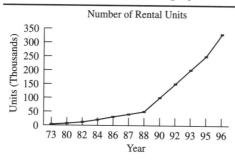

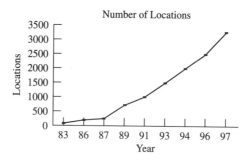

by setting up branches at airports to serve national travelers, Enterprise built an extensive network of neighborhood locations serving the "home-city" market—people who needed rental cars as replacements when their cars were wrecked or in the shop being repaired. Because these customers were often stranded at a body shop or repair garage and had no easy way to get to a rental office, Enterprise offered to pick them up. Enterprise's home-city strategy had been very successful—by 1997, the company captured more than 50 percent of the replacement car segment. In recent years, Enterprise had consistently led the industry in growth and profitability.

A Surprise Guest

Out of the corner of his eye, Dean saw two men getting out of a nearby car. Dean recognized Dan Miller, Enterprise's regional vice president who was responsible for operations in eastern North and South Carolina, and Andy Taylor, Enterprise's president

and chief executive officer. Andy had attended a management meeting in Raleigh the day before, and Dan had suggested they visit the new Durham branch this morning before Andy's plane left for St. Louis, where Enterprise still had its international headquarters.

Dan knew that Andy liked to visit branches whenever he had the chance. As the son of Enterprise's founder, Jack Taylor, Andy started working for Enterprise at the age of 16 in his father's first office. Like Enterprise's other top executives who had started as entry-level branch employees, Andy still had branch operations in his blood. He and other executives visited branches regularly to stay in touch with employees and customers, to learn about new ways to grow the market, and to offer whatever support they could to branch personnel. In fact, most Enterprise executives boasted that on occasion they still "got their ties caught in the vacuum cleaners" while cleaning cars and performing other chores to help out while visiting busy branches.

"Good morning!" Dean hailed across the parking lot.

"Hi, Dean," Andy responded as he threw up his hand. "Good looking new office. That's a nice suit. Is it new, too?"

"Yes. I needed some new suits to go with the office. Glad you were able to stop by Andy. I've scheduled an interview with a prospective employee this morning. Perhaps you'd like to sit in for a few minutes."

"That sounds great. Who's the candidate?"

"Her name is Rachael Van Doren. Based on her resume and a preliminary interview by one of our recruiters, she seems to be bright, ambitious, and not afraid of hard work. More importantly, she seems to be a real people person, someone who'd do well marketing to our referral sources and working with our customers. She also seems to be a team player with great management potential."

"I'd like to meet her," Andy responded. "Good people are the key to our business. As you know, we've got to hire a lot of new people this year if we are going to continue our rapid growth. In fact, recruitment may be the number one issue we face this year. We need to attract more employees with the right expectations and help them see that, although it may not seem as glamorous as some other careers, working at Enterprise offers real opportunity."

As the three men entered the office, Dean spotted Rachael in the waiting area. "Good morning, Rachael, I'm Dean Pittman. I hope you didn't have trouble finding the office."

"No, your directions were very good."

"I appreciate your coming for an interview on such short notice. As it turns out, we're going to have a special guest in your interview. Rachael Van Doren, meet Andy Taylor, Enterprise's president and chief executive officer. And this is Dan Miller, our regional vice president."

"Hello, Mr. Taylor, Mr. Miller. It's a pleasure to meet you." Rachael responded as she shook hands.

"Please call us Andy and Dan—we aren't very formal at Enterprise," Andy responded. "I hope we're not overwhelming you. Whenever I have the chance, I like to visit our branch offices. Do you mind us sitting in?"

"Oh, no. That's fine," Rachael answered. "I guess I'm lucky to get to meet the president of the company."

"Well, Rachael, the branch office is the key to our company's success—it's where all the important action takes place. So it's always exciting when I get to spend time at a branch. We've grown more than 25 percent in each of the past 11 years. Needless to say, a key factor in continuing such growth is developing quality employees who want to run their own branches."

The Interview

As they walked through the office, Dean introduced the group to the other branch employees and showed off the new office. They stopped by a break room to pick up coffee, and Dean pointed out pictures on the bulletin board from last weekend's New Year's party. The Durham and Chapel Hill branches had held a contest in December to see which branch could grow its business the most that month. The Durham branch had won, so the Chapel Hill group had arranged and paid for the party. "We're always competing like that," Dean noted. "It really adds excitement and challenge to our work."

The group moved to Dean's office, and he began the interview. "Rachael, we're interviewing you for a position in the Chapel Hill office. Normally, the branch manager, Sally Pinon, would be here, but she's on maternity leave now. Why don't you start by telling us a little about your background and how you came to apply at Enterprise?"

"I'm originally from Abington, Virginia," Rachael explained. "I graduated from the University of North Carolina at Greensboro last May with a degree in marketing. When I graduated, I wasn't sure what I wanted to do. I interviewed for a number of jobs, but didn't find anything that really appealed to me. So for the last few months, I've been working in a temporary administrative position at Duke University Medical Center while I continued looking for a permanent position.

"Last month, I went to a job fair in Raleigh and met one of your recruiters. I gave her my resume, and she gave me some information on the company. Apparently, she sent my resume to Hamilton Morales, your regional recruiter in Raleigh, and he called me for a preliminary interview last week."

"Did you know anything about Enterprise before you met our recruiter at the job fair, Rachael?" Andy asked.

"No, sir. I really didn't know much about the company. Once I looked at your materials, I did remember seeing some of your television ads with the wrapped car."

"After reading the brochures," Dan asked, "were you interested in the company?"

"To be honest, no," Rachael answered. "Enterprise seemed like a good company, but I had brochures from lots of companies at the job fair. I don't think I would've been interested if Hamilton hadn't called and invited me to the interview. My reaction was that a rent-a-car company didn't sound like a business that required someone with a college degree. I couldn't see myself renting cars like those uniformed people you see behind the counters at the airport."

"Did your interview with Hamilton change your opinion?" Dean asked.

"Yes. I could sense his excitement about working for Enterprise and his feeling that he had a real future with the company. I also met some of the other employees at the regional office, and I could tell they enjoyed their jobs. I learned that there's a lot more to this business than just working behind a counter."

Company Background

"I've also learned a lot about the company," Rachael continued, "but I'd be interested in your thoughts on why Enterprise has been so successful."

"Many factors have contributed, Rachael," Andy answered. "First, cars have become more important to people. People today just can't do without their cars, even for a day or two. And, as more and more families have both adults working or are single-parent families, there is often no one else in the family who can pick you up when you have car problems. Tied in to this, the courts ruled in the 1970s that insurance companies have to offer coverage so that insured motorists can rent a replacement car if they lose the use of their car. As a result, those insurance companies began to offer rental replacement coverage in their policies.

"But perhaps the most important reason for our success is that we've adhered closely to my father's initial beliefs about how we should run the business. First, and most importantly, we believe that we're here to serve the customer. That's why, from day one, my father urged his employees to do whatever they had to do in order to make the customer happy. Sometimes it means waiving charges. Other times, it means stopping everything and running out to pick up a stranded customer. Our employees know that they need to do whatever it takes to make customers happy.

"When my father first started this company, he also believed—and he still believes—that after customers come employees. If we're going to satisfy our customers, we need to have satisfied, challenged employees working as a team." Andy explained that all of Enterprise's branch employees, from assistant manager on up, earn a substantial portion of their pay based on branch profitability. In addition, the company has a profit-sharing plan for all employees. Enterprise hires primarily college graduates and promotes from within. Ninety-nine percent of its managers start as management trainees at the branch level. "As a result," Andy concluded, "they really know how our business works, and they understand our customer-centered culture."

Dean Pittman agreed. "That's really true. Jack Taylor believes that if you take care of the first two—customers and employees—profits will follow."

"A final piece of the puzzle," Andy continued, "is our conviction that Enterprise is a local-market business. We believe strongly that our branch employees know how best to respond to customer needs in their markets. We see our business not as a broad, national business, but as a network of small, independent businesses—more than 3,000 of them now.

"We let our managers run their businesses, and we like to create friendly competition between branches. For example, employees at each branch see revenue and profit information for neighboring branches. As a result, all of these locally managed operations come up with many ideas about how to expand their businesses and serve their customers better. We weed out the ideas that don't work and share those that do with other Enterprise operating groups.

"Enterprise is a highly decentralized operation with a very small corporate staff," Andy explained. "The corporation provides capital to help branches fund their growth and a national marketing program. The only other centralized component of our business is our information system." As of 1997, the company had 23 IBM AS/400 computers in St. Louis, connected in real time via satellites to each branch worldwide. At peak times, the system processed some 834,000 transactions an hour. Enterprise knew the status of every car in its fleet at all times and was the only home-city rental company with this capability. The system also gathered all the information that corporate and branch managers needed to monitor each branch's performance. Another system allowed customers around the country to call just one telephone number and be connected to their nearest Enterprise office.

Marketing Strategy

"You mentioned that Enterprise began its rental business by targeting the home-city replacement market. Are you targeting other market segments?" Rachael asked.

"Yes, Rachael," Andy answered. "Although the majority of our business is in the replacement market, we're in two other markets as well. In the replacement market, of course, our end customers are the individuals who rent the cars. However, our initial customer is often the referral source—the insurance agent or auto body shop employee who recommends Enterprise to the stranded customer. Few of our customers get up in the morning thinking they'll need to rent a car—but then they're involved in a wreck. So referral sources are extremely important to us.

"The second segment of the home-city market is the 'discretionary' or 'leisure/vacation' segment. Friends or relatives may visit and need a car, or the family may decide to take a vacation and feel that the family car is really not dependable. More and more people are renting for trips just to keep the extra miles off the family car. This is a rapidly growing segment for us as more people learn about Enterprise's nearby locations and low prices.

"Finally, we are seeing growth in our business from what we call the local corporate market. Many small businesses and some large ones have found that it's cheaper and easier for them to rent their fleets from Enterprise rather than trying to maintain their own fleets. For example, we do a lot of business with colleges and universities that have realized that it's cheaper to rent a 15-passenger van from us when the soccer team travels than to keep a van full time for only occasional use."

"How big is the home-city market?" Rachael asked.

"That's a good question," Andy responded. "It's very hard to define accurately, but the trade publication *Auto Rental News* has made some estimates and sees the market growing at 10 percent to 15 percent per year (see Exhibit 2). The entire rent-a-car market, including airport rentals—what we call the travel segment—is about $14.6 billion."

"I also read in several news articles that Enterprise's rental rates are about 30 percent lower than those of the rent-a-car companies that operate at airports. Is that true?" Rachael asked.

"Our local rates are much lower than those you typically find at the airport," Dean answered. "We tend to locate our offices where the rent is much lower than at the airport. We also keep our cars a little longer than the typical airport-rental company. These two factors, along with our efficient operations, help us to keep our rates lower." Because home-city market car rentals peak during the workweek, Enterprise experiences excess capacity during weekends. Therefore, it also offers attractive weekend promotional prices in most markets, Dean explained.

"Who is your competition?" Rachael asked.

"We have a greater share of the total home-city market than any other single competitor," Andy answered. "A handful of major regional competitors, such as Spirit and Snappy, when combined, capture an equivalent share of the market. The airport-rental companies, such as Hertz, Avis, and Alamo, get only a small portion of the home-city business. In fact, Hertz is just now starting a small operation that focuses on the home-city replacement market. Local 'mom-and-pop' firms that often have just one office and a few cars serve the remainder of the market."

"As I noted earlier," Rachael began, "I'd never really heard of Enterprise. I'm very impressed with what I have learned, but I must admit that I wonder why so few people seem to know about the company. When I told my friends I was coming for an interview, few of them recognized the company name until I mentioned your ads with the car wrapped in paper and the 'Pick Enterprise. We'll pick you up.' slogan."

"That's a problem," Dan agreed. "When our recruiters go to a university's career day, they often find that students sign up for interviews without knowing who we are. I'm sure even more would sign up if we were more widely known."

"We grew up as a very quiet company," Andy joined in. "We have always depended on word-of-mouth and our referral sources. It wasn't until 1989 that we did our first national advertising. At that time, marketing research showed that we had low awareness. If you showed people a list of company names and asked them to identify the rent-a-car companies, only about 20 percent picked us. We then started advertising nationally, but still kept our ads low key. Since then we have more than quadrupled our annual advertising and promotion spending."

"Our research shows that Enterprise's awareness is now up substantially. Still, only about one-third of those surveyed are aware of our pick-up service, and only about one-third are aware that we have branches nearby. Further, few college-age people

EXHIBIT 2   The Replacement Car Rental Market
Competitors, Revenue Estimates, and Other Market Data

I. Competitor	1996 U.S. Revenue	% Replacement[1]	Cars in Service (U.S.)
1. Enterprise Rent-A-Car	$2.61 billion[2]	78%	315,000
2. Ford and Chrysler Systems	$490 million	92	82,250
3. Snappy Car Rental	$100 million	100	15,500
4. U-Save Auto Rental	$115 million	60	13,500
5. Rent-A-Wreck	$85 million	35	10,942
6. Premier Car Rental	$66 million	100	9,500
7. Advantage Rent-A-Car	$76 million	33	9,000
8. Spirit Rent-A-Car	$50 million	100	7,500
9. Super Star Rent-A-Car	$43 million	100	5,250
10. Many independent companies	$750 million	53	
11. Airport-based companies: Hertz, Avis, Budget, Dollar, National, Thrifty, Alamo[3]	$360 million	100	—

II. Industry Average Pricing

Estimated industry average price per day for replacement rentals, not including additional insurance coverages or other rentals, such as cellular phones: Industry average daily rental is $23. Industry average rental period for replacement rentals is 12 days.

Additional insurance coverages produce about 5 percent of revenue, with other rental options producing about 2 percent of revenue. Per-day rental rates are often established through national contracts with insurance companies or automobile manufacturers' or dealers' warranty reimbursement programs.

There are approximately 150 major U.S. airport rental markets. Airport-based rental rates vary widely depending on competition. Airport rental companies also negotiate corporate rates with individual companies.

III. Overall Rent-a-Car Market

Overall 1996 U.S. market estimated at $14.62 billion broken down as follows: business rentals—40 percent; leisure/discretionary rentals—33 percent, replacement rentals—27 percent.

IV. Advertising

Advertising Age estimated that U.S. car rental companies spent $384.4 million in measured advertising in 1994, about 2.8 percent of revenue. It estimated that Enterprise spent $22 million in 1994, up from $13 million in 1993. Enterprise's 1994 spending compared with $47 million spent by Hertz, $31 million by Alamo, and $24 million by Avis (Sept. 27, 1995).

Source: *Auto Rental News*

Note: Estimates provided by *Auto Rental News*. Data are for case discussion purposes only. Use in case does not imply certification of estimates by Enterprise.

[1] Replacement market includes insurance replacement rentals, mechanical repair rentals, dealer loaner rentals, and warranty rentals.

[2] *Auto Rental News* estimate of U.S. rental revenue excluding leasing. Seven percent of revenue is from airport/traveler rentals and 93 percent is from local market rentals. Local market includes replacement, business, and leisure rentals, with business and leisure about equal for Enterprise.

[3] Includes the portion of airport-based companies' revenue from local market operations that target the replacement market, including Hertz H.I.R.E. operations with 70 locations and Alamo with 115 locations. Hertz total fleet included 250,000 cars; Avis, 190,000; Alamo, 130,000; Budget, 126,000; National, 135,000; Dollar, 63,500; and Thrifty, 34,000.

have direct experience with us, even though we are one of few companies that will rent to someone under 25 years of age. We realize that we still have a way to go in getting our name out."

The Management Trainee's Job

"I'd also like to know more about the management trainee position. Exactly what are the responsibilities of that position?" Rachael asked.

"When you come to work for Enterprise your goal should be to learn all aspects of developing a business. First, you're assigned to a branch," Dean answered. "After initial training and orientation, we continue your on-the-job training by putting you on the front line to work alongside the other branch team members, dealing with customers who are renting or returning cars. Besides the work at the computer terminal, this involves picking up customers. Even though many of our branches have employees called "car preps" who are assigned specifically to washing and preparing our cars for renting, all branch employees help prepare cars from time to time. They also check the repair status of customers' cars and inform insurance adjusters about how the repairs are coming along. In addition, they constantly monitor the branch's income statement and operating information to learn the logistics of running a business. This is exactly how Andy and our other senior managers started."

Dean went on to explain that aside from direct interaction with rental customers, the most important aspect of the trainee's job is managing relationships with referral sources. Each week, they spend time visiting the insurance agents, claims adjusters, and body shop and repair shop employees who generated much of the company's business by referring customers to Enterprise. "We visit these people every week, often taking donuts or pizzas, as a way of saying thank you for their business," Dean noted. In addition, trainees also make cold calls on referral sources and others who are not yet doing business with Enterprise. Building and maintaining these relationships is one of the most important parts of the job, he said.

"There is a lot of room for aggressiveness and creativity in this job, Rachael," Dean continued. "We need people who are willing to work hard for long hours (about 52 hours a week) while keeping a positive, friendly attitude toward customers and other employees. Our people must be dedicated to learning all aspects of branch operations, and they need to have good communication and interpersonal skills. They also need to be able to make decisions quickly, an important skill as they move up in management."

"What happens after the first few weeks?" Rachael asked.

"You spend several months learning how to run our business," Dan answered. "After six to nine months, your manager will give you what we call the Management Qualification Interview. Our employees call it 'the Grill.' The manager takes a couple of hours to ask you a full range of questions about every aspect of running a branch. If you pass this test, you get a raise and a promotion to management assistant; and you're on your way to becoming a manager." Dan explained that successful trainees move up quickly at Enterprise. Frequently within another six to nine months, they become the assistant manager of a branch. Then, within two to three years of joining the company, they are promoted to branch manager, assuming full responsibility for a branch with four to six employees and 100 to 150 cars. Within five to seven years, a successful employee could expect to become an area manager, with responsibility for two or more branches. Beyond that were positions as city managers, group rental managers, group managers, corporate vice presidents, and, of course, Andy Taylor's job as CEO.

"With advancement comes the opportunity for significant increases in income," Dan continued. "A management trainee starts at a competitive salary based on local market conditions, along with a full range of benefits and company profit sharing. Our typical branch manager is 27 years old and has doubled his/her initial salary. Managers continue to earn a percentage of the profits of the branches for which they are responsible as they move up in the organization.

"In my case," Dan noted, "I started with Enterprise 10 years ago in Southern California. In about two years, I became a branch manager with responsibility for satisfying customers, watching the bottom line, motivating employees, and managing more than $1 million in assets. Within seven years, I was a group rental manager in Birmingham, Alabama. Two years ago, I moved to Raleigh to become a regional vice president with responsibility for 30 offices and 4,000 cars, $60 million in assets, in eastern North and South Carolina. Our region grew 43 percent last year, creating lots of opportunities for advancement. One of my friends, Rob Hibbard, is now a corporate vice president after only 9½ years, at the ripe old age of 33! In fact, you'd be amazed at how young our corporate officers are."

"That's impressive," Rachael responded, "but I'm not sure I'm very excited about starting out at a retail salary, working such long hours, and having to wash cars. As I mentioned earlier, I've been working at Duke University Medical Center in a temporary position. The Center has offered me a permanent, full-time job with a higher starting salary and a more normal nine-to-five work schedule. I've also been interviewing with a large pharmaceutical firm that has outside sales positions starting at $30,000 with a company car. When I told my father that I was going to interview with you, he was a little skeptical. I'm not sure he sees working for a rent-a-car company as a good use of my college degree."

"We realize people like you have lots of options," Dean answered. "That's why we think it's important that you understand our job and expectations so that you can decide if there's a good fit. The Duke job sounds like a good opportunity, but Enterprise employees typically prefer moving about and working with people rather than working behind a desk all day. Outside sales jobs like the one you mentioned often come with lots of travel, and some require you to relocate periodically. Perhaps more importantly, at Enterprise, unlike many other jobs, your pay increases significantly because it reflects your increasing value to the company. Further, although you can apply for open positions anywhere in our system, we don't force you to relocate. I guess it comes down to your deciding what is most important to you."

"Well, I've been thinking about those issues. I was a waitress while I was in college, and I know that I like being active and working with people. It's also important to me that I enjoy what I do. One thing I've noticed is that the Enterprise people I met in Raleigh and here this morning seem to be happy and to enjoy their work."

Role Playing

"It seems to me that you've been doing a better job interviewing us than we have of interviewing you," Andy joked. "Let me ask you a question like one you might get in the 'Grill' exam we mentioned. This question is based on an actual incident that Dan told me about this morning—something one of our employees faced last Friday at the Chapel Hill office. A management trainee went to pick up a young man at the university hospital's main entrance in order to bring him to the branch to get a rental car. The customer was a third-year medical student whose car had 'died' several weeks earlier. He wanted to rent one of our cars for the weekend at our special weekend rates. It was about 4:30 on a cold, rainy afternoon with lots of traffic congestion. With four employees on duty, our office was extremely busy. When our employee, who'd been on the job only about seven weeks, arrived at the hospital, the customer informed her that he'd just realized that his license had expired. Of course, we can't rent to someone with an expired license. The customer said he'd just called the Department of Motor Vehicles office, located about three miles away, and the DMV officer had indicated that if he came over it would take only a few minutes to renew the license. The question is, if you were the employee, what would you do?"

Rachael thought for a moment. "Well, you said the office was very busy, and if I did what the customer asked I'd be away from the office longer than expected. So, I guess I'd call the office to see if it was okay to take the customer to the DMV office," Rachael answered.

"Okay," Andy replied. "Let's assume you can't locate a phone quickly. What then?"

This time, Rachael didn't hesitate. "You said earlier that customer satisfaction is number one. If I don't take the customer, he'll probably be without a car for the weekend. So, I'd take him to the DMV office and try to call our office from there to let them know that I'd been delayed. Hopefully, it wouldn't take the customer long to renew the license, and I'd wait and take him back to our office to complete the rental."

"Well done, Rachael! Great answer," Andy exclaimed. "That's exactly what we'd expect from an Enterprise employee."

Back to the Airport

Dan broke in. "Excuse me, Rachael, but I've got to get Andy to the airport now. We'll leave you with Dean to complete your interview. Thanks for letting us sit in."

"I enjoyed the discussion, Dan," Rachael answered. "I learned a lot about your company. It was nice to meet you, Andy. I hope you have a good trip back to St. Louis."

*****

"Rachael seemed very sharp," Andy observed as he and Dan walked to the car.

"Yes, I wish we could find more prospective employees like her. But we have awareness and image problems. In this economy, with good college grads having so many choices, we've got to deal with those issues."

"How's your recruiting coming?" Andy asked.

"Pretty well. Hamilton Morales, my regional recruiter, has been on the job for three months now. I created that job and promoted him from one of our branch offices. This gives me someone who concentrates full time on recruiting. We're doing all the normal recruiting activities, like going to college career days and advertising in the college newspapers. But we've got to find other sources and be creative if we are going to meet our hiring goals. We've got to hire about 75 college grads to meet our growth targets and cover normal turnover. I understand we need more than 5,000 recruits companywide."

"We learned last year," Dan continued, "how important it is to keep up the supply of good employees. Our demand skyrocketed. It's easy to add 40 to 50 cars to an office to meet demand, but we can't add people that fast.

"I've asked Hamilton to put together a recruiting plan for our region that outlines the general types of activities we should carry out. I've encouraged him to do some 'out-of-the-box' thinking. We've got to find new and more effective ways to recruit college grads if we're going to meet our growth goals."

Andy nodded. "I have just gotten some results from several recruitment studies that the corporate office commissioned. I think this information will be helpful to you (see Exhibit 3). I was surprised by the results, especially the reasons candidates turned

---

EXHIBIT 3 Enterprise Rent-A-Car Recruiting Study Results

1. Top eight messages to communicate in recruitment advertising:[1]
   a. Fun and friendly work environment.
   b. Great earning potential.
   c. Earnings and responsibility are performance-based.
   d. Great place to start.
   e. Perfect place for well-rounded people.
   f. Promote from within.
   g. Not a desk job.
   h. Run a business in two years.
2. Top six messages to communicate to prospective employees:[1]
   a. Opportunity to advance.
   b. Promotion from within.
   c. Future earnings potential.
   d. People you work with.
   e. Learn a business.
   f. Team environment.
3. Backgrounds of successful managers:[2]
   a. Active in extracurricular activities.
   b. Worked their way through school.
   c. Officers in clubs/organizations.
   d. Come from full-time job.
   e. Active in athletics.
4. Top reasons our offers are turned down:[2]
   a. Compensation.
   b. Prestige.
   c. Hours vs. pay.
   d. Don't see potential.
5. Why people leave[1]
   a. Long hours.
   b. Stress.
   c. Low pay.

Source: Enterprise Rent-A-Car.

[1] Based on a written questionnaire to 103 students and 53 graduates at 10 campuses.
[2] Based on a survey of 188 current Enterprise managers and 107 recruiters.

down our offers and why people chose to leave. It seems we aren't getting the word out about the future opportunities, both in terms of pay and prestige."

"Andy, I think we've got to understand that recruiting is a marketing problem," Dan said. "We can use marketing techniques to attack this problem just as we use them to develop strategies to serve our customers. We're selling a dream."

"Yes," Andy replied. "And good recruiting will be essential if we want to keep growing at our current pace. We think we can double revenues again by the year 2001, but we're wrestling with a number of growth-related issues. What markets should we target? How should we position ourselves? Are there new services that we might offer? Do we need to be doing more to get the Enterprise story out to customers? How are we going to respond when Hertz and others decide to attack our home-city markets? And how can we keep up this rapid growth without losing our focus, and without losing the wonderful culture we've developed?

"All of our growth is driven not to create notoriety and wealth for Enterprise, but to serve new customers and to create opportunity for our employees. You're right, Dan. We do have a dream to sell—my father's dream. The Enterprise dream."

CASE 1–2
COCA-COLA (JAPAN) COMPANY

It was October 1987. Arthur Grotz, brand manager, was pacing the floor in his Tokyo office. He was pondering whether he should recommend that Coca-Cola launch a ready-to-drink tea in Japan. Since 1981, four notable Japanese companies had entered the tea market. The decision needed to be made quickly and was critical to Grotz's career. For him it was "sink or swim." A success for Coca-Cola would mean career advancement; a failure could result in dire consequences.

Grotz's research and final suggestion would pass through many hands within the Coca-Cola Company. Approval would have to come first from the president of Coca-Cola (Japan). Ultimate approval would come from corporate headquarters in Atlanta, Georgia. Thus, the final decision would rest with Roberto C. Goizeuta, chairman and chief executive officer of the Coca-Cola Company. Grotz mused, Should Coca-Cola enter the tea market in Japan?

The Coca-Cola Company

The Coca-Cola empire was founded in 1886, when John C. Pemberton, an Atlanta, Georgia, pharmacist, developed Coca-Cola, a carbonated soft drink. Following a strategy of international and national expansion, the company, by the late 1980s, was the world's largest producer and distributor of soft drink syrups and concentrates. The company's products were sold through bottlers and fountain wholesalers and distributors in more than 155 countries. Soft drinks generated approximately 81 percent of operating revenues and 96 percent of operating income in 1987 (Exhibit 1 provides summary revenue and income information from 1984 through 1987.)

Coca-Cola operated two business sectors: the North American Business Sector and the International Business Sector. The North American Business Sector was comprised of Coca-Cola USA, Coca-Cola Ltd. (Canadian operations), and Coca-Cola Foods (juice drinks). The International Business Sector had four geographic-oriented groups: Greater Europe, Latin America, Middle and Far East, and Africa.

Japan

Japan, located in the Pacific Ocean, consisted of four main islands—Honshu (mainland), Hokkaido, Kyushu, and Shikoku—covering 145,856 square miles. Population in the late 1980s was around 123 million, of which 75 percent were urban dwellers.

The Japanese economy had improved considerably in the 1980s. Consequently, a growing number of Japanese enjoyed a rising standard of living with an annual income of US$25,000. This led to a boom in consumer spending for both durable and nondurable goods. The yen had been appreciating in value from 1985 to 1987. (See

This case was prepared by Laura Gow, MBA student, under the supervision of Victoria L. Crittenden, associate professor of marketing, Boston College, as the basis for class discussion rather than to illustrate either effective or ineffective handling of a managerial situation. Information was derived from secondary sources. Pseudonyms were used. Revised 1997.

EXHIBIT 1

Operating Revenues and Income
Soft Drink Products

	Revenues	Income
1984	67%	86%
1985	67	86
1986	81	89
1987	81	96

International Operating Revenues and Income
for Soft Drink Products

	Revenues	Income
1984	42	51
1985	42	50
1986	53	75
1987	55	74

Source: Coca-Cola Company annual reports.

EXHIBIT 2   **Average Exchange Rates, Japanese Yen/U.S. Dollar, 1970–87**

Year	Rate
1970	360
1975	297
1977	269
1980	227
1981	221
1982	249
1983	238
1984	238
1985	239
1986	169
1987	145

Exhibit 2 for exchange rates.) Economists were positive about the future, but consumers were guarding their purse strings carefully.

The 1980s Japanese consumer was more concerned with health issues than ever before. This was due in part to an aging population interested in longevity and feeling well. Additionally, it was aided by a desire to be fit and trim. This health trend appeared to be continuing, and possibly gaining in popularity, into the late 1980s. Along with this consumer interest came a proliferation of nutritious food and beverage products.

Japanese Beverage Market.   The Japanese beverage industry was worth US$18 billion by 1987. The market consisted of the following segments:

Colas	10%
Other carbonated drinks	9
Juices	26
Teas	9
Coffees	21
Waters	16
Sports drinks	9

Japanese Tea Market.   Originating in the 15th and 16th centuries when leaders in China began to boil tea leaves in water, tea preparation traditionally had been considered an almost ceremonial event. In the mid-1970s the founder of Ito En Ltd., a packager and wholesaler of dried tea, decided that the future for his company and its current product was limited. As such, Mr. Masanori Honjo decided to follow the trend toward more convenience-oriented products by developing an unsweetened tea packaged in a can. The product was introduced in Japan in 1981. By this time, a canned oolong tea was already available in China.

The ready-to-drink tea segment was comprised of three basic categories of tea: oolong (57 percent of the market), black (31 percent of the market), and green (12 percent of the market). From 1985 to 1987, oolong tea growth had averaged 42 percent annually and black tea growth had averaged 60 percent annually. Rapid growth was expected to continue in the canned black tea market. Western-style tea (tea with milk and/or sugar) was also experiencing strong growth of about 60 percent annually. Tea sold in cans (250 milliliters) for around 100 yen and also in larger PET containers (1,500 milliliters).

Tea, along with other beverages, was sold through grocery stores, convenience stores, restaurants, and vending machines. Grocery stores had experienced an annual average growth rate of 5.1 percent by the middle 1980s (1985 grocery store sales of 4.8 million yen). Convenience stores had an annual average growth rate during this same period of 15.8 percent (1985 convenience store sales of 3.4 million yen). Vending machine sales, which accounted for approximately 50 percent of beverage sales, continued to grow. In fact, a well-placed machine was expected to sell about 10,000 cans of beverage per year, similar to a convenience store. Japan had about 5 million vending machines, with 2 million selling canned drinks. The average drink machine had 20 spots in 250-milliliter or 350-milliliter sizes.

In crowded urban areas, a consumer usually had a choice among many machines and alternative products. Aside from canned drinks, vending machines offered everything from flowers to comic books to lingerie. Companies competed not only in vending machine accessibility, but also in machine appearance and interactive capabilities—a talking or singing machine was not uncommon. A downside to vending machine distribution, however, was vandalism.

The Coca-Cola (Japan) Company

The Coca-Cola (Japan) Company Limited (CCJC) was established in Tokyo in 1957. Since trade regulations prohibited Coca-Cola from expanding to other Japanese locations, company executives focused their attention on making local connections, assessing the competitive environment, and gaining a solid understanding of Japanese culture. This information and knowledge provided a strong foundation for future growth.

In 1961, when the Japanese government enacted trade deregulation policies, CCJC was ready to pursue expansion and unrestricted advertising.

A major part of CCJC's strategy was to form strategic alliances with powerful Japanese corporations. The three most notable partners were Mitsui, Mitsubishi, and Kikkoman. By forming strong relationships with these local bottlers, CCJC was able to reap immediate economies of scale and scope, as well as gain the Japanese consumer confidence and buy-in.

In the 1960s, Coca-Cola's sales in Japan soared, with revenues doubling every year, making Coca-Cola the best-selling soft drink in Japan by 1965. Important to CCJC's revenue figures was the return the company saw in concentrate prices. CCJC made four to five times as much on a gallon of syrup as did its U.S. counterparts. By 1985, CCJC had solidified its dominance in the market, becoming the industry leader in improving quality standards and introducing new products. To establish itself as an integral part of the Japanese lifestyle, CCJC actively promoted cultural, educational, and athletic activities.

CCJC Success. Two factors were thought to have contributed to the company's leadership position: (1) the company's direct marketing approach and (2) the company's distribution system of independent local franchisees. In addition to supplying bottlers with syrups and concentrates, the company provided support in distribution and the entire marketing effort—"from the TV set to the store shelf."

The Japanese market was divided into 17 regions serviced by 17 individual bottlers. (See Exhibit 3 for a geographic view of the market and the company's bottlers.) The direct sales concept (which was pioneered by Coca-Cola in its start-up operations in the United States) had encountered stiff resistance in Japan initially. Traditional Japanese business practices involved several wholesalers. However, the enthusiasm of the bottlers and strong sales of Coca-Cola eventually convinced local retailers of the benefits of the new system. A key element of the distribution system was that it generated activity in the local economy because CCJC's system established partnerships with local businesses. In principle, bottlers acted as independent corporations, sourcing their raw materials locally and completing all aspects of production on-site. The CCJC unified this assembly of disparate players through a carefully crafted strategy of aggressively monitoring all regional operations, creating all marketing strategies, and initiating new product development. By the end of the 1980s, however, CCJC had become worried about the diversification efforts of the bottlers. Non–Coca-Cola brands were accounting for 20 to 40 percent of total annual sales at some of the bottlers.

Although CCJC offered a variety of products (Exhibit 4), three products were Japan's favorites:

- *HI-C.* The HI-C line of products with 50 percent fruit content was introduced in 1973. The product line opened the way for a new fruit juice drink market, and, in the process, helped avert a crisis for Japanese citrus farmers. An overproduction of *mikan,* Japanese tangerines, had caused a serious problem for individual growers and agricultural cooperatives. Coca-Cola had stepped in and bought the bumper crop to produce its HI-C products. This led to a lasting relationship between CCJC and the growers.
- *Georgia.* In 1975, CCJC launched a ready-to-drink coffee, Georgia.[1] Although Japan was projected to become one of the largest canned coffee markets in the world,

---

[1] The name Georgia came from the home state of Coca-Cola's headquarters in the United States.

Exhibit 1–3 Individual Bottler Regions in Japan

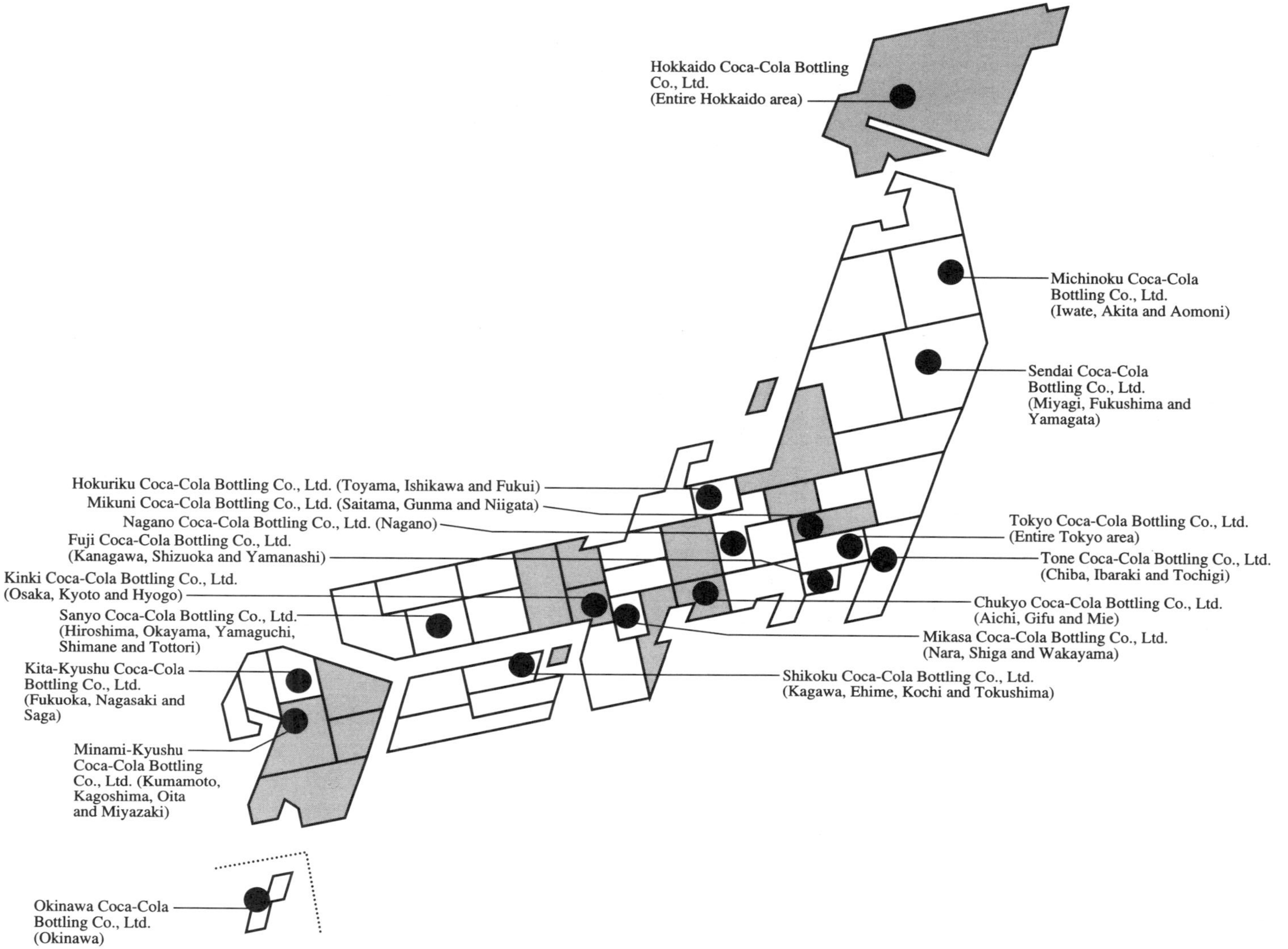

Michinoku Coca-Cola Bottling Co., Ltd. (Iwate, Akita and Aomoni)

Sendai Coca-Cola Bottling Co., Ltd. (Miyagi, Fukushima and Yamagata)

Tokyo Coca-Cola Bottling Co., Ltd. (Entire Tokyo area)

Tone Coca-Cola Bottling Co., Ltd. (Chiba, Ibaraki and Tochigi)

Chukyo Coca-Cola Bottling Co., Ltd. (Aichi, Gifu and Mie)

Mikasa Coca-Cola Bottling Co., Ltd. (Nara, Shiga and Wakayama)

Shikoku Coca-Cola Bottling Co., Ltd. (Kagawa, Ehime, Kochi and Tokushima)

Hokkaido Coca-Cola Bottling Co., Ltd. (Entire Hokkaido area)

Hokuriku Coca-Cola Bottling Co., Ltd. (Toyama, Ishikawa and Fukui)
Mikuni Coca-Cola Bottling Co., Ltd. (Saitama, Gunma and Niigata)
Nagano Coca-Cola Bottling Co., Ltd. (Nagano)
Fuji Coca-Cola Bottling Co., Ltd. (Kanagawa, Shizuoka and Yamanashi)
Kinki Coca-Cola Bottling Co., Ltd. (Osaka, Kyoto and Hyogo)
Sanyo Coca-Cola Bottling Co., Ltd. (Hiroshima, Okayama, Yamaguchi, Shimane and Tottori)
Kita-Kyushu Coca-Cola Bottling Co., Ltd. (Fukuoka, Nagasaki and Saga)

Minami-Kyushu Coca-Cola Bottling Co., Ltd. (Kumamoto, Kagoshima, Oita and Miyazaki)

Okinawa Coca-Cola Bottling Co., Ltd. (Okinawa)

Source: Coca-Cola (Japan) Company.

EXHIBIT 4   CCJC Product Line

Coca-Cola
Coca-Cola Light
Fanta
Sprite
HI-C
Aquarious
Ambasa Water
Georgia Coffee
Real Gold
Mello Yello

CCJC had taken several years to introduce a canned coffee product into the Japanese market. The lack of a canned coffee product had been the source of mild controversy between CCJC and its local Japanese bottlers. Once introduced, the Georgia brand quickly became the leading brand in this very competitive market segment, with 34 percent of the market by 1987. The young Japanese businessman was the primary target for the Georgia brand. The sweet, milky flavor deterred the female consumer, who preferred unsweetened, lower-calorie drinks.

• *Aquarious.* Soon after the 1983 introduction the Aquarius line of isotonic drinks, it became as popular as Georgia and HI-C. Touted as a health drink, it was ideal for replenishing fluid and electrolytes lost through perspiration.

CCJC commanded 90 percent of the cola market, slightly less than 60 percent of the noncola carbonated market, and approximately 10 percent of the remaining drink market. Coca-Cola beverage sales in Japan accounted for 21.5 percent of Coca-Cola's worldwide profits, compared with 18 percent for the United States, with profit per gallon four times higher than in the U.S. Gross sales in Japan were approximately US$195 million. CCJC owned and operated around 750,000 vending machines (accounting for almost 65 percent of canned beverage sales) and distributed to approximately 1 million retail stores and food service outlets. CCJC invested in around 100,000 new vending machines annually at a cost of US$4,000 per machine. Routine replacement was due to technology change and not the machine life, which was around 10 years. (Exhibits 5 and 6 provide select financial information.)

Competition

The soft drink industry was highly competitive, with up to 1,000 new product introductions each year and around 8,000 products in the marketplace. Competitors included producers of other nationally and internationally advertised brands, as well as regional producers and private-label suppliers. Other beverages competed with soft drinks. Advertising and sales promotional programs, the introduction of new packaging and new products, and brand and trademark development protection were important competitive factors. Ito En Ltd., Suntory Ltd., Kirin, Hitachi Zosen Corp., and Asahi Breweries Ltd. were the leading competitors in the tea market.

Ito En Ltd. was the leading Japanese canned tea marketer. The company initiated the canned tea boom in 1981 by marketing the first unsweetened tea in a can. In 1985, it introduced the first can of Japanese green tea, Ryokucha. Ito En spent months per-

EXHIBIT 5   **CCJC Financial Data: Summary of Operations, 1986–87**
(In U.S.$ millions)

	1987	1986
Net operating revenues	$7,658	$6,977
Cost of goods sold	3,633	3,454
Gross profit	4,025	3,523
S,G,&A	2,665	2,446
Provisions for restructured operations and divestment	36	180
Operating income	1,324	897
Interest income	232	154
Equity income	297	208
Other income (deductions)—net	113	152
Gain on sale of stock by former subsidiaries	—	35
Income from continuing operations before income taxes	40	375
Income taxes	1,412	1,405
Income from continuing operations	496	471
	916	934

Source: Coca-Cola Company annual reports.

EXHIBIT 6   **Coca-Cola Company Net Operating Revenues and Operating Income, 1986–87** *(In U.S.$ millions)*

United States	1987	1986
Net operating revenues	$3,459.1	$3,277.9
Operating income	384.5	273.8
Latin America		
Net operating revenues	558.0	555.5
Operating income	153.2	140.8
Europe and Africa		
Net operating revenues	1,709.5	1,628.9
Operating income	508.1	354.6
Pacific and Canada		
Net operating revenues	1,917.0	1,502.4
Operating income	453.3	352.4

Source: Coca-Cola Company annual reports.

fecting systems to manufacture and produce a canned tea that was free from oxidation and did not change color, taste, or aroma even when subjected to drastic temperature changes. While the company's focus was tea, there were rumors that the company had plans to enter the canned tea market.

Suntory Ltd. was Japan's largest distiller. The company was also gaining ground in its nonalcoholic divisions. In 1981, Suntory introduced a canned oolong tea called Tess. By 1987, Suntory held nearly 50 percent of the oolong tea market. Additionally, the company produced colas, green tea, and health tonics. The company planned to enter the canned coffee market by the end of the 1980s.

Kirin was the first to produce a canned black tea, called Afternoon Tea, in 1986. The fifth largest Japanese brewery, Kirin had 50 percent of the Japanese beer market. The company also was one of Japan's leading soft drink producers and marketers with canned soft drink sales of around US$1 billion. Kirin also produced fruit drinks, vitamin-enriched drinks, and sports drinks as well as posting brisk sales in its canned coffee.

Hitachi Zosen Corp. was a "Big Five" shipbuilder in Japan that diversified into biotechnology and developed a new tea from the Chinese tochu tree. In 1987, it introduced this "healthy" unsweetened tea in cans and bottles. For centuries, the Chinese had used the bark of the tochu tree in herbal medicine to treat high blood pressure as well as liver and kidney ailments. The bark was also rich in calcium, iron, and magnesium.

Asahi Breweries Ltd. was the first producer to market a Western-style canned tea with milk and/or sugar. Asahi was also a major player in the canned coffee market.

The Tea Decision

In the early 1970s, a Japanese company began marketing a canned ready-to-drink beverage that contained coffee, milk, sugar, and water. Served cold, it was considered a soft drink under Japanese food laws. For approximately 50 years, Coca-Cola had been looking into coffee-flavored technologies that would enable the canned coffee to be served hot or cold, depending upon the season, from a vending machine. Despite the fact that the technology was available and a sales opportunity existed, it took CCJC five years to arrive at the decision to enter the coffee market. It then took several years to capture a portion of the growing canned coffee market.

Would ready-to-drink tea, like coffee, be a success in the long term, or was it a passing fad? Would the Japanese truly embrace a canned version of their traditional beverage? Arthur Grotz knew this could make or break his career at Coca-Cola (Japan) Company. Should he recommend that Coca-Cola enter the ready-to-drink tea market? What were the pros and cons of this strategic move? Grotz knew that other soft-drink issues were simmering in Japan. For example, how would generic colas impact the Japanese cola market? Was the trend moving toward fruit-flavored drinks? These issues weighed heavily on his thinking. Should his attention be on products other than tea?

Whatever the decision, Grotz needed to present his recommendation to the vice president of marketing next week. What should he do?

Sources

Benjamin, Todd. "Ready-to-Drink Tea Catches On in Japan." *Cable News Network, Inc.,* October 13, 1992.

Beverage World. *Coke's First 100 Years.* Kentucky: Keller International Publishing, 1986.

Casteel, Britt. "Japan's Taste for Canned Tea Growing." *The Daily Yomiuri,* January 6, 1991.

Coca-Cola Company. *Annual Reports.*

Coca-Cola Company. *The Chronicle of Coca-Cola since 1886.*

Coca-Cola Company. Web site information.

Coca-Cola (Japan) Company, Limited. *The Coca-Cola Business in Japan.*

"Consumption of Upmarket Goods Booms in Japan," *Business Asia,* October 22, 1990.

"Drink Makers Read Tea Leaves, Discover Canned Teas are Trend." *Nikkei Weekly,* August 29, 1994.

Eisenstodt, Gale. "Japan's New Business Heroes." *Forbes,* July 4, 1994.

Fukui, Makiko. "At Your Convenience; 24-Hour Services Take Root in Urban Areas." *The Daily Yomiuri,* September 9, 1993.

Hideko, Taguchi. "Tea Reading." *Asia Inc.,* May 1994.

Hoover's Handbook of World Business. *Kirin Brewery Company, Ltd.* 1993.

Japan Economic Newswire. "Breweries Beefing Up Soft Drinks Divisions." March 8, 1991.

Karassawa, Kazuo. "Canned Coffee Sales Regain Two-Digit Growth; Japanese Coffee Sales." *Tea & Coffee Trade Journal,* March 1991.

Kilburn, David. "Pepsi's Challenge: Double Japan Share." *Advertising Age,* December 10, 1990.

Kilburn, David. "Suntory Splashes in Softer Drinks." *Advertising Age,* March 25, 1991.

Killen, Patrick. "Business Talk; Coca-Cola Light Bubbles to No. 2 in Cola Market." *The Daily Yomiuri,* February 20, 1990.

Killen, Patrick. "Coke Chief Sees Japan." *The Daily Yomiuri,* December 21, 1993.

Lin, Diane. "Canned Tea New Battleground in Japanese Food War." *The Reuter Library Report,* July 30, 1992.

Market Reports. "Japan—Health Foods." *1993 National Trade Data Bank,* October 15, 1993.

Mitari, Shin. "The Japanese Beverage Market." *Prepared Foods New Products Annual,* 1991.

Miyatake, Hisa. "Shipbuilder Berths in Tea Market and Sales Soar." *Japan Economic Newswire,* March 12, 1994.

Morris, Kathleen. "The Fizz Is Gone." *Financial World,* February 1, 1994.

Nakayama, Atsushi. "Canada Dry Rights Buy-Up Rattles Bottlers." *Japan Economic Journal,* September 8, 1990.

Nomiyama, Chizu. "Fickle Public Makes Japan Soft Drinks Tough Market to Tap." *The Reuter Library Report,* January 29, 1991.

Pepper, Thomas, Merit Janow, and Jimmy Wheeler. *The Competition Dealing with Japan.* New York: Praeger, 1985.

Reuter Textline. "Japan: Canned Tea New Battleground in Japanese Food War." *Reuter News Service,* August 10, 1992.

Reuter Textline. "Japan: Canned Tea Sales Look Set to Rise Further." *Nikkei Weekly,* October 13, 1990.

Reuter Textline. "Japan: Green Tea Making Comeback in Cans." *Nikkei Weekly,* May 24, 1993.

Reuter Textline. "Japan: Marketing Weekly Spotlight on Marketing and Media Information." *Marketing Week,* April 11, 1991.

Reuter Textline. "Japan: Producers Banking on Strong Sales of Canned Coffee." *Nikkei Weekly,* September 21, 1992.

Reuter Textline. "Japan: Soft-Drink Makers Focus on Blended Tea in Push for Share." *Nikkei Weekly,* February 21, 1994.

Reuter Textline. "Japan: Sugar-Free Tea Enjoys Revival." *Marketing Week,* September 20, 1991.

Stinchecum, Amanda. "The Where and Ware of Hagi." *The New York Times,* July 3, 1988.

The Nikkei Marketing Journal. "Rivals Thirst to Reduce Coca-Cola's Lead; Some Cautious, Other Bold—But All Challengers Are Still Far Behind." *The Japan Economic Journal,* April 27, 1991.

Thomson, Robert. "Setting Out to Get the Coffee Market in the Can." *Financial Times,* December 10, 1990.

Tsukiji, Tatsuro. "Tea Brings in Wave of Beverage Market Profit." *The Japan Economic Journal,* January 19, 1991.

"Unsweetened Soft Drinks Soar on Health Fad." Report from Japan, Inc., 1990.

Watters, Pat. *Coca-Cola.* New York: Doubleday, 1978.

Coca-Cola Company References

Mr. Jean-Michel Bock
Vice President
Coca-Cola International
Pacific Group
PO Drawer 1734
Atlanta, GA 30301

Mr. John Elwood
Assistant to President
Coca-Cola (Japan) Company, Limited
Shibuya PO Box 10
Tokyo 150
Japan

CASE 1–3
BATTERED WOMEN FIGHTING BACK!

Stacey Kabat, executive director and founder of Battered Women Fighting Back!, would always have a vivid recollection of the 1994 Academy Awards. She looked into the glaring lights and saw thousands of heads that resembled bobbing apples. As they received their Oscars for Best Short Documentary, *Defending Our Lives,* the other two filmmakers thanked everyone. Then Stacey said, "Domestic violence is the leading cause of injury to women in the United States, more than rapes, muggings, and automobile accidents combined. Please, we need all your help to stop this."

Stacey's comment was cited the next day in *The Los Angeles Times* as one of the most memorable moments at the Academy Awards. However, Stacey could not allow herself to sit back and enjoy this rare moment of glory. Battered Women Fighting Back!, a human rights organization, had been catapulted into a unique position to nationally frame the issue of domestic violence.

First and foremost, Stacey wanted to stop domestic violence. To do this, however, Stacey and Battered Women Fighting Back! needed funding. Stacey was not a businessperson, but she knew she had a big marketing job on her hands.

Domestic Violence

There were between 2 and 4 million victims of domestic abuse yearly in the United States.[1] Domestic violence was a crime that in most cases involved the assault of a woman by a man who was her spouse or boyfriend. A national crime survey had found that women were the victims of violent crime committed by family members at a rate three times that of men and that a woman was in nine times more danger at home than on the streets. By 1992, domestic violence occurred in one out of four American families.

Domestic violence was a leading cause of birth defects. Studies had even found that violence against women increased during pregnancy. Other statistics showed

- Over 80 percent of violent offenders in prison came from homes with histories of domestic violence. (Men who saw their parents attack each other physically were three times as likely to hit their wives as those who had not seen such violence at home, and sons of the most violent parents beat their wives at a rate 1,000 times greater than the sons of nonviolent parents).
- Sixty-three percent of boys under the age of 18 in prison for murder were jailed for killing their mother's abuser.

---

[1] This range was cited from "Domestic Violence: Help and Resources for Battered Women." *The Boston Parents' Paper,* October 1994. The Commonwealth Fund in New York reported that 3.9 million women had admitted being beaten by a husband or male friend during a 12-month period. This translated to a woman being beaten somewhere in the U.S. every nine seconds.

* The video for this case may be available at your local library.

This case was prepared by Jennifer Fraser, MBA student, and Victoria L. Crittenden, associate professor of marketing, Boston College, as the basis for class discussion rather than to illustrate either effective or ineffective handling of a managerial situation. Research assistance was provided by Stephanie Hillstrom, Boston College. Revised 1997.

- Seventy percent of men who abused their female partners also abused their children. (As violence against women became more severe and frequent, children experienced a 300 percent increase in physical violence and 30 percent of children from violent households became abusive parents.)
- Nationally, 50 percent of all homeless women and children were on the streets because of violence in the home.
- Sixty-three percent of abused women permanently left their partner.
- Seventy-three percent of women treated medically for abusive injuries were separated, single, or divorced, and 35 percent of hospital emergency room visits by women related to battering.
- Ninety-two percent of abused women did not tell their medical doctors.
- Businesses lost $3 to $5 billion yearly due to absenteeism from work because of domestic abuse. (This included women who were battered and men who battered and had to take time away from work for court appearances, etc.) Around 70 percent of battered women were employed when abused.
- Abusive men were as likely to be educated, middle-class, or employed as they were to be uneducated, poor, or unemployed.
- Fifty percent of abusive men were between 26 and 35 years of age, 26 percent were between 36 and 50 years old.
- Domestic violence against women was still considered acceptable in many countries.
- There were three times as many animal shelters in the United States as there were shelters for battered women and their children.

While the concentration of domestic violence occurred in women between the ages 15 to 35, domestic abuse crossed all monetary, geographic, and cultural stratospheres. (Exhibit 1.)

Awareness. Secretary of Health and Human Services Donna Shalala had called for a national awakening to "domestic terrorism," the "unacknowledged epidemic" in America.[2] During the 1990s, the domestic violence issue was magnified on a national and international scale by incidents such as those involving Charles Stuart in Boston, Massachusetts, and O.J. Simpson in Los Angeles, California.

The murder of Carol Stuart made international headlines in October 1989 when a white man, Charles Stuart, alleged that he and his pregnant wife had been shot by a black man following Lamaze classes at Beth Israel Hospital in Boston, Massachusetts. All evidence, however, suggested that Charles Stuart killed his wife. Stuart committed suicide in 1990 when the evidence became overwhelming to accuse him of first-degree murder.

The murders of Nicole Brown Simpson and Ronald Goldman in 1994 created chaos, confusion, and doubt among many communities and brought new attention to the issue of domestic violence. Several allegations against O.J. Simpson by Nicole Brown Simpson detailing domestic violence for several years had been recorded. Nicole Brown Simpson's telephone calls, however, did not instigate police investigation or action because the issue of domestic violence was considered a "private matter" and one that involved only a "certain population." As a result of the Nicole Brown

---

[2] Speech delivered before the American Medical Association (AMA) National Conference on Family Violence, Washington, D.C., March 11, 1994.

EXHIBIT 1   Victim Description

Demographics

Sex:	Female
Age:	15–35 years old
Income:	All levels
Occupation:	All types
Education:	All levels
Ethnic background:	All
Family life cycle:	All
Household size:	Any size

Psychographics

Social class:	All classes
Personality:	Compulsive

Geographic

Region:	All regions
City size:	All sizes

Simpson case, some prior negative conceptions and assumptions about individuals and families involved in domestic violence were challenged.

Legislation/Business Support. As early as 1948, The Universal Declaration of Human Rights, adopted by the United Nations, assured life, liberty, and security of person as well as freedom from torture and other cruel, inhuman, or degrading treatment. In June 1993, the United Nations World Conference on Human Rights was held. Additionally, the Global Tribunal on Violations of Women's Human Rights was held in 1993. This conference was sponsored by the Center for Women's Global Leadership at Douglass College in New Jersey. The aim of the conference was to draw international attention to gender-driven crimes.

The Violence against Women Act was part of the 1994 national government's crime bill. This act stipulated that gender-based crimes violated a woman's civil rights. This made women eligible for compensatory relief and damages. The act authorized $1.8 billion over five years to aid police, prosecutors, women's shelters, and community-prevention programs. The sponsor of the act was U.S. Representative Connie Morella from Maryland, who also sought $1 million to establish a national domestic violence hotline that would be operated 24 hours a day in more than two dozen languages. The U.S. Congress had also designated October as Domestic Violence Awareness Month.

A nonprofit organization, the Advertising Council, selected domestic violence as one of 28 national pro bono projects for 1994. This resulted in roughly $20 million in free ads. Corporations including DuPont, Ryka, Liz Claiborne Inc., and Polaroid had identified domestic violence as a major area of social responsibility as well.

DuPont offered workshops on spouse/child abuse and volunteers operated 24-hour rape hotlines. Ryka, a women's athletic shoe company, established the ROSE Foundation to end violence against women. The company pledged 7 percent of pretax earnings to the foundation. Also, along with Lady Foot Locker, the Ryka ROSE Foundation made grants to rape crisis centers and prevention programs. Liz Claiborne Inc.

supported the Women's Work Program, which consisted of community-based public art projects designed to heighten awareness of domestic violence. Polaroid donated $42,000 to seven battered women's shelters in Massachusetts as well as offering self-image groups for battered employees.

Intervention Resources. At the beginning of 1993, there were almost 550,000 U.S. charities eligible to receive tax-deductible donations.[3] This was an almost 50 percent increase since 1985 and a 71 percent increase since 1980. Included in these charitable organizations were intervention resources to assist victims of domestic violence.

Intervention resources were comprised of five common services. Battered women service providers could offer one or any combination of intervention resources. The five common resources were

- *Shelter.* This resource sought to provide a safe haven for the battered woman and her children. This was considered one of the most costly services provided by an intervention resource.

- *Hotline.* It was found that many battered women made their first contact or call for help via the crisis telephone line. The hotline volunteer had to make a quick judgment as to whether the caller was in immediate danger and/or needed emergency medical attention. Hotlines were operated 24 hours a day, seven days a week.

- *Emergency medical assistance.* This was a referral service in which the battered woman was referred to a hospital emergency room or private physician known by the referral service to be highly qualified to administer to a battered woman.

- *Financial assistance.* This program provided financial assistance to assist the battered woman with personal and children's needs and/or to aid the woman in meeting her needs for entering the work force.

- *Support services.* This all-encompassing program could provide counseling, legal assistance, employment information, child care, and other types of services.

Exhibit 2 lists intervention resources in the greater Boston, Massachusetts, area. The services offered by these organizations varied from counseling, support groups, and shelters to education and lobbying.

Battered women and their children could call the Brookline Women's Shelter in emergency situations. While many of the women were battered, many were homeless. This shelter did not receive any outside funding. Thus, the organization sheltered women and children on a temporary basis when funds allowed. Additionally, the shelter assisted the women and children in finding other places to go.

At Community Services for Women, one-half of the women who called were battered. The other half were substance abusers. The service counseled drug abusers and referred battered women to Battered Women Fighting Back! and/or RESPOND.

RESPOND offered counseling, support groups, and shelter for battered women. The organization was funded privately and by the Massachusetts Department of Social Services.

---

[3] In 1993, *Financial World* identified eight characteristics sought by grant givers when selecting charitable organizations to target their giving: (1) a focused mission, (2) results that could be evaluated, (3) inspired and dedicated leadership, (4) the organization's responding to a proven community need, (5) a board of directors that understood its role and reflected the diversity of those served, (6) money spent on programs exceeded administration and fund-raising costs, (7) training for volunteers and efforts to develop leadership skills, and (8) innovative, creative programs.

EXHIBIT 2 Domestic Violence Help Resources in the Greater Boston, Massachusetts Area

Alternative House
Asian Women's Project
Battered Women Fighting Back!
Battered Women's Hotline
Battered Women's Resources
Brockton Family and Community Resources
Brookline Women's Shelter
Casa Myrna Vasquez
Community Services for Women
Daybreak
Domestic Violence Program
Dove House
Elizabeth Stone House
FINEX House
Harbor Me
Help for Abused Women and Their Children
Independence House
Mary Forman House of CMV
Massachusetts Coalition of Battered Women Service Groups
My Sister's Place
Network for Battered Lesbians
New Bedford Battered Women's Project
New Hope Inc.
Our Sister's Place
Rosie's Place
Renewal House
RESPOND
Second Step Inc.
Services Against Family Violence
South Shore Women's Center
Transition House
Waltham Battered Women's Support Committee
Womansplace
Women's Center
Women's Crisis Center
Women's Protective Services
Women's Resource Center

Source: "Domestic Violence: Help and Resources for Battered Women," *The Boston Parents' Paper,* October 1994, p. 53.

The Massachusetts Coalition of Battered Women's Service Groups was neither a shelter nor a counseling service. Rather, the group provided referrals to shelters and counseling. The group's primary focus was lobbying for laws for battered women's rights.

Battered women and children could go to Services Against Family Violence for one-on-one counseling and support groups. The women who went there were emotionally and/or physically abused. This service had court advocacy in Woburn, Massachusetts and Malden, Massachusetts, and an advocate in the Malden police station. A 24-hour hotline and legal referrals were offered. Shelter was not provided, but the group did refer women to shelters.

At the national level, the National Resource Center on Domestic Violence (NRC) located at the Pennsylvania Coalition against Domestic Violence in Harrisburg, Pennsylvania, was funded in 1993 through a three-year grant by the U.S. Department of Health and Human Services. The NRC's goal was to strengthen existing support systems for battered women and their children in addition to identifying and filling information and resource gaps that tended to perpetuate domestic violence in U.S. communities. Three other national resource centers included Battered Women's Justice Project in Duluth, Minnesota, Resource Center on Child Protection and Custody in Reno, Nevada, and Health Resource Center on Domestic Violence in San Francisco, California.

In addition to organized resource groups, there were local events to raise awareness and funds for battered women's programs. One example was the Jane Doe Safety Fund's 10K Walk for Women's Safety. This walk served to increase domestic violence awareness, as well as raising funds for programs.

Battered Women Fighting Back!

Battered Women Fighting Back! (BWFB!) was a Boston, Massachusetts-based education and advocacy group that addressed the severity of domestic violence as a human rights violation. Its primary charge was to create and disseminate educational programs designed to eradicate domestic violence in society and to promote human rights for everyone.

Begun as both a prison support group for battered women who had defended their lives and a diverse grass-roots task force dedicated to raising community awareness on domestic violence, BWFB! was incorporated in Boston, Massachusetts in November 1992. BWFB!'s official 501(c)(3) agency status[4] was the culmination of work performed for years by over 100 volunteers dedicated to freeing the "Framingham Eight."[5] The goal of the new organization was to heighten community awareness around the indisputable fact that domestic violence was a direct violation of a person's fundamental human right as stated in the Universal Declaration of Human Rights. Stacey Kabat was the visionary and driving force behind BWFB!

In 1994, BWFB! operated on what Stacey referred to as "a shoestring" budget of approximately $150,000. The agency solicited and received funding from individual donors (usually people committed to the domestic violence cause), corporations (e.g., Reebok and Aveda), foundations (e.g., The Public Welfare Foundation), and sponsorship/events. Exhibit 3 breaks down sources of solicited funds.

The program was run by three full-time employees, three part-time staff members, and a group of volunteers. Volunteers answered the phones, did administrative work, networked, and/or assisted in writing grant proposals. Essentially, volunteers did whatever they were capable of doing at the time.

Stacey Kabat.   Stacey Kabat was the woman behind BWFB! whose spectrum of experience helped create the agency. Stacey was the daughter and granddaugher of battered women.

---

[4] Organizations with this status were charities that accepted tax-deductible donations. The organizations had to submit Form 990s to the IRS yearly, which detailed their finances.

[5] The Framingham Eight were eight women who had become famous for their cases involving the killing of their batterers. The cases became landmark political and social cases as it was the first item a Massachusetts governor had proposed pardoning prisoners based on evidence that the woman was a victim of battering. Each of the eight women testified that her partner abused her to the point that she feared for her own life and, in effect, killed in self-defense. As of June 1994, four of the eight were freed on parole, two were granted commutations, one persuaded a judge to revise her sentence, and one remained in jail.

EXHIBIT 3   Sources of Funding

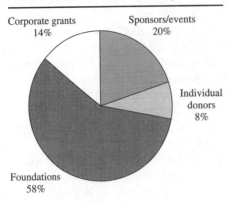

Corporate grants
14%

Sponsors/events
20%

Individual
donors
8%

Foundations
58%

Stacey began her human rights work by establishing an Amnesty International Campus Network while at Bates College in Maine. She later traveled to London to work for the International Secretariat. She worked for an anti-apartheid organization, IDAF, transcribing radio broadcasts out of southern Africa, and visited families in refugee camps in the Middle East. Upon returning to the United States, Stacey worked for two years at the Renewal House, a shelter for battered women in Roxbury, Massachusetts. Later, through her work at MCI–Framingham with battered women and substance abusers, Stacey and a group of eight women incarcerated for defending themselves from their batterers (the Framingham Eight) founded BWFB!. The organization was intended initially as a support group for women imprisoned for killing their batterers.

Local and National Recognition.   Both Stacey Kabat and the BWFB! agency had received local and national recognition. Stacey and her two other film comrades from Cambridge Documentary Films had won the 1994 Academy Award for Best Documentary for *Defending Our Lives*. The documentary exposed the severity of domestic violence in the United States. Along with winning a prized award, Stacey had made many Hollywood connections. Her office boasted many pictures of Stacey with such celebrities as Glenn Close, Angela Bassett, Nicole Kidman, and Steven Spielberg. The Academy Award, however, was not BWFB!'s only claim to fame. Stacey Kabat had won the Reebok Human Rights Award in 1992, and BWFB! was named one of "America's Best Run Charities" in 1993 by *Financial World*. As well, BWFB!'s documentation and publication of domestic violence homicides in Massachusetts had led Massachusetts Governor William Weld and Lieutenant Governor Paul Cellucci, in 1992, to declare a "state of emergency" in response to the ever-increasing cases of domestic violence.

Existing Violence Prevention Program.   The theme of BWFB!'s violence prevention program was "Peace in the World Begins at Home." The name of the program was based on the belief that everyone could help stop domestic violence if given the proper tools and information. The program was designed as a public awareness/education tool designed to both prevent and stop domestic violence by

1. Shattering myths about domestic violence.
2. Identifying warning signs.
3. Encouraging help for those who were victims of such violence.

Exhibit 4   Contents of the Booklet *Domestic Violence: The Facts*

Since receiving the 1992 Reebok Human Rights Award for my work on domestic violence I have created a grassroots public education campaign entitled 'Domestic Violence: The Facts' geared toward heightening cross-cultural awareness, providing tools for intervention and enlisting greater community involvement.

Stacey Kabat

Contained within *Domestic Violence: The Facts* you will find

1. Statistics
2. Myths and Facts
3. Controlling Behaviors Warning List
4. Violence Wheel
5. Cycle of Domestic Violence
6. Non-Violence Wheel
7. Basic Suggestions for Offering Help
8. Personalized Safety Plan
9. Excerpts from the Universal Declaration of Human Rights
10. Hotline Numbers
11. Bibliography and Resources

The materials for the "Peace in the World Begins at Home" program included the 1994 award-winning documentary *Defending Our Lives* and a booklet *Domestic Violence: The Facts*. (Exhibit 4 shows the contents of the booklet.) These items could be disseminated to places such as high schools, universities, places of worship, physician's offices, libraries, or any number of public places.

Current Situation

In June 1994, Stacey Kabat knew that the issue of domestic violence was in the public sphere. While telephone logs were not kept, Stacey felt certain that inquiries and calls had surged in the past few months. Requests for educational information and materials for awareness programs had quadrupled. Stacey had to capitalize on this level of interest. How could she most effectively obtain funding to distribute BWFB!'s materials and implement, worldwide, the "Peace in the World Begins at Home" program? While other resources were available for victims of domestic violence, Stacey felt that BWFB! was unique.

Stacey pondered her many marketing challenges:

- First and foremost, how could she get information to the people who needed it most?
- Could she market BWFB!'s idea and frame domestic violence as a human rights violation—not "just a women's issue"—to the public?
- Could she obtain funding for resources and education for domestic violence educational programs across the United States if not the world?
- Where should she start with each of these challenges?
- What did she need to do?

Sources

"Domestic Violence: Help and Resources for Battered Women." *The Boston Parents' Paper,* October 1994, p. 53.

Engelken, Cort. "Fighting the Costs of Spouse Abuse." *Personnel Journal,* March 1987, pp. 31–34.

Frum, David. "Women Who Kill." *Forbes,* January 18, 1993, pp. 86–87.

Giobbe, Dorothy. "Publicizing Domestic Abuse." *Editor & Publisher,* December 18, 1993, p. 13, 45.

Gold, Jacqueline S. "Finding Gems among the Rhinestones." *Financial World,* August 3, 1993, pp. 46–58.

Kessler, Hannah. "Washington Watch." *Working Woman,* June 1993, p. 16.

Marmon, Lucretia. "Domestic Violence: The Cost to Business." *Working Woman,* April 1994, pp. 17–18.

Miller, Cyndee. "Tapping Into Women's Issues Is Potent Way to Reach Market." *Marketing News,* December 6, 1993, pp. 1, 13.

National Resource Center on Domestic Violence. Harrisburg, PA.

Nichols, Paula. "Reaching the Compassionate Consumer." *American Demographics,* November 1993, pp. 26–27.

Sabatino, Frank. "Hospitals Cope with America's New Family Value." *Hospitals,* November 5, 1992, pp. 24–30.

Shalala, Donna E. "Domestic Terrorism." *Vital Speeches of the Day,* May 15, 1994, pp. 450–53.

"Too Much of It About." *The Economist,* July 16, 1994, p. 25.

"When Did You Stop Beating Your Wife? After Seeing All Those Ads, Doubtless." *Adweek,* August 1, 1994, p. 17.

Kevin Cage, general manager of Wind Technology, sat in his office on a Friday afternoon watching the snow fall outside his window. It was January 1991 and he knew that during the month ahead he would have to make some difficult decisions regarding the future of his firm, Wind Technology. The market for the wind profiling radar systems that his company designed had been developing at a much slower rate than he had anticipated.

Wind Technology

During Wind Technology's 10-year history, the company had produced a variety of weather-related radar and instrumentation. In 1986, the company condensed its product mix to include only wind-profiling radar systems. Commonly referred to as wind profilers, these products measure wind and atmospheric turbulence for weather forecasting, detection of wind direction at NASA launch sites, and other meteorological applications (i.e., at universities and other scientific monitoring stations). Kevin had felt that this consolidation would position the company as a leader in what he anticipated to be a high-growth market with little competition.

Wind Technology's advantages over Unisys, the only other key player in the wind-profiling market, included the following: (1) The company adhered stringently to specifications and quality production. (2) Wind Technology had the technical expertise to provide full system integration. This allowed customers to order either basic components or a full system, including software support. (3) Wind Technology's staff of meteorologists and atmospheric scientists provided the customer with sophisticated support, including operation and maintenance training and field assistance. (4) Finally, Wind Technology had devoted all of its resources to its wind-profiling business. Kevin believed that the market would perceive this as an advantage over a large conglomerate like Unisys.

Wind Technology customized each product for individual customers as the need arose: the total system could cost a customer from $400,000 to $5 million. Various governmental entities, such as the Department of Defense, NASA, and state universities, had consistently accounted for about 90 percent of Wind Technology's sales. In lieu of a field sales force, Wind Technology relied on top management and a team of engineers to call on prospective and current customers. Approximately $105,000 of their annual salaries was charged to a direct selling expense.

The Problem

The consolidation strategy that the company had undertaken in 1986 was partly due to the company's being purchased by Vaitra, a high-technology European firm. Wind Technology's ability to focus on the wind-profiling business had been made possible

This case was prepared by Ken Manning, Gonzaga University, and Jakki Mohr, University of Colorado at Boulder. This case is intended for use as a basis for class discussion rather than to illustrate either effective or ineffective administrative decision making. Some data are disguised. Copyright © by Jakki Mohr 1990. All rights reserved.

by Vaitra's financial support. However, since 1986 Wind Technology had shown little commercial success, and due to low sales levels, the company was experiencing severe cash flow problems. Kevin knew that Wind Technology could not continue to meet payroll much longer. Also, he had been informed that Vaitra was not willing to pour more money into Wind Technology. Kevin estimated that he had from 9 to 12 months (until the end of 1991) in which to implement a new strategy with the potential to improve the company's cash flow. The new strategy was necessary to enable Wind Technology to survive until the wind-profiler market matured. Kevin and other industry experts anticipated that it would be two years until the wind-profiling market achieved the high growth levels that the company had initially anticipated.

One survival strategy that Kevin had in mind was to spin off and market component parts used in making wind profilers. Initial research indicated that, of all the wind-profiling system's component parts, the high-voltage power supply (HVPS) had the greatest potential for commercial success. Furthermore, Kevin's staff on the HVPS product had demonstrated knowledge of the market. Kevin felt that by marketing the HVPS, Wind Technology could reap incremental revenues, with very little addition to fixed costs. (Variable costs would include the costs of making and marketing the HVPS. The accounting department had estimated that production costs would run approximately 70 percent of the selling price, and that 10 percent of other expenses—such as top management direct-selling expenses—should be charged to the HVPS.)

High-Voltage Power Supplies

For a vast number of consumer and industrial products that require electricity, the available voltage level must be transformed to different levels and types of output. The three primary types of power supplies include linears, switchers, and converters. Each type manipulates electrical current in terms of the type of current (AC or DC) and/or the level of output (voltage). Some HVPS manufacturers focus on producing a standardized line of power supplies, while others specialize in customizing power supplies to the user's specifications.

High-voltage power supplies vary significantly in size and level of output. Small power supplies with relatively low levels of output (under 3 kV)[1] are used in communications equipment. Medium-sized power supplies that produce an output between 3 and 10 kV are used in a wide range of products, including radars and lasers. Power supplies that produce output greater than 10 kV are used in a variety of applications, such as high-powered X-rays and plasma-etching systems.

Background on Wind Technology's HVPS

One of Wind Technology's corporate strategies was to control the critical technology (major component parts) of its wind-profiling products. Management felt that this control was important since the company was part of a high-technology industry in which confidentiality and innovation were critical to each competitor's success. This strategy also gave Wind Technology a differential advantage over its major competitors, all of whom depended on a variety of manufacturers for component parts. Wind Technology had successfully developed almost all of the major component parts and the software for the wind profiler, yet the development of the power supply had been problematic.

---

[1] V (kilovolt): 1,000 volts.

To adhere to the policy of controlling critical technology in product design (rather than purchasing an HVPS from an outside supplier), Wind Technology management had hired Anne Ladwig and her staff of HVPS technicians to develop a power supply for the company's wind-profiling systems. Within six months of joining Wind Technology, Anne and her staff had completed development of a versatile power supply which could be adapted for use with a wide variety of equipment. Some of the company's wind-profiling systems required up to 10 power supplies, each modified slightly to carry out its role in the system.

Kevin Cage had delegated the responsibility of investigating the sales potential of the company's HVPS to Anne Ladwig since she was very familiar with the technical aspects of the product and had received formal business training while pursuing an MBA. Anne had determined that Wind Technology's HVP could be modified to produce levels of output between 3 and 10 kV. Thus, it seemed natural that if the product was brought to market, Wind Technology should focus on applications in this range of output. Wind Technology also did not have the production capabilities to compete in the high-volume, low-voltage segment of the market, nor did the company have the resources and technical expertise to compete in the high-output (+ 10 kV) segment.

The Potential Customer

Power supplies in the 3–10-kV range could be used to conduct research, to produce other products, or to place as a component into other products such as lasers. Thus, potential customers could include research labs, large end users, OEMs, or distributors. Research labs each used an average of three power supplies; other types of customers ordered a widely varying quantity.

HVPS users were demanding increasing levels of reliability, quality, customization, and system integration. *System integration* refers to the degree to which other parts of a system are dependent upon the HVPS for proper functioning, and the extent to which these parts are combined into a single unit or piece of machinery.

Anne had considered entering several HVPS market segments in which Wind Technology could reasonably compete. She had estimated the domestic market potential of these segments at $237 million. To evaluate these segments, Anne had compiled growth forecasts for the year ahead and had evaluated each segment in terms of the anticipated level of customization and system integration demanded by the market. Anne felt that the level of synergy between Wind Technology and the various segments was also an important consideration in selecting a target market. Exhibit 1 summarizes this information. Anne believed that if the product was produced, Wind Technology's interests would be best served by selecting only one target market on which to concentrate initially.

Competition

To gather competitive information, Anne contacted five HVPS manufacturers. She found that the manufacturers varied significantly in terms of size and marketing strategy. (See Exhibit 2.) Each listed a price in the $5,500–$6,500 range on power supplies with the same features and output levels as the HVPS that had been developed for Wind Technology. After she spoke with these firms, Anne had the feeling that Wind Technology could offer the HVPS market superior levels of quality, reliability, technical expertise, and customer support. She optimistically believed that a one-half percent market share objective could be achieved the first year.

EXHIBIT 1   HVPS Market Segments in the 3–10-kV Range

Application	Forecasted Annual Growth (%)	Level of Customization/ Level of System Integration*	Synergy Rating**	Percentage of $237 Million Power Supply Market***
General/univ. laboratory	5.40%	Medium/medium	3	8%
Lasers	11.00	Low/medium	4	10
Medical equipment	10.00	Medium/medium	3	5
Microwave	12.00	Medium/high	4	7
Power modulators	3.00	Low/low	4	25
Radar systems	11.70	Low/medium	5	12
Semiconductor	10.10	Low/low	3	23
X-ray systems	8.60	Medium/high	3	10

* The level of customization and system integration generally in demand within each of the applications is defined as low, medium, or high.
** Synergy ratings are based on a scale of 1 to 5; 1 is equivalent to a very low level of synergy and 5 is equivalent to a very high level of synergy. These subjective ratings are based on the amount of similarities between the wind-profiling industry and each application.
*** Percentages total 100 percent of the $237 million market in which Wind Technology anticipated it could compete.
Note: This list of applications is not all-inclusive.

Promotion

If Wind Technology entered the HVPS market, they would require a hard-hitting, thorough promotional campaign to reach the selected target market. Three factors made the selection of elements in the promotion mix especially important to Wind Technology: (1) Wind Technology's poor cash flow, (2) the lack of a well-developed marketing department, and (3) the need to generate incremental revenue from sales of the HVPS at a minimum cost. In fact, a rule of thumb used by Wind Technology was that all mar-

EXHIBIT 2   Competitor Profile (3–10-kV range)

Company	Gamma	Glassman	Kaiser	Maxwell*	Spellman
Approximate annual sales	$2 million	$7.5 million	$3 million		$7 million
Market share	1.00%	3.00%	1.50%		2.90%
Price**	$5,830	$5,590	$6,210	$5,000–$6,000	$6,360
Delivery	12 weeks	10 weeks	10 weeks	8 weeks	12 weeks
Product customization	No	Medium	Low	Medium	Low
System integration experience	Low	Low	Low	Medium	Low
Customer targets	Gen. lab.	Laser	Laser	Radar	Capacitors
	Space	Medical	Medical	Power mod.	Gen. lab.
	Univ. lab.	X-ray	Microwave	X-ray	Microwave
			Semiconductor	Medical equip.	X-ray

*Maxwell was in the final stages of product development and stated that the product would be available in the spring. Maxwell anticipated that the product would call in the $5,000–$6,000 range.
**Price quoted for an HVPS with the same specification as the "standard" model developed by Wind Technology.

keting expenditures should be about 9 to 10 percent of sales. Kevin and Anne were contemplating the use of the following elements:

1. Collateral Material.

Sales literature, brochures, and data sheets are necessary to communicate the product benefits and features to potential customers. These materials are designed to be (1) mailed to customers as part of direct mail campaigns or in response to customer requests, (2) given away at trade shows, and (3) left behind after sales presentations.

Because no one in Wind Technology was an experienced copywriter, Anne and Kevin considered hiring a marketing communications agency to write the copy and to design the layout of the brochures. This agency would also complete the graphics (photographs and artwork) for the collateral material. The cost for 5,000 pieces (including the 10 percent markup for the agency) was estimated to be $5.50 each.

2. Public Relations.

Kevin and Anne realized that one very cost-efficient tool of promotion is publicity. They contemplated sending out new-product announcements to a variety of trade journals whose readers were part of Wind Technology's new target market. By using this tool, interested readers could call or write to Wind Technology, and the company could then send the prospective customers collateral material. The drawback of relying too heavily on this element was very obvious to Kevin and Anne—the editors of the trade journals could choose not to print Wind Technology's product announcements if their new product was not deemed newsworthy.

The cost of using this tool would include the time necessary to write the press release and the expense of mailing the release to the editors. Direct costs were estimated by Wind Technology to be $500.

3. Direct Mail.

Kevin and Anne were also contemplating a direct mail campaign. The major expenditure for this option would be buying a list of prospects to whom the collateral material would be mailed. Such lists usually cost around $5,000, depending upon the number of names and the list quality. Other costs would include postage and the materials mailed. These costs were estimated to be $7,500 for a mailing of 1,500.

4. Trade Shows.

The electronics industry had several annual trade shows. If they chose to exhibit at one of these trade shows, Wind Technology would incur the cost of a booth, the space at the show, and the travel and incidental costs of the people attending the show to staff the booth. Kevin and Anne estimated these costs at approximately $50,000 for the exhibit, space, and materials, and $50,000 for a staff of five people to attend.

5. Trade Journal Advertising.

Kevin and Anne also contemplated running a series of ads in trade journals. Several journals they considered are listed in Exhibit 3, along with circulation, readership, and cost information.

6. Personal Selling.

    a. Telemarketing (inbound/inside sales).[2] Kevin and Anne also considered hiring a technical salesperson to respond to HVPS product inquiries generated by prod-

---

[2] *Inbound* refers to calls that potential customers make to Wind Technology, rather than *outbound,* in which Wind Technology calls potential customers (i.e., solicits sales).

EXHIBIT 3   **Trade Publications**

Trade Publication	Editorial	Cost per Color Insertion (1 page)	Circulation
Electrical Manufacturing	For purchasers and users of power supplies, transformers, and other electrical products.	$4,077	35,168 nonpaid
Electronic Component News	For electronics OEMs. Products addressed include work stations, power sources, chips, etc.	$6,395	110,151 nonpaid
Electronic Manufacturing News	For OEMs in the industry of providing manufacturing and contracting of components, circuits, and systems.	$5,075	25,000 nonpaid
Design News	For design OEMs covering components, systems, and materials.	$8,120	170,033 nonpaid
Weatherwise	For meteorologists covering imaging, radar, etc.	$1,040	10,186 paid

Note: This is a partial list of applicable trade publications. Standard Rate and Data Service lists other possible publications.

uct announcements, direct mail, and advertising. This person's responsibilities would include answering phone calls, prospecting, sending out collateral material, and following up with potential customers. The salary and benefits for one individual would be about $50,000.

b. Field sales. The closing of sales for the HVPS might require some personal selling at the customer's location, especially if Wind Technology pursued the customized option. Kevin and Anne realized that potentially this would provide them with the most incremental revenue, but it also had the potential to be the most costly tool. Issues such as how many salespeople to hire, where to position them in the field (geographically), and so on, were major concerns. Salary plus expenses and benefits for an outside salesperson were estimated to be about $80,000.

Decisions

As Kevin sat in his office and perused the various facts and figures, he knew that he would have to make some quick decisions. He sensed that the decision about whether or not to proceed with the HVPS spin-off was risky, but he felt that to not do something to improve the firm's cash flow was equally risky. Kevin also knew that if he decided to proceed with the HVPS, there were a number of segments in that market in which Wind Technology could position its HVPS. He mulled over which segment appeared to be a good fit for Wind Technology's abilities (given Anne's recommendation that a choice of one segment would be best). Finally, Kevin was concerned that if they entered the HVPS market, that promotion for their product would be costly, further exacerbating the cash flow situation. He knew that promotion would be necessary, but the exact mix of elements would have to be designed with financial constraints in mind.

CASE 1–5
THE METROPOLITAN MUSEUM OF ART

The New York Metropolitan Museum of Art, or Met, ended the 1990–1991 fiscal year with an operating deficit of $2 million. The deficit occurred in part because of decreases in auxiliary revenue, increases in operation expenditures, and decreases in admissions revenue. Even though the base museum attendance figures exceeded those of previous years, the absence of large-scale ticketed exhibitions, or "blockbusters," curtailed admissions revenue in 1990. During 1991, however, admissions revenues increased due to rising admission prices and the return of large-scale exhibitions.

The Met is dependent on external sources of revenue including interest on endowments, gifts, governmental appropriations, and grants as well as internal sources of revenue from merchandising operations, auditorium rental, parking garage fees, restaurants, admissions, memberships, royalties, and fees. Operating expenses include the costs of the curatorial departments, educational programs, libraries, and public information programs; costs associated with development including marketing research, stocking merchandise inventories for auxiliary operations; and various additional administrative costs.[1] Because total expenditures are rising at a faster rate than total revenues, future deficits are predicted. Management of the museum must find creative and effective ways to sustain financial stability.

History

The state of New York established the museum on April 13, 1870, by granting a charter to a group forming a corporation in the name of the Metropolitan Museum of Art. The corporation was formed for the purpose of "establishing and maintaining in the city of New York a museum and library of art, of encouraging and developing the study of the fine arts, and the application of arts to manufacturing and practical life, of advancing the general knowledge of kindred subjects, and, to that end, of furnishing popular instruction and recreation."[2] The mission remains unchanged to date with one exception—the word "recreation" has been removed.[3]

City Support

The city of New York owns the building housing the museum, but the collections are the property of the corporation operating the Met. The city continues to appropriate funds to the museum to be used for maintaining the building as well as providing utilities at no charge to the Metropolitan. The allocations in 1991 totaled $15,633,609, which is 9.3 percent of the total operating revenue for the year; however, the allocations are increasing at a decreasing rate due to the fiscal instability of the city of New York. A history of support from the city of New York is included in the five-year summary shown in Exhibit 1.

This case was prepared by Marilyn M. Helms, Paula J. Haynes, and Tammy L. Swenson of the University of Tennessee at Chatanooga. This case is intended for classroom discussion only, not to depict effective handling of administrative situations. All rights reserved to the authors.

Collections

The Met is a nonprofit, tax-exempt [501(c)(3)] organization located on the east side of Central Park. Museum collections include ancient and modern art from Egypt, Greece, Rome, the Near and Far East, pre-Columbian cultures, and the United States. Exhibit 2 shows the Met floor plan. The Cloisters, a branch museum, houses the European medieval art collection. Opened in 1938, this gallery is located in Fort Tryon Park on the far north tip of Manhattan Island. The structure is constructed from parts of five European monasteries. The land and the building were donated to the city of New York and much of the art within was donated by John D. Rockefeller, Jr.[4] (See Exhibit 3.)

Facilities

The museum consists of many gallery wings, a 250,000-volume library of art and reference materials used by graduate students in accordance with the museum's affiliation

EXHIBIT 1   The Metropolitan Museum of Art: Five-Year Summary

	1991	1990	1989	1988	1987
Operating Fund: Revenue and Support					
Total income from endowment including The Cloisters	$ 14,169,461	$ 12,815,529	$ 10,838,371	$ 10,849,935	$ 9,912,411
City of New York					
Funds for guardianship and maintenance	9,645,657	10,193,481	9,892,601	9,970,936	8,339,423
Values of utilities provided	6,068,111	5,398,227	5,489,227	4,910,772	4,768,439
Memberships	11,723,453	10,809,726	10,557,710	9,732,467	9,674,124
Gifts and grants					
Education, community affairs, and special exhibitions	5,784,889	5,921,025	4,419,936	2,481,572	3,852,564
General-purpose contributions	15,864,740	14,126,525	11,492,125	9,862,288	9,596,497
Income for specified funds utilized	439,330	539,539	403,308	323,237	360,722
Admissions	8,621,001	7,304,343	10,032,361	6,588,169	8,343,996
Royalties and fees	1,814,579	1,222,951	1,438,572	878,547	838,063
Other	3,817,124	4,941,078	4,393,423	4,737,758	2,241,464
Gain on partial termination of pension plan	—	—	—	7,828,874	—
Income before auxiliary activities	77,948,345	73,272,424	68,957,634	68,164,555	57,927,703
Revenue of auxiliary activities	90,154,977	79,565,366	78,480,090	64,967,946	61,088,135
Total revenue and support	168,103,322	152,837,790	147,437,724	133,132,501	119,015,838
Expenses					
Curatorial					
Curatorial departments, conservation, and cataloguing	16,617,016	15,091,929	14,921,578	13,266,536	12,724,858
Operation of The Cloisters	3,253,558	2,913,132	2,801,680	2,484,003	2,322,191
Special exhibitions	5,789,990	6,242,448	5,061,807	3,407,668	5,056,044
Education, community programs, and libraries	5,300,858	5,104,734	5,700,470	4,351,743	3,641,121
Financial, legal, and other administrative functions	6,084,069	5,542,451	5,046,463	4,646,079	4,483,464

EXHIBIT 1   (Concluded)

	1991	1990	1989	1988	1987
Public information, development, and membership services	5,431,390	6,649,179	5,398,638	4,809,956	5,259,375
Operations					
Guardianship	15,404,915	14,981,129	13,497,933	12,305,602	12,434,875
Maintenance	9,994,162	8,460,979	8,075,233	7,284,095	6,721,522
Operating services	5,359,190	4,870,045	4,572,179	3,870,884	3,586,939
Value of utilities provided by the city of New York	6,068,111	5,398,227	5,489,227	4,910,772	4,768,439
Nonexhibition capital construction and renovation	2,088,713	2,530,557	1,163,930	—	—
Expenses before auxiliary activities	81,391,972	77,784,810	71,729,138	61,337,338	60,998,828
Cost of sales and expenses of auxiliary activities	88,672,214	77,647,773	72,223,048	61,555,170	53,968,101
Total expenses	170,064,186	155,432,583	143,952,186	122,892,508	114,966,929
Revenue and support (under) over expenses	(1,960,864)	(2,594,793)	3,485,538	10,239,993	4,048,909
Transfer of gain on partial termination of pension plan and net pension income to endowment funds	—	—	—	9,195,557	—
Net (decrease) increase in operating fund balance	$(1,960,864)	$(2,594,793)	$ 3,485,538	$ 1,044,436	$ 4,048,909
Additional information					
Endowment funds balance	$450,890,594	$425,725,761	$396,149,106	$331,790,406	$353,836,762
Capital construction expenditures	$ 22,978,339	$ 20,434,301	$ 15,476,598	$ 30,866,842	$ 22,299,538
Acquisitions of art	$ 16,945,340	$ 18,259,644	$ 17,107,754	$ 15,845,522	$ 7,000,695
Full-time employees	1,627	1,659	1,568	1,542	1,503
Visitors to the Main Building and The Cloisters	4,702,078	4,558,560	4,816,388	3,978,404	4,859,522

Source: The Metropolitan Museum of Art, *Annual Reports.*

with New York University; a 708- and a 246-seat auditorium; three classrooms; a restaurant and cafeteria; a parking garage; and a museum store. Ten other museum stores are operated by the Metropolitan off-site in New York City, Connecticut, California, Ohio, and New Jersey.[5]

Activities

Activities at the museum include guided tours, lectures, gallery talks, concerts, formally organized educational programs for children, intermuseum loans, and permanent, temporary, and traveling exhibitions.[6]

Management

Currently, the Met is operated by a dual management system, as shown in Exhibit 4. The president and the director report directly to the board of trustees. The dual management system was started in 1978, when the board decided the museum was too complex and large for one person to manage.[7] Prior to the board's action in 1978,

EXHIBIT 2   The Metropolitan Museum of Art: Floor Plan

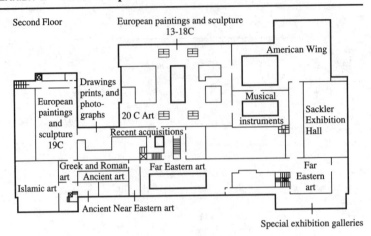

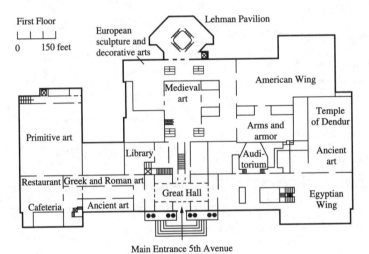

Ground Floor

Lehman Pavilion

European sculpture
and decorative arts

Ceramics, glass,
and metalwork

Public parking
garage

Enter from
5th Ave.

Ruth and
Harold D. Uris
Center
for Education

Costume
Institute

80th Street entrance   81st Street entrance

EXHIBIT 3   The Cloisters: Floor Plan

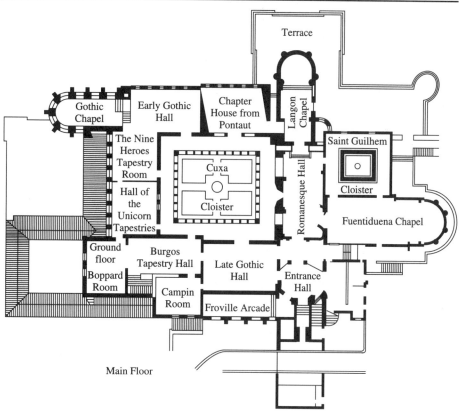

Thomas Hoving had been the chief executive at the museum since 1967. Often disparaged as a publicity-seeking showman, by 1971 Hoving had brought the museum to a fiscal crisis through his excessive acquisitions and expansion projects.[8] Some of these included the 1975 addition of the Lehman Wing, a glass-covered garden court; in 1978 the Sackler Wing, a climate-controlled glass-roofed room, housing the Temple of Dendur; and in 1980 the American Wing. Major renovations of the Great Hall and Costume Institute were completed in 1970 and 1971.[9]

Most of the controversy surrounding Hoving's tenure was due to his role in institutionalizing the "blockbuster" event at the Metropolitan as an answer to the financial crisis. Because the public is most attracted to temporary events, attendance figures were high at the large-scale ticketed events.[10] An example of these types of events was the "Treasures of Tutankhamen" show in 1978 and 1979 in which 1.2 million tickets were sold. Other examples of large-scale ticketed events include "The Great Age of Fresco," "Mexico: Splendors of Thirty Centuries," and the controversial "Harlem on My Mind."[11] The blockbuster issue has been intensely debated, however. Supporters of these events say the attraction of new audiences will diminish the elitist image of museums. Those against such exhibitions, such as Sherman Lee, director of the Cleveland

EXHIBIT 4 **The Metropolitan Museum of Art: Organization Chart, October 1990**

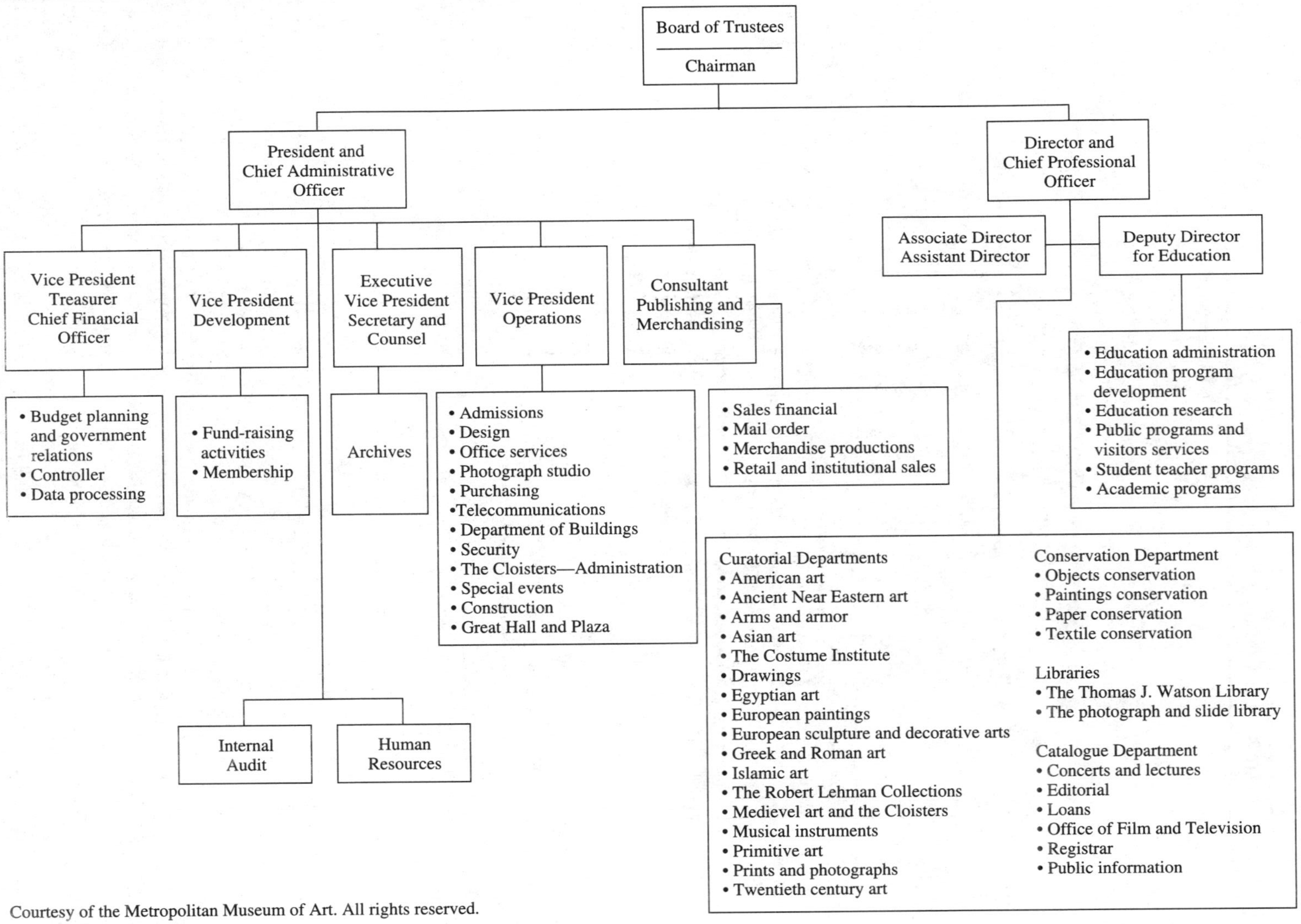

Board of Trustees
Chairman

Director and Chief Professional Officer

President and Chief Administrative Officer

Deputy Director for Education

- Education administration
- Education program development
- Education research
- Public programs and visitors services
- Student teacher programs
- Academic programs

Associate Director
Assistant Director

Conservation Department
- Objects conservation
- Paintings conservation
- Paper conservation
- Textile conservation

Libraries
- The Thomas J. Watson Library
- The photograph and slide library

Catalogue Department
- Concerts and lectures
- Editorial
- Loans
- Office of Film and Television
- Registrar
- Public information

Curatorial Departments
- American art
- Ancient Near Eastern art
- Arms and armor
- Asian art
- The Costume Institute
- Drawings
- Egyptian art
- European paintings
- European sculpture and decorative arts
- Greek and Roman art
- Islamic art
- The Robert Lehman Collections
- Medievel art and the Cloisters
- Musical instruments
- Primitive art
- Prints and photographs
- Twentieth century art

Consultant Publishing and Merchandising

- Sales financial
- Mail order
- Merchandise productions
- Retail and institutional sales

Vice President Operations

- Admissions
- Design
- Office services
- Photograph studio
- Purchasing
- Telecommunications
- Department of Buildings
- Security
- The Cloisters—Administration
- Special events
- Construction
- Great Hall and Plaza

Executive Vice President Secretary and Counsel

Archives

Vice President Development

- Fund-raising activities
- Membership

Vice President Treasurer Chief Financial Officer

- Budget planning and government relations
- Controller
- Data processing

Internal Audit

Human Resources

Museum, feel the values of the marketplace, if applied carelessly, may undermine public confidence in the museum's integrity.

Both of these views aside, the revenue earned from additional attendees has helped support all the museum's activities in the last 10 years. Since Lee's retirement from the Cleveland Museum, Philippe de Montebello, the current director of the Metropolitan and Hoving's successor, has taken on the responsibility of the antiblockbuster cause. Mr. de Montebello's position is to "lament the cost-effective mentality that places any museum activity that does not generate attendance or immediate income in jeopardy."[12] For the year ended June 30, 1990, there were no large-scale ticketed events at the Metropolitan, and the total revenue from admissions decreased by 27 percent.[13] However, during 1991 the museum's increased admission prices and large-scale exhibition offerings increased total admission revenues.

Currently, de Montebello and William H. Luers, the president, share the responsibility of managing the Met. Philippe de Montebello, a graduate of Harvard and New York University, is primarily responsible for all curatorial functions, conservation departments, libraries, and educational activities. William H. Luers, a former U.S. Ambassador to Czechoslovakia, is responsible for the business side of the Metropolitan. His basic responsibilities include daily operations, merchandising, development, human resources, internal auditing, and all financial matters including budgeting. Even though the president is responsible for development of the Metropolitan including fund raising, de Montebello is also involved heavily in this activity as well as in acquiring donations of works of art and money. Mr. Luers stated, "Phillippe should be perceived as the man who gives esthetic and artistic vision to the museum. And I am the manager, diplomat, executive, fund-raiser, and basically a communicator."[14]

Fund-Raising

In 1982, the Met began a public campaign to raise $150 million to offset operating deficits and enhance the endowment. Even though large gifts have been solicited for specific projects on several occasions, this campaign was the first formal fund-raising drive ever conducted. These funds were supposed to help the Metropolitan Museum achieve financial stability, to allow all galleries to stay open when the museum is open, and to finance the existing educational programs, the work of curatorship, and the conservation library.[15] This five-year drive was completed in 1987 and was successful in meeting the $150 million goal; however, the Metropolitan has experienced an operating deficit of $2.6 million for the 1989–1990 fiscal year and a $2.0 million deficit for 1990–1991 with future deficits predicted. The development staff at the Metropolitan has implemented the following fund-raising techniques in an attempt to offset deficits.

Endowed Chairs.   An effective fund-raising technique, borrowed from universities and hospitals, has been soliciting funds for existing curatorships in the form of endowed chairs. All major art dealers in New York as well as industry leaders are approached to solicit endowments. These chairs would carry the name of the donor, who would add to the endowment indefinitely. This drive was the first attempt to raise the salaries of curators so the Metropolitan could be competitive within the job market by attracting the best people and retaining the people they already have by increasing their existing salaries. Raises of this type would have not otherwise been possible due to the operating fund shortfalls.[16]

Corporate Sponsorships. As governmental funding decreases, corporations have come under increasing pressure to take the lead in funding social and community programs. Based on a 1991 study performed by *American Demographics,* the largest share of corporate support goes to education (38 percent), with health and human services (34 percent) following. The results of this survey do not present a promising future in corporate sponsorship of the arts because most corporations practice "strategic philanthropy," focusing philanthropic efforts to maximize their returns.[17] At the Metropolitan, great effort is given to matching the 30 annual special exhibits to corporations' activities to entice them to fund the exhibit; otherwise the exhibit might not be shown.[18] One example of matching a corporation's activities to an exhibit was a gift of $500,000 from the Hunting World Group of Companies to maintain a gallery displaying American arms.[19]

A corporate patron program is also available and requires an annual donation of $30,000. This membership level allows companies the right to have one party a year, at their own expense, in the Temple of Dendur, the American Wing, or the Medieval Sculpture Hall. Proceeds from this technique cover operating costs. Even though private use of public space is a controversial issue, it has proved to be a successful way to generate funding. Phillippe de Montebello said, "There is no ministry of culture in the United States. We don't receive a check from Washington, so we have to seek ways to provide revenues."[20]

Memberships. The museum has various levels of membership and councils. The chair's council members donate $25,000 annually and are included in the governance of the museum. Membership in this council is by invitation only. The Real Estate Council is responsible for raising money for special showings not fully financed. Each member is given 15 invitations to a special showing.[21] There are many memberships available to the public. Members enjoy free admission and receive the *Bulletin,* a quarterly magazine, and the bimonthly events listing, the *Calendar.* Also they receive catalogues of the museum at no cost and are given 10 percent off all merchandise. The Metropolitan Museum's membership is now over 100,000. In addition, the contribution levels required for all categories of membership were increased in 1991. See Exhibits 5 and 6 for a comparison of the number of members by category for 1987 through 1991.

Government Grants. For the year ended June 30, 1991, the Met received funding from the local, state, and federal governments. The city of New York provides the building that houses the museum, the utilities, and appropriate funds for maintaining the building. The state of New York provides an annual allocation from the New York State Council on the Arts for general operating and program support. Special capital funds from the National Heritage Trust were received for support of the special exhibitions programs. Federal agencies such as the National Endowment for the Arts and the Institute of Museum Services provided support for specific projects and general operations. Funds provided from governmental sources amounted to $17,059,604 for the year ended June 30, 1991. Most governmental support is appropriated on an annual basis; therefore, during recessionary periods this external funding is uncertain.[22]

Gifts. The 1986 Tax Reform Act (TRA86) curtailed donations of works of art to the Metropolitan and other museums. The change in the tax law reduced the tax deduction donors could take for appreciated art objects. This move resulted in many of these objects being sold to the highest bidder in auction houses.[23] A survey conducted by

EXHIBIT 5   Annual Members

Current Prices*	1991	1990	1989	1988	1987
Student ($30)	1,557	1,575	1,517	1,309	1,381
Individual ($70)	29,175	33,054	34,548	30,425	32,379
Dual ($125)	21,261	23,299†	24,485‡	22,440	23,826
Sustaining ($300)	6,539	7,329	7,729	6,486	7,047
Supporting					
Contributing ($600)	1,547	1,671	1,885	1,798	1,773
Donor ($900)	555	611	634	562	581
Sponsor ($2,000)	507	521	541	524	577
Patron ($4,000)	156	182	175	142	82
Upper patron ($6,000)	51	62	51	45	36
Nat'l asso. ($35)*	32,848	31,555	29,777	31,058	27,189
Total	94,196	99,859	101,342	94,789	94,871

Source: The Metropolitan Museum of Art, *1991 Annual Report.*

* Rates for all membership categories were increased an average of 21 percent in 1991.
† Includes life members.
‡ Nonresident membership.

American Demographics found that charitable giving by corporations fell by 12 percent after the 1986 Tax Reform Act became effective.[24] In March 1991, the Metropolitan received the largest gift it had received in over 50 years, probably due to a temporary "tax window," a one-year restoration of tax deductions for the full market value of art donated in 1991. Valued at $1 billion, the paintings donated by Walter Annenberg will not become the property of the Metropolitan until Mr. Annenberg's death.[25]

Admissions.   The Met is the number one tourist attraction in New York City. For the year ended June 30, 1991, there were 4,702,078 visitors to the museum and The Cloisters. (Refer again to the last line of Exhibit 1, p. 53, for attendance figures from 1987 through 1991.) Attendance decreased in 1990 because there were no large-scale ticketed exhibitions like the two in 1989. Because of this, revenue from admissions decreased by $2,728,000 (27 percent). This decrease is 3.7 percent of the total revenue

EXHIBIT 6   Members of the Corporation

	1991	1990	1989	1988	1987
Honorary fellows for life	3	3	3	3	4
Fellows for life	873	901	911	936	965
Fellows in perpetuity	329	336	342	349	357
Benefactors	355	389	372	364	334
Total corporation members	1,560	1,629	1,628	1,652	1,660
Total annual members	95,756	99,859	101,342	94,789	94,871
Grand total	97,316	101,488	102,970	96,441	96,531

Source: The Metropolitan Museum of Art, *1991 Annual Report.*

EXHIBIT 7   Museum Hours and Admission Charges

Hours of Operation	
Sunday, Tuesday–Thursday	9:30 AM–5:15 PM
Friday, Saturday	9:30 AM–8:45 PM
Monday	Closed
Donation for Admission	
Adults	$5.00
Students and seniors	2.50
Children under 12	Free

Source: *The Official Museum Directory 1990,* National Register Publishing Company.

before auxiliary operations. The management of the museum has decided to veer away from ticketing exhibitions in an effort to make special exhibitions more spontaneous and more rewarding for the frequent visitor.[26]

Hours of Operation

Evening hours were added on Friday and Saturday nights in place of opening on Tuesday evening in an attempt to increase attendance. Attendance on Tuesday evening averaged 2,500, while attendance on Friday and Saturday evenings is averaging between 3,500 and 5,000.[27] See Exhibit 7 for the hours of operation and the suggested donations for admission to the museum.

Target Customer

Many surveys are conducted by the Metropolitan each year to determine the key demographics of its visitors. See Exhibit 8 for the demographics of the average visitor to the Met. The Met's management feels that understanding the demographics of the current average visitor is the key to marketing the museum's services effectively. Of the 1,357 surveyed, 48 percent were New York City residents, 39.6 percent were residents of other areas of the United States, and 12.4 percent were foreign residents.[28]

EXHIBIT 8   Customer Demographics

Demographics	*Data*	*Percent*
Number of visits within 1 year	1–3 visits	32.8%
Time spent in museum	2 hours	36.0
Primary reason for visiting museum	Special exhibition	51.1
Median age of visitors	Age 38	
Sex of visitors	Female	57.0
Education of visitors	Baccalaureate	33.5
Occupation of visitors	Teachers/other professionals	47.5
Ethnicity of visitors	Caucasian	76.1
Museum membership	Member	15.5

Source: *The Metropolitan Museum of Art,* January 1991.

Volunteers

Approximately 800 volunteers work at the Metropolitan Museum. Three hundred of these are docents, or volunteers, who lead tours of school children and other groups.[29] Unfortunately, the Met's traditional volunteer pool is shrinking. According to a Census Bureau study conducted in 1989, 59 percent of the women in the United States are now employed. As women continue to enter the work force, nonprofit organizations are finding it difficult to attract volunteers to work during the daytime hours.[30]

Auxiliary Operations

Today, at the Metropolitan, there are a growing number of business executives on the board because of the recognition that the museum has evolved into a big enterprise with an investment portfolio and business activities such as a reproduction studio and retail outlets. Because external funds can no longer be relied on, greater emphasis must be placed on the generation of internal sources of revenue.

Museum Shops.   Retail shops are operated within the museum, at The Cloisters, and in 10 off-site locations. Four of these satellite shops are in New York: Rockefeller Center, New York Public Library, the Americana at Manhasset, and Macy's. Two are in Connecticut: Stamford Town Center and Westfarms Mall. Two are in California: Century City Shopping Center in Los Angeles and Southcoast Plaza in Costa Mesa. One is in Ohio at Columbus City Center, and one is in New Jersey at the Mall at Shorthills.[31] Because the Met is a tax-exempt, nonprofit organization, it does not have to pay taxes on profits realized from any retail operations; therefore, some feel it has an unfair advantage over other retailers selling similar goods.[32] The museum is only required to pay income taxes on all retail items unrelated to its mission, in accordance with section 511 (imposition of tax on unrelated business income of charitable organizations) of the Internal Revenue Code.

The purpose of the unrelated business income tax is to prevent tax-exempt organizations from competing unfairly with businesses whose earnings are taxed. Unrelated business income is any income derived from any unrelated trade or business. The term *unrelated trade or business* is defined in section 511 of the Internal Revenue Code as

> the case of any organization subject to the tax imposed by section 511, any trade or business the conduct of which is not substantially related (aside from the need of such organization for income or funds or the use it makes of the profits derived) to the exercise or performance by such organization of its charitable, educational, or other purpose or function constituting the basis for its exemption under section 501.[33]

The museum's stores sell greeting cards, posters, calendars, postcards, sculptures, glass, and jewelry. Nearly all the items offered are reproductions or adaptations from the museum's collections. These items are not available for sale at any other retail location. Items are sold in the museum shops or through mail order. The museum management contends the sale of the items in the shops falls within the mission of the museum in that the sale of an item makes people think about the museum outside its walls and it serves as an extension of their visit. Groups who represent small businesses are lobbying for changes in the tax code because some commercial ventures undertaken by nonprofit institutions compete unfairly with private companies who are selling nearly the same merchandise. These groups want the tax code rewritten detailing specifically which items would be considered tax-exempt.

The Metropolitan's merchandising activities resemble those of commercial businesses in some ways but are unique in others. The resemblances include the Met's desire to introduce such technology as a point of sale (POS) computerized inventory system into its stores. The differences include the requirement that all merchandise sold in the museum must reflect the permanent collection to preclude assessment of taxes on the earnings. Therefore, the decision on the types of items to sell does not necessarily reflect customer wants. Marketing research consists of showing pictures of items in the permanent collection to randomly selected customers in the museum shop to determine if the items should be reproduced for sale.

The museum almost never advertises except to invite people to join its catalog mailing list. Six catalogs per year are mailed out to members and other customers on the mailing list. The Christmas catalog is mailed out to 3 million people and the others are mailed to a smaller number. Some of the merchandising policies, such as buying large quantities of an item to get it at a lower price, have led to inventory storage problems. It is not unusual for an item to remain in the inventory for up to two years. The museum manufactures the molds to make the actual copies of art in its own reproduction studio. The art books are printed in the United States and around the world.[34]

The museum leases space for off-site retail stores and for the warehouse that serves as the headquarters for the mail order business and as a storage facility for inventory. Lease costs for all rented spaces used solely for the retail operation amounted to $1,456,295 and $1,675,519 for the years ended June 30, 1990, and 1991, respectively.[35]

Restaurants. The museum operates a restaurant, cafeteria, and bar. The restaurant and bar are open to accommodate the evening hours on Fridays and Saturdays. The museum has received approval to open a new restaurant to replace the current restaurant and cafeteria so that the space can be used for additional galleries.[36]

Other Auxiliaries. Other auxiliary operations at the Metropolitan are the parking garage and the auditorium. The parking garage is located adjacent to the museum for use by its patrons at the rate of $8.50 for the first hour, $1.00 for each additional hour up to the fifth, $17.50 for 5 to 10 hours, and $19.50 beyond 10 hours.[37]

Auxiliary Results of Operations. Net income from merchandising operations was $787,852 for the year ended June 30, 1991. Though sales from mail order were up 4 percent, the total revenue was less than forecasted. A general softening of the retail industry was thought to be the reason for this shortfall. The net contribution to the museum's operations from auxiliaries totaled $1.48 million in 1991. See Exhibit 9 for the balance sheet and Exhibit 1 for the five-year summary.

Future Outlook

The future financial stability of the Met is the key concern of management. The fiscal instability of the city of New York could lessen future city support. Threatened reductions in federal funding could also have an adverse effect on the museum's operations. The national recession could also affect the museum in terms of attendance and retail sales.

According to the book *Megatrends 2000,* researchers predict the arts will begin to replace sporting events as society's primary leisure activity. The authors cite a 1988 report by the National Endowment of the Arts calculating Americans spend $28 billion on sports events compared to $3.7 billion on art events. However, more than 500 mil-

EXHIBIT 9   The Metropolitan Museum of Art: Balance Sheet for the Years Ended June 30, 1987–91

	1991	*1990*	*1989*	*1988*	*1987*
Assets					
Cash	$ 606,396	$ 907,578	$ 395,529	$ 1,237,648	$ 1,915,744
Investments, at market	531,292,293	521,786,251	500,028,584	425,091,168	444,762,386
Receivables	41,046,111	33,443,105	34,426,235	26,112,389	13,697,322
Merchandise inventories	18,019,006	19,710,828	15,528,500	13,110,043	10,848,449
Fixed assets, at cost, net	18,609,096	13,413,486	9,953,319	8,580,484	8,548,091
Deferred charges, prepaid expenses, and other assets	7,042,756	5,622,154	4,092,675	4,900,913	4,510,822
Total assets	$616,615,658	$594,883,402	$564,424,842	$479,032,645	$484,282,814
Liabilities and Fund Balance					
Accounts payable	$ 21,631,963	$ 27,182,146	$ 27,075,186	$ 23,926,641	$ 16,527,236
Accrued expenses, primarily payroll, annual leave, and pension	14,112,100	14,363,817	13,080,930	9,636,881	6,003,065
Deferred income, principally memberships, gifts, and grants	11,038,712	10,700,500	9,801,820	8,716,301	7,533,288
Notes payable	15,800,000	7,750,000	8,000,000	10,400,000	8,000,000
Loan payable	46,915,000	47,655,000	48,260,000	48,260,000	44,990,000
Total liabilities	$109,497,775	$107,651,463	$106,217,936	$100,939,823	$ 83,053,589
Fund (deficit) balance	507,117,883	487,231,939	458,206,906	378,092,822	401,229,225
Total liabilities and fund balance	$616,615,658	$594,883,402	$564,424,842	$479,032,645	$484,282,814

Source: The Metropolitan Museum of Art, *Annual Reports.*

lion people visited American museums last year, far more than attended professional sporting events.[38]

Growth in the future must continue to come from individual and corporate donors. Statistics from *The Economist* show that while the French government spends approximately $30 per capita on the arts and the British $9, the U.S. federal and state governments together spend only about $2. This means others, including corporate America, will be required to help reduce this differential.[39]

Many believe the resurgent interest in the arts will bring success for the museum shops. Patrons want to support local culture and are spending generously on books, maps, models, posters, replicas, and other museum shop items. The Metropolitan sold more products than any other museum in 1991 and remains the only museum manufacturing its own line of merchandise. Second in sales was the Smithsonian Institution in Washington, D.C., which sells through its nine museum shops and catalog. Other shops with a minimum of $1 million in annual sales include the Museum of Modern Art and Whitney Museum of American Art in New York, Boston's Museum of Fine Art, the San Francisco Museum of Modern Art, the Art Institute of Chicago, the Los Angeles County Museum of Art, the Philadelphia Museum of Art, and the San Diego Museum of Art.[40]

Competition for museum shops is not solely limited to museum locations. The Museum Company, a retailer based in East Rutherford, New Jersey, has opened stores in seven states in two years and sells merchandise from the Louvre in Paris, the British Museum, and other art institutions and pays royalties to the museums. Its first-year revenues topped $10 million.

Other Museum Competition

Because there are multiple demands for the free time of museum visitors, many activities, outings, and other forms of recreation and leisure are potential substitutes. The direct competitors—other museums—are plentiful and many are in the New York area. These include the American Museum of Natural History, the Museum of Modern Art, the Whitney Museum, and the Museum of the City of New York.

Other activities and forms of available recreation range from sporting events to theatrical presentations. The New York metropolitan area is the home of two National Basketball Association teams; three National Hockey League teams; two National Football League teams; two baseball teams; and two race tracks. Broadway, the most celebrated street in America, offers daily productions in 40 theaters and numerous off-Broadway shows for the tourist or resident of New York.

In addition, each of the five New York boroughs has many attractions to choose from including the Statue of Liberty, the Bronx Zoo, and the National Historic Landmark district on Staten Island. Central Park and the World Trade Center are easily accessible to all visitors via the New York City subway.

End Notes

1. The Metropolitan Museum of Art, *1990 Annual Report.*

2. W. Howe, *A History of the Metropolitan Museum of Art* (New York: Arno Press, 1913), p. 125.

3. *The Metropolitan Museum of Art—Charter, Constitution, and By-Laws,* p. 3.

4. *Collier's Encyclopedia,* 1981, Volume 16, p. 70f.

5. *The Official Museum Directory 1990* (National Register Publishing Company, 1990), p. 581.

6. Ibid.

7. G. Glueck, "The Metropolitan Museum's Diplomat at the Top," *The New York Times,* May 2, 1988.

8. M. Conforti, "Hoving's Legacy Reconsidered," *Art in America,* June 1986, pp. 19–23.

9. *Collier's Encyclopedia,* 1981, Volume 16, p. 70f.

10. Conforti, "Hoving's Legacy Reconsidered," pp. 19–23.

11. C. Tomkins, "The Art World," *The New Yorker,* February 28, 1983, pp. 94–97.

12. Conforti, "Hoving's Legacy Reconsidered," pp. 19–23.

13. The Metropolitan Museum of Art, *1990 Annual Report.*

14. Glueck, "The Metropolitan Museum's Diplomat at the Top."

15. J. Russell, "Met Museum Opens 5-Year Drive for $150 Million," *The New York Times,* October 26, 1982.

16. G. Glueck, "A Raise for Met's Curators," *The New York Times,* November 14, 1990; "Met Museum Seeks Endowed Chairs," *The New York Times,* March 15, 1983.

17. B. O'Hare, "Good Deeds Are Good Business," *American Demographics,* September 1991, pp. 38–42.

18. S. Salmans, "The Fine Art of Museum Fund Raising," *The New York Times,* January 14, 1985.

19. "$500,000 to Met Museum," *The New York Times,* December 20, 1990.

20. J. Taylor, "Party Palace," *New York,* January 9, 1989, pp. 20–30.

21. Salmans, "The Fine Art of Museum Fund Raising."

22. The Metropolitan Museum of Art, *Annual Report.*

23. G. Glueck, "For Two Museums, a Very Good Week," *The New York Times,* March 1, 1991.

24. B. O'Hare, "Corporate Charitable Gifts Reached 5.9B in 1990," *American Demographics,* September 1990, p. 38.

25. Glueck, "For Two Museums, a Very Good Week."

26. The Metropolitan Museum of Art, *1990 Annual Report.*

27. Smith, "Weekends at Dusk, a New Met Museum," *The New York Times,* March 30, 1990.

28. The Metropolitan Museum of Art, Survey, December 1990 and January 1991.

29. The Metropolitan Museum of Art, *1990 Annual Report.*

30. P. Mergenbagen, "A New Breed of Volunteer," *American Demographics,* June 1991, pp. 54–55.

31. The Metropolitan Museum of Art, *1990 Annual Report.*

32. W. Honan, "Deciding Which Profits Should Be Tax Exempt," *The New York Times,* May 15, 1988.

33. Internal Revenue Code, Section 511.

34. B. Feder, "Metropolitan Museum Shows Retailing Bent," *The New York Times,* May 27, 1988.

35. The Metropolitan Museum of Art, *1990 Annual Report.*

36. Ibid.

37. Ibid.

38. J. Naisbitt and P. Aburdene, *Megatrends 2000* (New York: Wm. Morrow, 1990).

39. L. David, "Picture of Success: National Gallery of Art Celebrates 50th Anniversary," *International Washington Flyer,* 1992, V1, pp. 70–74.

40. S. Soltis, "Retailing Rodin: Museum Shops Carve a Profitable Niche," *International Washington Flyer,* 1992, V1, p. 73.

On a March night in 1988, Maxwell Jones, new products/special project manager for California Valley Wine company, leaned back in his chair in the office headquarters in Fresno, California. He glanced at the clock. It was already 10:30 PM on Wednesday. Max had been in the office since morning, but he was not sure that he was any closer to resolving the dilemma. Max had to make a recommendation which would shape the future of California Valley Wine Company (CVWC).

In recent years the company experienced diminishing sales and declining profitability (Exhibit 1). Several new product ideas were under consideration by CVWC management. Max received instructions to make a recommendation on what the new product was to be. For several months Max worked on the new product project and struggled with the decision. He gathered a large amount of information from trade sources, field salespeople, and executives at CVWC. By the end of the week, Max's recommendation was due to the New Product Evaluation Committee.

Background of California Valley Wine Company

CVWC was established in early 1934, shortly after the repeal of Prohibition. The founders, two cousins, George and Frank Lombardi, grew table grapes in Fresno, California, and saw the sudden demand in wine as a good opportunity to enter the wine business. The Lombardis purchased an old winery that had been vacated during Prohibition, and they began fermenting in the fall of 1934. In the early years they sold their wines mainly in barrels to restaurants, hotels, and liquor stores. In 1950 they constructed a major modern winery on the outskirts of Fresno and planted additional vineyards.

In 1988 CVWC owned 1,600 acres of grapes, mostly Chenin Blanc, Thompson Seedless, and Ruby Cabernet. They marketed the wines in 1.5 and 3.0 liter bottles which retailed for $3.59 and $6.79, respectively. The three wines sold were Chenin Blanc (a white wine made from Chenin Blanc grapes), Mountain Burgundy (a red wine made from Ruby Cabernet grapes), and Mountain Rose (a rose wine made from a blend of red wine and Thompson Seedless).

Contemporary Wine Industry Conditions

In recent years the wine business in California (where 90 percent of U.S. wine is produced) experienced particular difficulties. The so-called wine boom of the 1970s, when consumption levels of wine rose steadily, was over; per capita wine consumption recently declined (see Exhibit 2). The highest-ever consumption level occurred in 1985 and 1986, at 2.43 gallons per capita. However, in 1987 for the first time in 25 years, per capita consumption of wine decreased. Max knew well the reasons for the decline: growing health consciousness in society, greater awareness of physical problems asso-

This case was prepared by John E. Bargetto, MBA student, and Patrick E. Murphy, professor of marketing, University of Notre Dame. Copyright © 1990 by Patrick E. Murphy. Used with permission.

EXHIBIT 1   **Sales and Profit for CVWC, 1980–87 ($ millions)**

Year	1980	1981	1982	1983	1984	1985	1986	1987
Sales	18.2	19.6	21.9	22.0	21.1	21.2	20.9	19.5
Earnings before taxes	2.1	1.8	1.9	1.6	0.9	1.0	(0.5)	0.05

ciated with alcohol consumption, stiffer DUI laws and a rising drinking age, and the popularity of soft drinks with the younger generation. After 15 years of solid growth, total wine consumption (including coolers) in 1987 slipped to 581 million gallons.

During the 1970s, with its steady growth and romantic appeal, the wine industry drew many interested investors. The number of California wineries grew from 240 in 1970 to over 600 by 1980. While most of these were smaller wineries with whom CVWC did not compete directly, some aggressive competitors did enter the market. For example, in 1977 Coca-Cola purchased Taylor California Cellars and employed the same sophisticated marketing techniques—segmentation and slick advertising campaigns—used to sell Coke. (Coke sold Taylor to Seagrams in 1983, but Coke left behind the impact of much greater advertising expenditures by the entire wine industry.) With all of these new entrants, inventories swelled in most wineries and the industry suffered from excess supply.

To make matters worse, during the first half of the 1980s the dollar was overpriced in international markets. The wine market became flooded with inexpensive foreign wines, mainly from Italy, France, and Germany. In 1984, imports held 25.7 percent of the total wine market in the United States. Italian wines (such as the well-known brands of Riunite and Soave Bolla) dominated in the United States with 51 percent of the imported wine market.

EXHIBIT 2   **Apparent Wine Consumption in the United States, 1934–87**

Year	Population* 1,000 Persons	Population* Percent Change	Wine Consumption† 1,000 Gallons	Wine Consumption† Percent Change	Per Capita Wine Consumption Gallons	Per Capita Wine Consumption Percent Change
1934	126,374	—	32,674	—	0.26	—
1935	127,250	0.7%	45,701	39.9%	0.36	38.5%
1936	128,053	0.6	60,303	32.0	0.47	30.6
1937	128,825	0.6	66,723	10.6	0.52	10.6
1938	129,825	0.8	67,050	0.5	0.52	0.0
1939	130,880	0.8	76,647	14.3	0.59	13.5
1940	131,954	0.8	89,664	17.0	0.68	15.3
1941	133,121	0.9	101;445	13.1	0.76	11.8
1942	133,920	0.6	133,038	11.4	0.84	10.5
1943	134,245	0.2	97,501	–13.7	0.73	–13.1
1944	132,885	–1.0	98.955	1.5	0.74	1.4
1945	132,481	–0.3	93,975	–5.0	0.71	–4.1
1946	140,054	5.7	140,316‡	49.3	1.00‡	40.8
1947	143,446	2.4	96,660‡	–31.1	0.67‡	–33.0

Exhibit 2   (Concluded)

Year	Population* 1,000 Persons	Population* Percent Change	Wine Consumption† 1,000 Gallons	Wine Consumption† Percent Change	Per Capita Wine Consumption Gallons	Per Capita Wine Consumption Percent Change
1948	146,093	1.8	122,290	26.5	0.84	25.4
1949	148,665	1.8	132,567	8.4	0.89	6.0
1950	151,235	1.7	140,380	5.9	0.93	4.5
1951	153,310	1.4	126,514	−9.9	0.83	−10.8
1952	155,687	1.6	137,620	8.8	0.88	6.0
1953	158,242	1.6	140,796	2.3	0.89	1.1
1954	161,164	1.8	142,156	1.0	0.88	−1.1
1955	164,308	2.0	145,186	2.1	0.88	0.0
1956	167,306	1.8	150,039	3.3	0.90	2.3
1957	170,371	1.8	151,881	1.2	0.89	−1.1
1958	173,320	1.7	154,633	1.8	0.89	0.0
1959	176,289	1.7	156,224	1.0	0.89	0.0
1960	179,979	2.1	163,352	4.6	0.91	2.2
1961	182,992	1.7	171,632	5.1	0.94	3.3
1962	185,771	1.5	168,082	−2.1	0.90	−4.3
1963	188,483	1.5	175,918	4.7	0.93	3.3
1964	191,141	1.4	185,625	5.5	0.97	4.3
1965	193,526	1.2	189,677	2.2	0.98	1.0
1966	195,576	1.1	191,176	0.8	0.98	0.0
1967	197,457	1.0	203,403	6.4	1.03	5.1
1968	199,399	1.0	213,658	5.0	1.07	3.9
1969	201,385	1.0	235,628	10.3	1.17	9.3
1970	203,984	1.3	267,351	13.5	1.31	12.0
1971	206,827	1.4	305,221	14.2	1.48	13.0
1972	209,284	1.2	336,985	10.4	1.61	8.8
1973	211,357	1.0	347,481	3.1	1.64	1.9
1974	213,342	0.9	349,465	0.6	1.64	0.0
1975	215,465	1.0	368,029	5.3	1.71	4.3
1976	217,563	1.0	376,389	2.3	1.73	1.2
1977	219,760	1.0	400,972	6.5	1.82	5.2
1978	222,095	1.1	434,696	8.4	1.96	7.7
1979	224,567	1.1	444,375	2.2	1.98	1.0
1980	227,255	1.2	479,628	7.9	2.11	6.6
1981	229,637	1.0	505,684	5.4	2.20	4.3
1982	231,996	1.0	514,045	1.7	2.22	0.9
1983	234,284	1.0	528,076	2.7	2.25	1.4
1984	236,477	0.9	554,510	5.0	2.34	4.0
1985	238,736	1.0	580,292	4.6	2.43	3.8
1986	241,096	1.0	587,064	1.2	2.43	0.0
1987	243,400	1.0	580,933	−1.0	2.39	−1.6

* All ages resident population in the United States on July 1.
† All wine, including wine coolers, entering distribution channels in the United States.
‡ Figures reflect excessive inventory accumulation by consumers and the trade in 1946, and subsequent inventory depletion in 1947; therefore, data for these years do not accurately reflect consumption patterns.

Sources: Prepared by Economic Research Department, Wine Institute, on behalf of the California Wine Commission. Based on data obtained from reports of Bureau of Alcohol, Tobacco, and Firearms, U.S. Treasury Department, and Bureau of the Census, U.S. Department of Commerce.

EXHIBIT 3   **CVWC Market Share of Jug Wines, 1980–87**

Year	Share
1980	14.0%
1981	15.0
1982	15.1
1983	14.9
1984	14.1
1985	14.6
1986	13.2
1987	10.4

During the 1980s consumption of hard booze such as whiskey and vodka dropped significantly. At the same time, low-alcohol wines (7–9 percent) as well as nonalcoholic wines entered the market. These changes reflected a growing concern about the need for greater moderation regarding the consumption of alcoholic beverages. Increased desire for good health and concern about the high caloric content of alcoholic beverages also discouraged alcoholic beverage consumption in the United States during the 1980s. In fact, a Gallup Poll taken in 1987 showed that 63 percent of Americans "occasionally drink alcohol" while a 1989 poll indicated that the percentage fell to 56 percent.

Social activist groups had recently directed consumers' attention toward the need for more moderate alcohol consumption. The growing attention about the dangers of alcohol use while driving gave rise to organizations such as MADD (Mothers Against Drunk Driving) and SADD (Students Against Driving Drunk). One organization, Stop Marketing Alcohol on Radio and Television (SMART), embarked on a major lobbying effort to restrict advertising of beer and wine because of health problems associated with alcoholic beverages and the companies' appeal to younger and under-age drinkers.

From his vantage point within the industry, Max was clearly aware that all these factors pointed to the changing attitude that Americans had toward the use of all alcoholic beverages. CVWC's sales had been affected by all of these developments. The sales of its red, white, and rose table wines bottled under the brand name California Valley continued to lose market share (Exhibit 3). It was time that CVWC did something and it was Max's responsibility to evaluate new product possibilities. He had been with CVWC since 1962 when he joined as a sales representative. Over the years he was promoted to sales manager and eventually became the western states regional director of sales.

Two Possible Products

After considering several possible products, including sparkling wines, fruit wines, and blush wines, Max narrowed the field to two: a wine cooler or an inexpensive dessert wine. A wine cooler is a blend of carbonated water, fruit juice, and wine with an alcohol level of 4–6 percent. While wine coolers had been consumed for years, sometimes in the form of sangria, the surge in popularity had been a recent phenomenon (Exhibit 4). Coolers were first introduced as a commercial beverage in the early 1980s by California Cooler and there were numerous brands on the market. One concern expressed by the president at CVWC was the relatively high caloric content (225 per 12-ounce

Exhibit 4   Total Cases of Wine Coolers Sold, 1981–1987 (millions)

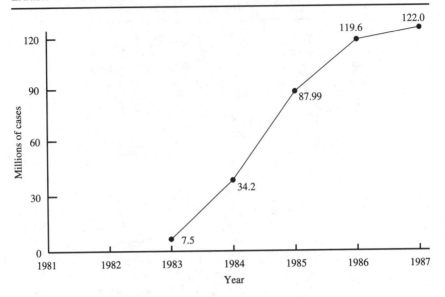

bottle) of the wine cooler. By 1987, the wine cooler segment of the wine industry had swelled to a $1.7 billion business representing 20 percent of the wine market.

The majority of the cooler market was divided between five market leaders. In 1987, Seagram's Wine Cooler and Gallo's Bartles and Jaymes together commanded nearly 48 percent of the market (Exhibit 5). Miller Brewing Company made a major product introduction of Matilda Bay malt-based cooler in 1987. Max was uncertain whether wine coolers were merely a fad or if they would become a permanent beverage option for consumers.

Although the rapid growth of the cooler market had ended, it represented a tremendous potential for sales. However, if CVWC were to enter this market, it would meet tough competition. A large advertising budget would be required to take market share from those brands already established, such as Bartles & Jaymes and Seagrams. For instance, Gallo allotted $80 million in 1985 to introduce its new cooler product.

CVWC could easily produce wine coolers from excess bulk wine. Other ingredients needed to make coolers are easily obtained. The same wine wholesalers through which CVWC sold its table wine could be utilized to distribute the cooler product. For example, the company used wholesalers and also sold directly to large retailers such as the Liquor Barn (a chain of California discount liquor stores) and out-of-state distributors in other places.

Exhibit 5   Wine Cooler Market Shares, 1987

Seagrams	24.0%
Bartles & Jaymes	23.4
California Cooler	13.1
Sun Country	9.2
White Mountain	7.1
All others	23.2
Total	100.0%

The Dessert Wine Option.   Wines containing more than 14 percent alcohol are known as fortified or dessert wines because brandy has been added during the fermentation process to yield a beverage with higher alcohol content than table wines. Dessert wines can be contrasted with table wines that usually have an alcohol content of 10–14 percent. The most important advantage of the fortified wine option is profitability; the 22 percent net margins on these wines were larger than the 13 percent net margin on wine coolers. The varieties of grapes that CVWC grew were ideal for fortified wines, both for making the wine and the brandy required. Max had estimated that for $20,000 CVWC could set up an in-house brandy distillery which could supply all the brandy required to make fortified wines.

Although the same distributors would be used to get this product onto the market, Max was aware that some of the biggest liquor stores in California refused to carry low-end dessert wine products. In the words of a manager at one Liquor Barn, "We don't carry those products because we do not want the clientele in our store."

Dessert wines included a whole range of products from high-end Portugese ports ($15/bottle) to low-end muscatels ($1.99 bottle). During the 1940s and 1950s, these sweet ports and sherries represented a sizable portion of the wine consumed and they continued to grow until about 1970. The tastes of typical wine consumers for these sweet wines moved to a preference to drier table wines, and the market for fortified wines began to erode. In recent years, the majority of the fortified wines consumed were inexpensive brown bag purchases by street drunks. Although the image of these wines has changed, dessert wines have a noble past.

History of Fortified Wines.   Fortifying wine with the addition of brandy is a practice that dates back to the Roman period. The fortification process solved a practical problem of wine spoilage in ancient times. Wine spoilage especially posed a problem for those traveling who did not have the luxury of a cool cellar to protect the wine from damaging heat. Winemakers of that early era discovered that if wine was fortified by adding a concentrated spirit (like brandy) it would age longer. This practice was copied by the British living in Madeira, Portugal, who found that this fortification process allowed the wine to hold up better for the long sea journey home.

During the decades following the repeal of Prohibition in 1933, fortified wines such as sherries and ports represented a major portion of the wine consumed in the United States. These wines were typically enjoyed as an aperitif or as a dessert. However, as tastes changed and the variety of wines available broadened, wine drinkers began to consume more table wines. In 1970 dessert wines represented 27.7 percent of the wine market, but by 1986 they accounted for only 7.5 percent of the total wine market. Inexpensive fortified wine products are classified as special natural wines. As measured in volume, consumption of this product has been quite steady during the years 1968–1986 (Exhibit 6). Table wines saw a big increase in consumption during the 1970s and represented the vast majority of the nearly 600 million gallons consumed in the United States.

The Dilemma

Max was well aware, however, of the problems involved with entering the fortified wine market. Fortified wines presently available in the market were typically associated with the type of wines consumed by the destitute alcoholics who roamed the streets. Max was struck by an article he read some time ago in *The Wall Street Journal.* He reached for a copy of the article he had placed in a file folder and reread it closely. (The text of the article is shown in Exhibit 7.)

EXHIBIT 6   Wine Consumption in the United States, 1968–86

Year	U.S.-Produced Other Special Natural Wine over 14 Percent Alcohol Consumed in the United States	All U.S.-Produced Wine Consumed in the United States (1,000 gallons)	Percent of Type
1968	12,591	191,447	6.6%
1969	12,221	210,936	5.8
1970	11,665	237,328	4.9
1971	11,631	269,065	4.3
1972	11,823	289,942	4.1
1973	10,944	292,041	3.7
1974	9,653	298,071	3.2
1975	10,918	318,071	3.4
1976	11,994	317,470	3.8
1977	12,396	331,766	3.7
1978	11,104	340,620	3.3
1979	10,084	352,206	2.9
1980	10,008	377,120	2.7
1981	10,288	390,971	2.6
1982	10,293	391,956	2.6
1983	11,055	397,070	2.8
1984	10,807	412,099	2.6
1985	11,724	441,034	2.7
1986	13,698	477,891	2.9

He was particularly sensitive about alcoholism because his father had suffered from the disease. He knew that many street drunks depended on these inexpensive fortified wines because it was the cheapest source of alcohol available. However, Max was not really sure what percentage of fortified wines were purchased by public drunks.

Max had wondered for some time about the ramifications of offering a fortified product to the market and whether or not it would add to the serious problem of alcoholism in this country. After reading *The Wall Street Journal* article, Max contacted the Wine Institute in San Francisco. The Wine Institute is an industry-funded organization whose purpose is to represent the California wineries and promote their wines. The reply regarding this question of the so-called misery market came in a written letter.

We reject the notion, however, that availability of "over 14 percent wine" encourages and/or causes abuse of the product. We know from a wide range of literature that alcohol abuse is a complex medical and social problem evolving from a vast array of genetic biochemical predispositions, cultural norms, behaviors, expectations, and beliefs. We believe the most effective way to address alcoholism is through intervention, education, treatment, and prevention programs.

In doing some more research about the social implications of fortified beverages, Max had found an article in the *British Journal of Addiction*.[1] The article was titled, "A Ban of Fortified Wine in Northwestern Ontario and Its Impact on the Consumption

---

[1] "A Ban of Fortified Wine in Northwestern Ontario and its Impact on the Consumption Level and Drinking Patterns," *British Journal of Addiction* 76 (1981), pp. 281–88.

EXHIBIT 7

Misery Market: Winos & Thunderbird Are a Subject Gallo Doesn't Like to Discuss

NEW YORK—In the dim light of a cold February morning, a grizzled wino shuffles into the Bowery Discount liquor store muttering, "Thunderchicken, it's good lickin'." Fumbling for some change, he says: "Gimme one bird." Raymond Caba, the store clerk, understands the argot and hands over a $1.40 pint of Thunderbird, the top seller in what he calls "the bum section."

The ritual is repeated a thousand times a day in dead-end neighborhoods across the country. Cheap wines with down-and-dirty names—and an extra measure of alcohol—are the beverage of choice among down-and-out drunks. But winos are a major embarrassment to the big companies that manufacture these wines. With rare exceptions, they aren't eager to acknowledge their own products.

Thunderbird and Night Train Express are produced by the nation's largest wine company, E. & J. Gallo Winery, though you'll not learn that from reading the label on the bottle. MD 20/20 is made by Mogen David Wine Corp., a subsidiary of Wine Group Ltd., which refuses to talk about its product. Richards Wild Irish Rose Wine, the very best seller in the category, is produced by Canandaigua Wine Co. Canandaigua is volubly proud of the wine but quick to point out that it enjoys wide popularity with people who aren't alcoholics.

The Biggest Bang

People concerned about the plight of street alcoholics are critical of the purveyors of dollar-a-pint street wines made with cheap ingredients and fortified with alcohol to deliver the biggest bang for the buck. At 18% to 21% alcohol, these wines have about twice the kick of ordinary table wine, without any of the pretension.

The consumption of alcohol in the U.S. is declining in virtually every category, but the best selling of the low-end brands keep growing, in large part because customers can't stop drinking. Says Paul Gillette, the publisher of the wine investor in Los Angeles: "Makers of skid-row wines are the dope pushers of the wine industry."

Vintners generally try hard to filter their wines through the imagery of luxury and moderation, stressing vintage, touting quality. So they are understandably reluctant to be associated in any way with what some call a $500 million misery market.

Suppliers deny that the most popular street wines sell as well as they do because they appeal to dirt-poor, hard-core drinkers. Companies contend that their clientele is not like that at all, and besides, any alcoholic beverage can be abused. (The wine people say they face stiff competition from high-alcohol malt liquor and 200-milliliter bottles of cheap vodka.) The future for the high-proof business, vintners say, isn't particularly rosy in any case. The wine category they call "dessert" or "fortified"—sweet wines with at least 14% alcohol—has lost favor with drinkers.

Markedly Profitable

Wino wines are inexpensive to produce. They come in no-frills, screw-top packaging and require little or no advertising. Although they generally aren't the major part of vintners' product lineups, they are especially profitable. All told, net profit margins are 10% higher than those of ordinary table wines, Canandaigua estimates. Gallo says that isn't true for its products, but it won't say what is true.

The wines are also a rock-solid business. Of all the wine brands in America, the trade newsletter *Impact* says, Wild Irish Rose holds the no. 6 spot, Thunderbird is 10th and MD 20/20 is 16th. In contrast to the lackluster growth of most other wine brands, unit sales of the leading cheap labels, Wild Irish Rose and Thunderbird, are expected to be up 9.9% and 8.6% respectively this year, *Jobson's Wine Marketing Handbook* estimates.

So unsavory is this market that companies go to great lengths to distance themselves from their customers. If suppliers are willing to talk about the segment—and few are—they still don't acknowledge the wino's loyal patronage. Gallo and Canandaigua leave their good corporate names off the labels, thus obscuring the link between product and producer.

The "No-Name Market"

"This is the market with no name," says Clifford Adelson, a former executive director of sales at Manischewitz Wine Co., which once made low-end wines and was recently acquired by Canandaigua. "It's lots and lots of money, but it doesn't add prestige."

Cheap wines typically aren't even sold in many liquor stores. For instance, Frank Gaudio, who owns the big Buy-Rite Twin Towers Wine & Spirits store in New York's World Trade Center, doesn't stock any of these

EXHIBIT 7   (Continued)

brands, though many homeless alcoholics spend their days just outside his door. "We don't want that clientele in our store," he says. "We could sell [fortified wines] and probably make money, but we don't." The wines, however, are staples of the bulletproof liquor stores of low-income neighborhoods. While you can't say the whole market for items like Thunderbird and Night Train consists of derelicts, down-and-outers do seem to be its lifeblood. Fifty current and reformed drinkers interviewed for this article claim to have lived on a gallon a day or more of the stuff.

"The industry is manufacturing this for a selected population: the poor, the homeless, the skid-row individual," says Neil Goldman, the chief of the alcoholism unit at St. Vincent's Hospital in Manhattan's Greenwich Village.

* * *

Dawn finds a small bottle gang near the Bowery, chasing away the morning shakes with a bottle of Thunderbird they pass from hand to hand. Mel Downing tugs up the pant leg of his filthy jeans to reveal an oozing infection on his knee. He is drinking, he says, to numb the pain of this "wine sore" and other ones on his back before he goes to the hospital later in the morning. "We're used to this stuff," the 39-year-old Mr. Downing quickly adds. "We like the effect. We like the price."

A cheap drunk is the main appeal of the wines that winos call "grape" or "jug," but most often just "cheap." Winos say that these wines, even when consumed in quantity, don't make them pass out as readily as hard liquor would.

Walter Single, a recovering alcoholic, recalls that on a daily diet of nine pints of Wild Irish Rose, he still was able "to function well enough to panhandle the money he needed to drink all day and still have enough left for a wake-up in the morning."

Some drinkers say the high sugar content of the wines reduces their appetite for food, so they don't have to eat much. Others say they still can drink wine even after their livers are too far gone to handle spirits. Still others appreciate the portability of pint bottles.

"I feel more secure with a pint," explains Teddy Druzinski, a former carpenter. "It's next to me. It's in my pocket." Canandaigua estimates that low-end brands account for 43 million gallons of the dessert category's 55 million gallons and that 50% is purchased in pints.

Many people in the wine industry eschew producing skid-row wines. "I don't think Christian Brothers should be in a category where people are down on their luck—where some may be alcoholics," says Richard Maher, the president of Christian Brothers Winery in St. Helena,

Calif. Mr. Maher, who once was with Gallo, says fortified wines lack "any socially redeeming values."

"The consumers are we alcoholics," agrees Patrick Gonzales, a 45-year-old wino who is undergoing a week of detoxification at a men's shelter on New York's Lower East Side: "You don't see no one sitting at home sipping Mad Dog [MD20/20] in a wine glass over ice."

Market Profile

Major producers see their customers otherwise. Robert Huntington, the vice president of strategic planning at Canandaigua, says the Canandaigua, N.Y., company sells 60% to 75% of its "pure grape" Wild Irish Rose in primarily black, inner-city markets. He describes customers as "not supersophisticated," lower middle-class and low-income blue-collar workers, mostly men.

Daniel Solomon, a Gallo spokesman, maintains that Thunderbird "has lost its former popularity in the black and skid-row areas" and is qualified mainly by "retired and older folks who don't like the taste of hard products."

According to accounts that Gallo disputes, the company revolutionized the skid-row market in the 1950s after discovering that liquor stores in Oakland, Calif., were catering to the tastes of certain customers by attaching packages of lemon Kool-Aid to bottles of white wine. Customers did their own mixing at home. The story goes that Gallo, borrowing the idea, created citrus-flavored Thunderbird. Other flavored high-proof wines then surged into the marketplace. Among them: Twister, Bali Hai, Hombre, Silver Satin, and Gypsy Rose. Gallo says that the Kool-Aid story is "a nice myth" but that Thunderbird was "developed by our wine makers in our laboratories."

Vintners advertised heavily and sought to induce Skid Row's opinion leaders—nicknamed "bell cows"—to switch brands by plying them with free samples. According to Arthur Palombo, the chairman of Cannon Wines Ltd. and one of Gallo's marketing men in the 1950s and 60s, "These were clandestine promotions." He doesn't say which companies engaged in the practice.

Today, such practices and most brands have long since died out. Companies now resort to standard point-of-sale promotions and, in the case of Canandaigua, some radio and television advertising. There still is an occasional bit of hoopla. In New Jersey, Gallo recently named a Thunderbird Princess, and Canandaigua currently is holding a Miss Wild Irish Rose contest. But to hear distributors tell it, word of mouth remains the main marketing tool.

The market is hard to reach through conventional media. Winos will drink anything if need be, but when they

Exhibit 7   (Continued)

have the money to buy what they want, they tend to hew to the familiar. (Sales resistance may help explain why the handful of low-end products that companies have tried to launch in the past 20 years mostly have bombed.) Besides, "it would be difficult to come up with an advertising campaign that says this will go down smoother, get you drunker and help you panhandle better," says Robert Williams, a reformed alcoholic and counselor at the Manhattan Bowery Corp.'s Project Renewal, a halfway house for Bowery alcoholics.

Companies see no reason to spend a lot of money promoting brands they don't want to be identified with. "Gallo and ourselves have been trying to convey the image of a company that makes fine products," says Hal Riney, the president of Hal Riney & Associates, which created the TV characters Frank Bartles and Ed Jaymes for Gallo's wine cooler. "It would be counterproductive to advertise products like this."

Richards Wild Irish Rose purports to be made by Richards Wine Co. The label on a bottle of Gallo's Night Train reads "vinted & bottled by Night Train Limited, Modesto, Ca." Gallo's spokesman, Mr. Solomon, says "The Gallo name is reserved for traditional [table] wines."

Industry people chime in that it isn't at all uncommon for companies to do business under a variety of monikers. But they also agree with Cannon's Mr. Palombo: "Major wine producers don't want to be associated with a segment of the industry that is determined to be low-end and alcoholic."

Winos have their own names for what they buy, Gallo's appellations notwithstanding. When they go to buy Night Train, they might say, "Gimme a ticket." They call Thunderbird "pluck," "T-Bird," or "chicken." In street lingo, Richards Wild Irish Rose is known as "Red Lady," while MD 20/20 is "Mad Dog."

If Skid Row wines are cheap to market, they are even cheaper to make. They are generally concocted by adding flavors, sugar, and high-proof grape-based neutral spirits to a base wine. The wine part is produced from the cheapest grapes available. Needless to say, the stuff never sees the inside of an oak barrel.

"They dip a grape in it so they can say it's made of wine," says Dickie Gronan, a 67-year-old who describes himself as a bum. "But it's laced with something to make you thirstier." Sugar probably. In any event, customers keep on swigging. Some are so hooked that they immediately turn to an underground distribution system on Sundays and at other times when liquor stores are closed. "Bootleggers," often other alcoholics, buy cheap brands at retail and resell them at twice the price. The street shorthand for such round-the-clock consumption is "24-7."

At nightfall, Mr. Downing, the member of the bottle gang with the leg infection, is panhandling off the Bowery "to make me another jug," as he puts it. As his shredded parka attests, he got into a fight earlier in the day with his buddy, Mr. Druzinski, who then disappeared. Mr. Downing also got too drunk to make it, as planned, to the hospital for treatment of his "wine sores."

A short while later, Mr. Druzinski emerges from the shadows. He has a bloodied face because he "took another header," which is to say he fell on his head. Nevertheless, in the freezing darkness, he joins his partner at begging once again.

"I'm feeling sick to my stomach, dizzy, and mokus," Mr. Downing says, "But I still want another pint." He scans the deserted street and adds: "Another bottle is—the biggest worry on our minds."

Level and Drinking Patterns." The article described an experiment in which fortified wines were removed from store shelves in 10 communities in Ontario. The brands removed were those in the lower-price category, and considered to be the more popular beverages of public inebriates, many of whom were Native Indians. The researchers sought to compare the drinking patterns of people living in these 10 delisted communities with those in 18 communities where these fortified wines continued to be available. The researchers found that the ban of these fortified wines only led to an increased consumption of table wines, vodka, and Liquor Board wines and in some cases created additional social problems. Max felt that the presence of fortified wines in the American market did not cause alcoholism, but felt bothered by the idea that a large proportion of the customers for a CVWC fortified product might be these public drunks.

Marketing Strategy

Whether Max recommended CVWC to enter the fortified wine market or the wine cooler market, he would be responsible for developing the appropriate marketing strategy. Max had a fairly clear vision in his mind of what the two potential products could be. In the case of the fortified wine, it would be made from the Thompson Seedless and French Colombard grapes and would contain about 15 percent sugar while having 18 percent alcohol. He thought perhaps the product could have an added orange or cherry flavor.

Given the potential image problems that a market for a fortified product could create for CVWC, Max felt that if they were to enter this market it would be best for CVWC to utilize an alternative brand name and a DBA (doing business as). The DBA is the name of the producer which, by law, has to be listed on the label. To protect the image of California Valley Wine Company, the bottom of the label could read "Produced and Bottled by CVWC Cellars," thereby disguising the producer of the wine. In addition to the DBA, as the *TWSJ* article mentioned, many wineries in California used second labels in order to protect the image of their main brand. For example, Gallo bottles its wines under a whole myriad of brand names: Carlo Rossi, Andre, and Polo Brindisi. Exhibit 8 lists the brand names, producers, and market shares of the leading fortified wine products. Although Max had not given much consideration to possible brand names for the fortified wine, Warm Nights had been tossed around by some of the salespeople.

Max felt that perhaps an upscale product with a distinctive label could be developed, one that commanded a higher price in the market and which in turn would yield a greater margin. It could be bottled in 750-milliliter bottles and positioned distinctively away from the low-end competition of MD 20/20 and Thunderbird. Certainly part of the reasons these wines were favorites of the public drunks was the inexpensive price. A 375-milliliter bottle of Night Train retailed for $1.09. The 750-milliliter bottles of Thunderbird and Wild Irish Rose could be purchased for as little as $1.99 and $2.32, respectively.

He wondered if the flat-shaped, pint-size bottle of Night Train had been intentionally designed to fit into a coat pocket. He thought that CVWC—in order to avoid the misery market—could market a product packaged with a fancy label in a corked

EXHIBIT 8   **U.S. Fortified Wine Industry (fortified wines are sweet wines with at least 14 percent alcohol)**

Wine	Producer	Market Share
Wild Irish Rose	Canandaigua	22%
Thunderbird	Gallo	18
All other Gallo dessert wines		16
MD 20/20	Wine Group Ltd.	7
Cisco	Canandaigua	4
Night Train Express	Gallo	3
All others: imported dessert wines, other domestic brands		30

Source: Industry estimates.

bottle, and sell it for a higher price, for example, $5.50. It could be positioned more as a sophisticated dessert wine. But then Max questioned whether or not customers would be willing to pay for this.

Max believed that the fortified wine was a liquor store item. Perhaps it would be feasible to selectively market this product, focusing on suburban stores. In this way the inner-city liquor stores, often frequented by public drunks, could be avoided. Max knew that once the product is out on the store shelves, the producer cannot influence who buys the product or how it is used. One idea that came to mind was that CVWC could print on the bottom of the labels "ENJOY IN MODERATION" like some other alcoholic beverage producers had done.[2] Perhaps this would help discourage abuse of the product. Max had bounced the idea off one of the salespeople, who replied, "Hey, Max, that's not our responsibility."

Promotion of fortified wines posed a particularly difficult problem. Max wondered how CVWC could promote the product and which product attributes could be highlighted. Max pulled out his *Code of Advertising Standards* that wine industry members were to voluntarily abide by. The following is a paragraph from the first section:

> Subscribers shall not depict or describe in their advertising: The consumption of wine or wine coolers for the effects their alcohol content may produce or make direct or indirect reference to alcohol content or extra strength, except as otherwise required by law or regulation.

There were certainly problems with promotion of this product, but one thing was certain. If CVWC was not able to promote the product, it would be difficult to take market share away from the competition.

Of course, if Max were to recommend entering the wine cooler business, the problems associated with fortified wines would be avoided. If CVWC was to be successful in the wine cooler business, it would require some innovation. Max had thought that CVWC could develop a cooler with new flavors, for example, pomegranate or wild berry. They could be packaged in six-packs potentially leading to greater sales over the typical four-pack. He believed women could be targeted for this new product which could be sold as low-calorie. Max considered whether CVWC might get some nationally known TV star to endorse the new product.

He turned on the PC near his desk and stared at the projections for both the fortified wine and wine cooler options. Exhibit 9 contains the actual numbers generated by the spreadsheet program. Both alternatives seemed to be viable and would help the bottom line of CVWC. He thought the numbers might even be a bit conservative.

Max was even more confounded by all of these considerations. But then again it was his responsibility to give the recommendation to the committee. Not only was he expected to present his recommendation regarding the new product to the New Product Evaluation Committee but he was also asked to discuss his strategy with the Social Responsibility Committee. This committee had been established in 1976 to oversee the activities of the various departments at CVWC because of its involvement in the alcoholic beverage industry.

When looking for some misplaced statistics on his cluttered desk, Max found a memo he had received from the vice president of marketing earlier in the day. The memo was marked "urgent" in red ink. It instructed Max to have his recommendation

---

[2] "Alco Beverage Company and Moderation Advertising," HBS case 9-387-070.

EXHIBIT 9   Projected CVWC Sales, 1989–91

	1989	*1990*	*1991*
Wine Cooler			
Sales (millions)*	5.00	6.00	7.00
Expenses			
Cost of goods sold	3.00	3.60	4.20
Selling and administrative	0.20	0.20	0.20
Salaries	0.15	0.17	0.19
Advertising	0.90	0.90	0.90
Interest	0.20	0.25	0.25
Total expenses	4.45	5.12	5.74
Earnings before taxes	0.55	0.88	1.26
Fortified Wine			
Sales (millions)†	2.50	3.50	5.50
Expenses			
Cost of goods sold	1.00	1.40	2.20
Selling and administrative	0.20	0.20	0.20
Salaries	0.10	0.11	0.12
Advertising	0.20	0.20	0.20
Interest	0.15	0.15	0.15
Total expenses	1.65	2.06	2.87
Earning before taxes	0.85	1.44	2.63

* Based on $11.42/case selling price.
† Based on $14.75/case selling price.

available by noon tomorrow. The memo concluded, "Are there any other new product options you haven't explored? Max, see me in the morning." Max took a long breath and reached for the articles on the wine industry that covered his desk. Thumbing through them, he hoped that a clear strategy would come to mind, one that he could sleep with.

PART

II

MARKET ORIENTATION AND ORGANIZATIONAL LEARNING

Market orientation highlights the central importance of the customer as the focal point of business operations. "A business is market-oriented when its culture is systematically and entirely committed to the continuous creation of superior customer value."[1] Unfortunately, the term *market orientation* often becomes confused with *marketing orientation* though the two are significantly different. A market orientation refers to everyone in the organization being committed to the customer and adapting in a timely way to meeting the changing needs of the customer.[2] A market*ing* orientation implies that the marketing function is the most important function within the organization and that all other functional areas are driven by the demands of the marketing department. Market orientation is an organizational rather than functional responsibility.

Today's globally competitive environment demands that companies, in order to survive, focus on meeting the needs of worldwide customers quickly and efficiently. A market orientation has helped companies such as Boeing, Dell Computer, Hewlett-Packard, and Southwest Airlines outperform their competitors. For example, in the design and manufacture of its 777 commercial airliner, Boeing utilized multifunctional teams including key customers to reduce development time and costs. The design and manufacturing processes were computerized, resulting in a paperless product development process. An evaluation by Singapore International Airlines compared the 777 against the Airbus 330, concluding that Boeing's aircraft offered superior value based on performance, purchase price, and operating costs.[3]

Becoming market-oriented does not happen overnight. To grow more market-oriented, managers must identify rapidly changing customer needs and wants, determine the impact of these changes on customer satisfaction, increase the rate of product and service innovation in business strategies, and develop strategies for competitive advantage. We first describe the characteristics and features of a market-oriented organization and consider the importance of becoming market-oriented. Next, the issues and hurdles confronting the transition to a market-oriented organization are discussed. Finally, we look at the role of organizational learning and its close relationship with market orientation.

What Is Market Orientation?

Achieving a market orientation involves obtaining information about customers, competitors, and markets; examining the information from a total business perspective; determining how to deliver superior customer value; and implementing actions to provide value to customers (Exhibit 1). Market orientation blends together a culture committed to customer value and a process of continuously creating superior value for buyers.[4] Market orientation requires a customer focus, competitor intelligence, and interfunctional coordination.

Customer Focus

The importance of the customer was first highlighted in the marketing concept articulated by a General Electric executive in the 1950s. In fact, there are many similarities between the marketing concept and market orientation. The *marketing concept* advocates starting with customer needs and wants, deciding which needs to meet, and involving everyone in the process of satisfying customers. The important distinction is that *market orientation* extends beyond the philosophy of the marketing concept, also offering a process for delivering customer value. The market-oriented organization understands customers' preferences and requirements and then combines and directs the skills and resources of the entire organization to satisfy customers.

"That model of competing, which links R&D, technology, innovation, production, and finance—integrated through marketing's drive to own a market—is the approach that all competitors will take to succeed in the 1990s," writes Regis McKenna.[5]

Achieving a customer orientation requires finding out what values buyers are looking for to help them meet their purchasing objectives. Their buying decisions are guided by the attributes and features of the brand that offers the best value. The buyer's experience in using the brand is compared to expectations to determine customer satisfaction.[6]

EXHIBIT 1   Components of Market Orientation

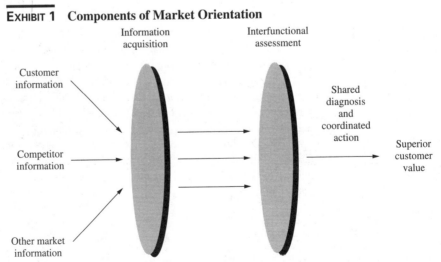

Source: Stanley F. Slater and John C. Narver, "Market Orientation, Customer Value, and Superior Performance," *Business Horizons,* March/April 1994, pp. 22–27, at p. 23.

Competitor Intelligence

Market orientation is about the competition as well as the customer.

The key questions are which competitors, and what technologies, and whether target customers perceive them as alternate satisfiers. Superior value requires that the seller identify and understand the principal competitors' short-term strengths and weaknesses and long-term capabilities and strategies.[7]

Complacency leads to disaster in today's turbulent marketplace. For example, Western Union failed to define its competitive area as telecommunications, concentrating instead on its telegraph services, and eventually was outflanked by fax technology. Had Western Union been a market-oriented company, its management might have better understood the changes taking place, seen the competitive threat, and developed strategies to counter the threat.

In the 1980s Wal-Mart's management recognized the changes taking place in retailing. By investing heavily in information systems technology, the power retailer was able to improve inventory management, lower costs, and increase customer satisfaction. Wal-Mart's private satellite system links retail stores, distribution centers, headquarters, and suppliers. Store reorders are sent direct to the supplier and shipped to distribution centers. Often the centers are able to unload and load for delivery to stores within 24 hours.

Interfunctional Coordination

Market-oriented companies are successful in getting all business functions working together to provide customer value. The tendency to "box" management functions so that manufacturing does not talk with R&D, R&D does not talk with marketing, marketing does not talk with manufacturing, and sales does not talk with anyone in the organization creates functions empty of responsibility and void of interaction. In contrast, interfunctional cooperation and shared decision making lead to achieving customer value objectives.

Becoming a Market-Oriented Organization

As shown in Exhibit 1, becoming a market-oriented company involves several interrelated requirements. These include information acquisition, interfunctional assessment, shared diagnosis, and coordinated action.

Information Acquisition

"A company can be market-oriented only if it completely understands its markets and the people who decide whether to buy its products or services."[8] For example, Wal-Mart's information system provides a wealth of information about popular store items, supplier responsiveness, and differences in customer preferences in various regions.

Interfunctional Assessment

Rubbermaid has overcome the hurdles of getting people from different functions to work together to conceive and develop new houseware products. It is important that new product planning involves all functions because they all contribute to customer satisfaction.[9] Rubbermaid's entrepreneurial teams seem to overcome problems with conflicting functional objectives and other differences.

Shared Diagnosis and Action

The remaining cornerstone of the market orientation paradigm is deciding what actions to take. This involves shared discussions and analysis of trade-offs.[10] An effective multifunctional team approach to decision making facilitates diagnosis and coordinated action. Rubbermaid's teams are empowered to make decisions and are responsible for results.

Becoming market-oriented is challenging and quite different from an organization that does not have close and shared responsibilities across business functions. Nonetheless, mounting evidence suggests that the market-oriented organization has an important competitive advantage in providing customer value and achieving superior performance.

Organizational Learning

Learning about markets requires developing a process throughout the organization for obtaining, interpreting, and acting on information from sensing activities. The learning processes of market-oriented companies follow four steps: open-minded inquiry, synergistic information distribution, mutually informed interpretations, and accessible memory usage.[11]

Open-Minded Inquiry

A danger to be avoided is not being open to exploring new views about markets and competition. Sometimes referred to as "out-of-the-box" thinking, the idea is to not be bound to past views about markets and how they are likely to change in the future. Search for information is of little value if management already has a view on which new information will have no influence.

The members of the market-oriented organization recognize the importance of market sensing and coordinated interpretation of market intelligence to guide strategies. Not all companies see the value in continuous learning about markets. Managers who are not part of market-driven cultures may be unwilling to invest in information for decision making. Unfortunately, these same companies often encounter problems because of faulty or incomplete market sensing.

Continuous learning allows firms to capture more information about their customers, suppliers, and competitors. This capability provides the potential for growth based on decisions made by open-minded managers taking into account a more complete representation of the competitive environment. Also, firms can respond much more quickly to competitors' actions and take advantage of situations in the marketplace.

Synergistic Information Distribution

This part of the learning process encourages the widespread distribution of information throughout the organization. The intent is to leverage the value of the information by cutting across business functions to share information on customers, channels of distribution, suppliers, and competitors. Traditional information processing in organizations allocates relevant information to each business function. Synergistic distribution works to remove functional hurdles and practices. Multifunctional teams help to encourage transfer of information across functions.

Mutually Informed Interpretations

The mental model of the market guides managers' interpretation of information. The intent is to reach a shared vision about the market and about the impact that new information has on this vision. The market-oriented culture encourages market sensing. But the process requires more than gathering and studying information. "This interpretation is facilitated by the mental models of managers, which contain decision rules for deciding how to act on the information in light of anticipated outcomes."[12] The model reflects the executives' vision about the forces influencing the market and likely future directions of change. Learning occurs as members of the organization evaluate the results of their decisions based on their vision at the time the decisions were made.

Accessible Memory Usage

This phase in the learning process emphasizes the importance of gaining access to prior learning. The objective is not to lose valuable information that can continue to be used.

Urban Outfitters, Inc., a successful specialty retailer, is guided by management's shared vision about the market. The company has an effective learning process. Fiscal 1995 sales were $110 million from 16 stores. The retailer's products include fashion apparel, accessories, household items, and gifts. Urban Outfitters' unique strategy is the shopping environment it provides to the 18-to-30 targeted age group. To stay ahead of its unpredictable buyers' whimsical tastes, management employs over 75 fashion spies who sense what is happening fashionwise in neighborhoods in New York, California, London, and Paris.[13] Salaries and expenses of this market-sensing team total $4 million annually. Market feedback guides new product decisions and signals when buyer interest is slowing down. Management is testing new retail concepts to appeal to its buyers when they move into an older age group.

Hewlett-Packard's Inkjet product strategy illustrates market orientation and organizational learning. In the early 1980s H-P's product team developed a shared vision about how the global printer market would change. The team believed that dot matrix technology would be replaced by a better method of printing that was less expensive than laser printers. H-P developed inkjet technology as an alternative to dot matrix printers. The team's decision to target the higher-volume dot matrix market instead of positioning against laser printers is an impressive example of higher-order learning. This strategy offered H-P a value proposition for differentiating the printer and lowering cost by serving the mass market instead of a high-end niche. Following the market-orientation process, H-P's product team made a major effort to sense market needs using information from customers, competitors, and distributors. These inputs guided design, production, and marketing decisions.

End Notes

1. Stanley F. Slater and John C. Narver, "Market Orientation, Customer Value, and Superior Performance," *Business Horizons,* March-April 1994, p. 22.

2. Thomas Bonoma, "A Marketer's Job Is to Self-Destruct," *Marketing News,* June 25, 1990; and Regis McKenna, "Marketing Is Everything," *Harvard Business Review,* January-February 1991.

3. Michael Mecham, "Year's Biggest Order Goes to Boeing 777," *Aviation Week & Space Technology*, November 20, 1995, pp. 28–29.

4. Slater and Narver, "Market Orientation."

5. McKenna, "Marketing Is Everything," p. 72.

6. Philip Kotler, *Marketing Management,* 8th ed. (Englewood Cliffs, NJ: Prentice-Hall, 1994), Chapter 2.

7. Slater and Narver, "Market Orientation," p. 23.

8. Benson P. Shapiro, "What the Hell Is Market Oriented," *Harvard Business Review,* November-December 1988, p. 120.

9. Ibid., p. 121.

10. Ibid., p. 122.

11. The following discussion is based on George S. Day, "The Capabilities of Market-Driven Organizations," *Journal of Marketing,* October 1994, p. 43. See also Stanley F. Slater and John C. Narver, "Market-Oriented" Isn't Enough: Build a Learning Organization, Report no. 94-103 (Cambridge, MA: Marketing Science Institute, 1994).

12. Day, "The Capabilities of Market-Driven Organizations," p. 43.

13. Robert La Franco, "It's All about Visuals," *Forbes,* May 22, 1995, pp. 108–12.

CASES FOR PART II

Becoming market-oriented is a challenging yet rewarding endeavor. The six cases in this part reflect the difficulty a firm has when attempting to adopt a market-oriented approach to conducting business. The cases encompass situations in areas such as consumer products, services, business-to-business, and international markets.

The video case, **Navistar International Transportation Corporation (Case 2–1),** focuses upon how a large corporation should implement a customer orientation program. Navistar is the largest truck manufacturer in the United States. However, competition is taking customer-oriented actions that threaten Navistar's market position. With international markets opening their doors to foreign truck manufacturers, Navistar has many decisions facing it. All the while, however, the company has been given a mandate to cut costs.

Floral Farms (Case 2–2) is a producer and distributor of fresh-cut flowers. The flowers are grown in South America and then marketed and distributed in the United States. The annual planning meeting between marketing and production has not gone well. While the marketing arm of the business (located in the United States) projects increased demand for most of the company's major products, the production arm of the company (located in South America) seems either unable or unwilling to alter its production plans. The company's owner has told the two groups to work toward an agreeable forecast.

Case 2–3, Quality Plastics International S.A. de C.V. (QPI), is a Mexico-based plastics manufacturer. It is felt that the company is successful because it gives customers what they want at a good price. However, the owner of the company is puzzled by comments from the plant manager and accountant. The owner's enthusiasm regarding QPI's growth opportunities is apparently not shared by the entire management team.

Case 2–4, Food Lion, Inc., is an interesting analysis of a successful regional supermarket chain. Management has developed a unique positioning concept. Deciding how to compete in the future is a vital concern to management. The case highlights several strategic analysis and planning issues.

The opening of borders has led to interesting issues at **Banco Nacional de Comercio Exterior, S.N.C. (BANCOMEXT) (Case 2–5).** As the Mexican bank charged with providing promotional services in support of Mexico's foreign trade,

BANCOMEXT is having a difficult time matching its notion of a market orientation with the way Mexico's small and medium-sized companies conduct business.

Optical Fiber Corp. (OFC) (Case 2–6) produces fiber optic materials for use in fiber optic cables for information transmission. In seeking to reduce its role as a captive supplier, OFC is trying to develop end user markets rather than being a supplier to cable companies.

CASE 2–1
NAVISTAR INTERNATIONAL TRANSPORTATION CORPORATION

A truck is a capital good. It's purchased to do a job. It's not purchased for esoteric reasons, it's only purchased to create value for the user. The buyer is a very professional person or company. They are looking for something that's going to create a return for them. [Our job] is understanding the needs of each one of those customers.

Gary E. Dewel

Gary E. Dewel, senior vice president of sales and marketing at Navistar, reflected upon the strategic intent that had been a major factor in the Fortune 500 company's turn-around. A descendant of International Harvester Corporation, Navistar was on the brink of bankruptcy in 1982. Heavy debt, rising interest rates, and a struggling agricultural business resulted in the loss of $3.4 billion between 1980 and 1985. New management, facing the task of transforming the stifling bureaucracy into a flexible organization with the ability to compete in an increasingly competitive trucking industry, had chosen to focus on reducing costs and increasing customer service. Management felt that a greater familiarity with the customer would result in a competitive advantage that had been lacking in Navistar's history. Management knew, however, that a customer orientation would have to go hand in hand with new avenues for cutting costs. At the same time, Navistar had to keep abreast of market changes as a result of the North American Free Trade Agreement (NAFTA).

The Company

History.   In 1831, Cyrus H. McCormick pioneered the first mechanical grain reaper, providing the foundation for International Harvester—a company specializing in the production of farm machinery. Trucks became part of Harvester's core business in the 1920s, as soldiers returning from World War I continued the industrialization of the United States. Perhaps beginning Harvester's troubles, Fowler McCormick, grandson of the late Cyrus, led the company into an era of haphazard expansion in the late 1940s, culminating in a devastating battle to dethrone Caterpillar's leadership of the construction machinery industry.

In the 20 years that followed Fowler's 1951 ousting, Harvester was hindered by an unmanageable variety of truck models. Attempting to provide such a wide product offering, Harvester ignored both production capabilities and marketing difficulties. At the same time, a lack of customer awareness resulting in gross underestimation of tractor demand severely limited Harvester's main business. Costs soared and profit margins disappeared.

The agricultural boom of the 1960s and 1970s provided cover for Harvester's rigid structure and rising cost base. The series of strikes and concessions to the United Auto Workers (UAW) through the early 1980s resulted in operating inefficiencies through-

This case was prepared by Victoria L. Crittenden, associate professor of marketing, Boston College, and John DeVoy, MBA student, Boston College, as the basis for class discussion rather than to illustrate effective or ineffective handling of a managerial situation. Research assistance was provided by David Angus, undergraduate research assistant, Boston College/Andersen Consulting Fund. All information was derived from secondary sources. Revised 1997.

out the corporation. Capital spending, aimed at the modernization of aging factories, was increased modestly, but barely offset administrative inefficiencies. The most agonizing union battle came at the start of the 1980 recession, resulting in a six-month strike. Lost sales, rising interest rates, and a growing debt left the company struggling for survival. Trying to keep the company afloat, Archie McCardell, who succeeded McCormick in 1978, sold the company's profitable Solar Turbines unit to Caterpillar in 1981 and disposed of several smaller businesses, including the company's unprofitable steel mill.

New management was brought in by early 1982. Donald Lennox (on the verge of retirement from International Harvester) began presiding over the company. Unfortunately, his tenure began at the start of four of the worst years in the company's history. Saddled with tremendous debt and outdated product lines, Lennox was forced to do everything possible just to keep the company from hemorrhaging cash.

With the sale of its losing agricultural business to Tenneco in 1985—along with the rights to the Harvester name—the company adopted the name Navistar and began to focus exclusively on manufacturing trucks.

Navistar International Corporation. Navistar International Corporation, with its world headquarters in Chicago, Illinois, was a holding company. The corporation was the leading producer of heavy and medium trucks and school buses in North America. The corporation's principal operating subsidiary was Navistar International Transportation. The products were sold to distributors in certain export markets. The company had financial services subsidiaries which provided wholesale, retail, and lease financing as well as commercial physical damage and liability insurance. Dealers and retail customers comprised the majority of the financial services customers.

In 1986, led by James C. Cotting as CFO, the company posted its first full-year profit since 1979, earning $2 million on sales of $3.4 billion. Cotting maneuvered the company through a vast restructuring during the mid-1980s and became chief executive officer in 1987.

Cotting's long-range plan was for half of Navistar's revenue to come from new businesses by 1997. These new businesses were to come from acquisitions related to Navistar's core truck business. While simultaneously seeking acquisitions, Cotting began cutting costs internally. For example, the plan was to trim 450 white-collar jobs and add more medical copayments on employee insurance by 1990.

Navistar International Transportation Corporation. The transportation subsidiary of Navistar operated in one principal industry segment—the manufacture and marketing of medium and heavy trucks. This included school bus chassis, midrange diesel engines, and service parts.

Led by Neil A. Springer and based in Chicago, Illinois, the company had introduced 22 new models by 1989. These models replaced S-Series units, which were introduced in 1977 and 1978. Additionally, the company began partnering with its customers and its suppliers.

In late 1987, when U-Haul International wanted to revamp its medium-size rental truck, it could not initially find a supplier that would agree to make the requested design changes. No one was interested because U-Haul was requesting some nontraditional ideas. However, Navistar began working with U-Haul and the result was that Navistar won an order for 5,400 trucks. U-Haul received a prototype five months after an agreement was reached with Navistar. Dana Corporation, Navistar's frame supplier and partner, brought the truckmaker and U-Haul together.

Started in 1986, the Navistar/Dana Corporation vertical partnership was one of the oldest and most fully developed partnerships between two companies.[1] Both companies felt that combining Dana Corporation's component design expertise and manufacturing capability with Navistar's ability to put the total system together and manage distribution would be an advantage for each firm. The success of the partnership led to partnering between Navistar and Goodyear and between Navistar and Caterpillar. As such, when Navistar introduced two dozen new models in late 1988, the product display included drive trains composed of Caterpillar engines, transmissions, clutches, drivelines, and axles plus Goodyear tires.

In 1987, top management supported a major cost-cutting proposal—electronic data interchange (EDI). In its simplest form, EDI involved the electronic exchange of business documents over a standard telephone line using computer information systems. Prior to EDI, Navistar's monthly needs were mailed to suppliers and daily production requirements were phoned in. With EDI in place, Navistar was able to instantaneously transmit and receive documents that had previously taken up to a week of processing time. As a result, inventories were reduced from 33 days' supply to an average of six days', and as little as four hours' inventory in some instances. Navistar was able to cut its inventory by $167 million (33 percent) in the first 18 months of EDI implementation.[2]

The U.S. Truck Marketplace

The beginning of the 1990s was not an easy time for truck manufacturers. The trucking industry was reeling from a business recession (which began for truckers around the middle of 1989) that meant both rising fleet expenses and sluggish freight traffic. The economy had posted a 1 percent decline from the third quarter of 1990 through the second quarter of 1991. Predictions were that the economy would begin working itself out of that decline, but the outlook was not good with growth rates maybe around 2 percent. This translated into expected sluggishness in the trucking marketplace.

Truck Class.   Several classes of trucks existed in the truck marketplace. Classes 1 and 2 were considered light-duty trucks. A rise in sales for Class 1 (under–6,000–lbs. GVW[3]) trucks was predicted at the beginning of 1990. Class 2 (6,001-to-10,000–lbs. GVW) sales were thought to have peaked in 1990 and declines were projected for the early 1990s. Vehicles sold for straight commercial fleet applications were expected to account for slightly over 10 percent of combined Classes 1 and 2 sales.

The emerging segment of the commercial market was Classes 3 and 4. Class 3 (10,001-to-14,000–lbs. GVW) was the only vehicle class to show growth in the early 1990s. Class 4 (14,001-to-16,000–lbs. GVW) showed signs of growth and the outlook was positive. The smallest commercial market class in annual sales, Class 5 (16,001-to-19,500–lbs. GVW) had peaked in sales in 1985 when over 8,000 units were sold.

The medium-duty trucks encompassed Classes 6 and 7. Class 6 (19,501-to-26,000–lbs. GVW) and Class 7 (26,001-to-33,000–lbs. GVW) showed signs of growth. Medium-duty truck sales were predicated on wholesale and retail traffic. Other factors had begun affecting sales in this category as well. One, there was a large number of

---

[1] Interestingly, the partnership did not include a written contract between Navistar and Dana. The deal was consummated on a handshake and a lot of trust.

[2] Prior to EDI, a one-day reduction in inventory was the largest the company had been able to achieve.

[3] GVW refers to Gross Vehicle Weight.

late-model used trucks in this range. Two, fleets had begun stretching replacement cycles due to increases in warranty mileage coverage.

Heavy trucks made up the Class 8 (over-33,000–lbs. GVW) market. The market for Class 8 trucks had been declining. Projections were that this market would not see an increase until 1992. There was concern that 1991 would be the worst year since the 1982–83 recession. The industry's replacement-demand pattern was being reshaped due to more productive trucks and an increase in warranty mileage. The trend in the heavy-truck market was toward trucks designed specifically for a single vocation.[4]

The outlook for the mid-1990s was better than for the beginning of the 1990s. The expected economic recovery would be further along, and carriers would begin replacing older trucks with newer-technology vehicles. Vocational or job-specific trucks[5] were increasingly being considered by buyers and sellers in Classes 3 through 8. Another trend was toward automatic transmissions. By the early 1990s, around 70 percent of Class 3 trucks sold were automatics.

Buying Behavior.   Fleet managers were bombarded daily with trade magazines[6] and factory mailings regarding product offerings. Additionally, OEMs and suppliers would often bring their product directly to the offices of larger fleets. The annual International Trucking Show, however, was the premier show for truck manufacturers and truck users to interact. The show offered a hands-on introduction to the newest in trucks and refinements to existing trucks. Another show in which suppliers of trucking equipment and OEMs exhibited was the beverage industry's premier show, the InterBev.

Order specifications from a fleet owner were so detailed they could fill several pages and include as many as 200 line items. Exhibit 1 provides an example of the types of specifications requested by a fleet owner. A large percentage of items might require a specific manufacturer's part. Additionally, there was some concern that many standard parts had not been tested sufficiently prior to becoming standard. In 1989, estimates were that 60 percent of fleets operating less than 10 trucks had Class 8 trucks built to order. The number increased steadily by fleet size, with 94 percent of fleets operating over 100 Class 8 trucks requesting built-to-order trucks. This was a 35 percent increase in built-to-order compared to 1985 figures.

Many truck manufacturers had begun focusing upon ways in which they could help the transportation industry address some of its most pressing concerns. A major industry concern was the turnover rate of drivers. It was not uncommon to hear of 80, 100, 110, and 200 percent annual turnover rates among U.S. private fleet owners. The turnover rate problem was compounded by an increasing driver shortage attributed primarily to low pay, long hours away from home, and uncomfortable equipment.[7] Another major industry concern was holding down costs for the fleet owner.

To address the driver shortage/turnover rate problem, truck makers were concentrating on improving the driver "environment." Manufacturers were providing high tech

---

[4] Some industry experts doubted that there would ever be the time when a *standard* model Class 8 truck would be popular.

[5] These were trucks tailored as much as possible to the job requirements of specific vocational applications in given market segments.

[6] Examples include *Fleet Equipment, Fleet Owner, Distribution,* and *Equipment Management.*

[7] The driver shortage problem was expected to be made worse in the short term by the Commercial Driver's License (CDL), which was to be phased in nationwide by 1991. The CDL would provide one national license instead of several state licenses for truck drivers. The short-term impact was expected to be a decrease in the number of drivers (both good and bad). The longer-term impact was expected to be an improved quality of truck driver.

EXHIBIT 1   **Example of Fleet Owner Specifications**

Category	Percentage of Total Items Ordered
Standard to manufacturer	27%
Improved maintenance	35
Operational requirements	11
Improved safety	8
Increased driver comfort	7
Improved appearance	7
Fuel economy	5

Source: "Spec'ed or Standard," *Fleet Equipment,* June 1989, pp. 38–42

features for comfort, maneuverability, safety, fuel economy, vehicle operation, and maintenance. Manufacturers of Classes 7 and 8 trucks were paying increased attention to drivability, ergonomics, and creature comforts.[8] Both truck manufacturers and fleet owners felt that a driver would treat the truck better if he or she was treated well.

To help fleet owners keep costs down, manufacturers were offering tremendous engineering advances with introductions of new aerodynamic and fuel-efficient designs. As well, durability had improved, with proper maintenance and repowering delaying capital expenditures for equipment replacement. There was even talk of the 1,000,000-mile truck.[9]

Industry Competitors

In the medium and heavy truck categories (principally Classes 7 and 8) there were seven leading manufacturers: Ford, Freightliner, Mack, Volvo, Peterbilt, Kenworth, and Navistar.

Ford.   Ford was the manufacturer of a complete line of light-duty through Class 8 trucks. It produced both diesel and gasoline-powered vehicles. Ford had traditionally been the industry leader in Class 7 trucks. Its major truck plant in Kentucky was dedicated to medium and heavy trucks. This facility operated a rapid scheduling system for special orders. An $18 million computer system allowed Ford to save weeks of special engineering by comparing current and historical orders as a way of utilizing existing designs to speed vehicle delivery time. The company operated 28 field locations in the United States. In 1990, Ford planned to spend three times as much money on its heavy-duty truck line as it had in the previous five years. The plans were to upgrade every piece of equipment by 1995.

Ford offered a long line of Classes 7 and 8 trucks. The LTLS-9000 was designed for the heaviest applications. The most appropriate Ford truck for long-haul cargo applications was the LTL-9000. Ford's L-Series included a broad range of other heavy-

---

[8] Ergonomics is the scientific study of human factors in relation to working environments and equipment design. Examples include dashboard layout, support and seating adjustments, and outside visibility. An example of a creature comfort is an oversized sleeper cab.

[9] The 1,000,000-mile truck would go 1,000,000 miles with good routine maintenance and without rebuilding major components.

duty trucks. In 1991, Ford was to offer its new AeroMax series. This aerodynamic series focused on fuel efficiency. Additionally, Ford planned to offer 24-hour emergency road service for the AeroMax.

Ford had conducted driver surveys at truck stops across North America. These surveys focused on driver comfort issues. As a result of the information gathered in these surveys, Ford had plans to offer convenience items such as a dash-mounted cup holder, lumbar support in the driver's seat, an innerspring mattress, and a television package.

Freightliner.   Of the seven leading heavy-truck manufacturers, Freightliner offered the broadest range of Class 8 equipment. In 1990, Freightliner began offering five new glider kits to complement its line of trucks. The glider kits provided an economical means for fleet owners to upgrade existing vehicles. The kits included the frame, finished cab, front axle with wheels, fuel tanks, steering systems, and electrical, cooling, and exhaust components. Basically, the kits enabled owners to turn an older truck into a new, customized truck with the high-tech features of Freightliner's new trucks.

Freightliner planned to introduce a new design focusing on interior comfort. Features to be included were an interior allowing occupants to stand anywhere in the forward compartment, a wide-open sleeper, and multiple shelves and storage units/closets in the sleeper. This new offering would provide an improved ride inside a lighter-weight, aerodynamically designed truck.

The company's production was 17,000 units in 1986 and remained relatively stable at 23,000 to 24,000 units from 1987 through 1991.

Mack.   "Built like a Mack truck" was a popular American saying. Trying to continue this tradition, Mack promoted its durability and technological innovation, particularly in its Class 8 CH600 series. The CH600 series, launched in 1990, was Mack's premier truck. The series introduced Mack's V-MAC electronics system.

V-MAC, an acronym for Vehicle Management and Control, was a fully integrated, all-vehicle electronic control system that aimed to optimize vehicle performance and driver efficiency. Mack believed that its V-MAC was the start of total vehicle management which would provide consistent vehicle performance through precise electronic control of fuel delivery and engine timing. The V-MAC offered several programmable options that would enable owners to adapt the truck to their particular needs and applications. The programmable options included cruise control, engine shutdown, idle shutdown, and variable engine speed limit. Mack felt that the V-MAC addressed the current and future needs of the industry.

Regarding creature comforts, Mack boasted that its Class 8 CH600 had the most comfortable ride of Class 8 trucks in the industry. This was attributed to its unique air-suspended cab/sleeper combination. The CH600 was also the roomiest and quietest model Mack had ever produced. Standard in the truck were a tilt-telescoping steering wheel and a two-piece, wraparound windshield. Options included power windows and door locks and a high-rise sleeper-cab configuration.

Mack's production had increased steadily from 1986 to 1988 (from 17,000 units in 1986 to 23,000 units in 1988). However, production had tapered off to 15,000 units in 1990 and 10,000 units in 1991. The company expected production to increase for 1992.

Volvo GM.   During the late 1980s, Volvo and General Motors (GM) formed a new company, Volvo GM, to develop Class 8 trucks. Volvo owned 76 percent and GM owned 24 percent of the new company. Volvo GM accounted for 34 percent of Volvo Truck Corporation's 1990 worldwide sales. Volvo's two product lines introduced in 1986, the FE Series Class 7 and Class 8 trucks, remained its two major lines at the beginning of the 1990s.

Both the Class 7 and Class 8 trucks featured dashboards, seating, and steering wheels designed to improve driver comfort and performance. The Class 8 models were designed to provide a high degree of fuel efficiency through advanced aerodynamics.

To better meet customer demands of flexibility and to appeal to a wider base of customers, Volvo began assembling its FE Series Class 7 trucks in its Ohio plant in 1991. The trucks had been assembled in its Belgium plant. In another move to push the company closer to the customer, Karl-Erling Trogen (president of Volvo GM) had plans to improve parts availability, increase training, enhance literature offerings, improve computer systems, and improve communications (via satellite) between headquarters and the company's 200 dealers. Trogen's goal was to increase the penetration of Volvo components in American trucks.

Peterbilt.   Peterbilt, a division of Paccar, offered a wide range of models in its Classes 7 and 8. Safety and driver concerns were major factors in the design of Peterbilt's newer models. To provide smoother ride quality, Peterbilt introduced its first front air suspension in 1990. To address safety concerns, the company provided a Bendix BPR-1 bobtail proportioning system as an option on its trucks. The Bendix BPR-1 was designed to prevent rear axle lockup. This, in turn, reduced stopping distances and decreased uneven wear on the truck's rear tires.

Peterbilt's Class 7 line of trucks shared the same name with its sister company, Kenworth. This Mid-Ranger series was designed for ease of maintenance, better visibility and maneuverability, and a tighter curb-to-curb turning circle than a conventional Class 7 truck.

Kenworth.   The Paccar division selling Class 7 and 8 trucks along with Peterbilt, Kenworth offered several models in its Class 8 line. The models offered improved aerodynamics, which boosted fuel economy. Kenworth attempted to target its Class 8 truck models to particular market segments. For example, its T400A was marketed to fleets transporting consumer and business-to-business products such as general freight, petroleum, food, and lumber. Its K100E was targeted toward moving companies, truckload carriers, and private fleets. The company's Class 7, Mid-Ranger series mirrored Peterbilt's.

Navistar.   With production averaging around 75,000 units a year from 1986 through 1991, Navistar was the nation's largest truck manufacturer.[10] The focus of the company's truck design at the beginning of the 1990s was ergonomics. The manufacturer planned to increase driver comfort through a new axle designed to improve driver maneuverability, increase aerodynamics and driver visibility, plus offer new interiors and more electronic controls (e.g., cruise control). The plan was to update 65 percent of the company's product line by the end of 1992.

Customer support also was the center of attention at Navistar. As part of the company's greatly expanded parts program, a new service maintenance kit for truck air conditioning systems was introduced in 1990. The kit contained all of the parts needed

---

[10] Production peaked in 1988 at 85,000 units, with a low of 63,000 units in 1991.

for the annual preventive maintenance of all makes of its International trucks. The kit was made available through Navistar's network of 900 North American dealers.

Many of Navistar's trucks carried the International name. However, the company also offered its 8000 (Class 7) and 9000 (Class 8) series. Like Freightliner, Navistar was strong on glider kits in 1990, with the kits available for its 8000 and 9000 series models. By the beginning of the 90s, the company had introduced 22 new truck models which replaced models brought to the market in the late 1970s. There were plans to introduce a limited-edition model focusing on the very best in driver comfort.[11]

The International Truck Marketplace

Mexico and South America were potentially large markets for truck manufacturers. With the passing of the North American Free Trade Agreement (NAFTA) in 1993, U.S.-based companies were presented with new challenges as well as new opportunities. In its purest form, NAFTA allowed products and services to cross borders just as easily as they moved within a nation. While NAFTA was drawing immediate attention, implementation of its components was expected to take as long as 15 years. Highlights of NAFTA included

- Greater access to the Mexican marketplace for U.S. and Canadian manufacturers.
- Tariff cuts on vehicles with substantial North American parts and labor.
- Equal treatment for international and domestic companies doing business in Mexico.
- Phasing out of barriers to investment in the Mexican trucking industry.
- Continuation of individual-country environmental, health, and safety standards.

Mexico's population was estimated to be 95 million in 1995. With its accelerated population increase and significant growth in its industrial sectors, Mexico, by the beginning of the 1990s, had a larger industrial base than Belgium, Spain, or Sweden. Mexico's government appeared adamant in expanding Mexico's infrastructure to continue to support the country's ongoing industrialization.

As part of the continued investment in infrastructure, the country's National Investment Program called for the construction of several major highways to connect industrial centers such as Kermosillo and Nogales, Monterrey and Tampico, Guadalajara, and the port of Mansanillo. One new major Mexican highway was complete by early 1993. This 163-mile toll route between Cuernavaca and Acapulco, however, cost around US$150 to travel round-trip. (There was concern that truckers would not use expensive toll roads but would instead stick to the older roads, especially since time was not considered to be worth as much as money.) In addition to new roads, Mexico had a young, cheap work force. A Mexican worker earned just US$10 to US$20 a day. Capital costs could be cut by using more of these workers and fewer robots and less expensive machinery.

The American Society of Transportation and Logistics estimated that 1.7 million truckloads of goods accounted for 85 percent of all freight moving between the United States and Mexico. This generated US$75 billion in annual revenue. The American Trucking Association estimated that 6,000,000 truckloads of goods would travel

---

[11] Only 250 units would be produced. The cabs would feature air-suspended, high-back leather seats with dual armrests, an easy-to-read instrument panel accented by genuine rosewood trim, and an upgraded stereo system.

between the two countries by the year 2000. Approximately 85 percent of total freight tonnage in Mexico was transported by truck. Achieving reforms instigated by NAFTA would allow private industry to expand their operations—allowing expanded operations in the trucking industry.

This industrialization and rapid GDP growth in Mexico had led to a sharp increase in sales of medium and heavy trucks (Classes 6 through 8). Annual truck sales in 1990 were around 6,000 units but had doubled by 1991. Expectations were that unit sales would hold near the 1991 total for three to five years. The Mexican truck fleet was very large with an estimated 550,000 trucks in operation at the beginning of the 1990s. The trucks had an estimated average age of 12 years—nearly twice the average for the U.S. truck fleet. Mathematically, industry sales would have to exceed 45,800 trucks a year to prevent further aging of Mexico's fleet.[12]

A Mexican company, Grupo Dina, dominated the Mexican truck market with close to 50 percent of the medium- and heavy-truck market. Kenmex, the Mexican division of Paccar, assembled Kenworth and Peterbilt trucks at a plant in Mexicali. While dominating the Mexican heavy-truck market for three decades, Kenmex had begun to face intense competition. Other truck manufacturers in Mexico in the early 1990s included Daimler Benz and Chrysler.

Projections were that the South American commercial vehicle market would be around 6,500 new trucks (4,000 heavy-duty trucks and 2,500 medium trucks) by the early to mid-1990s. In 1991, around 31 percent of Classes 6, 7, and 8 trucks shipped out of North America by U.S. producers were sold in South America. The relatively sound economy in Chile offered truck exporters a solid base from which to spread into nearby countries.[13] Additionally, Chile had no vehicle import restrictions, and there was no Chilean truck manufacturing industry.

U.S. companies that had entered Chile by the early 1990s were Ford, General Motors, Navistar, Kenworth, Mack, and Freightliner. There were also manufacturers from Europe and Asia. Russia's Kamaz truck had become the best-selling truck (medium-duty). The Kamaz had edged out Mercedes-Benz, which had truck assembly operations in Argentina and Brazil.

In addition to Chile, other South American countries such as Venezuela, Colombia, Brazil, and Argentina were becoming more industrialized. Although several of these countries were battling high inflation—2,937.8 percent in Brazil and 2,311.3 percent in Argentina in 1990—there were still South American countries with relatively stable economies. Chile's annual rate of inflation was 26 percent, Venezuela's was 40 percent, and Colombia's fell between the two.

A few of these countries were already producing commercial vehicles. Brazil, for instance, produced 251,600 units in 1990. However, many other South American countries were producing fewer. For example, Chile only produced 8,000 commercial vehicles in 1990. Colombia and Venezuela produced 17,700 and 21,600 units, respectively, in 1990.

As South American nations became more industrialized, they would need more commercial trucks. Usage of these trucks could be quite large considering that, in 1990, South America's total population was approximately 297.01 million people (over 20 million more people than found in the United States and Canada).

---

[12] Douglas Laughlin, "Automotive–Heavy Trucks: A Sunshine Industry in Mexico," *Institutional Investor* (June 1993), p. SS8.

[13] Peru was seen as the country to enter after getting established in Chile.

A Customer Orientation

Navistar was the largest truck manufacturer in the United States. But could it remain in that position long, given its competitors' customer-oriented actions? Dewel knew a customer focus was necessary to survive in the highly competitive truck marketplace. But, how could he implement this customer focus when he also had a mandate to cut costs? Weren't the two goals contradictory? Also, what about the international marketplace?

Sources

Baker, Stephen. "Detroit South—Mexico's Auto Boom: Who Wins, Who Loses." *Business Week,* March 16, 1992, n.3256 (Industrial/Technology Edition), pp. 98–103.

Birkland, Carol. "Gasoline Engine Update." *Fleet Equipment,* April 1992, pp. 14–17.

Burr, Barry B. "Navistar Joins Electronic Pay Age." *Pensions & Investment Age,* April 6, 1987, pp. 37–38.

Byrne, Harlan S. "They Almost Bought the Farm, But Navistar and Varity Are on the Road to Recovery." *Barron's,* May 2, 1988, pp. 6–7, 32–34.

Cullen, David. "Building Working Assets." *Fleet Owner,* August 1991, pp. 55–58.

Cullen, David. "The Long Pull Ahead." *Fleet Owner,* January 1992, pp. 30–36.

Darlin, Damon. "Maquiladora-ville." *Forbes,* May 6, 1996, pp. 111–12.

Deierlein, Bob. "The Next Best Thing." *Beverage World,* September 1992, pp. 92–96.

Deierlein, Bob, and Tom Gelinas. "Spec'ed or Standard." *Fleet Equipment,* June 1989, pp. 38–42.

Deveny, Kathleen. "Can the Man Who Saved Navistar Run It, Too?" *Business Week,* March 9, 1987, p. 88.

Dumaine, Brian. "How Managers Can Succeed through Speed." *Fortune,* February 13, 1989, pp. 54–59.

Duncan, Thomas W. "Adding Muscle to Light-Duty Trucks." *Fleet Owner,* August 1988, pp. 77–82.

Duncan, Thomas W. "Chile Emerging as Export Prize." *Fleet Owner,* December 1992, p. 12.

Gage, Theodore Justin. "Cash Makes a Comeback in Navistar Financing." *Cash Flow,* December 1987, pp. 53, 58.

Gonze, Josh. "EDI Users Anticipate X.12 Boost." *Network World,* November 30, 1987, pp. 2, 45.

Green, Larry. "Building the Best Business Partnership." *Equipment Management,* April 1991, pp. 18–23.

Green, Larry. "Staying Power." *Equipment Management,* June 1991, pp. 25–30.

Heinze, Bernd G. "Big Wheels Keep on Turning." *Business Mexico,* November 1995, pp. 42–43.

"Highway Tractors: Accent on the Creature Comforts!" *Traffic Management,* November 1992, pp. 49–52.

Kraul, Chris. "Hauling Down to Mexico." *Los Angeles Times,* April 11, 1996, section D, p. 1.

Laughlin, Douglas K. "Automotive—Heavy Trucks: A Sunshine Industry in Mexico." *Institutional Investor,* June 1993, p. SS8.

Martin, James D. "Attention Returns to Heavy-Duty Trucks." *Distribution,* November 1990, pp. 54–62.

Mele, Jim. "The 1,000,000 Mile Truck." *Fleet Owner,* April 1994, pp. 77–83.

Milbrandt, Ben. "EDI: A More Efficient Way to Operate." *Corporate Cashflow,* August 1990, pp. 34–35.

Milbrandt, Ben. "Making EDI Pay Off." *Corporate Cashflow,* December 1988, pp. 24–28.

Moore, Thomas L. "Forging Partnerships." *Fleet Owner,* May 1992, p. 4.

Moore, Thomas L. "New Volvo GM Head Pushes Customer Focus." *Fleet Owner,* February 1, 1992, p. 96.

Najlepszy, Frank. "Turnaround in Truck Design." *Machine Design,* April 7, 1988, pp. 40–48.

Navistar 1993 Annual Report.

"Navistar's New Lines of Medium-, Heavy-Duty Conventionals Replace S-Series Models." *Fleet Owner,* January 1989, pp. 58–61.

Palmeri, Christopher. "Bridge Financing," *Forbes,* November 8, 1993, pp. 43–44.

Stavro, Barry. "A Surfeit of Equity." *Forbes,* December 29, 1986, pp. 62, 64.

"Supplier Partnerships . . . Who Benefits?" *Fleet Equipment,* July 1989, pp. 43–45.

Teresko, John. "Speeding the Product Development Cycle." *Industry Week,* July 18, 1988, pp. 40–42.

"The Construction Market in Mexico." *Construction Review,* July-August 1991, pp. ix–xiv.

"Truck Makers Feature Safety, Driver Comfort." *Traffic Management,* October 1991, pp. 73–77.

Flowers are a perfect replica of human life: planting, growth, bloom and withering. I guess flowers say it best from birth to death.

Jim Moretz[1]

It was very late on an unusually warm, humid evening on January 29, 1998. Marketing executives at Floral Farms, a producer and distributor of fresh-cut flowers, were brooding over the day's planning meeting. Leslie Stair, marketing manager, and John August, vice president/sales manager, were sitting in Leslie's office discussing the exchange between the Miami-based marketing group and the Colombian-based growers.

Leslie and John had gone into the yearly planning meeting feeling better than ever! The 1998–99 marketplace looked good, resulting in an expected sales increase for all their products. Leslie and John had presented their sales projections (with reasons why) for all 11 of Floral Farms' major flower products. The euphoric feeling had lasted all day—while questions had been asked about how projections were derived, the meeting had appeared to be going smoothly.

However, after Leslie and John had completed their presentation, Carlos Diaz, vice president of production (headquartered in Colombia), commented, "You made a very nice presentation. It's too bad that we can't increase output by the amounts you projected for the June 1998–May 1999 time period. We can't change production for any of the products for the next 11 months. What is planted is planted. I will send you an overview of product availability for the upcoming fiscal period." After asking that marketing and production work toward an agreeable projection, Manuel Ortiz, the company's owner, adjourned the meeting.

The Fresh-Cut Flower Industry

Globally, annual retail sales of fresh-cut flowers were estimated at US$25 billion. While Europeans were the largest spenders when it came to fresh flowers, the decade of the 1990s opened with Americans increasing their spending for what had once been considered a luxury item. Americans had begun buying fresh-cut flowers like Europeans—for any occasion or no occasion. While changing consumer taste was one driver for the increased purchasing behavior, availability was thought to be a major driver. Americans no longer had to purchase fresh-cut flowers from a florist, as they were available in a variety of locations. For example, supermarkets, discount stores, department stores, corner pushcarts, electronic kiosks,[2] and catalogs had become popular

---

[1] As quoted in "Flower Power" by Anne Keegan, *Chicago Tribune Magazine,* February 16, 1991, sec. 10, p. 15.

[2] Electronic kiosks could be placed in shopping malls, airports, offices, and so on. Orders are placed by the press of a few buttons.

This case was prepared by Victoria L. Crittenden, associate professor of marketing at Boston College, and William F. Crittenden, associate professor of management at Northeastern University, as the basis for class discussion rather than to illustrate either effective or ineffective handling of a managerial situation. Research assistance was provided by David Angus, Boston College/Andersen Consulting Fund.

points of purchase, accounting for almost 50 percent of floral industry sales by the mid-1990s.[3] As well, American consumers could bypass FTD[4] (and the accompanying fee) by calling the toll-free telephone numbers of many large florist shops. The U.S. wholesale flower market was valued around US$600 million.

Changes in distribution were not the only modifications taking place in the floral industry. Flower growers had begun extending the lives of fresh-cut flowers by precooling them to 36 degrees Fahrenheit before shipment. With some flower varieties, this meant a 15-day life cycle after being cut. Six states (California, Florida, Michigan, Ohio, Pennsylvania, and Texas) were considered to be the top floriculture producers. While many flowers were grown in U.S. greenhouses, fresh-cut flowers were imported daily. These imports were said to be making fresh-cut flowers much cheaper.

Imports.   Fresh flower imports accounted for around 75 percent of the cut flowers sold in the United States. Carnations, pompons, and roses accounted for around 60 percent of imports.

In the late 1980s, American growers claimed that imports from 10 countries were injurious to the domestic fresh-cut flower market. These 10 countries included Canada, Chile, Colombia, Costa Rica, Ecuador, Israel, Kenya, Mexico, the Netherlands, and Peru. Additionally, American growers identified five types of imported flowers causing the most harm: carnations, chrysanthemums, alstroemeria (a type of lily), gypsophila (often called baby's breath), and gerberas (a daisy). Although the International Trade Commission did rule that imports might be causing harm to domestic products, feelings were mixed among members of national floral councils. Some industry spokespeople were unclear if it was imports or the change in farm size (e.g., major producers instead of small mom-and-pop producers) driving some companies out of business. While imported flowers were not produced much cheaper than flowers grown in the United States, they were easier to obtain year-round. Also, imported flowers arrived just as quickly as U.S. shipments.

The Dutch held a 20 to 25 percent share of the U.S. wholesale cut flower import market and were responsible for around 65 percent of world cut flower exports. The flower industry—one of the leading industries in the Dutch economy—consisted of around 11,000 growers and 5,000 buyers. Buyers participated daily in the Dutch flower auctions. While there were seven flower auctions in the Netherlands, the Verenigde Bloemenveilingen Aalsmeer (VBA) was the largest auction of its kind worldwide, with 43 percent share of the market. Around 14 million flowers were sold daily via the VBA. Mexico and Colombia were top exporters to the VBA. Largely due to strict laws regarding insects and soil particles, less than 5 percent of the VBA's business was shipped into the United States.

Most flowers sold in the United States were grown in Colombia (accounting for about 70 percent of U.S. flower imports). About 80 percent of carnations and 40 percent of roses sold in the States were from Colombia. Colombia's cut flower exports amounted to US$315 million by the mid-1990s. Accounting for 10 percent

---

[3] Additionally, with gross margins of 40 to 50 percent, floral products were some of the highest-margin items at these locations.

[4] Florists' Transworld Delivery Association (FTD), a member-owned group, linked approximately 23,000 independent flower shops in North America. This allowed a customer in Boston to easily send flowers to a friend in San Francisco. The FTD florist in Boston would receive approximately 20 percent of the price, the San Francisco FTD florist received approximately 73 percent, and the FTD association received 7 percent.

of the world's flower exports, the floral industry was Colombia's second largest employer.

Thailand was the leading orchid grower. Thailand's fresh flower exports, of which orchids were about 75 percent, equaled around US$80 million. The Japanese were the largest importers of Thai flowers (about 50 percent), with Europe importing around 25 percent of the country's flowers and the United States about 20 percent. Thai exports were about 1.5 percent of the total U.S. flower import market.

Floral Farms

Floral Farms grew and marketed fresh-cut flowers. The company's mission statement was

> We are in the business of growing floral products. We will grow high-quality products, of a wide variety, and distribute these products worldwide. We will have the reputation as a high-quality producer. As well, we will seek to optimize investments, maximize long-term profits, and develop human resources.

Exhibit 1 diagrams the company's organization. The company owned its own farms in Colombia. The marketing organization for Floral Farms was located in Miami, Florida.

Floral Farms had been in Manuel Ortiz's family for decades. As such, although Floral Farms was only a small portion of the Ortiz family wealth, Manuel maintained a strong interest in Floral Farms' success. However, he had turned active, daily responsibility and control over to Carla Williams. Manuel and Carla had met at an executive MBA program in the States. Their mutual interest in imports–exports and their South American heritages had made it easy for a friendship to develop. Their two families had grown close. Manuel's and Carla's daughters attended the same college in California.

Customers.   Floral Farms' customers included (1) local wholesalers in different cities (which accounted for 95 percent of Floral Farms' sales), (2) supermarket retail chains, and (3) the end-consumer (via the company's retail operation in New York). U.S. and Canadian sales combined represented 95 percent of the company's total sales. The remaining 5 percent of sales was to selected importers in Europe, the Caribbean, and South America.

Marketing.   The Miami-based marketing group was responsible for all U.S. and Canadian sales. Vice president/sales manager John August had been with the company for 10 years. He had 13 salespeople, with a goal of having at least 20 by the end of 1999. Leslie Stair, marketing manager, had been with Floral Farms for two years. Prior to Floral Farms, she worked as a buyer at a large retail chain in Florida.

Exhibit 1   Corporate Structure

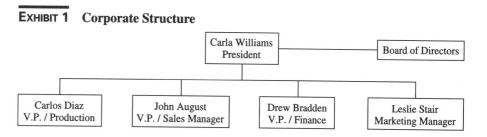

Products. The company had 11 major flower products:

1. alstromeria
2. carnations
3. miniature carnations
4. freesia
5. gerbera
6. gypsophila
7. lilies
8. pompons
9. roses
10. spider mums
11. statice

The quality of Floral Farms products was considered to be very high. Some lines had received various floral awards for consecutive years. Workers at Floral Farms took great pride in the care, handling, and sales of their products.

Distribution. All Floral Farms flowers were air-shipped from Colombia into Miami. The products would clear customs at the Miami airport and were then reshipped via airfreight or trucking companies to their next destination of wholesaler, supermarket, or the New York retail outlet. (While the company had operated five retail locations at one time, the differences in marketing products to distributors and end-consumers had proven to be too large for the company to manage effectively. Thus four locations had been closed, leaving only one operation, New York City's, to sell flowers directly to the public.)

Fresh-cut flowers were packed in cardboard boxes of 100 to 1,000 units depending upon the variety and packing size.

Prices. Fresh-cut flower prices followed a seasonal pattern. Moreover, in reality, prices fluctuated by the minute. The company's salespeople contacted customers via telephone from a large salesroom in the Miami office. The going rate for all fresh-cut flowers was posted constantly on the room's dry-erase board. A salesperson always had to be aware of the correct price for the products he or she was selling. For example, the salesperson could be talking to one customer in New York and quote a particular price for x number of stems of roses. Five minutes later, the salesperson might be talking to another customer in New York and quote a different price for that number of stems of roses.

However, historical pricing patterns did exhibit some yearly consistency. Rose prices were higher around February 14, carnation prices were highest around February 14, pompon prices were lowest during summer months (May–July), and there was an inverse relationship between industry/Floral Farms supply and prices for all products.

Marketing Communications. Buyers (wholesalers and supermarkets) seemed pleased with Floral Farms products. While the company did use Floral Farms as a brand name, there was no name recognition among end-consumers. Basically, final purchasers of fresh-cut flowers did not know if they were buying a Floral Farms product or not. The company did no trade or consumer advertising.

Production. Floral Farms owned three farms in Colombia. Each had a general manager, who reported to Carlos Diaz, vice president/production. While Carlos reported to Carla Williams, Carla's Miami-based location often meant that Carlos contacted Manuel Ortiz directly when something came up and/or he needed information or guidance.

Colombian farms were in Las Palmas and Jardines de Colombia. While Floral Farms was one of around 200 floral growers in the country, it was one of the largest and most respected operations, with approximately 175 hectares available for flower production. By the late 1980s, the Colombian government had stopped its low-cost financing for carnations, roses, and pompons.

Floral Farms was entertaining the purchase of farm land in both Ecuador and Peru. Diaz was looking at 100 hectares in Ecuador and 144 hectares in Peru.

Ecuador was considered the second-best production country behind Colombia. Environmental elements, such as better light and less temperature fluctuation, were thought to be important variables to consider in future production expansion possibilities. Additionally, import laws were fairly open and labor was cheaper than in Colombia. However, transportation was complicated due to altitude limitations in Ecuador's capital, Quito. Products would have to be shipped from the coast, a seven-hour drive from the company's farm.

There were three farms available in Peru, for a total of 144 hectares. Flowers slated to be grown in Peru, should the farms be purchased, were gypsophila, statice, minicarnations, and pompons. Additionally, Diaz thought Floral Farms could utilize the climate in Peru to experiment with some new types of roses and carnations.

Exhibit 2 provides the production cycle for the 11 major products grown by Floral Farms. Due to year-round demand for floral products and the company's reputation as a full-line supplier, production for any of the products could never be zero.

The January Planning Meeting

The January planning meeting was the first of its kind at Floral Farms. A consultant hired by the company owner had recommended that the production people travel to Miami once a year for a planning session. Additionally, the marketing group had made its first trip to visit the Colombian farm sites in November 1997. It was decided to

EXHIBIT 2   Production Cycle of Major Crops

Flower Crop	Vegetative Period (weeks)	Production Period (weeks)	Number of Plants per Square Meter	Production per Square Meter by Production Cycle
Alstroemeria	24	156	2.84	590 stems
Carnations	21	83	22.82	380 flowers
Minicarnations	21	83	21.64	42 bunches
Freesia	19	6	53.3	5.26 bunches
Gerbera	16	88	5.1	255 flowers
Gypsophila	13	10	3.42	9 bunches
Lilies	14	2	65	61 flowers
Pompons	12	1	68.9	9 bunches
Roses	18	520	5.58	900 flowers
Spider mums	12	2	58	5.6 bunches
Statice	16	36	4.62	24 bunches

make the trip an annual project. The idea behind annual on-site visits, according to the consultant, was that such cross-functional interaction was necessary for the company to become market-oriented.

As part of the attempt to implement a companywide market orientation, the consultant had expressed a desire that top management participate in the cross-functional interactions. As such, the Colombian owners, members of the board of directors, and the president of the Miami-based operations had participated actively in the November visit and were present at the January planning meeting.

Stair and August thought that they were well prepared for the meetings. They felt that their visit to the Colombian farms greatly added to their product knowledge. It had been exciting for them to see and experience hectare after hectare of floral products. As businesspeople, they sensed they would be better able to speak the language of the production people and also be in a better position to talk to their customers.

The marketing group had worked extremely hard in preparing for the January planning meeting. Stair and August had planned to use the meeting for two major purposes: (1) to orient the production people to the marketing side of the business and (2) to share with production and top management the vast potential in the marketplace.

All meeting participants had been provided with a notebook of information detailing the analysis the marketing group had gone through to reach its recommendations. The information included three years of historical company data regarding (for each product) hectares in production, Floral Farms' unit sales, Floral Farms' percentage of U.S. market, Floral Farms' percentage of Colombian exports to the United States, total amount sold to the United States, production costs (growing, freight, duty), average selling price, and return per square meter. Tables and graphs showed fiscal year 1997–98 monthly product quantity and monthly average price. (Exhibit 3 shows sales projections, production costs, and average selling price for each of the 11 products, as provided to meeting participants.)

Evening of January 29, 1998.   Leslie looked at the clock. It was 10:53 PM and she was exhausted! After going to dinner and having a couple of drinks, she and John had come back to the office. They had rehashed the meeting—who had said and done what? Leslie looked at John and asked, "What happens now? Should we call Carlos

EXHIBIT 3   Marketing/Production Projections

Flower Crop	1998–99 Sales Projection	Increase over Previous Season	Production Cost (U.S.$)[1]	Average Selling Price (U.S.$)
Alstroemeria	2,080,375	115%	$0.17	$2.71
Carnations	100,022,562	25	0.08	0.14
Minicarnations	2,367,000	21	1.02	1.79
Freesia	226,500	27	0.13	1.69
Gerbera	6,076,500	45	0.19	0.22
Gypsophila	454,290	97	1.41	2.76
Lilies	1,184,000	2	0.40	0.52
Pompons	6,453,750	14	0.72	1.26
Roses	26,235,775	46	0.17	0.32
Spider mums	1,465,350	20	1.25	2.50
Statice	555,750	166	0.95	1.62

Note: Sales projections are in units as are costs and average prices.

[1] Production cost includes growing cost, freight, and duty.

and plan to go to Colombia in the next couple of weeks? I don't know what it would accomplish. We really can't prepare any more marketing data. Should we wait for Carlos to call us? Manuel did say that production and marketing were supposed to work this out. So, that's him the same as us. I wonder if he is worrying tonight like we are. It really ticked me off that Manuel adjourned the meeting so quickly after Carlos's statement. It was almost as though he let Carlos close the meeting. In looking back over the last few minutes of the day, the way things were handled makes me very uncomfortable."

John agreed with Leslie. He reminded her that the consultant had told all of them that they had to begin communicating more (and better). That was one of the notions behind the cross-functional site visits. However, John thought that Carlos had been very uncommunicative that day, letting them go through the entire sales forecast and then making the comment that he did.

Leslie and John decided to revisit the issue the next day. Maybe they could both think better after a good night's rest. As they were leaving the office, John said, "What can we do to make Carlos see the importance of fulfilling our sales projections? Our recommendations take Floral Farms from 1998 fiscal year sales of slightly over US$50,000,000 to almost US$70,000,000 for the 1999 fiscal year. What's wrong with that? The market is out there. Floral Farms production only has to provide us with the correct amount of the right products at the right time!"

Sources

Bennett, Stephen. "Flower Power." *Progressive Grocer,* November 1994, pp. 105–10.

"Budding Battle over Cut Flowers." *The Nation's Business,* September 1986.

Caughey, Terry. "Dutch Treat; Away from Amsterdam, Holland Offers a Variety of Quaint, Scenic Charms." *The Patriot Ledger,* January 11, 1997, p. 36.

"Colombian Business, Fallow Ground." *The Economist,* October 23, 1993, p. 86.

Deveny, Kathleen. "Now the Flower Business Is Blooming All Year." *Business Week,* December 23, 1995, p. 59.

Driessen, Christoph. "Dutch Market's Flower Power Growing Daily." *Chicago Tribune,* May 10, 1993, p. 8.

Faber, Harold. "A Big Drop in Flower Sales May Prompt an Industry Recount." *The New York Times Metro,* May 22, 1994, sec. 1, p. 40, col. 1.

Gillis, Chris. "The Netherlands' 'Other Airline,' Martinair Holland." *American Shipper,* July 1996, p. 73.

Grier, Peter. "A Rose Is . . . Likely to Be from South America." *The Christian Science Monitor,* February 14, 1992, p. 1, col. 2.

"Halloween Boo-quets, Anyone?" *Forbes,* October 26, 1992, pp. 206–08.

Handley, Paul. "In the Pink." *Far Eastern Economic Review,* February 27, 1992, pp. 58–59.

Hill, Helen. "Flower Power: Budding Logistics for a Worldwide Market." *Air Cargo World,* October 1996, p. 34.

"Innovating to Be Competitive: The Dutch Flower Industry." *Harvard Business Review,* September–October 1995, pp. 130–31.

Juilland, Marie-Jeanne. "Melridge Is Bustin' Out All Over." *Venture,* June 1987, pp. 33–34.

Keegan, Anne. "Flower Power." *Chicago Tribune Magazine,* February 10, 1991, sec. 10, p. 10, col. 2.

Levy, Robert. "Flower Power in the Supermarket." *Business Month,* March 1997, pp. 62–63.

"Md.'s Flower Industry Continues to Blossom." *Washington Post,* August 26, 1991, sec. WBIZ, p. 43, col. 5.

Steinmetz, Greg. "FTD to Look at Bids to Make It Bloom Again." *The Wall Street Journal,* November 2, 1994, sec. B, p. 1, col. 6.

Woodward, Richard B. "Business Is Booming." *The New York Times Magazine,* May 9, 1993, pp. 33–36.

CASE 2–3
QUALITY PLASTICS INTERNATIONAL S.A. DE C.V.

Sergio Trevino de Elizondo was enthusiastic regarding the potential of his plastic manufacturing business, Quality Plastics International S.A. de C.V. (QPI). Company sales and profits had increased yearly (see Exhibit 1). Exports to Canada and the U.S. had grown to 45 percent of revenues. Numerous new customers were added each year and a number of North American firms were seeking quotes from QPI.

However, Trevino was puzzled by recent comments from two of his managers. Yesterday, plant manager Federico Gonzales Ojeda had grumbled about the demands being placed on manufacturing. Yet QPI had recently purchased another injection molding machine, and Gonzales had quickly and successfully brought it on line. And this morning, QPI's accountant, Rosa Maria Maldonado, voiced concerns with the record keeping and financing involved with having so many customers.

Background

Trevino founded the plastic molding concern in 1987 to fill the tubing needs of his former employer, a local refrigerator manufacturer. Acting when another supplier failed to provide needed components in a timely fashion, Trevino recognized that many firms in Nuevo Leon, Mexico, could use a local, reliable, low-cost alternative to suppliers from the United States, Europe, or the Far East. Outsourcing trends made QPI's strategy look good. An increasing number of firms were purchasing components and parts from outside suppliers in order to concentrate on product development, assembly, and other basic strengths.

Marco Aldana de Luna, director of business development and sales, believed success resulted from two key factors:

We give the customers what they want, and we do it at a good price.

EXHIBIT 1 QPI Operating Results
(Mexican new peso, figures in thousands)

	Sales	Net Profit
1993	8,304	298
1992	6,475	246
1991	4,385	193
1990	3,426	154
1989	2,741	110
1988	1,570	58
1987	821	<15>

Current (1993) exchange rate 3.21 pesos per US$.

This case was prepared by Associate Professor William F. Crittenden of Northeastern University as the basis for class discussion rather than to illustrate either effective or ineffective handling of an administration situation. Names and figures have been disguised. Key relationships have been preserved. Copyright July 1994.

EXHIBIT 2   QPI's Operating Policies

We will sell quality products to satisfy the needs of various consumer and industrial segments while offering efficient and accommodating service. Our customers always deserve a good price.
We are proud of our Mexican heritage and we want to remain an independent company.

We do not wish to be controlled by suppliers and wish to remain free to buy materials when and where we want to buy.

Single customers may not purchase more than 20 percent of our production capacity.

Excellent labor–management relations are our goal at all times. We deal with our workers each day so that all problems may be solved in an atmosphere of mutual understanding and respect.
We believe in the importance of personal and corporate integrity.

Although QPI had started as a component manufacturer, they had also been successful in cracking the market for finished products. Toy manufacturing was an especially successful segment. They also were involved with a promising insulated mug manufacturing venture; they would be marketing and distributing in Mexico and Central and South America.

Trevino believed his workers were instrumental in the growth of his firm.

We pay a good wage to attract workers, and we have a young productive work force. Our employees do not have a union and this has given us great flexibility.

With industrial wages and benefits averaging 7.3 new pesos per hour, Mexican workers earned less than many Asian workers (e.g., Hong Kong, 12.1 new pesos; and Singapore, 14.8).

Since its inception, QPI's management had developed a management philosophy that, accompanied by certain basic guidelines, governed the operations of the business and that Trevino believed had much to do with the steady progress of the firm. The guidelines are described in Exhibit 2. Key financial data for QPI are provided in Exhibits 3 and 4. Although Trevino owned most of the company (65 percent), his top managers shared 15 percent, and a Texas investment firm held the remaining 20 percent.

EXHIBIT 3   QPI's Income Statement Information
(constant Mexican new pesos, figures in thousands)

	1993	1992	1991	1990
Net sales	8,304	6,475	4,385	3,426
Cost of goods sold	6,228	4,662	2,937	2,261
Gross profit	2,076	1,813	1,448	1,165
Selling expenses	1,254	965	548	428
Administrative expenses	392	383	242	232
Operating income	430	465	658	505
Foreign exchange gain (loss)	28	–87	–361	–268
Income after foreign exchange	458	378	297	237
Taxes	160	132	104	83
Net profit	298	246	193	154

Source: Quality Plastics International S.A. de C.V. annual report.

EXHIBIT 4   QPI's Balance Sheets as of December 31
(constant Mexican new pesos, figures in thousands)

	1993	1992	1991	1990
Assets				
Cash and liquid securities	261	385	734	684
Accounts receivables	887	508	403	342
Inventory				
Raw materials	383	376	388	392
Work in process	269	247	186	174
Finished goods	423	412	317	298
Total current assets	2,223	1,928	2,028	1,890
Machinery and equipment	1,160	1,083	971	971
Furniture and fixtures	52	45	33	33
Vehicles	48	48	48	48
Less depreciation	181	158	108	108
Total long-term assets	1,079	1,018	944	944
Total Assets	3,302	2,946	2,972	2,834
Liabilities and Equity				
Current liabilities	915	837	688	613
Long-term liabilities	1,378	1,309	1,668	1,749
Total liabilities	2,293	2,146	2,356	2,362
Common stock	165	165	165	165
Retained earnings	844	635	451	307
Total equity	1,009	800	616	472
Total Liabilities and Equity	3,302	2,946	2,972	2,834

Note: Mexican Generally Accepted Accounting Principles (GAAP) require property, plant, and equipment depreciation, and materials and supplies to be stated at net replacement cost.

Source: Quality Plastics International S.A. de C.V. annual report.

Quality Plastics International is located in Escobedo, Nuevo Leon, Mexico. Nuevo Leon, in Northern Mexico, is known for its dynamic industrial activity. The industrial concentration, principally in the metropolitan area of Monterrey (Escobedo is part of the Monterrey metro area), has created a high level of diversification. Many of Mexico's most important industrial groups are located in this area, notably Alfa, producer of steel, synthetic fibers, paper, and foodstuffs; Visa, specializing in beer and processed foods; Vitro, manufacturer of glass and glass-related goods; and CYDSA, which concentrates on chemical products, petrochemicals, and synthetic fibers. A skilled work force, solid infrastructure, and close proximity to the United States contributes to Nuevo Leon's strong exports. The population is approximately 3.2 million. Approximately 30 percent of the employed work force is female. Organized labor accounts for 35 percent of the work force.

Mexico and NAFTA

Mexico is a federal democratic republic, with 31 states and the Federal District (the capital). With 1,972,550 square kilometers, Mexico is the thirteenth largest country in the world and third largest in Latin America. The economy of Mexico is mixed. The government, its agencies or government-owned/controlled companies, dominate in the areas of utilities, petroleum, and certain basic manufacturing. Private enterprise is the principal factor in manufacturing, mining, commerce, entertainment, and the service industry. Foreign investment is found most frequently in manufacturing and mining.

The United States is Mexico's largest trade partner, accounting for 70 percent of total exports. Conversely, Mexico is the United States' third largest trading partner, accounting for approximately $75 billion in total trade. Since the mid-1980s, imports from the United States have grown from $12 billion to over $40 billion a year. Canada, members of the European Community, and members of the Latin American Integration Association also do substantial international trade with Mexico.

Industrial production accounted for about 25 percent of Mexico's GDP and had an estimated growth rate of 4.5 percent. Principal manufacturing industries included the automobile and auto parts producers; steel manufacturers; the textile industry; food processing; breweries; glass; chemicals and petrochemicals; and cement and other materials for the construction industry. The Mexican plastics production industry represented 0.5 percent of Mexico's total GDP and was expected to grow 7 to 9 percent annually.

The North American Free Trade Agreement (NAFTA) presented Mexican companies with many new opportunities and challenges. Mexican firms faced expansion options in Canada and the U.S., while facing increased competition in home markets from Canadian and American firms. Ultimately, most goods and services will cross borders just as easily as they move within each nation.

Plastic Products

Plastic was cheap, light, corrosion-resistant, and easy to fabricate. The production process for most plastic shapes was well defined. Primary inputs (monomers and polymers) were reacted with chemical reagents to impart desired characteristics, and then processed using one or more methods such as coating, extrusion, molding, or laminating.

Consumption of plastic products was highest in the electronics, health care, construction, transportation and automotive, and food packaging industries. Material substitution (e.g., plastic for metal, wood, or glass) was not expected to contribute to growth, reflecting an already high level of substitution. However, new applications were emerging. These would place greater demand on convenience and safety features. Demand for recycled and biodegradable materials was expected to continue and drive development of more economical recycling technologies.

Plastic waste constituted a minor component of total North American solid waste collected; however, plastic waste was generally very visible and the percentage of total plastic recycled was low compared with total production. Efforts to develop environmentally safer products in response to public pressures were an industry priority.

Although the global economy appeared to be coming out of a prolonged slump, many economists suggested very low growth would be the norm. In addition, long-term interest rates appeared to be headed upward. Spokespersons for the North American plastics manufacturing industry indicated concerns with worldwide excess capacity.

Customers

Most customers used several criteria to determine from whom to purchase, yet Trevino believed the most important was price. Equipment capabilities and reputation for reliable delivery were other factors. Customers also considered continuity of relationships with sales representatives, although most multisourced.

EXHIBIT 5   **QPI's Major Accounts in Canada and the United States, 1993**
(U.S.$, figures in thousands)

Bombardier	$102
Carrier Air Systems	253
Fisher-Price	71
Ideal Toy	525
Little Tykes	26
Sears	32

QPI's customers were principally located in Mexico (especially Coahuila, Chihuahua, and Nuevo Leon), although the company has had significant sales in Canada (Ontario and Quebec) and the United States (Texas, Illinois, and New Jersey). Exhibit 5 lists QPI's major international accounts.

According to international sales manager Juan Luis Padilla Sanchez,

> Through our own five-person sales organization, our products are sold throughout Mexico. Outside Mexico, we use brokers, who have several noncompeting clients for whom they sell. We would like to have our own direct sales force in select North American markets.

Some customers ordered one-time only; others demanded a guaranteed price for a period of time. For example, a customer might plan to purchase a specific number of units every month for a year and would seek a guaranteed price for the year. However, the customer was under no obligation to actually make this purchase each month. In fact, actual purchases tended to be quite seasonal. This placed varying demands on manufacturing and on different types of equipment. For example, demand for toy manufacturing was strongest early to late autumn, while demand for air conditioning tubing was strongest late spring to early summer.

Padilla believed QPI had many advantages in the North American market:

> We are a very customer-oriented company. We are very flexible and will customize products based on market demands. Our manufacturing people do not always like it—but we have to give the customers what they want.

Except for repeat business, pricing was always unique to the needs of the customer. Quotes had to be approved by a regional sales manager. Quotes generally included product specifications, lot size, price, and date(s) of delivery. Often there were immense pressures to submit a quote by a specific time.

QPI operated in the highly competitive plastic injection molding and extrusion businesses. Worldwide, some 40,000 plastic injection molding companies are in operation. Hong Kong was estimated to have at least 5,000 such firms.

QPI performed little in-house R&D. The customer delivered product specifications and often developed and owned the individual molds required to produce the product.

Competition

QPI faced four types of competitors:

1. Firms that competed exclusively in injection molding. These firms tended to be very focused on a few well-defined customer segments.
2. Firms that competed exclusively in plastic extrusion. These firms were often "captive" or had strong strategic alliances with a few large customers.

3. Multiprocessing firms with molding, extrusion, and sometimes additional capabilities. These firms often had their own R&D capabilities and could work with customers to design molds, product graphics, packaging, and so on.

4. Large, vertically integrated manufacturers. These firms required large volumes of product and could support their own plastic processing operations. Competition resulted during slack periods when these large firms would "rent" unused capacity to other firms. This added capacity to the industry and depressed prices. These firms were principally in extrusion.

Raw material manufacturers seldom vertically integrated into the plastic processing business due to the need for very different capital investment and skills. Overall, injection molding was an approximately 203-billion–peso business worldwide, with 40,000 competitors. The U.S. was estimated to have some 2,800 molders, while Canada had fewer than 300. Hong Kong claimed 5,000. Extrusion constituted a 165-billion–peso global business and had some 15,000 competitors.

Suppliers

Raw Materials.   Between 1987 and 1993, Mexico's consumption of plastic resins increased at an average annual rate of 6 percent reaching 1.5 million tons. Imports were estimated to represent 35 percent of total consumption in terms of value and 24.8 percent in volume. For 1994, supply imports were estimated to exceed 2.1 billion new pesos, a 9 percent increase over 1993.

Raw material supplies from the U.S. dominated the Mexican import market with a 90 percent share. Mexican buyers were receptive to U.S. suppliers for several reasons: geographic proximity, familiarity with American resins and materials, perceived quality, reliability, and price competitiveness. In addition, many Mexican plastic processors were subsidiaries of U.S. companies and purchased from or through their U.S.-based counterparts.

German suppliers had approximately 4.6 percent of the market and Japanese firms less than 1.5 percent. However, for Japanese firms, this was an increase from less than 0.25 percent share in 1989.

Chronic worldwide overcapacity, particularly in Europe and Japan, depressed long-term prospects and had led to price declines. Plant closures and capacity cutbacks were expected to continue.

Equipment.   Plastics manufacturing was very capital intensive. However, fierce competition between Asian, European, and North American plastic molding machine builders had depressed some equipment prices. Japanese makers had not raised prices in three years, yet they continued to add features. A recently formed group calling itself the Coalition of North American Machinery Manufacturers gave notice that it was concerned with dumping. It was alleged that machines were discounted below cost to gain market share or to sell off excess production that the market could not absorb at normal prices. However, Trevino saw this as a boon to his business as he could purchase additional new machinery and pursue new business with much less investment than when he began QPI.

QPI plant manager Federico Gonzalez Ojeda worried about the machine purchases that were being made.

> Worker training and maintenance with many different machines could become a problem. Machine changeover, service delays, and an unreliable supply of spare parts could hurt our productivity.

EXHIBIT 6   QPI Machinery

Date Purchased	Manufacturer	Function	Purchase Price[1]
1987	Engel	Injection	$ 37,500 (used)
1988	Battenfelds	Extrusion	48,000 (used)
1989	Demag[2]	Injection	109,000
1990	HPM	Injection	46,000
1990	Battenfelds	Extrusion	52,000
1992	Toshiba	Injection	33,700
1993	Jinwa	Injection	24,250

[1] International purchases by Mexican firms are generally made in U.S. dollars.

[2] The Demag injection press was a multipurpose machine with broad product flexibility. Each extruder also could produce a fairly wide range of products.

QPI owned two extruders and five injection molding machines. The two extruders were made by the same manufacturer. Exhibit 6 identifies the major machinery owned by QPI.

Physical Distribution

Transportation: QPI owned two trucks that were used to make deliveries in Nuevo Leon, to pick up locally produced raw materials, or to transport goods between two manufacturing sites and a warehouse. Outside carriers handled deliveries to other Mexican states, the U.S., and Canada. If an order could not be completely filled by the deadline, partial shipments were made and the remainder sent as a back order. This generally increased shipping costs about 20 percent more than if the total order had been shipped on time. Border crossing delays had often been experienced in the past, chiefly due to inspections by U.S. immigration officials. Further, some local carriers were known for uneven or slow delivery, but had prices 30 percent below their competitors.

Inventory: Each manufacturing plant had modest storage area for raw materials and finished goods. The warehouse supported the bulk of raw material and finished goods storage, and all customer orders were shipped from the warehouse.

Conclusion

QPI had experienced tremendous growth in its seven-year history. An aggressive sales team had consistently added new customers. New equipment allowed diversification substantially beyond refrigeration tubing. More recently, the North American Free Trade Agreement had created increased visibility for Mexican suppliers. While changes in trade barriers were important to all of Mexico, QPI's record of customer satisfaction as a supplier to Canada and the U.S. created excellent opportunities to gain new customers in the North American continent. Trevino was excited about gaining new customers and showing the world what QPI could do for a customer. He wished he could extend his enthusiasm to his entire management team.

In 1957 three former Winn-Dixie employees opened their first supermarket in Salisbury, North Carolina, under the name Food Town. Cofounders Ralph Ketner, Brown Ketner, and Wilson Smith all had considerable retail experience in the grocery industry; however, Food Town struggled in its early years. Various marketing gimmicks were implemented (the company gave away trading stamps and even free automobiles), but the stores failed to win the loyalty of customers. In fact, Ralph Ketner had to close 9 of the 16 stores during the first 10 years of operation. He blamed much of this failure on the underpricing techniques of Winn-Dixie. By 1966, only seven Food Town stores remained.

In response to the problem, Ketner decided to slash prices on all items sold in the stores. He realized that a drastic increase in volume would be necessary to make this approach work and keep the company afloat. The company theme of LFPINC or "Lowest Food Prices in North Carolina" became popular as both customers and sales increased greatly. Sales rose 54 percent to $8.9 million, and profits rose 165 percent to $95,000 in the first year under the new pricing strategy.[1]

In 1970 the company went public. Établissements Delhaize Frères et Cie, a Belgium grocery chain, purchased 47.6 percent of the stock in 1974. Today, Delhaize controls 50.6 percent of the voting stock and has 5 of the 10 seats on the board of directors.[2] The company changed its name to Food Lion in 1983 to avoid confusion with another similarly named chain. Also, the company began implementing its expansion program.

Today, Food Lion operates in eight states, from Delaware to Florida, and is considered to be one of the fastest growing retail grocers in the country. (See Exhibit 1.) Food Lion President and CEO Tom E. Smith explains, "Our goal is to bring extralow grocery prices to as many people in the Southeast as possible."[3]

Food Lion has 27,000 employees, and continues to operate conventional-size stores (21,000–29,000 square feet) and to offer discount prices. The company remains committed to expansion throughout the Southeast and has avoided moving into the sales of general merchandise in its stores. A food consultant's comments highlight the company's success in the aforementioned areas. He states that Food Lion is "probably the best example of commitment to a format and operating style in the industry today. And although it is a conventional store operator, it also stands as an excellent practitioner of niche marketing. The stores aren't fancy, but beat everyone on price, and the company doesn't make many mistakes."[4]

---

[1] Richard Anderson, "That Roar You Hear Is Food Lion," *Business Week,* August 24, 1987, p. 66.
[2] Ibid.
[3] *1987 Food Lion, Inc., Annual Report,* p. 1.
[4] Richard DeSanta, "Formats: Growing Apart, Coming Together," *Progressive Grocer,* January 1987, p. 37.

Prepared by Janet L. Caswell under the direction of Professor Neil H. Snyder, both of the University of Virginia. © 1988 by Neil H. Snyder.

EXHIBIT 1   Store Distribution

Location	Stores	Percentage of Total
North Carolina	233	49.1%
Virginia	112	23.5
South Carolina	74	15.6
Tennessee	29	6.1
Georgia	19	4.0
Florida	6	1.3
Delaware	1	0.2
Maryland	1	0.2
Total	475	100.0%

Source: *Standard & Poor's Stock Report,* p. 3905.

Ralph Ketner.   Since cofounding Food Lion, Ralph Ketner has continued to be a force behind its success. In 1968 it was his idea to adopt the strategy of discount pricing and his LFPINC theme which promoted the company. He acted as chief executive officer until 1986, when he passed the reins to President Tom Smith. Despite giving up his CEO title, Ketner still exerts considerable influence over the operation of Food Lion. He remains chairman of the board of directors, and plans to retain this position until 1991. In addition, Delhaize signed an agreement in 1974 to vote with Ketner for 10 years. This agreement was later extended and was in effect until 1989.[5]

Tom E. Smith.   President and CEO Tom E. Smith is very much responsible for Food Lion's growth and success. This is largely attributed to his involvement with the company since his youth. At age 17, Smith began as a bag boy at Food Lion's first store. He attended night school at Catawba College and graduated in 1964 with a degree in business administration. He spent the next six years working for Del Monte. Then he was hired as Food Lion's sole buyer. Smith developed the successful strategy of stocking fewer brands and sizes than his competitors. He also took advantage of wholesaler specials by purchasing large volumes at discount prices. He was named vice president for distribution in 1974, and later became executive vice president in 1977. His continued success in these areas led to his promotion to president in 1981, at the age of 39. In 1986 he was named CEO.

Smith views himself as a planner who carefully molds the company's growth while keeping a close eye on the operations. This style has enabled him to react to and resolve any problems quickly and effectively. He has been a primary reason for Food Lion's constant commitment to its overall strategy of discount pricing and cost reduction. Smith has also become well known through his participation in over 50 percent of the Food Lion commercials. This media exposure has brought him recognition not only in the Southeast, but as far away as San Francisco and even Scotland from visiting customers.[6] These commercials portray Smith as a hard working and very trustworthy manager.

---

[5] "Ketner Gives Up Food Lion Reins," *Supermarket News,* January 6, 1986, p. 18.
[6] Anderson, "That Roar You Hear Is Food Lion," p. 65.

EXHIBIT 2   **Percentage of U.S. Retail Sales by Type of Establishment**

Type of Establishment	1983	1984	1985	1986	1987*
Food stores	22.0%	21.1%	20.6%	20.4%	20.3%
Eating and drinking	9.9	9.6	9.7	10.0	10.1
Drug and proprietary	3.5	3.4	3.4	3.4	3.6
General merchandise	11.1	11.0	10.9	10.7	11.0
Furniture and appliance	4.6	4.8	5.0	5.4	5.5
Auto dealers	19.8	21.6	22.6	22.9	22.2
Hardware and lumber	4.4	4.7	4.8	5.2	4.7
Clothing	5.3	5.3	5.4	5.5	5.8
Gas stations	8.5	7.8	7.3	6.1	5.7
All others	10.9	10.7	10.4	10.4	11.2

Source: Bureau of the Census (Revised) 1987.
*First six months.

Food Lion's Attitude toward Social Responsibility

Food Lion is recognized as a corporate neighbor, and it takes pride in performing charitable acts. In 1986 the company received the Martin Luther King, Jr., Award in recognition of its humanitarian efforts. Food Lion received the award for its role in donating trucks to aid southeastern farmers during a prolonged drought; the trucks enabled the farmers to transport hay from Indiana. Also, the company was cited for providing equal opportunity employment and establishing express lanes for handicapped customers.[7]

The Supermarket Industry

Several trends in the supermarket industry were of concern to many retail grocers. During 1987 there was a decline in the percentage of disposable income spent for food at home. After discounting inflation, real sales did not increase from 1986. As Exhibit 2 shows, food-at-home spending accounted for more retail sales than any other category in 1983. However, slow growth has caused a reduction in this percentage, leaving food stores in second place behind auto dealers. The percentage of retail sales for eating and drinking establishments during this same period has trended upward.

The grocery industry is also experiencing competition from other types of stores. Discount department and drug stores are starting to sell more packaged foods. Many fast-food restaurants continue to sell a larger variety of prepared foods for takeout. Sales from specialty shops, which concentrate on one particular type of food, have increased as well. Wholesale clubs have also been of concern to retail grocers. These clubs have been effective at luring many customers away from conventional supermarkets. Those supermarkets stressing discount prices have been hurt most by the emergence of the wholesale clubs.

In response to the trends, most grocery chains are stressing the idea of one-stop shopping. New store formats and product offerings are abundant. These ideas are an attempt to obtain a product mix that stresses higher margin items and services, as well as creating an atmosphere causing consumers to view the supermarket as more than a

[7] *1986 Food Lion, Inc., Annual Report*, p. 4.

EXHIBIT 3   Chain Executives' Opinions on Prospects for New Formats

	Excellent	*Good*	*Fair/Poor*
Superstores	56%	35%	8%
Combination	38	53	9
Convenience stores	26	39	35
Superwarehouse	22	39	39
Hypermarkets	10	33	57
Specialty	8	37	55
Wholesale clubs	6	30	62
Conventional	4	35	59
Warehouse stores	1	17	79

Source: *Progressive Grocer,* April 1988.

place to buy groceries. Items such as flowers, greeting cards, videocassettes, and pharmacy items are appearing more frequently in many supermarkets. There has also been a greater emphasis on stocking perishables.

However, the biggest trend in the industry is the shift to bigger stores. Several experts believe that increased size is necessary to provide the variety that many consumers desire. One chain president expressed this sentiment: "Customer satisfaction starts with the store design: one-stop shopping, complete service departments, and integrating a drugstore and pharmacy into the store."[8] Much of the one-stop shopping trend is a result of increases in the numbers of working women, dual-income families, single parents, and singles living alone. Time and convenience are two characteristics that consumers fitting into these groups often desire.

The one-stop shopping concept has resulted in several new store formats. Combination stores offer consumers a variety of nonfood items. These stores can be as large as 35,000 square feet, and 25 percent of the space is devoted to nonfood and pharmacy items. Superstores are similar to the combination stores in that they offer a wide selection of general merchandise items. These stores are all greater than 40,000 square feet, and are thought to be the strongest format for the near future. Exhibit 3 shows chain executives' views on the prospects for the various formats that exist today.

The newest and largest of the formats is the hypermarket. Currently, 55 of these stores exist in the United States. The typical hypermarket ranges in size from 125,000 to 330,000 square feet and requires $25 to $50 million in sales per year just to break even.[9] Normally, 40 percent of the floor space in hypermarkets is devoted to grocery items and the remaining 60 percent is used for general merchandise. Freeway access, population density, and visibility are all key variables contributing to a hypermarket's success. A majority of the stores are run by companies that are not U.S. food retailers. For example, Wal-Mart has opened several stores under the Hypermarket USA name. Also, Bruno's, a retail grocery chain, is teaming up with Kmart to build a store in Atlanta.[10]

Because of the trend to expand store size, the number of stores declined for the first

[8] "Retail Operations: The New Basics," *Progressive Grocer,* September 1987, p. 56.

[9] David Rogers, "Hypermarkets Need Something Special to Succeed," *Supermarket Business,* May 1988, p. 26.

[10] Ibid.

EXHIBIT 4   Store Attributes Desired by Consumers

Rank	Characteristic
1	Cleanliness
2	All prices labeled
3	Low prices
4	Good produce department
5	Accurate, pleasant clerks
6	Freshness date marked on products
7	Good meat department
8	Shelves kept well stocked
9	Short wait for checkout
10	Convenient store location

Source: *Progressive Grocer,* April 1988.

time in years. However, the larger store sizes resulted in an increase in actual square footage. Many small units have been closed due to the openings of larger stores. In many market areas, there continue to be too many stores and too few customers to support them. This is going to be an even bigger concern given the advent of the combination stores and hypermarkets, since they tend to attract customers from a wider area than the conventional stores.

Although the majority of retailers believe that the bigger stores are necessary to be successful in the future, there is a large group that believes the industry is going overboard in its attempt to provide one-stop shopping. Chain executive Carole Bitter believes that the emphasis on size is unfounded. "There has been an ego problem in the industry that has led to overbuilding and has driven up store sizes and has increased the number of formats."[11] Proponents of conventionals claim that the larger stores are too impersonal to be attractive to everyone. They also believe that many consumers desire the conventional type of store, and that this format will continue to be successful. Although many consumers claim that they want more service departments, studies have shown that the shoppers are not willing to pay enough for such departments to make them profitable. Exhibit 4 reveals what the average shopper desires. One-stop shopping capabilities rates only 26th on the list.

Competition

In recent years, competition in the Southeast has become quite intense. Previously, this area was characterized by predominantly conventional stores. Combination and superstores were scarce. However, many retailers realized that the Southeast was a prime location for the newer formats. In 1984 Cub Foods opened three large, modern stores in the Atlanta area in an attempt to challenge Kroger's dominance in the Southeast. This move marked the beginning of several competitive shakeups in the South.

Kroger.   Kroger operates 1,317 supermarkets and 889 convenience stores in the South and Midwest. In 1987 sales were nearly $18 billion. More than 95 percent of the floor space is either new or has been remodeled during the past 10 years.[12] This is a

---

[11] "Retail Operations: The New Basics," p. 62.

[12] *Standard & Poor's Standard Stock Reports,* p. 1318.

result of the chain's move to larger combination and superstore formats. Kroger has not been as successful as it would like. The company realizes a net profit margin of approximately 1 percent. This is partly due to its new outlets cannibalizing its existing stores and has caused same-store sales comparisons to be relatively flat.[13]

In response to the disappointing profit margins, Kroger is planning to decrease its capital spending plans by about $300 million. It is hoped that this will reduce interest costs as well as keep start-up expenses down. Also, the firm is cutting corporate overhead 20 percent. As for future store designs, Kroger is considering the curtailment of the new superwarehouse stores. These stores combine low grocery prices with high-priced service departments and have not appealed to a large segment of the market. Furthermore, the company is planning to reduce store remodeling in mature market areas.[14]

Winn-Dixie.   Winn-Dixie is the fourth largest food retailer in the country with sales of nearly $9 billion. The chain operates 1,271 stores in the Sunbelt area, with the heaviest concentration of stores located in Florida, North Carolina, and Georgia. During the past few years, Winn-Dixie has been hurt by the influx of competition in the Southeast. As a result, profit margins have dipped to just over 1 percent. Net income also declined in 1987. Management points to a lack of investment in new stores and a rather slow response to competitors' underpricing methods as the main reasons for the decline in profits.[15]

Management has adopted several new strategies to combat the competition. Foremost is the move to larger store formats. In the past, the chain operated mostly conventional stores and depended on operating efficiencies to realize sizable profits. However, management believes that it is now necessary to alter the stores in response to changing consumer needs. At the end of 1987, the average supermarket was 27,700 square feet. There are approximately 250 new stores in the 35,000–45,000-square-feet range, and they are expected to account for nearly half of all sales in the next five years.[16] The units in the 35,000-square-feet category are combination stores operated under the Winn-Dixie name. The 45,000-square-feet stores employ the superstore format and use the name Marketplace. Emphasis is being placed on service departments as well as price sensitivity.

Other changes involve management. Last year, the company eliminated a layer of management that resulted in 60 layoffs. The firm is also adopting a decentralized strategy that divides the company into 12 operating units. Each division is allowed to develop its own procedures and image. It is hoped that this will help the stores cater to the consumers in each market area more effectively.

Lucky Stores.   Lucky operates nearly 500 supermarkets throughout the country. The majority of these are located in California; however, the chain does operate 90 stores in Florida. In 1986 Lucky began a major restructuring. This resulted in the sale of all the nonfood businesses. Also, the company has concentrated on increasing store size to enable the sale of more service and nonfood items. The average size of the stores at the end of 1986 was 31,000 square feet.[17]

---

[13] *Value Line Investment Survey,* 1987, p. 1511.

[14] Ibid.

[15] *Standard & Poor's,* p. 2491.

[16] "Winn-Dixie Strategy," *Supermarket News,* March 3, 1987, p. 12.

[17] *Standard & Poor's,* p. 1387.

EXHIBIT 5   **Selected Statistics for Major Southeastern Supermarket Chains, 1987**

	Kroger	Lucky	Winn-Dixie	Bruno's	Food Lion
Stores	2,206	481	1,271	111	475
Employees	170,000	44,000	80,000	10,655	27,033
Sales ($ million)	$17,660	$6,925	$8,804	$1,143	$2,954
Sales/employee	103,881	157,386	110,049	107,265	109,267
Net profit ($ million)	$246.6	$151	$105.4	$31	$85.8
Net profit margin	1.4%	2.2%	1.2%	2.7%	2.9%
Gross margin	22.4	25	22	20.8	19.2
Current ratio	1.1	.83	1.65	1.63	1.41
Return on equity	24.5	46.3	15.2	15.4	25.3
Return on assets	5.5	11.8	7.9	10.3	10.6
Long-term debt/equity	0.69	0.38	0.03	0.04	0.26
Earnings per share	$3.14	$3.92	$2.72	$.79	$.27
Average price/earnings ratio	15.1	10.2	13.9	23.1	35.3

Source: *Standard and Poor's.*

At the end of the year, there was much speculation that American Stores Company would begin to pursue an unsolicited tender offer for all outstanding shares of Lucky common stock. American is a leading retailer in the country and operates mostly combination food and drug stores.

Bruno's.   Bruno's operates approximately 100 supermarkets and combination food and drug stores in the Southeast. This chain pursues a strategy of high-volume sales at low prices. Another strategy involves the use of four different formats under various names. Consumer Warehouse Foods stores are relatively small warehouse stores that emphasize lower prices and reduced operating costs. Food World stores are large supermarkets that offer a variety of supermarket items at low prices. Bruno's Food and Pharmacy stores promote the idea of one-stop shopping through the combination store format. Finally, FoodMax stores are superwarehouses that offer generic and bulk foods in addition to the national labels.[18]

The company is also well known for its innovative forward buying program. Bruno's is able to purchase goods at low prices because of its 900,000-square-feet distribution center which houses excess inventory. This strategy has been very successful as the company boasts high operating and net profit margins.[19] Exhibit 5 presents comparative statistics for Food Lion and its four major competitors.

Expansion at Food Lion

Food Lion has continued to grow and expand in the Southeast. During 1987 the chain opened 95 new stores while closing only 8, bringing the total to 475. With the exception of four supermarkets, Food Lion operates its stores under various leasing arrangements. The number of stores has grown at a 10-year compound rate of 24.1 percent.[20]

---

[18] Ibid., p. 3358M.

[19] John Liscio, "Beefing Up Profits," *Barron's,* May 25, 1987, p. 18.

[20] *1987 Food Lion, Inc. Annual Report,* p. 9.

EXHIBIT 6   **Food Lion's Growth and Expansion**

Year	Stores	Sales	Net Income
1987	475	$2,953,807	$85,802
1986	388	2,406,582	61,823
1985	317	1,865,632	47,585
1984	251	1,469,564	37,305
1983	226	1,172,459	27,718
1982	182	947,074	21,855
1981	141	666,848	19,317
1980	106	543,883	15,287
1979	85	415,974	13,171
1978	69	299,267	9,481

Source: Food Lion annual reports.

With this expansion has come a 29.7 percent compound growth rate in sales and a 30.9 percent compound growth rate in earnings—see Exhibit 6.[21]

The existence and further development of distribution centers serve as the core for continued expansion. At the end of 1987, four such centers had been completed. These are located in Salisbury and Dunn, North Carolina; Orangeburg County, South Carolina; and Prince George County, Virginia. Two additional centers are planned for Tennessee and Jacksonville, Florida. These distribution centers enable Food Lion to pursue expansion using its "ink blot" formula. Using this strategy, new stores are added to an existing market area in order to saturate the market. "If anyone wants to go to a competitor, they'll have to drive by one of our stores," explains CFO Brian Woolf.[22] Despite the emergence of new stores, cannibalization has not been a problem. In fact, same-store sales increase approximately 8 percent annually. When Food Lion enters a new area, the strategy of underpricing the competitors is employed. Such a strategy has caused average food prices to decline 10–20 percent in some parts of the country.[23] Every new store is constructed no farther than 200 miles from a distribution center. With continued expansion, new distribution centers whose radiuses overlap an existing distribution territory are erected to keep warehouse and transportation costs down.

Moreover, Food Lion continues to employ a cookie-cutter approach to its new stores. Rather than purchase existing stores, the firm much prefers to build new ones from scratch. All the stores fall into the conventional store category. The majority are 25,000 square feet and cost only $650,000 to complete. These stores emphasize the fruit and vegetable departments. Approximately 40 percent of the new stores are 29,000 square feet and contain a bakery/delicatessen. These are placed after careful consideration is given to the demographics and psychographics of the area. Normally, new stores turn a profit within the first six months of operation. In comparison, most competitors construct slightly larger stores which cost over $1 million to complete.[24]

The standard size of the stores has allowed the company to keep costs down while sticking to basics. Aside from the bakery departments, Food Lion has stayed away

---

[21] Ibid.

[22] Liscio, "Beefing Up Profits," p. 19.

[23] "Food Lion's Roar Changes Marketplace," *Tampa Tribune,* April 5, 1988, p. 1.

[24] Anderson, "That Roar You Hear Is Food Lion," p. 65.

from service departments such as seafood counters and flower shops. Such departments are often costly due to the increase in required labor. Also, Food Lion has remained a retail grocery chain, shunning the idea of moving into the general merchandise area.

With the steady increase in stores over the past 10 years comes an increase in the need for quality employees. In an interview last March, Smith expressed concern over the high dropout rate of high school students.[25] Food Lion relies heavily on recent graduates, and the current trend may signal a decline in the quality of the average worker. Food Lion has responded to the labor problem by setting up an extensive training program for its 27,000 employees. These programs range from in-store training at the operational level to comprehensive training programs for potential managers. In addition, the firm continues to offer programs at headquarters to upgrade the work of the upper staff. Management is also attempting to increase the use of computers within the company. More specifically, Smith is hoping to utilize computer systems to handle much of the financial reporting aspects in the individual stores in an attempt to lessen the need for more employees.

Advertising

Rather than employ costly advertising gimmicks, such as double coupon offers, Food Lion's advertising strategy combines cost-saving techniques with an awareness of consumer sentiment. Smith is the company's main spokesman, appearing in over half of the television commercials. Not only has this method kept advertising expenses down, but it has also made the public aware of both Smith and his discount pricing policy. By producing most of the ads in-house and using only a few paid actors, the cost of an average TV spot is only $6,000. Also, the company policy of keeping newspaper ads relatively small results in annual savings of $8 million. Food Lion's advertising costs are a mere 0.5 percent of sales, one-fourth of the industry average.[26]

The content of the ads is another reason for Food Lion's success. Many of the TV spots feature some of the cost-cutting techniques used by the firm. One often-mentioned theme at the end of ads is "When we save, you save." Another commonly used theme states, "Food Lion is coming to town, and food prices will be coming down." Before moving into the Jacksonville, Florida, area, Food Lion launched a nine-month advertising campaign. Many of these ads focused on innovative management methods that permit lower prices to be offered in the stores. For example, one ad demonstrates how a central computer is used to help control freezer temperatures. Other ads attempt to characterize Food Lion as a responsible community member. One such spot describes the importance that management places on preventive maintenance for its forklifts and tractor trailers.

Smith has also used the media to react to potential problems. For instance, Winn-Dixie launched an advertising attack against Food Lion reminding customers how competitors have come and gone. The company countered with an ad featuring Tom Smith in his office reassuring consumers. "Winn-Dixie would have you believe that Food Lion's low prices are going to crumble and blow away. Let me assure you that as long as you keep shopping at Food Lion, our lower prices are going to stay right where they belong—in Jacksonville."[27] Smith also reacted quickly to a possible conflict in

---

[25] "Food Lion, Inc.," *The Wall Street Transcript,* March 28, 1988, p. 88890.

[26] Anderson, "That Roar You Hear Is Food Lion," p. 65.

[27] "Food Lion, Winn-Dixie in Animated Squabble," *Supermarket News,* September 14, 1987, p. 9.

eastern Tennessee in 1984. Several rumors circulated that linked the Food Lion logo to Satanic worship. In response, Smith hired Grand Ole Opry star Minnie Pearl to appear in the Tennessee advertisements until the stories disappeared.[28]

Innovations

The grocery industry is characterized by razor-thin margins. While most retail grocery chains have failed to introduce new innovations in the industry, Food Lion has employed several techniques that enable the firm to offer greater discounts on nearly all its products. These innovations help Food Lion to realize a profit margin of nearly 2.9 percent, twice the industry average. The company's credo is doing "1,000 things 1 percent better."[29] Such a philosophy has resulted in keeping expenses at 14 percent of sales as compared to the industry average of 20 percent.

Examples of the company's cost-cutting ideas are abundant. Rather than purchase expensive plastic bins to store cosmetics, Food Lion recycles old banana crates. These banana boxes are also used for storing groceries in warehouses. These innovations save the company approximately $200,000 a year.[30] Furthermore, the firm utilizes waste heat from the refrigerator units to warm part of the stores. Also, motion sensors automatically turn off lights in unoccupied rooms. Costs are further reduced by Food Lion's practice of repairing old grocery carts rather than purchasing newer, more expensive models. Perhaps the greatest savings can be attributed to the carefully planned distribution system. This system allows management to take advantage of wholesalers' specials. The centralized buyout-and-distribution technique allows products for all stores to be purchased at one volume price.

Moreover, labor costs remain lower than those of many competitors. Smith is vehemently opposed to the use of unionized labor. Despite protests from the United Food and Commercial Workers International Union claiming that Food Lion's wages are well below union standards, management has continued to please its workers and avoid unionization. In fact, Smith believes its employee-benefit package is unequaled in the industry. A profit-sharing plan linking an employee's efforts in making Food Lion profitable with wealth accumulation for the future is already in use. Plans to improve long-term disability insurance benefits are underway.[31] In contrast, several other chains have experienced problems solving labor union problems. For example, a month-long strike by Kroger's Denver-area employees resulted in concessions on wages, benefits, and work rules. Safeway employees were also given quick concessions after threatening to close down several stores.[32]

Other innovations are designed to increase sales. Food Lion often sells popular items such as pet food and cereal at cost in an attempt to draw more customers into the stores. The company makes $1 million a year selling fertilizer made from discarded ground-up bones and fat. Lower prices are also feasible due to the policy of offering fewer brands and sizes than competitors. The company has increased its private label stock, which now includes at least one unit in every category. These two methods allow the company to price its national brand products below many competitors' private brands. As mentioned earlier, the smaller store size and sale of mostly food items have contributed to the high profit margin realized by the company.

---

[28] Anderson, "That Roar You Hear Is Food Lion," p. 66.

[29] Ibid., p. 65.

[30] "Ad Series Heralds First Florida Food Lion," *Supermarket News,* March 2, 1987, p. 12.

[31] *1986 Food Lion, Inc. Annual Report.*

[32] *Value Line Investment Survey,* August 28, 1987, p. 1501.

EXHIBIT 7   **Selected Financial Ratios for Food Lion, 1978–1987**

Year	Operating Margin	Net Profit Margin	Return on Assets	Return on Equity	Long-Term Debt as a Percent of Capital
1987	6.8%	2.9%	14.2%	32.4%	26.0%
1986	6.9	2.6	14.1	29.8	24.0
1985	6.3	2.6	14.4	29.1	20.5
1984	6.3	2.5	13.6	30.2	22.8
1983	5.9	2.4	13.0	28.3	25.9
1982	5.6	2.3	15.7	28.1	18.0
1981	6.7	2.9	18.1	32.3	12.4
1980	5.9	2.8	17.7	33.4	15.5
1979	6.7	3.2	20.0	39.0	19.0
1978	6.9	3.2	19.5	38.3	22.8

Source: *1987 Food Lion, Inc. Annual Report.*

Finance

Food Lion has been able to expand without becoming overextended or burdened with heavy debt repayments. The firm's capital structure consists of 26 percent long-term debt and 74 percent equity. The majority of growth has been financed through internally generated funds. The company does not want to grow at the expense of profits. Exhibit 7 presents selected financial ratios for the company.

The growth in Food Lion's stock price also reflects the sound financial position of the company. This growth illustrates the continued confidence of investors in the future productivity of the firm. In response to the rapid rise of Food Lion's stock price, management has declared two stock splits since late 1983, when the two separate classes of stock were formed from the previous single class. These splits are designed to keep the price of the stock low enough to be attractive and affordable to all investors. The price/earnings ratio indicates how much investors are willing to pay for a dollar of the company's earnings. In 1987 Food Lion's P/E ratio was the 83rd highest of all the companies listed in the Value Line Investment Survey.

Future

Next week, Tom Smith is meeting with the board of directors to discuss and present his ideas for the next few years. Given the recent troublesome trends in the grocery industry as well as the increasing competition in the Southeast, he is reviewing the future strategy of Food Lion. Foremost in his mind is the extent to which Food Lion should continue to expand operations of its conventional stores in this area. He is also pondering movement into other market areas. Smith wants to be sure that the company will be able to finance future growth without greatly changing its current capital structure. Although the current success of Food Lion is quite impressive, Smith realizes that other grocery chains have experienced problems by not responding to the changing environment. He wants to be certain that this does not happen to Food Lion.

CASE 2–5
BANCO NACIONAL DE COMERCIO EXTERIOR, S.N.C. (BANCOMEXT)

The prevailing business environment (globalization of the world economy, the free trade agreement among Mexico, the United States, and Canada [NAFTA]) was providing new and diverse trade and investment opportunities for Mexican companies. A primary player in this new environment was The Mexican Bank for Foreign Trade—BANCOMEXT. BANCOMEXT was the Mexican government's financial institution in charge of extending federal government credits, guarantees, and promotional services in support of Mexico's foreign trade.

Ms. Maria Rosa Gonzalez was in charge of coordinating the promotional services provided by the bank. The promotional services were designed to (1) consolidate Mexico's export capacity and (2) facilitate access and ensure availability of Mexican products in international markets. In 1991, Maria and her group defined their marketing strategy as one of "selective orientation." That is, the group decided to focus on identifying *segments* in various markets to promote *specific* products. A key aspect of the selective orientation strategy was the design of export projects with a market orientation.

Unfortunately, by 1993, Maria had encountered a major obstacle in implementing the new strategy. The bank placed special emphasis on promoting Mexico's small and medium-sized companies. However, none of these companies had a market-oriented culture. Maria saw her major challenge for 1994 as devising an alternative to the selective orientation strategy as a means to continue promoting and helping Mexican companies. How could BANCOMEXT follow a strategy driven by the central theme of a market orientation if the companies the bank worked with were not driven by the same customer focus?

Mexico[1]

Mexico is a federal democratic republic, with 31 states and the Federal District (the capital). See Exhibit 1 for a map of Mexico. With 1,972,550 square kilometers, Mexico is the thirteenth largest country in the world and third largest in Latin America. The economy of Mexico is mixed. The government, its agencies or government-owned/controlled companies, dominate in the areas of public utilities, petroleum, and certain basic manufacturing industries. Government financing of cooperative farms (*ejidos*) and purchases of crops at supported prices dominate a large part of the country's agriculture. Private enterprise is the principal factor in manufacturing, mining, commerce, entertainment, and the service industry. Foreign investment is found most frequently in manufacturing and mining.

---

[1] Source: Reference material prepared for the NAEP, International Marketing Institute, Boston College, 1993.

This case was prepared by Victoria L. Crittenden, associate professor of marketing at Boston College, and William F. Crittenden, associate professor of management at Northeastern University. Research assistance was provided by Stephanie Hillstrom at Boston College. The case is designed as the basis for class discussion.

Exhibit 1 Map of Mexico

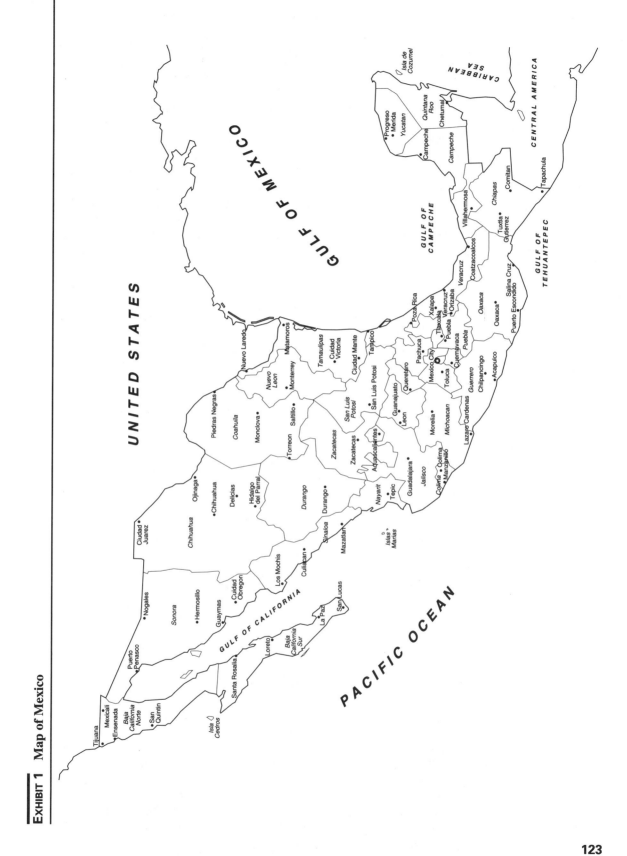

Economic Policy.   Mexico had steadily advanced its economic modernization and revitalization process as a result of ongoing policies adopted by the government in 1985–1986. After more than 20 years of growth dependent on oil exports, the drastic plummeting of oil prices in 1982 forced the country to face an economic situation seriously affected by ever-growing external debt and inflation rates. In response to this crisis, the government developed a long-term strategy that would encourage growth and give Mexico a competitive position within the world economy. Two goals of the 1989–1994 economic strategy were the gradual achievement of sustained growth in economic activity and price stability. Inflation fell from 11.9 percent in 1992 to 8 percent in 1993. This was the lowest inflation rate in 21 years.

Foreign trade was a foundation for Mexico's economic recovery, growth, and modernization. Mexico became a member of the General Agreements on Tariffs and Trade (GATT) in 1986 and the Andean Development Corporation and Permanent Committee of the Conference on Asian and Pacific Economic Cooperation in 1990. Foreign trade policy strengthened export promotion mechanisms through the adoption of measures concerning foreign exchange control, customs simplification, external restrictions, transportation, transit revision, phytosanitary restrictions, and registration of brands.

Direct foreign investment in 1992 was estimated at $43 billion. Approximately 51 percent of foreign investment was concentrated in the manufacturing industry (predominantly in textiles, chemicals, processed foods, transport, and electrical equipment). Services accounted for around 40 percent of foreign investment. The largest foreign investor was the United States, with 53 percent of foreign capital. Other countries expanding their investment in Mexico were Great Britain, Germany, France, Japan, and Switzerland. A new law, establishing clear rules and procedures, was passed in 1993 to promote foreign investment.

Mexican Exporters.   Non-oil exports were the main source of foreign exchange, representing 86 percent of total exports in 1993. Agricultural products were an important component of non-oil exports. The products experiencing the highest growth were tobacco, tomatoes, cattle, and fresh vegetables. Exports of manufactured goods were expected to continue increasing, particularly given the approval of the North American Free Trade Agreement. The automotive industry export market had an annual growth rate, in 1993, of 22 percent. After electrical and electronic equipment, the automotive industry was the number two ranking source of foreign exchange (replacing crude oil). Nonmetallic minerals, plastic and rubber products, and steel experienced export growth rates greater than 20 percent in 1993. Metallic products, machinery and equipment, and textile and leather saw export growth just under 20 percent. Additionally, the Mexican Congress approved the Foreign Trade Law in 1993 that included provisions for the promotion of non-oil exports and attempted to regulate/control unfair practices.

Around 90 percent of non-oil exports were sold to the United States, Canada, Spain, Japan, France, and Germany. Latin American countries received the remaining 10 percent of exports.

The Mexican government attempted to strengthen the export market by four major means. First, the Mixed Export Promotion Committee (COMPEX) worked on the development of export projects. Second, the Mexican System for External Promotion (SIMPEX) was established. SIMPEX identified and promoted trade and investment projects that had both Mexican and foreign company interests. Third, support was provided to the State Export Promotion Programs. These programs addressed issues such as deregulation, administrative issues, and coordination. Fourth, Banco Nacional de Comercio Exterior, S.N.C. (BANCOMEXT) was created by the Mexican government for the promotion of foreign trade and its financing.

Additionally, Mexico provided a number of incentives for exporters. The principal tax incentive was the zero rate of value-added tax (VAT) applicable to exports and the consequent right to the refund of VAT charged by others on materials, supplies, and services used in the production of exports. Exporters were required to convert export proceeds to pesos in the controlled exchange market, but were allowed to use a considerable portion of the foreign currency to pay their own liabilities in the controlled market.

Imports.   The majority of imported products (84 percent) came from the United States, Japan, Germany, Spain, and Canada. By 1993, a large majority of imported raw materials were used in products manufactured for the export market. The growth rate for imported products was slightly over 5 percent in 1993. This compared to 24 percent in 1992. Comprising this total decline in growth of imports were intermediary goods with a growth rate of 8.5 percent (compared to 20.5 percent in 1992) and capital goods at −4 percent (compared to 35 percent in 1992).

The North American Free Trade Agreement (NAFTA)

Approved in 1993, the North American Free Trade Agreement presented Mexican companies with many new opportunities and challenges. Mexican firms faced the possibility of expanding their markets to the U.S. and Canada. At the same time, these Mexican firms faced increased competition in their own market from American and Canadian firms.

In its purest form, NAFTA allowed products and services to cross borders just as easily as they moved within each nation. To be phased in over a 15-year period, highlights of NAFTA included

- Greater access to the Mexican market for U.S. and Canadian manufacturers.
- Tariffs cut on vehicles with substantial North American parts and labor content.
- Equal treatment for international and domestic companies doing business in Mexico.
- Trade barriers eliminated over a 10-year period for textile and apparel trade.
- Barriers to investment in Mexican trucking industry phased out.
- Continuation of individual country environmental, health, and safety standards.

Based on 1990 data,[2] population of the three countries totaled 370 million. Exhibit 2 provides population and labor force profiles for each of the countries.

BANCOMEXT

BANCOMEXT was founded in 1937 as a financial institution in charge of extending federal government credits, guarantees, and promotion services in support of Mexico's foreign trade. Headquartered in Mexico City, the bank had 43 regional and state offices, as well as a network of 28 representative offices in 20 different countries. See Exhibits 3 and 4 for national and international locations of each of these facilities.

Two main areas existed within the bank: financial services and promotional services. The major goal, for both areas, was to support Mexican companies in order to

---

[2] Sources: CIA, Knight-Ridder, Associated Press.

EXHIBIT 2   Country Profiles

Population

Country	Population
United States	253 million
Canada	27 million
Mexico	90 million

Labor Force

	Service	Industry	Agriculture	Other
United States	68%	27%	3%	2%
Canada	75	19	4	2
Mexico	25	38	3	34

EXHIBIT 3   National Offices

Headquarters
2 locations in Mexico City

Executive Regional Offices
• Metropolitana (Mexico City)
• Centro-Sur (Guadalajara)
• Norte (Monterrey)

Regional Offices
• Centro (Queretaro)
• Metropolitana (Mexico City)
• Noreste (Monterrey)
• Norte (Chihuahua)
• Occidente (Guadalajara)
• Oriete (Puebla)
• Pacifico Norte (Tijuana)
• Pacifico Sur (Tuxtla Guiterrez)
• Sureste (Merida)

State Offices
• Aguascalientes
• Ciudad Juarez
• Cuernavaca
• Culiacan
• Gomez Palacio
• Hermosillo
• Leon
• Mexicali
• Morelia
• Saltillo
• San Luis Potosi
• Tampico
• Tlalnepantla
• Tlaxcala
• Toluca
• Vallejo
• Veracruz

State Representatives
• Campeche
• Cancun
• Colima
• La Paz
• Los Mochis
• Mazatlan
• Oaxaca
• Pachuca
• Reynosa
• Tapachula
• Tepic
• Villahermosa
• Zacatecas

EXHIBIT 4 International Offices

United States of America	Asia
• Atlanta, Georgia	• Korea
• Chicago, Illinois	• Hong Kong
• Dallas, Texas	• Japan
• Los Angeles, California	• Taiwan
• Miami, Florida	
• New York, New York	**Latin America**
• San Antonio, Texas	• Argentina
	• Brazil
Canada	• Colombia
• Montreal	• Costa Rica
• Toronto	• Cuba
• Vancouver	• Chile
	• Guatemala
Europe	• Venezuela
• Germany	
• Spain	
• France	
• Holland	
• England	
• Italy	

increase their productivity and competitiveness. This included both financial assistance and promotional help for the increase of exports and inflows of foreign investment. Exhibit 5 provides an overview of the bank's organizational structure.

Services provided by the bank included export and import credit for non-oil goods and services, comprehensive financing to increase the country's range of goods available for export, guarantees to protect against nonpayment risks in foreign trade, and promotional, informational, and training/advisory services to facilitate trade and foreign investment. Companies served by the bank worked in industries ranging from agricultural commodities to electronic products and services such as tourism, engineering, and construction.

The opening of markets in the United States and Canada through the free trade agreement as well as markets in Central and South America, Europe, and Asia presented attractive trade and investment opportunities for BANCOMEXT.

Financial Services. New credit services were introduced and existing products were modified to meet changing requirements of Mexican companies in 1993. These products and services included the bank's role as a financial intermediary, financing by

EXHIBIT 5 Organizational Structure

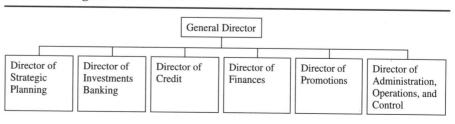

EXHIBIT 6   **Mexican Companies' International Projects Receiving Financial Support from BANCOMEXT**

Sector	Number of Projects	Countries
Electrical	11	Colombia, Costa Rica Guatemala, Honduras Nicaragua, Panama
Infrastructure	7	Brazil, Bolivia Guatemala, Dominican Republic
Oil	11	Bolivia, Brazil, Colombia, Cuba, Ecuador, Guatemala, Russia, Venezuela
Telecommunications	10	Bolivia, Colombia, El Salvador, Guatemala
Transportation	8	El Salvador, Guatemala, Nicaragua, Panama, Dominican Republic, Venezuela, Surinam
Tourism	6	Costa Rica, Guatemala, Dominican Republic

Source: *1993 BANCOMEXT Annual Report.*

market sectors (e.g., manufacturing, agriculture), export credit guarantees, financing of projects abroad, and financing of infrastructure projects in Mexico. Additionally, BANCOMEXT adjusted its export credit guarantee schemes to facilitate Mexican companies' access to credit services.

The bank granted credit, totaling $14.6 billion, to nearly 15,000 companies (mainly small and medium-sized firms) in 1993. Compared to 1992, this was a 47 percent increase in terms of credit and an almost 115 percent increase in the number of companies serviced. Manufacturing firms were the recipients of 63.3 percent of this $14.6 billion. The remaining was distributed among agricultural/agro-industrial firms (17.7 percent), mining/metallurgical (13.3 percent), and tourism and fishery (5.7 percent). BANCOMEXT provided financial support to Mexican companies for 53 international projects in 1993 (Exhibit 6).

Promotional Services.   In addition to the financial support needed to increase non-oil exports and inflows of foreign investment, BANCOMEXT offered a broad range of services to Mexican firms that assisted them in competing at both the national and international levels. These included agreements with promotional institutions, export development projects, investment projects, and information, counseling, and training services (which took place at the Foreign Trade Service Center built and owned by BANCOMEXT). As part of its selective orientation strategy, special attention was given to the identification of market niches with the greatest potential, the promotion of exportable goods and services with the highest value added, and the development of more efficient commercialization mechanisms. The promotional strategy took a proactive approach and focused on *generating* export supply, rather than just *identifying* the supply.

BANCOMEXT felt that Mexican companies needed to be promoted, not just by Mexican promoters, but also by institutions outside of Mexico. As such, BANCOMEXT entered into several *agreements with non-Mexican agencies* for the promotion of Mexican goods and services. Such agreements were made with the China External Trade Development Council of Taiwan, the Industrial Development and

EXHIBIT 7   **Major Export Projects Supported by BANCOMEXT**

Products	Markets
Mangoes	Benelux
Grapes	United Kingdom
Meat products	Japan
Foodstuffs	Southern United States
Frozen vegetables	Germany
Blown glass	Spain and Sweden
Textiles and apparel	Germany
Subcontracting of metal-mechanical goods	United States

Source: *1993 BANCOMEXT Annual Report.*

Investment Center of Taiwan, the Long Term Credit Bank of Japan, the Center for the Promotion of Developing Country Imports of Holland, the Belgian Foreign Trade Institute, and the General Department of International Economic Relations of the Chilean Ministry of Foreign Affairs.

Export development projects were a major means for increasing the sales of small and medium-sized Mexican companies. BANCOMEXT was involved in promoting such export projects. Export projects included agricultural and agro-industrial projects directed toward North American and European markets, textile and apparel projects targeted toward the United States and Canada, and automotive and auto parts focused on Latin America. Exhibit 7 identifies some of the major export projects promoted by the bank.

Sixty-five *foreign investment projects* were promoted in 1993. One of these promotional activities involved the First Mexican–European Agro-Industrial Forum in Mexico City. The Forum, intended to enhance/highlight strategic alliance possibilities between European and Mexican companies, was attended by representatives from 113 European and 200 Mexican companies.

Additionally, the bank offered *information, counseling, and training services* to its clients. A major means of providing information was through the Foreign Trade Service Center (CSCE). The CSCE provided access to national and international databanks, export guides, product classification systems, and domestic/import/export directories. The bank, through the CSCE, provided counseling services both in terms of programs/services/support offered by the bank to its client base and guidance to export companies in matters such as customs requirements, tariff regulations, and trade practices. The CSCE was expected to become the central focus for the bank's selective orientation strategy. The goal was to educate the Mexican businessperson in modern business techniques. In 1993, the bank provided 1,125 such consultations. To further facilitate the goal of the CSCE, the bank offered 188 training courses in 1993 in areas such as marketing, strategic planning, finance, negotiating, and logistics.

The Foreign Trade Service Center.   To complement the bank's promotional services efforts, the bank accumulated all of its available promotional services resources and housed them in the Foreign Trade Service Center (CSCE). The CSCE was the largest international trade information network in Mexico. It offered state-of-the-art communications technology, with access to domestic and foreign databases. Offered at the CSCE were advisory services (technical, commercial, legal, financial), information services (product, market, import, export data, and information related to international business issues), and a technical training institute (training programs).

The CSCE offered a number of publications. The BANCOMEXT *Trade Directory of Mexico* (both in printed and electronic form) contained information on Mexican companies with export experience. The *Trade Opportunity Bulletin* compiled data on world demand for products and services. Several "how to" series were offered in areas such as world geographic market profiles and procedures for exporting to different countries. Additionally, staff of the technical training institute had developed computer-based simulations as training aids.

Other Development Banks.   BANCOMEXT was not without competition. Major competitors included[3]

- Nacional Financiera (NAFIN)
  [National Financing Company]
- Banco Nacional de Comercio Interior (BNCI)
  [National Bank of Interior Commerce]
- Fondo de Operacion y Financiamiento Bancario a la Vivienda (FOVI)
  [Operational Funds and Financial Banking for Housing]
- Fideicomisos Instituidos en Relacion con la Agricultura (FIRA)
  [Commissions Instituted in Relation to Agriculture]
- Fondo para el Desarrollo Comercial (FIDEC)
  [Funds for the Commercial Development]

Other sponsoring institutions were

- Banco Nacional de Credito Rural (BANRURAL)
  [National Bank of Rural Credit]

- Banco Nacional de Obras y Servicios Publicos (BANOBRAS)
  [National Bank of Public Works and Service]

- Banco Nacional del Ejercito, Fuerza Aerea y Armaa (BANJERCITO)
  [National Bank of Army and Air Force]
- Financiera Nacional Azucarera (FINA)
  [National Sugar Financing Company]

Competing development banks had begun to offer high-volume/low-cost products, such as credit cards and automatic access loans. These banks tended to advertise extensively with the small to medium-size companies as their main targets. The competition could offer dollar-denominated loans at competitive rates and had the full-faith and credit support of the Mexican government, but not a strong financial position. The competition generally had a larger Mexican network than BANCOMEXT, but not international offices.

Promotional Services at BANCOMEXT

The promotional services group, based at BANCOMEXT headquarters in Mexico City, had both national and international counseling offices. The international representatives worked in collaboration with Mexico-based offices to identify host country

---

[3] English interpretation in brackets.

market opportunities and create favorable conditions for stable, long-term trade between Mexican and host country companies. Marketing and information services were provided "free of charge" by this worldwide network of electronically connected offices. (Operational costs of the international offices were estimated at $10 million in 1990; costs of promotional events and services provided in Mexican territory were estimated to be at least three times that amount.)

Having counseling offices domestically and internationally allowed BANCOMEXT to (1) identify both producers and consumers in Mexico and the foreign market of interest, (2) speed the internationalization of Mexican companies, and (3) strengthen the development of potential exporters. National and international offices worked closely with foreign banks and trade offices. Additionally, the bank, in partnership with Mexico's Ministry of Trade and Industrial Promotion, provided information regarding specific investment opportunities in Mexico.

Current Situation.   For two years, Maria and her group had been working on specific projects to promote Mexican exports. Considering the efforts of both national and international promotional offices, BANCOMEXT had 50 export projects and special initiatives as part of the 1994 program.

In an increasingly competitive environment, Maria needed to promote and help Mexican companies. However, she was concerned that the selective orientation strategy which BANCOMEXT had chosen to pursue was not working properly. How could, or should, Maria create a market-oriented culture in the small and medium-sized businesses that BANCOMEXT worked with? Were more business training/educational programs for these businesses the key? Or should BANCOMEXT just forget about the selective orientation strategy and determine an alternative strategy for its services?

CASE 2-6
OPTICAL FIBER CORPORATION

The business year had just ended and Edward Porter, president and CEO of Optical Fiber Corporation (OFC), was reviewing the financial results with pleasure and concern. It had been a successful year with record sales and earnings and the addition of 30 percent more manufacturing capacity. The expansion was timely because the sales report that accompanied the financial statements indicated that the order backlog for the company's optical glass fiber products had already reached $20 million and was steadily increasing. Yet, Porter was concerned about the ability of the company to continue its successful growth. Several years ago OFC had entered the fiber optics industry by obtaining patent licenses that allowed it to manufacture and market optical fiber and cable. In return, the license agreement obligated OFC to pay royalties to the patent holders based on its sales of the licensed products. Beginning in 1989 and continuing into 1997, some of the basic patents on the optical fiber technology would begin to expire, enabling the entry of new competition to manufacture and market some of the same products that OFC was successfully marketing.

The threat of new competition caused Porter to reflect on how OFC should be strategically positioned for the next five years. Several opportunities were under review by Porter and Paul Harriman, the vice president of marketing:

1. Over the past two years, OFC had been successful in developing optical glass fibers for a number of small specialized markets. They included medical, military and commercial aircraft, aerospace, and specially coated fibers for installation in severe environments. Additional product development and marketing would enable OFC to expand its sales of fibers to specialty markets.

2. Recently, engineers had been successful in reducing the costs to manufacture OFC optical fibers. Improvements in technology and manufacturing had made it possible to lower the costs on several important OFC products. With continuing expenditures for research and development (R&D), it was likely that further cost reductions could be achieved.

3. Historically, OFC's expertise has been in the production of multimode optical glass fiber for short-distance, high-speed data communications. Recently, the company had been contacted by prospective customers interested in a source for singlemode fiber to be used in long-distance communications systems.[1] OFC believed it had the expertise to manufacture singlemode fiber and was considering the development of a product line.

---

[1] *Singlemode:* an optical fiber that allows only one light to travel through the fiber. Singlemode fibers have very small cores (diameters) and are widely used in long-distance communications. *Multimode:* an optical fiber that allows several light rays to travel through the fiber simultaneously. Multimode fibers have larger cores and wide application in data communications networks that connect electronic equipment.

4. Although OFC had obtained the necessary patent licenses to produce fiber optic cable from strands of optical fibers, it had chosen not to do so. Instead, it had pursued the strategy of selling optical fibers to the companies that assembled them into cables. Some executives believed that OFC should integrate forward and begin selling cable in addition to glass fiber.

Each opportunity was being carefully considered by the company and, hopefully, one or more would eventually make sense. However, it was not entirely clear to management which opportunities would place the company in the strongest competitive position. A number of factors would need to be considered as the company attempted to develop a corporate marketing strategy for the future.

History and Development of Optical Fiber Corporation

OFC was founded in 1980 by four engineers to participate in the fast-growing fiber optics industry. The founders had been successful in negotiating patent licenses that enabled OFC to manufacture and market optical glass fiber subject to restrictions on production volume. For a few years, the company struggled to survive because the optical fiber and the electronic equipment necessary to make it work were too expensive for most businesses to consider. But as fiber prices dropped and communication systems became more data intensive, the economics of optical glass fiber began to be competitive with other means of transporting information such as copper wire cable, microwave transmission, and satellite. Initially, the company focused its resources on developing a product line of multimode optical fibers for use in data communications. Although the data communications market was substantially smaller than the telecommunications market, it was growing rapidly and enabled OFC to avoid competing with the larger companies that specialized in manufacturing optical fiber for telecommunications applications. The company was successful with its strategy and within eight years, sales had increased to more than $20 million and employment had grown to 110. OFC markets included military, aerospace, communications, computers, and process control.

In 1989, OFC moved into a larger facility in a new industrial district of Minneapolis to accommodate its expanding engineering and manufacturing operations. At the same time, OFC began to pursue R&D to reduce manufacturing costs and achieve technical breakthroughs that would lead to new products. The R&D commitment, which amounted to about 2.0 percent of sales was quite successful, and by 1990, the company had applied for seven patents covering the development of special performance optical fibers and fiber coatings for use in a variety of emerging specialty markets. Management was confident that the patents would be awarded over the next few years.

In 1991, OFC was successful in extending the earlier license agreements which had enabled the company to enter the market. The new licenses provided for an immediate increase in the quantities of optical fiber licensed for manufacture and also provided for annual increases through the year 2000. In return for the extended license, the company agreed to pay an additional $3.0 million in 1993 for the license as well as a royalty fee of 9.0 percent of net sales of OFC products manufactured under the agreements. Approximately 85 percent of the company's sales were subject to the license agreement.

During 1992, OFC expanded its manufacturing capacity and extended its line of multimode fiber optics products with three specialty optical fibers used in military

EXHIBIT 1 Income Statement (Year Ending 12–31–92)

Net sales	$48,764,000
Cost of sales	30,475,000
Gross profits	18,289,000
Marketing and administrative expenses	7,575,000
Research and development costs	975,000
Income (loss) from operations	9,739,000
Other income (expense):	
Interest income	737,000
Interest expense	(245,000)
Income (loss before taxes)	10,231,000
Income tax	4,092,000
Net income (loss)	$ 6,139,000

missile guidance systems, nuclear power plants, and other military applications. Additionally, the data communications markets were strong, reflecting the growth in computers, peripheral equipment, and local area networks. OFC sold multimode fibers to these markets through cable manufacturers who assembled the optical fibers into cables jacketed with a protective covering and resold them to original equipment manufacturers and cable distributors. The three largest cable companies that OFC supplied with optical fiber accounted for over 70 percent of the company's revenues. By the end of 1992, OFC sales had reached $48.8 million and the company had 250 employees in manufacturing, marketing, administration, R&D, and quality assurance. Additionally, OFC generated over $8.0 million in cash flow from operations during 1992, up substantially from the prior year. Exhibits 1 and 2 contain the financial statements for the year ending December 31, 1992.

Fiber Optics Technology

Fiber optics is a new technology that uses rays of light instead of electricity to transmit information over optical fibers at very high speeds. The optical fibers are usually thin strands of glass that are combined into cables and used to send information and computer data in the form of pulses of light. The optical fibers provide much clearer and faster transmission than conventional copper cable and satellite links.

An optical fiber consists of a core of high-purity glass encased in a coating of optical cladding to reduce signal loss through the side walls of the fiber. The information to be transmitted is converted from electrical impulses into light waves by a laser or light-emitting diode. At the point of reception, the light waves are converted back into electrical impulses by a photo-detector. Exhibit 3 shows a basic fiber optic system connecting two electronic circuits.

Communication by means of light waves guided through glass fibers offers a number of advantages over other methods of communication. Signals of equal strength can be transmitted over longer distances through optical fibers than through metallic conductors such as copper wire cables. Fiber optic cables are substantially smaller and lighter than metallic cables of the same capacity, they can be installed more rapidly and used in confined spaces, and they are often less expensive. Optical fibers also have other advantages over satellite and line-of-sight transmissions such as microwave. Fiber optic cables provide interference-free communications that offer a high degree of security.

EXHIBIT 2   Balance Sheet, Year Ending December 31, 1992

Assets	
Current assets:	
Cash	$11,894,000
Marketable securities	4,574,000
Accounts receivable	7,392,000
Inventories	6,656,000
Prepaid expenses	506,000
Total current assets	31,022,000
Property, plant, and equipment:	
Land	991,000
Buildings	7,042,000
Machinery and equipment	25,349,000
Less accumulated depreciation	13,352,000
Other assets:	
License agreements	5,424,000
Total assets	56,476,000
Liabilities and Stockholders' Equity	
Current liabilities:	
Long-term debt	2,310,000
License for payable	3,000,000
Accounts payable	1,149,000
Income taxes payable	1,405,000
Accrued liabilities	4,629,000
Total liabilities	12,493,000
Stockholders' equity:	
Common stock	1,500,000
Paid-in capital	50,153,000
Retained earnings (deficit)	(7,670,000)
Total stockholders' equity	43,983,000
Total liabilities and stockholders' equity	$56,476,000

Optical fibers are manufactured using expensive, precisely engineered equipment. Gaseous vapors of varying chemical composition are introduced into a glass tube in a clean, controlled environment. The glass tube, which will form the optical cladding, and the vapors are heated; and the oxide particles, which are formed through a reaction of chemical vapors with oxygen, are deposited on the inside of the tube. As the particles attach to the tube wall, they are fused to create a layer of high-purity glass. Succeeding layers of glass are deposited in this fashion to permit the transmission of light in accordance with the desired specifications. The glass tube is then collapsed into a rod consisting of a deposited core and the optical cladding. The glass rod, called a *preform,* is placed at the top of a fiber drawing tower and heated until it softens, after

EXHIBIT 3   Fiber Optic Transmission

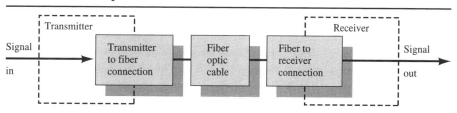

EXHIBIT 4   Singlemode and Multimode Optical Fiber

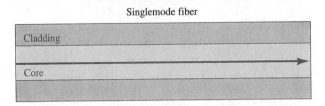

Singlemode fiber

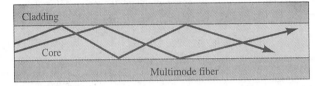

Multimode fiber

which it is drawn into a fiber of predetermined diameter. Exhibit 4 illustrates the core and cladding of singlemode and multimode glass fiber.

Before an optical fiber can be used, it must be converted into a cable by a manufacturing process called *cabling* to apply an outer protective covering around the fiber to protect it during installation and use. Important characteristics of optical cables are strength, flexibility, environmental resistance, and appearance. The importance of these features depends on how the cable will be used. An outside telephone cable, for example, must endure extremes of temperature, ice deposits that cause it to sag on a utility pole, high winds that buffet it, and rodents that chew on it underground. Similarly, a cable running under an office carpet has different requirements than a cable running within the walls of an office. Cable design and construction can be simple or complex, depending on the cable's intended use and desired performance. Aerial cables that are strung between buildings may contain only one or two optical fibers, while other cables may carry several dozen fibers if they are used in local area networks. About 20 companies are involved in the manufacture of optical cable in the United States. It is a highly competitive industry requiring sophisticated design and engineering capabilities. And, as the market for optical fiber expands, copper cable manufacturers will extend their product lines to include fiber optic cable. Facing increasing competition, these cable companies will prefer extremely responsive optical fiber suppliers. The ability of OFC to provide excellent customer service has enabled it to establish business relationships with some copper cable manufacturers.

An Example Application of Fiber Optics

Local area networks which connect office computers, factory workstations, and peripheral equipment are an example of an important application for optical fiber cables. Such cable networks improve productivity and quality by enhancing the speed, accuracy, and capacity of data transmission.

In a business involving multiple locations, there are three applications for optical fiber links. Optical cables designed for aerial or underground installation are used between buildings to connect main distribution panels, sometimes as replacements for copper wire cables.

Individual workstations on a particular floor within a building may also be connected by fiber optic cable. Here, networks employing optical fiber cable connect workstations to a central processing unit and to other stations through a communications panel.

In the third application, the communications panel on each floor is linked with the main building distribution center using multiple vertical cable runs through elevator or other shafts forming the communications backbone of the building. The information capacity and resistance to electrical interference provided by optical transmission are distinct advantages in this application. Fiber optic cable designs for office-floor and between-floor connections meet building safety codes, so the optical cable for these applications will often replace conventional copper wire cables.

Local area networks present a significant long-term opportunity for OFC. It is estimated that more than 50 million workstations are now installed in the United States, and continued growth and rapid technological change is expected. Many companies are increasing productivity by networking individual workstations, while others are converting existing systems from copper to fiber optic cables. Although the market for optical communications systems has been growing over the past several years, the majority of optical cable penetration of local area networks has yet to be realized. OFC has about a 30 percent share of the U.S. market for optical fiber installed in local area networks.

The Market for Optical Fiber and Cable

The world market for optical fiber continues to grow rapidly, with shipments increasing 14 percent from an estimated 7.0 million kilometers of fiber in 1990 to approximately 8.0 million in 1991. The United States enjoys a 40 percent share of the world market and a surplus in the international trade of optical fiber and fiber optic cable. In 1992 the trade surplus amounted to $303 million, a 43 percent increase from the previous year. However, some foreign-based companies produce fiber, cable, and fiber optic components in U.S. facilities, which increases the competition faced by OFC and other domestic businesses in the industry.

In the United States, the total 1991 optical fiber market has been estimated at 3.5 million kilometers, comprised of approximately 3.2 million kilometers of singlemode fiber valued at $320 million and 330 thousand kilometers of multimode fiber valued at approximately $65 million. This represents a growth in demand for multimode fiber in the United States in excess of 20 percent from 1990 to 1991. As shown in Exhibit 5, the demand for multimode fiber is predicted to continue to expand through the mid-1990s, with some market analysts indicating that 15 to 20 percent annual growth over the next three years is reasonable. Strong demand is expected for singlemode and multimode fiber to be used in cables for local area networks, telecommunications, cable television (CATV), and transoceanic fiber optic systems.

Local Area Networks.   The local-area-network segment of the U.S. fiber optics market is expected to grow 20 percent annually through the first half of the 1990s. Ease of connection, compatibility with cost-effective electronics, and multimedia applications that combine text, voice, and video at a workstation make multimode fiber attractive for local area networks. Industry analysts expect new installations to continue to drive the growth of multimode fiber in data communication markets such as business, banking and financial services, government facilities, universities and hospitals, and other industries with high-volume data or security requirements.

EXHIBIT 5   U.S. Multimode Cabled Fiber Market

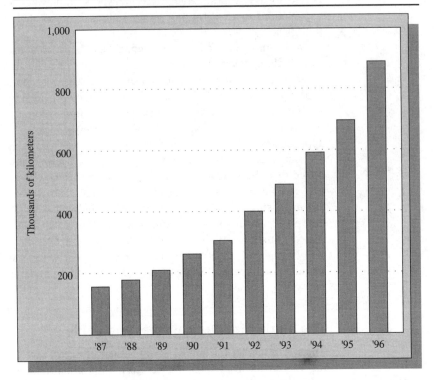

Telecommunications. Telecommunications companies such as AT&T, Sprint Corporation, and MCI Communications Corporation are still installing fiber optic cable throughout their long-distance systems. Presently, about 80 percent of the long-distance network is fiber optic cable and 60 percent of the network between the long-distance system and local telephone offices is cabled with optical fiber.

Strong interest by the federal government in constructing a telecommunications network that will enhance the nation's ability to compete with foreign countries is expected to stimulate the development of fiber optic telecommunications. A goal of achieving a nationwide fiber optic network by the year 2015 has been mentioned by government sources. Singlemode optical fiber is usually preferred because it can transmit signals at very high rates over long distances without regeneration. This information-carrying capacity and low signal-loss make singlemode fiber well suited to very-high-speed, long-distance applications.

Recently, attention has turned to fiber optic installation from the local telephone office to the residential customer where less than 5 percent is fiber optic cable. For these "fiber-to-the-home" and "fiber-to-the-curb" applications, cost is still an issue. While fiber optics is competitive with copper cable on a technical basis, it is still not economical to install fiber in all cases. That economic "crossover" point should be achieved by the mid-1990s. It is expected that these shorter-distance communications applications will be served with singlemode and multimode cable.

Cable Television (CATV). An area of dramatic growth for fiber optics in the United States is cable television. The market is growing rapidly because cable television companies are installing new fiber optic CATV systems to increase channel

EXHIBIT 6   **Installed Base of Fiber Optic Cable in the CATV Industry**

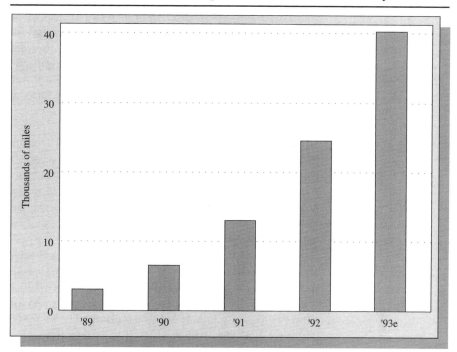

capacity and to upgrade existing systems to provide consumers with more sophisticated two-way services, including telecommunications. The National Cable Television Association estimates that the CATV operator's use of fiber optics has increased 400 percent since 1988 and will continue to increase by 25 percent annually through the 1990s. Industry plans call for spending $18 billion during the next 10 years to upgrade plant and equipment and rebuild more than 60 percent of existing systems. As Exhibit 6 illustrates, the installed base of fiber optic cable in the cable television industry was estimated to be 40 thousand miles in 1993. Both singlemode and multimode fibers will be used to produce the cables needed by this industry. Some cable producers have established separate divisions specifically dedicated to the needs of CATV customers.

Undersea Cable Systems.   The next several years could see an explosion of capacity for international communication if the transoceanic fiber optic systems being planned during 1991 and 1992 are constructed. Many of the plans involve linking or extending international fiber optic cable systems. Most are expected to be completed between 1993 and 1998 and they will link the United States with Europe, Asia, and South America. Transoceanic systems will feature transmission speeds up to 5 billion bits per second using both singlemode and multimode fiber optic cable. The total investment in currently installed and planned undersea fiber optic cable may exceed $12 billion by the time of its completion in the late 1990s.

Marketing Strategy and Product Lines

OFC primarily markets its optical fibers through direct sales made by a small sales and marketing staff located at the corporate offices in Minneapolis. The company also advertises in trade publications, distributes product brochures and other technical material to its mailing list of potential customers, and demonstrates its products at technical conferences and trade shows. All of its present customers are cable manufacturers that purchase optical fibers and assemble them into fiber optic cables for resale to manufacturers, distributors, and other customers such as government and military facilities, colleges and universities, CATV, and telecommunications and broadcasting firms. In 1992, approximately 70 percent of the company's sales were made to three large cable manufacturing companies, one of which was a firm that was licensing OFC to produce and market optical glass fibers.

Standard Multimode Optical Fibers. OFC specializes in multimode fiber for data communications and telecommunications markets. The markets are extremely competitive and OFC's main rivals are the two licensors to whom it pays royalties. Each has substantially greater resources and operating experience. To date, OFC has been successful because of the licensing requirements that limit competition and because of its competitive advantages of outstanding customer service, product performance, and competitive pricing.

The multimode product line is very profitable and accounts for most of the firm's profits. It consists of six products, each designed for specific communications requirements. Four products, OFGI-100, OFGI-110, OFGI-120, and OFGI-130, are optical fibers with different core diameters designed for telecommunications and local area networks requiring high-speed data transmission. Two products, OFSI-200 and OFSI-210, have other uses such as short-distance data links, electronic instrumentation, and process control. Technological change in fiber optics is rapid, so improvement in the performance characteristics of multimode fiber is a frequent occurrence. Both OFC and its competitors offer product revisions and line extensions that improve the performance of multimode fibers in customer applications. OFC, for example, has recently developed a process to apply a metallized coating to the end of its multimode fiber so it could be soldered to a semiconductor laser light source and other electronic components. To keep abreast of changing technology and competition, OFC was required to maintain an expensive, ongoing R&D program.

Product quality was also essential to the success of OFC's multimode optical fibers. Quality control programs were designed to maintain strict tolerances during the manufacturing process and to assure compliance with the customer's requirements. Each product was 100 percent tested for quality and performance using standard industry test procedures before it was shipped. Careful attention to product quality was an important factor in establishing OFC as a major supplier to three of the leading manufacturers of optical cable.

Specialty Optical Fiber. During 1992, OFC was successful in the development and introductory marketing of three optical fibers for application in niche markets. OFC-SF100 was a radiation-resistant optical fiber designed for cables that would be installed in radioactive environments such as nuclear power plants, missile silos, and naval vessels. A hermetically sealed optical fiber, OFC-SF200, was specially coated to withstand air, moisture, and water for cables to be used in underwater and harsh outdoor environments. OFC-SF300 was a coated fiber developed for cables used in high-temperature environments such as heating ducts and other locations where fire was a threat. Exhibit 7 summarizes the standard and specialty optical fibers marketed by OFC during 1992.

Specialty fibers were an attractive marketing opportunity for OFC because the sales

EXHIBIT 7   OFC Fiber Optic Products

Product	Type	Recommended Application
OFGI-100	Multimode	Telecommunications and local area networks
OFGI-110		
OFGI-120		
OFGI-130		
OFSI-200	Multimode	Electronic instrumentation, data links, process control
OFSI-210		
OFC-SF100	Multimode	Radioactive environments
OFC-SF200		High-moisture and wet environments
OFC-300		High-temperature environments

of these products were frequently not covered by the patent licenses. Although the markets were usually small and the fibers required marketing research and product development, the profit margins were substantially larger than those for the standard multimode products. OFC was regularly contacted by manufacturers' representatives and cable companies requesting special fibers for cables to be installed in severe environments around chemical and petroleum plants, at military installations, and in equipment for the defense and space programs.

Recently, OFC had successfully experimented with a fiber capable of transmitting ultraviolet light and another fiber made of fluoride glass that had promise in laser surgery and other medical and scientific applications. However, if OFC were to continue to pursue optical fibers for niche markets, an additional annual R&D expenditure of $400,000 would be required and several organizational changes would be necessary. The present marketing staff was not adequate to conduct the market research needed to identify prospective customers, define their special needs, and complete the sales process. Paul Harriman estimated that OFC would need a sales manager, a product manager, and a marketing assistant. Experienced sales managers were paid an annual salary of $140,000, typically, while product managers with experience earned around $110,000 a year. One or more marketing assistants were usually employed to assist product management, and trained personnel expected a salary of $75,000 a year.

The marketing organization would also have to be restructured so the specialty optical fiber products would receive the necessary attention. Whatever organizational changes were made, it would be necessary to make some arrangement for sales personnel to represent the product line. Consideration was being given to using salaried employees as either sales representatives or manufacturers' representatives. Recently, OFC had been contacted by a business in Oakland, California, about representing the specialty fiber products in the western region of the United States. The company employed four salespeople and specialized in selling the optical and electronic components of manufacturers for a sales commission of 10 percent. Paul Harriman believed that until the necessary marketing organization and strategy were formalized for the products, additional product development expenditures could not be justified.

Product Development of Singlemode Optical Fibers.   Recent improvements in the technology for producing singlemode fibers has made it possible to produce them as economically as multimode fibers. In applications involving the transmission of information over short distances, both fibers were acceptable substitutes. However, because of their desirable optical properties and high transmission rates, it was expected that the next generation of fiber optic cable for the CATV and long-distance telephone industry would be made using singlemode fibers. Although the change would occur slowly, it would be significant because these industries were the largest users of fiber optic cable.

During 1992, OFC was contacted by cable companies and requested to become an alternate supplier of singlemode fiber. OFC had not responded to the opportunities because it had not developed singlemode fibers for marketing. Management estimated that if OFC were to market singlemode fiber, two products would be necessary. Product development would require a year and an expenditure in R&D of $2,500,000. In addition, new manufacturing equipment would be needed to produce the smaller-diameter fibers to the exacting specifications of the cable producers. New equipment would take a year to install and test before acceptable fiber could be produced for marketing. A capital investment of $4 million (not including the R&D expenditure) would be necessary to enter the market.

The marketing strategy and personnel presently used to market the standard multimode fibers could also be used for singlemode fiber products. Direct sales by the existing OFC corporate marketing staff would be made to the cable producers. Still, the market would be very competitive because one of the OFC licensors owned a large subsidiary that produced singlemode cable for the long-distance telephone industry and was a leading supplier. Management reasoned that OFC could be successful as a secondary supplier of singlemode fiber and eventually sell a large quantity at modest profit margins.

Vertical Integration.   Several times over the past few years, management had considered the possibility of producing optical cable with its fibers. Two of the company founders had been previously employed in the optical cable industry, and they believed that OFC should diversify its business by forward integration. They persuasively argued that since most of the OFC multimode fiber business was with three cable companies, it would be possible to expand the sales of optical fiber by producing cables for OEMs and cable distributors. They also noted that the patent licenses recently negotiated authorized not only the production of optical fiber, but also the conversion of the fiber into optical cable. It was the opinion of some that forward integration into cable production would enable OFC to add more value to its products and enhance the profitability of the company. Two strategic approaches were being evaluated by OFC management.

One strategy was to enter the optical cable business through internal product development. In this instance, OFC would expand its R&D department to develop a line of optical cable products. Management estimated that ongoing R&D costs would increase by $500,000 annually when the necessary personnel and prototype equipment were added to conduct the development and testing. OFC planned to focus initially on developing cable products that used its specialty optical fiber. This approach was considered attractive because royalties would not have to be paid on the cable produced with the specialty fibers and they would be protected from competition if the OFC patents were awarded. About two years would be needed to develop and test the products. If the development effort was successful, equipment would have to be purchased to manufacture the optical cable. It was estimated that a capital investment of $5 million would have to be made in manufacturing equipment and facilities. Management believed that the optical cables produced with the specialty fibers could initially be sold by the corporate marketing staff to OEMs and military installations and through optical cable distributors to other users. As the cable business expanded, OFC would add marketing staff as necessary.

A second integration strategy under consideration was the acquisition of an optical cable manufacturer for cash. Management was confident that an excellent business could be located that would permit OFC to quickly enter the cable market with products and the necessary manufacturing and marketing capability. Rapid expansion of the cable industry over the past several years and a weak economy had resulted in a temporary oversupply of cable. As a result, a number of good businesses were looking for buyers to avoid bankruptcy or liquidation. Some executives favored an acquisition as the avenue for growth because it was likely that a producer of both singlemode and multimode cable could be purchased which would enable OFC to completely integrate its business if it desired to do so. Others argued against the acquisition because it would immediately place OFC in competition with its existing cable customers.

If OFC were to proceed with an acquisition, 18 months would be needed to locate an acceptable company, borrow the money and complete the negotiations, and combine the business operations. Industry experts estimated the cost to acquire a cable manufacturer at between $10 million and $15 million. Of course the price would probably increase as the economy recovered and the supply of fiber optic cable came back into balance with demand.

Developing a Corporate Marketing Strategy

As Edward Porter and Paul Harriman considered the future marketing strategy, they were reminded once again of the importance of protecting OFC's enviable market position. Success had not come easily and it had only been achieved with the dedication of loyal employees and carefully planned and executed strategic decisions. Yet, expiration of the basic fiber optics patents over the next several years posed a serious threat. It would certainly mean new businesses offering comparable fiber-optic products and competing for the same customers. Both executives wondered what OFC could do to continue to differentiate its products and preserve its competitive advantage in the marketplace.

Continued growth was also an important priority of management. However, selecting the most desirable combination of marketing opportunities was somewhat complicated because of a recent regulatory development. In 1992, a landmark decision by the FCC allowed CATV operators to provide telecommunications services, bringing them into direct competition with the telephone companies. The decision was expected to encourage CATV operators to upgrade and build fiber optic networks to handle telecommunications. In response, the telephone companies were acquiring CATV systems as a way of offering video services to preserve and expand their market position. Most industry experts, including Harriman, thought that in a few years, after the acquisitions, joint ventures, and strategic alliances were completed, little distinction would exist between the companies in the two industries.

Porter and Harriman strongly believed that in addition to protecting its existing business, OFC must carefully select new marketing opportunities that would enable it to continue to achieve record levels of sales and profits without exposing the company to unnecessary risk. Because resources were limited, the selection of an inferior marketing strategy would have serious consequences for OFC's ability to remain an industry leader. Porter wasn't even willing to consider this as a possibility.

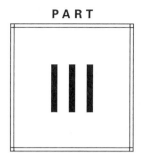

PART

III

GROWTH STRATEGIES

In this part we examine growth strategies from two perspectives. First, we explore alternative directions of growth that may be taken from a company's core (initial) business. Second, we examine strategic challenges and opportunities in growth markets.

Company Growth Strategies

A business can achieve growth by marketing current or new products in existing or new markets. Management must be aware of any marketing opportunities, strategic windows, or potential differential advantages. A useful tool to help identify alternatives is the strategic opportunity matrix in Exhibit 1. The matrix organizes opportunities into four categories based upon product and market considerations.

Market Penetration. A firm pursuing a market penetration strategy tries to increase market share among existing customers. If Kraft General Foods started a major promotional campaign for Maxwell House coffee, with aggressive advertising and cents-off coupons to existing customers, it would be following a penetration strategy.

Market Development. Market development entails attracting new customers to existing products. Ideally, new uses for old products stimulate additional sales to existing customers while also bringing in new buyers. McDonald's, for example, has opened restaurants in Russia, China, and Italy and is eagerly expanding into Eastern Europe. In the nonprofit area, the growing emphasis on continuing education and executive development by colleges and universities is a market development strategy.

Product Development. A product development strategy entails the creation of new products for present markets. The "eating healthy" trend of the early 1990s led

EXHIBIT 1 **Strategic Opportunity Matrix**

Present Products	New Products
Market penetration	Product development
Market development	Diversification

ConAgra—maker of Banquet, Morton, Patio, and Chun King frozen dinners—to develop Healthy Choice frozen dinners, which are low in fat, cholesterol, and sodium. Responding to the same trend, Kraft General Foods introduced no-cholesterol mayonnaise, and General Mills and Kellogg brought out high-fiber, low-fat, and low-sodium cereals. Managers following this strategy can rely on their extensive knowledge of the target audience. They usually have a good feel for what customers like and dislike about current products and what existing needs are not being met. In addition, managers can rely on the established distribution channels.

Diversification. Diversification is a strategy of increasing sales by introducing new products into new markets. For example, LTV Corporation, a steel producer, diversified into the monorail business. Sony practiced a diversification strategy when it acquired Columbia Pictures; although motion pictures are not a new product in the marketplace, they were a new product for Sony. Coca-Cola manufactures and markets water-treatment and water-conditioning equipment—a challenging task for the traditional soft-drink company. A diversification strategy can be quite risky when a firm is entering unfamiliar markets. On the other hand, it can be very profitable when a firm is entering markets with little or no competition.

Movement beyond the core business is not unusual as businesses grow and mature. Several factors may influence the rate and direction of company growth strategies including available resources, management's preferences, pending opportunities and threats, and the desire to reduce dependence on the core business. For example, when growth in the apparel market began slowing in the late 1980s, Benetton grew by acquiring sporting goods firms. Nordica Spa (ski equipment), Prince (tennis rackets), and Rollerblade (inline skates) now account for about one-fifth of Benetton's worldwide sales.

Sometimes a company relies on its own expertise to grow. At other times it uses the expertise of others. Three primary ways of accomplishing a growth strategy include leveraging a core competency, engaging in mergers and acquisitions, and establishing a joint venture or strategic alliance.

• *Leveraging a core competency.* A company may use its own expertise in a particular field to grow. For example, Honda's diverse line of products—including cars, garden tillers, motorcycles, lawnmowers, snowblowers, snowmobiles, power generators, and outboard motors—seems to be a growth strategy of diversification into unrelated markets. However, Honda has simply exploited its core competency in small-engine technology and manufacturing and its brand recognition to leverage growth into diverse power equipment markets.

• *Engaging in mergers and acquisitions.* In the past decade, this method has been a leading growth strategy of companies in a variety of industries. Toymaker Mattel acquired Fisher-Price to gain entry into the preschool and infant markets. Disney acquired Capital Cities/ABC to expand movie and TV producers' ability to distribute their products. Ernst & Young, the Big Six accounting firm, acquired Kenneth Leventhal & Company, a smaller CPA firm specializing in real estate, to grow in that industry.

• *Establishing a joint venture or strategic alliance.* Companies often form partnerships with other corporations to develop products. One example is the partnership between Apple, IBM, and Motorola to develop the PowerPC microchip. Another reason to form an alliance is to vertically align with specific suppliers or customer groups. An example is Boeing Corporation developing long-term relationships with a core group of suppliers and involving its customers in designing products.

Marketing Strategy in Growth Markets[1]

Growth markets are typically characterized by escalating industry sales, many competitors entering the market, large companies acquiring pioneering firms, and healthy industry profits. The strategic focus shifts from stimulating generic or primary demand to aggressive selective or brand demand stimulation. Large firms are likely to enter markets at the growth stage, utilizing superior skills and resource advantages to overcome some of the timing advantages of market pioneers. Large firms also have the advantage of evaluating the attractiveness of product markets during initial development. The uncertainties about the size and scope of the emerging market may encourage a wait-and-see position by large potential competitors.

Procter & Gamble, for example, sometimes enters growth markets dominated by well-entrenched competitors. Instead of launching me-too or single-segment products, P&G introduces a succession of products aimed at different segments. Each entry creates a loyal following and takes some business away from the competitor. Soon, the competitor is surrounded, its revenue is weakened, and it is too late to launch new brands at outlying segments. This presents an opportunity for P&G to introduce a brand to compete head-on in the major market segment dominated by the competitor. This approach has been labeled an "encirclement" strategy.[2]

Growth markets present interesting strategic challenges and opportunities. Key issues that marketing managers must consider include market segmentation, targeting, and positioning.

Market Segmentation. If not already defined in the emerging market, segments should be defined, described, and analyzed in the growth stage. Identifying customer groups with similar needs improves targeting, and "experience with the product, process, and materials technologies leads to greater efficiency and increased standardization."[3] The market environment moves from highly uncertain to moderately uncertain during growth. Further change is likely, but information is available about the forces that influence the size and composition of the product market. Analysis of existing buyers' characteristics and preferences yields useful guidelines for estimating market potential. Anticipating the directions of change is important in developing or maintaining a competitive advantage. The potential for segment growth, profitability, and stability must be evaluated by management.

Targeting. The major influences on targeting decisions in growth markets include (1) the capabilities and resources of the organization, (2) the competitive environment, (3) the extent to which the product market can be segmented, (4) the future potential of the market, and (5) the market entry barriers confronting potential competitors.

A concentrated or niche targeting strategy may be appropriate when buyers' needs are differentiated or when product differentiation occurs. A new market entrant may identify segments that are not served by large competitors. These segments provide an opportunity for the small firm to gain competitive advantage. The market leader(s) may not find small segments attractive enough to allocate the skills and resources necessary to gain a position in them.

A company that seeks to appeal to multiple market segments using a differentiated targeting strategy must determine how much variation exists in buyers' needs and wants. During the growth stage of the business market for personal computers, the three major segments were small-, medium-, and large-size companies. Microsegmentation (many segments) in a growth market is typically not necessary. A small number of segments can be identified by one or a few general characteristics (e.g., size of business). When no segments are apparent, undifferentiated targeting is guided by a general profile of buyers. This average-buyer profile becomes the target.

Positioning Strategy. As product markets shift from emerging to growth, positioning strategies typically change. Exhibit 2 shows some positioning strategies found in emerging, growth, and mature product markets. These strategies are illustrative because many factors influence the choice of a strategy.

As product markets shift from emerging to growth, the strategic focus shifts from stimulating generic or primary demand to aggressive selective or brand stimulation. The expanded number of models and competitors contributes to this shift. Another reason for this shift in strategies is that most potential customers and distributors are aware of generic product features, advantages, and benefits. Promotion emphasis changes from education, product awareness, and primary demand stimulation to developing brand loyalty.

Distribution becomes a major key to success in growth markets. Manufacturers scramble to sign up dealers and distributors and to begin building long-term relationships. Without adequate distribution, it is impossible to establish a strong market position.

Toward the end of the growth phase, profits normally begin falling from the peak level. Price reductions result from increasing economies of scale and rising competition. Also, most firms have recovered their development costs by this time, and their priority is in increasing or retaining market share and enhancing profits.

Intuit Corporation found success in the growth stage of what otherwise might have become a commodity market.

> Intuit makes microcomputer software. Its flagship product is Quicken, a program that allows consumers and small businesses to write checks and keep track of their finances on a personal computer. Quicken is probably the most successful personal finance program ever written, holding a market share estimated at 60 percent.[4]

EXHIBIT 2   Illustrative Positioning Strategies in Emerging, Growth, and Mature Markets

Positioning Strategy Component	Emerging Markets	Growth Markets	Mature Markets
Product strategy	Limited number of models; frequent product modification	Expanded number of models; frequent product modifications	Large number of models
Distribution strategy	Distribution usually limited, depending on product; intensive efforts and high margins often needed to attract distributors	Expanded number of distributors; margins declining; intensive efforts to retain distributors and shelf space	Extensive number of dealers; margins declining; intensive efforts to retain distributors and shelf space
Promotion strategy	Develop product awareness; stimulate primary demand; use extensive personal selling to distributors; use sampling and coupons to consumers	Stimulate selective demand; advertise brand aggressively; promote heavily to retain dealers and customers	Stimulate selective demand; advertise brand aggressively; promote heavily to retain dealers and customers
Pricing strategy	Prices are usually high to recover development costs.	Prices begin to fall toward end of growth stage as a result of competitive pressure.	Prices continue to fall.

Intuit's secret formula? A faster, cheaper, hassle-free, and, above all, easy-to-use program supported by extensive and continuous product development, testing, customer research, and technical support representatives who share management's obsession with customer satisfaction. Intuit's success is frequently linked to its corporate philosophy of doing whatever it takes to satisfy a customer.

End Notes

1. Much of the material in this section is from David W. Cravens, *Strategic Marketing,* 5th ed. (Burr Ridge, IL: Irwin/McGraw-Hill, 1997), pp. 195–97.

2. Philip Kotler, *Marketing Management,* 8th ed. (Englewood Cliffs, NJ: Prentice-Hall, 1994), p. 376.

3. Mary Lambkin and George S. Day, "Evolutionary Processes in Competitive Markets: Beyond the Product Life Cycle," *Journal of Marketing,* July 1989, p. 14.

4. John Case, "Consumer Service: The Last Word," *INC.,* April 1991, p. 89.

CASES FOR PART III

Growth occurs in various forms of product development and market development. The six cases in this part portray growth strategies in small, entrepreneurial organizations as well as growth options in larger corporations. Products examined in these case scenarios range from popcorn to computer software.

Case 3–1, Golden Valley Microwave Foods, Inc, a video case, presents a situation in which an entrepreneur has been successful with one product and now must consider introducing more products. The company needs to introduce new products into its current market and needs to develop new markets.

The leader in the video-rental industry, **Blockbuster Entertainment Corporation (Case 3–2)** has achieved $1 billion in annual revenues in a relatively short time. However, there is concern that the market is entering the maturity stage of its life cycle. The company needs to formulate its marketing strategy for the 1990s and beyond.

SystemSoft Corporation (Case 3–3), a provider of system-level software, has been very successful with its core product lines. The company has to decide if it should push into new product categories and segments by entering the call avoidance software business. Rewards for pioneering a new product category could be tremendous. Yet pursuing this opportunity could stretch SystemSoft's resources at a time when the company has to begin to understand and manage growth.

Case 3–4 involves **Angostura Bitters, Inc.,** a small, privately held company on the islands of Trinidad and Tobago. Its flagship product, Angostura Bitters, is the world leader in aromatic bitters. The company wants to globalize and is contemplating a number of growth options.

The Bacova Guild Ltd. (Case 3–5) is an innovative, fast-growing U.S. company. The firm has expanded operations to accommodate sales growth and now must develop and market a steady stream of new products to cover overhead and maintain profitability. The case focuses on a new consumer product called Signmaster™.

An entrepreneurial start-up, **The Faith Mountain Company (Case 3–6)** distributes gifts, apparel, and home accessories through its mail order catalog, catalog customer list, and retail store. The company has experienced rapid increases in sales and profits. The key strategic question facing the company is how to grow. Company owners recognize that growth will have both managerial and personal implications.

CASE 3–1
GOLDEN VALLEY MICROWAVE FOODS, INC.

Jim Watkins, president and chief operating officer of Golden Valley Microwave Foods (a division of ConAgra Inc.), was in a market where repeat business was key. Consumers would buy novelty microwavable items. However, the key was getting these consumers to continue to buy the products. The challenge to Golden Valley was to link technology, quality, convenience, and price into a product that consumers would buy on a regular basis.

The company was experiencing considerable success with its Act II microwavable popcorn. However, the jury was still out regarding the company's move into microwavable french fries and breakfast items.

The microwave food market had experienced ups and downs. To remain successful, Golden Valley had to continue to introduce new products into its current markets, while at the same time educating new markets to the notion of microwavable food items.

The Company

Jim Watkins was the founder of Golden Valley Microwave Foods, Inc. (GVMF). Watkins worked for Pillsbury from 1971 to 1978 as a member of a research team developing foods for microwave ovens. Pillsbury was not as enthusiastic about microwave oven foods as the team, including Watkins, would have liked. Watkins quit Pillsbury when the company refused to focus efforts on the microwave food market. Watkins started Edina, Minnesota-based Golden Valley Microwave Foods with $250,000 in venture capital in 1978.[1] GVMF was founded upon Watkins' strong belief that every family in the United States wanted to cook entire meals in a few minutes.

Watkins felt certain that the microwave market was lucrative. By the end of the 1970s, only 12 percent of U.S. households owned microwave ovens, but projections were for rapid growth.[2] Aspiring to pioneer in this high tech market, Watkins set out to sell microwavable frozen, ready-to-eat dinners through supermarket chains. An outside firm was hired to make dinners under the Golden Valley label in 1980. Watkins met with difficulty. GVMF was a new company with minimal marketing or business clout, a new unrecognized product, and no formal channels of distribution. The new product introduction failed.

Watkins decided that the product failure was not due solely to the product and market, but also to the mode of distributing the product. Supermarkets were in a highly competitive arena that GVMF was not able to penetrate. Watkins then began to pursue vending machines as a way to distribute microwave food items. Microwave ovens had

---

[1] The company went public in 1986.

[2] One percent represented approximately 800,000 homes.

This case was prepared by Victoria L. Crittenden, associate professor of marketing at Boston College, as the basis for class discussion rather than to illustrate either effective or ineffective handling of a managerial situation. Research assistance was provided by Jennifer Fraser and David Angus, Boston College. All material was from secondary sources. Revised 1997.

started to appear in cafeterias and office suites next to vending machines stocked with ready-to-heat foods.

Watkins thought distributors should be ripe for more snack items to place in vending machines. Deciding the popcorn market was a great microwave food opportunity, Watkins hired five people to find the best kernels and develop bags that would actually pop all of the kernels. Golden Valley microwavable popcorn was born. In 1983, one year after introduction, Golden Valley had almost $7 million in popcorn sales. The initial popcorn product (Act I) was a frozen version. The shelf-stable popcorn (Act II) was introduced in 1984. GVMF concentrated its efforts on vending machines and mass merchandisers. The company licensed its packaging technology to General Mills to use in the grocery store market.

With more than 80 percent of American households having at least one microwave oven by the 1990s, approximately 90 percent of GVMF's $170 million in revenues came from the sale of its microwave popcorn. The remaining 10 percent of revenues were from the Microwave Morning line of waffles, pancakes, and french toast.

By the end of the 1990s, GVMF was the largest manufacturer of microwave popcorn in the world. Its popcorn products were sold in over 20 countries. Additionally, GVMF was the parent company of Vogel Popcorn, a leading producer of bulk popcorn. Vogel Popcorn had high-capacity plans in the United States and Argentina. Shipping to over 55 countries worldwide, Vogel grew approximately 25 percent of the total annual popcorn production in the United States.

ConAgra Inc.   Founded in 1919 in Nebraska, ConAgra was the second largest food processor (after Philip Morris) in the United States. The company operated in three market segments: Food inputs and ingredients (crop protection chemicals, fertilizers, seeds), refrigerated foods (beef and pork products, deli meats, chicken and turkey products, cheese products), and grocery/diversified products (tomato-based products, oils, popcorn, beans, frozen foods). The corporation employed around 100,000 people worldwide by the 1990s, with annual revenue of around US$24 billion.

ConAgra acquired Golden Valley Microwave Foods in 1991 in a stock swap valued at US$436 million. The GVMF acquisition followed acquisition of Beatrice, Inc., and Armour Foods. Such acquisitions had provided ConAgra with brands such as Butterball turkey, Orville Redenbacher popcorn, Peter Pan peanut butter, and Armour luncheon meats. Motivation for the GVMF acquisition included gaining the company's leading edge microwavable food research, tapping the company's ability to sell outside grocery stores, and control of the company's potato-products supplier.

The Snack Food Market

The snack food industry was comprised of many different types of products, with an estimated market size ranging from $10 to $15 billion.[3] Major categories included in these estimates were chocolate candies, nonchocolate candies, gum, nuts, granola, salted snacks, meat snacks, ice bars, fruit snacks, and baked snacks. However, the range on market size was indicative of the fact that the snack food market was ill-defined in that many different products could possibly be included in some estimates

---

[3] With over 33 million children between the ages of 4 and 12 in the United States, the buying power of children was thought to have a strong impact on consumption/purchase of snacks in the future. The most popular expenditure for children's wealth (valued at US$9 billion), aside from saving about 30 percent of this money, was snack food at a rate of about US$2 billion per year.

but not in others. (For example, drinks such as beer, colas/noncolas, and wine were included in some estimates.) Needless to say, snacks were a sizable market in the 1990s.

The size and growth of the snack foods market had resulted in the introduction of around 500 new snack products (including reformulations) each year. By the mid-1990s, however, predictions were for the start of an industry shakeout. With healthy snacks the fastest growing segment in the snack category, industry survivors were expected to be companies with "healthier" product offerings (low-salt, low-fat). Healthy snacks accounted for 4 percent of the annual US$6.2 billion spent on salty snacks. Growth projections were as much as 25 percent for the end of the 1990s. The Frito-Lay division of Pepsico, Inc., had reportedly planned investments of around US$200 million to speed up production of reduced-fat products. Gourmet snacks were also in vogue.

Keebler Co. introduced eight new products in the early 1990s, including cookies, pretzels, and additional varieties in its well-established lines such as Town House Crackers and Club Crackers. Frito-Lay (which was estimated to have over 40 percent of the salty snack market) invested heavily in its Rold Gold brand of pretzels, while buying out the SunChips brand of multigrain chips.[4] In the early 1990s Terra Chips sold an estimated $10 million of its chip made from taro and flavored with beet juice, yucca, sweet potato, batata, and parsnip. Other new chip flavorings included jalapeno, cheddar, and chile cheese. Party mixes (premixed batches of assorted snacks) and the snack cracker/chip (baked instead of fried) were other growth areas. The one product category experiencing flat growth was nuts.

Popcorn.   Popcorn had moved from "junk food" status to health food which is low in calories and high in fiber. Per capita consumption of popcorn in the United States was approximately 50 quarts in the 1990s.[5] Excluding movie sales of popcorn, Americans were spending $1 billion for popcorn annually, with slightly over $600 million on microwavable popcorn. U.S. retail sales of popped and unpopped popcorn had experienced annual growth rates of 25 percent. Some industry experts predicted that the microwave popcorn market was matured, resulting in a plateauing of sales for the future. Contrary to this prediction, Golden Valley believed that it would see annual growth rates of 15 percent.

The microwavable popcorn market was dominated by two extremes in the mid-1990s. One major product in the category was butter-flavor popcorn, the other being reduced-fat popcorn. Leading brands in the market by the beginning of 1996 were Orville Redenbacher (39 percent share) and Golden Valley's Act II (14 percent share). The microwavable popcorn category was promoted heavily to the consumer. (A common promotion was the two-for-one deal.) The level of promotion was thought to be a major factor in keeping private-label brands out of the market.

Flavor was seen as strong direction for category growth for the latter half of the 1990s. Going along with the flavor trend, Golden Valley had introduced varieties such as Ranch, White Cheddar Cheese, Caramel Glaze, Cinnamon Toffee Glaze, and Santa Fe Butter (jalapeno peppers, onions, and garlic). While active in the flavored popcorn market, GVMF had not overlooked the two dominant category extremes. The Act II

---

[4] Multigrain chips were derived from rice, corn, wheat, and oats. Some industry experts predicted that these chips had the potential to be a $300 to $400 million annual business by the end of the 1990s.

[5] This was equivalent to almost 13 billion quarts.

Theatre Style/Movietime popcorn product satisfied the creamy butter consumer, and the Act II 96% Fat-Free product targeted the health-conscious consumer.

The global market was open to popcorn as a snack. However, the international version of popcorn was not the butter-and-salt version found in the United States. The Swedes liked their popcorn very buttery, the Germans and French sprinkled sugar on their popcorn, Europeans had a strong preference for goat cheese on their popcorn, and Mexicans liked jalapeno-flavored popcorn. The British, however, perceived popcorn as child's food or candy rather than a salty snack product. Additionally, usage patterns in microwave ovens, lack of microwave oven capability (for example, microwaves in Japan had a metal base and microwavable popcorn could not perform on a metal surface), and government regulations (for example, labeling) were potential obstacles in an international expansion program.

Microwave Ovens

Microwave oven penetration of the U.S. home market soared from 0.1 percent in 1971 to 85 percent by 1995.[6] As consumers became used to microwave ovens in their homes, usage extended to the away-from-home market. As such, microwave ovens (which were smaller than those found in the home) began appearing in cafeterias, workplaces, dormitory rooms, and anywhere else a person might spend time away from her primary residence. A study by the Campbell Microwave Institute reported that women used microwave ovens 2.6 times a day, children used them twice a day, and employees used office microwaves 17 times a month. The trend was toward using microwave ovens to warm rather than cook food.

Internationally, microwave ovens were found in approximately 40 percent of Japanese homes and 30 percent of homes in the United Kingdom. Microwave ovens were the fastest-growing home appliance market in Western Europe.

Microwave Food Consumption.   Americans tended to search continually for a convenient meal. By the early 1990s, the fast-food market was estimated to be around US$55 billion. Of this, around 75 percent was fast food consumed in the home (e.g., carryout and delivery items). This was a 55 percent increase over fast-food consumption in the 1980s. This search for convenience led to an increased use of the microwave oven,[7] which in turn led food manufacturers to provide microwave-ready food items. However, average household expenditures for food for the microwave were only US$15 in the first half of the 1990s. Microwaves had not been utilized as supermarkets would have liked. According to the Supermarket Business' 1990 Consumer Expenditures Study, a large percentage of microwave food sales came from snacks and occasion foods. Sales of unpopped popcorn increased almost 10 percent in grocery outlets. This was double the growth for frozen dinners and entrees. Single-serve microwave meals for children represented a growing segment of the market by the 1990s.

Not every product was microwavable (e.g., bagels). Developing microwavable products that tasted good, did not pick up any packaging odors, and cooked evenly was difficult. The key to preparing food in the microwave tended to rest with packaging the product.

---

[6] One study reported that almost 92 percent of mature consumers (ages 55+) used a microwave oven.

[7] The barbecue grill had experienced increased usage as well. By 1992, 32 percent of U.S. households used their grill for at least one meal during a two-week period. This compared to 22 percent in 1984.

Packaging.   Microwavable containers were a "hot" topic among packaging experts. Package forms ranged from traditional plates/bowls/cups to pouches/bags to boards to packages with visual indicators for doneness. Materials included plastic, paperboard, and molder pulp. There was concern in the industry, however, that food packagers and package suppliers were not working together to make the proper package for the designed type of food.

Two major issues focused upon taste and technology arose surrounding packaging. First, the package material and form had to be such that the food cooked properly (e.g., thoroughly, crispy, browning, crunchy). Second, the packaging had to be safe for the consumer. Serious burns had occurred from collapsing packages and from the eruption of superheated liquids. Additionally, food packages had to be made of such material that they would not ignite in the oven during the cooking cycle. Environmental concerns also were directed toward the type of material used in microwavable products. Clear labeling of cooking directions was a must on the microwave package.

Microwavable Foods.   Microwavable food items introduced included dessert mixes, instant potatoes, frozen pizza, frozen pies, bacon, popcorn, vegetables, cake mixes, sandwiches, and french fries. Most of these products were considered under-performers compared to other items in their product categories. A major problem in the microwave food market was product quality. Novelty tended to fascinate consumers enough to purchase the food item initially. However, repeat purchase failed to materialize because the products did not meet consumers' expectations. Yet with repeat business a must, microwave foods tended to experience increased quality problems as production levels increased.

Companies that introduced products into the microwave market included Pillsbury (cake mixes), Pitaria Products Co. (sandwiches), J. R. Simplot Co. (sandwiches), Geo. A. Hormel & Co. (sandwiches, single-serve meals, french fries), Quaker Oats Co. (sandwiches), Hershey Foods Corp. (pasta), Dial Corp. (single-serve meals), and Golden Valley Microwave Foods (popcorn, french fries, pancakes).

The U.S. frozen potato market consisted of around 7.5 billion pounds annually. French fries accounted for approximately 85 percent of this market. Frozen potato exports totaled around 250 million kilograms annually. Less than 1 percent of the retail frozen potato volume was served in a single, snacking package.

By 1995, Golden Valley had refined its microwave french fry technology to enter the product into mass production. While introduced in the late 1980s, the unique packaging of Fries-To-Go Microwave Fries presented production challenges. Fries-To-Go came in a paper box with compartments. (The surface material was the same as used in the company's popcorn.) Basically, potatoes were mashed, shoved through an extruder, fried to two-thirds done, and then placed singularly in each of the package's compartments. GVMF offered three french fry varieties: regular, zesty-seasons, and cheese-flavored. The product's suggested retail price for a three-pack container was around $1.99.

A potentially strong contender in the french fry single-serve market was Ore-Ida. Ore-Ida had introduced its Snackin' Fries in about 20 percent of the United States by the end of 1994. Other leading brands of frozen potatoes included McCain Foods and Universal Foods.

Tapping into the convenience market for breakfast items, GVMF introduced its Act II Microwave Buttermilk Pancakes in 1995. The single-serving frozen pancake came in a choice of three toppings (blueberry, maple, apple-cinnamon) in three-count heat and serve boxes. Promotion involved a "buy one Fries-To-Go, get one pancake free" coupon.

Golden Valley's Marketing Strategy

Golden Valley's marketing strategy was twofold. First, the company wanted to find new markets for its current products. Second, the company knew that it would have to develop new products for its current and future markets. The challenge was to use technology to produce microwave products that were convenient, high-quality, and priced appropriately.

Within this twofold marketing strategy existed three arenas: international markets, vending machine distribution, and frozen dinners. From an international perspective, ConAgra owned major international operations such as ConAgra Asia-Pacific (retail/foodservice in the Far East, food processing in Australia and Thailand), ConAgra Latin America (poultry and corn food processing/distribution), and meat and chicken processing in Europe. The president of ConAgra International had begun looking for additional opportunities in Eastern Europe where the company already marketed the Golden Valley line of popcorn.[8]

A $25 billion a year business in the United States, the vending machine market was dominated by candy, snacks, cigarettes, and soda. The vice president of sales and marketing at ConAgra Frozen Foods predicted that vending machines would replace convenience stores in the consumer's quick-stop for frozen prepared meals. With an expected 25,000 frozen food vending machines by the year 2000, ConAgra had begun aggressive pursuit of products suitable for this marketing channel.

Worth about $2.4 billon by 1996, the low-calorie, low-fat, low-sodium frozen dinner entree market was one of the hottest areas of competition. The products were purchased by both men and women. A *Consumer Reports* test, however, revealed that most of the 800 frozen meals/entrees in the "light" category fell short of consumer's traditional expectations for foods either prepared at home or purchased at a deli or coffee shop.

As a division of ConAgra, Golden Valley Microwave Foods did not face the same risks as it had when it was started by Jim Watkins with his microwave popcorn. However, a solid growth strategy was imperative for GVMF to remain a profitable division of the corporation.

---

[8] The popcorn was sold by street vendors using old-fashioned theater poppers imported by Golden Valley.

Sources

"Act II Microwave Heat & Serve Buttermilk Pancakes." *Product Alert,* May 15, 1995.

"Act II Microwave Popcorn—Low Fat–Butter Flavored." *Product Alert,* May 23, 1994.

Balzer, Harry. "The Ultimate Cooking Appliance." *American Demographics,* July 1993, pp. 40–44.

Berman, Bonnie. "Candy & Tobacco Supplement: Holidays Are Happy Times for Candy Industry/Value-Priced Cigarettes Capture Industry Attention." *Discount Merchandiser,* September 1987, pp. 69–77.

ConAgra Corporate Offices. Web site information.

Donlon, J. P. and Joseph L. McCarthy. "A Healthy Choice for Transition." *Chief Executive (U.S.),* November 1992, p. 32.

Doyle, Kevin. "Snack Makers Feel the Crunch." *Incentive,* November 1991, pp. 50–52.

Duff, Mike. "Making More out of the Microwave." *Supermarket Business,* April 1991, pp. 45–48, 89.

Dwyer, Steve. "'Healthy' or Traditional, Snacks Maintain Their Customer Appeal." *National Petroleum News,* July 1992, pp. 38–41.

Erickson, Greg. "For One on the Run." *Packaging,* March 1991, pp. 26–28.

Forest, Stephanie Anderson. "Chipping Away at Frito-Lay." *Business Week,* July 22, 1991, p. 26.

Fredrickson, Tom. "Golden Valley Microwave Finesses French Fry Science." *Minneapolis–St. Paul City Business,* December 17, 1993, p. 7.

Golden Valley Microwave Foods. Web site information.

"Growing Markets: Grain Processing Companies Target Eastern Europe, F.S.U., Former Soviet Union." *Milling & Baking News,* March 16, 1993, p. 1.

Kim, James. "Stock Swap Bodes Well for ConAgra." *USA Today,* April 23, 1991, p. 3B.

Larson, Melissa. "Microwave Packaging Cooks Up Conflict." *Packaging,* October 1988, pp. 60–62A.

Larson, Melissa. "Microwave Technology Heats Up." *Packaging,* June 1988, pp. 66–69.

Larson, Melissa. "Taste and Value Drive Microwave Foods." *Packaging,* February 1991, pp. 32–36.

Lewis, Leonard. "Will Vending Machines Make a Good Home for High Quality Frozens?" *Frozen Food Age,* March 1993, p. 35.

Liesse, Julie. "Microwave-Only Food Market Loses Steam." *Advertising Age,* July 16, 1990, pp. 3, 40.

Lubove, Seth. "Report from the Front." *Forbes,* September 13, 1993, p. 220.

Madonia, Moira. "Snack Foods." *Supermarket Business,* September 1992, pp. 134–35.

McNeal, James. "Children as Customers." *American Demographics,* September 1990, pp. 36-39.

Menzie, Karol V. "Frozen Dinners Are Sizzling in the '90s." *The Arizona Republic/The Phoenix Gazette,* February 10, 1993, p. FD1.

Remich, Norman. "High Tech Wins Vote of Mature Consumers." *Appliance Manufacturer,* March 1991, pp. 62–63.

Riell, Howard. "Consumer Expenditures Study: Snack Foods." *Supermarket Business,* September 1991, pp. 172–73.

Roman, Mark. "Renegades of the Year 1987." *Success,* January-February 1988, pp. 43–49.

Ryan, Nancy. "Race Heats Up to Zap More Flavor into Microwave Products." *Chicago Tribune,* January 6, 1991, p. 1.

Savitz, Eric J. "This Spud's for You? Or, Are French Fries the New Popcorn?" *Barron's,* October 23, 1989, pp. 20, 51–53.

Scarpa, James. "Piece Meal: Munching Madness." *Restaurant Business,* July 20, 1992, pp. 127–28.

"Snack Food Industry Finds Itself in the Midst of Radical Change." *Chain Drug Review,* February 13, 1995, p. 16.

Spethmann, Betsy. "ConAgra Onslaught Reaches Bread, Popcorn." *Brandweek,* October 2, 1995, p. 1.

Sternman, Mike. "Keeping Popcorn Hot: Challenged by Snack Aisle Competitors, Microwave Popcorn Makers Are Still Popping Out New Ideas." *Supermarket News,* January 9, 1995, p. 25(3).

Tierney, Robin. "Pop Culture." *World Trade,* October 1993, p. 20.

Vogel Popcorn. Web site information.

Wellman, David. "Operation Global Valley; Golden Valley Microwave Markets Microwave Popcorn Worldwide." *Food & Beverage Marketing,* May 1991, p. 56.

Wold, Marjorie. "Nuts Can't Crack the Snack Market." *Progressive Grocer,* May 1992, pp. 179–80.

Zbytniewski, Jo-Ann. "A Snack Food Free-for-All." *Progressive Grocer,* September 1992, pp. 121–22.

CASE 3–2
BLOCKBUSTER ENTERTAINMENT CORPORATION

On May 9, 1991, Wayne Huizenga, chairman and CEO of Blockbuster Entertainment Corporation, convened a regularly scheduled management committee meeting of top Blockbuster executives at its Fort Lauderdale corporate headquarters. An important subject at the meeting was the May 3 announcement by one of Blockbuster's largest franchisees, Cox Enterprises Inc., that it intended to sell its 82 Blockbuster Video stores. Blockbuster had a disappointing first quarter and was faced with a significant drop in its stock price (stock had fallen to $10, almost 30 percent below its price of $14 just two months earlier). Wayne Huizenga was concerned not only with the immediate defection of one of Blockbuster's main franchise partners but also with the general conditions of the video-rental marketplace which were causing some observers to state that the "bloom was off the rose" in the video-rental business.

In its relatively short history, Blockbuster Video had experienced dramatic growth and success which propelled it to $1 billion in annual revenues after only five years (for example, it took the McDonald's chain 17 years to arrive at $1 billion in revenues). Blockbuster had 19 stores in 1986. It ended 1990 with almost 1,500 video-rental "superstores," which were company-owned and franchised. Blockbuster had become the undisputed leader in the video-rental industry, a status earned as a result of its energetic executive leadership and its aggressive expansion strategy.

In calling this particular meeting of his top executives, Wayne Huizenga was concerned with the perception that the video-rental market was entering a stage of maturity. The decision by Cox Enterprises to sell all of its stores was disturbing, not because of any significant impact on revenues (Blockbuster would still collect its royalties from the new owners), but because of the perceived reasons for Cox's decision to bail out. Cox executives had determined that its resources could be more profitably utilized in other ventures. After several years of high, double-digit growth, industry revenues appeared to be leveling off at a more moderate rate. According to consultants Alexander and Associates, growth rates in videocassette rentals were also slipping. This view concerning market maturity was further supported in a *Business Week* quote from Jules Gardner, vice president of West Coast Video Enterprises, the number two chain of video-rental stores. According to Gardner, "The business matured real fast. It is still a great business, but we have to work for our money." Such observations provided little encouragement to potential franchises whom Blockbuster depended upon for its continued growth in store units.

Huizenga was not inclined to panic. Blockbuster had experienced fluctuations in its stock prices before. Also, some of the leveling off of business in the spring of 1991 could have been directly attributed to temporary changes in viewing habits brought about by the Gulf War and reduced franchise growth due to recessionary factors. He believed that Blockbuster executives should step back at this important juncture to review market conditions and to formulate its competitive strategies for the 1990s. Al-

This case was prepared by Patrick M. Quinn, Marnie L. Cameron, and Raymond Keyes, professor of marketing, Boston College. This case was written to facilitate classroom discussion rather than to illustrate effective/ineffective corporate decision making.

159

though Huizenga did not think that the industry had reached its mature stage, he knew that maturity was a future reality. Therefore, he wanted his staff to plan its strategies with this contingency in mind.

Blockbuster's strategy for growth was fairly simple and straightforward:

1. Open new stores.
2. Acquire stores in key growth areas.
3. Enhance store revenues.
4. Expand internationally.

The international strategy, the most recent initiative, directly addressed the potential saturation in the domestic market. The company operated 27 superstores in the United Kingdom and 51 in Canada. Additionally, the company had signed letters of intent for development of Blockbuster Video Superstores in Mexico, Australia, Venezuela, Spain, and Japan. The joint venture with Fujita & Co., Ltd. of Japan positioned Blockbuster to enter the Japanese market, the second largest home video market after the United States. Fujita was half-owner of McDonald's of Japan, which owned or franchised more than 730 McDonald's restaurants throughout Japan.

At the conclusion of the strategy session, Wayne Huizenga asked senior vice president of marketing Tom Gruber to gather information on Blockbuster's current situation and to identify and evaluate alternative growth strategies as a basis for an executive staff discussion at its next meeting.

Company Background

Blockbuster, formerly Cook Data Services, Inc., had been in the business of providing software and remote computing services to oil-and-gas–related businesses. The company discontinued these activities in July 1985 and entered the videocassette rental business. Blockbuster was the brainchild of David P. Cook, a Dallas computer whiz, whose idea was to create a big, bright, computerized video store. In 1985, Cook opened his first Blockbuster store in Dallas, Texas. He stocked 8,000 tapes, which was an enormous selection for those days. The store consisted of 8,500 square feet with computerized sales and inventory management. Eighteen similar stores were added in 1986. Although Cook sold some franchises, money was not coming in fast enough to support expansion.

Huizenga was the co-founder, former president, and CFO of Waste Management Inc., which he built into the world's largest waste collection and disposal company. His strategy consisted of building and expanding a chain through acquisitions of smaller, more vulnerable companies. At one point, 90 garbage companies were added to the Waste Management portfolio in just nine months. Waste Management Inc. became the largest waste disposal company in the world with revenues of over $6 billion.

In the spring of 1987, John Melk, a Blockbuster franchise investor and former Waste Management executive, convinced Wayne Huizenga and Don Flynn, another former associate at Waste Management, to make a visit to a Chicago Blockbuster Superstore. Melk had hopes of adding them as franchisees in the Blockbuster system. Instead, the three men—Melk, Huizenga, and Flynn—decided to buy the entire operation. They saw the opportunity to replicate the Waste Management Inc. strategy in the video-rental industry. Waste disposal had been a highly fragmented, "mom and pop" business until Huizenga came along. In April of 1987, the three-person investment group, led by Mr. Huizenga, assumed control of Blockbuster for $18.6 million. Soon

EXHIBIT 1   **Blockbuster System Video Store Count**

Year	Total	Company-Owned	Franchised Outlets
1985	1	1	0
1986	19	11	8
1987	133	77	56
1988	415	239	176
1989	1,079	561	518
1990	1,467	769	698
1991(E)	1,849	914	935
1992(E)	3,000		

Note: Store counts were for Blockbuster Video stores only. Acquired stores, not yet converted, were not included.

after gaining control of the company in 1987, Huizenga and his associates set out to assemble a management team with the skills necessary to operate a much larger company, eventually on an international scale.

Having learned from his experience in building the world's largest waste management company, Huizenga was willing to pay the premium to attract seasoned executives from such companies as McDonald's, Kentucky Fried Chicken, and Waste Management. He also sought the talents of others who had built successful regional chains. For example, Tom Gruber began his management career at McDonald's and spent 14 years as the director of international marketing at the Golden Arches. Luigi Salvaneschi, Blockbuster's president and CEO, was formerly in charge of real estate development and construction at Kentucky Fried Chicken and McDonald's. Many others like Gruber and Salvaneschi worked in the corporate management of Blockbuster.

Shortly after the purchase, Blockbuster engaged in a massive growth strategy that took the company from 19 stores in 1986 to 1,467 outlets in 1990 (Exhibit 1). At one time the company was opening a store almost every 17 hours and went on a growth campaign of 400 units per year, or one store every 22 hours for four years. Blockbuster planned to have 3,000 stores in their system by the end of 1992.

The company's growth was achieved through three procedures: new company stores, new franchise outlets, and buy-outs. The company's basic operating strategy was to expand nationwide by building company-owned stores in midsized and large cities and by franchising stores in smaller towns. Much like Huizenga's construction of the Waste Management empire, the Blockbuster chain was partially assembled from a collection of regional chains. For example, Blockbuster purchased five chains and a number of mom-and-pop operations. Some of the companies purchased by Blockbuster and their store counts are shown in Exhibit 2.

EXHIBIT 2   **Blockbuster's Major Purchases**

Date	Company	Number of Stores	Market
May 1987	Movies-To-Go, Inc.	29	St. Louis
March 1988	Video Library, Inc.	42	San Diego
January 1989	Major Video Corporation	175	Las Vegas, New England
August 1989	Video Superstore M.L.P.	106	Chicago, Milwaukee
April 1991	Erol's	208	Washington, D.C.

EXHIBIT 3   Blockbuster Company and System Revenues (in millions)

Revenue	1990	1989	1988	1987	1986	1985
Rental revenue*	$ 468,207	$283,933	$ 87,299	$19,009	$ 2,893	—
Product sales†	129,005	101,268	41,452	21,546	4,247	—
Royalties and other fees‡	35,378	17,337	8,142	2,673	298	—
Total	$ 632,670	$402,538	$136,893	$43,228	$ 7,438	$119
Systemwide (Included Franchises) Revenue	$1,133,150	$663,475	$283,691	$98,218	$25,155	—

*Rental revenue included revenues from videocassette rentals in company-owned stores.

†Product sales consisted of revenue generated from (1) the sale of products to franchise owners, including initial videocassette inventories, computer hardware, software, and other supplies, (2) product sales at company-owned stores, including ancillary product sales such as confection, popcorn, and blank tapes.

‡Royalties and other fees were derived from the 3 to 8 percent royalties charged on franchisees' revenues and software fees for ongoing software support.

Source: *Blockbuster Annual Reports,* 1988 and 1991; and Form 10K, December 1989, 1990.

Blockbuster's strategy for national expansion through the purchase of regional competitors, franchises, and new stores contributed to significant revenue and market share growth. Tom Gruber was quick to point out that "we want to be the McDonald's of this industry and we are well on our way—what took them 15 years to achieve ($1 billion in sales), Blockbuster has done in five." Exhibit 3 outlines the tremendous revenue growth experienced by Blockbuster Entertainment Corp. and its franchises.

Dave Cook, the company founder, created the superstore concept for Blockbuster. The video-rental industry mainly consisted of small, 1,500-to-3,000–square-foot stores that offered about 3,000 films. Cook believed that a store of 5,500+ square feet with over 8,000 titles would better serve the needs of America's growing video market. Cook also left the dark, dingy image behind and created the concept of having brightly lit, freshly painted stores. "The 100-watt light bulb is one of our best marketing tools," says J. Ronald Castell, senior V.P. programming and communications. This store format would offer a wide selection to the consumer in an ambient, family atmosphere that better served the target audience. Huizenga and the Blockbuster team stuck to this original strategy, while increasing the number of outlets in a McDonald's-like fashion. (Blockbuster's financial figures are in Exhibits 4 and 5.)

Videocassette-Rental Industry

The prerecorded videocassette-rental business began in the mid-1970s with the introduction of the videocassette recorder (VCR) to the consumer market. VCR sales rose from a level of 800,000 in 1980 to 9.5 million in 1990. The average price of a VCR declined significantly from 1980 to 1990, with moderate-quality VCRs available for less than $200. The technological advances added to these machines improved dependability, portability, picture quality, and convenience. With these improvements in the VCR, consumer purchasing had increased. Exhibit 6 outlines VCR penetration of U.S. households from 1985 through 1995 (expected).

The consumer market for prerecorded videocassettes was comprised of the rental and purchase of feature-length and other films. Consumers typically rented recent hit movies and other releases, while purchases were made of instructional and children-oriented videos. Both segments were expected to grow as VCR penetration climbed, but rentals would remain the dominant revenue generator in the industry, as shown in

EXHIBIT 4

Blockbuster Entertainment Corporation and Subsidiaries
Consolidated Statements of Operations
for the Years Ended December 31, 1988–1990
($ thousands, except per share data)

	1990	1989	1988
Revenue			
Rental revenue	$ 468,287	$283,933	$127,023
Product sales	129,005	101,268	46,460
Royalties and other fees	35,378	17,337	6,296
	632,670	402,538	179,779
Operating costs and expenses			
Cost of product sales	91,904	71,391	34,784
Operating expenses	344,394	207,760	90,103
Selling, general, and administrative	77,062	47,246	25,076
Operating income	119,310	76,141	29,816
Interest expense	(14,212)	(11,039)	(3,711)
Interest income	2,970	1,283	1,213
Other income—net	43	3,380	1,026
Income before income taxes	108,111	69,765	28,344
Provision for income taxes	39,457	25,613	10,818
Net income	$ 68,654	$ 44,152	$ 17,526
Net income per common and common share equivalent	$ 0.43	$ 0.28	$ 0.12
Net income per common and common share equivalent—assuming full dilution	$ 0.42	$ 0.28	$ 0.12

System sales (Blockbuster plus its franchises)
1987	$ 98,218,000
1988	283,691,000
1989	663,475,000
1990	1,133,150,000

Exhibit 7. Additionally, growth in the industry was expected as a result of the changing entertainment habits of Americans. The industry would benefit from the increased number of hours spent at home, the increased amount of at-home entertainment, and the increased number of families. This was attributable to the "graying" of America—50 percent of the U.S. population was between the ages of 35 and 59 and held over 60 percent of the nation's disposable income.

The level of at-home entertainment was increasing. Justifiably, video rentals and sales compiled revenues of over $10.6 billion in 1990, while movie theater box office receipts totaled $5 billion. The typical family outing to a theater would run $28 for tickets (assuming four individuals at $7 per person) and $10+ for popcorn, soda, and so on. In comparison to the $40+ trip to the movies, the family could spend $3 on the video rental and $5+ for popcorn and soda. Thus, more families were expected to view movies in the economical surroundings of home, except in those cases where the movie was a "must see" at the theater.

After deciding to rent a movie, consumers would seek three distinct attributes from the video store: greater title selection, convenience (based on store location, extended hours, parking facilities, and transaction time), and rental rate. Because consumers

EXHIBIT 5

Blockbuster Entertainment Corporation and Subsidiaries
Consolidated Balance Sheets
as of December 31, 1989–1990
($ thousands, except share data)

	1990	1989
Assets		
Current assets		
Cash and cash equivalents	$ 49,300	$ 39,790
Accounts receivable, less allowances	23,345	15,954
Merchandise inventories	36,448	29,455
Other	6,444	7,393
Total current assets	115,537	92,592
Videocassette-rental inventory—net	183,438	133,041
Property and equipment—net	194,671	132,544
Intangible assets—net	68,709	38,509
Other assets	45,859	20,628
	$ 608,214	$ 417,314
Liabilities and Shareholders' Equity		
Current liabilities		
Current portion of long-term senior debt	$ 4,489	$ 19,030
Accounts payable	71,143	42,564
Accrued liabilities	20,191	11,140
Income taxes payable	9,720	3,724
Advance payments from franchise owners	4,171	6,899
Total current liabilities	109,714	83,357
Long-term senior debt, less current portion	67,927	24,218
Subordinated convertible debt	101,378	93,729
Other noncurrent liabilities	14,431	7,821
Commitments		
Shareholder's equity		
Preferred stock, $1 par value; authorized 500,000 shares; none outstanding	—	—
Common stock, $0.10 par value; authorized 300,000,000 shares; issued and outstanding 149,167,614 and 143,472,116 shares, respectively	14,917	14,347
Capital in excess of par value	170,526	133,175
Retained earnings	129,321	60,667
Total shareholders' equity	314,764	208,189
	$ 608,214	$ 417,314

viewed many movies over the course of a year, they desired a wide title selection. Consumers rented an average of 56 movies at 2.8 tapes per visit in 1990, up from 48 a year at 2.2 tapes per visit in 1985. Convenience was one of the least satisfied attributes in the industry. The "typical" video store operated with inefficient manual check-out systems that led to long waits and customer frustration. Location was a critical factor as a competitive weapon; in some areas of the country there were six rental stores within a three-mile radius of one another, which led to saturation. One video chain president stated, "The business is location, location, location." The average rental price in the industry was $2 per night per film. Additionally, the customer's viewing habits reflected seasonal patterns. Revenues declined in April and May with the change to

EXHIBIT 6 VCR Penetration

Year	Cumulative Households with Television Sets (thousands)	Cumulative VCR Penetration of TV Households (%)
1985	84,900	30%
1986	85,900	42
1987	87,400	53
1988	88,600	62
1989	90,400	68
1990	92,100	72
1991(E)	93,900	77
1995(E)	97,600	91

Source: *1991 Annual Report,* Form 10-K December 31, 1990, 1992.

Daylight Savings Time. They also declined during the fall months because the children returned to school and the new network programs were being aired.

Competition. The video rental industry was a highly fragmented and competitive business with over 29,000 units in operation nationwide. Over 26,000 of these were mom-and-pop stores, meaning that they were under 3,000 square feet, offered about 3,000 movie titles, and did not utilize computerized check-out. Also included in this grouping were the convenience stores, drug stores, supermarkets, and mass merchandisers that engaged in video rentals and sales. The average inventory of these outlets was between 200 and 500 videocassette titles with an emphasis placed on sales rather than rentals.

The remaining 3,000+ stores were controlled by Blockbuster and a number of regional chains across the country that operated under the superstore concept. In building its network of 1,620 stores, Blockbuster had purchased three of its top four competitors. Blockbuster's annual sales were greater than the combined figures for the second through sixteenth largest competitors. West Coast Video, a national chain concentrating on smaller suburban markets, was the largest competitor with 710 stores and sales of $180 million. Exhibit 8 provides the industry's top chains. Though Block-

EXHIBIT 7 Estimated Industry Revenues ($ billions)

Year	Rental	Sales	Total
1985	$ 2.9	$0.7	$ 3.6
1986	4.2	0.9	5.1
1987	5.2	1.1	6.3
1988	6.4	1.6	8.0
1989	7.1	2.2	9.3
1990	7.6	2.7	10.3
1991(E)	8.1	3.1	11.2
1992(E)	8.6	3.6	12.2
1993(E)	9.3	4.1	13.4
1994(E)	10.0	4.6	14.6
1995(E)	10.8	5.0	15.8

Source: Blockbuster Entertainment Corporation, Form 10-K, December 31, 1990.

Exhibit 8   **Top Video Rental Chains (1990)**

Company	Headquarters	Number of Stores		Sales ($ millions)	
		1989	*1990*	*1989*	*1990*
Blockbuster	Ft. Lauderdale, FL	862	1435	$664	$1,038
Erol's	Springfield, VA	198	210	138	133
West Coast/National	Philadelphia, PA	702	610	165	130
Tower Video	West Sacramento, CA	50	56	50	63
RKO Warner	New York, NY	31	36	40	42
Palmer Video	Union, NJ	124	93	38	42
Video Central	San Antonio, TX	23	29	15	25
Video Galaxy	Rockville, CT	43	43	27	24
Video Connection	Toledo, OH	80	85	18	24
Video Express	Birmingham, AL	76	85	24	24

Source: *Video Store Magazine,* December 1990 and December 1991.

buster had encountered a considerable level of competition on the local scenes, it expected to see more contenders on a national level. Fran Bernstein of Merrill Lynch stated, "Blockbuster stands alone in the video rental market in both size and ambition. They wonder where is the Burger King to their McDonald's?"

The videocassette-rental business was highly competitive. Blockbuster believed that the principal competitive factors in the videocassette-rental business were title selection, number of copies of titles available, location, customer convenience, and rental rates. The company and its franchise owners competed with video retail stores, supermarkets, drug stores, convenience stores, book stores, mass merchandisers, and others. Video retail specialty stores had grown from approximately 7,000 outlets in 1983 to approximately 29,000 outlets in 1989. The company believed that its success lay on its large, attractive company-owned and franchise-owned superstores that offered a wider selection of movie titles and larger and more accessible inventories of videocassettes than its competitors. The superstores also had more convenient store locations, faster and more efficient computerized check-in/check-out procedures, extended operating hours, and competitive pricing.

In addition to competing with other retailers of rental videocassettes, Blockbuster competed for consumers' entertainment dollars and time with movie theaters, network television, sporting events, and other leisure activities. The company also competed with cable television, which included movie channels and pay-per-view (PPV) channels that ran newly released films. PPV offered first-run movies transmitted via telephone lines or cable in the comforts of home for a fee of around $8 per film. However, PPV movies had to be watched when they were offered, not on demand. Also, PPV movies did not include VCR utilities to start, stop, and pause. PPV was exploring a number of technological advances that would result in greater viewing flexibility for a wider audience. PPV captured $330 million in consumer entertainment expenditures, and sales were expected to grow with the introduction of technological advances. "I think Blockbuster will do just fine for the next few years," said Robert Whistler, president of Comsat PPV Company. "Whether they will still be around 10 or 12 years from now, that's another question!"

The Company

Blockbuster's corporate objective was "to provide customers with entertainment, instructional, and cultural videos in pleasant, family-oriented, and spacious surroundings." Blockbuster had developed the "superstore" concept on the premise of large title selection and convenience, with rental rates as a less important factor. The typical store had 8,000 to 10,000 square feet of selling space and stocked an average of 10,000 tapes. The videocassettes were arranged alphabetically within more than 30 categories—comedy, drama, mystery, classics, and such—for easy shopping. The videos were "faced" so that the customer saw not just the title, but also the tape cover. The facing of videos was extremely important because many customers may not remember the movie by reading the title, but will by seeing a picture of the actors on the tape cover. The facing of the films also encouraged customers to pick up more than one film as they browsed through the selections. Since the actual movies were displayed with their descriptive boxes on the showroom floor, the customer knew immediately if the selection was available for rental. This helped the sales personnel by not making them search for the titles behind the counter or in the back room. Once the customer made the selection, proprietary computer software allowed store personnel to process transactions rapidly.

Customers received free membership. When applying for membership, their genre preferences and other demographic information were put into the database. Blockbuster developed a laser barcode scanner system, which sped up the transaction time while also providing management with a database on customer addresses, customers' buying habits, rental activity by tape, and so on. This database allowed Blockbuster to develop more effective marketing/promotional activities. In 1990 there were 12 million members in the Blockbuster system, and this number grew at a rate of 300,000 new members per month.

In addition to broad title selection and convenience factors, all Blockbuster Superstores conformed to standardized design specifications and operating procedures, much like the McDonald's chain. Blockbuster's tag line was "America's Family Video Store"—they did not stock X-rated films and they allowed parents, through their membership account, to prevent their children from renting R-rated films. All Blockbuster Superstores offered extended business hours from 10 AM to midnight, seven days a week. Most stores were highly visible, located in free-standing structures or at the end of strip shopping centers, and had plenty of free parking. They were designed to be destination points and did not rely on traffic drawn by neighboring stores. In keeping with its emphasis on customer service, many stores had exterior drop-off boxes, provided a child's play area, and sold movie-oriented food products.

Franchise Development.   Blockbuster believed that the penetration of available markets in a short period of time was a critical success factor in competing in the videocassette market; therefore, they employed a strategy of franchise development. The ratio between corporate-owned and franchise locations was 50:50. Blockbuster aimed to run the operations in major markets while franchising out those locations in smaller, less dominant markets. By the end of 1995, the company hoped to reduce this 50:50 ratio to 40:60 as Blockbuster expanded further into the smaller markets.

Opening a Blockbuster Video Superstore generally required between $425,000 and $700,000, exclusive of any franchise fee or development fee. In many cases, the ability of a prospective franchise owner to meet these large financial requirements was contingent on the availability of outside financing. Each franchise owner had the sole responsibility for all financial commitments relating to the opening and operation of super-stores in the franchised territory, including rent, utilities, payroll, and other relevant expenses. The typical franchise agreement called for a $55,000 initial fee for the right to operate under the Blockbuster Video name, a fee in the amount of up to $30,000 for the required proprietary software, and a continuing monthly payment of $650 for the maintenance of the software. Additionally, the franchisee had to pay (1) a continuing royalty and service fee equal to a certain percentage of gross sales, ranging from 3 percent to 8 percent, (2) a percentage of gross revenue for national advertising and marketing programs, approximately 0.5 percent, and (3) an additional percentage of revenue for local advertising.

Franchise owners were generally required to have an opening inventory of 5,000 to 7,000 tapes. They were not required to purchase their initial inventories from the company (used tapes could usually be purchased at lower prices) but, because of barcoding and packaging requirements, many chose to do so because it was much easier and more efficient. The company priced videocassettes competitively with major cassette distributors and charged a packaging and handling fee. Franchisees were not allowed to place any tape in inventory that had not been previously approved by the company.

The company's franchise agreement required the franchise owner to participate actively in the operation of the franchise. To assist its franchisees, the company offered a wide range of services including site selection and lease negotiation assistance, construction assistance, employee training, and computer hardware and software support on a fee basis. All franchise owners and managers, in typical McDonald's fashion, had to attend a program at Blockbuster University that trained them in the standard operating procedures and practices of the company.

Pricing.   The average videocassette cost Blockbuster $40 to purchase, package, and deliver to its store locations. Blockbuster then charged customers $3 for each tape, which they were allowed to keep for three evenings. The pricing structure was used to encourage multiple rentals per visit by the customer, as Blockbuster customers averaged two tapes per visit. This liberal three-day policy could be disastrous, though, because the big hits were rarely available for Friday or Saturday rental. "Whenever I go to Blockbuster they don't have the movies I want," said a customer in Atlanta. Company officials stood by the policy for customer convenience and marketing reasons. Though the $3 pricing structure was above the industry average of $2 per night, Blockbuster believed that the consumer was willing to pay the premium for the services and selection.

Distribution.   Blockbuster operated an 80,000–square-foot distribution center in Dallas, Texas, through which it supplied new stores with videocassettes and other necessities. The facility had storage capacity of 400,000 cassettes and was used for shipping, receiving, and packaging rental videocassettes according to the company's uniform standards. This process involved removing each rental from its original carton, applying barcode labels to the video, and placing the cassette into its hard plastic case. The display carton was created for each cassette by inserting a foam device into the original carton and shrinkwrapping it. The end result of this process was a shipment that arrived at the store alphabetically sorted within categories and ready to be placed on display shelves. All stores received their initial titles from a preselected inventory compiled by this facility, alleviating the store manager from the tedious task of selecting 8,000 titles. This system at Blockbuster greatly contributed to the efficiency of videocassette selection and distribution nationwide.

Advertising and Promotion.   The company advertised the Blockbuster Video Superstore on television, radio, newspapers, and billboards and through direct mail. Blockbuster's corporate marketing department, with the assistance of national advertising agencies, developed advertising campaigns for implementation systemwide. Along with its explosive store growth, Blockbuster's advertising expenditures increased from $25 million in 1989, to $60 million in 1990, to over $90 million in 1991. One of Blockbuster's marketing themes, "WOW! What A Difference," incorporated the competitive standing of the company. Blockbuster believed it offered a combination of variety, convenience, and service that no other firm could provide. In response to this belief and the consumer's perception of these attributes, Blockbuster said, "WOW! What A Difference."

As part of their marketing program, Blockbuster began running McDonald's-like promotions. In 1990, they launched the Blockbuster Video $10 million game which was the largest promotional event ever in the video industry. The game utilized game pieces and a variety of prizes ranging from free rentals to $100,000 in cash. Plans called for another such promotion in the summer of 1991. The company also sponsored a college football game in 1990 with the introduction of the Blockbuster Bowl, the sixth largest college bowl game. Both programs were expected to be repeated in future periods. Blockbuster's advertising and promotions were founded on the belief that an effective advertising umbrella would increase store sales by a significant amount. Additionally, the marketing clout established by Blockbuster offered them advantages and economies of scale over competitors on a national basis.

Preparing for the Meeting

Tom Gruber, the chief marketing officer for Blockbuster, was the logical person to pull together the various growth alternatives for review at the upcoming management committee meeting. Prior to joining Blockbuster, Tom had spent 19 years with McDonald's, most recently as vice president of international marketing. This background positioned him to know a great deal about the franchising business in terms of both domestic operations and international expansion. However, as he identified and evaluated strategic options, he felt that the appropriate response should consider a broad range of opportunities rather than adhering too closely to Blockbuster's existing and admittedly successful strategies. As he thought about it, he concluded that this was the ideal time to think about and plan for the future. He needed to consider long-range market conditions and opportunities in an open-minded, creative way. As he saw it, the key question was "What major directions and what strategies should Blockbuster pursue in order to sustain its record of growth and success through the 1990s?" This question opened up a number of avenues for consideration and it occurred to him that a useful framework for exploring alternatives could be found in the traditional Product/Market Expansion Grid which identified four major categories:

	Existing Products	New Products
Existing Markets	Market Penetration	Product Development
New Markets	Market Development	Diversification

Using this framework, Gruber proceeded to jot down some preliminary thoughts concerning the various alternatives for consideration of the executive staff.

1. **Market Penetration:** Consisted of a company seeking increased sales from its current products in its current markets through more aggressive marketing effort. This included increasing market share from competitors going out of business.

   - In this category, he could identify several possibilities. One was the use of promotions or incentives to get customers to increase their rental usage. Blockbuster had already launched a $10 million McDonald's-style promotional game in which customers pasted stamps to make pictures and win prizes ranging from a free rental to $100,000. He knew that there were many other promotional incentives that could be used, including points, coupons, bonus tapes, price breaks, quantity discounts, and midweek pricing reductions.

   - Another idea that had been discussed involved the possibility of developing a mail-order business to build sales of videotapes, using a catalog and 800 phone number.

2. **Product Development:** Consisted of a company seeking increased sales by developing new or improved products for its current markets.

   - In considering product/service opportunities, one possibility involved the design of a smaller retail store model for use in less densely populated areas. A streamlined version of the superstore concept could utilize the successful systems developed for the superstore, but the requirements for retail space and tape inventories would be reduced with smaller demands.

   - There was also the possibility of designing a retail outlet model for supermarkets. Again, a streamlined model would utilize considerably less space and fewer titles but could be made more efficient than existing approaches by virtue of the Blockbuster systems.

   - The recent success of Domino's Pizza chain with its home delivery service suggested that offering home delivery and pickup might increase sales.

3. **Market Development:** Consisted of a company making increased sales by taking its existing products into new markets.

   - Blockbuster could continue to expand its international operations. The company operated superstores in the United Kingdom and in Canada, and they were exploring opportunities in Japan, Australia, Mexico, Chile, Spain, and Venezuela. Generally, operations in foreign markets were franchised stores.

   - Blockbuster could expand more aggressively into market areas with lower populations. As mentioned previously, store design, film inventories, and support systems could be adapted for lower usage rates, either through freestanding units or through leased departments in supermarkets, sundries stores, and other local retail outlets.

   - A less desirable but potentially lucrative approach for expanding its market involved entering the adult film market with the addition of X-rated films on a limited, controlled basis.

4. **Diversification:** Consisted of a company seeking increased sales by seeking new products for new markets where it could use its distinctive competencies.

   - This category presented the biggest challenge for Blockbuster. Gruber was seeking opportunities to move into new business areas where Blockbuster could utilize its particular knowledge and experience. This would involve a clear identification of the particular strengths and capabilities of the company. This would involve searching out broad opportunities or industries in which existing marketing activities were both fragmented and inefficient. He could identify several such possibilities, including amphitheaters and other entertainment-oriented venues and products, all of which fit under the Blockbuster Entertainment corporate umbrella. Tom realized that the real challenge was in identifying and evaluating the company's opportunities that appeared to represent the best strategic fit for Blockbuster. He recognized this as a critical stage in the company's strategic planning, and he felt that it was his responsibility to initiate the thinking that would launch the company in a broad-based review of its current position and its future business directions.

As Gruber considered the various alternatives, he was mindful of the fact that there were many possibilities that he had not identified in his preliminary review. However, he felt comfortable with this as a first effort. In organizing his own thinking regarding the different options available to Blockbuster, he found it useful to consider the strategy question at two levels. First, it was important to devise a realistic marketing strategy to position the company to operate effectively in a mature market situation characterized by slower growth and more aggressive competition. At another level, he recognized the importance of planning a long-range strategy for the company, including the serious evaluation of the different business opportunities and directions. In short, he appreciated the fact that Wayne Huizenga's assignment to him for the next executive meeting could, in fact, represent an initial step in the formulation of Blockbuster's major business strategies for the years ahead.

Sources

Corporate

Blockbuster Entertainment Corp., *News Release: Company Background,* March 18, 1991.

Blockbuster 1988 Annual Report.

Form 10-K, Securities and Exchange Commission, December 31, 1989; December 31, 1990.

Form 10-Q, Securities and Exchange Commission, September 30, 1990.

Financial

Advest Financial Services. Research Brief. March 12, 1991.

Merrill Lynch, January 29, 1991.

Merrill Lynch, February 7, 1991.

Periodicals

"Blockbuster CEO Has Giant Plans." *Billboard Magazine,* June 16, 1990.

"Blockbuster Looks beyond Retail." *Billboard Magazine,* May 26, 1990.

"Blockbuster vs. the World." *Los Angeles Times,* July 22, 1990.

"Blockbuster's Grainy Picture." *Business Week,* May 20, 1991.

"Meet the King of Video." *Fortune,* June 4, 1990.

"Slower Forward: After Frantic Growth, Blockbuster Faces Host of Video Rental Rivals." *The Wall Street Journal,* March 22, 1991.

"Video Chain Aims to Star as Industry Leader." *USA Today,* July 22, 1988.

Research Groups

The Chicago Corporation, April 27, 1990.

Kidder, Peabody Equity Research, October 26, 1990.

Montgomery Securities, May 22, 1990.

Southeast Research Partners, June 19, 1990.

CASE 3–3
SYSTEMSOFT CORPORATION

William O'Connell, senior vice president, strategic accounts and business development at SystemSoft Corporation, sat in his office and contemplated his company's future direction. SystemSoft had experienced tremendous growth since its founding in 1991 and was now the world's leading supplier of PC Card software.[1] SystemSoft had gone public in August 1994 and now, just one year later, O'Connell faced a difficult decision regarding the company's growth strategy.

SystemSoft developed system-level software allowing the operating system of a PC to interface with the hardware. The company had been highly successful in its core product lines of BIOS (basic input/output system), PC Card, and power management software. SystemSoft operated in a highly competitive environment in which technological innovation was a key driver of success. O'Connell had to decide whether to proceed in developing a new "call avoidance" product category.[2] Call avoidance software had a significant market potential and there was no comprehensive problem resolution software on the market.

O'Connell knew that SystemSoft must continue to innovate and push into new categories and segments, but he was concerned that the call avoidance software was too different from the company's core product mix. While rewards for pioneering a new product category could be tremendous, pursuing this opportunity could also stretch SystemSoft's resources too far at a time when the company had to begin to understand and manage its growth. Pursuing growth through a strategy of product development would have far-reaching effects within SystemSoft. For example, O'Connell would have to decide whether the salespeople should be organized by product line or whether they should be generalists, representing all of SystemSoft's products to an account. Some questioned whether SystemSoft should delve into this new category, given that it differed from its core product lines in many ways. O'Connell wondered, Was market penetration a safer route?

Company Overview

SystemSoft was co-founded in 1991 by four people from Phoenix Technologies as a developer of system-level software. SystemSoft's mission was to become the leading provider of connectivity and other system-level software for microprocessor-based devices. Its strategy was focused on technological leadership, strategic alliances, key cus-

---

[1] Formerly termed PCMCIA (Personal Computer Memory Card International Association). This is the industry standard for expansion slots on portable computers. PCMCIA slots accept a variety of PCMCIA cards from a variety of manufacturers. They can be used to add things such as memory, modem, fax, or LAN cards.

[2] Call avoidance software is intended to solve user problems on a PC, reducing the number of technical support calls to manufacturers.

This case was prepared by Lisa Robie Adam, graduate assistant, Boston College, under the supervision of Victoria L. Crittenden, associate professor of marketing, Boston College. This case was written to facilitate classroom discussion rather than to illustrate effective or ineffective corporate decision making.

EXHIBIT 1

SystemSoft Corporation Consolidated Balance Sheet, January 31			
Assets	**1995**	**1994**	**1993**
Current assets:			
Cash and cash equivalents	$ 7,716,687	$ 2,758,318	$ 696,249
Restricted cash	—	—	125,000
Marketable securities	4,885,069	—	—
Accounts receivable, net of doubtful accounts	4,572,757	2,423,612	1,439,477
Receivable from related party	73,500	89,950	43,082
Prepaid and other current assets	481,626	298,142	62,761
Deferred income taxes	1,218,812	—	—
Total current assets	18,948,451	5,570,022	2,366,569
Property and equipment, net	1,060,048	521,437	447,595
Purchased software, net	—	—	575,293
Software development costs, net	1,088,926	1,302,990	429,148
Total assets	$ 21,097,425	$ 7,394,449	$ 3,818,605
Liabilities and Stockholders' Equity (Deficit)			
Current liabilities:			
Accounts payable	$ 614,501	$ 354,259	$ 1,032,226
Accrued expenses	302,392	284,229	208,927
Income taxes payable	391,143	7,000	—
Accrued commissions	734,715	339,752	318,846
Accrued compensation and benefits	622,470	563,502	205,797
Accrued royalties	237,707	122,263	318,591
Deferred revenue from related party	260,000	540,000	—
Notes payable, current portion	—	359,123	189,901
Total current liabilities	$ 3,162,928	$ 2,570,128	$ 2,274,288
Notes payable, net of current portion	—	60,045	183,943
Deferred income taxes	276,600	—	—
Commitments			
Redeemable convertible preferred stock	—	12,080,511	8,656,702
Warrant	—	500,000	—
Stockholders' equity (deficit)			
Common stock	98,611	29,393	28,997
Paid-in capital	22,453,812	—	—
Less treasury stock	(128,696)	(128,696)	(105,596)
Accumulated deficit	(4,765,830)	(7,716,932)	(7,219,729)
Total stockholders' equity (deficit)	17,657,897	(7,816,235)	(7,296,328)
Total liabilities and owners' equity	$ 21,097,425	$ 7,394,449	$ 3,818,605

tomer relationships, further expansion into the desktop market, and finding additional markets for PC Card software and power management technology. Exhibits 1 and 2 show SystemSoft's balance sheet and income statement for the past several years.

System-level software provides a layer of connectivity and ease of use for personal computers by allowing the operating system to recognize, configure, and communicate with the system hardware, including the peripherals. (Exhibit 3 describes system-level software.) The end user typically is not familiar with system-level software because it operates between the computer chips and the operating system. In 1995, SystemSoft

EXHIBIT 2

SystemSoft Corporation Consolidated Statement of Operations, January 31				
	1995	1994	1993	1992
Revenues				
Software license fees	$ 10,223,294	$ 6,281,190	$ 4,425,216	$ 2,188,881
Engineering services	2,532,588	1,279,630	1,153,129	481,575
Related party	2,419,298	1,077,408	711,488	260,251
Other	46,077	515,364	—	—
Total revenues	15,221,257	9,153,592	6,289,833	2,930,707
Cost of Revenues				
Software license fees	1,303,769	850,006	960,202	808,084
Engineering services	951,023	1,046,140	1,028,102	837,465
Related party	1,817,343	616,093	513,776	276,517
Other	40,181	455,977	—	—
Total cost of revenues	4,112,316	2,968,216	2,502,080	1,922,066
Gross profit	11,108,941	6,185,376	3,787,753	1,008,641
Operating Expenses				
R&D	2,252,491	1,506,891	1,076,379	709,301
Sales and marketing	5,073,194	2,685,619	2,250,633	1,750,793
General and administrative	1,900,779	1,579,877	1,782,670	1,593,646
Litigation settlement	—	—	1,019,225	—
Total operating expenses	9,226,464	5,772,387	6,128,907	4,053,740
Income (loss) from operations	1,882,477	412,989	(2,341,154)	(3,045,099)
Interest income	298,726	15,857	28,480	41,417
Interest expense	(10,005)	(38,164)	(37,092)	(12,432)
Income (loss) before income taxes	2,171,198	390,682	(2,349,766)	(3,016,114)
Provisions for income tax	125,798	160,340	242,495	157,185
Net income (loss)	2,045,400	230,342	(2,592,261)	(3,173,299)
Accretion of preferred stock	(412,640)	(759,378)	(497,986)	(144,246)
Net income (loss) available to comm. shareholders	$ 1,632,760	($529,036)	($ 3,090,247)	($3,317,545)
Net income (loss) per share	$ 0.22	($0.15)	($0.87)	($0.93)
Weighted average number of shares outstanding	7,342,619	3,559,074	3,554,381	3,568,687

offered three categories of software products: PC Card, power management, and BIOS. The company dominated the mobile computer market, but its share of the desktop computer market remained negligible.

Products and Competition

The advent of mobile computers had dramatically changed the way people worked and communicated by the mid-1990s. Rapid development of mobile devices created a need for additional technologies that addressed the limitations of mobile computers. For example, PC Cards provided expanded memory and increased flexibility/functionality, while power management lengthened life between battery charges. Power management had also become more important on desktop PCs due to rising energy costs and

EXHIBIT 3   System-Level Software

SystemSoft is a supplier of PCMCIA and other system-level software to the rapidly growing market for mobile computers, comprised of laptops, notebooks, subnotebooks, and personal computing devices. PCMCIA is a published industry standard which enables PCs and electronic devices to automatically recognize, install, and configure peripherals (including, for example, modems, flash memory, and network cards) incorporated in credit-card–sized PCMCIA cards. System-level software provides both a connectivity layer, which facilitates the addition, configuration, and use of peripheral devices, and a hardware adaptation layer, which comprises the communication link between a PC's operating system software and hardware. Each new version of hardware or operating system software generally requires new system-level software. PC manufacturers are able to offer enhanced functionality, flexibility, and ease of use by using the company's software in their products.

System-level software is one of the four basic technologies in the architecture of a PC: application software, operating system software, system-level software, and hardware.

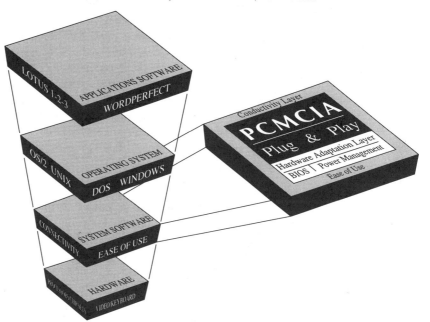

Application software is designed to perform end user tasks, such as word processing and data analysis. WordPerfect and Lotus 1-2-3 are examples of widely used application programs. Operating system software allows PC hardware to control the sequencing and processing of applications and respond to a PC user's commands, such as storing data, displaying data, and running an application program. Microsoft's DOS and Windows are the dominant operating systems in the IBM-compatible PC market. System-level software is a necessary component in every PC, enabling the computer's operating system to recognize, configure, and communicate with the hardware including peripherals. PC hardware consists of microprocessors, also known as central processing units (CPUs), CPU-support chipsets, memory, input–output devices (such as monitors and keyboards), and various other peripheral devices (such as printers, modems, and CD-ROM drives). Intel's $x86$ and Pentium chips are the leading CPUs in the PC market.

the Environmental Protection Agency's (EPA's) Energy Star Program.[3] The next page shows a brief description of the functionality of SystemSoft's core product lines:

---

[3] Energy Star is a voluntary program between the U.S. EPA and computer, monitor, and printer manufacturers that was developed in 1992 to conserve energy. To qualify for the Energy Star program, a computer must have a "sleep" feature that powers down the computer when not in use. This feature can cut the power usage by up to 75 percent.

EXHIBIT 4   Market Share by Product Category, 1995

Product	Market Share
BIOS and power management	
Notebook market	20% of available market,* 10% of overall market
Desktop market	Negligible
PC Card	64%

* The available market refers to personal computers that shipped with third-party BIOS and power management software. All OEMs used third-party manufacturers for PC Card software.

- *BIOS (basic input/output system)* software enables PC hardware components to accept commands from and deliver commands to the operating system software.
- *PC Card* software gives users immediate access to the features contained in add-on peripheral cards. Users insert credit-card–sized cards into sockets built into PCs in a manner similar to the insertion of a floppy disk. PC Card software enables a computer to identify the inserted card and reconfigure and allocate system resources without manual intervention by the user (such as setting jumper switches or configuring operating system software). PC Cards incorporate a standard published by the Personal Computer Memory Card International Association.
- *Power management* software reduces the power consumption of PCs by slowing or stopping the operation of specific system components when not in use.

SystemSoft had different competitors in each type of software it developed. Phoenix Technologies was the only competitor that developed software in all of SystemSoft's product categories. American Megatrends (AMI) was a leading competitor in the BIOS segment. Award competed with SystemSoft in the PC Card segment.

SystemSoft's greatest success was its dominance of the PC Card market. The company had approximately a 64 percent market share in 1995 and it supplied 14 of the top 15 notebook vendors. Its BIOS and power management software were also highly successful, with approximately a 20 percent share of the available notebook market in 1995.[4] (See Exhibit 4.) Phoenix was the leader in the notebook BIOS and power management market; AMI was second. SystemSoft's share of the desktop BIOS and power management market was small, but the company was looking to expand it.

Companies in the mobile computer industry operated in a highly competitive, rapidly changing technological environment. Innovation and the ability to change rapidly drive success. In addition to the leading direct competitors, there was always the competitive threat that operating system vendors would enter the market or incorporate enough features so as to decrease SystemSoft's revenues from original equipment manufacturers (OEMs).

Sales and Marketing

SystemSoft's sales and marketing efforts were focused on personal selling and attending trade shows. The company distributed data sheets on its products, but did little ad-

---

[4] The available market refers to notebooks that ship with a third-party BIOS. The available market is approximately 50 percent of 10 million units.

vertising and promotion. (Exhibit 5 shows a sample data sheet.) SystemSoft's sales were driven by a direct sales force, complemented by independent manufacturers' representatives for international sales. SystemSoft had a national sales office in California and international offices in Taiwan and Japan (the international headquarters). The software was licensed to OEMs, and SystemSoft received royalties on systems shipped. There was no initial charge for the software, unless SystemSoft customized or made adjustments to the software for the customer.

Revenues from BIOS software ranged from US$0.10 to US$1.00 for every unit shipped. Power management software was typically sold along with BIOS software, and it added about 20 to 50 percent to the BIOS revenue. PC Card software generated approximately US$1 to US$3 for each unit shipped, and the proposed call avoidance product was expected to generate US$3 to US$7 per unit.

Customer Base

SystemSoft licensed its products to OEMs, including PC manufacturers, hardware component manufacturers, PC Card manufacturers, and operating system software companies. The company had licensed its software to more than 100 PC manufacturers and more than 45 PC Card manufacturers. Exhibit 6 lists a number of SystemSoft clients in various segments.

Much of SystemSoft's success was attributed to a number of key customer relationships and strategic alliances that it had developed over a few short years. In 1993, SystemSoft entered into a Development and License Agreement with Intel, whereby Intel licensed certain technologies to SystemSoft. SystemSoft, in turn, developed these technologies into products marketed under the SystemSoft name. The Intel Agreement stipulated that the two companies would meet quarterly to identify new product opportunities. In addition to this agreement, Intel had around 10 percent equity ownership in SystemSoft. The agreement with Intel was the most comprehensive agreement for SystemSoft. However, the company also worked with other companies, such as Microsoft, to co-develop software.

The Call Avoidance Marketplace

When an end user has trouble with her personal computer, she frequently calls the manufacturer's technical support line. This call involves an "interview" stage in which the technical support representative asks a series of questions to diagnose the problem. Many of these calls are for routine problems, yet the sheer volume of calls is quite costly to the manufacturer. SystemSoft's goal was to develop an expert system to diagnose and solve common PC problems. The proposed product was expected to solve many problems, including scanning for and repairing viruses as well as remedying general protection faults, resource conflict, and configuration problems. Automating this process would significantly decrease the number of calls to technical support centers, reducing both the cost to manufacturers and the number of unanswered technical support calls.

The idea for the new product was a result of SystemSoft's huge success with CardWizard, a product launched in early 1995 to solve problems with PC Cards. CardWizard enabled mobile computer users to change PC Cards without having to stop what they were doing, an ability called hotswapping. Prior to the release of CardWizard, users often had to restart Windows or even reboot their computer with a different configuration to change cards. CardWizard simplified changing PC Cards because it automatically solved configuration problems, allowing PC Cards to be recognized upon in-

EXHIBIT 5   **Sample Data Sheet**

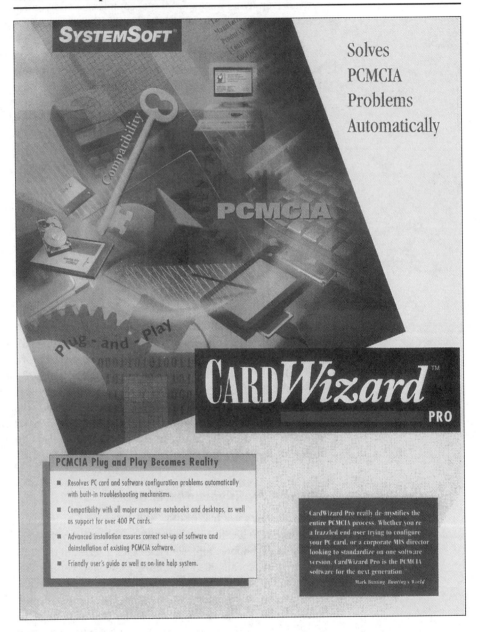

sertion. SystemSoft assumed that if it could develop a successful product to solve problems on a specific part of the PC, it could expand the concept of CardWizard to the PC as a whole.

The market research firm Dataquest estimated that more than 200 million calls would be received at technical support centers nationwide in 1996, more than 67 percent increase from 1992. Dataquest attributed this rise to the dramatic increase in the complexity of new hardware, operating system, and application software products. With the average cost per call exceeding $20, the PC industry would spend nearly $4

EXHIBIT 5   (Continued)

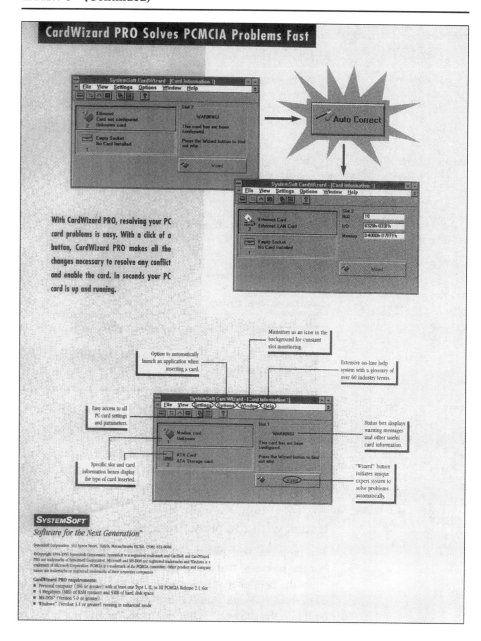

billion on "help desk" support in 1996. SystemSoft's proposed call avoidance software would help the PC industry handle its increasingly large number of customer support calls, significantly decreasing the enormous expense of technical support to PC manufacturers.

CyberMedia was the largest competitor in the call avoidance product category. CyberMedia had a call avoidance software package, First Aid 95, in the retail channel, but the company did not have an OEM presence. First Aid 95 automatically caught problems with PCs and it offered a variety of diagnostic programs that let the user

EXHIBIT 6   Sample Customer List by Segment

Hardware Component Manufacturers
Intel
Advanced Micro Devices (AMD)

PC Manufacturers

Acer	Hewlett-Packard	NCR/AT&T
AST Research	Hitachi	NEC
Citizen	Hyundai	Seiko Epson
Clevo	IBM	Sotec
Compaq	ICL	Twinhead
Dell	Inventec	Wacom
Digital Equipment	LiteOn	
Gateway 2000	Mitsui	

Operating System Software Companies
Microsoft
Geoworks

PC Card Manufacturers

Adaptec	Megahertz
Advanced Micro Devices	Motorola
AMP	National Semiconductor
Epson America	New Media
Hayes	Qlogic
Integral Peripherals	Standard Microsystems
Kingston Technology	US Robotics

pinpoint the cause of other problems, such as the wrong drivers for a sound card. While CyberMedia's product detected common problems, SystemSoft's new product entry would detect and remedy such problems on the spot. No company had developed such complete problem resolution software.

Issues with the New Product

The proposed new product raised both engineering and sales issues for SystemSoft. For the proposed call avoidance software to be successful, SystemSoft would need to enlist the help of many players in the PC industry. The company would need knowledge from software vendors, hardware vendors, and OEMs regarding what should be built into the software. While SystemSoft had established relationships and experience with OEMs, the company did not have experience with either hardware or software vendors. As such, SystemSoft approached Intel and Digital Equipment Corporation (DEC) to solicit feedback on the new product idea and request development assistance. Intel was excited about the possibilities of call avoidance software, and it provided SystemSoft with access to relevant patent portfolios to develop the product. DEC was also excited about the possibilities that call avoidance software offered. DEC's service arm, Multivendor Service Customer Support, expressed interest in helping SystemSoft determine product requirements and develop the product.

It was also clear that SystemSoft would need to hire additional engineers and create a separate engineering group for the new product. The company had two engineering groups: one dedicated to BIOS software and the other dedicated to PC Card software. These two groups required similar skill sets and experience, and engineers could easily be transferred from one group to the other. However, the proposed product would run off servers and builders; therefore it would require different engineering skills than SystemSoft's line of system-level software.[5] SystemSoft would have to hire engineers with the appropriate skill sets and create a separate engineering group to maintain and enhance the call avoidance product.

If O'Connell decided to pursue the new product, he must recommend whether SystemSoft should market it to OEMs as it did its current products or launch it to the retail trade to compete directly against CyberMedia. While CyberMedia's call avoidance software was distributed through the retail channel, SystemSoft lacked a retail presence.[6] The retail channel was different than the OEM channel, particularly with regards to co-op funding and advertising. SystemSoft was an engineering-driven company and large dollar outlays for such expenses did not fit with its core competencies or corporate strategy.

Selling the call avoidance product through the OEM channel required a very different sales process than that used for SystemSoft's other products. Basically, every PC needs BIOS software and all notebooks need PC Card software. As a result, the decision for OEMs is simply a make-or-buy decision—they either purchase the software from another company or develop it themselves. Almost all OEMs purchase BIOS and PC Card software as opposed to developing it on their own. Engineering departments typically decide which software to put into the PC; therefore SystemSoft's sales force had experience in selling solutions directly to the engineers.

Call avoidance software, on the other hand, was not a necessary product. Thus, the sales force would have to convince companies of the benefits of this new product, rather than simply convincing them to purchase SystemSoft software. Furthermore, the product was more complex than system-level software and the decision making power did not rest with engineers. The technical support center would need a server with special software to run the call avoidance system, and the software would have to be included on each individual PC.

The complexity of the call avoidance system required that the product be sold to several people. SystemSoft's sales force would first have to convince the OEM call center that this product could significantly reduce the amount of calls it received and demonstrate the cost savings that would result from this product.[7] Second, the product manager for the PC line had profit-and-loss responsibility. Therefore, SystemSoft must convince the product manager to invest in the product to include it in the PCs. In effect, SystemSoft would have to sell both the call center and product manager, a time-consuming process given that the call center and headquarters of many OEMs are located in different areas of the country.

If O'Connell recommended pursuing the call avoidance market through the OEM channel, how should the sales force be structured? Selling the call avoidance product was more complex and required a different skills set than selling system-level

---

[5] Servers are the hardware and software to which all machines on the network are connected. They run the network and store shared information. Builder software is a developmental tool for engineers that allows them to program new information into the knowledge base. It is used to enter information on new problems to keep the problem resolution software updated.

[6] SystemSoft launched its CardWizard PC Card product into the retail channel in mid-1995 and, while it received strong product reviews, retail was not a successful distribution channel for the company.

[7] An OEM call center is the facility at which technical support calls from customers are received.

software. O'Connell could take the most successful salespeople from the PC Card and BIOS software and have them sell the new product, but he was unsure how that would affect the current business. Furthermore, this would result in two SystemSoft salespeople calling on each account, which could confuse the customer.

The Decision

The call avoidance market represented a tremendous opportunity for SystemSoft to further its reputation as a technology leader. A successful new product could propel the company into new segments and help stimulate growth in the coming years. On the other hand, the risks were numerous. In addition to organizational issues surrounding engineering and sales, another factor complicated O'Connell's decision. The stockholders were pressuring SystemSoft to lower its rising software capitalization costs. Software companies are permitted to capitalize R&D expenses once a product reaches technological feasibility. O'Connell knew that pursuing this new product would boost the software capitalization even higher for up to two years. The capitalized costs threaten future earnings because they eventually will have to be expensed through amortization. Would the stockholders accept that or would many begin to sell shares, causing a decline in the valuation of the company?

Should O'Connell pursue this opportunity or should he recommend that System-Soft focus on pushing its core products into emerging technologies and further developing SystemSoft's presence in the desktop PC market?

Case 3–4
Angostura Bitters, Inc.

Think back to the early 1800s and imagine a young man named Dr. Johann Siegert. First he serves in the Prussian Army during the Battle of Waterloo, then he leaves his homeland of Germany to fight for freedom. This departure from home leads to his becoming a surgeon for Simon Bolivar's army. Stationed in Angostura, the troops are fighting for Venezuelan independence against the Spanish throne. While serving Bolivar, Siegert spends many hours studying botanicals and herbs from all around the world. He hopes to find a natural cure for stomach disorders that plague Bolivar's troops. After four years of trial and error, Siegert creates a blend of herbs and spices that is Angostura[1] aromatic bitters.

Now put yourself in July 1991 and imagine Carl Ambrose, the brand manager for Angostura Bitters, Ltd. Siegert's research led to the development of the company, and now Ambrose's research needs to globalize the company. Although Siegert's and Ambrose's goals differ greatly, their research is what links them and the two centuries together. Ambrose is contemplating a number of growth options. The most popular idea floating around Angostura is that of launching a new bottled rum under the Angostura name. Other ideas evolve around the liquid flavor sauce market. One option being discussed is the development of new sauce products. However, some people at Angostura think the company should expand on its flagship product, bitters, by creating new uses for the product.

The Company

The name, Angostura, was recognized around the globe as the leader in the market for aromatic bitters. The product had been around since 1827 and was distributed in over 140 countries. No less than six monarchs appointed Angostura as the royal purveyor of aromatic bitters. Among them were the King of Prussia, Alfonso XIII of Spain, Britain's Kings George V and VI, Queen Elizabeth II, and Sweden's King Gustav. Angostura's bitters achieved worldwide acclaim as a stomachic, a pick-me-up, and an important ingredient in innumerable mixed drinks.

By modern day standards, Angostura was a very small, privately held company. Located on the islands of Trinidad and Tobago, the company had 210 employees, with sales of TT\$163 million.[2] Although bitters was the flagship product, the majority of company sales and profits was derived from bulk rum and bottled rum. Angostura products reached consumers through the use of distributors all over the world, except in the U.S. where Angostura International Ltd.'s USA Division operated out of New Jersey.

---

[1] Angostura was the name of the town on the banks of the Orinoco River that served as Bolivar's headquarters.

[2] TT\$4.25 was approximately equal to US\$1.00 in 1990.

This case was prepared by Victoria L. Crittenden, associate professor of marketing at Boston College, and William F. Crittenden, associate professor of management at Northeastern University. Research assistance was provided by Karen Bickmore at Northeastern University. The case is designed as the basis for class discussion. All material was obtained from secondary sources.

Angostura began buying bulk rum from distributors and blending/bottling the rum under its own name at the beginning of the 1900s. By the early 1940s, the company had become a substantial buyer of bulk rum. In 1949, Angostura erected its first distillery, thereby making Angostura a major rum producer. By the 1990s, Angostura operated one of the most modern rum distilleries in the world and was a major exporter of bottled and bulk rum. Bacardi & Co. held a 43 percent share in Angostura Bitters, Ltd.

Trinidad and Tobago

As the two southernmost West Indian islands of the Caribbean, Trinidad and Tobago (T&T) are just 11 kilometers east of the South American coast of Venezuela (see Exhibit 1). Grenada, the closest neighboring Caribbean island, is located about 120 kilometers to the northwest. Trinidad is the larger of the two islands at 1,864 square miles, while Tobago is 116 square miles in area. Slightly over 1 million people inhabit T&T.

Trinidad and Tobago are part of the 13-member Caribbean Community and Common Market (CARICOM) pursuing the creation of a single Caribbean market. Efforts to implement a common external tariff, to remove regional trade barriers, and to allow free movement of skilled workers had worked well. On January 1, 1984, the Caribbean Basin Initiative was implemented by the U.S. This initiative helped attract new investment and aided Caribbean exports by allowing duty-free access to the U.S.

The U.S. was the largest importer of T&T goods, with a 55.5 percent share of T&T exports. The U.S. was also the largest exporter to T&T. Approximately 40 percent of T&T imports were from the U.S. While T&T was a principal trading partner with other countries, such as Canada, Japan, and the United Kingdom, none of these countries came close to matching T&T's relationship with the U.S. in either imports or exports. The principal cash crops were sugar cane (largest cash crop), coffee, cocoa, and citrus fruits. T&T was also producing slightly over 3 million gallons of rum yearly in the early 1990s.

Liquid Flavorings

Bitters.   Bitters were a liquid blend of herbs and spices, generally alcoholic, used to accentuate mixed drinks or to flavor salad dressing, stews, soups, and sauces. Bitters were often confused with vermouth. The main difference was that vermouth was based on wine, not "spirits" (alcohol).

The linkage between bitters and spirits was strong. There were around 100 recipes for cocktails which called for "a dash of bitters." This included such well-known drinks as the Manhattan and the Bloody Mary. As such, a change in the consumption of spirits was reflected in the sale of bitters.

In addition, bitters was thought to be an aid to digestion by stimulating the secretion of various digestive juices. Anecdotal evidence suggested that bitters could cure dyspepsia, colic, dysentery, nausea, seasickness, flatulence, and hangovers. For example, a dash of bitters in orange juice was suggested as a way for people, troubled by acidity, to enjoy such a citrus drink.

Sauces.   Sauces and dressings accounted for almost 1.6 percent of U.S. supermarket sales in 1990, for a category total of $4,331 million. While this category was comprised of at least 10 kinds of sauces, three major liquid flavoring sauces existed: soy, teriyaki, and worcestershire.

EXHIBIT 1 **Location of Trinidad and Tobago**

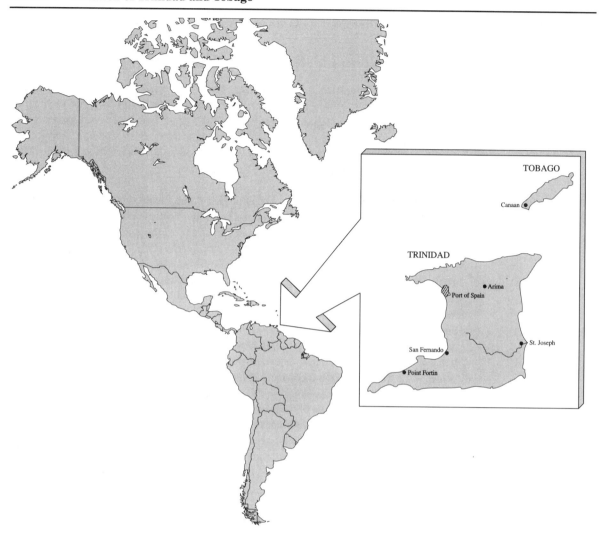

Soy sauce is made by fermenting soybeans, wheat, yeast, and salt. It is very salty and could contain 14–16 percent salt by weight. One tablespoon usually contains about 1,000 milligrams of sodium. Light versions contain 30 to 50 percent less sodium, but still average 600 milligrams per tablespoon. The three most popular types of soy sauce are Chinese, Japanese, and American. The Chinese have both a light- and a dark-colored sauce. Dark soy sauce is aged longer and accented with molasses. Japanese soy sauce is slightly sweeter than Chinese sauce because it has a higher wheat-to-soybean ratio. American-style soy sauce is not aged as long as other types and, on occasion, might be chemically processed.

Teriyaki sauce is based on soy sauce, with added fruit and sweetening agents. It is used for marinating, as well as enhancing the flavor of a teriyaki dish.

Worcestershire sauce is based on the flavor of the anchovy. Other ingredients include soy, various fruits, vinegar, salt, and sweetening agents.

Supermarket sales of soy and teriyaki sauce totaled $87.49 million in 1990. This was a 4 percent increase over 1989. Soy sauce alone was estimated to have generated $34 million in sales for 1990, a 2 percent increase over 1989. The reduced salt sauce segment grew 28 percent in 1990 to approximately $11 million.

Spirits

Most producers categorize spirits as either "brown" or white." Brown spirits include scotch and whiskeys, with rum and vodka known as white spirits. Another distinction made is "neutral" versus "noble" spirits. Neutral spirits (like vodka and gin) are distilled continuously and are usually flavorless or have taste added to them. Sold immediately upon creation, neutral spirits mix well with other beverages. Noble spirits (like cognac and malt whiskey) are made in batches and need to age in oak casks for as long as 50 years.

All spirits are made from sugar. For example, brandy is produced from the sugar of the grape, whiskey with the sugar produced from the conversion of the starch in barley, corn, or rye, and rum from the fermented products of the sugar cane (usually molasses).

World spirit consumption in 1990 was 525 million cases,[3] a 1 percent decline from 1989. Despite the obvious decline in world consumption, many industry leaders experienced healthy profits. In fact, the market contracted 6 percent in 1989, yet sales of the top 100 brands grew 4 percent. Sales of premium-priced brands, selling for more than $10 per bottle, rose 5 percent between 1985 and 1990. The increase in profits was attributed to several factors. A major factor was the opening of new markets. Trade barriers to Spain fell when it joined the European Community, and tax barriers to Japan were lifted in 1989. The rising affluent communities in Thailand, Greece, and Brazil opened the doors for spirit sales. As well, industry leaders experienced market growth by promoting global brands, controlling pricing and distribution, and cooperating with each other in countries where it was difficult to distribute.

The spirits market was rather highly concentrated among several transnational companies. Four companies (Int'l. Distillers & Vintners owned by Grand Metropolitan, United Distillers owned by Guinness, Seagram, and the Hiram Walker Group owned by Allied-Lyons) controlled around 35 percent of the spirits market, owning 40 percent of the top 100 brands. Exhibit 2 provides a listing of brands owned by each of these four companies. Seagram, for example, produced whisky, rum, gin, vodka, and liqueurs. However, none of these top four companies owned the number one top brand in spirit sales. This spot was held by Bacardi, the world's brand leader in spirits sales with its Bacardi rum.

Most of the large spirits producers were integrated vertically, from raw material processing through marketing of their products. In addition, many were linked contractually to large multicommodity traders as their distributors in foreign countries. For example, E. D. and F. Man, one of the world's largest sugar traders, was also a major distributor/shipper of rum.

Market surveys during the late 1980s suggested that spirits consumption per head was greatest in Hungary and the former East Germany (15.8 bottles), followed by Poland (14.2 bottles), Czechoslovakia (11.75 bottles), and Canada (11.3 bottles). Overall, drinking was predicted to be on the increase in Greece, Spain, and Japan and on the decline in the United States.

---

[3] A case contains nine litres.

EXHIBIT 2 Brands Owned by Top Four Companies

Int'l. Distillers & Vintners (GrandMet)
- Smirnoff (vodka)
- J&B Rare (Scotch)
- Popov (vodka)
- Baileys (liqueur)
- Dreher (brandy)

United Distillers (Guinness)
- Gordon's Gin (gin)
- Johnnie Walker Red (Scotch)
- Bell's (Scotch)
- Dewar's (Scotch)
- Johnnie Walker Black (Scotch)

Seagram
- Seagram's 7 Crown (American blended)
- Seagram's Gin (gin)
- Chivas Regal (Scotch)
- Seagram's VO (Canadian whiskey)
- Crown Royal (Canadian whiskey)

Hiram Walker Group (Allied-Lyons)
- Ballantine's (Scotch)
- Canadian Club (Canadian whiskey)
- Kahlua (liqueur)
- Beefeater (gin)
- Teacher's (Scotch)

Source: Jennifer Reese, "Liquor Profits Runneth Over," *Fortune,* November 4, 1991.

The liquor business enjoyed high status in Britain, which was the home to three large multinational liquor companies: Guinness, Grand Metropolitan, and Allied-Lyons.

U.S. Spirits Market. Experiencing one of the worst years since Prohibition, the U.S. liquor industry fell 5.6 percent to 147 million cases in 1991. Industry observers claimed the decline was a result of price increases,[4] tax hikes (a $1 per gallon increase in federal excise tax was instituted), the recession, and U.S. consumers' moderation in drinking alcoholic beverages (a moderation driven by concern with personal health and fitness). The average yearly decline in spirits sales was expected to be around 3 percent over the next several years. Spirits' low status in the U.S. market was suggested as a major reason that none of the big multinational spirits companies were American. Still, the U.S. accounted for almost one-half of all liquor imports in the world.

"White" goods held the largest share of the U.S. market at 45 percent, with "brown" goods accounting for about 40 percent of the market. Total gallons of spirits consumed in 1990 in the U.S. market was 365.6 million, with a wholesale value of $12,372.3 million and a retail value of $19,349.7 million. Bacardi, the world leader in spirits sales, ranked number one in the U.S., with 5 percent market share. The four largest geographic areas of spirits consumption in the U.S. were South Atlantic, Pacific, Middle Atlantic, and East North Central.

---

[4] The price of premium goods was expected to rise in greater percentages than the price of medium- and lower-priced goods.

Angostura's Markets

Liquid Flavorings. The U.S. market was the single largest market for Angostura bitters. Sales of bitters and sauces in the U.S. accounted for approximately 30 percent of the company's exports. It was estimated that U.S. annual sales of both bitters and sauces ranged somewhere between $15 million and $20 million in 1990.[5]

Bitters. Used in dashes, bitters was plagued by the fact that the product just lasted too long in the bottle. When asked about bitters, a typical consumer response was, "Yes, I have a bottle of that somewhere in my cupboard." Consumer research in 1990 found that product awareness declined amongst younger age groups (18–24 year olds). Three out of 10 consumers, however, equated Angostura with bitters. A closely guarded secret, only four people in the world had the recipe for Angostura bitters (and these four people were never allowed to travel together).

While expected to level off in 1991, Angostura bitters U.S. sales slipped from a peak of 80,000 cases in 1980 to 50,000 cases in 1990. The drop in sales was attributed to the U.S. economic recession coupled with consumer moderation in alcoholic consumption.

In 1990, Angostura launched a worldwide advertising and promotional campaign in an attempt to increase awareness, and encourage usage, of Angostura bitters. Since many T&T consumers used Angostura bitters in preparing Caribbean recipes, the 1990 campaign focused upon the many uses for the product (e.g., cooking as well as drink preparation) and began touting bitters as an ingredient of nonalcoholic drinks (i.e., picking up on the "healthful" drink theme of health-conscious Americans).

Specifically, the company began promoting the "Charger," a low-calorie, low-sodium beverage which consisted of club soda (or sparkling soda water) and bitters with a wedge of lemon or lime. According to Angostura U.S. President Robert Hanson, Angostura had to make sure that its product was a part of the current trend of changes in tastes in order to remain successful in the flavor business.[6] There were other nonalcoholic drinks in which bitters could be added, such as lemonade, ginger ale, coffee, and tonic water.

In promoting its bitters product, Angostura offered a professional mixing guide (which could be obtained from the company for a $1 postage-and-handling charge). Recipes and suggestions included mixing with orange juice and melted butter for a carrot glaze, flavoring for homemade milkshakes, and a substitute for vanilla extract in baked goods.

Traditionally, bitters had not been advertised globally. This led to basically regional or national bitters. These included Tennent's Special, McEwan's Export, Tetley Bitter, John Smith's Yorkshire Bitter, Stones Bitter, Webster's Yorkshire Bitter, and Whitbread Best Bitter. However, as the leading maker of bitters, Angostura really experienced no competition. Other manufacturers (e.g., Germany's Underberg) were unable to compete with Angostura on a global basis.

Sauces. By 1990, sauces and dressings comprised a multimillion-dollar business in the U.S. Supermarket sales of soy and teriyaki sauces accounted for almost $90 million in 1990. Kraft and Beatrice's La Choy were major names in this marketplace.

In 1986, after having invested throughout the years in advertising bitters as a food flavoring in addition to a beverage flavoring (with themes such as "a shelf of spices in

---

[5] As a privately held company, Angostura did not release numbers.

[6] As reported in Patricia Winters, "Bitters' New Bit: Angostura Ads Tout No-Alcohol Mix," *Advertising Age,* February 27, 1989.

a bottle" and "Angostura flavors the world"), Angostura began test marketing brand extensions in the U.S. Three such liquid flavoring extensions were introduced by the 1990s. Angostura soy sauce and worcestershire sauce were introduced first, followed later by a teriyaki sauce. All were specifically formulated with the unique selling appeal of "low sodium." Angostura's strategy was to identify a niche in the marketplace, which major manufacturers found too small to bother with.

By 1991, around 150,000 cases of these Angostura brand sauces had been sold in the U.S., with an expected annual growth rate of 20 percent.

Rum.   Rum's share of the U.S. spirits market was around 8.5 percent in 1989. This was double its 1975 market share. When the spirits market experienced a considerable drop in consumption, sales of rum remained fairly strong due largely to the fact that rum was used in more mixed drinks than any other spirits.

The market leader in rum sales, Bacardi experienced a decline in growth of almost 1 percent in 1990, yet posted record profits. Bacardi, reportedly, spent over $22 million in advertising its rum in 1991. While there were no close competitors to Bacardi in the rum category, by 1991 Smirnoff had begun battling Bacardi for the number one brand in the U.S. liquor industry (Smirnoff held around 0.1 percent less market share than Bacardi in the spirits market). Other rums included Castillo, a budget brand by Bacardi, which ranked 44th in the liquor industry in 1989, and Ronrico, a Seagram's rum, which ranked 57th in 1989.

For many years, Angostura introduced bottled rums into the U.S. market via its facility in New Jersey, but with little success. These rums were marketed under various brand names, such as Old Oak and Vat 19. Consumer research found that Angostura's brand names held no meaning with the U.S. rum consumer. This was very unlike the Trinidad and Tobago rum marketplace where Angostura held around 95 percent market share. The backbone of Angostura's export business was its bulk rum sales to many large rum producers, the majority of whom were Puerto Rican manufacturers.[7] Angostura's annual distilling capacity in Trinidad was 4 million gallons.

The Situation

Ambrose needed to make a decision soon. Unlike Dr. Siegert, he did not have four years, nor could he risk a trial-and-error approach, to make a recommendation to top management.

Was now the time for Angostura to strike again with its bottled rum? Consumers appeared ripe to try new drinks. Jack Daniels was launching a bourbon lemonade, Seagram's had introduced Gin and Juice, Jim Beam & Cola was very popular in Europe, and Bacardi Breezer (low alcohol, light rum, and natural fruit flavor) was one of the best selling spirits brands in the U.S. Should Angostura pursue brand extension of the Angostura name with a bottled rum? Despite the downward trend in consumption, industry experts were saying that there was a lot of potential in the spirits market. The key, said the experts, was to accept the fact that consumers were drinking less and focus attention on getting these consumers to drink better.

Or should Angostura focus its efforts on the liquid flavoring market? Was there a niche market for Angostura in the sauce category? Could the brand name be extended? Could more be done with bitters?

---

[7] Due to initiatives at the Caribbean Basin Institute, all Caribbean rums could be fairly matched in price with the branded Puerto Rican rums.

Sources

"Beverage Market Index for 1991," *Beverage World,* May 1991, pp. 29–34.

"Cheers through the Tears," *The Economist,* April 16, 1988, pp. 77–78.

Clairmonte, Frederick F.; and John H. Cavanagh. "TNCs and the Global Beverage Industry," *The CTC Reporter,* Autumn 1990, pp. 27–33.

Hollreiser, Eric. "Mellow Booze," *Adweek's Marketing Week,* December 16, 1991, p. 24.

Kochilas, Diane. "Soy Sauce," *Restaurant Business,* May 20, 1991, p. 195.

Lampert, Hope. "Bacardi Runs after Affluent Drinkers," *Adweek's Marketing Week,* May 7, 1990, pp. 28–29.

Lazarus, George. "Bitters Firm Finds a Low-Sodium Niche," *Chicago Tribune,* October 28, 1987, p. 4.

—. "Bush Blessing Not Exactly Sales Tonic," *Chicago Tribune,* September 19, 1991, p. 4.

Leatherbee, Lucy. "The Art of Drinking," *Chicago Tribune,* May 6, 1990, p. 26.

"Miscellaneous Grocery," *Progressive Grocer,* July 1991, pp. 74–76.

Pritchard, Barry. "Scotland Heads Bitter Brands, as Yorkshire Taps into Northern Tastes," *Marketing,* November 15, 1990, p. 21.

Reese, Jennifer. "Liquor Profits Runneth Over," *Fortune,* November 4, 1991, pp. 172–184.

"Sauces," *Institutional Distribution,* May 15, 1991, pp. 110ff.

"What's Mine?" *The Economist,* December 22, 1984, pp. 3–18.

Wiltz, Teresa Y. "It's Enough to Drive the Distillers to Drink," *Business Week,* June 25, 1990, pp. 98–99.

Winters, Patricia. "Bitters' New Bit: Angostura Ads Tout No-Alcohol Mix," *Advertising Age,* February 27, 1989, p. 26.

CASE 3–5
THE BACOVA GUILD, LTD.

As the director of marketing for the hardware division of the Bacova Guild, Ltd., John Walters was facing some decisions on new products that were not meeting expected sales. The disappointing sales were of concern to senior management because the firm's growth was driven by the successful development and marketing of new products. The Bacova Guild was an innovative company, winning two *Inc.* awards in the 1980s as one of the 500 fastest-growing small companies in the United States. The firm had expanded operations to accommodate the sales growth and it now faced a situation of having to successfully develop and market a steady stream of new products to cover a higher level of overhead and maintain profitability.

John Walters knew he faced a challenge. Product life cycles were getting shorter as competitors copied the Bacova products. In addition, the product categories that Bacova had entered with new products were proving to be susceptible to changing consumer tastes and economic conditions.

The hardware division, which had been very successful marketing decorative mailboxes, was also experiencing some problems with maturing markets. Division sales had fallen from $5.3 million in 1989 to $3.6 million in 1990. In response to the declining sales, the hardware division marketing group was beginning to market two new products designed to extend an existing line of outdoor decorative products for homeowners.

Postmaster, marketed in late 1989, was a complete mailbox system that could be purchased in one location to simplify the task of installing a rural mailbox. SignMaster, the newest product and the subject of this case study, is shown in Exhibit 1. It was a decorative house sign that could be used to identify a residence. Constructed of plastic in different shapes and decorative designs, it was sold with SignMaster house numbers made of peel-and-stick outdoor vinyl that the customer purchased separately and installed on the sign. Introduced during the National Hardware Show in August 1990, the product had received favorable reviews from the trade. Later in 1990, it was market-tested by a mass merchandiser and a home center store. The consumer sales had proven to be disappointing.

Bacova management believed that it was necessary to review SignMaster and its marketing strategy. Certainly changes would be made, but what was needed was not clear. Some Bacova employees believed that SignMaster had been priced improperly, while others felt that the packaging for the product did not have strong enough appeal for a self-service environment. Walters reflected that SignMaster had been introduced without trade or consumer promotion. With the end of 1991 approaching, Bacova

This case was written by Lawrence W. Lamont, Timothy J. Halloran, and Thomas D. Lowell, all of Washington and Lee University.

Property of the Department of Management, Washington and Lee University. Case material is prepared as a basis for class discussion and not designed to present illustrations of either effective or ineffective handling of administrative problems. Copyright © 1992 by Washington and Lee University.

The authors gratefully acknowledge the cooperation and assistance of Mr. Ben Johns and Mr. Patrick Haynes, senior management of The Bacova Guild, Mr. John Walters, director of marketing for the Hardware Division, and the employees of The Bacova Guild, Ltd.

Postmaster™, SignMaster™, and Accentbox™ are registered trademarks of The Bacova Guild, Ltd., Bacova, Virginia.

EXHIBIT 1   The SignMaster™ Decorative House Sign

Shown: (top left to right) Ivy, Cardinal Chickadee, and Decoy; (bottom left to right) Floral, Classic Border, and Country House.

management knew that decisions had to be made to finalize the marketing strategy and determine the role of SignMaster in the company's future.

History of The Bacova Guild, Ltd.

The Bacova Guild, Ltd., traces its origins back to 1963, when Grace Gilmore and her husband, William, began a small company known as Gilmore Designs, in New Bern, North Carolina. Grace was an artist and the business centered around silk-screening her wildlife drawings onto paper which was laminated between fiberglass surfaces to form a flexible decorative panel. The panels were then used for TV trays, card tables, and other gift items.

In 1957, Malcolm Hirsh, a retired businessman from New Jersey, purchased a "company town" located in the Allegheny Mountains of Virginia. The town was named Bacova, an acronym for Bath County, Virginia. Later, in 1964, Hirsh purchased Gilmore Designs, relocated the business to Bacova, and renamed it The Bacova Guild, Ltd.

Hirsh transformed Gilmore Designs from a mom-and-pop operation into a small company that found its niche selling to retail gift shops and mail-order companies. In the late 1960s he recognized that the fiberglass panels, originally used for indoor products, would also withstand the outdoor environment. This discovery led to the development of the Classic Bacova Mailbox, a product that would eventually become the cornerstone of the business. The Bacova Guild mailboxes were constructed with fiberglass covers attached to standard rural mailboxes. They utilized the original Gilmore wildlife designs and could be personalized with the name and address of the purchaser. Exhibit 2 shows the Classic Bacova Mailbox.

EXHIBIT 2   The Classic Bacova Mailbox

Source: The Bacova Guild, Ltd.

Financial difficulties led Hirsh to put The Bacova Guild up for sale in 1980. The Guild was sold in 1981 to Patrick R. Haynes, Jr., and Benjamin I. Johns, Jr., two former tennis professionals looking for a business opportunity. At the time of the purchase, there were 25 employees, a small building, and 900 customers.

The business was unprofitable in 1980, losing $40,000 on sales of $550,000. To become profitable, the partners aggressively pursued market penetration and product and market development. Bacova marketed ice buckets, waste baskets, utility barrels, and outdoor window thermometers using the wildlife designs and the fiberglass lamination process that worked with the mailboxes. Haynes and Johns also developed additional customers through increased participation in gift trade shows and dealer recruitment. The firm achieved profitability in 1982, and by 1983 sales had grown to $1.7 million, while earnings reached $98,016.

In 1984, Bacova diversified into the textile industry. The firm developed inks and a printing process that enabled it to print the same traditional wildlife designs on indoor/outdoor doormats. The mats were an instant success with gift shops and mail order businesses that sold them with the decorative mailboxes.

The success with wildlife designs printed on doormats led Bacova to develop a line of products for mass merchandisers. The new line, branded Accentmats, used similar wildlife designs, but the mats were smaller and priced for a market of lower income consumers. Within a short time, the sales of Accentmats made it the leading product

EXHIBIT 3   Sales and Profit History, 1981–90

Year	Sales	Net Income
1990	$ 13,371,093	$ 39,539
1989	14,380,456	(301,914)
1988	15,766,699	866,314
1987	19,090,441	1,821,085
1986	9,599,765	807,943
1985	3,808,209	242,569
1984	2,420,683	150,197
1983	1,681,189	98,016
1982	1,116,058	64,637
1981	776,282	(10,840)

Source: The Bacova Guild, Ltd.

line. A similar strategy was followed with mailboxes. In 1986, Bacova was successful in developing an inexpensive decorative mailbox that could be sold through the same retail outlets at prices considerably lower than the price of the original Bacova Classic Mailbox. The new mailbox line was branded with the name Accentbox. Like the door-mats, the product was very successful and Bacova discovered the enormous sales and profit potential of distribution channels that reached the majority of American consumers.

Sales and profits grew rapidly and employment and production capacity was expanded to meet the growing demand for Bacova products. The original Bacova facility was doubled in size, a new manufacturing facility was constructed across the street, additional production capacity was leased in a nearby village, and a small carpet plant was opened in Dalton, Georgia. At the end of 1987, sales reached $19 million, profits stood at $1.8 million and about 200 people were employed at Bacova.

Bacova's success drew the attention of competitors and they quickly copied its designs and products. During 1989 through 1990, sales declined as Bacova faced a slowing economy, maturing markets, and aggressive price competition in both hardware and textile products. The firm responded with new-product development and added a product line of printed cotton throw rugs, molded plastic mailboxes, decorative mailbox cover kits that could be applied to existing mailboxes, Postmaster post kits and accessories, and SignMaster house signs. The new products helped, but as the sales and profit history in Exhibit 3 indicates, the problems persisted. For the 1990 business year, Bacova's sales had fallen to $13.4 million and the firm reported a profit of $39,539. Exhibits 4 and 5 contain the financial statements for the year ending December 31, 1990.

Bacova Marketing and Product Lines

The textile and hardware divisions of The Bacova Guild market the product lines which account for a majority of company sales. Additionally, Bacova has a gift line that includes some hardware and textile products marketed to retail gift shops and mail-order companies at higher prices. However, management responsibility for the gift line falls within either the textile division or the hardware division depending on the product.

The textile product lines include floor mats and rugs for indoor and outdoor use, while the emphasis of the hardware line is on outdoor products such as mailboxes. In

EXHIBIT 4   Income Statement Year Ending December 31, 1990

Net sales	$ 13,371,093
Cost of sales	9,537,692
Gross profit	$ 3,833,401
Selling, general, and administrative	3,486,321
Operating income	347,080
Other income (expense)	
Interest expense	(338,585)
Interest income	13,556
Other, net	17,488
Net income	$ 39,539

Source: The Bacova Guild, Ltd.

EXHIBIT 5   Balance Sheet, Year Ending December 31, 1990

Assets	
Cash	$ 1,131,840
Accounts receivable	2,173,248
Inventories	1,437,035
Prepaid expenses	64,886
Total current assets	$ 4,807,009
Net fixed assets	2,518,282
Total assets	7,325,291
Liabilities and Equity	
Current installments	315,546
Accounts payable	590,413
Accrued expenses	139,221
Current liabilities	1,045,180
Long-term liabilities	2,151,792
Total liabilities	3,196,972
Stock	12,000
Paid-in capital	396,049
Retained earnings	3,720,270
Total equity	4,128,319
Total liabilities and equity	7,325,291

Source: The Bacova Guild, Ltd.

1990, the textile division accounted for 55.3 percent of Bacova sales, while the hardware division's sales were 28.1 percent. Sales of hardware and textile products to the gift and mail-order trade were 16.6 percent of total sales. Exhibit 6 provides a percentage breakdown of textile, hardware, and gift sales by product line.

Product development is conducted in Bacova, Virginia, where the firm maintains a design facility and support staff. When appropriate, Bacova also contracts with other firms for assistance with market research, product design, packaging, and the preparation of promotional materials.

Approximately 31 manufacturer's representative firms with a total of 75 salespeo-

EXHIBIT 6   1990 Sales by Product Line

Hardware Product Lines	*Percentage of Sales*
Accentbox	4.2%
Postmaster	15.3
Hearth Mat	6.6
Auto Mat	0.9
SignMaster	0.1
Other	1.0
Total	28.1%
Textile Product Lines	
Accentmat	33.2%
All American Rug	19.5
Braided Rug	1.2
Other	1.4
Total	55.3%
Gift and Mail Order	
Classic Mail Box	5.0%
Bacova Guild Mat	7.3
Other	4.3
Total	16.6%

Source: The Bacova Guild, Ltd.

ple sell Bacova products to mass merchandisers, home center stores, hardware stores, do-it-yourself lumber yards, department stores, retail gift shops, and mail-order firms. Manufacturer's representatives earn sales commissions averaging 5.0 percent on sales of Bacova products. They are managed out of Bacova's New York sales office and showroom by a vice president of marketing and sales with assistance from three sales managers located in the Eastern, Midwestern, and Western regions of the United States. Bacova also directs promotional literature, catalogs, and sales promotion to middlemen and is regularly represented at the major trade shows attended by its customers. Historically, Bacova has used trade shows to introduce new products such as SignMaster.

Textile Products.   The textile division markets decorative indoor/outdoor mats, and cotton, braided, and berber rugs. The products are usually printed with attractive wildlife and contemporary designs and purchased as a decorator item. The textile business is quite seasonal, and the majority of sales occur in the last quarter of the year. Popular designs are quickly imitated by competitors, and aggressive pricing is important to success. Bacova believes that its success in the textile market also depends on its design capability, printing technology, and ability to respond quickly to changes in consumer tastes. These unique strengths have enabled Bacova to market superior products at competitive prices.

Product Lines.   Accentmats, the best-selling product line in the company, are decorative doormats featuring the original Bacova designs printed on the mat. They are targeted to lower- and middle-income consumers looking for attractive prices. Distribution is through mass merchandisers, home center stores, and retail hardware stores.

The "All American" cotton rug is a line of indoor rugs printed with a variety of original Bacova designs. Available in four popular sizes, the rugs are made of 100 percent cotton with a nonskid backing so they can be used in a kitchen, bathroom, or hallway. The cotton rugs have been on the market since 1989 and are distributed through department stores and gift shops.

Two other product lines are the braided rugs and berber rugs. Braided rugs are made of 100 percent cotton, oval shaped, and available printed with Bacova designs or unprinted. The berber rug is a new line made of synthetic fibers. It is also available with Bacova designs and a nonskid backing.

Hardware Products.   The hardware division markets mailboxes and accessories, specialty mats for automobiles and fireplace hearths, and house signs. With the exception of the mats, most of the products are used as outdoor accents for residences. The specialty mats are marketed by the hardware division because the buyers for these products purchase primarily hardware items.

Mailboxes and accessories are the hardware division products accounting for the majority of sales. Bacova competes with three competitors whose products have low prices, comparable designs, and widespread retail distribution. Bacova believes it retains a competitive advantage because of the quality of its mailboxes, but competition has been successful in penetrating the market for decorative mailboxes. Bacova is moving to strengthen its position by marketing a full line of mailboxes and accessories.

Product Lines.   Accentbox is a line of metal mailboxes with a decorative plastic panel permanently attached to the cover. Fifteen decorative designs are available for the Accentbox and personalization is available by special order. The Accentbox line is distributed through gift shops and specialty stores to consumers preferring an inexpensive decorative mailbox.

Postmaster is the newest line of mailboxes in the hardware division. The line includes plastic mailboxes with and without decorative covers, snap-on mailbox cover kits to enable the purchaser to select and change the design on the mailbox, mounting plates, plastic posts, and an easy-mount stake that eliminates the need to dig a posthole. Postmaster is designed to be merchandised as a complete modular system and is distributed through mass merchandisers, home center stores, and hardware stores.

Hearth and automobile mats complete the product lines of the hardware division. Hearthmats are used to protect surfaces in front of fireplaces and doorways. Automats are sold in sets of two and are designed to fit most automobile floorboards. The products are constructed of synthetic fibers and are available in sporting, wildlife, and designer motifs.

Retail Gift Store and Mail-Order Products.   Historically, sales to retail gift shops and mail-order companies were the foundation of the Bacova customer franchise. As new products were developed and distribution channels were expanded, the gift market became a smaller part of the firm's business. However, Bacova continues to market mailboxes and indoor/outdoor doormats to consumers interested in purchasing higher quality, more expensive products through retail gift shops and mail-order catalogs. The business is attractive because of the higher profit margins available through these distribution channels.

Product Lines.   The Classic Bacova Mailbox and the Bacova Guild Mat line are the most important product lines marketed as gifts. The Classic Bacova Mailbox has a handcrafted decorative fiberglass cover permanently applied to a sturdy steel mailbox. About 35 different decorative designs featuring animals, wildlife scenes, birds, flowers, and sports motifs are available to consumers. The Bacova Guild Decorative Door-mats are large rugged indoor/outdoor carpets with a nonskid rubber backing. The mats are available in different colors with a variety of attractive designs. If desired, the mail-boxes and doormats can be personalized with the purchaser's name, address, or other message and drop shipped from the Bacova facility in Virginia to the consumer after the retailer has made the sale.

The mailboxes and doormats have strong appeal as gifts where consumers are look-ing for top quality and price is not a major consideration. Both products are distributed through retail gift shops and mail-order firms.

SignMaster—a New Bacova Product

The most recent addition to the hardware division is SignMaster, a home identification product that enables consumers to identify residences with house numbers mounted on a decorative sign. SignMaster house signs are available in rectangular, oval, and tavern shapes with three Bacova designs for each shape. Three-inch house sign numbers made of weather-resistant peel-and-stick vinyl are displayed with the signs and se-lected at the time of purchase. Enclosed in the package is an alignment guide and di-rections to assist in applying the numbers to the sign. The house sign is 1/8-inch thick and is attached to the residence by using the double-sided adhesive mounting tape in-cluded in the package. Exhibit 7 illustrates a SignMaster Classic Border installed at a residence.

Development of SignMaster began in the spring of 1990 when management was looking for new products to extend the hardware division's line of outdoor accents. Following a three-month period involving a collaborative effort between the hardware division marketing group and a firm contracted to provide product development assis-tance, SignMaster was ready for marketing in August 1990.

SignMaster offered a new approach to identifying a residence. Decorative house signs were generally not available to consumers except through a few mail-order cata-logs. The closest competitive products were the plastic, wood, aluminum, and brass numbers which consumers attached individually to their residence. The inexpensive plastic numbers were available individually or in packages of 25 or more, while the wood, aluminum, and brass numbers could generally be purchased individually from a point-of-purchase display. A consumer using the conventional method of numbering a residence with three numbers could expect to invest between $1.20 and $18 in house numbers depending on the size and type of product selected.

Pricing and promotion of SignMaster house sign and numbers were important deci-sions. Bacova management reasoned that if the price of SignMaster to retailers was lower than it needed to be, Bacova would receive a low profit margin and fail to maxi-mize the profits on the product. On the other hand, if a high price was established, there was a risk that it would not be acceptable to consumers and the product would not sell. Complicating the decision was the retail markup that the retailers in the distri-bution channels would apply to the product. Previous experience indicated that hard-ware chains, home center stores, and mass merchandisers usually used markups of about 40 percent.

Consumer behavior would also influence the pricing decision. Consumers purchas-ing the product at retail were required to make two purchasing decisions. First, the consumer had to select the preferred shape and decorative design, and then one to four numbers depending upon the residence address. Thus, the cost to the consumer for the house sign and numbers was the total of the two purchase decisions. A second consid-

EXHIBIT 7   SignMaster Installed at a Consumer Residence

Shown in Rectangular—Classic Border.

eration centered around the fact that comparable products did not exist in the channels being considered for SignMaster. It was not clear whether consumers would simply compare the cost of installing SignMaster with the conventional approaches to numbering a residence or whether the product would be perceived as an entirely new and better solution to the problem. If the product was viewed as new, then it was likely that consumer promotion would be necessary to develop an understanding of what SignMaster was before it would sell.

Costs would also be a factor in arriving at Bacova's selling price. Based on minimum production runs, the total cost for the house sign was $3.15, comprised of $2.60 variable costs and $0.55 fixed overhead. The house numbers had a cost of $.109 each, including variable costs of $.096 and fixed overhead of $.013. Management believed that these costs would remain unchanged over the next few years, unless substantial changes were made in product design or packaging.

SignMaster was introduced without consumer or trade promotion in August 1990, at the National Hardware Show in Chicago. Bacova priced the house sign at $8.50 and the numbers at $0.50 each. Initial distribution was achieved in 10 Target stores, a discount department store chain owned by Dayton-Hudson, and in one Lowe's store, a specialty retailer pursuing the home-center do-it-yourself business. Sales for the period September–December 1990, were $14,000. Consumers purchased an average of three numbers with each house sign.

Retail pricing was believed to be partly responsible for the disappointing sales. Pricing for SignMaster at the Target Stores was approximately $15.95, while Lowe's priced the product at $13.47. The house numbers were priced at $0.79. Late in 1990, both retailers reduced the price of the house sign to $9.95 in an attempt to stimulate sales.

Review of SignMaster Marketing Strategy

In January of 1991, management decided to review SignMaster and its marketing strategy. After reflecting that consumer research had not been conducted prior to market introduction, management decided to retain an independent marketing research organization to survey consumers and determine their reaction to the new product. At the same time, management moved to address the pricing issue by using the research organization to assist the hardware division marketing group in the design and implementation of a test market. SignMaster was placed in retail hardware stores located in six Virginia cities where three prices could be tested for consumer acceptance. The consumer survey research was completed by March. The sales results from the test market became available in November of 1991.

Research Methodology for Consumer Research.   A sample of 79 homeowners consisting of married couples and singles representing 46 different homes in 13 states was surveyed using personal interviews. The average age of survey respondents was 46, and the median market value of the homes was $140,000. After respondents had examined the house sign and numbers, they were asked a series of open-ended questions.

Survey Results.   The research confirmed that most consumers viewed SignMaster as a new product. Only 23 percent of the sample had ever seen a similar product. Most respondents believed that SignMaster would be purchased primarily by a female, although as indicated in Exhibit 8, it was also cited as a product that might be purchased

EXHIBIT 8   Expected Purchaser of SignMaster

Purchaser	Number	Percent
Female	44	60.3%
Male	15	20.5
Joint	10	13.7
For others as gift	4	5.5
Total	73	100.0

Source: Independent market research.

EXHIBIT 9   **Expected Retail Outlets for SignMaster**

Retail Outlet	Number	Percent
Hardware store	42	31.3%
Home-center store	30	22.4
Mass merchandiser	27	20.1
Gift shop	13	9.7
Department store	6	4.5
Mail-order catalog	5	3.7
Craft store	3	2.2
Lumberyard	3	2.2
Other	6	4.5
Total	134	100.0

Multiple response: Totals may not equal 100% due to rounding.

Source: Independent market research.

by a male or jointly, or given as a gift. When asked to name the retail stores where they would expect to find SignMaster, respondents mentioned hardware stores, home-center stores, and mass merchandisers most often as indicated in Exhibit 9. After examining the house sign in its package and the house numbers, respondents were asked what retail prices they would expect for each item. Exhibit 10 summarizes the responses for the survey sample. The significant difference in the expected price between male and female respondents was quite remarkable.

Preferred sign shapes and decorative designs were also examined in the survey research. Consumers were asked to express a preference for the shapes and decorative designs available for each shape. The most popular items were oval-Decoy, oval-Floral, tavern-Country House, and the rectangle-Classic Border. Less preference was expressed for the other combinations, although some had sold well during the market introduction in 1990.

In an effort to identify promotion opportunities, consumers were asked where they would expect to find advertising for SignMaster. Magazines were cited most frequently by both female and male respondents, although direct-mail and newspaper advertising was also mentioned. The responses are shown in Exhibit 11.

At the end of the interview, survey respondents were asked to remove the house sign from its package and carefully examine the product and instructions. Once again, consumers were asked to provide an expected retail price for a SignMaster house sign. The median price changed, with males now reporting $7.95 and females $10. In short, the perceived value of the product declined after the product was removed from the

EXHIBIT 10   **Expected Retail Price (Median) of SignMaster House Sign and Numbers**

Product	Respondents		
	Male	Female	Combined
House sign	$7.99	$10.99	$10.00
House numbers	0.59	0.79	0.69

Source: Independent market research.

Exhibit 11 Advertising Media Mentioned for SignMaster House Sign and Numbers

	Respondents		
Advertising Media	*Male*	*Female*	*Total*
Magazines	39.1%	38.7%	38.9%
Mail-order catalog	13.0	16.1	14.8
Direct-mail flier	15.2	11.3	13.0
Newspaper supplement	10.9	8.0	9.3
Newspaper print	6.5	9.7	8.3
Television	6.5	9.7	8.3
Point of purchase	8.7	6.5	7.4
Total	100.0%	100.0%	100.0%
Number of responses	46	62	108

Multiple response: Totals may not equal 100% due to rounding.

Source: Independent market research.

package and carefully inspected. Upon further questioning, respondents expressed concern about the strength of the adhesive mounting tape used to attach the sign to the residence, the complicated instructions and multiple-step procedure for attaching the numbers, the durability of the product, and the time and patience required for installation. Respondents even suggested that the house numbers be included in the house-sign package to simplify the purchasing process. Management acknowledged that this would be possible, but to do so would require the inclusion of many more numbers than would be needed to identify a residence.

Some survey respondents also reacted negatively to the packaging used for the house sign. They asserted that it concealed the product and restricted the ability of a purchaser to determine the material used in construction and its thickness. Others felt that the light gray color of the package did not enhance the image of the product and would not be visually appealing at the point of sale.

The research was successful in identifying target markets for SignMaster. Although the findings are preliminary, three possibilities emerged when consumers were asked who they believed would purchase the product. First, young low-income couples who were owners or renters of inexpensive residences in suburban locations were mentioned as attractive prospects. Second, older retired middle-income couples living in traditional country homes in rural areas and small communities were mentioned as likely to be interested in SignMaster. Finally, the product was viewed as a decorative accent for second residences such as cottages, chalets, beach houses, townhouses, and condominiums located in vacation and recreational areas.

The SignMaster Test Market. In March 1991, John Walters decided to incorporate some of the consumer research findings into the design of an attractive display that would hold up to 12 house signs and allow consumers to visually inspect Sign-Master prior to purchase. The point-of-purchase display, shown in Exhibit 12, was designed to display a house sign with the numbers installed and feature three popular shapes and decorative designs. It was loaded with 12 SignMaster house signs and 100 house numbers and market tested in six hardware stores located in small and medium-sized cities in the state of Virginia. The test was designed to determine the sales re-

EXHIBIT 12 **SignMaster Point-of-Purchase Display**

Source: The Bacova Guild, Ltd.

sponse to three different SignMaster retail prices and the acceptability of the display as a point-of-purchase merchandiser in hardware stores. Exhibit 13 summarizes the demographic characteristics of the test market cities and Exhibit 14 describes the experimental design used to test retail prices of $8.95, $9.95, and $10.95 for the house sign and $0.69 for the numbers. The market test began in May 1991 and lasted six months. Each SignMaster price was tested in each store for a two-month period and the sales made at each retail price were recorded.

Test Market Results.   The test market for the SignMaster conducted in retail hardware stores was reasonably successful. The new product sold best during the July–August test period when consumers were likely to be making exterior home improvements. Exhibit 15 summarizes the results for each two-month period of the test. The Country House was the most popular sign in the display and a $9.95 retail price

EXHIBIT 13   Population Characteristics of Test Market Cities

	Covington	Waynesboro	Harrisonburg	Buena Vista	Staunton	Lexington
Population (in thousands)	7.6	18.1	29.5	6.5	22.7	6.8
Median age	38.2	36.6	27.8	34.1	37.6	24.6
Age distribution (%)			30.2	10.2	10.9	39.0
18–24 years	9.7	9.3				
25–34 years	14.8	15.3	14.5	16.0	15.6	10.2
35–49 years	18.4	21.8	15.6	22.4	21.3	13.4
50 and over	35.7	30.7	23.9	26.1	32.5	24.2
Median household income	$20,113	$26,028	$20,047	$23,493	$24,726	$24,053
Income distr. (%)						
$10,000–19,999	28.7	22.5	28.0	24.6	22.9	22.4
20,000–34,999	29.8	30.5	24.6	35.4	28.6	24.2
35,000–49,999	13.9	17.4	13.9	17.2	17.7	13.3
50,000 and over	6.6	15.9	11.8	7.6	14.4	21.5

Source: *Sales and Marketing Management,* 1989 Survey of Buying Power, August 13, 1990.

resulted in the most sales. Seventy-seven percent of the consumer purchases were made in the communities of Buena Vista, Covington, and Waynesboro, cities in which the economic base was primarily manufacturing and blue-collar employment.

Looking Ahead—1991 and Beyond

As John Walters and the hardware division marketing group pondered the future of SignMaster, they reflected on the brief history of the new Bacova product. In many ways, substantial progress had been made. SignMaster had achieved retail distribution and even though the 1990 sales had proven to be disappointing, the trade had reacted favorably to the product. The consumer research, although conducted after the product had been introduced to the market, had been useful in developing a display that responded to some of the consumer questions at point of purchase. The market test, conducted during the middle of 1991, seemed to indicate that the product would sell in a retail hardware store if it was properly priced and displayed. Yet to be considered was the desirability of offering retailers advertising allowances to build consumer awareness of SignMaster prior to the retail shopping experience. If management decided to add this promotional enhancement to the marketing strategy for SignMaster, the costs would result in a lower before-tax profit margin on sales for the product. The display (excluding house signs and numbers) cost Bacova $7.52, while advertising allowances of $1.15 per sign would probably be necessary to motivate retailers to advertise the product.

EXHIBIT 14   Retail Pricing of SignMaster in Test Market Cities

Test Period	Covington	Waynesboro	Harrisonburg	Buena Vista	Staunton	Lexington
May–June	$10.95	$10.95	$ 9.95	$ 9.95	$ 8.95	$ 8.95
July–August	8.95	8.95	10.95	10.95	9.95	9.95
September–October	9.95	9.95	8.95	8.95	10.95	10.95

House numbers priced at $0.69 each during entire test market.

EXHIBIT 15   **SignMaster Sales in Test Market Cities**

	Unit Sales in Test Period			
Retail Price	*May–June*	*July–August*	*September–October*	*Sales (Units)*
$ 8.95	0	5	2	7
9.95	3	3	5	11
10.95	5	3	0	8
	8	11	7	26

Source: Independent market research.

Most of the information had now been collected, and it was time to reconsider the marketing strategy for the balance of 1991 and beyond. John Walters reflected that the market research would be helpful in improving the marketing strategy. It was obvious that some changes were needed because the 1991 SignMaster sales forecast of $250,000 (30,000 signs) would be difficult to achieve. Through the first nine months of 1991, sales were approximately $100,000 (11,338 signs).

Pricing was an important decision that needed to be finalized. The marketing group had to decide on an acceptable trade price for the house sign and numbers that would result in an attractive retail price for consumers. Promotion was another area of special concern. Research indicated that a point-of-purchase display was helpful, but it also seemed that some consumer promotion prior to the shopping experience would be desirable. Advertising allowances for retailers were one possibility, and if necessary, they could be combined with the point-of-purchase display that had proven successful in the market test. Whatever pricing and promotion methods were used, they had to be carefully considered because management was concerned that the house sign and numbers provide a profit margin on sales of at least 30 percent.

Packaging for the house sign was also a troubling issue. The consumer survey research seemed to indicate that improvements could be made to enhance the visual appeal of the product and simplify the application of the numbers. On the other hand, the market test results indicated that the product would sell at retail if it was properly priced and displayed.

Regardless of the marketing decisions on SignMaster, the hardware division marketing group knew that new products would be needed to meet the division's goals for sales and profitability. Experience with SignMaster seemed to indicate that a different approach to product development might be appropriate to assure success in the future.

Having passed the $5 million mark in annual sales, the Faith Mountain Company recorded its first profit in July 1991. According to industry norms, it was right on schedule, but it still came as something of a surprise to Cheri and Martin Woodard. It had been a remarkable year on several counts: the all-important catalog customer list had grown 31 percent, to 251,771 names; despite the recession, sales were up 41 percent; and, best of all, from a loss of $185,791 in fiscal year 1990, the company had posted a new profit of $161,476 for fiscal year 1991.

By December 1991, it was clear that Faith Mountain was on its way to another record-breaking year. When they stopped to reflect on the growth of their business, however, Cheri and Martin admitted they faced some tough questions. What next? Could they count on continued growth at this rate, and if so, could they manage it and remain profitable? Where should they grow, and how? What financial and human resources would be required, and would this small company in the Blue Ridge Mountains be able to attract and retain them?

In their first business plan, completed only last year in conjunction with a major effort to raise capital, they had set ambitious goals: by the year 1995, $10 million in sales from the Faith Mountain catalog, $5 million from the retail division, and an additional $10 million from acquisitions or development of another catalog company. Even as they struggled to keep pace with customer demand in their busiest time of the year, they knew they soon would have to find the time to review that plan, examine their goals, and renew their efforts to make them reality.

History of the Faith Mountain Company

Cheri Faith Woodard.   Cheri Faith Woodard grew up, in her own words, "a product of the 70s—I wasn't a radical, but I had a vision of a better society, and a belief that things could be different." She left college before graduating, married, had a son, and helped found a cooperative natural foods store near College Park, Maryland. After a divorce in 1974, she moved to Sperryville, Virginia, a small town of about 500 people at the foot of the Blue Ridge Mountains. Only 69 miles from Washington, D.C., the natural beauty and very low cost of living in Rappahannock County attracted many young people to the area.

To support herself and her young son, Cheri worked in an antique shop. At the time, the best connecting route between two major state highways went through Sperryville, right around the corner from the antique shop. During vacation seasons, with heavy tourist traffic to and from the Shenandoah National park, the shop did extremely good business. Cheri learned much about antiques and furniture restoration, and she enjoyed bargaining with customers.

This case was prepared by James J. Dowd, Michael D. Atchison, and John H. Lindgren, Jr., University of Virginia, for the 11th McIntire Commerce Invitational (MCI XI) held at the University of Virginia on February 13–15, 1992. The authors gratefully acknowledge the General Electric Foundation and the McIntire School of Commerce for their support.

Soon after arriving in Sperryville, Cheri met Florence Williamson, known throughout the area as "the herb lady." She knew how to grow all kinds of herbs and how to use them in recipes, medicines, and gardens. Many people, from local families to the directors of the National Herb Garden in Washington, D.C., sought her advice.

Cheri became interested in herbs while working at the natural foods store in Maryland, and she was eager to learn more. Mrs. Williamson was always busy, but as she approached 75, she decided she needed a helper, so she was willing to teach Cheri. The two began working together as teacher and apprentice.

In 1975, Cheri met Martin Woodard at a square dance. Martin had graduated from Vanderbilt University with a degree in sociology and history. He too was drawn to the quality of life in Rappahannock County and had established a successful masonry contracting business. In 1977, they were married.

Opening the Store.

Meanwhile, Cheri began contemplating opening her own business. She had learned a great deal about herbs, and she sensed that more and more people were becoming interested in growing and using them. She also wanted to work at home to be near her son. She decided she would open a store to sell herbs, related products, and antiques. She discussed her ideas with Martin and Mrs. Williamson, and both gave their full support. Cheri remembered,

> Martin and I had faith in each other and in ourselves—we said, "We can do this!" And we were here in the Blue Ridge Mountains—so that's how we got our name. A business started on faith at the foot of the mountains: The Faith Mountain Herbs and Antique Shop.

The Woodards found a house for sale on Main Street in Sperryville, just a block down the street from the antique shop in which Cheri had worked. The front part of the house was built in 1790 and had been used as a doctor's office, a tavern, and a guest house. There was room in the backyard for an herb garden, and there were small outbuildings for storage or workshops. Even better, the house was big enough to serve as both home and store. With owner financing, the Woodards bought the house for $26,000, assumed a $200 monthly mortgage, and set about restoring the old house.

The family lived in the back of the house and used the four front rooms for the store. Cheri grew her own herbs in the backyard and bought others locally to sell in the store. The business grew slowly; herbs were inexpensive, and small amounts lasted a long time. Local businesspeople, suspicious of herbs and of the young couple, predicted the store would fail. With the full support of "the herb lady," however, Cheri began to establish a strong reputation as an "herb lady" in her own right, giving local talks and workshops on cooking with herbs, making wreaths of dried flowers, and the like.

Between 1977 and 1980, she slowly increased the variety of products offered, adding herb blends, dried flowers, simple garden supplies, books, kitchen tools, preserves, and handicrafts. She displayed the products on antique furniture she bought, restored, and offered for sale. Encouraged by praise from customers who had driven from Washington, D.C., for a day in the country, Cheri purchased her first ads in the *Washington Post* in 1979.

Birth of the Mail-Order Business

In 1980, construction was completed on Interstate 66, a highway connection eliminating most of the east–west traffic passing through Sperryville. Like the other businesses in Sperryville, Faith Mountain suffered, and its antique sales all but disappeared. Even though Cheri kept the store open all weekend to capture any possible business, she could not make the store profitable.

Faith Mountain was no longer merely an interesting way for Cheri to be able to work at home. She felt she deserved more reward for all her hard work, and she began to consider a mail-order catalog.

Tourists from around the country had stopped to shop at Faith Mountain on their way to Shenandoah National Park, so she knew her products appealed to a wide market. Further, more and more customers were writing to her, asking if she could send them a wreath or another product they remembered seeing in the store.

Confident that she had a market, she created the first Faith Mountain Herbs and Antiques catalog in the spring of 1980. The 12-page catalog offered mostly herbs and herbal products and featured simple line drawings and text. She was able to get the catalog printed and copied for free as a test of new machines by a friend who worked for Xerox Corporation. Her greatest difficulty was with the local post office, which had never worked with bulk mailings before. With advice from a cousin in the mail-order business, she obtained bulk rate permit No. 1 from the Sperryville post office and mailed her first 1,000 catalogs.

As the mail-order business began to grow, the Woodard family realized they had to move out of the house. They bought a local farm, grew more than 20 kinds of herbs and flowers, and dried them in their barn. Cheri hired part-time employees to help with the store and the catalog. In 1983, the first color photo catalog was mailed, with a press run of 110,000 copies.

Incorporation and Growth. Until that time, Martin Woodard had concentrated on his masonry business, helping out occasionally with the store and the catalog. Increasingly frustrated by problems with his employees and aware of the growing burden on Cheri, he began thinking about working with Faith Mountain full time.

By 1984, Faith Mountain's annual sales had reached $400,000. At a Direct Marketing Association meeting in Washington, D.C., the Woodards were referred to Don Press, director of the Smithsonian Museum Gift Catalog and part-time mail-order consultant. They asked him two questions: "Does our business have a future? If so, what is our next step?" Martin recalled what happened next:

> Don looked at everything, and then he told us: "Yes, you have something here. It's not going to be easy, but you do have a future with this business." So there was the validation, and I had to make a decision. I sold the masonry business and came on full-time at Faith Mountain in the fall of 1984.

Martin became catalog director, with responsibility for merchandise selection, catalog production and marketing, and also financial planning. Cheri retained responsibility for the store, manufacturing and warehouse operations, customer service, and all personnel matters. Martin was very clear from the start he wanted no responsibility for people.

Working closely with their consultant, Cheri recalled, "We really started to get serious about the business and slowly put together a real company." They incorporated in 1985 and offered Don Press a seat on the board of directors. He referred them to more professional services for catalog production and helped them manage their finances by teaching them benchmark ratios for catalog operations' budgets and income statements. They bought some small buildings in 1985 to accommodate the growing business and rented additional space as needed.

In the same year, Cheri was elected to a three-year term as president of the Sperryville Business Council. She organized a Sperryville Spring Festival to correspond with the anniversary of the Faith Mountain Herbs and Antiques Store, and it became an annual event, drawing thousands to the town. That year, Faith Mountain printed 500,000 catalogs and annual sales exceeded $1.5 million.

By 1988, Faith Mountain was running out of room, and there was no more space to rent. Later that year, the Woodards' barn burned. It was clear that the company needed more space, and it would improve operations if all parts of the business, now scattered in several buildings throughout Sperryville, could be brought together under one big roof.

At the suggestion of their banker, the Woodards applied for funding from the U.S. Small Business Administration under a special loan program assisting small business expansions. With a "504 loan," the SBA would finance 40 percent of the expansion project, secured by a second deed of trust. A conventional lending institution would finance 50 percent of the project, with a first deed of trust, and the company would pay the remaining 10 percent.

The Woodards located a 1.75-acre site on Route 211 that would support construction of a 10,000-square-foot facility for offices, a warehouse, and possibly a retail outlet. The SBA loan package would include the land and the building, the warehouse equipment and shelves, the phone system, hardware and software improvements, and office furniture and partitions, for a total cost of $425,000. Cheri remembered,

> It was a *big leap* to spend that much money. We hadn't had much of a business plan, and now we had to show one to get the money. We had to get the site rezoned for commercial use, and then we just went ahead. In April 1989, we signed contracts to buy the land and contracts to begin construction on the building—this was before we had even gotten approval on the SBA loan! I remember Martin said, "We have to have faith." Almost a full month later, on May 10, we got the call from the SBA: We had the loan. Thank God—we had already spent it!

The Faith Mountain Company in 1991

Location. In 1991, the Faith Mountain Company operated out of that 10,000-square-foot site. The building had about 4,000 square feet of office space and 6,000 square feet of warehouse space. The company was then paying about $5,000 per month in principal and interest for the facility. The roof was constructed to permit addition of a mezzanine level, which would double the storage space in the warehouse area, and the entire building was designed to facilitate an addition of 10,000 to 15,000 square feet. The retail store still operated in its original location, about two miles away.

Organization and Staffing. As the company ended its 1991 fiscal year, it employed 39 people, 25 of those full-time. The organization chart (Exhibit 1) shows that Cheri and Martin still shared responsibilities as they had in 1984.

As chief financial officer, Martin supervised Debbie Jenkins, the accounting supervisor. With one full-time clerk, Jenkins took care of day-to-day financial bookkeeping, including payables, receivables, and all internal financial reports. Payroll was handled by an outside firm. Martin was responsible for long-term financial planning. The current fiscal year (1992) was the first year in which monthly and year-to-date budget reports were created and used.

As catalog director, Martin was responsible for all aspects of the Faith Mountain Company catalogs. The past year was the first in which Faith Mountain had produced four different catalogs, one for each season; previously, the summer catalog had been essentially the spring catalog with sale prices. The 1991 spring catalog, featuring Easter gift items, was 40 pages and mailed at the end of December 1990. The summer catalog, at 32 pages, was mailed in mid-April. The 40-page fall catalog, featuring Halloween, Thanksgiving, and some Christmas items, was mailed at the end of June. And the Christmas catalog, at 48 pages their biggest ever, was mailed in mid-September.

Kim Baader, merchandising manager, was charged with selecting and promoting

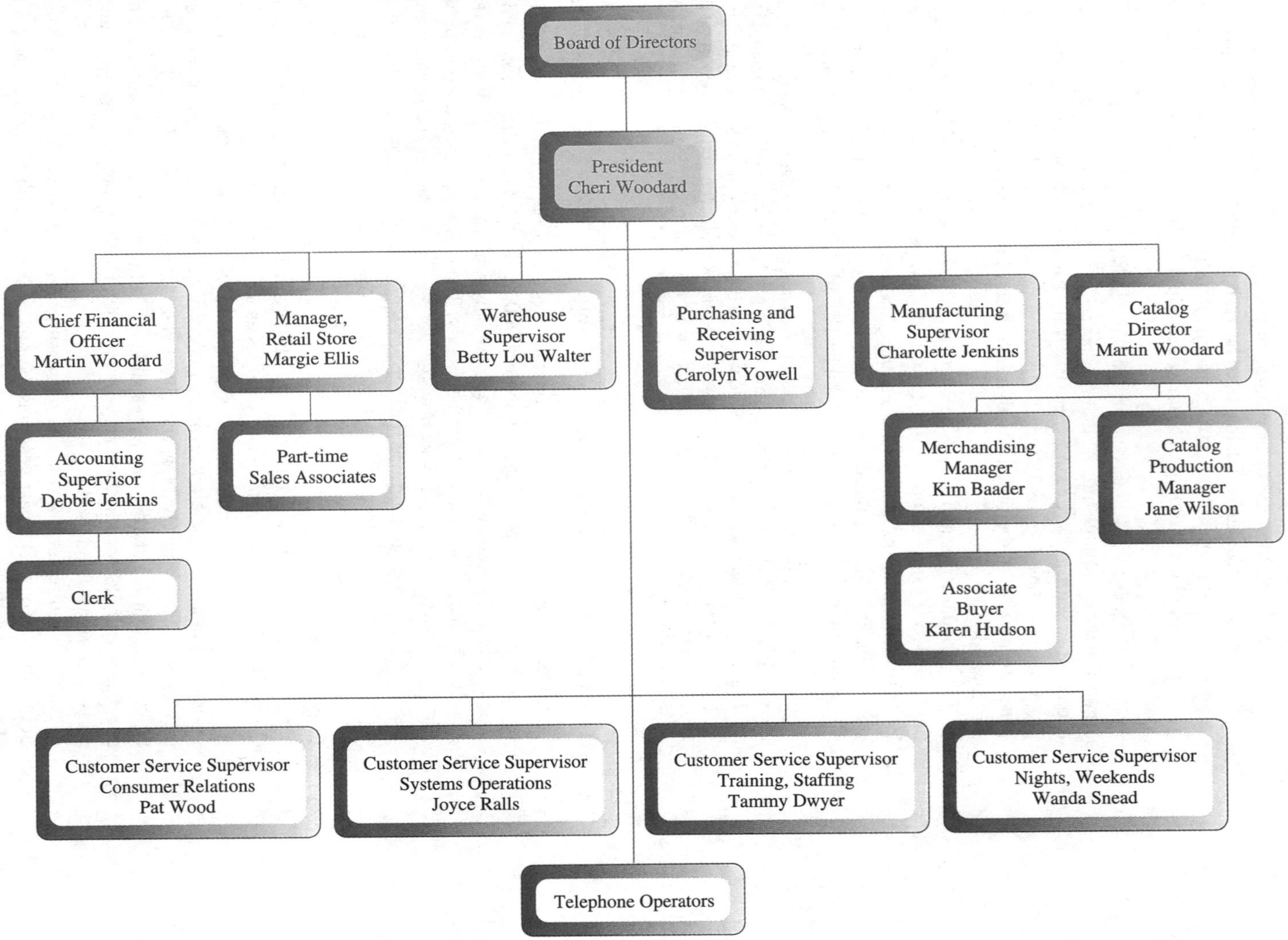

EXHIBIT 1 Organization Chart for the Faith Mountain Company, 1992

items for the catalogs. She and Martin went to gift, apparel, and other trade shows throughout the year, seeking vendors with quality products and a reputation for reliability in shipping. They brought potential catalog items back to the office, where Martin and Cheri, Baader and her assistant, and Margie Ellis, the store manager, would examine each piece and argue for or against offering it to Faith Mountain customers.

Having selected the catalog merchandise, under Martin's direction, Baader worked closely with a contract copywriter while Martin worked with the professional service firms contracted to design and produce the catalog, including layout, photography, and printing. Interviewing, inspecting, selecting, negotiating, and managing these vendors demanded so much time that in the summer of 1991, the former accounting clerk was promoted to catalog production manager to assume primary responsibility for these areas. Finally, before catalogs were mailed, Baader briefed the customer service and telemarketing staff on each catalog item, and she prepared summary product descriptions for easy reference on the automated entry system. By the time a catalog was mailed, work was already under way on the next.

As president, Cheri was responsible for overall direction of the company, and she was involved in all major decisions in all areas. Responsible for all aspects of human resource management in the firm, Cheri decided all personnel policies and practices and described them all in the Faith Mountain employee handbook. She had hired every employee in the company until September 1991, when the store manager hired a part-time sales associate, with Cheri's knowledge, but without her prior approval. Cheri stated, "That was a funny feeling, and I'm not sure I like it."

As director of operations, Cheri supervised the following people and areas:

- **Margie Ellis,** manager of the retail store, responsible for store sales, merchandising, staffing, and customer service.
- **Betty Lou Walter,** warehouse supervisor, responsible for product flow and shipping accuracy and timeliness.
- **Carolyn Yowell,** purchasing and receiving supervisor, responsible for receiving merchandise, forecasting, and managing back orders and overstocks.
- **Charolette Jenkins,** manufacturing supervisor, responsible for design and production of Faith Mountain products (wreaths, herb mixtures, etc.), including purchasing, scheduling, and inventory control.

In addition, Cheri supervised the customer service and telephone operations areas. Four customer service supervisors rotated primary responsibility for customer service calls each day, and each had her own special area of responsibility:

- **Pat Wood,** customer service supervisor responsible for Wednesday and Friday, handled all customer correspondence (not including mail orders).
- **Joyce Ralls,** customer service supervisor responsible for Tuesday, handled system hardware and software, including local maintenance and system planning.
- **Tammy Dwyer,** customer service supervisor responsible for Monday and Thursday, was responsible for training and staffing of telephone operators.
- **Wanda Snead,** customer service supervisor responsible for customer service in the evening (5–8:30) and on weekends, generated day-end activity reports.

Finally, Cheri also directly supervised the telephone operators. Eight regular part-time employees (more part-timers were hired for peak season) were responsible for taking customer orders by phone, referring any customer complaints or problems to the customer service supervisor. The phone operators also opened and sorted mail

Exhibit 2

Balance Sheet of the Faith Mountain Company, 1987–91
(Fiscal Years Ending June 30; Dollar Amounts in Thousands)

	1987	1988	1989	1990	1991
Assets					
Cash	$ 3	$ 3	$ 15	$ 1	$ 48
Net accounts receivable	8	14	26	25	55
Inventories	114	176	183	320	410
Unamortized catalog costs	32	53	150	198	400
Total current assets	$ 157	$ 246	$ 374	$ 544	$ 913
Net property	35	69	203	511	489
Intangibles				10	9
Other noncurrent assets			3	2	4
	$ 192	$ 315	$ 580	$ 1,067	$ 1,415
Liabilities and Net Worth					
Bank loans—short-term (see Note 1)	$ 42	$ 46	$ 114	$ 212	$ 333
Current maturities of long-term debt				30	29
Other notes payable			135		
Accounts payable	60	84	113	321	304
Accruals	3	4	3	11	11
Advance from stockholder				15	
Total current liabilities	$ 105	$ 134	$ 365	$ 589	$ 677
Long-term bank debt (see Note 2)		42	28	417	399
Total liabilities	$ 105	$ 176	$ 393	$ 1,006	$ 1,076
Preferred stock	42				
Common stock (see Note 3)	92	264	310	370	518
Capital surplus					
Retained earnings	(47)	(125)	(123)	(309)	(179)
	$ 192	$ 315	$ 580	$ 1,067	$ 1,415

Note 1: Notes Payable, Bank

Notes payable, bank at June 30, 1991, consists of $333,000 drawn from an available line of credit of $350,000 with C&S/Sovran Bank.

The note is secured by a first security interest in all accounts receivables, inventory, and property and equipment and bears interest at C&S/Sovran Bank's prime rate plus 1½% (10.0% at June 30, 1991). The note is payable on demand, with interest payable monthly. The line expires on October 30, 1991.

Under the requirements of the note agreement the company has agreed, among other things, to (1) maintain its ratio of debt to net worth at no more than 5 to 1, measured at fiscal year end, (2) maintain all of its primary deposit relationships with C&S/Sovran as long as this commitment is outstanding, and (3) not incur any indebtedness so long as this commitment remains outstanding without the prior written consent of the bank. The note is guaranteed by Martin Woodard and Cheri Woodard, shareholders of the company.

orders each day, forwarding checks to the accounting department and verifying order forms for entry into the system.

Financial Position.   Exhibits 2 and 3 provide information on the company's financial position in 1991. Other than the Small Business Administration loan described earlier, financing was primarily short-term. R. R. Donnelley, the catalog printer, extended the firm $350,000 in credit with lenient terms. Inventory moved through the warehouse quickly, and trade payables to vendors were small. About 10 percent of catalog orders were handled as "drop shipments," where vendors shipped directly to the customer. Inventory financing was handled through a line of credit, recently increased from $350,000 to $500,000.

EXHIBIT 2   (concluded)

Note 2: Long-Term Debt

A summary of the company's long-term debt, and collateral pledged thereon, consists of the following:

	June 30	
	1991	*1990*
C&S/Sovran Bank, note due in monthly installments of $456.00, including interest at 12.5% through January 1995, collateralized by truck	$ 15,903	$ 18,906
Signet Bank, capitalized lease obligation, discounted at a rate of 11.5% due in monthly installments of $1,034 to October 1993	24,356	24,163
Marathon Bank, note due in monthly installments of $944, plus interest at Marathon Bank's prime rate plus 1 through November 1999, collateralized by real estate	208,510	220,242
Virginia Asset Financing Corporation, note due in monthly installments of $1,741, including interest at 8.9% through January 2010, collateralized by the personal guarantees of Martin Woodard and Cheri Woodard, shareholders of the company, and a second deed of trust on real estate	179,439	183,110
Other	107	667
	$ 428,315	$ 447,088
Less current maturities	29,483	29,610
Long-term portion	$ 398,832	$ 417,478

Aggregate maturities required on long-term debt at June 30, 1991, are due in future fiscal years ending June 30 as follows:

1992	$ 29,483
1993	30,224
1994	24,933
1995	19,435
1996	16,580
Thereafter	307,660
	$ 428,315

Interest expenses for the years ended June 30, 1991, and 1990, were $65,824 and $35,297, respectively.

Note 3: Stockholders' Equity

For year ended June 30, 1991, the company issued 1,150 units which comprised 1,150 shares of common stock and 1,150 warrants to purchase common stock. The gross proceeds of the issue was $115,000. Each warrant entitles the holder to purchase one share of common stock at a price of $90 per share, subject to certain conditions through June 30, 1992.

New Products

The Faith Mountain Mail-Order Strategy   In 1991, the Faith Mountain Company developed, manufactured, and marketed high-quality gifts, apparel, and home accessories, distributing them through its mail-order catalog and its retail store.

The company focused on the needs of women between ages 30 and 50 who owned their own homes and had family incomes of $40,000 to $60,000. Faith Mountain believed female homemakers sought traditional, nostalgic, whimsical, and romantic gifts, apparel, and home accessories to enhance the quality of their homes and family lives. Although increasing numbers of these women balanced their family responsibilities with work outside the home, they held traditional family values, and time spent at home with their families dominated their nonworking hours. Even as they sought products and gift items that reflected those values, they were reluctant to spend time driving through congested urban or suburban areas to shop in glitzy commercialized malls. Instead, these women were increasingly likely to turn to mail-order catalogs, which offered the option of shopping at their own convenience, in their own homes, 24 hours a day.

Competition.   The Woodards estimated approximately 50 catalog companies sold gifts, apparel, or home accessories. Within its own niche of "traditional" products in those categories, Faith Mountain had targeted four significant competitors. Based on knowledge they had gained from industry analysts and other sources, the Woodards described them in their 1990 business plan as follows:

EXHIBIT 3

Income Statement for the Faith Mountain Company, 1987–91
(Fiscal Years Ending June 30; Dollar Amounts in Thousands)

	1987	1988	1989	1990	1991
Net sales	$1,234	$1,654	$2,429	$3,554	$5,025
Less: Cost of sales	496	780	1,249	1,936	2,900
Gross profit	$ 738	$ 874	$1,249	$1,936	$2,125
Percentage of net sales	59.81%	52.84%	51.42%	54.47%	57.71%
Less: Operating expenses	366	247	545	835	1,030
Catalog production and promotional expense	382	705	753	1,346	1,784
Depreciation		23	25	33	44
Operating profit	(10)	(101)	(74)	(278)	42
Other income	14	40	88	127	185
Less: Interest expense		11	12	35	66
Net profit before tax	4	(72)	2	(186)	161
Profit after tax	4	(72)	2	(186)	161
Net profit (loss)	$4	$(72)	$2	$(186)	$161
Net after dividends	4	(72)	2	(186)	161
Add: Beginning retained earnings	(51)	(47)	(125)	(123)	(340)
Less: Other		6			
Ending retained earnings	(47)	(125)	(123)	(309)	(179)

Potpourri: Founded in the late 1960s and run by Bill and Sue Knowles and their two sons, the company is an institution in the industry. Industry sources estimate Potpourri prints 40 million catalogs per year, with annual sales in the $50 million range, and an average order size of $60. Bill and Sue are widely respected for their business sense and marketing/merchandising abilities, but as they approach their 70s, it is unclear whether the sons will be able to carry on their successful merchandising. We believe the quality of Potpourri's merchandise and customer service is inferior to Faith Mountain's.

Charles Keath: With sales estimated in the $35 million range, this company is also widely respected for its excellent merchandising. It is owned by Charles Edmundson, who has built the company from the ashes of a failed catalog company. We believe Faith Mountain's catalog features higher-quality photographs and copywriting and we rate Faith Mountain's customer service more highly than that offered by Charles Keath.

W.M. Green: Only seven years old, the company is run by two sisters, Marianne Carson and Beth Everitt, and their brother, Mark Green, out of North Carolina. Annual sales are estimated at $4.5 million, with an average order size of about $110. Like Faith Mountain, this company features handmade traditional gifts, with some home accessories, but W.M. Green does not sell apparel. We respect the quality and customer service of W.M. Green but believe Faith Mountain's experience with a broader product line is a distinct advantage.

Sturbridge Yankee: Offering home accessories with a distinct American "country" flavor, this company has about $8 million in annual sales. It has opened three retail stores in New England, leading many to believe the company will emphasize retail stores over catalog operations. In any event, we believe the narrow focus on "Americana" will limit the company's growth.

For its own part, Faith Mountain adopted a mail-order strategy that focused on three key areas: merchandise, quality, and service.

Merchandise. Faith Mountain offered a broad range of high-quality products to its customers, united by "a lifestyle theme of traditional, cozy, and family-oriented life." In 1991, the company rotated over 500 products through its catalogs, including its own manufactured products, herbs and floral arrangements, sportswear, jewelry, gifts, and home and garden decorations. Exhibit 4 provides summary product line descriptions as contained in Faith Mountain's 1990 business plan.

Merchandise selection was a critical ingredient in the success of the company. The Woodards attributed their success in this area to the fact that they both "lived the lifestyle" of their customers and to the contacts they had developed in the gift industry over the past 14 years. They sought exclusive marketing rights for products and had begun to move more aggressively to private labeling. Finding and developing quality

---

EXHIBIT 4   **Summary Descriptions of Faith Mountain's Major Product Lines**

Faith Mountain herb and floral arrangements, designed by Cheri Woodard and staff and created in the Sperryville studio, were the traditional core of the business. Faith Mountain was one of the original manufacturers of these products, and its creations were regularly copied for sale in other catalogs. Especially popular were the chain of flowers, eucalyptus arrangements, and the herb wreath, the best-seller in every fall catalog since 1981.

Updated casual sportswear, including sweaters, skirts, dresses, and novelty items, appealed to women who sought high-quality classic designs with a stylish flair, suitable for entertaining, parties, church, and weekends, and to a limited extent, for work. Obtained from vendors such as Lanz, Susan Bristol, and The Eagle's Eye, these products were not exclusive to Faith Mountain, although the Woodards knew of no other catalog devoted to such "country fashions."

Unique jewelry, such as pins, earrings, belts, necklaces, and bracelets, sold well as impulse purchases. They were price-blind and were easy to ship and warehouse.

Children's products, including puzzles, toys, and mazes, were selected to appeal to mothers, grandmothers, or other relatives who sought "wholesome, old-fashioned fun with educational value" as gifts for children age 2–8. In addition, the company sold lamps, rugs, and other accessories to bring a traditional or nostalgic appearance to children's bedrooms.

Seasonal decorative accessories, especially items for Halloween, Thanksgiving, Christmas, and Easter, were offered to help families decorate their homes for these holidays, according to old traditions and to create new ones. The line excluded "cheap plastic decorations, glitzy tinsel, or poorly constructed merchandise" to focus on long-lasting, high-quality items to keep and use every year, such as evergreen wreaths, advent calendars, and centerpieces.

Collectibles, limited-edition series of handcrafted figurines, plates, dolls, cottages, and the like were increasingly popular among Faith Mountain customers. These items were created in series to inspire collecting every individual item in the set. Secondary markets sometimes developed for these items, which could bring prices far above the original purchase price. The items were ideal for catalogs because these generated repeated purchases, enhancing the responsiveness of the customer list, but manufacturers were selective in choosing catalog outlets.

Gifts, especially sentimental, inspirational, or symbolic items that reflect the customer's traditional values, were selected for the catalog. Faith Mountain did not offer "standard giftware" of silver, china, or glass, as these were easily available in many retail outlets. Instead, the catalog featured unusual items.

American crafts, or artistic handmade goods, were another way in which Faith Mountain could distinguish itself from ordinary retail outlets. To source and offer these goods, the company had to deal with artists, not vendors, and because the items were one-of-a-kind, customers had to be educated about the use and value of these pieces. Because Faith Mountain was itself a small manufacturer, it was able to work effectively with artisans other outlets viewed as difficult or unreliable, and it offered these crafts as gifts and as decorative accessories.

Home and garden accessories, or items to decorate and personalize one's "living space," were sold to help customers create "comfortable, secure, cozy home environments." The vast array of items were available through manufacturers' representatives, trade shows, and personal contacts.

merchandise before the competition did was the driving force of the merchandising function at Faith Mountain.

Quality. The Woodards prided themselves on offering the best-quality herb and floral products in America, and they sought to offer only merchandise of the highest quality, representing the best value available. Because Faith Mountain manufactured approximately 20 percent of the merchandise it sold, it could personalize and customize products to individual customer needs. Cheri and Martin stressed the importance of doing a quality job in all aspects of the company, from producing the catalog through taking, packing, and shipping an order. Incentive plans for both warehouse and customer service employees rewarded error-free performance. Even more important, however, the Woodards believed their own dedication to quality in all phases of the company resulted in a highly motivated staff who took great pride in their jobs. The pride and quality, they believed, would show through to customers and make them believe they were dealing with a first-class organization.

Service. Finally, Faith Mountain set for itself the goal of quality customer service unsurpassed in the mail-order industry. The company had a toll-free telephone number for placing orders and for customer service inquiries and complaints. Its telephone system, a Siemens 20/40, could support 20 incoming lines and 40 phone sets and had automatic call distribution features and activity reporting capability. Order entry and product inquiry were handled on an ADDS minicomputer with the on-line Nashbar QOP system. Designed by a mail-order bicycle company, the system allowed for speedy order placement and easy access to product reference guides, so operators could answer questions with the customer still on the phone.

The phones in Sperryville were staffed from 8 AM to 8:30 PM seven days a week. After 8:30 PM, calls were switched to a vendor who followed Faith Mountain protocol, took orders, and sent completed order forms to Sperryville by Federal Express the next morning. The average Faith Mountain order was about $75. Operators answered calls, "Faith Mountain; this is [first name]. May I help you?" They would place orders directly on the system, and if callers wanted customer service, they would transfer the call to the customer service supervisor on duty. The system was designed to answer 90 percent of all customer inquiries within two minutes, and customer service supervisors were authorized to do whatever was necessary to keep a customer happy.

From their research and experience in the industry, the Woodards knew the biggest obstacle to catalog shopping was the question of what to do with an order if the customer didn't like it. In such cases, after a customer service supervisor had talked with the customer, and if the customer was still dissatisfied, Faith Mountain would send United Parcel Service to the customer's home to retrieve the order at company expense. This policy was extremely rare in the industry and cost Faith Mountain approximately $8,000 in 1991. Other customer service policies included guaranteed lowest prices, optional Federal Express delivery, and extremely quick shipping from receipt of the order. Faith Mountain also enclosed coupons and the company history with every order.

The Faith Mountain Retail Store Strategy. Although small in comparison to the catalog business, Faith Mountain's retail store revenues totaled almost $300,000 in fiscal year 1991. The store was run by a full-time manager, Margie Ellis. She ordered merchandise for the store, hired, scheduled, and supervised the sales help, and made all the operating decisions at the store. The store employed two women and three high school girls, who all worked part-time including weekends. The store was open from 10 AM to 6 PM seven days a week.

The store had about 2,000 square feet of selling space on two floors. Its merchandise reflected the same product lines featured in the catalog, but not all items from the catalog were sold in the store, and about 20 percent of the store merchandise was not offered in the catalog. (There was some storage space in an attic and in a back-room office that the store manager rarely used.)

Customers walked in the front door of a very old house filled with antiques and the smell of herbs. The front room of the store was the "food room," with the herbs and oils, potpourri, and jewelry. Straight ahead to the right was the breezeway, where collectibles and dolls were kept. In the back and side rooms, customers found clothes, books, lotions, and products made in Virginia. Upstairs were two rooms—a year-round Christmas room and a room for children's products. One of the outbuildings on the property was used as an outlet for catalog overstocks, which were sold at a slightly lower price.

By 1991, the store had become an important part of the town. Where once Faith Mountain had hoped to capitalize on traffic drawn to the area, it had become a draw in its own right, and other businesses hoped to grow from the Faith Mountain traffic. Local people shopped at Faith Mountain, too. Margie Ellis described the store's community role in this way:

> There are lots of tourists in the fall—the peak weekend is in October, and then people might grumble a bit about the traffic, but there is no real resentment. This store is very important to the town. This is one of the few stores in the area you can *count on* being open. That doesn't mean much in some areas, but here it means a lot. A lot of local people know about it, depend on it for birthday presents, for clothes, for herbs.
>
> You know, in terms of volume or of profit margin, those herbs are nothing. I had moved them out of the front room back into the kitchen, and you should have seen the customers react! "How could you move them to the kitchen? You can't do that!" So now we know: In the front room we have to have the herbs.
>
> The biggest sellers are the clothes and gifts. For the most part, the clothes are bought by local people. Busy tourists coming through won't buy an outfit; they might buy a sweatshirt. For the local people to get this quality apparel, they would have to drive to a mall in Culpeper or to Manassas, and they *do not* want to drive in northern Virginia traffic.

The Woodards believed the store served another valuable but intangible purpose—it gave Faith Mountain credibility and integrity. Customers who would not buy from the company by mail were able to drive to the store and see and touch products before ordering them; traffic in the store always surged after a catalog mailing. The location of the store—in Sperryville, in Rappahannock County, Virginia, at the foot of the Blue Ridge Mountains—gave an aura of authenticity to the products offered in the catalog. Being able to give directions to the store and to invite customers to visit was part of the company's image as a good, hardworking, honest family business. Many customers arrived and asked people to point out which of the Blue Ridge peaks was "Faith Mountain."

In September 1991, Margie Ellis and Martin Woodard developed the first annual budget for the retail store. Because the previous year had been so good, but the economy was not strong, they agreed to set the previous year's numbers for the current year's targets. Margie reported directly to Cheri, but met monthly with Martin to review progress against the budget. Summary budget data appear in Exhibit 5.

The Mail-Order Industry

The Market in 1990.   The July 1991 issue of *Direct Marketing* magazine reported highlights of the *1990 Guide to Mail Order Sales,* the 10th annual study by Arnold Fishman of Marketing Logistics. According to that study, the total mail-order sales in the United States in 1990 topped $200 billion, with consumer mail order at $98.2 billion, business mail order at $43.5 billion, and charitable contributions by mail at $49 billion. The consumer mail-order total was further defined as follows: $40.7 billion on services, $44.5 billion on products from specialty merchandisers, and $13 billion on products from general merchandisers.

According to the Fishman study, total mail-order sales for 1990 reflected 10.1 percent of general merchandise sales, 3.2 percent of retail sales, 2.1 percent of consumer services, and 1.8 percent of gross national product for the year. The following data on growth in the industry are excerpted from the same study:

- Overall growth for consumer mail order in 1990 is between 4 and 8 percent in money (current dollar) terms and –1 percent to +3 percent in real (adjusted for inflation) terms, somewhat higher than growth in overall retail or in department store chain sales.

- Among specific sales segments, growth was above average for sportswear (apparel), videocassettes (audio/video), libraries and schools supplies (business specialties), television and videotex (general merchandising), and drugs/vitamins and physical fitness (health).

- Growth was below average for footwear (apparel), auto clubs, automotive–aviation, full-line business supplies, consumer electronics products, continuity cosmetics, crafts, catalog retailers (general merchandise), low-end gifts, hardware/tools, fashion jewelry, photofinishing, photographic equipment, and apparel-oriented sporting goods.

- Among individual companies, major-size companies with 20 percent growth included American Association of Retired Persons Insurance, Cabela's, CompuServe, J. Crew, Current Domestications, Frederick's, Hamilton Mint, Home Shopping Network, International Masters Publishers, Medco Containment, Prodigy, Tweeds, United Services Automobile Association, and Viking Office Products.

EXHIBIT 5   Faith Mountain Company's Store Budget, 1992 Fiscal Year

	First Quarter	*Second Quarter*	*Third Quarter*	*Fourth Quarter*	*Total*
Sales	$79,861	$99,284	$41,494	$77,059	$297,698
Cost of goods sold	35,770	44,469	18,586	34,515	133,340
Gross profit	44,091	54,815	22,908	42,544	164,358
Promotional costs:					
Retail advertising	1,650	2,300	1,650	1,500	7,100
Special events	250	2,000	200	1,400	3,850
Catalog costs	14,434	15,378	8,815	7,926	46,553
Total	16,334	19,678	10,665	10,826	57,503
Operating expense	4,114	6,303	3,275	2,481	16,173
General and administrative	18,653	21,741	20,114	20,148	80,656
Net income	$ 4,990	$ 7,093	$ (11,146)	$ 9,089	$ 10,026

EXHIBIT 6   U.S. Mail-Order Sales Growth, 1981–90

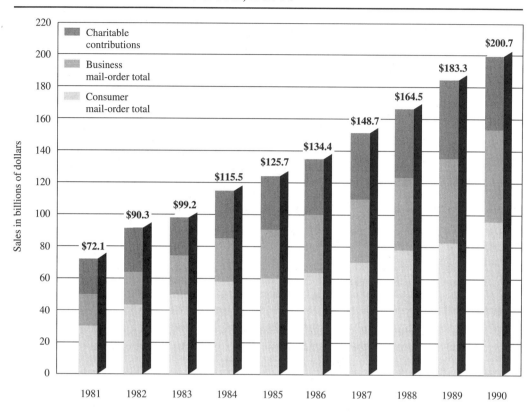

- Limited growth was experienced by L.L. Bean, Cincinnati Microwave, Collector's Guild, Cosmetique, GRI, Horchow, Quill, Reliable, Royal Silk, Sears, Roebuck & Company, Shopsmith, and Warshawsky.

Additional data from the *1990 Guide to Mail Order Sales* excerpted from the *Direct Marketing* article appear as Exhibits 6 through 8.

Trends for the Future.   Over 100 years ago, Sears, Roebuck & Company set the industry standard for general merchandise marketing through catalogs. As Exhibit 6 shows, the continuing growth through the 1980s enticed many entrepreneurs to enter the industry. In addition, several retailers had responded to the mail-order threat by developing their own catalogs. In 1986, the U.S. Postal Service sent out 11.8 billion copies of 8,500 different catalogs. In the same year, the Direct Marketing Association surveyed these catalogers and found that 93 percent were increasing their mailings.

Some marketers argued the catalog industry was peaking. One 1984 study pointed to the fact that although the number of catalogs issued in the United States increased 68 percent in 1983, the customer base increased only 24 percent. It seemed unlikely that this customer group would increase its consumption sufficiently to support the additional catalogs entering the market and sustain the growth rates of current catalog companies.[1] In addition, a 1983 Stone-Adler market study had found that 43 percent of

---

[1] Maggie McComas, "Catalog Fallout," *Fortune,* January 20, 1986, pp. 63–64.

EXHIBIT 7   Facts about the Mail-Order Catalog Business in the United States, 1990

- On a per capita basis, Americans spent an average of $393 on mail-order purchases in 1990.
- Specialty mail-order vendors enjoy a substantially greater share of consumer mail-order product sales (77 percent) than do general merchandising mail-order vendors (23 percent).
- U.S. business mail-order sales in 1990 were $53.4 billion and charitable contributions were $45.9 billion. The total of U.S. mail order/sales and contributions was $200.3 billion.
- While U.S. consumer mail-order product sales may appear modest on the overall scale of gross national product, retail sales, or general merchandise sales, they are immense as a source of sales. Consumer mail-order product sales are equivalent to 82% of sales of the top 100 department stores ($70 billion), more than catalog showrooms, direct selling, and vending machines combined ($45.7 billion), and as much as any single consumer selling channel except mass general merchandisers and supermarkets. It is a leading consumer selling channel for specialty merchandise with prices under $1,000.
- U.S. consumer mail-order sales of products and services were $98.2 billion in 1990: $57.5 billion in products and $40.7 billion in services. This represents
  - 1.8 percent of gross national product.
  - 10.1 percent of general merchandise sales.
  - 3.2 percent of retail sales.
  - 2.1 percent of consumer service sales.

Source: *Direct Marketing,* July 1991.

all U.S. households were against catalogs. Some experts expected this number to increase as mail-order companies continued to trade customer lists and a select number of people received an inordinate number of catalogs.

On the other hand, population projections for the United States (Exhibit 9) seemed to support those who predicted continued strong growth in the industry. Although many older people were not accustomed to credit card use, today's younger generations have been exposed to credit cards all their lives. As these generations grow older and their income increases, the ease of making credit card purchases through the mail would certainly improve the prospects of catalog purchasing. A 1989 study reported that 7 out of 10 families had no adult buyer home during the day to go shopping.[2] Jay Walker, chairman of Catalog Media Corporations, stated

> Only 5 percent of retail sales are through catalogs. Now it is hard for you to tell me that a channel is mature at 5 percent penetration, when the underlying demographics of the population at large favor the channel. More working women, less time, more credit cards, 800 numbers—all of these things favor the catalog industry continuing as a major growth trend.[3]

"Specialogs."   One significant trend in the industry was the increasing use of "specialogs"—catalogs focused on a particular market segment. During the 1980s, many large, general merchandise catalog companies like Alden's and Montgomery Ward went out of business. In 1987 J.C. Penney began to provide catalogs targeted at petite women, extra-size women, tall women, big and tall men, nurses, brides, and other special groups. Advanced computer technology allows companies to identify, target, and track the purchases of their customers and then to develop special catalogs for groups sharing key characteristics. Then, highly sophisticated printing technology permits companies to prepare customized catalogs for particular clients. Some analysts pre-

---

[2] Rayna Skolnik, "Selling via Catalog," *Stores,* October 1989, pp. 47–50.

[3] Janice Steinberg, "Special Report: Direct Marketing," *Advertising Age,* October 26, 1987, pp. 51–51G.

EXHIBIT 8   Specialty Vendors of Consumer Products

	Sales (Millions)	Number of Vendors	Percent of Sales
Animal care	$ 70	120	0
Apparel	4,250	570	10
Audio/video	630	370	1
Automotive aviation	620	540	1
Books	2,760	—	6
Collectibles	1,690	520	4
Consumer electronics/science	710	100	2
Cosmetic/toiletries	450	110	1
Crafts	840	780	2
Food	1,310	940	3
Gardening	850	700	2
Gifts	2,020	630	5
Hardware/tools	530	240	1
Health products	2,480	410	6
Home construction	310	490	1
Housewares	1,220	820	3
Jewelry	500	150	1
Magazines	6,020	5,000	14
Multiproducts	7,410	340	17
Newspapers	3,020	1,700	7
Photographic products	410	90	1
Records	780	—	2
Sporting goods	3,460	1,140	8
Stationery	440	80	1
Tobacco	30	30	0
Toys/games/children's products	710	380	2
Computer software	650	60+	1
Computer hardware	350	100+	1
Total	$ 44,520	16,410+	100%

Consumer products specialty vendor sales segments (vendors classified by major product category) fall into three tiers:

Top Size ($1 Billion+)	Middle Size ($0.5 Billion–$1 Billion)	Moderate Size (Less than $0.5 Billion)
Multiproducts, gifts, collectibles, magazines, books, apparel, food, newspapers, housewares, health, sporting goods	Automotive/aviation, gardening, children's products, toys/games, records, computer software, jewelry, hardware/tools, audio/video, consumer electronics/science, crafts	Cosmetics/toiletries, computer hardware, stationery, tobacco, photographic products, home construction

Excluding books, magazines, newspapers, computer software, computer hardware and records, 9,520 businesses account for $30.9 billion in sales, or an average of $3.25 million in sales per business.
Source: *Direct Marketing,* July 1991.

dicted it would soon be common—and cost effective—for a mail-order company to send two different catalogs to neighboring households, depending on their past purchasing patterns.[4]

Credit Card Competition.   Increased competition between Visa USA and Master-Card for the mail-order market in 1991 resulted in new inducements to consumers who shop by mail. For example, Visa announced in June it would be offering a "Visa Catalog Collection": Consumers would be offered 40 catalogs at a nominal fee, and those who ordered catalogs through Visa would receive certificates good for up to 20 percent

---

[4] Ibid.

EXHIBIT 9   **Actual and Projected Population of the United States, 1990, 1995, and 2000**

	1990	1995	2000
Male (in Thousands)			
Under 5	9,426	9,118	8,661
5–17	23,377	24,787	25,027
18–24	13,216	12,290	12,770
25–34	22,078	20,579	18,662
35–44	18,785	21,104	21,945
45–54	12,406	15,292	18,296
55–64	10,103	10,149	11,557
65–74	8,171	8,476	8,242
Over 74	4,681	5,326	6,032
Total	122,243	127,121	131,192
Female (in Thousands)			
Under 5	8,982	8,681	8,237
5–17	22,253	23,587	23,788
18–24	12,924	11,991	12,461
25–34	21,848	20,384	18,487
35–44	19,112	21,233	21,966
45–54	13,081	16,005	18,927
55–64	11,260	11,175	12,601
65–74	10,201	10,454	10,001
Over 74	8,505	9,507	10,607
Total	128,166	133,017	137,075
Total (in Thousands)			
Under 5	18,408	17,799	16,898
5–17	45,630	48,374	48,815
18–24	26,140	24,281	25,231
25–34	43,926	40,963	37,149
35–44	37,897	42,337	43,911
45–54	25,487	31,297	37,223
55–64	21,363	21,324	24,158
65–74	18,372	18,930	18,243
Over 74	13,186	14,833	16,639
Total	250,409	260,138	268,267

off their purchases. In response, MasterCard announced its "Forests for Our Future" green marketing approach: Trees would be planted in the consumer's name for merchandise bought through certain catalogs. This promotion was designed to downplay the image of catalogers as tree killers. In essence, both companies were to provide free advertising for catalog companies, and the support of these two financial giants would likely boost sales.[5]

Government Regulations.   Catalogs remained vulnerable to the increasing costs of paper and postage. According to the *1990 Guide to Mail Order Sales,* a 1989 postage rate increase for third-class mail was still being felt in 1990. In addition, re-

---

[5] Alison Fahey, "Credit Cards Tie in with Catalogs," *Advertising Age,* June 3, 1991, p. 50.

cent rulings from the Federal Trade Commission had increased legal risks for catalog companies. Previously, the FTC had held that manufacturers were liable for false product claims; in 1990, the FTC shifted that responsibility to the mail-order firms.[6]

On another front, mail-order firms awaited a decision from the U.S. Supreme Court concerning state taxes on mail-order goods. Targeting mail-order firms in particular, the state of North Dakota was attempting to collect sales taxes from any company that "regularly and continuously" solicited business in the state. Current practice, established by a 1967 Supreme Court case (*National Bellas Hess, Inc.* v. *Department of Revenue,* 386 U.S. 753), prohibited states from collecting taxes on companies without a physical presence in the state. The Direct Marketing Association and many mail-order firms had filed briefs arguing against the North Dakota standard, citing the excessive administrative burden such a change would impose on them. Oral arguments were scheduled for January 22, 1992.

Catalog Company Failures.   Even in a growing market, mail-order firms failed. A 1984 study of 35 failed catalog companies cited the following key contributing factors:

- Lack of market research; failure to evaluate the market and offer desired goods.
- Overusage of popular mailing lists.
- Undercapitalization.
- Oversaturated marketplace.[7]

Most industry experts pointed to merchandise selection as the *sine qua non* of success in the mail-order business. Harold Schwartz, president of Hanover House Industries, noted that you cannot "fall in love with your catalog."[8] Mail-order firms had to be objective in determining what worked and then be able to change their catalogs to meet new demands and to exit saturated markets.

The Future of the Faith Mountain Company

Confident that fundamental market forces were very positive for their company, Cheri and Martin Woodard believed the key strategic question for Faith Mountain was how to grow.

Overall Company Goals.   The Faith Mountain Company intended to establish itself as the industry leader in quality, high-value gifts, apparel, and home accessories. To that end, top management had set for itself the overall goal of $25 million in annual sales by 1995, with $10 million from the Faith Mountain catalog, $5 million from the retail division, and an additional $10 million from the acquisition or development of another catalog company. The Woodards intended to achieve these targets and at the same time accomplish the following objectives:

- Grow as quickly as possible, yet maintain profitability.
- Grow at a rate that does not hurt product quality and customer service.

---

[6] Laurie Freeman and Janet Meyers, "FTC Gets Tough on Catalog Claims," *Advertising Age,* November 12, 1990, p. 73.

[7] New York University Advanced Catalog Seminar, "Successes and Failures Examined by Catalog Leaders," *Direct Marketing,* July 1984, pp. 98–101.

[8] Ibid.

EXHIBIT 10 Catalog Sales Forecast for Faith Mountain Company, Fiscal Years 1991–95

Season	Source of Names for Catalog Mailings	Quantity of Catalogs Mailed	Projected Sales
Fall 90	Rented lists	825,000	$ 990,000
	In-house	242,600	477,922
Holiday 90	Rented lists	980,000	1,244,600
	In-house	267,300	526,581
Spring 91	Rented lists	637,000	713,440
	In-house	295,750	553,052
Summer 91	Rented lists	300,000	276,000
	In-house	200,000	200,000
Totals	Rented lists	2,742,000	$ 3,224,000
	In-house	1,005,650	$ 1,757,555
1991 Total		**3,747,650**	**$ 4,981,595**
Fall 91	Rented lists	990,000	$ 1,188,000
	In-house	322,095	653,852
Holiday 91	Rented lists	1,080,000	1,371,600
	In-house	351,500	713,545
Spring 92	Rented lists	765,000	856,800
	In-house	385,500	744,015
Summer 92	Rented lists	360,000	331,200
	In-house	300,000	318,000
Totals	Rented lists	3,195,000	$ 3,747,600
	In-house	1,359,095	$ 2,429,412
1992 Total		**4,554,095**	**$ 6,177,012**
Fall 92	Rented lists	1,200,000	$ 1,584,000
	In-house	414,260	969,369
Holiday 92	Rented lists	1,300,000	1,820,000
	In-house	449,660	1,052,204
Spring 93	Rented lists	920,000	1,030,400
	In-house	490,560	995,836
Summer 93	Rented lists	300,000	276,000
	In-house	300,000	330,000
Totals	Rented lists	3,720,000	$ 4,710,400
	In-house	1,654,480	$ 3,347,409
1993 Total		**5,374,480**	**$ 8,057,809**

- Aggressively develop new products and exclusive vendor relationships.
- Stay close to our customers through surveys, the store, and personal contact.
- Provide the best quality and value in unique and unusual products.
- Be the best company to do business with.
- Provide a work environment that allows employees personal and professional growth, to insure the highest levels of motivation and knowledge among our people, and therefore the highest level of quality in all aspects of the company.

Growth for the Faith Mountain Catalog. Performance projections for the Faith Mountain catalog through 1995 appear in Exhibits 10 and 11. Martin estimated capital expenditures of $350,000 to $400,000 would be needed to increase catalog sales to $10 million.

EXHIBIT 10 (concluded)

Season	Source of Names for Catalog Mailings	Quantity of Catalogs Mailed	Projected Sales
Fall 93	Rented lists	1,400,000	$ 1,848,000
	In-house	519,000	1,245,600
Holiday 93	Rented lists	1,500,000	2,100,000
	In-house	566,400	1,359,360
Spring 94	Rented lists	1,020,000	1,142,400
	In-house	620,200	1,290,016
Summer 94	Rented lists	300,000	276,000
	In-house	450,000	513,000
Totals	Rented lists	4,220,000	$ 5,366,400
	In-house	2,155,600	$ 4,407,976
1994 Total		**6,375,600**	**$ 9,774,376**
Fall 94	Rented lists	1,400,000	$ 1,848,000
	In-house	651,000	1,562,400
Holiday 94	Rented lists	1,500,000	2,100,000
	In-house	698,286	1,675,887
Spring 95	Rented lists	1,020,000	1,142,400
	In-house	742,086	1,543,539
Summer 95	Rented lists	300,000	276,000
	In-house	500,000	570,000
Totals	Rented lists	4,220,000	$ 5,366,400
	In-house	2,591,372	$ 5,351,826
1995 Total		**6,811,372**	**$ 10,718,226**

The typical percentage breakdown of a catalog company's income statement in 1991 was as follows:

Net sales	100%
Cost of goods sold	45%
Gross margin	55%
Promotional costs	30%
Operating expenses	19%
Net profit	6%
Other income	1–3%

The relationship between net sales and promotional costs was the most important dynamic in the catalog business. Promotional costs include design and layout of the catalog, photography, color separations, printing and mailing, postage, list rental, and associated computer costs. Based on his experience, Martin worked by rule of thumb requiring that increases in promotional costs increase sales by more than three times the additional cost.

Increasing the "House List." Growth in the mail-order catalog industry was fueled by the company's customer list. An industry rule of thumb required a catalog company to mail 1,250,000 catalogs four times a year to reach critical mass and attain profitability. Accordingly, each mail-order company sought to build its "house list"—names and addresses of customers who had actually purchased product(s) from the

EXHIBIT 11   Projected Income Statements, the Faith Mountain Company, Fiscal Years 1992–95

	1992		1993		1994		1995	
	($)	(%)	($)	(%)	($)	(%)	($)	(%)
Gross sales	$6,433,012	107.5	$8,325,809	107.5	$10,056,616	107.5	$11,014,578	107.5
Returns and allowances	482,476	7.5	624,436	7.5	754,246	7.5	826,093	7.5
Net sales	5,950,536	100.0	7,701,373	100.0	9,302,370	100.0	10,188,485	100.0
Cost of goods sold	2,814,604	47.3	3,645,587	47.3	4,390,719	47.2	4,798,776	47.1
Gross profit	3,135,932	52.7	4,055,786	52.7	4,911,651	52.8	5,389,709	52.9
Promotional costs	1,951,776	32.8	2,502,946	32.5	2,995,363	32.2	3,250,127	31.9
Operating expense	720,015	12.1	931,866	12.1	1,125,587	12.1	1,232,807	12.1
General & administrative	410,000	6.9	475,000	6.2	565,000	6.1	615,000	6.0
Operating income	54,141	0.9	145,974	1.9	225,701	2.4	291,775	2.7
Other income	230,000	3.9	250,000	3.2	270,000	2.9	310,000	3.0
Net income	$ 284,141	4.8	$ 395,974	5.1	$ 495,701	5.3	$ 601,775	5.9

Includes catalog and the Sperryville retail store.

catalog. Most smaller companies supplemented their house list by renting (for one-time use) outside lists, the house lists of other companies (through a broker), at an average price of $110 per thousand names. Any person from the rented list who purchased a product automatically went on the house list. Even the best outside list, however, was not as responsive to a mailing as the company's house list. When measured on a dollar-income-per-catalog-mailed basis, the response of the house list would be three to four times greater than any outside list.

The larger the house list, the less the company needed to rent other lists. Companies with larger lists exchange lists with each other rather than pay each other rental fees. Accordingly, as the house list grows, promotional costs decrease as net sales increase. (In addition, the company earns additional money from the rental of its own house list; in fiscal year 1991, Faith Mountain earned $130,000 in this way.)

The most marketable segment of any list was the group who had purchased product(s) within the previous six months. A key component of Faith Mountain's growth strategy was to increase its six-month buyer list to 60,000 names. Martin explained the logic:

> We regularly exchange lists with approximately 15 other catalog companies. Assuming a mailing of 1 million catalogs and an entire house list of 150,000 names, we need to use 850,000 names from these other companies. A six-month buyer list of 56,700 names would allow us to incur no rental fees (850,000 names divided by 15 companies equals 56,700 names).
>
> Our six-month buyers typically respond with $4 in sales for every catalog mailed versus the outside response of approximately $1.10 per catalog mailed. In the most recent catalog promotion, we had approximately 20,000 six-month buyers. If this segment were tripled, we would see approximately $50,000 in savings due to exchanging lists rather than renting and $120,000 in increased sales from the larger number of responsive buyers. Assuming four such catalog promotions per year, Faith Mountain would realize $200,000 in savings and $480,000 in increased sales solely from the larger six-month-buyer house list.
>
> To increase the buyer list, we will have to increase the catalog circulation to approximately 7 million every 12 months. Working with our list brokers, we can develop mail plans—testing list segments by monitoring coded responses—to raise the rate of response and reduce the number of catalogs required for circulation.

Moving to Private-Label Sportswear. A second strategy for growth in the Faith Mountain catalog was to change the merchandise mix, particularly in the apparel lines, to reflect half Faith Mountain designs with private labels, and half items from better manufacturers, to retain the quality brand name recognition. Martin gave an example of the benefits of this strategy:

> In general, the apparel industry has *no* flexibility on price, but smaller companies will do lots of deals if you are willing to commit to large quantities. For example, a vest: we paid $24 each and sold a *bunch*—somewhere between 750 and 1,000 of them—in last year's catalog for $49. The company we bought them from went out of business this year, taken down when the Sporting Life catalog went under. So Cheri called this guy, and he set her up with the factory in China where he had bought them. Now they have our own label, and they cost us $12.50. It's not easy to do that—you have to take a substantial position—but on this vest, we were willing to, due to last year's sales.

Growth through Acquisition of Another Catalog. Demand for the gifts, home accessories, and apparel carried in the Faith Mountain catalog was seasonal. There were two peaks in the sales calendar. The first began in September and dropped off in late December, and the second began in January and ended in February. Although the company did significant business in the other months, this seasonality caused rapid shifts in demand on the company's staff and system capabilities and depressed overall operating earnings.

Cheri and Martin knew they could make more efficient use of company facilities, systems, and human resources if they could acquire or develop another business countercyclical to the existing catalog. Fixed costs would be amortized over a larger and more constant flow of business. Acquiring another catalog would be the quickest and safest method to realize these efficiencies. They believed the ideal acquisition would offer small, easy-to-handle products, whose sales would peak in the first half of the year.

Growth in the Retail Division. In 1991, the retail division consisted of the one original store on Main Street in Sperryville, but Cheri and Martin had discussed opening additional retail outlets. Martin favored active exploration of possible sites. Referring to Williams Sonoma, Eddie Bauer, The Sharper Image, and other retailers that had taken this route, he stressed the synergy between the catalog and retail outlets, especially as the mailings continued to increase. Cheri was slightly less sanguine about opening additional stores. Margie Ellis, the store manager in Sperryville, also had doubts:

> This store was really the birthplace of the company—here since 1790, here in the Civil War, right by the Blue Ridge Mountains—you can't recreate that. You can buy an old house somewhere and put herbs in it, but that won't be Faith Mountain.

Based on casual discussions with real estate specialists, the Woodards estimated the cost of building out a "high-end" store (gutting the inside) at approximately $18 a square foot. The average space in a shopping center mall was 1,600 to 2,000 square feet. Simply taking over an existing space and doing minor leasehold improvements might cost as little as $3,000, however; and in the 1991 market, many of these costs could be negotiated with landlords. For example, the Woodards had heard of one outlet chain that had recently spent $18,000 to open a store in Norfolk, Virginia, and the landlord reimbursed them $15,000.

Managing Projected Growth: Issues for Management

Financial Implications.   The continuing economic recession in late 1991 seemed to have little effect on Faith Mountain sales, but in dealings with suppliers, Faith Mountain could feel the economic pinch. As Martin put it,

> Companies that used to offer terms of 75 to 90 days now insist on 30 days net, but we still try to negotiate terms. It's really hard to get anyone to listen to you in the apparel industry—you have to be *golden* to get those guys to listen. The name of the game for survival in this business is *credit rating*. We can't be turned in, we can't be late, we can't be delinquent.

Achieving the sales goals would require additional capital, but it was not clear where this capital would be best obtained. In November 1991, Sovran Bank increased the company's line of credit to $500,000. To increase its equity capital, in the spring of 1991, the company had offered 1,500 shares and sold 1,150. The Woodard family retained 55 percent interest in the company, but Prime Capital Group, a venture capital firm, was now the largest shareholder outside the family. Cheri and Martin were aware that outside shareholders would place different pressures on them; already Martin sensed some pressure from stockholders to start paying dividends. Exhibit 12 describes the company's board of directors.

Support Systems Implications.   Faith Mountain's current hardware configuration was capable of supporting 96 terminals with two simple upgrades—an additional 380 megabyte disc drive and a 4 megabyte RAM unit. The upgrade cost was $28,319 and was scheduled to occur in 1992. Additional workstations were available for $400. With these upgrades, the computer system could support projected growth through

---

EXHIBIT 12   Board of Directors and Supporting Professional Services

Faith Mountain Board of Directors

Mr. Peter Elliman, a partner in Prime Capital, a private venture capital fund in Warrenton, Virginia, brought over 25 years of financial and corporate development experience to the board.

Mr. Don Press, past director of the Smithsonian Museum Gift Catalog, currently a catalog consultant, had helped the Woodards since 1984.

Ms. Joan Litle, a catalog consultant specializing in the creative and merchandising aspects of the industry.

Mr. James Jamieson, a member of the board of directors of several companies, had extensive experience in corporate finance and investment banking.

Ms. Linda Dietel, a local community activist with many business and community contacts.

Ms. Cheri Woodard, president of Faith Mountain.

Mr. Martin Woodard, secretary/treasurer of Faith Mountain.

Supporting Professional Services

Legal: Bill Sharp, senior partner of Kates and Sharp, in Front Royal, Virginia, sat in on all board meetings.

Accounting: Gary Lee, of Yount, Hyde and Barbour in Winchester, Virginia, assisted in monthly accounting and performed a year-end financial review.

Banking: Marathon Bank in Stephens City, Virginia, held company accounts in connection with the SBA loan, and Sovran Bank in Charlottesville, Virginia, extended the company a $500,000 line of credit.

Advertising: Forgit & White of New Hampshire designed the catalog, and Faith Mountain operated an in-house advertising agency named Telesis.

Printing: R. R. Donnelley, the largest commercial printer in the world, had printed the company's catalogs since 1988.

1995. It appeared the Siemens phone system would be adequate through 1993. Finally, with the addition of a mezzanine level and with some new equipment and technical improvements in the warehouse, the current building would also support the projected $10 million in catalog sales by 1995.

Human Resources Implications. Cheri and Martin agreed that one of the greatest challenges facing Faith Mountain was in hiring, training, and managing the new people: operators, customer service supervisors, buyers, warehouse people, and managers necessary to achieve their goals. Even now, the two knew they were working at capacity. Martin described the situation this way:

> We need to identify the key positions and put good people in them. There are lots of little jobs that go begging now, but little things become much more important with size—if you can get 0.5 percent of sales with *X* change, that's a lot more significant at $10 million than at $500,000 in sales. For example, that might pay a salary—that person could add to the bottom line *and* carry his or her own weight. You have to think about who, and when, and how much more we can do of this before we can't do any more of it.
>
> I have people reporting to me now, but I still have a tendency to tell them what I want them to do and then expect them to go do it. Cheri has to tell people who work for me that they need to be self-starters, motivated people. I want to be able to tell them, "Go to the show and find me stuff that will sell"—not "Go find me six mugs and four blankets."

Cheri took her responsibility for all human resources matters very seriously. She had established the company's employee evaluation/self-evaluation process, initiated the training program, and prepared the company handbook of personnel policies. In 1991, she had started a new program for ongoing education and training through a local community college, and at year-end she was developing the company's first pension plan and an employee stock option program. At the same time, however, she had misgivings about continuing to handle all aspects of human resource management as the company grew. She said,

> For a long time, people answered only to me—Martin didn't want to deal with them. Now he has people who report to him. There's a changing orientation now to *us,* not just to *me.* Martin made me the president. He said, "You're so good with people, with public relations—you be the figurehead." So *Working Woman* did a feature story on me, and there is just my picture in the catalog—we're selling to women, and he said they would relate better to me. And I've grown into that role, and now I like it, provided he gets the recognition he deserves in public—and that's *my* job.
>
> Martin is more the gambler, more of a risk taker, a visionary, while I'm more of a people person—I run the business; I see that the orders go out the door; I manage the order flow. But as we get ready to add more positions—add more people—I ask myself, what about initiation and indoctrination? I can't train them all—the management people need to be trained, too. How do you get that management time?

The Woodards had had their first serious personnel problem in 1991. In January 1991, they had hired an assistant buyer to work for the merchandising manager. In late August, they had to fire her. Martin explained,

> It just didn't work out. She was not working as hard as what we were used to, and she was more of a drain on people's time than a help. It wasn't clear to this person who her boss was—I should have told Kim, "Look, this is your assistant, you tell her what to do," but she didn't want to have Kim for a boss, either. We also couldn't pay her what she thought she was worth—and even then what we did pay was too close to Kim's salary, and Kim wasn't happy about that because she was doing *far more.*
>
> So we sat down with her, both Cheri and I, after three months, and we said we were

having troubles. We talked things through with her, had her sign papers acknowledging the evaluation, and then we told Kim, "Look, you have to be the boss." Three months later, this person still wasn't coming around. We sat down with her again then and told her she had three more months, and if she hadn't improved by the end of October she'd have to leave. One month later I said, "Look, this isn't working, it's never going to work, let's get rid of her. We don't have that many people here, we might as well have the best." It was clear she was never going to be the best. We gave her four months' severance pay—so she ended up with a year's salary for eight months of work.

As Cheri and Martin considered adding staff in the company, Cheri emphasized the importance of strong human resources systems to train and support the new hires, while he stressed simply hiring the right people. They talked frequently about hiring an operations manager or a marketing manager to handle order taking, data processing, the warehouse, and human resources, including hiring, compensation, education, and morale. Cheri knew she would find it hard to give up responsibility in those areas. Martin described the requirements for such a person:

> They'd have to come in and work hard and fast. They'd have to have the entrepreneurial spirit and be willing to get out there and pack boxes with us on Saturdays, get their hands dirty. And they'd have to be willing to work for nothing, move out here in the middle of nowhere, and have an office in the corner in a warehouse.

Personal Implications.   As they considered their own futures with Faith Mountain, both Martin and Cheri realized the projected growth of their business would have significant implications on their own lives. Martin described their work/family life together:

> I don't know what's work and what's not. We work a lot—we're in the building from 8 AM to 7 PM and on Saturday and Sunday. It's unusual for us to take an entire day off. Now that our son is away from home, half of our home conversation is about work. Who should we keep when we have to lay off the seasonal phone operators after Christmas? Should we do *X* or *Y?*
>
> Every now and then, Cheri and I take off an entire day, not coming in. And we try to take an extra day on business trips. And two times a year we get away for four to six days.
>
> In the long run, I'll still be involved with the business, but I'd like something without so much stress—there are times when cash is tight, people call and ask why they can't be paid right now—I'd like to avoid those pressures. I'd like to not be so hands-on, to be able to step back and know that the wheels won't fall off the wagon. We need some cushions, though— so we can ride through hard times. Right now we don't have the cushion. There is no margin for error, no room for major mistakes.
>
> I enjoy all this on a theoretical level, though. There's something about keeping score. What are your greatest strengths? What are your weaknesses? Adults can compete in the business world—that appeals to me—there's something about keeping score.

For her part, Cheri had many questions about the future.

> I see a goal for the business as making us a life—a lifestyle better than our parents'. But money is now what drives us. We want to avoid worries and be comfortable. But if we wanted money, we wouldn't have settled in Rappahannock County.
>
> What I really like is growing a business and feeling like I can make a difference in the lives of our employees and the lives of our customers. The challenge to me is building a corporate structure that allows the individual to excel and yet be part of the team. If we get very large, will we be able to have the same esprit de corps?

MARKET TARGET STRATEGIES

Choice of the market target(s) is a critical business decision. Should a company attempt to serve all customers who are willing and able to buy, or selectively go after one or more subgroups (segments) of customers? Understanding the product market is essential in selecting the market target strategy. The targeting process consists of

- Deciding how to form segments.
- Describing the people or organizations in each segment.
- Evaluating market target alternatives.
- Selecting a market target strategy.

The possibilities for targeting range from attempting to appeal to most buyers in the market to concentrating on one or a few segments within the market.

The logic of market segmentation is that buyers within a product market will vary in their responsiveness to any marketing program because their needs and wants vary. The objective is to identify two or more subgroups within the product market. Each segment contains potential buyers who respond similarly to a marketing offer.

Finding and Describing Segments

Segmentation may enable a company to gain worthwhile advantages—including higher profitability and strength over competition—through better use of the firm's capabilities and resources. By selecting segments of the product market (each containing people or organizations that exhibit some degree of similarity in their needs and wants), management can gain greater customer responsiveness from effort expended than by directing the same marketing effort to the whole product market.

First, we identify possible segments and then, for each segment of interest, determine which marketing program positioning strategy will obtain the most favorable market response (e.g., profit contribution, net of marketing costs). Because there are many ways to divide a product market and several marketing program combinations that might be used for each segment, finding the very best (optimal) market target and marketing program strategy is probably not feasible. Instead, the objective should be to improve the sales response and cost results through effective targeting and positioning strategies.

Criteria for Segmentation

Five criteria are useful in deciding whether segmentation is worthwhile. First is determining the segment's responsiveness to a company's efforts. If little or no variation in responsiveness exists between segments, then the way they respond (e.g., the amount of and frequency of purchase) to any given marketing program should be the same. If segments actually exist, their responses will be different—and a different marketing program strategy will work best for each group.

After meeting the first condition—measuring responsiveness to a company's efforts—the other requirements come into play. Second, it must be feasible to identify two or more customer groups; and third, a firm must be able to aim an appropriate marketing program strategy at each target segment. It must be accessible through marketing activities such as advertising. Fourth, in terms of revenue generated and costs incurred, segmentation must be worth doing. Fifth, the segments must exhibit enough stability over time so that the firm's efforts via segmentation will have enough time to reach desired levels of performance.

If we fail to meet the five requirements, a segmentation strategy may be questionable. The ultimate criterion is performance. If a segmentation scheme leads to improved performance (profitability) in a product market, it is worthwhile. The advantage of meeting the requirements for segmentation is that we are more certain the strategy will lead to improved performance.

Forming and Describing the Segments

Much of the information obtained from market analysis can be used in describing market segments. The starting point in describing segments is the definition and analysis of the product market (customer profiles). The objective is to identify key characteristics that will be useful in distinguishing one segment from another.

It is important to identify key characteristics of the people or organizations that occupy each segment. Factors such as those used in dividing product markets into segments are also helpful in describing the people in the segments. The following information is used to describe market segments:

- Market profiles of customers (e.g., demographics, lifestyles).
- Size and growth estimates (forecasts and growth rates).
- Distribution channels (e.g., direct to end user, wholesalers, retailers).
- Nature of key competitors.
- Product- or brand-positioning strategy.

This information is needed for each segment of interest to better evaluate its potential value.

Microsegmentation

Computerized databases offer powerful capabilities for identifying and communicating with customers. This information enables companies to target individuals or small segments of people. The systems are very useful in sales and sales management support and for direct marketing programs. Database marketing has three main benefits: (1) strategic advantage through the more effective use of marketing information internally, (2) improvement in the use of customer and market information, and (3) a basis for developing long-term customer relationships.[1] The systems can be applied to mail order marketing, telemarketing, and support of personal selling activities. A major objective of database marketing is to find and develop strong relationships with the customer base that accounts for a large portion of a firm's annual sales.

Another form of microsegmentation is mass customization, which offers a process for serving the unique needs and wants of individual buyers. Mass customization employs information technology and production efficiencies to design and produce products to meet individual buyers' requirements at prices comparable to mass-produced products. For example, Motorola is able to offer organizational buyers customized pagers with an incredible array of alternative features at prices comparable to mass-produced pagers.

Evaluating Market Target Alternatives

Market target alternatives consist of strategies directed toward one, more than one, or all segments. The marketing program positioning strategy used for a segment may be totally different from that used for other segments, or each program may overlap to some extent programs aimed at other segments. Thus, a firm may use a unique combination of the product offering, distribution approach, price, advertising, and personal selling to serve each segment, or some of the marketing mix components may be used for more than one segment. For example, the same airline services are used to appeal to business and pleasure travelers, although different advertising and sales efforts are aimed at each user group.

Selecting a Market Target Strategy

Assuming that segments can be identified, management has the option of selecting one or more as market targets. Several factors often affect this decision.

Factors Impacting the Targeting Decision

Product Market Characteristics.   The market that a firm decides to serve has a strong influence upon the choice of a market target strategy. When buyers' needs and wants are similar, there is no real basis for trying to identify segments. Market complexity is another consideration, overlapping to some extent the other factors. The more complex the market situation as to competing firms, variety of product offering, variation in user needs and wants, and other factors, the more likely that a useful segmentation scheme can be found.

The maturity of the market is relevant in guiding the targeting decision. Defining segments in a new market may be difficult since buyers' needs and preferences are not clearly established. In contrast, a mature market is likely to include several segments.

Competitive Advantage.   A firm's market share may be an important factor in deciding what market target strategy to use. Low–market-share firms can often strengthen their position over competition by finding a segment where they have (or can achieve) an advantage over that competition.

The success of small–market-share firms such as Southwest Airlines lends strong support to this position. Also important in choosing a market target strategy are the firm's resources and capabilities. With limited resources a segmentation strategy may be essential, as is also the case when the firm's capabilities correspond best to a subset of buyers in the market.

Other Considerations.   Selection of an appropriate strategy must also take into account the number of competing firms and the capabilities of each. Intense competition often favors segmentation and selective targeting, particularly for low-share firms. Finally, production and marketing scale economies may influence management in choosing a strategy. For example, large sales volume may be required to gain cost advantages, and scale of production may also affect marketing and distribution programs.

Segmentation, Targeting, and Positioning

The interrelationships between segmentation, targeting, and positioning are shown in Exhibit 1. The process begins by defining and analyzing the product market to be segmented. Application of segmentation methods seeks to identify market segments as shown by segments A through E in Exhibit 1. Next, management must decide which (and how many) segments to target. The positioning strategy determines how management wants the buyers in a particular market target to perceive the organization's offering. For example, Nike uses symbolic positioning for its athletic shoes, featuring sports celebrities to promote Nike products.

Finally, the marketing program spells out the product, distribution, pricing, and promotion strategies intended to position the product with the buyers in the market target.

The market target decision sets into motion the marketing strategy as shown in Exhibit 1. Choosing the right market targets is a most important decision affecting the enterprise. This decision is central to properly positioning a firm in the marketplace. Locating the firm's best competitive advantage may first require detailed segment analysis. Market target decisions are central to business and marketing planning. These

EXHIBIT 1   **Segmentation, Targeting, and Positioning**

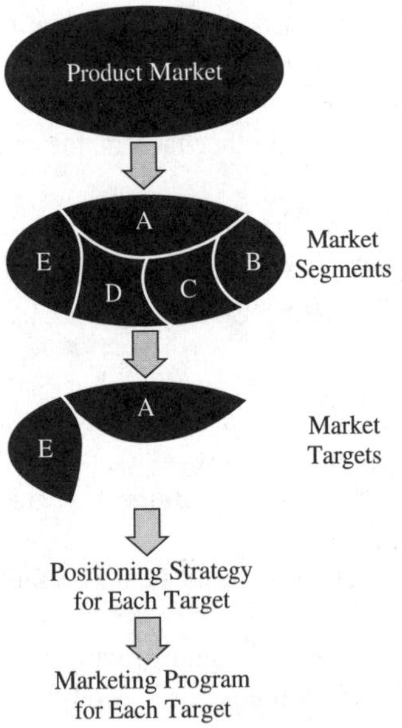

decisions establish key guidelines for planning, and the market target decision provides the focus for the remaining marketing strategy decisions.

End Notes

1. Keith Fletcher, Colin Wheeter, and Julia Wright, "The Role and Status of U.K. Database Marketing," *Quarterly Review of Marketing,* Autumn 1990, pp. 7–14.

CASES FOR PART IV

The six cases in this part consider the challenges many companies encounter in identifying target markets and in formulating strategies for penetrating selected markets. In addition to the marketing issues faced by consumer and business-to-business organizations, the companies examined in this part include both high technology and public utilities.

The video case, **Amtech Corporation (Case 4–1),** covers a rapidly growing international company and a leader in advanced transportation electronics. The company has reached a critical juncture in that its two markets are not growing and/or mature enough to provide a steady revenue stream. Amtech operates in two areas of transportation electronics. The company, however, is at a crossroads. It needs to decide whether to continue operating in both markets or focus solely on one of the two markets. Competition has become strong due largely to alliances between powerful companies.

Düring AG (Fottle) (Case 4–2) is a new product situation in an international environment. Targeting and other strategic issues must be evaluated.

Murphy Brewery Ireland, Limited (Case 4–3) is a brewery faced with developing a global strategy in a very competitive environment. Murphy has become a recognized international brand while maintaining a unique identity in Ireland.

Case 4–4, Shorin-Ryu Karate Academy, examines the challenges and opportunities of managing a small business. The owner has collected market research and must decide whether growth entails opening new facilities and/or expanding its current facility.

LoJack Corporation (Case 4–5) markets a method to track and recover stolen automobiles. Customers have voiced interest in a LoJack-type system for various applications such as child safety, keeping tabs on furloughed prisoners, and high-valued item protection. The company needs a growth strategy that will help it continue in its profitable stream. Market selection seems critical to this growth.

In **Case 4–6, Algonquin Power and Light Company** is a metropolitan gas and electric utility. The company is considering whether to begin manufacturing compost for sale from tree and shrubbery trimmings. Management needs to decide whether to pursue this business opportunity and, if they do, whether to target the retail market, the wholesale market, or both.

CASE 4–1
AMTECH CORPORATION

Amtech Corporation, a leader in advanced electronics to improve the world's transportation system, had reached a critical junction by the beginning of 1995. With disappointing 1994 profits and unsuccessful bids for new contracts, the company had experienced a US$300 million drop in market value. Share price had tumbled from US$33 per share in March 1994 to less than US$10 per share by the end of that summer. Amtech Corporation operated in two areas of transportation electronics. The company was a pioneer in the intelligent vehicle highway systems (IVHS) market including electronic toll and traffic management systems. The company also operated in the transportation market including automatic equipment identification (AEI) for the rail, intermodal, shipping, and fleet market segments. Prior to 1992, most of Amtech's revenues had come from the IVHS market. In 1992, however, the transportation segments (AEI) accounted for 62 percent of revenues, with the IVHS market holding the remaining 38 percent. However, Amtech had completed delivery of its AEI tags to North American railroads by the end of 1994, and other new business prospects had not developed to replace the AEI railroad revenue stream.

G. Russell Mortenson, Amtech's president and CEO, was under intense pressure from shareholders to implement strategies designed to maximize stockholder value.[1] At the heart of this strategy implementation was the identification of appropriate market targets for Amtech. Had the company reached an either/or situation with the IVHS and AEI markets? With the current level of shareholder dissatisfaction, Mr. Mortenson knew that he had little time to make public his plans for Amtech.

Company Background

Amtech Corporation, a leader in IVHS (Intelligent Vehicle Highway Systems) and AEI (Automatic Equipment Identification), had come a long way from the origination of its name, Animal Management Technology. Originally creating a product used to monitor livestock, Amtech got its start in 1983 when the U.S. Department of Agriculture released the patents on an 11-year-old radio beam system. David Cook and Kenneth Anderson (Blockbuster Entertainment co-founders) were convinced of the commercial viability of radio frequency technology. Cook and Anderson put up the seed money for the venture, with Texas billionaire Ross Perot later joining the Blockbuster duo. American President (a shipping concern) and Mitsubishi invested in Amtech as well.

Initial use of the technology was in inventory management as an electronic bill of lading (AEI). A radio frequency tag was developed to track equipment movement of rail and shipping containers. The technology had been adopted by many trucking com-

---

[1] Amtech went public in 1989.

This case was prepared by Victoria L. Crittenden, associate professor of marketing, Boston College, as the basis for class discussion rather than to illustrate either effective or ineffective handling of a managerial situation. Research assistance was provided by Stephanie Hillstrom and David Angus, Boston College. All information was derived from secondary sources. Revised 1997.

EXHIBIT 1   Five-Year Financial Summary (in thousands, except per share data)

	Year Ended December 31				
	1994	*1993*	*1992*	*1991*	*1990*
Statement of Operations Data					
Sales	$ 61,457	$59,424	$ 39,856	$ 18,748	$ 14,770
Operating costs and expenses:					
Cost of sales	31,288	28,678	20,190	11,563	10,123
Research and development	6,222	4,407	2,562	1,963	2,835
Marketing, general, and					
administrative	13,991	13,978	10,960	10,640	10,654
	51,501	47,063	33,712	24,166	23,612
Operating income (loss)	9,956	12,361	6,144	(5,418)	(8,842)
Interest income			1,261	433	1,181
Contract settlement	—	—	—	—	687
Provision for income taxes	4,398	3,729	132	—	—
Net income (loss)	$ 7,662	$16,367	$ 7,273	$ (4,985)	$ (6,974)
Earnings (loss) per share	$ 0.52	$ 0.70	$ 0.64	$ (0.50)	$ (0.71)
Shares used in computing					
earnings (loss) per share	14,799,782	14,855,323	11,359	9,927	9,760
Balance Sheet Data					
Working capital	$ 64,200	$52,263	$ 41,492	$ 13,554	$ 13,566
Total assets	80,622	76,720	57,445	22,991	22,269
Total stockholders' equity[1]	75,336	66,805	48,821	15,965	18,925

[1] The company completed an initial public offering in November 1989 by selling 2,760,000 shares of common stock for net proceeds of $21,552,000. Additionally, in May 1992, the company completed a follow-on public offering of 1,250,000 common shares for net proceeds of $24,884,000.

Source: Amtech Corporation, 1995 Annual Report.

panies and, by 1992, railroads had adopted the technology in all their 1.4 million rail cars.

A byproduct of Amtech's AEI project was toll-road tags (IVHS). With this system, commuters had a credit-card–size tag on their car which emitted a signal at the toll-gate. Transceivers, installed at toll plazas, bounced radio beams off these tags. Instantly, the tag identified the motorist, and her toll account was debited for the toll charge.

With corporate headquarters in Dallas, Texas, Amtech's product development and manufacturing groups operated out of the company's ISO9001-quality–certified facility in Albuquerque, New Mexico. The company was involved in a joint venture in Europe with Alcatel AVI S.A. in which Amtech products were marketed and serviced. (Named Alcatel Amtech S.A., the firm was 51 percent owned by Alcatel AVI S.A. and 49 percent by Amtech.) Mitsubishi Corp., which owned a 5 percent share of Amtech, marketed Amtech products in Asia. In early 1995, Amtech had agreed to form a joint venture, Sino-Amtech, Inc., which would market and support state-of-the-art radio frequency identification technology in the People's Republic of China. In the United States, Amtech and Motorola Inc. were involved in a joint venture to develop technology for the traffic management and electronic toll collection markets.

Exhibit 1 provides a five-year financial summary for Amtech.

EXHIBIT 2   The AEI Process

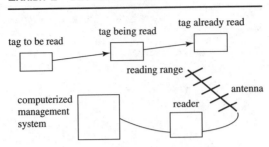

Automatic Equipment Identification

The Automatic Equipment Identification system was a scanning system for capturing cargo location information from all vehicles and sending this information directly to a mainframe computer. The bottom line was that a customer (and the shipper) would always know where the shipment was in the transit process. The AEI system eliminated the manual recording of identification numbers. The AEI provided continuous monitoring of rolling stock by sensors which scanned electronic tags containing identification information. The tags, which could be written on as well as read, allowed for locating where a container was in the shipping process as well as identifying what was in the container. As most cargo involved some interchange (i.e., different carriers handling the cargo before it reached its final destination), an AEI system virtually eliminated "lost" cargo.

AEI tags were electronic transponders that emitted radio signals. The tags could be attached to rolling stock containers (e.g., rail cars, trucks) and also to every piece of equipment handling the container. For example, if a crane placed the wrong container on the wrong carrier, the computer would signal the crane operator to remove the container.[2] Basically, the transponder was coded with a serial number that corresponded with a cargo container. The transponders were interpreted by a transceiver using radio frequency waves. The serial number was transmitted when the device was polled by the transceiver, and the data was routed from the transceiver to a processor that collected the data (a mainframe computer). Exhibit 2 diagrams the AEI process.

Rail.   The AEI had been sanctioned by the American Association of Railroads as a mandated standard reporting method.[3] It was felt that AEI usage would offer the following major benefits to railway users. *Customer satisfaction* would be higher due to reduced cost in shipment tracing/expediting, real-time exception reporting (deviations from train schedule), reduced billing errors, reduced claim filing, reporting accuracy, enhanced electronic data interchange capability, improved scheduling, enhanced rail competitiveness, seamless transportation (carrier interchange would not matter), and support for shipper quality programs. Regarding *inventory control,* there would be reduced inventory carrying cost,[4] support for just-in-time capability, improved production scheduling, reduced need for premium transportation, accurate and timely report-

---

[2] Error rates for the AEI system were predicted to be one in 800 million.

[3] Tests showed accurate readings at up to 180 miles per hour, with tags read as far away as 100 feet. Additionally, the system was reliable in harsh conditions such as snow, rain, and extreme dirt and dust.

[4] One study indicated a cycle time reduction of 4 to 5 percent, generating inventory cost savings in excess of the tagging costs.

ing of weights, and real-time control. *Equipment and other asset productivity gains* would be realized from private fleet size reduction (due to improved productivity of every car) and improved utilization, management, control, and operation of assigned cars and private fleets, plus reduced facility requirements for storage, tracks, tanks, and warehouses. *Information systems* benefits would result from worldwide standardization, support for service measurement in quality programs, minimized clerical rework and audit, support for a paperless environment, and improved data quality on private fleet mileage payments. Finally, *safety* would be enhanced, particularly in regards to the movement of hazardous materials. Dollarwise, estimates were that railway companies could save $56 to $75 million annually in fuel, maintenance, and personnel costs.

The Association of American Railroads' mandate required all rolling stock in North America to be equipped with electronic tags.[5] The mandate covered 1.4 million railcars, locomotives, and other equipment in Canada, the United States, and Mexico. The association's mandate standards were adopted as the European standard in 1993, affecting 32 railroads across the width of the continent. The European railroad market was estimated to be five times bigger than the U.S. market.

Railway usage of AEI opened up the need for complementary new products. Such potential products included tags that could interface with on-board devices such as fuel, temperature gauges in refrigerated railcars, and fluid levels, portable readers that would allow a person to retrieve and display data from individual tags (e.g., special handling instructions on a hazardous shipment), and improved tag programmers to make field programming of tags more efficient.

Fleet.   Trucking was another area of use for the AEI system. Trucking companies were more numerous, but smaller in size. Trucking firms received $100 billion of the $130 billion spent annually in the United States on the transportation of goods. Exhibit 3 lists the top 20 "Common General Freight" truck carriers.

Technology was transforming the way long-distance truck drivers in the United States did business. AEI technology not only allowed truck headquarters to monitor truck location at all times, but also resulted in better fleet asset management as drivers would not have to stop and call the dispatch center to report status or receive instructions. Additionally, trucks equipped with IVHS would benefit from nonstop trips on toll roads which would reduce cycle time. As well, many truck and trailer fleets ended up as piggy-back traffic on railroads. Basically, the same advantages found with rail usage would result with fleet usage.

Trucking companies were also evaluating another technology. Satellite-based networks forged data links between dispatch centers and terminals located in truck cabs. Two vendors (Geostar Corp. of Washington, D.C., and Qualcomm, Inc. of San Diego, California) were vying for this market. By 1998, 74 percent of the major U.S. trucking companies used computers to help plan truck routes. Fifty-seven percent of U.S. truck companies had computers on board each rig.

Intermodal.   Intermodal shippers were the largest customers of the railroad.[6] Several million intermodal containers traveled North America annually. AEI-tagged containers would be advantageous for intermodal shipping containers as more and more North American railroad reader systems were installed.

---

[5] European railroads endorsed the system in 1993.

[6] Intermodal shipping took place when more than one type of carrier was used to deliver the product. For example, a container might arrive via water travel and then be transported via rail.

EXHIBIT 3   **Top 20 Common General Freight Fleet Carriers**

Rank	Carrier	Location
1	United Parcel Service, Inc. (OHIO)	Atlanta, GA
2	United Parcel Service, Inc. (NY)	Atlanta, GA
3	Yellow Freight System, Inc.	Overland Park, KS
4	Roadway Express, Inc.	Akron, OH
5	Consolidated Freightways Corp.	Portland, OR
6	Schneider National Carriers, Inc.	Green Bay, WI
7	J.B. Hunt Transport, Inc.	Lowell, AR
8	Overnite Transportation Co.	Richmond, VA
9	ABF Freight System, Inc.	Fort Smith, AR
10	Con-Way Transportation Services	Portland, OR
11	Carolina Freight Carriers Corp.	Cherryville, NC
12	Ryder Dedicated Logistics, Inc.	Miami, FL
13	Werner Enterprises, Inc.	Omaha, NE
14	Missouri Nebraska Express (MNX)	St. Joseph, MO
15	TNT Holland Motor Express, Inc.	Holland, MI
16	Watkins Motor Lines, Inc.	Lakeland, FL
17	Preston Trucking Company, Inc.	Preston, MO
18	Nationsway Transport Service	Commerce City, CO
19	American Freightways, Inc.	Harrison, AR
20	Central Transport, Inc.	Warren, MI

Source: *Commercial Carrier Journal,* August 1994 (Fredericksburg, VA: Transportation Technical Services).

Security Access Market.   Another market that opened up for AEI was not part of the traditional transportation segment. The security market, particularly regarding walled communities, was a strong candidate for AEI.[7] The same concept as with transportation segments applied in the security market. An antenna would send out radio signals near the property entrance. As a vehicle approached the gate, the signal reflected off the tag. The computer-based system immediately looked up the tag's vehicle information in the community's database. Residents would be allowed to drive through security. Others, such as contractors, visitors, and service providers, would have to stop. The system allowed for monitoring the movement of contractors and service people around the community (as the contractor/service providers would be provided a temporary transponder while on the site).

Intelligent Vehicles and Highway Systems

Traffic congestion cost American businesses around US$100 billion in lost productivity annually. This US$100 billion estimate did not include costs associated with the billions of gallons of fuel wasted and the tons of pollutants spewed while sitting in traffic jams. Nor did the US$100 billion include the US$70 billion annual cost of traffic accidents that would be reduced if traffic congestion was decreased. Americans were expected to spend 7 billion hours in traffic jams in the year 2005. By 1997, the

---

[7] Walled communities were those communities that logged traffic in and out to control access to the facility within the secured area (e.g., apartment complexes, specific neighborhoods within larger cities, country clubs, military installations, corporate R&D labs).

Clinton administration was expected to announce legislation aimed at revamping federal road spending. This legislation in part would allow states to charge new tolls on existing interstate highways.

The U.S. Intelligent Vehicles and Highway Systems was a public–private research project with the objective of improving the U.S. road-based transportation system. The key IVHS products and services were transportation management, traveler information systems, productivity enhancements, and safety and driver assistance. The overall market for IVHS technologies was estimated to total US$210 billion from 1992 through 2011. However, estimates were that more than US$450 billion would be spent during this time period for R&D and test development. IVHS American was the nonprofit, scientific organization serving as the IVHS advisor to the U.S. Department of Transportation.

There were several foreign programs similar to the IVHS. The Program for European Traffic with Highest Efficiency and Unprecedented Safety (Prometheus) was a safety research project supported by the automotive companies in Europe and 50 research institutes. Japan had its Road Automotive Communications Systems and the Advanced Mobile Traffic Information System. At least 400,000 cars in Japan had navigation systems in place. In England, Trafficmaster was used to notify drivers of accidents, construction problems, or other traffic delays. Additionally, the European DRIVE (Dedicated Road Infrastructure for Vehicle Safety in Europe) project had 70 initiatives directed toward integrating the road transport environment. Amtech was working with Integra Ingenieria to install Amtech's IVHS system in the close to 200 toll road lanes in Mexico.

Through the development, testing, and deployment of advanced electronics using computers, communication, positioning, and automation technologies, IVHS contained five applications: advanced traffic management systems (ATMS), advanced traveler information systems (ATIS), advanced vehicle control systems (AVCS), advanced public transportation systems (APTS), and commercial vehicle operations (CVO). (These applications are described in the case appendix.)

Sales

Amtech sales were US$59,424,000 in 1993 and US$61,457,000 in 1994. Shipments to the rail industry decreased from US$33,438,000 in 1993 to US$30,506,000 in 1994. This was primarily due to a substantial completion of tag deliveries for the implementation of the Association of American Railroads mandated standard (and expectations were for a close to 75 percent drop as the project wound down in 1995). At the same time, research and development almost doubled (US$1.8 million in 1993 to US$3 million in 1994).

In 1992, Amtech had four major customers who accounted for 21, 13, 12, and 10 percent of sales, respectively. The company had two major customers accounting for 25 and 14 percent of sales in 1993, and two major customers in 1994 accounting for 21 and 13 percent of sales. Export sales declined from US$14 million in 1993 to US$12 million in 1994.

Prices for both the railway and electronic tolls started at US$2,600. Prices varied depending upon the customer's specifications. The tags for both systems ranged from US$18 to US$250 each, with the price dependent upon the sophistication of the tag. The US$18 tag, typically used for gate access applications, complemented the US$2,600 system and was the least sophisticated tag. The US$250 tag was almost like a minicomputer. However, most tag sales were in the US$35 to $60 range.

EXHIBIT 4   IVHS/ATMS Toll Collection Process

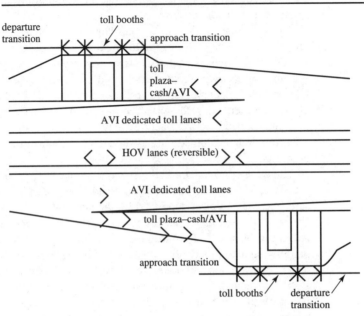

AVI dedicated lanes allow nonstop, high-speed passage, while patrons of the conventional toll plaza exit the main line to a parallel roadway to pay.

The electronic toll systems were sold to the toll authorities. These toll authorities then leased tags to patrons at tag stores owned by the toll authority. At the tag store, the patron opened an account for tag usage and received a tag. When the tag was used (i.e., went through a toll booth), the toll charge was deducted from the patron's account.

The IVHS market at Amtech was almost synonymous with automated toll plazas. (Exhibit 4 diagrams a toll area using IVHS/ATMS technology.) Amtech expected an increased number of toll roads in the future. This was based on the belief that the federal and state governments would not have the money to continue funding road construction at the demanded level. Both the North Dallas Tollway and the entire Oklahoma turnpike system used Amtech technology. Oklahoma's 561-mile system resulted in the purchase of more than 100,000 transporter tags. The North Dallas Tollway, with 15,000 issued tags, had been the largest in terms of number of transponders prior to the Oklahoma project. Amtech also operated its toll systems in parts of Louisiana and Georgia in the United States and in Mexico, France, Spain, and the United Kingdom. U.S. toll road agencies expected to decide upon IVHS technology included one in California and a group of seven toll road agencies in the Northeast serving New York, New Jersey, and Pennsylvania.

The toll tags, scanners, and related equipment market was expected to total US$5 to US$10 billion by the year 2000. Most of the systems would be sold in Europe and the Far East, where toll roads were more common than in the United States.

Amtech had received a major boost when the Association of American Railroads gave final approval for automatic equipment identification (AEI). This US$100 million revenue opportunity required that all 1.4 million rail freight cars in interchange service have identification tags (two tags per car) compatible with Amtech technology by the beginning of 1995.

The first international, intermodal carrier to begin outfitting its container fleet with AEI was American President Companies. American President expected to invest US$15 to $20 million in the installation of Amtech AEI tags on its domestic and international fleet and reader systems at 130 facilities in North America, Asia, and the Middle East.[8]

Amtech's Canadian distributor was working on a joint effort with a Canadian carrier, Sultran, to adapt the company's AEI technology to Sultran's requirements. A highly specialized company, Sultran moved 5 million tons of dry formed sulphur for 22 owners. The company worked from 17 origins feeding into two terminals in Vancouver. Sultran owned or leased over 1,500 freight cars.

Also in the AEI market, truckload carrier J.B. Hunt began installing Amtech tags in its 5,800-unit tractor fleet in 1992. The installation would allow J.B. Hunt rigs to participate in the New Mexico Port of Entry inspection bypass and weigh-in-motion program. The system also allowed the rigs to participate in the Oklahoma Turnpike automatic toll system (IVHS).

Competition

The IVHS market was not lacking in competitors for Amtech. Many large companies from the cutback-ridden defense industry and several key members of the Fortune 500 were entering the IVHS market. As well, several alliances were formed that contributed to the strength of even the already powerful companies. Examples of such ventures included alliances between American Telephone & Telegraph (AT&T) and Mark IV Industries, between Lockheed and AT&T, and between Texas Instruments and MFS Network Technologies.

Regarding *electronic tolls,* Mark IV Industries Inc. (an Amherst, New York, maker of electronic industrial equipment) and AT&T had formed a joint venture to compete in this market. The venture was thought to be a strong competitor for Amtech for seven toll road agencies' contracts in the Northeast. Other entrants in this market included General Motors Corp.'s Hughes Aircraft unit and AT/Comm Inc. (a hardware and software system supplier distributing its equipment either directly to the end user or through contractors such as Westinghouse, Cubic Corp. and Kiewit Technologies). Both Hughes and AT/Comm were competing for the $2 million system that would eliminate weigh station waits along Interstate 75 between Florida and Ontario, Canada. Additionally, Rockwell International had announced its intention to focus upon new markets in automated road and public transportation systems.

In other areas, Lockheed Corp. (a company already involved in electronic toll collection systems in some states) and AT&T had joined to create new *traffic-management systems.* Hughes, Westinghouse, and TRW were hoping to supply everything from *digital maps to collision-avoidance radars.* Texas Instruments and the MFS Network Technologies subsidiary of Peter Kiewit Sons' Inc. had signed a co-development agreement to *integrate telecommunications and highway systems.* Etak Inc. (a Menlo Park, California, company which made digital maps for navigation systems) was working on *electronic yellow pages for car computers.* As well, the three major U.S. auto manufacturers were entering the competition by bidding on a federally sponsored automated-highway test project. (Exhibit 5 lists these competitors.)

In the AEI market, Amtech was the only company producing equipment that met the Association of American Railroads' mandated standard. The American Trucking

---

[8] This included containers, chassis, tractors, railcars, and other equipment.

EXHIBIT 5   IVHS Competitors

Mark IV Industries Inc. and American Telephone & Telegraph (AT&T)
General Motors Corp.'s Hughes Aircraft unit
AT/Comm Inc.
   electronic toll market

Rockwell International
   new markets in road and public transportation system
   (also involved in the FAST-TRAC project)

Lockheed Corp. and AT&T
   traffic management systems

Hughes
Westinghouse
TRW
   everything from digital maps to collision-avoidance radars

Texas Instruments and MFS Network Technologies
   work toward integrating telecommunications and highway systems

Etak Inc.
   electronic yellow pages for car computers

General Motors, Ford, Chrysler
   federally sponsored automated-highway test project
   (GM was a sponsor in the TravTek project.)

Association was studying the railroad's standardization effort. The group was working with the railroads and maritime shippers to ensure that all could agree upon a standard that trucking, rail, and maritime could use for intermodal purposes.

The Situation

By the beginning of 1995, Amtech had amassed US$50 million in cash and marketable securities with no long-term debt. While CEO G. Russell Mortenson claimed to "have no itch to spend" the money, shareholder pressure was mounting for the company to identify its future direction. Market studies confirmed the potential for the AEI and IVHS markets. However, it was becoming more and more clear that many of the foreseen markets were not growing and/or mature enough to provide a steady/growing revenue stream for the company. Such a revenue stream was necessary for enhancing shareholder value in both the short and long terms. Mr. Mortenson knew that he was responsible for directing the company toward the right markets.

Appendix A–1
IVHS Applications

Advanced Traffic Management Systems (ATMS). ATMS comprised methods for integrating the management of various roadway functions. These functions included freeway surveillance and incident detection, changeable message signs, electronic toll collection, and the coordination of traffic signal timing over wide areas in response to real-time conditions. Additionally, real-time data from ATMS could be used as input to the ATIS.

Combining ATMS and advanced traveler information systems (ATIS), FAST-TRAC involved coordinating 1,000 intersections in Oakland County, Michigan.[9] Infrared beacons were used to provide real-time traffic and route guidance information. And, electronic toll collection was a growing trend in the ATMS realm of activity, with systems in Texas, Oklahoma, and the northeastern United States. (The case's Exhibit 4 diagrams a toll area using ATMS technology.)

System operators in Canada, using ATMS technology, monitored traffic flow via sensors or detectors embedded in the pavement and television cameras installed along highways. The central computers continuously ran an incident detection algorithm. When the computer alarm indicated a problem, the operator analyzed the situation via the computer readings. The system allowed operators to control road signs to inform motorists of problem areas.

A growing trend in the ATMS segment of IVHS was the adoption of regional technology specifications. In 1992, California set a statewide specification for the technology (modulated-backscatter technology) to be used in electronic toll collection. Another regional trend was the formation of toll agency coalitions which selected a technology for a specific region/area (e.g., seven toll agencies in the northeastern United States).

Advanced Traveler Information Systems (ATIS). ATIS was a system designed to aid the individual driver. An ATIS system could assist the private vehicle or public transit in reaching specific destinations without encountering long traffic delays. Recommended routes would be adjusted via the on-board navigation system, based on input from the ATMS regarding accident locations, weather conditions, road conditions, and/or lane restrictions.

"TravTek" and "ADVANCE" were ATIS research projects.[10] TravTek involved 100 Oldsmobile Toronados in the Orlando, Florida, area equipped with a communications system for receiving traffic data and conveying vehicle information, as well as an onboard computer loaded with Orlando-area tourist information. ADVANCE, evaluated in the Chicago, Illinois, area, involved 5,000 vehicles equipped with navigation and

---

[9] Rockwell International designed the traffic operations center for FAST-TRAC.

[10] TravTek was sponsored by General Motors, the Federal Highway Administration, the Automobile Association of America, the Florida Transportation Department, and the city of Orlando. The Federal Highway Administration, the Illinois Department of Transportation, and Motorola were sponsors of ADVANCE.

route guidance systems that provided real-time traffic information to a traffic information center.

Advanced Vehicle Control Systems (AVCS).   AVCS was created to assist drivers with vehicle control. This would help avoid accidents and could lead, ultimately, to fully automated chauffeuring capabilities. Inventions in this area included the antilock braking system, collision warning devices, and intelligent cruise controls that would automatically adjust speed according to distance and speed of the vehicle being followed.

Antilock braking systems were available in some automobiles. Other AVCS programs were to be developed in three stages over the 1992–2011 time period: (1) advice and warning systems, (2) support systems, and (3) automatic control systems.

Advanced Public Transportation Systems (APTS).   APTS was aimed at users of high-occupancy vehicles such as car pools and transit buses. A key behind APTS was the lack of exchange of cash. Such usage would allow consumers to board transit vehicles without paying cash. Additionally, APTS was designed to allow transit vehicles to pay tolls and parking fees without cash. ATIS was a part of the APTS system as well.

Commercial Vehicle Operations (CVO).   The CVO system was designed for commercial vehicle fleets. CVO would eliminate truck stoppage for weight measurements or state border inspections. As well, automated vehicle identification systems would allow automated toll collection for fleets, and automated vehicle location systems would allow dispatchers to locate vehicles immediately.

CVO programs included trucks equipped with electronic locator systems and two-way digital satellite communications systems that linked drivers and dispatchers and trucks traveling the Interstate 75 corridor from Florida to Ontario, Canada, equipped with transponders that allowed them to bypass weigh stations and state border inspection stations.

Sources

Amtech Annual Reports.

"Amtech Corporation Reports First Quarter Results and the Formation of a Joint Venture in the People's Republic of China." *Southwest Newswire,* May 12, 1995.

Amtech NonStops News, Fall 1996.

"Amtech's Earnings Up, 1995 Looks So-So." *Advanced Transportation Technology News,* March 1995.

"APC Will Equip Its Fleet with AEI." *Railway Age,* April 1993, p. 25.

"Automatic Equipment Identification—A Rail Industry Quality Improvement Program." July 1991, pp. 1–17.

Bary, Andrew. "Not-So-Fast-Lane; A Few Potholes for Maker of High-Tech Toll Device." *Barron's,* December 7, 1992, pp. 22–28.

Bergoffen, Gene S. "A New Agenda for Private Fleets." *Transportation & Distribution,* April 1991, pp. T4–T8.

Carey, Patricia M. "The Top 100 Fastest-Growing International Companies." *International Business,* December 1991, pp. 35–48.

Clark, Kim. "How to Make Traffic Jams a Thing of the Past." *Fortune,* March 31, 1997, p. 34.

Cullen, David. "Traveling the Electronic Road." *Fleet Owner,* February 1993, pp. 38–42.

Desmond, Paul. "Advanced Networks Keep Freight Industry Moving." *Network World,* August 14, 1989, pp. 1, 26–30, 34.

Eaton, Leslie. "Know Your Stocks." *Barron's,* September 28, 1992, pp. 12–14.

French, Robert. "Transportation Comes of Age." *American City & County,* December 1992, p. 10.

Gerlin, Andrea. "Amtech, a Hot Technology Stock, Encounters Glitches." *Boston Globe,* June 22, 1993.

Gerlin, Andrea. "Mark IV's Toll Plan Is Backed; Amtech's Stock Falls 34.2%." *Boston Globe,* March 22, 1994.

Hartje, Ronald L. "Tomorrow's Toll Road." *Civil Engineering,* February 1991, pp. 60–61.

Herst, Eric R. "AEI Adds Accuracy to JIT Logistics." *Global Trade & Transportation,* November 1993, p. 58.

Koelper, Jim A. "Railroad Streamlines Operation with CTI and IVR." *Communication News,* January 1994, pp. 25–27.

Mathews, Anna Wilde. "New Gadgets Trace Truckers' Every Move." *The Wall Street Journal,* July 14, 1997, p. B1.

"Network with Shortlines." *Transportation & Distribution,* January 1993, p. 15.

Nomani, Asra Q. "White House to Announce Transit Bill." *The Wall Street Journal,* March 12, 1997, p. A3.

"Officers Know Who's Coming with Auto ID." *Security,* September 1992, p. 20–21.

"One Mystery, No Panic." *Railway Age,* August 1992, pp. 91–93.

Oppel, Richard. "Amtech Shareholders May Push for Changes." *The Dallas Morning News,* December 19, 1994, p. 1D.

Ridings, Richard L., and Quinn, Stephen. "Life in the Fast Track." *Civil Engineering,* April 1992, pp. 46–49.

Riley, Kristyn. "Selling Automation to Toll Collectors." *New England Business,* April 1992, pp. 44–45.

Rourke, John. "Radio That Can Read—And Write." *Communications,* December 1992, pp. 24–25.

Sager, Ira. "The Great Equalizer." *Business Week: The Information Revolution 1994,* pp. 100–7.

Schine, Eric. "Here Comes the Thinking Car." *Business Week,* May 25, 1992, pp. 84, 87.

"Selling Automation to Toll Collectors." *New England Business,* April 1992, pp. 44–45.

Sheeline, William E. "Ten Ways to Bet Your Mad Money." *Fortune 1993 Investor's Guide,* pp. 72–76.

"Smart Highways . . . Slow Governments." *Distribution,* December 1993, pp. 18, 20.

Studt, Tim. "Smart Vehicles, Smart Highways Roaring down the Pike." *R&D Magazine,* October 25, 1993, pp. 14–18.

Sullivan, R. Lee. "Fast Lane." *Forbes,* July 4, 1994, pp. 112, 114.

"Tags Hold Data and a Glimpse of the Future." *Distribution,* May 1993, p. 16.

Weber, James. "Ministry Turns to Visuals in Attempt to Help Motorists." *Computing Canada,* April 25, 1991, pp. 17–18.

Wexler, Joanie M. "Conrail Revamps Architectures." *Computerworld,* May 25, 1992, p. 6.

Zipser, Andy. "Positive Identification." *Barron's,* December 2, 1991.

Zipser, Andy. "Watch the Steak, Not the Sizzle." *Barron's,* November 8, 1993.

In the early summer of 1994, Walter Düring, manager and owner of Düring AG, faced one of the toughest challenges of his career. Within three years of patenting the Fottle, Düring's latest development in liquid packaging, he had contributed to its licensing by over 30 leading detergent producers across Europe. Düring's challenge now was to replicate this successful market entry in the much larger and potentially more lucrative noncarbonated beverages market.

The Fottle is an easily foldable plastic bottle that uses less materials than most plastic bottles and, due to its foldability, less landfill space in garbage dumps. Its concept appealed to a growing number of detergent producers concerned with ecological and economical packaging. In 1994, the Fottle counted among its licensees major branded consumer goods giants such as S.C. Johnson & Son and Colgate-Palmolive. Nevertheless, the beverage market was considered very different from the detergent market in terms of the production environment, the competition, and the promotional strategy and pricing policy that would be required.

Düring was encouraged by the fact that an increasing number of European liquid milk producers had already switched to plastic as an alternative to carton packaging. This was the case in markets such as Switzerland where ecological awareness was strong,[1] but also in larger and more competitive markets such as France where product differentiation and innovation were crucial to market leadership. With this in mind, Düring was considering the French liquid milk market as a point of entry for the Fottle in beverage packaging. In this market, the Fottle would compete against the currently dominant carton packaging used for most liquid milk products.

Depending on the market segments targeted, the Fottle had to communicate to varying degrees the benefits of cost reduction, ecological soundness, differentiation through design, and convenience of production and use. In this respect, Düring needed to decide on a segmentation of dairy corporations, or attempt to market the Fottle in an undifferentiated manner to all dairy producers. Obviously, such segmentation also had implications for how Düring would define its offering and the positioning of this offering in the market.

Düring AG: Four Decades of Innovation

Zurich-based Düring AG was founded in 1951 when Maria Düring-Keller, a Swiss entrepreneur, developed a ready-to-use descaler.[2] Her own experience as a housewife made her realize the difficulty of manually removing calcium residuals from utensils. Maria began by producing small batches of her descaler in her garage. This was sold,

---

[1] Durisch, Guido and Johansen, Ragnvald. "Andere Laender—Andere Praeferenzen," *Pack Aktuell*, October 15, 1994, pp. 14–29.

[2] Descalers are acids that dissolve calcium residuals contained in tap water.

This case was prepared by Niraj Dawar, assistant professor, and Carlo Mobayed, research associate at INSEAD. It is intended to be used as a basis for class discussion rather than to illustrate either effective or ineffective handling of an administrative situation.

under the brand name Durgol, directly to institutional users such as schools, businesses, factories, and drugstores.

In 1963, Düring AG was incorporated and Maria's son Walter grew the business by extending the customer base to private households, still supplied exclusively through drugstores. Walter also actively invested in the development of new products. Some met with little success, but others such as a toilet cleaning detergent with descaling properties and a descaler for metal surface treatment opened new markets. In 1973, Düring AG sought new distribution channels as sales through drugstores became sluggish. The move allowed Düring AG to establish itself through large retailers as the undisputed market leader in Switzerland for descalers and toilet cleaning detergents. Partnerships with companies in other European countries and the development of new products for toilet maintenance led to further expansion.

In 1980, Walter Düring invented the "Toilet Duck," a detergent whose revolutionary bottle design offered the potential for global-scale marketing (Exhibit 1). Through licensing agreements with consumer companies, the largest of which is S.C. Johnson & Son., Düring AG products gained a strong presence in over 40 countries.

Düring AG, rather than focus on production, concentrated on worldwide marketing of its ideas and patents, mainly in the field of packaging solutions. It had an obsession with remaining small and nimble. In 1994, Düring AG had fewer than 40 employees and defined itself as an "ideas" company.

The Fottle®

The Fottle® is a very thin walled plastic bottle produced by extrusion blow-molding.[3] It was originally developed as a refill package for Toilet Duck, but soon proved useful as a regular bottle for a wide range of products. The Fottle base can be hexagonal, square, round, or oval, with sizes ranging from 20 cl to 3 liters. When empty, the Fottle can be easily folded down to 10 percent of its original volume due to its patented design. The special geometry of the bottom allows for a uniform distribution of the blown material, making it easily foldable.

In their drive for cost saving and ecological packaging, many large consumer goods companies in the late 1980s had introduced lightweight refill packs for detergents which were sold alongside original products. Refill packs, however, presented two major problems. First, they were often more expensive to produce than the original pack; and second, retailers could often not afford to offer enough shelf space to accommodate both the refill and original pack. The idea behind the Fottle was to resolve both problems. The Fottle was less expensive to produce, providing both the functionality of an original pack and the ecological soundness of a refill pack. The Fottle provided consumers with the convenience of use through a bottle-shaped, rigid package that still could be collapsed. (Exhibit 2 gives the weight of the Fottle versus other packages.)

PE (polyethylene) and PP (polypropylene), the raw materials of the Fottle, were some of the most commonly used and easily available plastic packaging raw materials. They did not, however, have the characteristics of traditional PVC[4] or the newer PET[5] packages, such as stiffness and transparency.

The packaging of food is subject to stricter regulations than the packaging of

---

[3] A heated plastic tube is "blown" through air pressure against the inner walls of a mold.

[4] PVC, polyvinyl-chloride, is the most commonly used plastic material for bottling still mineral water.

[5] PET, polyethylene-terephtalat, competes with glass for the bottling of fizzy soft drinks and mineral water.

EXHIBIT 1   Toilet Duck and Fottle Refill

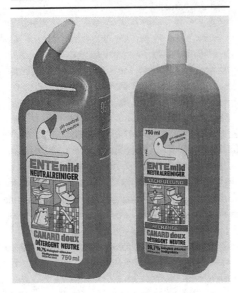

nonfood items. The sensitivity of food to humidity, external odors, and UV light raises additional requirements on packaging. Düring surveyed European regulations concerning the packaging of various noncarbonated beverages and concluded that the Fottle could definitely be used for liquid milk, yogurt drinks, juices, and nectars. At about the same time, ELF-Atochem introduced on the market a new quality of PP that could potentially be used for the Fottle.[6] The new PP could further improve the Fottle's transparency and barrier properties to external odors, and increase its chances of being used as an alternative to traditional plastic materials such as PET or PVC. However, for now the Fottle could serve most noncarbonated, still drinks and focus on the liquid milk market in France.

The French Market for Liquid Milk

In 1994, France was the third largest producer of liquid milk in Europe. As in the rest of Europe, milk production in France had been growing only marginally over the past decade and had in fact declined in 1992 (Exhibit 3). Consumption was, however, expected to expand in coming years due to a number of factors. One was the forecasted end of a three-year recession in the processed food market toward which dairy products had a substantial contribution. Another was the French market trend toward higher-value light and fresh food products. A variety of new specialty milk drinks enriched with vitamins and flavoring for niche markets such as newborns and pregnant mothers were introduced. Some leading innovative brands, such as Candia's Viva, Grand Vivre, and Lactel's Eveil, underlined national brand producers' drive to reposition milk as a high-value drink, not just for children and youngsters, but also for adults. Packaged in both carton and plastic bottles, Viva dominated about 80 percent of

---

[6] ELF-Atochem, a subsidiary of France's largest oil company, ELF, was one of Europe's largest producers of plastic polymers in 1994.

EXHIBIT 2 **Packaging Weights, 1993**

Type of Packaging	Bottle Volume (ml)	Bottle Material	Total Weight (g)
Fottle	1,000	PE coextruded	26
Biona	1,000	PE white	45.9
GF Multiblow	1,000	PE white	37.5
Schwyzer Milchhuus (CH)	1,000	PE white	38.2
Paturages de France	1,000	PE transparent	34.9
Candia	1,000	PE transparent	39.8
Candia	1,500	PE transparent	51.83*
Lactel	1,500	PE transparent	66.6
Yovol	1,000	PE transparent	33.4
Candia	1,000	PE transparent	34.8
Continent	1,000	PE transparent	37.6
Gervais	1,000	PE transparent	34.06*
Desserta Berghof (A)	1,000	Polycarb.	83.9
Fuchs etc. (CH)	1,000	Polycarb.	75.20*
Plastic Pouch	1,000	PE transparent	8
Conventional plastic bottle	1,000	PE transparent	37
Carton box	1,000	Carton laminated	32

*Cap not included.

the specialty milk segment (*lait élaboré*). The declining consumption of milk in terms of volume had prompted dairy producers to reposition milk from a nutritional necessity for children to a healthy drink for adults. Another factor related to the increased consumption of cereals in France, through which milk was gaining acceptance as an ingredient of the French breakfast culture.

Liquid milk products could be divided into several subcategories. Long conservation (so-called UHT milk) had a shelf life of up to three months.[7] Most flavored milk drinks were UHT. Pasteurized or fresh milk had a shorter shelf life (seven days). Despite indications of consumption trends toward fresh dairy products, UHT still dominated the market due primarily to its convenience and long storage life (Exhibit 4). Fresh pasteurized milk was not favored by large retailers due to its shorter shelf life and more complex storage requirements. The growing demand for half-creamed milk reflected consumers' increased preference for milk with lower fat content versus richer, tastier milk (Exhibit 5).

If the image of milk was to become less that of a nutritional necessity for children and more that of a beverage, Düring believed that bottle-shaped packaging design would become increasingly important. At about this time, TetraPak, the largest supplier of brick-shaped packaging, had made an acquisition of plastic packaging technologies for markets where its share had been eroding to the advantage of plastics.[8]

Players in the French Milk Industry. The French milk industry marketed three types of brands: national brands, private labels, and the *premiers prix* (discount brands).

---

[7] UHT-milk stands for milk processed at ultrahigh temperature.

[8] Johansen, Ragnvald, "Tetra Pak stieg ins PE-Milchbeutelgeschäft ein," *Pack Aktuell,* Sept. 1, 1994, pp. 1–6. Also "Einstieg der Tetra Pak in das PET-Geschäft," *Neue Zürcher Zeitung,* Oct. 7, 1994, p. 23.

EXHIBIT 3   Production of Liquid Milk in the European Union, 1982–92

Billions of liters

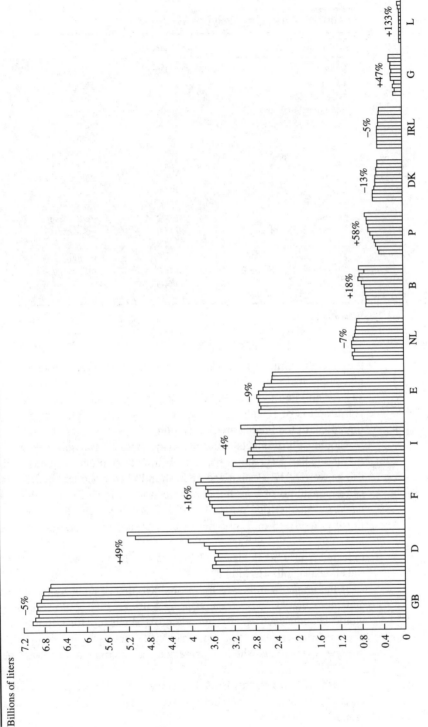

Source: Syndilait, from Eurostat.

Exhibit 4   **Evolution of Conditioned Liquid Milk's Market Shares, 1983–93**

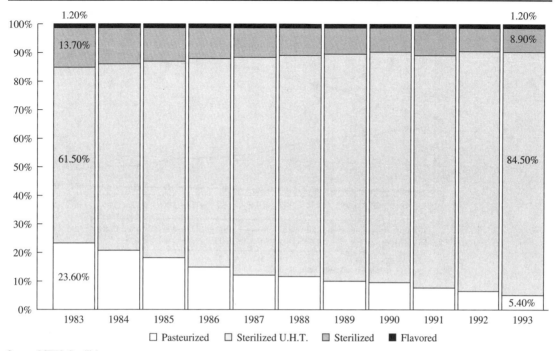

Source: SCEES, Syndilait.

For national brands, the market was dominated by Sodiaal and Besnier, which together accounted for about 42 percent of total FF (French franc) sales (Exhibit 6). Sodiaal was the umbrella brand for various products and producers. Its leading brands, Candia and Yoplait, were supported by heavy communication campaigns throughout Europe (e.g., Sponsorship of Winter Olympics 1992). Promotional expenditures in the industry were evaluated at FF14 million annually. Both brands projected a fitness image. Besnier operated in a wide variety of milk markets in France as well as in other European countries. Lactel was its best known brand. Compagnie Laitiere Européenne was the third largest dairy company in France.[9] It grouped together a number of cooperatives of producers in the Northwest. Its best known brand was Elle & Vire.

Producers of national brands concentrated on differentiated products and the building of strong brands. The rest of the market was shared between private labels and *premiers prix*. Private labels were exclusively distributed through owner retailer chains such as Groupe Intermarché and Leclerc. *Premiers prix* were sold by hard discounters who often subcontracted the filling of largely discounted milk production to small regional producers. With lower production costs and a competitive pricing policy favored by the sourcing of discounted milk, *premiers prix* were gaining a significant market, largely at the expense of private labels.

In 1991, in response to declining market share, private labels introduced plastic bottling of milk in addition to the already existing carton package. Product differentiation was clearly becoming the main competitive driver as French consumers enjoyed a

---

[9] In 1994 Compagnie Laitiere Européenne was in the process of being acquired by Bongrain, another large milk products company.

EXHIBIT 5   **Market Share Evolution of Liquid Conditioned Milk by Fat Content, 1980–92**

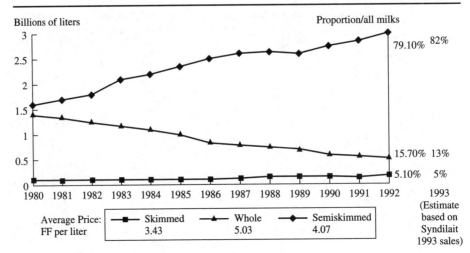

Billions of liters   Proportion/all milks

| Average Price: FF per liter | ■ Skimmed 3.43 | ▲ Whole 5.03 | ◆ Semiskimmed 4.07 |

1993 (Estimate based on Syndilait 1993 sales)

79.10% 82%
15.70% 13%
5.10% 5%

Source: SCEES, industry interviews, February 1995.

EXHIBIT 6   **Brand Value and Volume of Milk Sold through Mass Distribution in France, 1993**

Brand	Value in FF (millions)	Volume in Liters (millions)	% of Total Value	% of Total Volume
Premiers Prix	3,886	1,173	31%	39%
Candia	3,899	720	32	24
Private labels	2,673	696	22	23
Lactel	1,176	225	10	8
Other brands	408	105	3	4
Gervais & Nactalia[1]	334	81	3	3
Base of panel in millions	12,376	3,000		

[1] In 1994, BSN-Danone, owner of the Gervais brand, acquired Nactalia. Taken together, Gervais–Nactalia became France's third largest national brand.

greater variety of milk drinks than any other consumers in Europe. Innovation was the distinctive strength of large national brand producers. The three largest milk conditioning firms produced over 2,600 million liters of conditioned milk in 1994. They outspent their competitors on research, product development, and advertising. (Exhibits 5 and 7 show average milk prices.) Regional, medium-sized dairy producers supplied most of their milk to private labels and averaged an annual production capacity of around 70 million liters (Exhibit 8). One of the largest in this category was Laiterie St-Père, which produced about 200 million liters annually and allocated most of its capacity to the Intermarché retailing group. Many felt the pressures of the escalating price war between large French retail chains and hard discounters. Hard discounters had gained market share with lower prices during the 1991–94 recession. The main losers of the price battle were the many small to medium-size milk producers whose sales margins shrank dramatically. The full utilization of their packaging capacity of

EXHIBIT 7   **Cost Structure of Liquid Milk Industry**

	Carton			Plastics		Fottle
	National	*Private Labels*	*Discount Brands*	*National*	*Private Labels*	
Avg. retail price of 1 liter	4.76	3.76	3.31	5.89	4.64	—
VAT	0.25	0.20	0.17	0.31	0.24	—
Margin of distributor	1.65	0.77	0.37	2.14	1.00	—
Total unit cost to distributor	2.86	2.79	2.77	3.44	3.4	—
Distribution and transport. costs	0.35	0.35	0.35	0.44	0.44	0.35
Margin of producer	0.13	0.06	0.04	0.2	0.16	
Total unit cost to producer	2.38	2.38	2.38	2.8	2.8	2.26
Cost of pack	0.58	0.58	0.58	0.8	0.8	0.5

Note: Numbers are disguised.

EXHIBIT 8   **Contribution of Conditioning Firms to Brands and Retail Channels**

Capacity in Millions of Liters	*Number of Firms*	*National Brands*	*Private Labels*	*Discount Brands*	*Export Small Retailing*	*Total Vol. Produced*
Cedilac–Candia		720	90	180	110	1100
Besnier–Lactel		225	208	417	0	850
Gervais & Nactalia		81	190	379	50	700
> 50	8	95	198	110	160	563
> 10, < 50	48	10	10	87	880	987
Total		1,131	696	1,173	1,200	4,200

Source: *Official Journal of European Community,* August 9, 1994, and industry interviews, February 1995.

almost exclusively carton systems became key to their financial survival since most had leasing arrangements for their carton-based machinery. Small dairy producers often balanced the capacity of their carton packaging line by filling packs of milk or juice for retailers' private brands.

Sales levels of national brands were maintained mainly through numerous product innovations, in terms of both content and packaging. While continued innovation from the producers would contribute to growth, it was expected that growth would also come from changing consumption habits of consumers (e.g., breakfast cereals and adult consumption).[10]

Packaging Materials.   In 1993, France led Europe in the use of plastic packaging for milk. With over 18 percent of liquid milk sold in plastic bottles, France was also leading a Europewide trend away from the still-dominant brick-shaped carton, as Exhibit 9 shows.

One reason for the increased use of plastics was large dairy producers' attempt since 1986 to diversify their supply of packaging material and technology. Their goal was to gain some degree of freedom from market-dominant carton packaging suppliers in the choice and cost of materials.

[10] *Marketing in Europe,* Economist Intelligence Unit, Oct. 1993.

Exhibit 9   Packaging Materials Used for Milk Retailing
in Different Countries in Europe, 1993

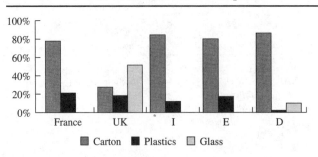

Glass and plastic bottles had been withdrawn from the French market in the 1970s after rapid loss of market share. This loss had been driven by the success of carton packaging, which offered greater convenience, reliability, and economy to both producers and retailers. Plastic packaging was revived in 1986 by Sodiaal, Europe's largest producer of conditioned milk, with the launch of a 1.5-liter plastic jug of UHT milk. The introduction of milk in a plastic bottle, an innovative differentiation, allowed Candia, Sodiaal's leading brand, to regain market share in a stagnant market with tough competition from private labels and hard discounters. (See Exhibits 6 and 10.) This introduction provided evidence that differentiation through packaging was a key factor in this market. While carton packaging carried an image of economy, national brands were able to gradually capitalize on the more convenient plastic bottle to capture high-value, premium milk segments. Despite Sodiaal's move in 1986, followed by other national brands in 1988, private labels and regional producers maintained carton packaging until 1991, when a continuous sharp decline in their market share prompted them to follow suit.

In Düring's view, a reliable, inexpensive bottling system such as the Fottle could be attractive for the dairy industry, where small gains in margins per unit were crucial. Nevertheless, he realized that the brick-shaped carton packages did have a competitive cost structure relative to traditional plastic bottles (Exhibit 7). Düring's challenge also lay in the fact that carton packaged milk was still strongly embedded in consumers' purchasing behavior. Distributors and retailers had to be convinced that the Fottle's benefits such as weight, design, and ecological performance could outweigh the storage and transportation advantages offered by the brick.

Dairy producers in France also faced increased price competition from cheaper East European imports, which had gained market share in recent years and stood at 2 percent of the market. Through increased spending on advertising, large producers were clearly aiming for differentiation through high-value branded products. Exhibit 11 shows the packaging-product situation in 1993.

UHT volume increased steadily between 1987 and 1993 at the expense of pasteurized and sterilized milk (Exhibit 4). In late 1993, Sodiaal followed the example of soft drink manufacturers by introducing "single-shot" plastic bottles of 50 cl. The introduction of the first six-pack of milk in Europe met with great success.[11] It also confirmed forecasts that adults would be drinking milk as a nutritious alternative to soft drinks. These developments in the French milk market prompted Walter Düring to consider France as a potential entry point for the Fottle.

---

[11] Company literature.

Exhibit 10   Top 10 Companies' Turnover in FF and Liters of Milk Transformed

Company (Brands)	Million FF	Billion Liters[1]
Besnier (Lactel, Bridel, Roquefort Société, Unicolait)	19,158	4.11
Sodiaal (Yoplait, Candia, Yop)	17,500	2.50
CLE[2] (Elle & Vire)	10,990	
Bongrain (Bresse Bleue, Grieges)	9,706	1.20
Fromageries BEL (BabyBel)	7,107	
BSN–Danone (Danone, Gervais, Nactalia, Eurial)	6,713	0.62
Nestlé (Chambourcy)	5,900	0.85
Groupe Entremont	4,000	
Groupe Laita	3,900	0.98
3A	3,539	0.56

[1] Includes milk products (cheese, yogurt, etc.).

[2] CLE (Companie Laitiere Europeene) was formerly known as ULN (Union Laitiere Normande).

Exhibit 11   Market Shares and Packaging Trend by Type of Milk

Product	% of Total Market	Carton	Plastic	Packaging Trend
UHT	78.3%	88%	12%	Plastics ↑
Pasteurized	5.8	48	52	Plastics ↑
Sterilized	7.4	66	34	Stable
Flavored	1.3	22	78	Plastics ↑
Specialty	7.2	65	35	Plastics ↑
Total	100%	82%	18%	Plastics ↑

Source: Industry interviews, Paris, June 1994.

Additionally, many producers had successfully introduced a wide range of packages with sizes differing from the one-liter standard. Examples are Candia's six-pack 50-cl bottles, and 1.5-liter plastic jug. This type of innovation in packaging, while commonplace in the highly competitive detergents business that Düring was used to, was just emerging in the milk market.

Packaging Technology

Turnkey solutions for liquid milk were first provided by TetraPak, a Swedish multinational, in the late 1960s and proved to be spectacularly successful. The carton-based packaging employed by TetraPak quickly became the dominant type of package for milk (and later fruit juice and nectars) worldwide. One reason for TetraPak's success was its ability to provide dairy producers with integrated in-house packaging systems that are reliable, inexpensive, and easy to handle. Beverage producers, however, often found themselves dependent on TetraPak's supply of packaging material and know-how. In July 1991, the European Court of Justice imposed on TetraPak the EC's highest fine ever for "abuse of market power and restraint of competition."[12]

---

[12] *Official Journal of European Community,* "Commission decision of 24 July 1991 relating to a proceeding pursuant to Article 86 of the EEC Treaty," Legislation L072, Mar. 18, 1992.

EXHIBIT 12   The Process of Milk Packaging with the Fottle System

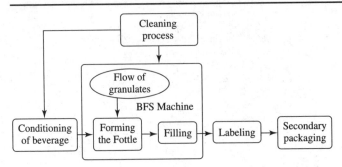

One option for Düring was to introduce the first turnkey solution for plastic bottling on the market. Since Düring AG only provided the know-how on packaging materials and design, it was considering a partnership with technology suppliers who could provide the forming, filling, and sealing technologies for production of the Fottle. While most plastic-based technology could not match the ease and convenience of the turnkey solution proposed by Tetrapak, Düring did find some engineering firms that could integrate the forming, filling, and sealing of the Fottle. (See Exhibit 12.) The integrated process by which this could be achieved was in itself a technical innovation. However, this form–fill–seal technology was not unique to the Fottle and could potentially be used for any PE bottles. The milk producer's investment to acquire such machinery would be equivalent to the cost of acquisition of a carton packaging system.

This solution not only integrated several operations, but also eliminated the need for preproducing empty bottles. Bottles could be simultaneously formed, filled, and sealed in a single operation. Plastics being a commodity, beverage producers could purchase their raw materials at market prices and avoid dependence on a single materials supplier. This process was also less labor-intensive than traditional bottling systems and required less factory space.

A second option for Düring was to license the Fottle directly to dairy producers with the engineering capability of installing Fottle molds on existing bottling lines. While having few competitors in the creation of package designs, Düring's licensing capability was limited to a few large beverage producers that would then have exclusive rights for marketing the Fottle under their own labels. One advantage of this system was that Düring had experience with similar contracts in the detergent business. However, unlike the detergent business (which was heavily dependent on packaging innovation), most milk producers were only now beginning to pay attention to the market value of innovative packaging. Only the largest milk producers had the engineering capability to adapt the Fottle molds to their packaging machinery; most producers subcontracted the handling of the machinery to engineering firms. An average mold would cost Düring approximately FF300,000.

A third option was to license the Fottle directly to engineering firms that provided the bottling technology to beverage producers. Many such firms, being interested in boosting their sales, would consider marketing proprietary packaging designs in addition to their machinery. The Fottle's success would then depend on the market position and future success of these firms. This solution would require the least long-term investment of time and resources on Düring's part. Licensing to engineering companies would be easier if a marketing plan were prepared to demonstrate to these companies that demand existed for the Fottle in France's milk market.

Pricing Policy

Düring was reluctant to consider a price-driven marketing strategy. Price competition in packaging technology could upset the existing transfer pricing equilibrium along the chain of dairy farmers, technology suppliers, milk producers, and retailers with unpredictable consequences. The current pricing structure in the industry had helped technology suppliers and retailers maintain above-average returns, usually at the expense of milk producers battling fierce competition and low margins. Many producers did not survive the extensive consolidation that took place through the 1980s around national producers and small, capacity-driven producers (Exhibit 8).[13] Packaging technology prices to milk producers were structured along three main elements: purchase or leasing of the packaging machinery, maintenance agreements, and sourcing of packaging raw material. If price competition were to be considered, Düring felt that—the first two elements being comparable between the Fottle and its competitors—the Fottle system could potentially outbid the low-priced carton-based packaging on materials to justify the switching costs for producers. In 1994, the average retail price of milk in plastic bottles was higher than for the same milk in carton package. (Exhibit 7 provides data on the estimated cost structures for different packages.) Producers were in fact ambivalent toward carton packaging. While the advantages of efficiency of packaging, transportation, and storage were clear, consumers complained of the carton being messy to open and—once it was opened—of the difficulty of preserving its contents from outside odors. The logistics and transportation of plastic bottles are less efficient than cartons'. The Fottle solution, however, could offset this disadvantage. While offering substantial cost reductions with respect to the existing plastic packaging systems, the Fottle was estimated to save up to 15 percent on materials compared to cartons. Moreover, if Düring opted to provide a turnkey solution to milk producers, the Fottle technology would offer a simplified packaging process, eliminating the need for aseptisation (the cleaning of the package and purchase of preproduced plastic bottles).

Consumer Behavior and the Ecology Factor

While research found over 62 percent of French consumers were aware of environmental problems and in favor of ecological regulations, French public opinion remained divided over the extent to which households should carry the burden of sorting their garbage. Reasons included the space required within the household, particularly in urban areas, to separately dispose of various packaging materials. The majority of consumers favored a more important role by large public utility companies in the sorting of waste.

In 1993, most beverage producers in France had ecology on their agenda due to Europe's increasing number of environmental regulations on packaging. However, they had not yet been proactive in promoting ecological packaging to consumers. Environmental consciousness among producers had gained momentum in 1991 after Germany imposed a hefty tax on beverage producers using nonreturnable packaging. In Switzerland, households were already taxed on the volume of garbage they generated. In France, however, the government's environmental campaign had suffered a serious setback with the onset of one of the nation's toughest recessions in 50 years. Environmental regulations implied high switching costs for beverage producers. For example, mineral water bottlers using PVC, a material already banned in Scandinavia and

---

[13] Most small producers were regional and sold their capacity to large retailers and hard discounters.

German-speaking Europe, were actively seeking and investing in new forms of packaging.[14] The French government's response to the new German-sponsored EU regulations was to launch 14 experimental sites for collecting and recycling packages. Results from these test sites were inconclusive. Further, no clear government agenda that would significantly stiffen the ecological requirements on packaging was in sight for the next three years. Producers also felt that while French consumers were aware of environmental issues, few were ready to adjust their buying behavior accordingly. Producers recognized the importance of the environmental issue due to France's increasing liquid milk and mineral water exports to other European countries.

Environmental concerns were also affecting competitive packaging. Carton packages were laminated with a plastic film and aluminum. Recycling the carton material and the aluminum involved the onerous tasks of separating the various materials and cleaning them before reconversion to raw composites. The Fottle had the advantage of being entirely manufactured of one material, PE, the same used for laminating carton. In contrast to aluminum, carton, and PET, however, PE was only recycled for limited use, such as piping.[15] However, PE was one of the cheapest raw plastic commodities and presented no environmental side effects during incineration.[16]

In 1991, carton technology suppliers TetraPak and PKL reacted to an increasing share of plastics and glass packaging by introducing a plastic lid meant to improve the convenience of opening and pouring the drink out of a carton.[17] As a result, carton packages became costlier to produce and recycle due to the increased amount of plastics in them. Also, as the use of plastics in a carton package became more obvious to the consumer, the long-advocated argument for carton as a "natural" substitute to plastics became less credible.

Furthermore, Europe was still divided as to whether one-way or returnable packages for drinks such as milk were more environmentally sound. Opinions were split as to whether recycling programs such as the German "Duales System," which involved the recovery of composite packaging materials, offered a more ecological solution than incineration. Some studies argued that recycling through energy recovery (incineration) was more ecological in the case of most one-way packages. Using either method, however, recycling complex packages such as layered cartons was found to be costlier than monomaterial packages such as polyethylene plastic bottles.[18]

The Future

With 9 to 14 years (depending on the country) left on the patent of the Fottle, there was a pressing need for Düring to capture as large a market share as feasible. In the short term, faced with the challenge of introducing the Fottle into the French milk market, Walter Düring needed to define the scope of his product concept and its market. The options of offering a turnkey solution, licensing the Fottle directly to dairy producers, or licensing it to engineering firms that provided bottling technology carried very different implications for segmentation and positioning as well as for the

---

[14] PVC is blamed for issuing chlorine fumes during combustion.

[15] PE, like PET, had been shown to be chemically reconverted, but the procedure had not been commercialized as yet.

[16] Market prices for PE and PP granulate in 1993 averaged ca. 1.28 Marks per kilogram.

[17] PKL ranked second to TetraPak in the world supply of aseptic carton packaging technology.

[18] Union Centrale des Producteurs Suisses de Lait, *Studie Milchverpackungen: Oekologie,* Oct. 1991, pp. 10–11.

company's long-term profitability. Düring needed to think through the consequences in terms of risk and profit sharing.

Düring also had to position the Fottle with respect to other packaging systems. Depending on the product definition and the market segments targeted, the Fottle had to communicate one or more of the following benefits: cost reduction for producers, ecological soundness, differentiation through design, and convenience of use. In this respect, Düring needed to assess the entry barriers for the targeted segments. The cost of switching from one packaging system to another was central to producers and the various benefits of the Fottle needed to reflect the benefits of switching. As part of this choice, the pricing policy also needed to be clarified.

CASE 4–3
MURPHY BREWERY IRELAND, LIMITED

Patrick Conway, marketing director for Murphy's, picked up his issue of the *Financial Times* and read the following headline on May 13, "Grand Met, Guinness to Merge," and pondered its impact on his firm. Guinness was Murphy's most formidable competitor, not only in Ireland but also worldwide. Since a staff meeting was already scheduled for later Tuesday morning, he decided to examine the article closely and discuss it with his team. As he read on, the £22.3 billion merger between two of the four largest distillers (Seagram's headquartered in Canada and Allied Domecq, another British company, were the other two) appeared to have much synergy. The article pointed out that the geographic and brand fits were good between the two companies. The new firm which will be called GMG will be approximately equal in size with such major multinationals as Unilever, Procter & Gamble, and Phillip Morris.[1]

During the 11:00 AM staff meeting, Patrick brought the merger to the attention of his colleagues. His company was in the midst of preparing its 1998 global marketing plan and this news brought some urgency to the task ahead. Patrick stated that he felt a major assessment of Murphy's status in the worldwide market was needed. He called upon David Ford, his export manager, to examine Murphy's position in the UK and European markets. He said he would phone Michael Foley of Heineken USA (distributor of Murphy's in the states) to report on Murphy's progress there and asked Dan Leahy to look into Murphy's status in Ireland. He asked each to report back to him within a week.

As part of his personal preparation, Patrick decided to dig into the files and reacquaint himself with the company history, since he had joined the firm only a few years previously. He also wanted to find out more about the merger. So, he rang the communications department to clip and route all articles from business publications on this topic to him. Patrick considered the impact that these developments would have on the Murphy's brands.

In 1997, Murphy's had become a truly international brand that maintained a unique identity in Ireland. The name Murphy, the most frequent surname in the entire country, is recognized internationally for its Irish heritage. Exhibit 1 shows that about 85 percent of Murphy's sales came from export business in 1996 and the company now employs 385 people. He located a report from several years previously that provided an historical perspective of the company.

Historical Background

James J. Murphy and Company Limited was founded in 1856 in Cork City, Ireland, by the four Murphy brothers—James, William, Jerome, and Francis. In 1890, they were described as follows: "These gentlemen applied themselves with energy and enterprise

This case was prepared by Patrick E. Murphy, professor of marketing, University of Notre Dame in Indiana, and former visiting professor of marketing at University College Cork in Ireland, and Don O'Sullivan, lecturer in marketing, Department of Management and Marketing, University College Cork.

This case is intended to serve as a basis for a class discussion rather than to illustrate either effective or ineffective handling of a business situation. The authors would like to thank Patrick Conway, David Ford, and Dan Leahy of Murphy Brewery Ireland and Michael Foley of Heineken USA for their assistance in writing this case.

EXHIBIT 1   Export Sales versus Total Company Volumes

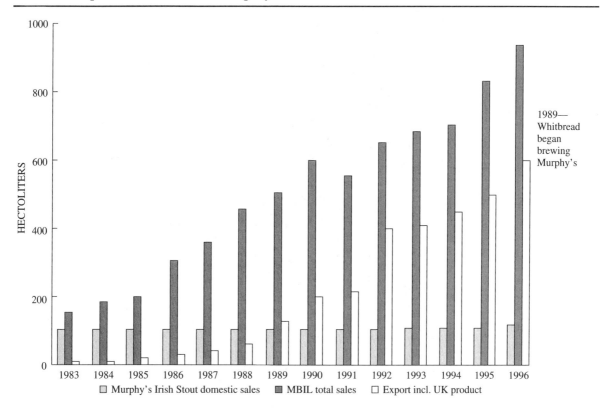

□ Murphy's Irish Stout domestic sales   ■ MBIL total sales   □ Export incl. UK product

to the manufacture of an article, the reputation of which now extends far beyond the South of Ireland where the firm's stout and porter have been long and favorably known and where they command a very exclusive sale."[2]

James J. Murphy inherited the family business skills. His grandfather, also called James, had founded, with his brothers, the distillery James Murphy and Company in Midleton, County Cork (15 miles to the east of Cork City) in 1825. These Murphy brothers prospered as ship owners and tea importers and had been paid quite a sum of money prior to founding their distillery. This company experienced significant growth and in 1867 amalgamated with four Cork distilleries to create Cork Distilleries Company Ltd. The firm in turn enjoyed great success over the following century and in 1966 joined with the Dublin distillery, John Jameson and Son, and John Power and Son to create Irish Distillers Limited.

The Murphy Brewery is located at Lady's Well in Cork which derives its name from a celebrated well on the hill opposite of the premises. It was dedicated to Our Lady and believed to possess miraculous properties. To the present day, pilgrimages take place to the shrine every year in the month of May. During the 19th century Lady's Well was one of Cork's largest breweries and was mentioned in the 1890 publication *Noted Breweries of Great Britain and Ireland,* which indicated that Murphy's Stout had become a formidable rival to Guinness in the South of Ireland.[3]

Initially, Murphy's brewed porter but switched exclusively to stout (the name *stout* denotes strong beers—see Exhibit 2 for description of the product) and this remained

---

EXHIBIT 2   What Is Stout and How Was It Promoted?

Stout is a black beer with a thick white head. The black color is due mainly to the fact that it contains malted barley which is roasted, in a similar way to coffee beans. The creamy white head is created from the "initiation" and "surging" of bubbles of nitrogen and carbon dioxide gas as the beer is poured. The gas enters the keg and forces the beer out. It is actually the nitrogen which causes the tight, creamy head.

The word *stout* has long been used to describe strong beers; it also meant stout as in stout ale. The strength may have been in terms of taste or alcohol or both. Standard stout ranges in alcohol content from 4 percent to 5 percent. The word *stout* gradually made the transition from adjective to noun. The basic constituent of stout is barley which consists mainly of starch. The barley becomes a malt and during this process it is converted to sugar which is fermentable. When the malt is roasted beyond the normal limits, this gives the stout its unusual dark hue. The highly roasted dark malt is 500 times darker than a pale malt and adds its distinctive color as well as flavor.

The resulting sugary liquid, called wort, is eventually formed. At this stage hops are added and boiled with wort to produce the liquid. When boiled for an hour or two, the hops release oils and resins which produce characteristic bitterness and aroma. A comparison of the bitterness level among the leading brands of stout conducted by the European Brewery Convention found that Guinness rates 45–48 European units of bitterness, Beamish 40, and Murphy's 36 to 38.

Stout is synonymous with Ireland and nowhere is stout as popular or as intrinsically part of everyday life. The criterion by which a pub is often judged is likely to be whether or not it sells a good pint of stout. In the pub, pouring pints of stout is an activity full of tradition and custom. The pouring of the product is seen as having a major impact on product quality. Stout is poured in two stages. First the glass is filled to 75 percent capacity and allowed to "settle" so that the creamy head will separate from the dark body. To top off the pint, the tap is pushed forward slightly until the head rises just below the rim. This activity takes a minute or two and results in stout taking longer to pour. Interestingly, the product is poured in one go/pull outside Ireland.

Stout has its roots in colder climates in Ireland and Scandinavia, and traditionally, it has been a winter brew. Comments, such as "typically consumed in the dark winter months" or "a seasonal beer brewed only in the winter" are regularly used by stout breweries worldwide. Stout is thought to be a drink suited to quiet, reflective sipping. Both in Ireland and worldwide, it is now a year-round drink.

To return to the definition, stout is often considered a strong drink. Therefore, both Murphy's and Guinness have extensively used strength in their marketing and advertising. Murphy's utilized a circus strongman who was shown lifting a horse off the ground with the label "Murphy's Stout gives strength" for many years in the late 1800s and 1900s. Guinness has utilized posters throughout Ireland depicting superhuman strength achieved by drinking Guinness with the moniker "Guinness for strength."

Source: Partially adapted from Brendan O'Brien, *The Stout Book* (Dublin: Anna Livia Press, 1990).

its sole beer product until 1965. Over the years the brewery acquired a number of licensed products and developed a wholesale spirits and soft drinks bottling business.

Although Murphy's opened up trade in London, Manchester, South Wales, and other parts of England early this century, the company began experiencing financial problems in the 1960s. There was considerable anxiety among the staff of 200 in Murphy's Brewery Cork concerning the continuity of their employment in the early 70s. At that time they had an English partner (Watney and Mann), who wanted to dissolve the partnership. Colonel John J. Murphy, chairman of Murphy's, stated that "we are confident that we can satisfy" certain financial conditions to meet the demands of the creditors. The company at this time was well over 100 years old and had overcome difficult periods in the past.

In February 1975 Murphy's approached Heineken N.B. (the Amsterdam-based brewery which had been founded by Garard Adriann Heineken the same year that the Murphy brothers opened their brewery in Ireland) with a proposal to begin a licensing

EXHIBIT 3 World's Largest Brewers, 1994

Company	HQ	Prod./Vol.[1]	World Share	% of Sales in Exports
Anheuser-Busch	United States	105.1	9%	6%
Heineken	Netherlands	59.6	4.8	89
Miller	United States	50.1	3.9	5
Kirin	Japan	35.1	2.7	5
Foster's	Australia	34.7	2.7	73
Carlsberg	Denmark	30.4	2.3	82
Danone Group	France	27.7	2.4	65
Guinness	UK	24.2	2.1	84

Source: Havis Dawson, "Brand Brewing." *Beverage World,* October 1995, p. 52.

1994 is latest year available.

[1] Production/volume is measured in hectoliters: 1 hectoliter = 26.4 gallons or .85 barrels.

Strategic Alliance

operation for Heineken in Ireland. Heineken examined the possibilities of the Irish market, found them favorable, and a license agreement was signed. A marketing company, Heineken Ireland Limited, was set up as a fully owned subsidiary of Heineken N.B. Heineken was well known for its lager beer that complemented the Murphy's Irish Stout offering.

Murphy's new policy of expanding as a broad-based competitor to the leading brands (e.g., Guinness and Beamish and Crawford) worked well at first. However, the company was hit by recessionary problems and J.J. Murphy and Company Limited went into receivership in 1982. At that time the company employed 235 people. On July 14, 1982, the Cork Examiner confirmed a commitment from the Dutch brewing company Heineken to invest 1.6 million pounds in the brewery.

In 1983 Heineken International purchased the assets of James J. Murphy and Company Limited, then in receivership. Murphy Brewery Ireland Limited became a wholly owned subsidiary of Heineken International, a move which gave a new lease on life to Murphy's Brewery. This development preserved the long and respected tradition of brewing in the Cork area and the well known brand name. Since then Murphy Brewery Ireland Limited has continued its brewing and marketing of Murphy's Irish Stout and Heineken. The adoption of Murphy's Irish Stout by Heineken International as one of its corporate brands meant that the brand became available to drinkers worldwide.

Global

The Heineken Era

Heineken International is the world's second largest brewer (see Exhibit 3) and a private company. Its flagship Heineken lager, the world's most exported beer, and the Amstel brand are also brewed under license by third parties. They are produced in over 100 plants and sold in 170 countries on all continents. The Heineken brand is sold in the same green bottle, promoted with the same brand imagery in the same price tier in China, Spain, the U.S., and elsewhere. Heineken was the first beer to be imported into the United States after Prohibition was lifted in 1933. The United States is now its largest market.

Murphy's management during the Heineken years has been led by four managing directors. Currently, Marien Kakabeeke, a native of Holland, serves in that position. He assumed the post in August 1993. Heineken has demonstrated its commitment to Murphy's by opening a new office complex in the old Malthouse at the brewery.

Murphy's became accredited in 1992 with the ISO 9002 mark for all aspects of operations—the first brewery in Europe to achieve this distinction.

Murphy's Brands and Packaging

Internationally, Murphy's Irish Stout (MIS) is now available in 63 countries worldwide, up from only 20 in 1992. Export sales of the brand grew by almost 200 percent during 1996. Growth markets include the United States, where MIS increased 163 percent, and Germany, France, Spain, Italy, and the Netherlands, where sales volumes grew by 82 percent. MIS's output has grown by 700 percent in the last decade. Most of this increase was fueled by international consumption with sales in Ireland only increasing 10 percent over that time (see Exhibit 1).

This growth is reflected in an increased turnover for MBI from Ir £125 million to Ir £140 million. The total company volume now stands at almost 950,000 hectoliters.

For most of its first 135 years, Murphy's Irish Stout was only available in draft form in pubs throughout Ireland. A packaging innovation (draughtflow cans) was launched in October of 1992. A plastic device (called a widget) is fitted into the bottom of the can which nitrates the liquid after the can is opened, creating the famous creamy head and giving the product a publike taste. Consumer acceptance of the can is reflected in the distribution growth of the product which makes it available in off-licenses/liquor stores. Within Europe a 330-milliliter cream-colored can is sold, while in the United States, a 14.9-ounce can is marketed. One distinguishing feature of the can in Europe is the message, "Chill for at least two hours. Pour contents into glass in one smooth action. Best before end—see base," reprinted in four languages on the cans.

Another packaging innovation for MIS was developed in 1995. A draught flow bottle is now available in both the United States and European markets. The 500-milliliter (16.9-oz.) bottle has a long neck and is dark brown in color. It is used as a powerful unique differentiating point for the brand. The back labels acclaim the benefits of the draughtflow technology. Warning labels concerning alcoholic beverages are shown on the U.S. labels.

Murphy's Irish Amber, a traditional Irish ale, was launched in 1995 as Murphy's Irish Red Beer in Germany and France. It is brewed in Cork but not available domestically in Ireland. In the United States, Murphy's Irish Amber was introduced in both draft and 12-ounce bottle during September 1996. The bottles are amber in color. The label's dark blue and red colors accented by gold signal a high-quality product. Compelled by the need for a stronger Murphy's portfolio due to increased interest in genuine red beers, the company believed this product would be successful. Thus far, Murphy's Irish Amber's success has far exceeded expectations.

Murphy's also offers Heineken's low-alcohol beer called Buckler. It contains ½ of 1 percent alcohol and about half of the calorie content of normal beer. It sells in 330-milliliter bottles in bars, off-licenses, and supermarkets in the served markets.

The Competition

After returning from a business trip to the continent a week later, Patrick Conway found on his desk a stack of articles sent to him from the Communications Department discussing the Guinness–Grand Met merger. Before turning his attention to them, he reflected on what he knew regarding the Guinness brand both in Ireland and elsewhere. Guinness Stout was the pioneer in this category and even an older firm than Murphy's. It was founded in 1759 by Arthur Guinness in Dublin. It was now the eighth largest brewer in the world in terms of volume with over a 2 percent market share. Murphy's parent, Heineken, is in second place worldwide. (See Exhibit 3.)

Guinness is brewed in almost 50 countries and sold in over 130.[4] In the stout category, it is the proverbial "500-pound gorilla" in that it commands a 70 to 90 percent share in almost all markets. When it moves, Murphy's and other competitors invariably pay close attention. The Guinness name defines the stout market in most countries and is the "gold standard" against which all other competing brands are measured. The company's marketing prowess is well known in that Guinness Stout is positioned as "hip in the United Kingdom," "traditional in Ireland," and a source of "virility" in Africa, and a special microbrew is aimed at "creating a new generation of beer snobs" in the United States. Guinness plans to continue targeting continental Europe, the United States, and Asia in a bid to expand its markets and grow its business.

Guinness has been very successful in building its stout brand around the world. The company is identified with its quirky advertising campaigns in Ireland and its high profile regarding other marketing and promotional endeavors. One significant effort involved the Irish national soccer team, who endorsed Guinness as their official beer for the 1994 World Cup. Sales of Guinness Stout rose dramatically in the United States during the World Cup finals. Another U.S.-based promotion program designed to appeal to the over 40 million Americans of Irish descent was the "Win Your Own Pub in Ireland" contest. This competition has been going on for several years and is featured in Guinness's Web page currently. Third, the huge development of the Irish pub concept around the world helped Guinness brands abroad and contributed to an increase in export sales of 10 percent in 1996. The company launched the Guinness pub concept in 1992 and there are now 1,250 "Guinness" Irish pubs in 36 countries. Four hundred more are expected to open in 1997.[5]

Patrick turned his attention to several articles about the Guinness and Grand Met merger. A rationale for the merger was that these firms could acquire new brands easier than they may be able to find new consumers in the U.S. and European marketplace where alcohol consumption is falling, population is aging, and concerns about health rising. The new firm will be a formidable force in the race to open up new markets in liquor and beer. The companies have complementary product lines and will be divided up into four major divisions (see Exhibit 4). The Guinness Brewery worldwide divison will feature its signature stout, Harp (a lager), Kilkenny (a red ale), Cruzcampo (a Spanish beer), and Red Stripe.

The Economist noted that even though GMG will be the seventh largest company in the world, it faces major obstacles. One is that even though its brands are very well known, the combined company will lack focus. Grand Met has a long history of trying its hand at different businesses but has done so with mixed success. Guinness, however, has an even longer history of not doing much besides brewing beer and its spirits business has been a struggle for the firm. *The Economist*'s conclusion gave Mr. Conway encouragement and reflected his own impression when the magazine stated: "Unless GMG manages to show very rapidly that they can mix these ingredients into something fairly tasty, then pressure will grow on it to simplify itself."[6]

Patrick recalled that Guinness is not the only competitor of Murphy's. Beamish & Crawford, also located in Cork, was founded in 1792 and currently employs about 200 people. In 1987, the company joined the Foster's Brewing Group. The primary brands offered by the company are Beamish (stout), Foster's (lager), and Carling Black Label (lager).

Beamish stout is available in most pubs throughout the South of Ireland. The brand is positioned on its Irishness, heritage of Beamish Stout, and the fact that it is the only

EXHIBIT 4   GMG Brands

Division	Turnover (millions)	Pretax Profit (millions)
Guinness Brewing Worldwide: Guinness Stout, Harp, Cruzcampo (Spanish), Red Stripe	£2,262	£283
United Distillers & Vintners (Guinness Brands) Dewar's, Gordon's Gin, Bell's, Moet Hennessey, Johnnie Walker, Black and White, Asbach	£2,468	£791
(Grand Met Brands) Smirnoff, Stolichnaya, J&B (whisky), Gilbey's Gin, Jose Cuervo, Grand Marnier, Bailey's, Malibu, Absolut	£3,558	£502
Pillsbury Pillsbury, Green Giant, Old El Paso, Häagen-Dazs	£3,770	£447
Burger King	£859	£167

Source: "GMG Brands: What the Two Sides Will Contribute," *Financial Times,* May 13, 1997, p. 27.

Note: Turnover and pretax profit numbers denote millions of pounds Sterling.

Irish stout exclusively brewed in Ireland. In the last three years, Beamish has been marketed in Europe (Italy and Spain mostly) and North America (Canada and the United States). It is distributed through the Foster's Brewing Group in these markets.

The Irish Market

Dan Leahy sent Patrick the following report on the market for Murphy's in Ireland. His memo discussed both the importance of pub life in the country as well as the competitive situation. Patrick read with interest Dan's assessment of the Irish market:

> With a population of less than 4 million people, the Irish market is small in international terms. However, it is the market in which stout holds the largest share at nearly 50 percent of all beer sales. With one of the youngest populations in the developed world and one of the fastest growing economies, it is an important and dynamic market for all stout producers. This is added to by the fact that the three competitors—Murphy's, Guinness, and Beamish—all use their Irishness as a key attribute in product positioning. A presence in the Irish market is viewed as being central to the authenticity of the Irishness claim.
>
> Pubs have long been a central part of Irish life, particularly in rural areas where pubs are semi-social centers. Irish pubs are regularly run by owner-operators who buy products from different breweries. This is quite different from most international markets where pubs tend to be run by or for the breweries. For example, in the Dutch market Heineken has 52 percent of outlets. Partly as a result of this, Irish consumers are highly brand loyal. Also, in the Irish market, breweries engage in higher levels of promotion.
>
> Irish pubs are perceived very positively in many parts of the world. They are seen as being places which are accessible to all the family. Irish pubs are intimately linked with musical sessions and viewed as being open, friendly places to visit. This positive perception has resulted in a proliferation of Irish-themed pubs, particularly in the last decade. This development has been used extensively by Guinness and, lately, by Murphy's as a means of increasing distribution.
>
> Guinness dominates the Irish stout market with 89 percent market share. Murphy's and Beamish have roughly equal shares of the rest of the market. Guinness' dominance of the market is reflected in the fact that the term *Guinness* is synonymous with stout. In many parts

of the country it is ordered without reference to its name simply by asking for "a pint." Similarly in Britain 1 million pints of Guinness are sold every day, with 10 million glasses a day sold worldwide.

Guinness Ireland turned in a strong performance in 1996 with sales up 8 percent to 764 million pints.[7] The company began a 12-million–pound advertising campaign last year called "The Big Pint" and engaged in extensive billboard advertising emphasizing the size and strength of the brand.

In Ireland, Beamish Stout is positioned as a value for money, Irish Stout selling at 20 pence (10 percent) lower than the competitors. It is slightly ahead of Murphy's currently in the race for second place in Ireland. As with Murphy's, Beamish's traditional base has been in the Cork area market. Today, one in every four pints of stout consumed in Cork is Beamish and one in every 14 pints in Ireland is Beamish.

Within the lager market in Ireland, Heineken dominates with nearly 40 percent of the market while Budweiser and Carlsberg (both distributed by Guinness) each have just over 20 percent market share. Harp, which once held an overwhelming 80 percent share, now accounts for only 8 percent.

Murphy's is priced on a par with Guinness in all markets in the country. The average price of a pint of stout in the market is Ir £2.00.

In parts of the market where demand for the brand is low, Murphy's has begun selling the product in an innovative 3/5-keg (a keg is a barrel containing 50 liters) size. This ensures that the product reaches the customer at the desired level of quality.

Murphy's has pursued market growth through the development of export markets and development of the take-home market. The development of these markets is driven by the fact that the domestic draught market is mature with static sales over the last number of years. In 1995 pub sales fell by almost 2.5 percent, while off-license sales grew by 37 percent. The growth in the off-license business is due in part to the impact of the new stronger drunk-driving legislation and in-home summer consumption.[8]

Both of these markets rely heavily on canned and bottled packaging for the product. Traditionally this has posed a difficulty for stout products as there is a perceived deterioration in quality compared to the draught version. Murphy's is selling its product in bottles and dedicating some advertising to the superior bottled taste and using it as a differentiating feature for all Murphy's products and using the draught bottle as a brand icon for the firm.

Conway thought about the report on the Irish market and how difficult it was to compete against Guinness and the extreme brand loyalty of the Irish consumer to it. He thought about the new three-year 5-million–pound advertising campaign launched in 1996 and hoped that the unique approach would win new customers. One memorable TV ad featured a group of Japanese Samurai warriors who arrive in a line at a bar, knock back bottles of Murphy's, and leave, while a Guinness drinker drums his fingers on the counter waiting for his pint to settle. Conway believed that brand awareness was growing. One successful promotional endeavor is the company's sponsorship of the Murphy's Irish Open which was part of the PGA European Golf Tour.

He knew that strides were being made in the distribution network outside its traditional stronghold of Cork City and County. One of the inducements the company was using was a lower trade price to the pubs so they made more on each pint sold. The company followed this philosophy internationally as well in the effort to compete with Guinness.

He also recalled two *Irish Times* articles that gave his and Kakabeeke's views on the importance of the Irish market to the company. He asked his secretary to retrieve them from the files and routed them to the marketing group. Conway was quoted as saying, "Murphy's believes it has to have an advertising spend comparable to Guinness if it is ever to achieve a critical mass in Ireland. We have to differentiate ourselves, and there's no use doing it with a whisper. A better market share in Ireland would also provide Murphy's Irish Stout with a backbone from which to grow exports."[9] Mr. Kakebeeke said that "the brewery is not happy with the 5 percent position in the Irish market and with the level of domestic growth being achieved by Murphy's Irish Stout. I feel that sales can be improved in Ireland."[10]

The UK and Continental European Markets

The United Kingdom (England, Scotland, Wales, and Northern Ireland), Ireland's closest neighbor, represents the world's largest stout market in terms of consumption at 60 million hectoliters. The total population of the UK is approximately 60 million consumers. Murphy's market share stands at 15 percent while Guinness (78 percent) and Beamish (6 percent) are the other two major competitors. MIS was launched in the UK in 1985 and has enjoyed continued growth in that market since then. The reason for Murphy's success in the UK may be attributed to several factors.

Distribution Network

First, Heineken and Murphy's are distributed in the UK through the Whitbread Beer Company located in Luton. Whitbread has an association with over 27,000 pubs in the country which translates to an automatic distribution network for Murphy's products. Recently, Whitbread has opened a series of themed bars under the banner "J. J. Murphy and Company" throughout the country. These outlets reflect the desired image for Murphy's and help raise the profile of the brand in the UK. As a point of comparison, Beamish is distributed in 10,000 outlets in Britain.

Second, Murphy's has also been successful with their advertising in the UK. Their continuing advertising theme "Like the Murphy's, I'm not bitter" campaign is a tongue-in-cheek poke at Guinness' taste. The campaign has received several awards and has resulted in a unique identity developed for the brand (see Exhibit 2 on stout). The firm has also sponsored the Murphy's English Open Golf Championship for five years.

Third, the brand has gained momentum since it was voted product of the year by the UK Vintners in 1990. Murphy's has a strong position in the minds of the British who prefer darker ales. The brand represents a viable option to those who do not like the taste of Guinness and/or seek an alternative to their favorite UK-based brands such as Thomas Hardy, Newcastle, Samuel Smith, Watney's, and Young's.

MIS is available in all Western European markets. It has excellent distribution in the Netherlands, where Heineken is headquartered. Guinness' recent Irish pub expansion program has also helped raise awareness for all entries in the Irish stout category. Murphy's experienced dramatic growth in volume and market share across Europe in 1996.

In Germany, the establishment of Murphy's Trading GmbH, a wholly owned subsidiary of Murphy Brewery Ireland, allows for greater focus and control of the Murphy's brands within this critical market. 1996 also saw Murphy's gain the exclusive beer rights to Paddy Murphy's, the largest chain of Irish theme pubs throughout Germany. Also, in Denmark MIS is distributed in the Paddy Go Easy chain in several Danish cities.

In 1996 new markets were developed in Eastern Europe including Hungary and the Czech Republic. The potential of the emerging Russian market is also anticipated. With the introduction of the brand in Finland, Murphy's is now available throughout all the Nordic countries.

The American Market

As he reached for the phone to ring Michael Foley, current CEO of Heineken USA (Van Munching & Co. is the importer's name) and former managing director of Murphy Brewery Ireland from 1989 to 1993, Patrick thought about the United States. He knew that the United States with its 270 million consumers and general high standard of living, represents the most lucrative beer market in the world. The $40 billion beer market in the United States is dominated by the "giants" of Anheuser Busch (10 brands and 45 percent market share), Miller (9/23 percent), and Coors (7/11 percent).[11]

Michael gave Patrick a status report on the Murphy's brand in the United States as of June 1997. Michael reiterated the U.S. strategy is to "build slowly" and gain acceptance of Murphy's products by endorsement of customers rather than attempting to buy market share with mass advertising. The plan is to "keep off TV because it is too expensive." Murphy's is seeking a premium brand positioning aimed at the specialty imported niche rather than the mass market.

Promo STR

Foley indicated he was very optimistic about the Murphy growth possibilities in the United States. "Our 1996 sales were up 180 percent and our target is 1 million cases by mid-1998," he said. Both Murphy's Irish Stout and Irish Amber are meeting expectations set for them by Heineken USA.

Murphy's Irish Stout has been available in the United States since 1992 and has experienced steady growth since then. MIS has been on a gradual progression, from 100,000 gallons in 1992 to 400,000 gallons in 1994 and 600,000 gallons in 1995. It is now on tap at over 5,000 bars and pubs throughout the country. The distribution tends to be concentrated in the Eastern corridor running from Boston through New York City (the largest market) to Washington, D.C. Another area of intense distribution is in South Florida. The "gold coast" area running from Miami to Fort Lauderdale is a stronghold for Murphy's partially due to its attraction to British tourists who are already familiar with the brand. Other areas of focus for MIS are the major metropolitan areas of Chicago, Los Angeles, and San Francisco.

For the off-premises/carryout market, MIS has been available in cans since 1993. Their size is 14.9 ounces and they are cream colored (like the "head" of the drink) and are priced relative to domestic U.S. beers at a premium level—$1.76 versus $1.99 for Guinness in the same size can. Foley stated that cans generally signify a "down market product" and the company would like to present more of a prestige image. Therefore, in September of 1996 Murphy's introduced the draughtflow bottle in the United States. While Foley believes the glass package is "more premium," the company has experienced a problem with it in the United States. The serving size of 16.9 ounces is not correct for the market since most beer glasses are only 12 ounces. The usual price is $1.99 per bottle. The size is not that important for in-home consumption, but in bars where MIS is sold by packages rather than on draught, this is a significant issue for the company. Another issue that has arisen is that the thick brown bottle takes substantially longer to cool than a can.

Murphy's Irish Amber was introduced into the American market in late 1996. Its on-premise penetration has exceeded company expectations and according to Foley, "the product is doing very, very well. It is the 'real deal' and replacing nonauthentic Irish products such as Killian's in many areas." The product is available in six-packs for off-site consumption. The rich-looking green-and-red package makes it attractive. The company has positioned it against Bass Ale and other premium-quality ales. Its price is in the $7.50 range which is substantially higher than many of the specialty imports which are in the $4.00 to $6.00 per six-pack. Killian's is sometimes sale priced as low as $3.99, but its regular price is in the $5.50 to $6.00 range and Sam Adams Red and Pete's Wicked Ale are priced at $5.49 and $5.99, respectively. Bass Ale, however, carries an even higher price ($7.79) than Murphy's.

Conway thanked Foley for his update on the status of the Murphy's brands in the

United States and asked if Michael could spend a few minutes discussing trends in the beer market within the country. "I know import sales are increasing about 7 percent a year in the United States and that Heineken is the leading import brand," said Conway, "But where does Guinness fall?" Foley responded that they were in tenth place while Bass Ale held down the eighth spot and beer imports from Ireland held sixth position among all countries (see Exhibits 5 and 6). Foley said that he recalled reading that the top 20 brands (out of a total of 400 import brands) account for 90 percent of the U.S. import sales.

Patrick asked about trends in the U.S. beer market. "It has been flat the last several years," said Foley. "The most significant recent trend domestically is the growth in microbreweries." Michael said he remembered seeing on a Web site that microbreweries, brewpubs, and regional specialty breweries totaled almost 1,300 in early 1997.[12] The microbrewery category has grown tenfold to 500 in 10 years. However, they still only accounted for a paltry 2 percent of the U.S. market in 1995.

Conway said good-bye and was just about to hang up when Foley said, "I almost forgot but someone passed an article from *The Wall Street Journal* by me a few weeks ago that talked about Guinness and the microbrewery boom. I will send it to you with the other material." (See Exhibit 7.)

Murphy's World Market Positioning and Marketing

Dan Leahy stopped by Patrick Conway's office and handed him the information requested on Murphy's status in the world market. Patrick glanced at the statistics assembled by Dan and noticed that the specialty category (into which MIS and MIA

EXHIBIT 5   Leading Imported Beer Brands in the United States (Thousands of 2.25-Gallon Cases)

Brand	Importer	Origin	1992[1]	1993	1994[2]	% Change 1993–1994
Heineken	Van Munching & Co.	Netherlands	26,700	29,200	31,200	6.8%
Corona Extra	Barton/Gambrinus	Mexico	13,000	14,000	16,000	14.3
Molson Ice	Molson USA	Canada	—	3,000	10,000	—
Beck's	Dribeck Importers	Germany	9,650	9,700	9,720	0.2
Molson Golden	Molson USA	Canada	8,500	8,600	8,700	1.2
Amstel Light	Van Munching & Co.	Netherlands	5,500	6,000	7,500	25.0
Labatt's Blue	Labatt's USA	Canada	5,900	6,200	6,500	4.8
Bass Ale	Guinness Import Co.	United Kingdom	2,850	3,390	4,160	22.7
Tecate	Labatt's USA	Mexico	2,900	3,400	4,000	17.6
Guinness Stout	Guinness Import Co.	Ireland	3,100	3,650	3,970	8.8
Foster's Lager[3]	Molson USA	Canada	3,500	3,700	3,800	2.7
Moosehead	Guinness Import Co.	Canada	3,400	3,350	3,340	–0.3
Molson Light	Molson USA	Canada	1,900	2,000	2,200	10.0
Dos Equis	Guinness Import Co.	Mexico	1,900	2,060	2,120	2.9
St. Pauli Girl	Barton Brands	Germany	2,200	2,000	2,000	0.0
Labatt's Ice	Labatt's USA	Canada	—	845	1,910	—
Molson Canadian	Molson USA	Canada	1,640	1,690	1,710	1.2
Labatt's Light	Labatt's USA	Canada	1,100	1,020	1,100	7.8
Corona Light	Barton/Gambrinus	Mexico	1,100	1,000	1,000	0.0

[1] Revised.

[2] Estimated.

[3] The gradual production switch from Australia to Canada began in April 1992.

EXHIBIT 6   Imported Beer Market
Market Share by Supplier, 1994 (Estimated)

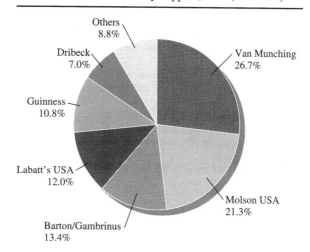

both fell) had grown over the last few years (see Exhibit 8). He was concerned that it was the second smallest of the five categories.

Dan left a revision of the Murphy's Positioning Statement on which Patrick and his colleagues had been working for several months. It read:

> Murphy's is a symbol of everything authentically "Irish." Its warm history takes time to discover but its taste is easy to appreciate.

Supporting this positioning was the image of Ireland that Murphy's planned to convey in its marketing strategy (see Exhibit 9). While the words in the exhibit are a bit stereotypical, they describe the perception of both the country and its people. It is in this context that Irish products are viewed by consumers in other counties. The elements of the marketing mix were summarized by Dan in several accompanying pages.

The product consists of the two brands—Murphy's Irish Stout and Murphy's Irish Amber/Red Beer. It is sourced in Ireland except for the UK and New Zealand markets. Ongoing new product development continues in line with positioning, umbrella branding, and premium packaging.

The distribution objective is one of controlled distribution growth. The focus is on quality Irish bars/pubs and specialty beer outlets. Package variants are available in low-volume outlets. Dual stocking of MIS and MIA/RB will occur wherever possible. Exclusivity is a goal but not a prerequisite for stocking. The existing Heineken distribution network will continue to be used wherever possible.

The pricing strategy is one of price parity with major specialty competitors. A reasonable margin is being offered to the trade. In fact, the company prices its products slightly below the competition to the trade as an enticement for them to carry the products.

The promotion and communications strategy is multipronged. The brands' Irish heritage and origin continue to be reinforced. The company engages in tactical advertising and promotion rather than larger-scale strategic campaigns. For example, St. Patrick's Day and Irish Music Nights are exploited. The communication focus is on both brands in most markets. The company plans to use still rather than electronic media to convey the authentic Irish image of the brands.

EXHIBIT 7 **Buoyed by Boom in Microbrews, Guinness Pours Its Cash into TV**

Guinness Import Co. poured about 33 percent more of its signature dark draft stout in the United States last year, as the microbrew boom helped lift import sales by creating a new generation of beer snobs. Now Guinness hopes to keep the beer taps flowing with its first large-scale U.S. TV ad campaign for the Irish-brewed brand, breaking today.

At a time when sales of all beer in the United States rose just 1 percent last year, several of Guinness Import's major brands, including Harp lager and Bass ale, posted double-digit gains. Overall, sales of Guinness Import's brands (including Moosehead, whose distribution rights Guinness is shedding, effective at the end of March) grew 20 percent to about 17 million cases last year, according to Guinness.

The company's success is one of the factors that contributed to an estimated 10 percent rise in the sale of beers last year, according to Frank Walters, senior vice president of research at M. Shanken Communications, publisher of *Impact*, which tracks beer sales. Final numbers on sales of domestic beers are expected to be flat, although it's estimated that the tiny microbrewery and specialty segment jumped more than 20 percent. "It's a good economy and people are indulging themselves more," says Mr. Walters of the sales of more-expensive imports.

Guinness stout's fast sales pace in bars and stores lifted it to the no. 6 or 7 ranking among imports, up from ninth place in 1995, according to Mr. Walter's estimates. Guinness Import, a unit of Guinness PLC of London, itself attributes its success to changing consumer tastes in the wake of the microbrew explosion and a more intense distribution and marketing effort. "People are getting more into beers with taste," said Sheri Roder, marketing development director for Guinness Import, "and at the same time, we've gotten behind our brands more."

There have been eye-catching promotions, such as annual "Win Your Own Pub in Ireland" contest, now in its fourth year. A "Great Guinness Toast," on Feb. 28, hopes to get into the *Guinness Book of World Records* for the largest number of people making a toast. And the number of outlets selling the brand jumped by 20 percent in 1996.

Even more unusual, Guinness has been sending out a force of "draft specialists" armed with thermometers and training brochures to visit bars and make sure they're serving Guinness under the best possible conditions. Brewers can't own bars, so they can't control whether tavern owners serve the product in sparkling clean glasses or how often they flush out built-up yeast in the lines that carry the beer from the keg to the tap.

With distribution and the quality program in place, Guinness decided the time was right to launch the TV campaign. "There's no point in advertising a lot when people can't find you," says Ms. Roder. "There's a likelihood now that people will be able to find a pint of Guinness, poured well to our exacting standards. You don't want to get people too excited about something they can't find."

The TV ad campaign, with the tag line, "Why Man Was Given 5 Senses," will air through St. Patrick's Day, March 17, in 18 major markets including New York, Los Angeles and Atlanta. Guinness won't say what it is spending on the ad campaign, which will run in late prime-time and sports programs, but calls it a significant media buy. Chicago viewers of the Super Bowl saw the ad run twice; Guinness also has spots in NBC's high-rated Thursday prime-time lineup.

The quirky ad, which goes through the ritual of ordering a pint of Guinness, from the nod to the bartender to the long wait for the beer to settle, was created by Weiss, Stagliano of New York City. It got a five-week tryout in Chicago and Boston last fall with convincing results: Sales of Guinness in Boston were up 24 percent in December over a year earlier, compared with just an 11 percent gain for the rest of the Guinness portfolio, while in Chicago, sales are up 35 percent from a year ago, with distribution up 22 percent.

Source: Elizabeth Jensen, *The Wall Street Journal*, February 10, 1997, p. B2.

Murphy's Future Direction

Patrick Conway assembled the reports on the Irish, UK, European, and American markets as well as the world positioning and strategy. He circulated them to the members of his group with a memo calling a meeting in early June of 1997. Conway indicated that he wanted to develop a longterm strategy for the Murphy's brand to take to

EXHIBIT 8 World Beer Market

Category	1994	1995	1996	Volume (Hectoliters)
Specialty	6.5%	7.4%	8.2%	103,000,000
Sophistication	11.9	12.4	12.9	162,000,000
Standard savings	63.3	62.7	61.2	763,000,000
Stay fit	15.9	15.5	15.8	189,000,000
Stay clear	2.1	2.0	2.1	24,000,000
Total	100	100	100	1,250,000,000

EXHIBIT 9   Image of Ireland

Perception of Country	Personality of People
Green	Relaxed
Environmentally friendly	Sociable
Natural	Friendly
Unspoiled	Different
Lost Arcadia	Humorous/witty
Underdeveloped	Pub atmosphere

Heineken management, rather than to develop a knee jerk reaction to the Guinness–Grand Met merger.

He believed that Murphy's reputation was improving both in Ireland and throughout the world. He did not want to jeopardize the gains made in the last several years. However, he was concerned with the stagnant nature of the beer industry in Europe and North America. He called a meeting for June 10, 1997, to discuss the marketing strategy for Murphy's.

Before he met with the Marketing department members, he stopped by Marien Kakebeeke's office. The managing director reminded him of the corporate goal for Murphy's, which is 20 percent of the world's stout market by the year 2000. "I know that is ambitious, Patrick, but I am confident you and your staff can achieve it."

"Do you realize that the Cork Brewery is almost at capacity now?" asked Patrick. "Even if we stimulate demand, how will we be able to meet it with production limits? Also, recall that we expanded the brewery in 1995."[13]

When Patrick, D. Ford, and Dan Leahy sat down that morning to discuss the future of Murphy's, they considered several questions:

How important is a strong showing in the Irish domestic market to Murphy's? Must they make a strong showing there to be successful worldwide?

Should Murphy's employ a global rather than local marketing strategy worldwide? The "I'm not bitter" campaign has been successful in the United Kingdom, so should several possible strategies be used especially in the large markets of the United States and continental Europe?

Is Murphy's destined to be a "niche" product forever? Will these brands ever reach the place where they command a substantial market share?

Should the company continue to make the two brands only at the Cork brewery for the lucrative U.S. market or should they consider making the product in that country? It worked for automobiles, why not beer?

Will Murphy's ever be able to achieve the status of other products that are famous for their Irish heritage such as Guinness, Bailey's Irish Cream, Jameson Irish Whiskey, Waterford Crystal, and Belleek China?

End Notes

1. John Willman and Ross Tieman, "Grand Met, Guinness to Merge," *Financial Times,* Tuesday, May 13, 1997, p. 1.
2. *Murphy Brewery Limited: A Profile,* undated.
3. Company sources.
4. Company fact sheet.
5. Barry O'Keeffe, " 'Black Stuff' Underpins Profit Raise at Guinness," *The Irish Times,* March 21, 1997.
6. "Master of the Bar," *The Economist,* May 17, 1997, p. 73.
7. Barry O'Keeffe, " 'Black Stuff' Underpins Profit Raise at Guinness."
8. Paul O'Kane, "Murphy Boosts Exports," *The Irish Times,* March 7, 1996.
9. Paul O'Kane, "Murphy's Aims to Double Its Sales in Three Years," *The Irish Times,* June 14, 1996.
10. Paul O'Kane, "Murphy Boosts Exports."
11. "Domestic Beer Shipments Drop 2.1% in '95 While Volume Dips 1.7%," *Beverage Industry,* January 1996, pp. 24–32.
12. "Craft-Brewing Industry Fact Sheet—February 1997," http://www.Beertown.org/craftbrew.html.
13. Paul O'Kane, "Murphy's Plans Major Expansion," *The Irish Times,* August 16, 1995.

CASE 4–4
SHORIN-RYU KARATE ACADEMY

Classes were over for the day at the Shorin-Ryu Karate Academy in Waltham, Massachusetts, and Sensei[1] James True (owner) had just received a call from one of the MBA students who had been working with him for the past four months. Eric had called excitedly to tell Jim that he and his MBA consulting team had just won the finals of the consulting project presentation competition. The team of MBA students had contacted Jim in January 1996 to see if they could work with him as partial fulfillment of their degree program. Jim had jumped at the chance to have a team of outsiders take a look at his business and the issues he was just starting to address.

Sensei Jim had started the academy in 1980 in the garage of his home. The academy was now located in a state-of-the-art training facility in Waltham and had a customer base of 324 active students. Jim had reached a point in both his business and karate careers in which he felt the need to grow. Jim had identified five areas that the student consulting team had focused on in their project. One, could he develop a better sense of managing the karate business? Two, could he increase the number of students at the academy? Three, were his students (and their parents) becoming dissatisfied with his use of student instructors? Four, was his advertising effective? Finally, was he at the point where he could and/or should open a second location?

Jim was excited for the student consulting team. He thought they had worked hard over the past few months, and they were a nice group of people. (One of the consulting team members had even started karate classes during the consulting project.) The team had provided Jim with some interesting information and recommendations. It was up to Jim, however, to ensure the steady growth of his business.

The Martial Arts Industry

While the origins of karate date back to around the 17th century, martial arts were not popularized in the United States until the late 1940s. By the middle 1990s, the U.S. commercialized martial arts instruction market was estimated to be a $1.5 billion business (the first karate school in the United States opened in 1956) and was second only to computer networking services in its 1994 growth rate.[2] While interest in the martial arts had grown substantially in the United States, Japan had experienced an equally substantial decrease in demand. Apparently, Japanese youth regarded karate as a sport for the poor, with foreign sports such as football and basketball taking precedent.

The martial arts arena was comprised of many disciplines, each representing various styles, forms, and techniques:[3]

---

[1] *Sensei* means teacher or instructor.

[2] Ferguson, Tim W. "Let's Talk to the Master." *Forbes* (October 23, 1995): 138–42.

[3] Much of this information was taken from Bob Condor, "Spirited Workout," *Chicago Tribune* (March 7, 1996): section 5, p. 4.

This case was prepared by Victoria L. Crittenden, associate professor of marketing at Boston College, and William F. Crittenden, associate professor of management at Northeastern University. Research assistance was provided by David Angus, Boston College/Andersen Consulting Fund. The case is designed as the basis for class discussion.

- *Karate,* developed in Okinawa in the 17th century, was an ancient Japanese tradition comprised largely of punching and kicking in a linear fashion.
- *Aikido* ("aye-key-doe") was also a Japanese practice and incorporated a Zen philosophy in its doctrine. The practice was based on the use of the opponent's energy to defeat.
- *Judo,* also stemming from the Japanese culture and developed in 1882, consisted of grappling or wrestling the opponent.
- *Taekwondo* (the form used in the Olympic Games) was a Korean discipline. While similar to karate, taekwondo involved more spinning and back kicks. While potentially the most deadly of the arts, taekwon do was thought to be the most popular of the martial arts in the United States.
- *Hapkido* was also a Korean discipline. Considered the least "spiritual" of the art forms, this form placed emphasis on the fighting aspect.
- *Tai chi* had its origins in China. Considered more meditative than most martial arts, it was gaining favor in the United States due to its gentle orientation (although in China the form could be very violent).[4]
- *Kung fu* was very intense and involved many blocks and retaliation techniques in its fighting. Kung fu was popularized in the United States via Hollywood (e.g., the "Kung Fu" television series in the 1970s with David Carradine).

Self-defense and concerns about children's safety fueled interest in the martial arts. Classes were dedicated to safety tips and demonstrations of physical tactics children and adults could use to thwart assault or abduction. As well, the media had done a good job of plugging martial arts with movies and television series such as *Karate Kid, Mortal Kombat, Teenage Mutant Ninja Turtles,* and "Mighty Morphin Power Rangers." Some estimates suggested that in the early stages of market development, close to 99 percent of all students enrolled in martial arts classes did so to learn to protect themselves.

However, personal discipline had become a driving force in martial arts instruction by the mid-1990s. In particular, karate combined the mastery of combat skills with the mastery of self-protection and the development of character and virtue. Martial arts training could help build a person's confidence and self-esteem, which could also aid in resisting the forces of violence. The physical fitness boom in American society had also fueled interest in the martial arts. Martial arts enhanced hand–eye coordination and flexibility and conditioned the body for other sporting activities.

There were thousands of martial arts businesses throughout the United States. While the typical academy had 75 to 100 students, there were operations boasting several hundred students and multiple locations. Such large chains included Y.H. Park with seven locations in the New York area and around 3,500 students, Master Glazier's Karate International based in New Jersey and similar in size to Y.H. Park, and East West Karate with 1,200 students. Additionally, there were several professional associations. The National Association of Professional Martial Artists (NAPMA) was headquartered in Florida, and the World Traditional Taekwondo Union was based in Arkansas.

Many companies were able to capitalize on the fragmented martial arts industry. Both Education Funding Co. (Chevy Chase, Maryland) and United Professionals, Inc.,

---

[4] While *tai chi* was practiced by more people, worldwide, than any other martial art, it was not as popular among Americans as *karate* and *judo.*

(Coral Springs, Florida) were in the billing business. United Professionals was reported to have collected around $18 million in 1994 by handling the billing for almost 500 schools. The largest martial arts uniform and equipment manufacturer in the United States was the Century Martial Art Supply of Oklahoma with yearly sales around $40 million. The second largest supplier was Macho Products of Florida.

The Marketplace.   Before the mid to late 1980s, about 90 percent of martial arts enrollees were between ages 16 and 25. By the middle 1990s, however, students spanned all ages. The American Taekwondo Association offered "Tiny Tigers" classes for students ages 3 to 5 all the way to "Silver VIP's" for those age 50 to 75 (and sometimes older). However, there were no national statistics on the number of children or adults taking martial arts lessons.

The lack of national statistics made it difficult to segment the market by age. However, estimates were that preteens accounted for about 40 percent of martial arts students in the United States. Parents were enrolling their children in martial arts classes for discipline training, self-defense, and physical fitness. As mentioned earlier, the influence of television and movies had spurred children's interest in the martial arts also. Martial arts programs were found in affluent suburbs and in the inner city. (Many inner city programs were the result of larger antiviolence programs.) Martial arts training was thought to be of special value to children with physical or mental disabilities, with these students seeing improvements in physical coordination (particularly relating to their motor skills) and self-confidence. Additionally, there appeared to be growing interest in parent/child martial arts classes.

Regarding older Americans, the Dallas area's Steel Magnolias was a karate demonstration group comprised of four women over age 62. The group performed at nursing homes, store openings, ceremonial events, and karate tournaments. The women in the group credited karate with multiple benefits, such as improved balance, stronger bodies, and increased self-confidence.

While considered a traditionally male preserve, the martial arts were increasingly focused on by women. Female membership in various martial arts associations was increasing steadily. For example, the U.S.A. Karate Federation of New Jersey tripled its female membership from 1988 to 1993, and the United States Tae Kwon Do Union had seen steady growth in female membership. Factors contributing to this increase were the physical fitness boom, crumbling cultural barriers, self-defense, and perceived psychological benefits related to careers. Women reported that the martial arts changed their personality, making them more assertive in all areas of their lives (e.g., home, workplace). The major stumbling block for women in the early stages of their martial arts training was fighting (called *kumite*). Initially, women were reluctant to fight, but typically lost this inhibition as training continued.

The martial arts had also entered the American workplace. Business organizations such as the Trump Taj Mahal Casino Resort, Cigna, and Peco Energy Company sponsored in-house martial arts lessons. Workplace benefits were thought to be improved physical fitness, relief from stress, enhanced teamwork skills, better personal relations skills, and humility.

In response to the growing adult interest in the martial arts, classes were being offered such as "cardio-karate," which combined karate movement with aerobic exercise. Cardio-karate focused on strengthening the heart muscle, making the class particularly valuable for people with heart conditions. Classes such as this did not follow the same regimen as typical karate classes in that the student did not wear the martial arts uniform and no self-defense training was involved.

Leisure Time. Leisure was one of the biggest growth industries for the 1990s. It was estimated that the average household spent anywhere from $1,500 to $3,500 a year on entertainment.[5] Middle-aged Americans were the largest group when it came to spending money on leisure time. In the 1990s, this group consisted of the baby boomers so leisure time was devoted toward family-oriented activities. However, this group was experiencing a decline in the amount of leisure time.

The Americans' Use of Time Project grouped leisure activities into 13 categories: adult education, religious services, other organizational (club) activities, going to entertainment places, visiting, conversing, sport and outdoor activities, hobby/craft/game activities, watching TV, reading, listening to the radio/recordings, thinking/relaxing, and travel to/from leisure activities.[6] Of these, adult education was one of the fastest growing areas. Additionally, time spent on sports and outdoor activities had more than doubled in a 20-year period, with TV watching and family conversations also showing increases. These gains appeared to come at the expense of newspaper reading and visiting.

From a gender perspective, the time project found that men spent more time than women on sport and outdoor activities and adult education. However, the two sexes spent almost equal time on activities in the other 11 categories.

Concerns about children's health had begun creeping into the leisure time of both children and their parents. In the early 1990s, the President's Council on Physical Fitness reported that 40 percent of children between the ages of five and eight were overweight, had high blood pressure, or had high cholesterol levels. This led to a huge increase in the number of health clubs offering children's fitness programs. As well, child care and sports programs began addressing the health and fitness concerns of children in their programs.

Instruction. Students of the martial arts generally attributed their selection of techniques, not to the technique itself, but to the instructor. Reinforcing this selection process, tae kwon do instructor Charlie Lee said that it did not matter what form of martial arts a student took since the basic principles of martial arts were the same (discipline, respect, confidence, self-defense).[7] He said that what was important was the instructor.

Basically, the "right" martial arts school used positive reinforcement, emphasized education, and focused on self-control (not confrontation). Suggested selection criteria when looking at martial arts programs included parental access to lessons, free or cheap introductory lessons, willingness of the head instructor to discuss teaching methods prior to student's enrollment, whether the head instructor actually taught classes, willingness of the head instructor to allow the potential student access to current students and their opinions, proof of liability insurance, and language skills (strong English-speaking skills).[8]

---

[5] Cutler, Blayne "Where Does the Free Time Go?" *American Demographics* (November, 1990): 36–38; Robinson, John P. "As We Like It." *American Demographics* (February 1993): 44–48; "That's Entertainment!" *American Demographics* (July 1993): 16. Exact numbers were difficult to calculate for the entertainment/leisure industry since estimates could include everything from clothes to cable TV.

[6] Robinson, John P. "The Leisure Pie." *American Demographics* (November 1990): 39.

[7] McManus, Kevin. "Karate Chops for Children." *Washington Post* (August 21, 1992), sec. NJ, p. 1, col. 3.

[8] Ibid.

A typical martial arts class was attended twice a week and consisted of stretching, arm and leg movements,[9] *katas* (choreographed movements designed for offensive/defensive postures), and sparring (fighting). Respect was a dominant theme in any karate class. The teacher was always addressed as "Sensei," and students and instructor bowed as a show of mutual respect at the beginning and ending of every class, as well as at the beginning and end of a sparring match. This respect extended beyond the dojo (training room) to both school and home. Many instructors expressed interest in school events and in grades.[10] At home, parents might suggest asking Sensei to help resolve a disagreement.

Participant ranking in a martial arts class was denoted by belt color. A beginning student was awarded a white belt after a few weeks of instruction. A black belt was the highest belt ranking that could be achieved. Colors in between were typically orange, gold, purple, green, blue, and brown. (There were several degrees of both brown and black belts.) In class, students gathered according to rank—highest belts in the class lined up first, then descending order to white or no belt.

From the school owner's perspective, there were some standards or benchmarks regarding the number of students at the school. A rough barometer was 100 to 150 students per 1,000 square feet of space. The number of "active students" was an important measure. Basically, active students could be broken down into three components: active paying students, active nonpaying students, and nonactive paying students. The active paying student measure was the number of students paying monthly tuition (and attending classes). The gauge was that this would be about 80 percent of the active students. Active nonpaying students were those who had paid in full or had bartered services for tuition remission (e.g., helped around the academy either through assisting with class teaching or office/maintenance activities). Nonactive paying students were students on the monthly payment plan but not attending classes. Owners could not depend on these students as long-term revenue generators unless the owner did something to get the student to attend classes again.

American Shorin-Ryu Karate Association

The American Shorin-Ryu Karate Association (ASKA) was a nonprofit 501(c)3 organization under the guidance of Papa Paul Keller, Papa Christopher Clarke, Papa Joe Hays, Shihan Dai Jules Pomier, and Dai Sempei James True. The association studied the Matsubayashi style of Shorin-Ryu karate. The Matsubayashi Shorin-Ryu Family Tree is shown in Exhibit 1.

The ASKA was a nationally prominent karate association that sponsored clinics and camps for all levels of students. President of the ASKA was Paul Keller. Papa Keller, a former U.S. weapons champion, was a leader in the field of VIP protection. The head instructor of the ASKA was Christopher Clarke. Papa Chris, who worked for the U.S. Department of State, was regarded as an expert on martial arts history. He spoke and read Chinese. There were three ASKA Massachusetts schools: the Shorin-Ryu Karate

---

[9] These exercises were typically done to the count of 10 in Japanese. *"Ichi! Ni! San! Shi! Go! Roku! Shichi! Ha-chi! Ku! Ju!"* After saying *"go"* and *"ju,"* students yell *"Kiai!"* The *kiai* was the expelling of breath from the inner soul and was thought to provide the martial arts student with greater strength.

[10] The American Taekwondo Association offered the "Karate for Kids" program which rewarded victory patches to children who displayed growth in three areas: (1) making the honor roll or making grade improvements in school, (2) participating in extracurricular activities, and (3) good conduct at home and working in the community.

EXHIBIT 1 **Matsubayashi Shorin-Ryu Family Tree**

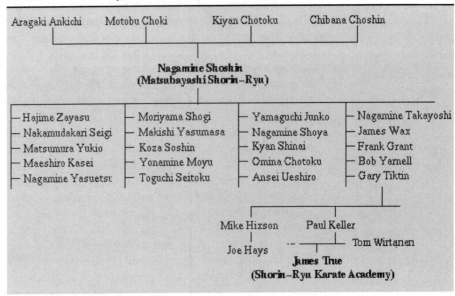

Academy in Waltham, the Northeast Shorin-Ryu Karate Academy in Andover, and the Academy of Traditional Karate in Wilmington.

The Shorin-Ryu Karate Academy in Waltham was led by Sensei James True. Sensei Jim was head instructor and had achieved the rank of 5th-degree Black Belt as well as 4th-degree Black Belt in Kobudo (Okinawan weapons). Sensei Jim was assisted by Sensei Michael Pepe, 4th-degree Black Belt. The school offered a wide variety of classes for ages four years and up.

The Northeast Shorin-Ryu Karate Academy in Andover was led by Sensei Dick Wolnik, who was a 3d-degree Black Belt and had assistant instructor certification. The school was run through the Andover Department of Community Service and met twice a week at a local elementary school. Youth classes started at eight years of age, and adult classes were held for students 12 years and older. Sensei Wolnik was assisted by Sensei Thomas Wirtanen, 4th-degree Black Belt.

The Academy of Traditional Karate in Wilmington was led by Sensei Todd Keane. Sensei was a full instructor and held the rank of 3d-degree Black Belt. The Wilmington school offered a wide variety of classes for all ages.

Students in the association participated at the following ranks (designated by belt color): no-belt, white, orange, gold, purple, purple with green stripe, green, blue, brown, and black.[11]

The Shorin-Ryu Karate Academy

The mission statement of the Academy was

> to develop and build an individual's confidence, discipline, respect, and achievement, while offering an opportunity to enrich a person's inner and outer life by the short-term accumula-

---

[11] According to the rules of Shorin-Ryu, students could not attain the status of black belt until the age of 16.

tion of physical stamina and coordination and the long lasting benefit of inner strength and peace.

Sensei Jim was a 1980 graduate of Bentley College in Waltham. He held a bachelor of arts in education and the social sciences. Jim began his karate training in 1975 and completed his black belt training in 1979. It was during this four-year training process that Jim decided that he wanted to own a karate academy.

In addition to owning, managing, and instructing at the academy, Jim was active in taking karate into the Waltham community. Jim held classes for the Waltham YMCA (for all ages), the Greater Waltham Association of Retarded Citizens, and the Waltham High School Adult Evening Division.

Location.   After an initial start-up in Jim's garage, the academy moved to a 2,500-square-foot, custom-designed facility in Waltham. The facility included three dojos (training rooms), male and female locker rooms, a small retail counter, an observation area (where visitors could observe classes), and Jim's office.[12]

Waltham, Massachusetts, was located in the middle of several affluent Boston-area suburbs. Seventy-seven percent of the academy's customer base resided in Waltham (56%), Watertown (12%), and Newton (9%). Newton was the largest and wealthiest of the three suburban communities with a 1990 population of 82,585 and 58.9 percent of its annual household incomes over US$50,000. Waltham's 1990 population was 57,878, with 43.9 percent of its annual household incomes over US$50,000. The smallest of the three communities was Watertown. Its 1990 population was 33,284 and 24.7 percent of its households had annual incomes over US$50,000.

Students.   Youth members of the academy fell into four major groups: (1) Pee Wee Beginners were called *Little Dragons* (ages 4 to 6), (2) Junior Youth Beginners were called *Junior Ninjas* (ages 7 to 9), (3) Youth Beginners were called *Samurais* (ages 10 to 14), and (4) Youth Intermediate to Advanced were called *Daimyos* or *Shoguns* (ages 8 to 14, with the group depending upon belt color). Also, there was a fifth group, *Teen Class* for ages 13 to 17. The youth market comprised 65 percent of the academy's membership base.

Adults attended class in the evenings with the appropriate level of student. For example, a beginning adult could attend class 7 to 8 PM on Tuesday or Thursday or 6 to 7 PM on Wednesday. Adult membership ranged in age from 21 to 50, with the majority of students in their 20s and 30s.

Jim used a software package, Black Belt Management, to maintain information (e.g., enrollment, advancement) on each of his students. Black Belt Management was designed specifically for karate institutions.

To gather additional information about youth students, the MBA consulting group had administered a survey to parents and guardians of students attending the youth classes. The survey was based on a convenience sample. (The survey was administered to adults watching youth classes at various times during a one-week period.) Exhibit 2 shows quantitative and qualitative results of the survey from parents of 66 of the youth.

---

[12]Retail sales accounted for around 4 percent of 1995 revenue. In addition to purchasing all necessary equipment (e.g., protective fighting gear), students could buy sweatshirts, T-shirts, jackets, duffel bags, and patches from the academy.

Programs and Pricing.   Most karate students attended two classes a week at the academy. However, the school did allow students to attend one class a week, and members of one of the Black Belt Clubs attended classes three times per week. The academy was open from 3 to 10 PM weekdays and 9 AM to 1 PM Saturdays. Children's

---

EXHIBIT 2   **MBA Consulting Team's Youth Survey Results**

1. How did you hear about Shorin-Ryu?

Child's friend	33%
Other parent	14
Advertising	21
YMCA program	32

2. If you looked at other schools, why did you choose Shorin-Ryu?

Jim/instruction	32%
Recommendation/reputation	14
Other	12
Didn't look at other schools	42

3. Why does your child take karate?

Likes it	13%
Self-esteem/confidence	43
Discipline	27
Fun/new skills	07
Other	10

4. What is your town of residence?

Waltham	56%
Newton	09
Watertown	12
Belmont	06
Other	17

5. What is your annual income?

Less than $20,000	06%
$21,000–30,000	13
$31,000–40,000	05
$41,000–50,000	18
Greater than $50,000	58

6. Do you have dual income in your household?

Yes	53%
No	47

7. Would you like to see the range of classes expanded?

Yes	39%
No	50
Undecided	11

8. Would you like to see the range of hours expanded?

Yes	27%
No	62
Undecided	11

9. How do you feel about the current size of classes?

Too small	00%
Too large	45
Just right	55

10. How does karate compare to other activities costwise?

Much less	34%
Less	21
Same	12
More	15
Much more	08
Undecided	10

11. How does karate compare to other activities timewise?

Much less	06%
Less	21
Same	42
More	26
Much more	01
Undecided	04

12. Does your child participate in other sports?

Yes	89%
No	11

13. Did you consider any other school(s) before joining Shorin-Ryu?

Yes	29%
No	71

14. Was Shorin-Ryu (as a style) important in your decision to join?

Yes	11%
No	89

15. Whose decision was it to join karate?

Parent	36%
Child	32
Both	32

16. Has either parent ever taken karate lessons?

Yes	15%
No	85

Qualitative Comments

"Jim is wonderful . . . he is inspirational, but he is the school. When he is not here the level of instruction is not the same."

"I like the idea that the school is like a community with the kids getting involved in the parties, movies, and car washes, and participating in Walk-a-Thons and Bike-a-Thons. It's great that the kids don't just go to and from classes and that's [the extent of their involvement]."

"Jim is wonderful!"

"I worry that my child will get bored with being a brown belt for so long."

EXHIBIT 3   Student Enrollment per Program, January–April, 1996

Program	Number of Students
Introductory special	0
3-month	10
6-month (1 class/week)	62
6-month (2 classes/week)	20
6-month family (1 class/week)	32
6-month family (2 classes/week)	2
12-month (1 class/week)	49
12-month (2 classes/week)	32
12-month family (1 class/week)	16
12-month family (2 classes/week)	17
Junior black belt (18 months)	16
Adult black belt (18 months)	13
24-month black belt	13
36-month black belt	3
Black belt, 18-month family	39

Source: Consulting report.

classes were taught in the afternoons and Saturday mornings; adult classes were taught in the evenings.

Regular programs included introductory special, three- and six-month trials, 12-month martial arts, black belt and junior black belt clubs, spring/summer vacation camps, women awareness, and private lessons. Monthly payment schedules were possible for all but the introductory offering. However, to encourage payment in full, a 10 percent discount was offered if full tuition was paid at the start of the program. Additionally, upon request Sensei Jim offered various demonstrations and martial arts talks to particular interest groups.[13] Birthday parties (including a martial arts demonstration) could be held at the academy. Exhibit 3 provides an overview of the number of students enrolled in various programs in the first half of 1996.

Introductory Special.   The $19.95 introductory special included a karate gi (uniform), a 30-minute private lesson, and a beginner's group lesson (with an appropriate age group). This introductory offer was designed to provide the prospective student with a sense of karate. Participation also allowed Sensei Jim to gauge the student's level of interest and maturity, which was particularly important with very young students.

Three- and Six-Month Trials.   These programs were available to the student who (or whose family) did not feel comfortable making a long-term commitment to learning karate. The three-month program was priced at $120, and the six-month program was $390 for two lessons a week and $240 for one lesson a week. To encourage family member participation at the academy, the second family member received a 20 percent discount off the regular price, with each additional member receiving a 50 percent discount.

Twelve-Month Martial Arts Program.   This 12-month program was offered for the

_____

[13] For example, Sensei Jim provided a martial arts demonstration to one student's Cub Scout troop. In addition to demonstrating various katas and weapons, Jim talked to the group about how to defend themselves against bullies. This demonstration resulted in one of the Cub Scouts becoming an active student at the academy.

student who knew that she wanted to learn karate and advance through the various levels. The program was priced at $720 for two lessons per week and $420 for one lesson per week. Family memberships were $1,020 for two lessons per family member a week and $750 for one lesson per family member per week.

Black Belt Clubs.   The Black Belt Clubs consisted of junior and adult academy members. Students in these clubs were required to attend three classes per week. Club members were eligible to join the SWAT (**S**tudents **W**orking **A**s **T**eachers) and demonstration teams and could participate in extra fighting and weapons classes.[14] Membership fees were $1,260 for 18 months, $1,560 for 24 months, and $1,980 for 36 months. An 18-month Family Black Belt program was priced at $1,800.

Spring/Summer Vacation Camps.   The academy offered week-long spring and summer vacation camps (9 AM to 2 PM) for youth students aged six and above. Daily programs were designed to be both entertaining and a learning experience. A typical day included kata, kumite, karate kick ball, and karate stories. Price of the camp was $75 for one child per family, $135 for two children per family, and $185 for three children per family.

Women Aware.   This was a four-week program focusing upon physical and psychological techniques designed to stop an attacker. The course was offered twice a year (October and May) at a price of $75.

Private Lessons.   Students could sign up for private lessons, which Sensei would give at a mutually convenient time. A 30-minute private lesson was $20, with a one-hour lesson priced at $35.

Extracurricular Activities.   Jim felt that even non–karate-practicing parents would want to participate in activities at the academy. The academy had a parent organization that planned and coordinated monthly events for the youth members. Examples of such activities included movie nights, holiday parties, pool parties, picnics, and field trips for the older youth.

Marketing Communications.   A major promotional event held at the academy was the "Bring a Friend" Week. During this week, each student was asked to bring a friend to class.[15] The friend participated in all class activities and at the end of the session was recognized by Sensei Jim and provided with a packet of information about the academy. (The packet also included a karate belt key chain.) Historically, there had been 20 to 25 friends attending the academy during the promotional week. However, no follow-up or tracking of the program was conducted.

Consistent with most martial arts programs, Shorin-Ryu ran promotional events such as a free introductory lesson, half-price tuition for additional family members, and a free uniform with enrollment.

In 1995, the Shorin-Ryu Karate Academy spent $11,910 advertising in local newspapers, the yellow pages, on cable TV, on shopping carts, and through direct mail. Exhibit 4 breaks down expenditures for each medium.

The MBA consulting group working with Sensei Jim had utilized the information stored in Jim's student database to obtain an overall idea of student responsiveness to the academy's marketing communications effort. Exhibit 5 provides this overview. Additionally, the consulting team had tracked the communication mediums in relation to the geographic density of the academy's student base. Exhibit 6 relates this spending to customer attraction in Waltham, Newton, and Watertown.

---

[14] Kobudo, the study of weapons, is considered to be karate's sister art.

[15] The friend (or parent) had to fill out and sign a Disclaimer of Liability (which included address and other demographic information) before participating in the class.

EXHIBIT 4   **Advertising Expenditures by Medium, 1995**

Shopping cart	$ 1,310
Cable TV	1,667
Newspaper	3,811
Direct mail	2,501
Yellow pages	2,263
Other	358
Total	$11,910

Source: Consulting report.

EXHIBIT 5   **Student Responsiveness to Marketing Communications**

Medium	Percentage of Student Base Response
Referral	45%
Newspaper	19
Yellow pages	15
YMCA program	11
Direct mail	05
Bring-a-Friend Week	03
Other	02

Source: Consulting report.

EXHIBIT 6   **Student Responsiveness to Marketing Communications by Town**

Medium	Waltham	Newton	Watertown
Referral	48%	46%	38%
Newspaper	21	23	28
Yellow pages	2	—	7
YMCA program	24	23	10
Direct mail	2	8	7
Bring-a-Friend Week	1	—	4
Other	2	—	6

Source: Consulting report.

Internal Operations.   Three major operating areas of the Academy were staffing, financial management, and the membership renewal process.

Regarding staffing, Sensei Michael Pepe assisted Jim with classes whenever possible.[16] Other than Sensei Mike's help, Jim relied on students to help him with classes. Typical to all martial arts training programs, students worked as nonpaid instructors as part of their advanced training. Because of the volunteer nature, however, there was a lack of consistency in both the availability and quality of help.

The academy utilized a cash basis of accounting. Under this method, revenues were recognized when cash was received and expenses were recognized when cash was expended. Company finances were maintained with the use of the QuickBooks software package. (See Exhibits 7 and 8 for the company's 1994 and 1995 financial statements.)

---

[16] Mike was a firefighter; karate was his avocation.

EXHIBIT 7   Profit and Loss Statement, 1994–First Quarter 1996

	1994	1995	1st Quarter 1996
Income			
After school	$ 3,420.00	$ 3,595.00	$ 7,420.34
Camps	—	—	—
Vacation camp	—	$ 1,015.00	$ 510.00
Other	—	$ 2,220.00	—
Total camps	$ 1,485.00	—	—
Deposit 95	$ 10.00	$ 21,946.12	—
Reirrb Exp	($299.00)	—	
Sales	$ 7,320.59	$ 6,653.56	$ 1,187.37
Seminars	$ 4,028.39	$ 3,645.00	—
Services	$ 296.16	$ 463.08	$ 63.00
Special rates	—	$ 792.00	—
Testing	$ 5,575.93	$ 3,645.00	$ 1,410.00
Tournaments	$ 7,445.49	$ 4,672.68	—
Tuition	—	—	—
ASKA Fee	—	$ 360.00	$ 150.00
Intro. lesson	$ 892.50	$ 439.05	$ 179.60
Down payments	$ 21,295.50	$ 21,666.00	$ 7,215.00
Monthly dues	—	$ 142.45	$ 13,307.35
Other	$ 99,598.44	$ 74,929.25	$ 7,407.00
Woman Aware	—	$ 375.00	$ 300.00
Total Income	$ 151,069.00	$ 146,559.19	$ 39,149.66
Expenses	—	$ 126.00	—
Accounting services			
Advertising	—	—	—
Newspaper ad	—	—	$ 939.78
Shopping cart sign	—	—	$ 177.50
Sign fee	—	$ 18.00	$ 9.00
Yellow pages	—	—	$ 788.00
Other	—	$ 11,891.95	$ 200.00
Total advertising	$ 14,318.85	—	—
Auto	—	—	—
Auto gas	—	$ 919.79	$ 221.07
Jeep expense	—	$ 445.77	—
Registry renewal	—	—	$ 30.00
Other	—	$ 6,248.13	$ 1,474.25
Total auto	$ 17,474.12	—	—
Charges	—	—	—
Bank	$ 110.50	—	—
Other	$ 0.50	—	—
Total charges	—	—	—
Business expense	$ 1,517.44	$ 4,692.46	$ 1,352.52
Cleaning	$ 644.81	$ 616.05	$ 106.52
Contributions (donations)	$ 532.98	$ 382.29	—
Customer satisfaction	$ 195.00	—	—
Deposit correction	$ 14.55	($3.00)	—
Donation	$ 460.00	$ 321.48	$ 25.10
Dues	$ 2,302.73	$ 1,980.00	$ 500.00
Equipment rent	$ 334.00	$ 634.60	—
Giveaway	$ 1,527.42	$ 3,954.42	$ 498.22
Home insurance	$ 495.00	—	—

EXHIBIT 7   Profit and Loss Statement, 1994–First Quarter 1996

	1994	1995	1st Quarter 1996
Insurance	—	—	—
Insurance—building con't.	—	$ 318.00	—
Life Insurance	—	—	$ 156.60
Other	—	$ 1,808.96	$ 316.74
Total insurance	$ 2,781.89	—	—
Interest expense	—	—	—
Loan	($ 11,369.26)	($246.50)	—
Total interest expense	—	—	—
Magazine subscription	—	$ 28.94	—
Miscellaneous expense	—	$ 109.42	$ 10.35
New car	$ 1,615.00	$ 751.16	—
New home	$ 14,809.73	$ 7,178.85	—
Office supplies	$ 2,138.20	$ 4,780.58	$ 374.75
Payout fees (travel)	—	$ 1,245.67	—
Personal C.C.	$ 3,909.72	$ 13,399.72	$ 6,400.00
Printing	$ 148.03	$ 801.15	$ 221.88
Professional fees	$ 1,823.00	$ 907.76	$ 50.00
Refund	$ 45.00	$ 1,025.00	$ 95.00
Rent	$ 19,349.98	$ 25,899.96	$ 6,474.99
Repairs	—	—	—
Building	—	$ 122.97	—
Other	—	$ 666.51	—
Total repairs	$ 3,719.76	—	—
Returned check	$ 928.95	$ 366.47	$ 50.00
School equipment	$ 8,316.37	$ 6,452.42	$ 267.88
Shipping and handling	$ 89.70	$ 463.82	$ 127.09
Special	$ 23,433.70	$ 4,509.00	$ 600.00
Supplies	$ 509.52	$ 6,619.13	$ 1,728.73
Travel and entertainment	—	—	—
Meals	$ 84.58	$ 620.13	—
Travel	$ 357.00	$ 1,026.87	$ 1,597.50
Other	$ 511.50	$ 1,006.60	—
Total travel and entertainment	—	—	—
Taxes	—	—	—
Federal	$ 6,000.00	—	—
Local	$ 50.55	—	$ 73.81
Property	—	$ 21.31	—
State	$ 1,910.00	$ 2,960.00	$ 1,452.00
Other	$ 28,044.27	$ 32,187.87	$ 184.21
Total taxes	—	—	—
Telephone	—	—	—
Car phone	—	$ 708.02	$ 137.05
Local	—	—	$ 109.27
Long-distance	—	—	$ 47.18
Other	—	$ 1,585.79	$ 45.39
Total telephone	$ 3,335.30	—	—
Uncategorized	$ 6,634.48	—	—
Utilities	—	—	—
Electric	$ 1,979.24	$ 2,856.54	$ 733.03
Total Utilities	—	—	—
Wages	—	$ 5,800.00	$ 1,100.00
Total Expense	$ 161,084.11	$ 158,210.06	$ 28,675.41
Net income	($10,015.11)	($11,650.87)	$ 10,474.25

EXHIBIT 8 Balance Sheet, December 31, 1994, 1995, 1996

	1994	1995	1996
Assets			
Current assets			
Checking/savings Shorin-Ryu	$ 24,575.50	$ 14,918.99	$ 27,235.47
Accounts Receivable	$ 1,626.00	($214.90)	($2,258.00)
Total current assets	$ 26,201.50	$ 14,704.09	$ 24,977.47
Total assets	$ 26,201.50	$ 14,704.09	$ 24,977.47
Liabilities & equity			
Liabilities			
Current liabilities			
Sales tax	$ 110.50	$ 238.71	$ 268.64
Total current liabilities	$ 110.50	$ 238.71	$ 268.64
Total liabilities	$ 110.50	$ 238.71	$ 268.64
Equity			
Earnings	—	($10,015.11)	($21,895.98)
Net income	($10,015.11)	($11,650.87)	$ 10,474.25
Open bal. equity	$ 36,106.11	$ 36,131.36	$ 36,130.56
Total equity	$ 26,091.00	$ 14,465.38	$ 24,708.83
Total liabilities & equity	$ 26,201.50	$ 14,704.09	$ 24,977.47

EXHIBIT 9 Renewal Letter

Dear Parents of _____ ,

I am writing to you as a reminder to let you know that your current karate program will be completed on the 30th of this month, 1996.

DON'T DELAY, take time NOW to decide on your next KARATE PROGRAM to further your KARATE EDUCATION!!!

I have enclosed a copy of our current karate programs and have highlighted the one that I feel would best help you maintain and achieve your short and long term goals of becoming a BLACK BELT.

If you have any questions, please feel free to call and discuss them with me. Thanks for your help and support in making the students and instructors of the SHORIN-RYU KARATE ACADEMY the BEST THAT THEY CAN BE!!!

YOURS IN KARATE-DO

SENSEI JAMES A. TRUE

Membership renewal was an important component of the academy's operational process. In the middle of each month, Jim used his student database to sort and develop a list of students whose memberships expired at the end of the month. Jim would print a hard copy of the renewal list. A renewal letter (Exhibit 9) and a listing of current karate programs were then handed to each of these students when they attended their next class. (Jim would highlight the program that he felt best suited the needs of the individual student.) Once a renewal letter was distributed, Jim would highlight (on his hard copy), in yellow, the name of the student who had received the letter.

Memberships were renewed at the student's own pace. Basically, students could re-

EXHIBIT 11 Local Competition

School	Martial Arts	Monthly Price	Promotions	Student Enrollment
Waltham				
Bushido-Zen Martial Arts	Karate	$ 60	Free introductory lessons	15+
Chung Do Kwan-Tae Kwan Do	Tae kwon do	65	None	65
Integrated Martial Arts Development Center	Mixture	70	Free introductory lessons	<100
Masters Self Defense Center	Karate, tai chi, judo	50	2 weeks free & ½ off for 2d family member	200
Savoy School of Self Defense	Mixture	70	None	150
Villar's Self Defense Center	Mixture	35	2 weeks free & ½ off for 2d family member	65
Newton				
Chos Olympic Tae Kwon Do	Tae kwon do	90	1 month free introductory lessons	200
Chung Moo Doe	Chinese American	90	2 free lessons & free uniform for 3-month introductory lessons	100
Esposito's Academy of Self Defense	Karate	50	None	120
Masters of Karate	Karate	57	Free introductory lessons	150
Ye-Sheu Way of the Fist	Mixture	30	None	100
Watertown				
American Karate Academy	Karate	120	None	150
DiRico's Rocky School of Kempo Karate	Karate	60	2 half-hour private lessons for beginners	55
Tokyo Joe's Studio of Self Defense	Mixture	60	2 free introductory lessons & ½ off for 2d family member	65
Wah Lum Kung Fu Academy	Kung fu	50	Free introductory lessons	160

Source: Consulting report.

new their membership, students could fail to renew and tell Sensei Jim that they would not be continuing in the program, or students could fail to respond. Students who renewed membership or told Jim that they were not renewing were crossed off Jim's renewal list. Students whose names were not crossed off the renewal list were eventually transferred to the inactive student file. Jim estimated that about one-half of his students renewed their membership through this process.

Competition. The MBA consulting group had identified 15 direct martial arts competitors in the three communities from which Shorin-Ryu derived a majority of its customers. Exhibit 10 identifies each of these 15 competitors along with the type of martial arts instruction received, the monthly price, regular promotions offered, and the reported student enrollment.

The Academy's Future

Jim felt that, with the help of the MBA consulting group, he had a lot of valuable information. Additionally, the consulting group had made some recommendations based on their survey and secondary research.

A major recommendation was that, to achieve Jim's objective of increasing enroll-ment by 175 students by the year 2000, Jim should target the youth segment (ages 5 through 17). The student team had gone so far as to provide information for this age group for Waltham, Newton, and Watertown. Basically, there were 6,119 individuals in Waltham, 10,887 in Newton, and 3,124 in Watertown in this age category. Of youths in these towns, 0.25 percent (Newton), 2.30 percent (Waltham), and 0.93 percent (Water-town) were active students at Shorin-Ryu.

Jim wondered, however, if he could further penetrate this youth market. If so, what was the best approach? Also, should he focus on growing this market base and just try to maintain his adult market or should he be doing something in the adult market as well?

A related issue was what (if anything) Jim needed to be doing to better manage his current (and future) business. Also, should he begin looking into that second location he had started dreaming about? If so, what communities would make sense?

The consulting team's information would go far in helping Jim look at the market-place and issues that he needed to address. Sensei Jim was happy for the team and glad they had won their presentation competition. He had watched them in the preliminary round of the competition. The quality of their presentation had made him proud of them and, also, very proud of his business.

Sources

American Taekwondo Association. "Taking Martial Arts into the 21st Century to Set the Standard for Others to Follow." *Arkansas Business* (July 31, 1995): S18(1).

Cimons, Marlene. "A Mesmerized Mom Jumps into the Act." *Los Angeles Times* (September 26, 1995), sec. E, p. 1, col. 4.

Cimons, Marlene. "Kick Backs." *Los Angeles Times* (September 26, 1995), sec. E, p. 1, col. 1.

Condor, Bob. "Spirited Workout." *Chicago Tribune* (March 7, 1996), sec. 5, p. 4, col. 1.

Cutler, Blayne. "Where Does the Free Time Go?" *American Demographics* (November 1990): 36–39.

Dickey, Linda. "My Son, the Black Belt." *New York Times* (January 2, 1994), sec. CY, p. 11, col. 2.

Dolan, Carrie. "Health: Concern about Kids' Safety Spurs Rise in Karate and Other Fitness Programs." *The Wall Street Journal* (April 12, 1993), sec. B, p. 1, col. 3.

Ferguson, Tim W. "Let's Talk to the Master." *Forbes* (October 23, 1995): 138–42.

Fields, Suzanne. "Karate for Hansel and Gretel." *Washington Times* (April 19, 1993), sec. E, p. 1, col. 3.

Goodrich, Robert. "Heart Patients Take to Karate." *St. Louis Post Dispatch* (November 14, 1994), sec. I, p. 1, col. 5.

Graden, John. *Black Belt Management: Learn to Run a Highly Profitable School.*

Kadaba, Lini, S. "New Corporate Kicks." *Chicago Tribune* (July 10, 1995), "Evening" sec., p. 7, col. 3.

Kata Consulting Group. "Shorin-Ryu Karate Academy" (May 1996), n.p. (used with permission of Sensei James True).

"Kicking the Habit." *The Economist* (November 20, 1993): 37.

Linke, Denise. "Families That Kick Together Stick Together." *Chicago Tribune* (February 26, 1993), sec. 2D, p. 1, col. 2.

McManus, Kevin. "Karate Chops for Children." *Washington Post* (August 21, 1992), sec. WW, p. 52, col. 1.

Mitchell, Kent. "Martial Art Tai Chi 'Meditation in Motion.' " *Atlanta Constitution* (August 30, 1991), sec. H, p. 4, col. 3.

Musante, Fred. "Where Discipline and Confidence Meet." *New York Times* (April 4, 1993), sec. CN, p. 12, col. 3.

Robinson, John P. "As We Like It." *American Demographics* (February 1993): 44–48.

Shaheen, Jacqueline. "Whether for Exercise or Self-Defense, More Women Take Up the Martial Arts." *New York Times* (November 7, 1993), sec. NJ, p. 1, col. 3.

"That's Entertainment." *American Demographics* (July 1993): 16.

Wexler, Natalie. "Karate Kids." *Washington Post* (July 7, 1996), sec. WMAG, p. 5, col. 1.

CASE 4–5
LoJack Corporation

It was February 15, 1994. Dan Michaels, vice president of sales for the LoJack Corporation of Dedham, Massachusetts, was reflecting on the future. One year ago, LoJack had reached an important milestone in that the firm had generated positive earnings of $817,000 before interest, depreciation, and amortization. According to the firm's annual report, this was "the first such earnings in its history." Michaels looked forward to finishing the fiscal year in two more weeks on February 28, 1994. LoJack appeared to be on track toward a profitable year.

Michaels was assessing several strategic challenges faced by LoJack. As the automobile antitheft market continued to grow and the competitive environment became more intense, he needed to evaluate several issues and make recommendations to his boss, Sal Williams, chairman, president, and CEO of LoJack. Michaels needed to evaluate whether the present sales, distribution, and pricing strategies were adequate for future growth. He also had to make recommendations concerning the product line, which was currently limited to one product. Should LoJack diversify, expand within the product category, or find new applications for the product?

The Product

LoJack marketed the LoJack System, a proprietary method used to track and recover stolen automobiles. The LoJack System, LoJack Retrieve priced at $595, was a transmitter the size of a blackboard eraser, hidden by LoJack technicians in one of 30 locations in a vehicle. State police cruisers and municipal police cars in LoJack markets were equipped with scanning units that were used to track and recover stolen vehicles.

When a LoJack-equipped vehicle was stolen, the owner contacted the police. Law enforcement authorities then tracked the car's location, using scanning units in the police cruisers that communicated with the transmitter in the stolen vehicle. Each scanning unit/transceiver covered a distance of 12 to 15 square miles. Multiple cruisers equipped with LoJack equipment provided overlapping coverage and allowed a stolen vehicle, identified by its vehicle identification number, to be tracked within a metropolitan area.

Only 64 percent of stolen cars were recovered nationally. LoJack, however, claimed a 95 percent recovery rate, with most recoveries within two hours of the reported theft. If a stolen vehicle was not recovered within 24 hours, LoJack refunded the cost of the system to the vehicle owner. Vehicles equipped with the LoJack System sustained average damages of $200 to $500, much lower than the national average of $5,000. LoJack's marketing emphasized that the system used only law enforcement personnel in its tracing mechanism, a reflection of the company's beginnings.

This case was written by Cathy Leach Waters under the supervision of Victoria L. Crittenden, associate professor of marketing at Boston College, as a basis for class discussion rather than to illustrate either effective or ineffective handling of an administrative situation. The material was taken from secondary sources. Pseudonyms are used throughout the case.

The Company

LoJack was formed in 1978 by Lewis McMahon, a former police commissioner in Medfield, Massachusetts. Without a working prototype, the firm was taken public in 1983 to raise funds for product development.

LoJack began marketing the LoJack System in its home state of Massachusetts in 1986. The company knew that before it could offer its antitheft device to the end user (the car owner), it had to have the cooperation of the local police. The nature of the product rendered it useless unless the police had the monitors necessary to track stolen cars. LoJack donated 250 of these necessary tracking units (at a value of $1,750 each) to the Massachusetts State Police. In July 1986, the Massachusetts State Police began using and testing the LoJack System in conjunction with early sales of the product to car owners. The statistics established during this test were later used to promote the success of the product.

The same year, Sal Williams, an early investor in the firm and a LoJack director since 1981, became chairman after Lewis McMahon resigned when the board pressured him to bring in new management. At the time, the company's financial position was tenuous. Williams had run a sizable nursing home business which he subsequently sold after becoming chairman of LoJack.

In February 1994, LoJack operated in Massachusetts, parts of California, Florida, Michigan, Illinois, Georgia, Virginia, and New Jersey. The firm intended to establish an East Coast corridor by entering four new markets in 1994: Rhode Island, Connecticut, New York, and Washington, D.C. Exhibit 1 provides a map of LoJack's U.S. oper-

EXHIBIT 1   LoJack Corporation Geographic Presence in the U.S.A.

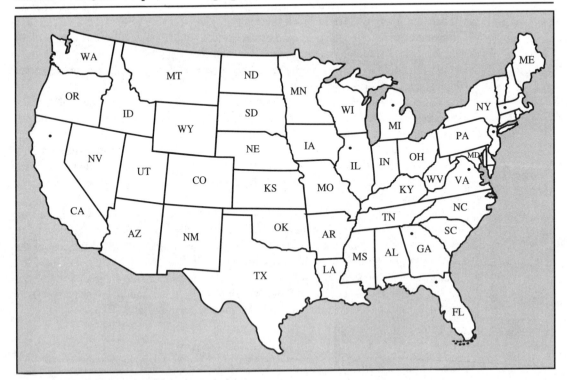

• *Represents LoJack locations in 1993.*

EXHIBIT 2

LoJack Corporation
Selected Financial Information

	Year Ended ($000)		
	2/28/93	*2/28/92*	*2/28/91*
Revenues	$23,346	$17,535	$14,056
Cost of goods sold	12,689	9,520	7,723
Gross margin	10,657	8,015	6,333
Costs and expenses:			
Marketing	5,748	5,202	6,261
Research and development	725	524	215
General & administrative	3,750	3,748	4,066
Depreciation & amortization	1,808	1,856	1,131
Total	12,031	11,330	11,673
Operating loss	(1,374)	(3,315)	(5,340)
Other income (expense):			
Interest expense	(381)	(1,425)	(1,368)
Interest income	14	101	448
Total	(367)	(1,324)	(920)
Net loss	$ (1,741)	$ (4,639)	$ (6,260)

ations. Additionally, LoJack had signed licensing agreements in the Czech Republic, Slovakia, Greece, the United Kingdom, Latin America, and Hong Kong in fiscal year ending February 28, 1993, which were worth $2,162,000 in revenue.

At the end of fiscal year 1993, the firm employed 203 people and planned to add 70 during 1994. Exhibit 2 provides financial information on the company.

The Environment

Auto theft was the second fastest growing area of crime in the United States and the riskiest crime for law enforcement officers. In 1990, 1.6 million cars were stolen in the United States with an increase of 1.6 percent in 1991. After increasing for seven years, auto thefts decreased 3 percent in the United States in 1992. Reduction in theft stemmed from three main factors: increased public awareness prompting better habits, better coordinated law enforcement, and increased use of antitheft devices.

In Boston, Massachusetts, the "car theft capital of the world" in the mid-1980s, auto theft decreased more than 25 percent from 1987 to 1992, due in part to penalties and incentives offered by the insurance industry for the use of antitheft devices. Owners of selected high-priced cars were subjected to a surcharge of as much as 50 percent of their comprehensive (fire and theft) insurance coverage if they did not have an antitheft device. Furthermore, the insurers offered discounts of up to 35 percent off the annual comprehensive premium if a policyholder installed a recovery device and an alarm or ignition disabler.

Auto theft is not unique to the United States. Budapest, Hungary, had experienced an epidemic of auto theft, and auto theft was rampant in Kenya. Government officials in the United Kingdom, reacting to the 575,000 cars stolen in 1991, had declared 1992 as Car Crime Prevention Year.

In addition to the theft of unattended cars, carjacking became a major concern in the early 1990s. *Carjacking* is the term used when a car thief confronts the driver of a vehicle and, by using force or threat, demands that the driver surrender the car. Several carjackings that resulted in the death of the driver received enormous media attention in the early 1990s. From 1991 to 1993, there were 40,000 carjackings in the United States, with a predicted 500 percent increase per year.

The Automobile Theft Deterrent Industry.   Sales of antitheft devices were expected to grow by 9 percent a year through 1998. In 1992, Americans spent $500 million on antitheft devices for their automobiles. The automobile antitheft device industry included systems both for theft prevention and automobile tracking and recovery. Preventive devices included ignition disablers, steering wheel locks, audible alarms, and motion sensors, all of which were usually enough to deter joyriders. (*Joyriders* are car thieves who steal a car not to dismantle it and sell the parts but for the thrill of the act.) Tracking and recovery devices were more costly and aimed at professional thieves.

Preventive Devices.   Preventive devices tended to fall into three categories: alarms, locks, and immobilizing devices. Using an alarm as a sole means of prevention was not advised because people (those people walking or driving down the street) tended to ignore them. However, alarms were still used as one "layer" in a strategy advocated by the New York City police, who recommended installing a visible preventative such as a sign or steering wheel lock, backed up by an alarm.

Steering wheel locks, a visible locking device, were considered to be the fastest growing category within the automobile theft prevention segment. Of the $500 million spent on antitheft devices in 1992, 20 percent went toward steering wheel locks. Visible locking devices included The Club, by Winner International, which retailed for $59.95. The Club was a bar-type steering wheel lock that prevented the wheel from turning. The driver had to remember to lock such devices across the steering wheel before leaving the car. Thieves could outwit steering wheel locks by cutting the steering wheel. Winner International had been very successful at gaining a strong low-cost position in the antitheft device market. Over 10 million Clubs, according to Winner's promotional campaign, had been sold.

The Malvy Lock by Malvy Technology, priced at $600 to $800, disengaged the steering wheel from the steering column so it spun freely and no one could drive the car. It reengaged the wheel only after a special ignition key had been inserted. The company boasted that the key had 4 billion possible combinations and could not be duplicated. A similar product called The Blocker, costing $85 to $125, was an electric device that was wired into the ignition and required a proper ignition key to start the car.

Another technique used to prevent would-be thieves from moving a car was electric shock. Secure Products manufactured a device that gave a thief a 5,000-volt shock and shut off the car engine.

Many antitheft devices focused on making a vehicle difficult for a thief to operate after it was stolen. Over two dozen manufacturers marketed electronically operated antitheft devices that generally shut off the engine from afar. The Blackjack ($160) by Clifford Automotive, shut down the automobile engine when the car slowed to three or four miles per hour, if the system had not been deactivated with a private code. Frequently, thieves could duplicate private codes to bypass such systems; Clifford's was advertised as more complex and harder to duplicate. Beeping horns and flashing lights also accompanied the engine shut down.

Other manufacturers sold similar systems that required the owner to punch a private code into a remote "key-ring" transmitter to disable the system before she could drive the car. Directed Electronics Inc. marketed the Viper 500 Plus system for $299, which included a shock sensor and electronic means of disabling the ignition. For an additional $59, the system could be equipped to prevent the car engine from starting after the owner had alerted the company's dispatch center. Directed Electronics reported sales of $47 million in 1992.

Tracking and Recovery Devices.   Professional thieves, headed for a "chop-shop" where car parts were worth three times the market value of the car itself, required extra measures. Tracking and recovery systems appeared to be the best means of fighting the professional, who accounted for 80 percent of stolen vehicles.

Some systems required the owner of a stolen car to call a centralized dispatch center where the alarm company sent out a command to the car that stopped the vehicle. The Posse by Audiovox ($599) gave clients a 24-hour toll-free number to call after they discovered their car had been stolen. The dispatcher sent a signal anywhere in the United States via their Sky Tel satellite paging network that disabled the car after it had been turned off. A touted second-generation possibility of the Posse was the ability to locate vehicles using satellite-based global positioning.

Some remote shut-down devices were tied into cellular phones. When sensors determined that a vehicle had been stolen, the owner could dial a monitoring station that sent a stop command to the cellular phone in the stolen car. Code Alarm's Intercept, at $1,495 and monthly monitoring charges of $15, was one such system. It could also be used to track the car location anywhere cellular phone service was available. The tracking was done by the monitoring station and police were later alerted as to the car's whereabouts. Code Alarm made a variety of antitheft devices which were available on Chrysler, Ford, General Motors, and Mitsubishi automobiles. The company had a three-year, $21 million agreement with Ford to supply security devices and keyless entry systems. Code Alarm got about 40 percent of its revenue from sales through manufacturers. The firm's products were available through 10,000 domestic and foreign auto dealers.

In 1994, LoJack's chief competitor in vehicle recovery was International Teletrac of Inglewood, California. When a car equipped with a Teletrac transmitter was started without disarming the system, a signal was immediately sent to the Teletrac monitoring operation. The company tracked the vehicle location and notified police. The system cost $599 in addition to a $15 per month monitoring fee. The Federal Communications Commission (FCC) had approved licenses for Teletrac to operate in 140 of the largest United States metropolitan areas.[1] Teletrac quoted a 95 percent recovery rate of stolen vehicles and professed to be installed in over 8,000 cars. The system was sold mainly by accessory firms (retailers of automotive parts and supplies) who also installed the system. An alarm used to request roadside assistance could be purchased as an optional feature.

Teletrac had over 500 fleet customers and experience in fleet management. Teletrac's management system, installed in vehicles belonging to a fleet, such as a trucking

---

[1] The FCC is an independent regulatory body that oversees domestic and foreign communications by radio, television, wire, and cable.

company, was used to keep track of vehicle location for dispatching and routing purposes, among others. Teletrac also offered fleet drivers a remote panic button to ensure worker safety during long road trips and to thwart hijacking attempts. Teletrac used a land-based communications system to track vehicles.

Pinpoint Communications of Dallas, Texas hoped to begin offering low-cost vehicle location services through Value Added Remarketers in 1994.

Exhibit 3 summarizes some of the competitive data.

Technology.   The technology used to communicate with vehicles was a key driving force in automobile tracking and recovery. There were four basic technologies used for vehicle tracking and recovery: radio communications, land-based positioning, satellite-based positioning, and cellular communications. Radio frequency communications, used by LoJack, was a mature, simple, and inexpensive technology that worked. The technology, as implemented by LoJack, was not as precise as the other three methods regarding vehicle tracking. LoJack's stolen vehicle network allowed a vehicle to be tracked to within one city block. Radio frequency systems, used by police departments for dispatching and communications for years, could support communication from a vehicle to a monitoring site for applications like roadside assistance. However, LoJack's system did not support such applications in 1994, and there were questions about how such services would be handled, given that LoJack's system was "piggy-backed" on the law enforcement's Police Broadcasting Network.

Land-based systems (one version was used by Teletrac) and satellite-based systems allowed more precise tracking of vehicles, as the software that supported the systems allowed metropolitan maps and grids to be displayed at a monitoring station so dispatchers could literally "see" the route that a vehicle followed. Such systems could be temporarily defeated when vehicles were driven into underground parking garages. Both land and satellite-based systems could be used to provide additional applications besides tracking and recovery, such as roadside assistance and paging.

Most satellite-based systems used Global Positioning Systems (GPS), which sometimes encountered "interruptions" in urban environments where buildings could block communications signals. GPS was more expensive than land-based systems. One fleet-management firm, Qualcomm, charged $4,000 per truck, in addition to computer charges, to perform fleet management activities over their satellite-based communication system. Other satellite-based competitors were Motorola's "Coverage PLUS" fleet-management offering, and Orbcomm, which planned to offer stolen vehicle recovery service for under $500 early in 1994.

EXHIBIT 3   LoJack Corporation Selected Competitive Data

Company	1992 Revenue ($ millions)	Product	Category	Price
Winner International	$ 100*	The Club	Steering wheel lock	$60
Directed Electronics	$ 47	The Viper	Prevention, remote shutdown	$359
Audiovox	$344†	The Posse	Remote engine shutdown	$399
Code Alarm	$ 45.7	Intercept	Recovery system	$1,495 + $14 monthly
International Teletrac	$ 31	Teletrac	Recovery system	$540 + $15 monthly

Revenue data from Infotrac; and Jennifer Reese, "How Crime Pays," *Fortune,* May 31, 1993, p. 15.

* Winner International's 1991 Sales: $8 million.

† Includes business from cellular telephones, automotive sound equipment, automotive accessories, and consumer electronics.

Data transmission over cellular networks (or CDPD—Cellular Digital Packet Data) was expected to become one of the predominant means of transmitting mobile data. McCaw Cellular planned to implement CDPD throughout its network by 1994. Along with providing cellular telephone communications and tracking and recovery via the cellular phone, CDPD also could provide applications such as emergency roadside assistance, data messaging services, fax capability, and paging facilities.

LoJack's Strategy

LoJack's market strategy was to expand the use of its technology into U.S. and international markets where the combination of population density, new car sales, and vehicle theft was high. Population growth statistics showed that Florida, where LoJack had operations, reflected the major growth in the U.S. during the 1970s and 1980s. Exhibit 4 lists the top 40 ranking of metropolitan statistical areas by population change from 1970 to 1990. Exhibit 5 shows a geographic breakdown of the U.S. resident population.

The world's 10 most populous nations included China, India, Soviet Union, United States, Indonesia, Brazil, Japan, Nigeria, Bangladesh, and Pakistan. Fourteen European countries were projected to not increase in population through 2025: Austria, Belgium, Denmark, Finland, Germany, Greece, Ireland, Italy, Netherlands, Norway, Portugal, Sweden, Switzerland, and the United Kingdom. However, some countries, such as Ethiopia, Kenya, Tanzania, Iraq, Libya, and Saudi Arabia, were expected to triple in population between 1987 and 2025. Exhibit 6 lists the United States' top export markets.

U.S. new cars were running at an annual rate of 13 million in January 1994. This compared to slightly less than 12 million in January 1993. The three largest U.S. domestic brands were General Motors, Ford, and Chrysler. The largest noncaptive imports included Toyota (24 percent), Honda (17 percent), Nissan (16 percent), and Mazda (10 percent). (These percentages represent the company's portion of total noncaptive import new car sales in the U.S.) The largest-selling luxury cars in the U.S. were represented by such European companies as Volvo, BMW, and Mercedes-Benz. As a whole, U.S. brands held the largest percentage (around 65 percent) of new car sales in the United States, with Japanese brands at about 30 percent of U.S. new cars sales, followed by European brands with 4 percent and Korean brands with 1 percent.

Within the United States, California represented around 10 percent of all new car sales. Rental companies purchased about 20 percent of the U.S. new car volume, with Florida rental agencies representing close to 5 percent of U.S. new car sales. There were around 25,000 car dealerships in the United States in the early 1990s.

Exhibit 7 lists the top 25 U.S. cities for motor vehicle theft when theft is adjusted for population.

New Market Entry. The first step in entering a market involved convincing the state police of LoJack's value as a tool in stolen automobile recovery. Concurrent to the process of convincing state police of LoJack's effectiveness, the firm also called on other groups who influenced law enforcement decisions. For example, state insurance commissioners, other government and municipal officials, and insurance company executives were called on by LoJack government affairs personnel to help influence the law enforcement decision-making process.

Once a state's police force agreed to use LoJack systems in their cruisers, an agreement was signed to use LoJack, exclusively, for auto recovery. The agreement was

EXHIBIT 4   Population Growth (1970–1990):
Metropolitan Statistical Areas

1.   Naples, FL
2.   Fort Myers–Cape Coral, FL
3.   Fort Pierce, FL
4.   Ocala, Fl
5.   Las Vegas, NV
6.   West Palm Beach–Boca Raton–Delray Beach, FL
7.   Orlando, FL
8.   Sarasota, FL
9.   Riverside–San Bernardino, CA
10. Daytona Beach, FL
11. Phoenix, AZ
12. Bradenton, FL
13. Austin, TX
14. McAllen—Edinburg–Mission, TX
15. Reno, NV
16. Bryan–College Station, TX
17. Olympia, WA
18. Fort Collins, Loveland, CO
19. Fort Lauderdale–Hollywood–Pompano Beach, FL
20. Las Cruces, NM
21. Provo–Orem, UT
22. Modesto, CA
23. Tucson, AZ
24. Santa Rosa–Petaluma, CA
25. Redding, CA
26. Tampa–St. Petersburg–Clearwater, FL
27. Bremerton, WA
28. Santa Cruz, CA
29. Vancouver, WA
30. Brownsville–Harlingen, TX
31. San Diego, CA
32. Boise City, ID
33. Laredo, TX
34. Vallejo–Fairfield–Napa, CA
35. Anchorage, AK
36. Chico, CA
37. Lakeland–Winter Haven, FL
38. Brazoria, TX
39. Oxnard–Ventura, CA
40. Sacramento, CA

Source: American Business Climate and Economic Profiles.

valid for anywhere from 5 to 10 years. LoJack donated the tracking systems, each worth $1,750, to the police. For example, LoJack donated 450 tracking units (valued at almost $1 million) to the Los Angeles police department, and installed and serviced the units as well.

LoJack also had to interact with the Federal Communications Commission. In 1989, the FCC had allowed LoJack to use radio frequency 173.075 MHz nationwide to operate their tracking network. LoJack used existing police antennas to install the equipment needed to communicate over the radio-based Police Broadcasting Network.

After appropriate law enforcement officials had agreed to use LoJack and after Lo-Jack trained police officers to operate the tracking system, the LoJack System was

EXHIBIT 5   U.S. Resident Population (thousands)

	1990	1991	1992
Northeast			
Maine	1,228	1,234	1,235
New Hampshire	1,109	1,104	1,111
Vermont	563	567	570
Massachusetts	6,016	5,996	5,998
Rhode Island	1,003	1,005	1,005
Connecticut	3,287	3,289	3,281
New York	17,990	18,055	18,119
New Jersey	7,730	7,753	7,789
Pennsylvania	11,866	11,882	12,009
Midwest			
Ohio	10,847	10,941	11,016
Indiana	5,544	5,610	5,662
Illinois	11,431	11,541	11,631
Michigan	9,295	9,380	9,437
Wisconsin	4,892	4,956	5,007
Minnesota	4,375	4,432	4,480
Iowa	2,777	2,795	2,812
Missouri	5,117	5,157	5,193
North Dakota	639	635	636
South Dakota	696	704	711
Nebraska	1,578	1,593	1,606
Kansas	2,478	2,495	2,523
South			
Delaware	666	680	689
Maryland	4,781	4,859	4,908
Washington, D.C.	607	595	589
Virginia	6,187	6,280	6,377
West Virginia	1,793	1,803	1,812
North Carolina	6,629	6,736	6,843
South Carolina	3,487	3,560	3,603
Georgia	6,478	6,623	6,751
Florida	12,938	13,266	13,488
Kentucky	3,685	3,713	3,755
Tennessee	4,877	4,953	5,024
Alabama	4,041	4,091	4,136
Mississippi	2,573	2,593	2,614
Arkansas	2,351	2,373	2,399
Louisiana	4,220	4,254	4,287
Oklahoma	3,146	3,175	3,212
Texas	16,987	17,348	17,656
West			
Montana	799	809	824
Idaho	1,077	1,040	1,067
Wyoming	454	460	466
Colorado	3,294	3,378	3,470
New Mexico	1,515	1,549	1,581
Arizona	3,665	3,748	3,832
Utah	1,723	1,770	1,813
Nevada	1,202	1,283	1,327
Washington	4,867	5,012	5,136
Oregon	2,842	2,922	2,977
California	29,760	30,380	30,867
Alaska	550	570	587
Hawaii	1,108	1,137	1,160

Source: U.S. Bureau of the Census, *Statistical Abstract of the United States: 1993*
(113th edition), Washington, D.C.

Exhibit 6   The United States' Top Export Markets

Canada
Japan
Mexico
United Kingdom
Germany
Netherlands
France
Saudi Arabia
Benelux
Venezuela

marketed to vehicle owners. It sometimes took up to four years to "sign up" a new market.

Ninety-five percent of LoJack's sales were through new car dealers. Over 3,000 dealers had been signed to sell the LoJack system. However, the firm was happy to install a LoJack system if a new car buyer requested it, regardless of whether the dealer was a designated LoJack dealer. Consumers could call LoJack directly via a toll-free telephone number to arrange for the installation of the LoJack System at their home, office, or dealership. LoJack installation technicians drove company vans to install the LoJack System wherever it was needed.

Licensing.   In November 1993 the firm had agreed to license the LoJack recovery system to Clifford Electronics, a major competitor based in California. The nonexclusive license allowed Clifford to sell the LoJack System as "Intellisearch," via aftermarket automotive retailers. Intellisearch used LoJack's established tracking network for vehicle recovery. The agreement was viewed as a test of retail distribution for the product. Retail outlets, typically automotive shops that stocked parts and accessories, tended to sell many antitheft devices aimed at "DIYs" (Do It Yourselfers).

Pricing.   LoJack's Prevent option provided an alarm and starter-disabler for $100 that could be purchasd on top of the basic $595 LoJack Retrieve system. To many customers, "their LoJack" was the remote starter-disabler attached to their key-ring, the only visible part of the LoJack system. LoJack felt strongly about not charging monthly fees for tracking and recovery services since many customers never had to actually use their LoJack System. The company did not want a customer's only perception of LoJack to be a bill that had to be paid every month, like an insurance premium, for monitoring services. Furthermore, LoJack Corporation was not equipped to operate the billing and payment processing system needed to support monthly monitoring fees.

Advertising and Promotion.   Radio advertising was the company's dominant form of communication with the marketplace. Ads featured true success stories and were a "play by play" format documenting what happened from the moment the owner of a LoJack-equipped car discovered his or her car had been stolen to the time the car was recovered by the police. The ads had an official tone to them, reminiscent of a news story or an official police bulletin. LoJack had experimented with limited television advertising outside the Massachusetts area. Approximately 25 cents out of every dollar of revenue was spent on advertising.

EXHIBIT 7   **Motor Vehicle Theft: 1991**

U.S. Cities	Offenses Known To Police per 100,000 Population
Newark, NJ	5,049
Fresno, CA	3,184
Fort Worth, TX	2,946
Detroit, MI	2,774
Atlanta, GA	2,732
Dallas, TX	2,439
Houston, TX	2,411
Boston, MA	2,350
Jersey City, NJ	2,350
Miami, FL	2,347
St. Louis, MO	2,313
Kansas City, MO	2,256
Memphis, TN	2,159
Milwaukee, WI	2,133
Tampa, FL	2,113
Cleveland, OH	2,085
Pittsburgh, PA	2,008
Sacramento, CA	2,004
New Orleans, LA	1,975
Los Angeles, CA	1,929
Oakland, CA	1,916
New York, NY	1,904
San Diego, CA	1,872
Stockton, CA	1,780
Chicago, IL	1,686

Source: U.S. Federal Bureau of Investigation, *Crime in the United States.*

LoJack received a significant amount of publicity from news releases that documented successful vehicle recoveries that were attributable to the LoJack System. In addition, whenever a new market was opened, newspapers usually featured prominent local officials praising LoJack.

LoJack periodically motivated car dealers to sell LoJack Systems by offering discounts. Since dealers usually sold a variety of theft prevention products, LoJack found that the dealers invariably sold whatever product was being discounted.

The Future

Dan Michaels was thankful to be involved with such an exciting product in a growing market. He could not help wondering if he should listen to comments made by LoJack customers and others about additional uses for the LoJack transmitter. Applications including child safety, furloughed prisoner and parolee tracking, and high-valued item protection were just some of the ideas interested parties had brainstormed for LoJack. He needed to consider whether the firm was ready to take on the added complexity of new product applications, in addition to addressing the issues already posed by the existing product. He picked up his telephone to schedule a meeting with Sal Williams to discuss the future marketing strategy for LoJack.

Sources

Alster, Norm. "A Car Thief's Nemesis." *Forbes,* 149 (10) May 11, 1992, pp. 124–125.

American Business Climate and Economic Profiles.

Beck, Ernest. "Budapest's Car-Alarm Entrepreneurs Capitalize on City's Easy-Street Image." *The Wall Street Journal,* October 25, 1993, p. A5A.

Blauth, John. "Ringing the Alarm on Soaring Car Crime." *The Accountant's Magazine,* September 1992, p. 31.

Bohon, C.D. "Just How Bad Is It?" *Auto Age,* August 1993.

Candler, Julie. "Ways to Outsmart Vehicle Thieves." *Nation's Business,* July 1993, pp. 35–36.

Chappell, Lindsay. "Program Cars Turns Quagmire." *Advertising Age,* March 30, 1992, p. S51.

Coeyman, Marjorie. "Automotive Market Firms Up—But So Do Competitive Pressures." *Chemical Week,* March 2, 1994, p. 9.

Cohen, Jeffrey. "Making Car Theft More Difficult." *The New York Times,* October 28, 1993. p. C2.

Coxeter, Ruth. "Hey Car Thieves, Try to Drive This One Off." *Business Week,* November 8, 1993, p. 99.

"Directed Electronics Viper Line Adds Anti-Carjacking System." *HFD,* December 13, 1993, p. 105.

Driscoll, Clement. "Automated Vehicle Location Increases Productivity & Security." *Automotive Fleet,* September 1993, pp. 74–79.

Exportise: An International Trade Source Book for Small Company Executives. Boston, MA: The Small Business Foundation of America, 1987.

"Fall & Winter Selling Guide: Security Products." *Automotive Marketing,* July 1993, p. 67.

"FCC Allocates Spectrum . . ." *FCC News,* August 29, 1989.

Hass, Nancy. "Deal Them In." *Financial World,* September 3, 1991, pp. 20-22.

Hovelson, Jack. "High-Tech Systems Help Thwart Car Thieves." *USA Today,* October 1, 1993.

Kindleberger, Richard. "Top Stolen Cars to Be Costly." *The Boston Globe,* August 1, 1990, pp. 55–56.

Kott, Douglas. "LoJack Puts Police on the Offensive to Recover Stolen Cars." *Road & Track,* November 1989, p. 133.

LoJack Annual Report—1993.

"LoJack License Pact with Clifford for Stolen Vehicle-Recovery System." *HFD,* November 29, 1993, p. 75.

Martin, Mary. "Reporting a Recovery." *The Boston Globe,* February 6, 1994, pp. A4–A5.

Mwangi, Patrick. "Car Thefts Hit Kenyan Insurers." *African Business,* April 1993, p. 40.

Olenick, Doug. "Ford, GM Canada in Code Alarm Deal." *HFD,* September 13, 1993, p. 98.

———. "Audiovox Corp. Shipping POSSE." *HFD,* November 15, 1993, p. 104.

Ryan, Ken. "Auto-Security Business Booms." *HFD,* April 12, 1993, p. 145.

Serafin, Raymond; and Horton, Cleveland. "GM Claims the Inroads in California." *Advertising Age,* January 31, 1994, p. 36.

Sinanoglu, Elif. "Stop Carjackers in Their Tracks." *Money,* September 1993, p. 20.

Terpstra, Vern; and Sarathy, Ravi. *International Marketing.* Chicago: The Dryden Press, 1991.

Torcellini, Carolyn. "To Catch a Thief." *Forbes,* April 17, 1989, p. 202.

———. "Beep, Beep." *Forbes,* December 25, 1989, p. 10.

Ward's Automotive Yearbook—1993.

Woods, Bill. "Bad News for Crooks, Good News for You . . ." *Corvette World,* August 1990, p. 24.

CASE 4–6
ALGONQUIN POWER AND LIGHT COMPANY

Background

Allan Beacham is the marketing director for the Algonquin Power and Light Company, a large public utility providing gas and electric service to a major metropolitan area whose market is more than 1.5 million people.

Beacham is studying a report sent to him by Donald Orville, the company's forester. Orville is employed by Algonquin Power and Light to manage reforesting and reseeding of company construction projects. Possessing a degree in forestry from Syracuse University, Orville is acknowledged as a real authority in the forestry community.

Like many other public utilities across the country, Algonquin Power and Light Company conducts a maintenance program on its existing power lines. Trees, shrubs, and scrub are cut away from the lines to prevent chances of damage and subsequent power shortages. This maintenance program is directed by Donald Orville, and he estimates that the company's maintenance crews collect 100 tons of waste wood residue (cuttings) each week as a result of the line-clearing program.

Orville has developed a compost from these tree and shrub cuttings in his company laboratory. In his mind, this compost provides an organic soil amendment that is in much demand in the county. In his report, Orville states, "Waste wood-chip residue can be converted into a humus material superior in quality to the organic peats, leaf molds, and composted redwood products being marketed in the county. An accelerated composting process will convert this waste material into a marketable soil amendment in a matter of 6 to 10 weeks." The Orville report continues, "Composted trimming wastes have properties superior to the various redwood products. Leafy vegetative matter is included in the chip residue resulting in a more complete composting of the material. This product has a low carbon to nitrogen ratio, which is desirable in composts." Orville firmly believes the compost can be marketed profitably and this is the reason he has submitted his report to Allan Beacham.

Past Company Tree Cuttings Disposal Practices

Up to this time, the company has simply taken its line maintenance cuttings to county-operated dumps or disposal sites. An average of 50 loads of wood chips is produced each week by the cutting crews, and the county assesses a dump charge against each truckload of waste hauled to the dump. This amounts to an annual disposal charge of $3,000.

In addition, each time a trip is made to the dump, an average of one hour of productive crew time is lost. Based on 50 such trips a week, crew time involved costs the company an additional $55,000 annually.

Orville contends that these costs could be eliminated if the waste wood material was processed into the soil amendment compost. Line-clearing equipment would then

Reprinted by permission from Robert W. Haas and Thomas R. Wotruba, *Marketing Management: Concepts, Practice and Cases* (Homewood, Ill.: Richard D. Irwin/Business Publications, Inc., 1983), pp. 324–32.

be based at the processing site or sites. The company would realize a profit on its sales of such compost.

Reading through Orville's report, Beacham is impressed with the logic of Orville's argument. To date, Algonquin Power and Light Company has paid money to dispose of product components that may be in great demand. In addition, Beacham believes such a program may have ecological advantages to the utility—the company would be converting a previously wasted resource into a valuable soil amendment.

Costs of Operating a Compost Operation

In his report, Orville foresees the need for two pieces of equipment to convert the waste wood residue into marketable humus composting material. Equipment required will be: (1) a 75-cubic-yard-per-hour shredder. Waste materials will pass through the shredder and would then compost in long windrows on a packed earth surface. After composting, the material will be reshredded and screened. Such a shredder costs $15,000; (2) a size 1½-cubic-yard loader will be needed to load the wood chips into the shredder and the compost into waiting trucks. The cost of this loader is $25,000.

Labor studies conducted by Orville indicate that a single man working with the mobile processing equipment can operate the compost program. In his report, Orville outlined what he believes the annual cost of operation to Algonquin Power and Light Company would be. His estimate of $46,786.16 is derived in the manner shown in Exhibit 1.

In his report, Orville estimates that the 100 tons of waste wood residue collected each week will convert into 10,000 to 15,000 cubic yards per year of marketable compost. He also believes that a "virtually unlimited market exists for all locally produced humus material at a bulk price of $8.50 per cubic yard." Using a 10,000–cubic-yard forecast, he computes the return to the company from such a program to be $96,000 based on the following:

$ 85,000	10,000 cubic yards of finished compost @ $8.50/yard
–47,000	Operation expenses of a subsidiary operation
$ 38,000	Direct profit from sale of compost
+58,000	Savings in residue hauling and dumping fees
$ 96,000	Return to the company

While Beacham is impressed with Orville's report, he is suspicious of some of the figures. He is particularly concerned with Orville's demand computations. For example, he questions Orville's contention that the compost could be sold at a bulk price of $8.50 per cubic yard. He also wonders if 10,000 cubic yards could in fact be sold in a year. Before he makes any decision regarding the compost program, Beacham wants his concerns to be addressed. He respects Orville's cost and technical expertise, but he questions his market knowledge and expertise. In short, Beacham requires more information before he makes a decision.

Marketing Organization

Algonquin Power and Light Company's marketing organization is headed by Allan Beacham who holds the position of director of marketing. Reporting to Beacham are three marketing program managers: Bob Morton, Ed Walton, and Carlos Berlozzi. These marketing program managers function very much like product managers—each

Exhibit 1 Annual Cost of Operation of the Compost Program

Capital Base	Annual Capital Cost Factor*	Equipment Operation Expense	Annual Revenue Requirements
Land			
($60,000) (0.1969)†	$11,814.00		$11,814.00
Loader			
($25,000) (0.3251)†	8,127.50	(1,500 hrs.) ($1,197) = $1,795.50	9,923.00
Shredder			
($15,000) (0.2626)†	3,939.00	(1,000 hrs.) ($1.197) = $1,197.00	5,136.00
Land and equipment revenue requirements			$26,873.00
Labor (special equipment operator)			
Annual labor factor		Overhead (33% of base labor)	
$10,836.96		$3,576.20	$14,413.16
Insurance estimate (from company insurance department)			500.00
Miscellaneous expense factors:			
Supervision, sales, etc.			5,000.00
Total annual return requirements, including return on equity			$46,786.16

* Levelized annual capital cost factors include a return on equity of 15 percent.

† Rates used by the company to compute annualized capital costs.

is responsible for developing and implementing assigned specific marketing programs. For example, Berlozzi has responsibility for the utility's energy-conservation program while Walton manages the industrial-applications program. In addition to these three marketing program managers, the department includes Marjorie Haskins, the marketing research manager, who supervises a staff of three research analysts, and Edward Robinzes, the advertising manager. Both Haskins and Robinzes provide staff assistance to Beacham and the three marketing program managers. Beacham decides to give the compost project to Bob Morton and calls him to his office.

The Meeting between Allan Beacham and Bob Morton

Allan Beacham briefed Bob Morton on Orville's findings and recommendations and handed him a copy of the forester's report. "Bob," Beacham said, "I would like you to check this out. Orville may have something here, but we need more definitive market information. Look into it, and get back to me with a feasibility report and a strategy recommendation either to enter or not to enter this compost business. Back up your recommendation with some research data so that we will have some facts to fall back on. I will alert Marjorie Haskins so that she knows you need her help. Get with her as soon as you can and then get back to me. In the meantime, I will put Orville on hold." With that, Bob Morton returned to his office to study Orville's report. From the tone of Beacham's conversation, he knew this was a high-priority project and that he would have to act soon. After thoroughly studying Orville's report, he scheduled a meeting with Marjorie Haskins, the marketing research manager.

Research Requirements

In his meeting with Haskins, Morton outlined what he thought were his research requirements. Specifically, he wanted to know:

1. The approximate size of the total county compost market, both for commercial and residential users.
2. Competitive prices in both the commercial and residential markets.
3. Present producers of compost sold in the county and their locations.
4. Resellers and/or middlemen involved in marketing compost in the county.
5. The willingness of prospective customers to switch to Algonquin's compost from their present product.

Morton outlined these requirements to Haskins and impressed upon her the need for prompt information. She knew of the project's priority because Allan Beacham had briefed her, too. She promised Morton she would schedule a meeting with her staff immediately and would have information back to him within a month. Morton was pleased with Haskins's cooperation, and he left the meeting with a positive feeling that Haskins would provide him with the type of information he needed.

Research Findings

About three weeks after their meeting, Haskins called Morton to inform him that the research had been completed by her department. Through the use of a "build-up" research methodology, Haskins had discovered seven basic markets for compost in the county. These are shown in Exhibit 2, which also indicates estimates of annual compost demand for each market. She considered the estimate of 78,641 cubic yards to be conservative yet realistic.

Breaking down the markets into retail and wholesale/user segments, she provided Morton with information showing brands and products presently being purchased,

EXHIBIT 2 Estimates of County Demand for Compost by Type of Customer

Customer Type	Estimate of Cubic Yards Used per Year
Topsoil companies	36,800
Retail nurseries:	
Specialty nurseries	11,400
Chains and discounters	4,816
Growers: Farms, orchards, etc.	19,200
Landscape contractors and gardeners	6,425
Manufacturers and distributors	Unable to ascertain
Government	Unable to ascertain
Total demand	78,641

Note: A limited number of manufacturers did use compost, but it was often purchased indirectly through landscapers, topsoil companies, etc. Local distributors also handled compost, but since they resold to other demand components (retailers, etc.), much of their demand was also duplicated in the demand of other components. Interviews with government buyers at city, county, and state levels indicated that government did at times purchase quantities of compost from outside suppliers. However, they also composted their own trimmings. Thus reliable estimates of compost purchased from outside suppliers could not be obtained. In view of these considerations, the estimate of 78,641 cubic yards is viewed as a conservative estimate.

EXHIBIT 3   Potential Competition in the Wholesale and/or User Market Based on Selected Field Interviews

Business Operation Interviewed	Products Presently Being Purchased	Quantities Purchased Annually	Sources and Locations of Suppliers	Present Price Being Paid
Maynard Sand and Material Company (topsoil company)	Douglas fir wood chips 3/8″ or less in size	24,000 cu. yd.	Local county distributor	$2.50 per cu. yd.
	Redwood shavings 3/8″ or less in size	3,600 cu. yd.	Local sawdust company (in county)	$4.50 per cu. yd.
Dave Parker Supplies (topsoil company)	Used sawdust	500–1,500 cu. yd.	Stall sweepings from local horse ranches	$1.00 per cu. yd.
	Nitrolized fir compost 1″ or less in size	250–750 cu. yd.	Both bought from out-of-county distributor 200 miles away	$5.50 per cu. yd. + 3.00 per cu. yd. freight
	Redwood compost 1″ or less in size	250–750 cu. yd.		$6.00 per cu. yd. + $3.00 per cu. yd. freight
Green Thumb Nursery (wholesale nursery grower of small ornamentals)	Redwood compost 1/8″ or less in size	100 cu. yd.	Local sawdust company (in county)	$4.50 per cu. yd.
Marlowe's Nursery (wholesale nursery grower of trees and large shrubs)	Redwood compost 1/4″ or less in size	1,000 cu. yd.	Local sawdust company (in county)	$3.50 per cu. yd. bought on a 40–cu.-yd. basis
Garden Valley Nursery (wholesale nursery grower of 1- and 5-gallon plants)	Nitrolized redwood and fir compost 1/4″ or less in size	2,000–3,000 cu. yd.	Local sawdust company (in county)	$4.00 per cu. yd.
County government	Redwood R.S.A. nitrogen-treated compost bulk	Unable to determine	Local county distributor for small orders	$5.75 per cu. yd. delivered on a 35–cu.-yd. basis
			Out-of-county sawdust company for large orders	$4.90 per cu. yd. delivered on a 60–65-cu.-yd. basis

their sources and suppliers, and prices paid. These data may be seen in Exhibits 3 and 4.

From field interviews with prospective customers, Haskins developed a list of product specifications that the compost must meet if customers were to seriously consider Algonquin compost as a substitute for existing competitive products already on the market. These specifications may be seen in Exhibit 5.

The field research also revealed some concerns or fears expressed by potential users. Some of the most commonly expressed fears were:

1. Could Algonquin Power and Light provide compost in the required quantities over time? Many prospective customers were reluctant to switch because they were afraid they might later find that the utility could not provide quantities required. This was a particular concern of large growers and topsoil companies

EXHIBIT 4   Potential Competition in the Retail Nursery Business Based on Selected Store Samplings

Type of Store	Brand Name of Competitive Product(s) Presently Stocked	Producer and/or Supplier of Present Products	Form in Which Product Is Sold to Consumers	Retail Price Charged
Discount Store A	Hawaiian Magic (redwood compost)	Out-of-county fertilizer Producer A	70-lb. bags	$1.19 per bag
	Garden Pride redwood soil conditioner	Out-of-county fertilizer Producer B	2–cu.-ft. bags	$1.99 per bag
Specialty Nursery A	Garden Humus Bark Compost	Out-of-county fertilizer Producer C	3–cu.-ft. bags	$2.49 per bag
Specialty Nursery B	Redwood Garden Mulch	Local fertilizer Producer A (in county)	4–cu.-ft. bags	$4.00 per bag
Discount Store B	University Formula Redwood Compost	Out-of-county fertilizer Producer D	60-lb. bags	$2.17 per bag
Department Store A	Redwood Compost	Private brand—no producer listed on bags	60-lb. bags	$2.49 per bag
Chain Drug A	Hawaiian Magic (redwood compost)	Out-of-county fertilizer Producer A	70-lb. bags	$2.29 per bag
	Organic compost	Out-of-county fertilizer Distributor A	65-lb. bags	$2.49 per bag
Specialty Nursery C	Redwood Garden Mulch	Local fertilizer Producer A (in county)	4–cu.-ft. bags	$2.97 per bag
Discount Store C	Viva Redwood Compost	Local fertilizer Producer A (in county)	4–cu.-ft. bags	$2.99 per bag
Discount Store D	Viva Redwood Compost	Local fertilizer Producer A (in county)	4–cu.-ft. bags	$2.99 per bag
Specialty Nursery D	Bandini 101 Redwood Compost	Bandini (national producer and sold through local distributor)	4–cu.-ft. bags	$3.79 per bag
Discount Store E	Red Star Redwood Compost	Out-of-county fertilizer Producer E	4–cu.-ft. bags	$2.26 per bag

mainly because the utility company's policy of underground power lines in new areas would in the long run reduce the source of compost materials.

2. How good would Algonquin's quality control be? The utility was seen as a novice in the soil amendment business. Many potential buyers expressed a fear concerning the company's production and quality-control capabilities.

3. How would the Algonquin compost compare to redwood compost? Most of the prospective customers interviewed did not think the compost would be as good as redwood compost, despite Orville's contentions that it was. The major concern was that the Algonquin compost would break down quicker than redwood compost. This was a particularly big point with growers of trees and large ornamental shrubs who use exclusively redwood compost. They argued that redwood compost allowed them to grow their plants in a pot to the desired sale size with a single planting because the break-down period of the redwood was the same as the growing time. If they switched to the Algonquin compost, they would have to replant during the growing period because the new compost's break-down period was considerably shorter. This, of course, meant increased cost to these growers. Growers of small plants expressed no such concerns.

EXHIBIT 5   Required Product Specifications for Compost Soil Amendment

Based on field interviews with such potential customers as topsoil companies, retail nurserymen, growers in the nursery industry, landscaping personnel in city, county, and state governments, and others, the compost produced would have to meet the following specifications if it is to be seriously considered as a substitute for existing competitive products already on the market:

- Its ability to sustain and stimulate plant life must be demonstrated.
- It should contain 1 to 2 percent nitrogen content.
- It should be a dark earthy color.
- It should be fine in content. Nursery customers would like compost to be capable of passing through a 1/4″ screen and preferably through a 1/8″ screen. Topsoil companies require a compost that will pass through a range of 1/2″ to 3/8″ screen, preferably the latter.
- It must be free of weed, seed, dust, and other objectionable materials.
- It must be friable—properties that allow it to be easily crumbled.
- It must be stable over time. Changes in content because processing batches were different would have adverse effects in all markets.
- Its source of supply must be reliable over time.
- It must hold moisture well.
- It must not contain any cuttings such as oleander, eucalyptus, and hardwoods, that might be harmful to plant life.
- It may contain other ingredients, such as peat moss and leaf mold, but it must *not* contain steer manure.
- It must be bagged and labeled for the retail-nursery business but can be sold in bulk for growers and topsoil companies.
- It must be certified by an independent laboratory.

Despite the concerns, most prospective customers who were interviewed were interested. All were concerned about future sources of redwood compost as the supply of redwood is limited, and all were looking for comparable competitive products that could be purchased at lower prices.

In summary, Haskins felt the compost market for Algonquin looked promising and she told that to Morton. After receiving Haskins' research findings, Morton called Donald Orville on the phone. He wanted to hear the forester's reaction to the required product specifications that the research uncovered. Specifically, he wanted to know if Orville's compost could meet those specifications. Orville's reaction was most positive. While the compost's present form did not meet those exact specifications, there was little problem in changing it to meet them. The present compost is light brown but could easily be given a dark earthy color. It could easily be nitrolized to meet the 1 to 2 percent nitrogen content requirement, and it could also be screened to any size desired. Other than that, the present compost could support plant life, and Orville had evidence of that in his laboratory. The certification requirement was no problem, and Orville had already met with a local chemical lab on such certification. Orville believed the compost could meet the required specifications with very little modification.

Armed with the research findings provided him by Haskins' department and Orville's positive reaction, Bob Morton starts to prepare the feasibility report that Beacham requested, and he considers strategy recommendations he would make for Orville's compost. Based on the research findings, Morton believes that any strategy recommendations must consider both the retail and the wholesale-user markets. Advise Bob Morton on what strategy approach is most appropriate.

PART

V

MARKETING RELATIONSHIP STRATEGIES

The use of marketing relationship strategies expanded rapidly during the 1990s. An organization may greatly enhance its value offering to customers by coupling its unique competencies with those of one or more internal or external partner organizations. Relationship strategies also enable companies to share risks and cope with environmental changes.

Relationship strategies may be developed between companies and end user customers, suppliers and manufacturers, distribution channel members, companies at the same level in the value chain, and different business functions within the organization. The purposes underlying these strategic relationships include gaining access to new markets, reducing the risks characteristic of the rapidly changing business environment, obtaining needed skills and resources, and reducing the time necessary to develop and implement business and marketing strategies.

The rapid growth of Tommy Hilfiger illustrates the benefits of partnering with suppliers, channel members, and industry members. The apparel company has fewer than 1200 employees and should generate nearly $1 billion in sales in 1998, nearly 10 times greater than 1991 sales. Hilfiger's profits have chalked up similar growth records. The company manages a network of relationships with other organizations. Hilfiger's competencies include very successful product designs and effective strategic partnering. The company has leveraged its powerful brand image by licensing its name to companies in related product categories like Estée Lauder, which produces Tommy fragrances.

What Are Relationship Strategies?

While there are several views of the nature and scope of relationship strategies, all place the customer at the center of the relationship paradigm. The objective is achieving high levels of customer satisfaction through collaboration of the partners involved. Tommy Hilfiger's network of relationships with apparel producers, transportation providers, and retailers illustrates how relationship marketing works.

Relationship marketing gained new importance in the 1990s as customers became more demanding and competition became more intense. Building long-term relationships with customers and others involved in providing value to buyers offers companies a way to build competitive advantage. Moreover, the consequences of not providing superior customer value are lower sales and profits.

**EXHIBIT 1
Growth in Strategic
Relationships among
Companies**

The chart shows the results of a 1993 Conference Board survey of 350 chief executive officers from the United States, Europe, Canada, and Mexico. Growth in all forms of strategic relationships is indicated by the executives surveyed.

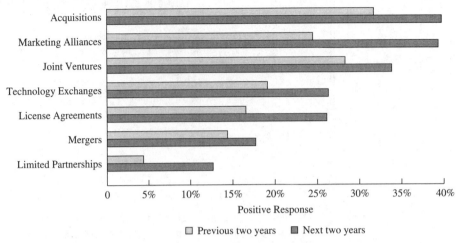

Note: Data show combined responses from all surveyed regions.

Source: Margaret Hart and Stephen J. Garone, *Making International Strategic Alliances Work* (New York: The Conference Board, Inc., 1994), p. 18.

Perhaps the most significant implication of the widespread use of relationship strategies is the reality that the potential advantages from partnering are much greater than trying to compete as a lone-wolf corporation. While maintaining strategic relationships with other organizations presents some challenging coordination and management issues, partnering can greatly increase an organization's competitive advantage.

As shown in Exhibit 1, marketing alliances are one of the most popular forms of strategic relationships. Gaining access to international markets is an important reason for partnering across national boundaries. For example, the strategic alliance between American Airlines and British Airlines awaiting regulatory approval in 1998 will provide both partners access to international air routes and airport gates.

Types of Relationships

Various types of strategic relationships may be formed within the value added system from suppliers to consumer and organizational end users. Relationships may also be formed horizontally between companies in the same industry or across related industries. For example, several strategic alliances exist among international airlines such as the one among Delta Airlines, Austrian Airlines, and Swissair. Although building collaborative relationships may not always be the best course of action, this avenue for gaining a competitive edge is growing in popularity.

Customer Relationships

Relationship marketing starts with the customer—understanding needs and wants and how to satisfy customers' requirements and preferences.

Customers think about products and companies in relation to other products and companies. What really matters is how existing and potential customers think about a company in relation to its competitors. Customers set up a hierarchy of values, wants, and needs based on empirical data, opinions, word-of-mouth references, and previous experiences with products and services. They use that information to make purchasing decisions.[1]

Understanding customers' needs and wants encourages developing long-term collaborative relationships. Driving the necessity of staying in close contact with buyers is the reality that customers often have several suppliers of the products they wish to purchase. Customer diversity compounds the competitive challenge. Developing a customer-oriented organization includes

- Instilling customer-oriented values and beliefs supported by top management.
- Integrating market and customer focus into the strategic planning process.
- Developing strong marketing managers and programs.
- Creating market-based measures of performance.
- Developing customer commitment throughout the organization.[2]

Supplier–Manufacturer Relationships

The relationships between suppliers and customers range from transactional to collaborative partnerships.[3] Collaboration may include product and process design, applications assistance, long-term supply contracts, and just-in-time inventory programs. While supplier–producer collaboration is employed by companies in various industries, the logic of these relationships needs to take into account the following factors:[4]

1. *Philosophy of doing business.* The partner's approach to business should be compatible. For example, if one firm has adopted a Total Quality Management (TQM) philosophy and the other partner does not place a high priority on TQM, conflicts are likely to develop in the working relationship.
2. *Relative dependence of the partners.* Collaborative relations are more likely to be successful if the dependence is important and equivalent between the two organizations.
3. *Technological edge contributions.* The buyer may represent an opportunity for a supplier to improve its product or process because of the customer's leading-edge application of the supplier's product or service. For example, collaborative co-design of industrial equipment can increase the supplier's competitive advantage.

Collaborative relationships require trust and commitment by both partners, since a considerable amount of proprietary information is shared. Evaluating the extent that a supplier or manufacturer should enter into a collaborative relationship is an important concern for both partners. Several companies have drasticaly reduced the number of suppliers from which they purchase and are working more closely with each supplier. For example, by the early 1990s Xerox had reduced its suppliers by 90 percent, from 5,000 to 500.[5]

Distribution Channel Relationships

Distribution channel relationships may involve transactional ties between producers, wholesalers, retailers, and consumer and industrial end users. Alternatively, more collaborative relationships may be developed through ownership, contractual commitments, or power and influence exercised by one of the channel organizations. For example, Wal-Mart has established strong relationships with producers of the products it sells in retail stores.

Coordinating relationships with distribution channel members is an important responsibility for each of the organizations involved. The role of a channel member may be to direct and coordinate the activities of the entire channel or instead to be managed by the firm that has gained control of the entire channel. Channel relationships vary from one organization managing the channel to situations where no channel member manages the channel.

Joint Ventures and Strategic Alliances

The alliance requires collaborative participation on a strategic project such as developing, producing, and marketing a new product. The joint venture involves creating a new organization to carry out the objectives of the venture partners. Collaboration among independent companies that are often competitors became popular in the 1990s. For example, a drug producer in one country may establish a marketing alliance with a drug producer in another country (or region). Each firm may market the other partner's products in its home country. Alliances and joint ventures are also used to develop and produce new products.

The drivers of the interorganizational collaborative relationships are (1) environmental complexity and risk and (2) skill and resource gaps.[6] Rapid changes in markets greatly increase the complexity and risks of competing. For example, many companies use alliances to enter new global markets. Similarly, the know-how and resources necessary to develop new products may exceed the capabilities of one company. When these requirements exceed the capacity (or willingness) of a single firm, it may seek one or more partners. Either an alliance or joint venture may be used.

The Conference Board reported in 1995 that 20,000 strategic alliances were formed by U.S. companies between 1987 and 1992, compared to 5,100 between 1980 and 1987. Creating and sustaining successful alliances is difficult. Many alliances fail or do not measure up to the expectations of the partners. Nonetheless, properly conceived and executed, the strategic alliance can substantially expand the capabilities of a single company and help to overcome the risks and uncertainties of the business environment.

The objectives in forming strategic alliances may be to expand an organization's capabilities, markets, and/or resources. Frequently cited objectives by companies employing alliances include lowering new market costs and risks, expanding market and technology bases, improving manufacturing utilization, speeding up new product development, reducing legal and trade barriers, reducing costs, and gaining scale economies.[7]

Internal Relationships

The redesign of internal organizations to focus on management of processes such as new product development requires creating strong internal relationships that cut across functional boundaries. Companies like Boeing, Hewlett-Packard, and Rubbermaid form teams of people from different business functions (e.g., accounting and finance, marketing, manufacturing, and research and development). These teams are responsible for identifying new product ideas, developing the products, and moving the products into commercialization.

Developing Effective Relationships

Executives from marketing and other business functions may be responsible for managing relationships with customers, suppliers, producers, internal functions, and partner organizations. The success of these relationships is enhanced by spelling out the objective(s) of the relationship and developing relationship management guidelines.

Relationship Objectives.   Objectives need to be developed for each of the major types of relationships. Included in these guidelines is establishing how much collaboration will be involved. In some situations, close collaboration may not be of interest to either party involved in the relationship. For example, if the partners differ concerning the type of relationship they seek, this issue must be resolved. Unless both partners develop trust and commitment in the relationship, it will not be successful. The partners must have compatible objectives.

Relationship Management Guidelines.   Guidelines are available for managing relationships between buyers and sellers, channel members, and internal departments. Perhaps the most challenging relationship management situation is the strategic alliance. Collaboration among competitive firms is contrary to the traditional view of competition. The starting point is making a good choice of a partner. These relationships require careful planning, trust, willingness to share information, conflict resolution processes, leadership structure, recognition of interdependence and cultural differences among the partners, decisions as to how to transfer technology, and means of learning from partners' strengths.[8]

Successful strategic alliances offer powerful advantages to the participants, but many alliances are not successful. Different cultures, lack of trust and commitment, and poor matching of shared competencies create problems between partners. Northwest Airlines and KLM Royal Dutch Airlines formed a successful alliance in the early 1990s that generated substantial profits for both partners. Nonetheless, by 1997, lack of trust and conflicting objectives threatened the future of the alliance.

After each partner yielded to the concerns of the other partner, they agreed in 1997 to extend the alliance for 10 years. KLM sold its Northwest Airlines stock to Northwest, more than doubling the investment. The initial alliance allowed either partner to exit after giving 12-months notice.

End Notes

1. Regis McKenna, *Relationship Marketing,* (Reading, MA: Addison-Wesley, 1991), p. 43.
2. Frederick E. Webster, Jr., "The Rediscovery of the Marketing Concept," *Business Horizons,* May–June 1988, p. 37.
3. James C. Anderson and James A. Narus, "Partnering as a Focused Market Strategy," *California Management Review,* Spring 1991, pp. 96–97.
4. Ibid., pp. 100–3.

5. John R. Emshuiler, "Suppliers Struggle to Improve Quality as Big Firms Slash Their Vendor Roles," *The Wall Street Journal,* August 16, 1991, p. B1.

6. David W. Cravens, Shannon H. Shipp, and Karen S. Cravens, "Analysis of Cooperative Interorganizational Relationships, Strategic Alliance Formation, and Strategic Alliance Effectiveness," *Journal of Strategic Marketing,* March 1993, pp. 55–70.

7. Julie Cohen Mason, "Strategic Alliances: Partnering for Success," *Management Review*, May 1993.

8. Timothy M. Collings and Thomas L. Dooley, *Teaming Up for the 90s* (Homewood, IL: Business One Irwin, 1991), pp. 101–2.

CASES FOR PART V

The seven cases in this part examine various types of relationships surrounding marketing's interactions with its constituencies. The cases involve diverse products—from ice cream and home appliances to tire production and trains—in countries such as the Philippines, Czech Republic, India, and Hungary. The broad range of case scenarios offers vast opportunity to explore a multitude of marketing relationships.

Case 5–1, ABB Tractions Inc., a video case, describes the formidable task ABB Traction has in convincing Amtrak officials that ABB's high-speed rail technology is the best choice for Amtrak. ABB needs to identify distinctive competencies that make it a prime partner for Amtrak and then must market itself to Amtrak.

Several foreign companies are courting **Ambrosia Corporation (Case 5–2)** with the notion of licensing Ambrosia to produce and distribute ice cream products in the Philippines. Ambrosia has to decide if it needs a foreign partner. If so, it can select from the three companies expressing interest in a partnership or it can pursue relations with other companies.

In **Case 5–3, Electro-Products Limited (EPL)** is a manufacturer of small home appliances. Located in a semirural area of the Czech Republic, the company exports a large portion of its production under an exclusive agreement with a large European-based international electronics manufacturing and marketing firm. EPL would like a closer working relationship with this European firm; however, the export company is not interested.

A modular home construction/sales company, **Southern Home Developers (Case 5–4)** has been in business less than a year. Potential for the company's modular homes was strong as was nationwide demand. However, the company was beginning to experience potential conflict between customer expectations and the operational side of the business.

Case 5–5, Konark Television India, considers the distribution strategy for a medium-sized manufacturer of television sets in India. A slowing market growth rate is complicated by dealer activities thought to be damaging to Konark. Immediate actions need to be taken with respect to dealer relations. However, selecting the appropriate action is difficult without a long-term distribution strategy.

A privately held company, **Powrtron Corporation (Case 5–6)** was grappling with an unprecedented problem of constrained capacity. Top management had to immediately resolve capacity, delivery, and customer problems. Exacerbating these problems was the high tension between the sales & marketing manager and the manufacturing manager. Manufacturing felt that Sales & Marketing was making unreasonable delivery commitments, while Sales & Marketing blamed Manufacturing for customer dissatisfaction problems.

Taurus Hungarian Rubber Works (Case 5–7) has decided that it needs to diversify away from its traditional dependence on truck and farm tires. The company's strategy is to seek cooperative strategic alliances to accelerate growth. Taurus must now determine the appropriate grouping of its current product lines. These changes will help define the company's attractiveness in terms of future relations with other companies.

CASE 5–1
ABB TRACTION INC.

Three hours, origination to destination, seemed to be the limit for the business traveler. This time constraint had given airlines a major competitive advantage in the transportation industry. Amtrak, a U.S. railroad giant, was very concerned about the uncertainty surrounding the future of the American railroad system. High-speed trains appeared to be the solution to enabling train transportation to remain competitive with other modes of travel, particularly air transportation. U.S. transportation experts expected that high-speed rail service would reduce the need to build new airports and interstate highways. Also, the U.S. government was very favorable toward high-speed rail service as the way to improve the nation's railway transportation system.

The National Railroad Passenger Corp. (Amtrak) operated the only high-speed rail service in the United States on its Washington–New York Metroliner route (226 miles). The trains on this line were Swedish-designed AEM-7 locomotives attached to conventional passenger cars. The trains proved very effective, traveling at speeds as high as 125 mph. Completing the trip in under three hours, the trains had become competitive with the air shuttle services, claiming 41 percent of the available market share. The AEM-7 was well suited to travel the fairly straight Washington–New York route, but its conventional cars did not handle curves well. The New York–Boston route (231 miles) contained many curves and lacked electrification over part of the route. Amtrak president W. Graham Taylor was looking for a long-term relationship with a supplier of equipment that could satisfy needs of the entire Metroliner route along the Northeast Corridor, the route between Washington, D.C., New York, and Boston. By 1997, Amtrak planned to offer a full schedule of high-speed trains along the corridor.

Several companies were vying for a working relationship with Amtrak for its high-speed rail business. Amtrak planned to select a partner by late 1994. ABB Traction Inc. wanted and needed the alliance with Amtrak. ABB management thought it had the best company, as well as the best trains, for Amtrak's rail needs. Naturally, however, ABB's competitors felt their offerings were superior. ABB not only needed to distinguish its product's virtues from its competitors' offerings, it also needed to communicate its internal and external characteristics that would make Amtrak see that ABB was the best possible partner.

ABB (ASEA Brown Boveri)

ABB Traction Inc., headquartered in Elmira Heights, New York, designed and manufactured passenger rail transportation systems for North America. Regional offices existed in New Jersey and California. The company had rebuilt and retrofit Arrow III commuter cars for the New Jersey Transit and had filled an order of light rail vehicles for the Baltimore, Maryland, MTA. As well, ABB had undertaken a joint venture in

This case was prepared by Cynthia Jaffe, MBA student, and Victoria L. Crittenden, associate professor of marketing, Boston College, as the basis for class discussion rather than to illustrate either effective or ineffective handling of a managerial situation. All information was taken from secondary sources. Research assistance was provided by Stephanie Hillstrom and David Angus, Boston College. Revised 1997.

the late 1980s with Amtrak (and later subcontracted to Morrison Knudsen) to build rail transit cars for a high-speed line.

ABB Traction Inc. was a part of the Transportation Segment of ABB Inc. in the United States. ABB Inc., headquartered in Stamford, Connecticut, provided products and services for the power, process, industrial automation, environmental control, and mass transit markets. ABB Inc. employed around 27,000 workers in the United States.

On a global scale, ABB Inc. was the U.S. operations of the ABB Group, a global electrical equipment giant. ABB was the result of the 1987 merger between the Electrotechnical group of ASEA, a Swedish engineering group, and Brown, Boveri & Company, Ltd, a Swiss competitor to ASEA. The electrotechnical segment of ASEA included power plants, power transmission systems, power distribution, transportation equipment, environmental controls, and finance services. Brown, Boveri's businesses were similar to ASEA's electrotechnical segment with power supply, installations, and industrial products accounting for a majority of the company's business.

The merger allowed ABB to become the largest supplier to the world's electricity industry, as well as a leading world supplier of robots, process automation systems, locomotives, and air pollution control equipment. ABB's 1,300 companies generated annual revenues in excess of US$30 billion during the early part of the 1990s, employed approximately 240,000 individuals, and operated in 140 countries.

Percy Barnevik, president and CEO of ABB, was the visionary behind ABB. He created a multidomestic enterprise that could maintain both a global perspective and deep local roots. After the 1987 merger, he ordered massive restructuring, layoffs, and plant closings to transform the new ABB Group into a streamlined, aggressive force within the complacent power and transportation industries.

In the years that followed the merger, Barnevik applied a specific acquisition formula that proved effective and profitable. ABB Group acquired reputable competitors. The acquired companies were restructured to streamline operations, excess layers of managers were removed, and ABB's global–local philosophy was instilled. Barnevik's methods were considered "tough," but he realized that ABB's operations had to be lean in order to operate efficiently and profitably. In the seven years following the merger, ABB acquired over 70 companies throughout Europe, North America, South America, Asia, Australia, and India.

ABB employed a matrix structure with worldwide business activities grouped into seven business segments which comprised 65 business areas. Each business area was responsible for global strategies, business plans, allocation of manufacturing responsibilities, and product development. At the next level there were geographical subgroups or companies. Companies had two supervisors: the local-country supervisor, who was responsible for employees and customers, and the business area supervisor, whose focus was regional profits, research and development, capacity, and product design.

ABB was a rather unique global company as it managed to find a balance between radical decentralization of its operations and centralized reporting and control. Barnevik's ruling philosophy was to balance the contradiction of being both local and global. He encouraged local managers to cultivate a local customer base. Meanwhile, the local company was able to benefit from ABB's global economies of scale, worldwide coordination, and the R&D and technological support systems of any ABB company.

Amtrak Specifications

Amtrak hoped to match, or beat, flying and driving times from city to city. Unlike Europeans, Americans did not have a tradition of riding trains. Proficient critics of different modes of transportation, Americans traveled a great deal for both business and vacation.[1]

Amtrak was looking to purchase 26 high-speed trains for use in the Northeast Corridor, with the option to purchase 25 more. They expected to spend in excess of US$400 million on the initial order. The goal was to reduce the trip time between Boston and New York from four and a half to three hours. They were also looking to increase passenger capacity utilization from 265 persons to 300 to 350 persons per train set. Beyond the technical specifications of the order, Amtrak wanted to work with a company that understood the needs of the rail system in the next century.

Amtrak had received US$1.3 billion in funding through the Northeast High-Speed Rail Improvement project to facilitate the electrification of the rail route between New Haven, Connecticut, and Boston, Massachusetts. However, ultimately, Amtrak wanted to offer high-speed rail service anywhere in the United States. The major constraint in fulfilling this objective was that many existing routes were either nonelectrified (trains ran on diesel engines) or were electrified but ran on DC rather than AC power.

Amtrak requested that companies bidding for the contract be able to supply power units that would allow the high-speed train to run on diesel engine or a 650-volt DC rail. Additionally, the selected train would have to be able to negotiate curves at high speeds without exceeding standards of passenger comfort. (Slowing down for curves increased travel time and would not allow for competing with airline travel.)

Basically, Amtrak selected bidders for the high-speed train business based on the following criteria:[2]

- Since Amtrak was subject to "Buy American" requirements, the bidder must own or be able to lease fabrication, production, and final assembly facilities in the United States.

- The bidder must be able to deliver two preproduction train sets by January 1996 and have the capacity to produce two production units a month.

The X2000

Several years ago the Swedish railroad faced a question similar to Amtrak's. It hoped to reduce the travel time between two main Swedish city centers, Stockholm and Goteborg, a frequently traveled business route, in order to make the rails competitive with air travel. They could have replaced the country's existing century-old tracks and laid new lines to run high-speed trains like the French TGV or Japan's Shinkansen Bullet train. However, the cost of constructing the special tracks required for these trains and purchasing the land for right-of-way could have exceeded US$100 million per mile. Instead, the Swedish railroad chose to make improvements to the existing rail infrastructure and purchased ABB's X2000, which could maneuver the existing track at high speeds.

---

[1] Many factors went into selecting the proper mode of transportation. Speed and safety were major buying criteria. Other decision variables included interior accommodations, food service, seating arrangements, communication services offered during travel, and price.

[2] While these were criteria surrounding the selection of the high-speed train bidder, there were other issues regarding the use of high-speed rail that would have to be addressed. Mechanical features of importance included tilt or nontilt, propulsion systems, horsepower, acceleration, and braking. Other concerns centered around issues external to the high-speed train itself, such as improved grade crossing warning systems, protection for the "lightweight" train if an accident did occur, and extra maintenance costs due to the requirement to maintain rail to a higher standard.

The X2000 began operating in Sweden between Stockholm and Goteborg, cutting the rail time from four and a half to three hours. Until the X2000 began running in 1990, the route had been dominated by airlines. By reducing the travel time from city center to city center (so that it matched the door-to-door travel time of flying between airports and commuting into the city center), rail travel became competitive with traveling by plane. Within two years the rail market share increased from 38 to 52 percent.

The X2000 utilized a unique flexible steering system which allowed it to follow curved tracks at much higher speeds than conventional trains. The flexible steering was mounted to the railcar trucks.[3] The front and rear axles of the X2000 trucks moved independently, which enabled them to maneuver curves better than the wheels of conventional trucks, which were locked parallel to each other. At high speeds, the rigidity of conventional trucks could cause the wheels to jump off the rail, but the X2000's flexible mounts that connected the train's axles to the trucks expanded and contracted with the curves in a track. The X2000 traveled 40 percent faster than conventional trains and could take a curve at 125 miles per hour, something that would force a conventional train to slow to 80 miles per hour. The X2000 also had a computer-controlled hydraulic tilting mechanism, which improved passenger comfort and alleviated the lateral sway and jolting that occurs when trains travel at high speeds on curves. The tilt technology kept passengers and their tables level while the exterior of the train banked around curves. The X2000s that operated in Sweden ran on AC electric power. Since most of the U.S. rail system was not electrified, ABB was developing a diesel engine that could run on nonelectric U.S. routes.

The X2000 offered business and vacation travelers first-class passenger accommodations. The plush interiors with spacious single or side-by-side seating were far superior to what was offered in air or other rail travel. The train offered amenities such as outlets for PCs, phones, and fax machines. Each car offered complimentary drink service and optional meal service.

The rail project using the tilting X2000 train, including the expense for improving existing rails and signals, was still less costly than building a new dedicated rail system that would be required for a train that ran on a single versus double rail. Price of the X2000 ranged from US$13 million to US$20 million per train. ABB Traction high-speed trains were to be manufactured in Elmira Heights, New York.

ABB's Competition

The rail industry was somewhat complicated in that, for example, two, three, or more major competitors often worked in conjunction with one another on a particular project. Another project, however, might have seen these same two, three, or more companies competing among each other and/or working with other competitors in the industry. For example, ABB Traction had worked with Morrison Knudsen on the SEPTA's Norristown High Speed Line project, yet was competing directly with Morrison Knudsen for the Amtrak project. In another example, Morrison Knudsen and GEC Alsthom had formed the Texas TGV Corporation in a bid for a Texas high-speed rail project.

The four major competitors for the Amtrak contract were

- ABB Traction
- Siemens Transportation Systems (STS)

---

[3] Railcar trucks are the steel frames that support the rail cars.

- GEC Alsthom
- Morrison Knudsen (MK)

Siemens Transportation Systems (STS).   STS, a German company, teamed with General Motors' Electro-Motive Division (EMD), its partner in AC traction (STS and EMD provided locomotives for the Burlington Northern Railroad) and with AEG Westinghouse, its partner in the InterCityExpress (ICE) train, to compete for the Amtrak project. The ICE train tested at speeds in excess of 250 miles per hour in Germany and was used to transport both German and Swiss passengers. The ICE began operation between Hannover and Wurzburg in Germany in late 1991 and had been successful at stealing market share in the intercity business travel market.

The ICE had an asynchronous motor which recycled energy otherwise lost in deceleration. Its air-pressurized coaches were made of lightweight aluminum (as opposed to steel) to increase speed and save energy.

The ICE was the only train, other than the X2000, to have demonstrated its capabilities to Amtrak by late 1993. The demonstration ICE, with passenger capacity of 285, was equipped with two power units (totaling 13,000 horsepower), a restaurant car (general seating of 24 and a Bistro section accommodating 26), an ICE Deluxe car (a European first-class with two-and-one seating and a reservable conference room), and four ICE Coaches (European second-class with two-two seating, with one of the coaches having a reservable conference room). The ICE came with many amenities: fax machine, copier, three-channel audio entertainment system, and color video screens on some seatbacks. The steering system was conventional so the train could not tilt.

STS was headquartered in New York. It operated a U.S. sales office in Oregon and had manufacturing facilities in Georgia, North Carolina, and Ohio.

GEC Alsthom.   GEC Alsthom was the principal French manufacturer of the French high-speed *Train a Grande Vitesse* (TGV). The TGV ran at speeds of up to 186 miles per hour and held the world speed record on rail at 320 miles per hour. GEC Alsthom also built the Eurostar trainsets for use in the Chunnel lining England and France. The company planned to offer Amtrak a high-speed train set based on the TGV technology. GEC Alsthom had not lined up a U.S. partner for the Amtrak proposal by mid-1993.

Three TGV lines were operating in France by mid 1993: TGV-Sud-Est (Paris–Lyon), TGV-Atlantique (Paris–Bordeaux), and TGV-Nord (Paris–Lille). An additional line, TGV-AVE in Spain between Madrid and Seville, was the first to use the TGV technology outside of France.

TGVs reportedly ran fastest on straight tracks tailored to TGV use. However, operation was feasible on standard rails at reduced speed. The TGV's traction mounts (under the body of the power car instead of directly on the support trucks) allowed it to climb steep slopes without a dramatic decrease in speed.

The TGV was supposedly the fastest train in service and boasted an accident-free record in its over 10 years of operation.

Morrison Knudsen (MK).   In the late 1980s, Morrison Knudsen was a floundering Boise, Idaho, business operating mainly in construction and engineering services. Yet, with a 77-year history of building rails, the company decided to become a builder of the cars that ride such rails. By 1992, MK had contracted with U.S. projects for the Chicago Transit Authority, New York's Metro-North Commuter Railroad, Metra

(Chicago's commuter line), Caltrans (California Transportation Dept.), and BART (San Francisco's bay area rapid transit) for construction of new railcars. Some predicted that Morrison Knudsen aspired to join the ranks of General Motors' Electro-Motive Division (EMD) and General Electric Transportation Systems.[4]

Morrison Knudsen was the lead company in the consortium, Texas TGV Corp. (which included GEC Alsthom's North American licensee, Bombardier), to provide high-speed rail service in Texas. The Texas high-speed rail project was a US$6 billion, 469-mile, state-of-the-art, high-speed rail system connecting seven major Texas cities. However, after over two years of work with the Texas TGV Corp., Morrison Knudsen withdrew its US$200 million debt-equity issue for the project in December 1993. The reported reason behind MK's withdrawal was that MK shareholders would be bearing the brunt of the risk behind the project since Texas law prohibited federal help from the U.S. Department of Transportation. There was concern that the Texas high-speed rail project was dead after MK's withdrawal.

Morrison Knudsen joined with Fiat Ferroviaria for the Amtrak project. Italy's Fiat Ferroviaria was builder of the active-tilt Pendalino train in use in Italy, Germany, and Finland. The diesel-electric train for use in Germany was a venture between Fiat and Siemens.

Bombardier.   Montreal (Canada)-based Bombardier had emerged as a global powerhouse by 1994 with a diverse product mix of aerospace, rail transportation equipment, motorized consumer products (for example, Ski-Doo Snowmobiles), and financial services. Located in Bensalem, Pennsylvania, Bombardier's Transportation Equipment Group was North America's leading manufacturer of rail transit equipment.

A tentative joint venture agreement was reached with the China National Railway Locomotive & Rolling Stock Industry in 1994 in which Bombardier would manage China's largest passenger rail factory near Qindao and bring the factory up to world-class standards. Bombardier had also won a US$400 million contract to build a 20-mile light-rail system in Kuala Lumpur (Malaysia) and had built the high tech railcars hauling cars and buses through Europe's Chunnel.

Other Possible Contenders.   There were other likely contenders for the Amtrak bid. GE Transportation Systems was considered one of the "Big Two" in the rail business. GE's Erie, Pennsylvania, facility included some of the most skilled engineers and technicians in the business and one of the most comprehensive four-mile test tracks. Ansaldo Transporti, based in Italy, had a North American operation, Union Switch & Signal, which was rumored to be thinking about entering the competition for the bid. Union Switch & Signal was headquartered in South Carolina, with systems and research operations in Pennsylvania and distribution operations in South Carolina. Mitsubishi Corp. of Japan provided the Shinkansen ("bullet train"), which was known for its accident-free operation and a maximum speed of 270 kmph. The Spanish Talgo from Renfe Talgo of America was tested between Seattle, Washington, and Portland, Oregon. The train was an articulated, tilt-body Talgo Pendular 200 with diesel-electric motive power. Amtrak was operating the Talgo as an extra train on one of its runs.

---

[4] EMD and GE were considered the "Big Two" in building locomotives. GE produced propulsion systems, dynamic braking systems, auxiliary power conversion equipment, and on-board diagnostic instrumentation for use on light-rail and rapid transit vehicles in addition to locomotives.

EXHIBIT 1   High-Speed Rail Systems in the United States

Project	Connection	Projected Annual Passengers	Projected Completion	Projected Cost (before Interest)
The Northeast Corridor	231 miles	n.a.	1997	$400 million
The High Roller	270 miles	6.5 million	1998	$3.5 billion
The Golden Palm	325 miles	2 million	1995	$2.5 billion
The Magnetic Mouse	20 miles	n.a.	1995	$700 million
The Longhorn Limited	280 miles	3.5 million	1998	$2.2 billion
The Buckeye Bullet	250 miles	4 million	2000	$2.2 billion

The Strategic Issue

ABB Traction Inc. had the formidable task of convincing Amtrak officials that an investment in their high-speed rail technology was the best choice. What kind of strategic marketing advantage did ABB have over other companies competing for the Amtrak contract?

This was a major step in the continuation of ABB Traction's role as a major player in the high-speed train arena. Similar projects were active in both the United States and other parts of the world. The "High Roller" connecting Anaheim, California, and Las Vegas, Nevada, the "Golden Palm" connecting Miami, Orlando, and Tampa, Florida, the "Magnetic Mouse" connecting Orlando Airport with Orange County, Florida, the "Longhorn Limited" connecting Houston and Dallas, Texas, and the "Buckeye Bullet" connecting Cleveland, Columbus, and Cincinnati, Ohio, were all prospective high-speed rail systems discussed in the United States. Exhibit 1 provides mileage estimates and other information for these routes as well as the Northeast corridor route. Basically, the United States was mapped with planned or proposed high-speed rail lines. The cost to improve existing tracks, upgrade crossings, and buy new equipment was estimated to run into the billions of dollars. The future of high-speed rail revealed an innovative magnetic levitation technology (maglev). It was predicted that maglev could propel trains at up to 300 mph.

Internationally, South Korea and Taiwan had proposed new systems. Japan, France, and Germany planned expansions on existing lines. Spain had opened its first high-speed rail line. France planned to extend its high-speed network into England, Belgium, and Germany.

What variables would make ABB Traction Inc. attractive as a prospective partner in the high-speed rail market? How could ABB Traction Inc. market itself and its X2000 to Amtrak?

Sources

"ABB's 1993 U.S. Results Announced," *Business Wire,* March 15, 1994.

"ABB Poses a Problem, Then Delivers the Solution," *Business Marketing,* April 1993, p. 58.

"ABB Sharpens Its Focus on Metals," *Iron Age New Steel,* November 1993, p. 9.

"Advanced Fixed-Block: The Los Angeles Green Line," *Railway Age,* October 1993, p. 46.

Agres, Ted, "Asea Brown Boveri—A Model for Global Management," *R&D,* December 1991, pp. 30–34.

Barnard, Bruce, "Inside Europe: Business Briefs," *Europe,* April 1993, pp. SS3–SS4.

"Big Switch at Switch," *Railway Age,* March 1992, pp. 39–40.

Byrne, Harlan S., "Morrison Knudsen: Mega-Projects, Growing Earnings," *Investment News and Views,* December 23, 1991, pp. 31–32.

Davis, L.J., "Born Again," *Business Month,* January 1990, pp. 22–34.

Dooling, Dave, "Transportation," *IEEE Spectrum,* January 1993, pp. 68–71.

Fairweather, Virginia, "A Supertrain Solution?" *Civil Engineering,* February 1990, pp. 50–53.

Frey, Sherwood C., Jr., and Schlosser, Michael M., "ABB and Ford: Creating Value through Cooperation," *Sloan Management Review,* Fall 1993, pp. 65–72.

"GM Calls Off Search for an EMD Partner," *Railway Age,* November 1993, p. 15.

Hofheinz, Paul, "Europe's Tough New Managers," *Fortune,* September 6, 1993, pp. 111–16.

Hughes, David, "Raytheon Pursues Tilt Train, Rapid Transit Systems," *Aviation Week & Space Technology,* December 13, 1993, pp. 59–61.

"ICE: High Speed and High Hopes for Siemens," *Railway Age,* May 1993, p. 52.

Joyce, Romy, "Global Hero," *International Management,* September 1992, pp. 82–85.

Ju-Hyeok, Nam, "Supertrains to Blow Off Korean Traffic," *Business Korea,* March 1992, pp. 62–64.

Jurgen, Ronald K., "Transportation," *IEEE Spectrum,* January 1992, pp. 55–57.

Kapstein, Jonathan, and Reed, Stanley, "The Euro-Gospel according to Percy Barnevik," *Business Week,* July 23, 1990, pp. 64–66.

Kennedy, Carol, "ABB: Model Merger for the New Europe," *Long Range Planning,* October 1992, pp. 10–17.

Klebnikov, Paul, "The Powerhouse," *Forbes,* September 2, 1991, pp. 46–52.

"Korea Picks TGV Technology," *Railway Age,* September 1993, p. 56.

Kruglinski, Anthony, "Looking Ahead with Bill Agee," *Railway Age,* November 1992, pp. 71, 90.

Kruglinski, Anthony, "No One Wants to Pay GM's Price for EMD. Why?" *Railway Age,* October 1993, p. 12.

"Market Outlook," *Railway Age,* January 1993, pp. 8–9.

McGough, Robert, "The Buckeye Bullet," *Financial World,* December 12, 1989, pp. 26–28.

McGough, Robert, "The Texas Cannonball," *Financial World,* August 6, 1991, pp. 20–22.

Middleton, William D. "Baltimore: Up and Running," *Railway Age,* June 1992, pp. 50–51.

Miller, Luther S., "France Gets It Together," *Railway Age,* July 1993, pp. 56–57.

O'Connor, Lee, "French TGV Making Tracks in Spain," *Mechanical Engineering,* November 1992, pp. 52–55.

O'Connor, Lee, "Tilting Train Smooths Out the Curves," *Mechanical Engineering,* February 1993, pp. 62–65.

Palef, B. Randall, "The Team and Me: Reflections of a Design Group," *Personnel Journal,* February 1994, p. 48.

Pennino, Thomas P., Ptechin, Jamey, Boothroyd, Geoffrey, and Knight, Winston, "Bringing Costs Down," *IEEE Spectrum,* September 1993, pp. 51–62.

Rapoport, Carla, "A Tough Swede Invades the U.S.," *Fortune,* June 29, 1992, pp. 76-79.

Reier, Sharon, "Silver Award Winners in the FW CEO of the Year Contest in Europe," *Financial World,* October 13, 1992, pp. 38–43.

Rochester, Jack B., "Using Information Systems for Business and Competitor Intelligence," *I/S Analyzer,* May 1990, pp. 1–12.

Rubin, Debra K., "Slow Going for Firms in Heavy Construction," *ENR,* May 24, 1993, pp. 68–69.

Schares, Gail E., "Mr. Barnevik, Aren't You Happy Now?" *Business Week,* September 27, 1993, p. 128L.

"Swedish Firms Set Sail for Europe,' *Economist,* September 1, 1990, pp. 59–60.

Symonds, William, Nayeri, Farah, Smith, Geri, and Plafker, Ted, "Bombardier's Blitz," *Business Week,* February 6, 1995, p. 62.

Taylor, Brian, "Trinova on Track with High Speed Rail," *Toledo Business Journal,* October 1993, p. 1.

Taylor, William, "The Logic of Global Business: An Interview with ABB's Percy Barnevik," *Harvard Business Review,* March-April 1991, pp. 90–105.

"The ICE Train Cometh," *Purchasing,* November 11, 1993, p. 45.

"TGV: 11 Years, 250 Million Riders, No Accidents," *Railway Age,* May 1993, p. 40.

"Trains: Faster than a Speeding Bullet," *Economist,* April 4, 1992, pp. 87–88.

"Turnkey Contract Goes to Ansaldo," *Railway Age,* June 1993, p. 28.

"Urban Rail Planner's Guide 1994," *Railway Age,* February 1994, pp. G41–G48.

"US&S Will Equip BN Centralized Dispatch Facility," *Railway Age,* September 1993, p. 18.

Vantuono, William C., "Amtrak Pre-Qualifies Teams, Sets FY1994 Funds," *Railway Age,* November 1993, p. 30.

Vantuono, William C., "Despite Setbacks, High Speed Rail Moves Ahead," *Railway Age,* April 1994, pp. 57–66.

Vantuono, William C., "Getting the NHSL Up to Speed," *Railway Age,* October 1992, p. 108.

Vantuono, William C., "ICE Makes U.S. Debut on Amtrak's Northeast Corridor," *Railway Age,* August 1993, p. 24.

Vantuono, William C., "North American Intercity Passenger Rail," *Railway Age,* April 1994, pp. 57–66.

Vantuono, William C., "The Contenders Line Up," *Railway Age,* June 1993, pp. 47–48.

Welty, Gus, "Engines of Change," *Railway Age,* July 1993, pp. 33–39.

Welty, Gus, "From Big Two to Big Three?" *Railway Age,* January 1994, pp. 48–53.

Welty, Gus, "MK's Move into OEM," *Railway Age,* July 1993, pp. 59–61.

Welty, Gus, "Mid-Range Power: How Big a Market?" *Railway Age,* November 1993, pp. 79–80.

Welty, Gus, "Precision Train Scheduling?" *Railway Age,* August 1991, pp. 27–34.

"What Happened (and What Didn't Happen) in Texas," *Railway Age,* February 1994, p. 24.

"Wheel/Rail Force Measurements on High Adhesion Locomotives," *Railway Age,* June 1993, pp. 74–77.

Woolsey, James P., "'Swedish Steel' Is Tested in U.S.," *Air Transport World,* July 1993, p. 100.

"World Update," *Railway Age,* March 1994, p. 100.

Yang, Dori Jones, and Kelly, Kevin, "Why Morrison Knudsen Is Riding the Rails," *Business Week,* November 2, 1992, pp. 112–16.

Yoo-Lim, Lee, "France's TGV Selected for High-Speed Railway Project," *Business Korea,* September 1993, pp. 14–17.

CASE 5–2
AMBROSIA CORPORATION–SAN AUGUST

"I've done some initial analysis/data gathering. The easy part is putting together the information on 'what' is going on in the frozen desserts and snacks marketplace in the Philippines. My problem is not so much with the 'what,' but with 'how' to maintain our market dominance," said Andrea Bratten, senior assistant vice president and operations director of the Frozen Desserts and Snack business of Ambrosia Corporation of the San August Group. She was facing an unfamiliar competitive situation in the ice cream marketplace. Ambrosia was the Philippines' first and only name in ice cream and frozen confections. Even with prices slightly higher, generally, than competitors', Ambrosia's market share in 1991 was around 77 percent. Suppliers of major raw materials for ice cream (e.g., Universal Flavors, Inc.) and manufacturers of dairy equipment (e.g., Alfa-Laval and APV) advertised Ambrosia in the same league as Häagen-Dazs and Baskin-Robbins as "world class" users of their products. However, the Philippines' continuing import liberalization program was broadening the competitive arena. Non–ice cream food items from foreign brands had high acceptance in the country, and consumers appeared willing to pay a premium for imported products. Ambrosia Corporation's domestic competitors expressed interest in having some sort of "tie-ups" with foreign brands.

Foreign companies were courting Ambrosia Corporation with the notion of licensing Ambrosia to produce and distribute the foreign company's products in the Philippines. But, if Ambrosia was already "among the world's best," did it need a foreign brand segment? Would Ambrosia lose its place in the premium segment to its own foreign brand segment? In short, should Andrea, and Ambrosia management in general, consider (and possibly accept) any offers from foreign investors?

San August Corporation

Founded in 1890 and incorporated in 1913, San August Corporation manufactured, distributed, and sold food products, beverages, packaging products, and animal feeds throughout the Philippines. San August Corporation was the Philippines' largest publicly held food and beverage company. It generated about 4 percent of the country's gross national product and contributed about 7 percent of the government's tax revenues. In 1993, San August was rated number 27 in the top 100 emerging market companies. Exhibit 1 shows San August's fundamental and historical philosophy, with major milestones of the San August Corporation included in Exhibit 2.

The San August Corporation did business in four major market segments: (1) beverages, (2) food and agribusiness, (3) packaging, and (4) property development. The beverage segment consisted of five companies, with a contribution to sales of 69 percent and contribution to operating income of 70 percent. The food and agribusiness

This case was prepared by Victoria L. Crittenden, associate professor of marketing and Erin L. Quinn, of Boston College and William F. Crittenden, associate professor of management at Northeastern University as the basis for class discussion rather than to illustrate either effective or ineffective handling of a managerial situation. Ambrosia and San August are pseudonyms, and some data have been disguised. All relevant relationships remain constant. Revised 1997.

EXHIBIT 1   Fundamental and Historical Philosophy

Profit with Honor

The following objectives are indivisible and together represent the broad aims of the Corporation and should be interpreted in the light of this philosophy.

Objectives

To be constantly aware of the aspirations of the people and of the nation, and to ensure that San August continues to make a major contribution towards the achievement of these aspirations.

To manufacture, distribute, and sell throughout the Philippines, food products, beverage, packaging products, and animal feeds; being ready at all times to add, modify, or discontinue products in accordance with changes in the market.

To diversify into fields that will ensure optimum utilization of management resources and a substantial contribution to corporate profits.

To seek and develop export markets for new products as well as for those already being produced by the Corporation.

To generate a return on funds employed sufficient to ensure an adequate rate of growth for the Corporation, and to provide satisfactory returns to stockholders.

To provide an environment that is conducive to the development of the individual and that encourages employees to realize their full capabilities.

To maintain the highest ethical standards in the conduct of our business.

To adopt a flexible and objective attitude toward change and to pursue an active policy of innovation.

EXHIBIT 2   Milestones in San August's History

1890	San August Brewery is founded.
1895	San August Beer wins its first well-deserved recognition when it is named the "product of the highest quality" in the Exposicion Regional de Filipinas.
1913	The enterprise becomes a corporation.
1925	The Ambrosia Ice Cream Plant is founded.
1927	San August Brewery secures exclusive rights for bottling and distributing Coca-Cola in the Philippines.
1938	The pilot glass plant starts operations, manufacturing beer bottles at first and later bottles for other San August products.
1942–45	Operations of the corporation are interrupted by the Japanese occupation of Manila and the seizure as enemy property of San August Brewery including all its plants, equipment, and inventories.
1954	San August enters poultry and livestock feeds processing.
1963	San August Brewery changes its name to San August Corporation.
1973	Sales exceed P1 billion and net profits are over P100 million for the first time.
1977	The company celebrates the 50th anniversary of the Coca-Cola bottling franchise in the Philippines.
1978	Construction of the new Ambrosia chicken processing plant begins at Cabuyao, Laguna.
1981	San August Beer firms up its worldwide reputation for excellence when it wins four of the top awards in the prestigious Monde Selection held in Brussels. Pale Pilsen Regular, Pale Pilsen Export, and Dark Beer won gold medals and Lagerlite won a silver medal.
1982	The company's highly automated and efficient brewery at San Fernando, Pampanga, commences operations in July.
1991	Ambrosia Division spins off as a separate corporation.

EXHIBIT 3   **Ambrosia Corporation Financial Overview**

	1991	1990	1989	1988
For the Year[1]				
Net sales	53,332	43,815	36,714	30,866
Income from operations	5,556	4,303	3,860	3,611
Net income before nonrecurring items	2,519	1,880	1,858	1,895
Earnings per share before nonrecurring items[2]	1.77	1.32	1.31	1.35
Net income after nonrecurring items	2,812	1,796	2,431	2,052
Earnings per share after nonrecurring items[2]	1.97	1.26	1.72	1.46
Cash dividends	432	432	417	374
At Year-End[1]				
Working capital	7,247	5,411	3,569	2,962
Total assets	42,338	35,684	29,554	23,893
Property, plant & equipment-net	17,880	15,514	12,287	8,766
Stockholders' equity	14,916	12,633	10,866	8,401

Source: Annual report.

[1] Pesos in millions (except per share).

[2] Based on the average number of shares outstanding during each year with retroactive adjustments for the stock split/stock dividends.

segment consisted of eight companies, with a sales contribution of 21 percent and operating income contribution of 16 percent. Packaging included five companies, with a sales contribution of 10 percent and operating income contribution of 14 percent. The property development segment began operation in 1991 and was managed by one company.

San August believed that strategic alliances were important due to the increasingly competitive global environment. Examples of such partnerships included relations with Conservera Campofrio S.A. of Spain, Yamamura Glass Co., Ltd., of Japan, and Guangzhou Brewery of China. It was believed that substantial benefits could be attained from synergies and the sharing of the cost of research and development.

Exhibit 3 provides a financial overview of the firm.

The Philippines

An island country of Southeast Asia, the Philippines lay on the western edge (about 600 miles or 960 km) from mainland Asia. Its 1992 population was around 62,000,000. The capital and largest city was Manila, with around 8,000,000 inhabitants in metro Manila.[1] There were two major airports in the Philippines: one in Manila and one in Cebu (population around 1,000,000). Exhibit 4 provides a geographic look at the country. Major storms approached the Philippines from the southeast. Most products were distributed by sea from Manila.

The Philippine economy contracted in 1991. The effects of the Gulf War, restrained government spending, the full implementation of an ad valorem tax on beer, the impo-

---

[1] The latest published census report was dated 1991 with population data for 1980; however, country spokesperson provided estimates for 1992 population data. This was almost a 30 percent increase in population from 1980 to 1992.

EXHIBIT 4
The Philippines

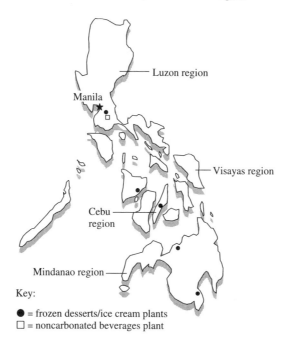

Key:

● = frozen desserts/ice cream plants
□ = noncarbonated beverages plant

sition of additional indirect taxes such as the import levy, high interest rates and inflation, and the damage caused by the eruption of Mount Pinatubo and other natural
calamities weakened consumer demand and set back employment opportunities as
well as investment and industrial activity. Additional factors that were expected to affect economic conditions included the government's continued implementation of fiscal and monetary measures aimed at economic stabilization, the ramifications of severe drought in Mindanao, the critical water supply situation, and increased power
rates that would add to industrial costs. Additionally, there were no antitrust laws in
the Philippines.

As a result of increased travel, improved communications, and the homogenization
of consumer tastes, a universal lifestyle appeared to be emerging in the Philippines.
Foreign food and beverage companies, technology, and financial resources were expanding and globalizing their operations. With the easing of trade and investment barriers, the availability of more foreign products was expected. As such, foreign companies—alone or in partnership with local firms—were taking advantage of business
opportunities in the Philippines.

Ambrosia Corporation

In 1925, San August Corporation bought the trademark "Ambrosia" when it purchased a
small ice cream plant on Aviles Street in Manila. In 1969, the Ambrosia Dairy Products
Plant was established on Aurora Blvd. in Quezon City just north of Manila. In 1981, a
joint venture with the New Zealand Dairy Board formed the Philippine Dairy Products
Corporation (PDPC). The PDPC, managed by Ambrosia, was 70 percent owned by San
August. PDPC's businesses were butter, margarine, and cheese. The Ambrosia Division
was transformed into a wholly owned subsidiary of San August Corporation in 1991. Exhibit 5 provides an overview of the organization structure in Ambrosia.

EXHIBIT 5 Organization Structure

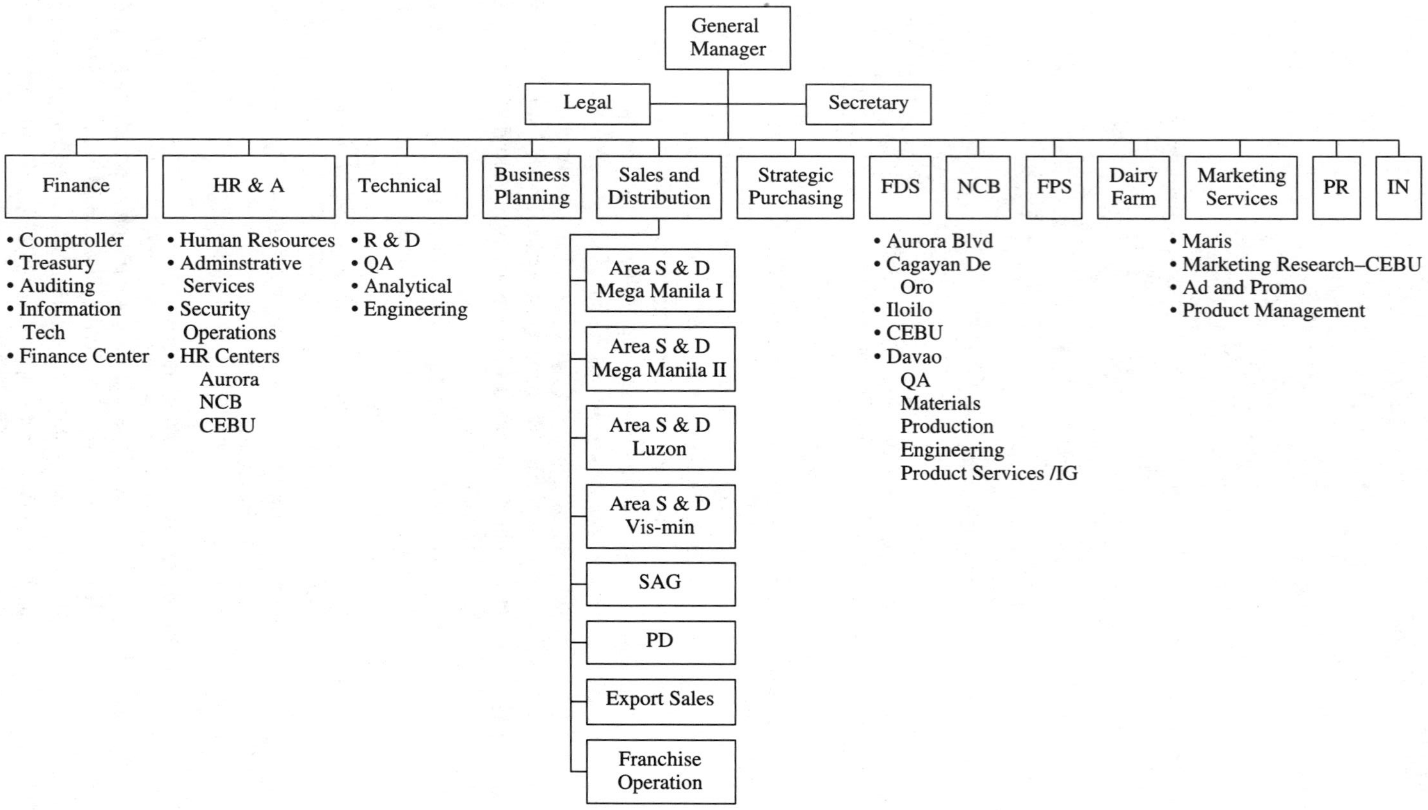

```
                              General Manager
                    Legal                    Secretary

Finance   HR & A   Technical   Business   Sales and   Strategic   FDS   NCB   FPS   Dairy   Marketing   PR   IN
                               Planning   Distribution Purchasing                    Farm    Services
```

Finance
- Comptroller
- Treasury
- Auditing
- Information Tech
- Finance Center

HR & A
- Human Resources
- Adminstrative Services
- Security Operations
- HR Centers
  Aurora
  NCB
  CEBU

Technical
- R & D
- QA
- Analytical
- Engineering

Sales and Distribution
- Area S & D Mega Manila I
- Area S & D Mega Manila II
- Area S & D Luzon
- Area S & D Vis-min
- SAG
- PD
- Export Sales
- Franchise Operation

- Aurora Blvd
- Cagayan De Oro
- Iloilo
- CEBU
- Davao
  QA
  Materials
  Production
  Engineering
  Product Services /IG

Marketing Services
- Maris
- Marketing Research–CEBU
- Ad and Promo
- Product Management

EXHIBIT 6
Business Portfolio

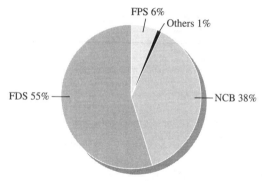

total revenue: P2.830 billion

Ambrosia was the only dairy manufacturer in the Philippines with its own dairy farm. The Ambrosia Dairy Farm in the hills of Alfonso, Cavite (just south of Manila), was at the forefront of a major effort to develop, through computerized breeding, a dairy herd suitable to the tropics. Besides being the biggest in Southeast Asia, the farm boasted being one of the most modern and advanced in the whole of Asia.

Ambrosia Corporation's businesses included frozen desserts and snacks (FDS), noncarbonated beverages (NCB), and food preparation and supplements (FPS), with a 1991 total revenue of P2.83 billion.[2] Fifty-five percent of Ambrosia's revenue came from its frozen desserts and snacks, 38 percent from noncarbonated beverages, and 6 percent from food preparation and supplements (Exhibit 6).

The frozen desserts and snacks product line consisted of three major line offerings (Bulk Ice Cream, Single-Serves, and Soft-Serve Ice Cream/Others) with wide variety in each. Exhibit 7 lists the offerings within each line. Ambrosia launched new products and flavors consistently in the frozen desserts and snacks category. Sixteen new products were at some stage of development and were expected to be introduced between 1993 and 1997. Between January and July 1992, the company introduced five new flavors of Gold Label and All Time Favorities (Swisse mocha, mangoes n' cream, double cheese supreme), and two Sorbetes flavors (sesame karoy espesyal, tsohalle real), as well as a new Sorbet in five flavors. In the Single-Serves category, Ambrosia introduced a fruit bar in four flavors (nangha, ube, sweet corn, orange). Additionally, Ambrosia Ice Cream Special in two flavors and five new single-serves were proposed for introduction between August and December 1992.

Exhibit 8 shows the product offerings in the noncarbonated beverages line. Exhibit 9 lists the food preparation and supplements offerings.

Ambrosia had six manufacturing plants. A major capacity expansion to be completed by the beginning of 1993 was expected to almost double current capacity. The Aurora Plant in Quezon City produced items for the frozen desserts and snacks and food preparation and supplements lines, with the Mandaluyong plant producing noncarbonated beverages. Four ice cream plants had opened since the early 1980s. The Ceba Ice Cream Plant opened in 1983, the Davao Ice Cream Plant in 1989, the Cagayan Ice Cream Plant in 1990, and the Iloilo Ice Cream Plant in 1991. Eighteen sales offices were located in Luzon, eight in Visayas, and nine in Mindanao. (Exhibit 4 gives

---

[2] P = peso.

EXHIBIT 7 Frozen Desserts and Snacks
Product Lines

Bulk Ice Cream
Ambrosia Gold Label (Premium and Super Premium)
Ambrosia Flavor-of-the-Month
Ambrosia All Time Favorites
Ambrosia Sorbetes
Ambrosia Lite n' Creamy (sugar-free ice cream)
Ambrosia Ice Cream Cakes and Moulds

Single-Serves
Ambrosia Chocolate Pinipig Crunch (stick bar)
Ambrosia Twin Popsies (stick bar)
Ambrosia Ice Drop (stick bar)
Ambrosia Drumstick
Ambrosia Crunchies (ice cream bar)
Ambrosia Ice Cream Sundae (cup)
Ambrosia Ice Cream Cups
Ambrosia Chocolait Bar

Soft-Serve Ice Cream and Others
Ambrosia Curly Creams Soft-Serve Ice Cream
Ambrosia Soft-Serve Ice Cream Mixes (powdered and liquid)
Ambrosia Ice Cream Cones
Ambrosia Soda Fountain Syrups
Ambrosia Frozen Yogurt (customized)

plants' locations.) With its expensive geographic spread, Ambrosia was able to ship from various locations throughout the Philippines, unlike its competitors, which distributed from Manila only. Thus, inclement weather did not pose a threat to maintaining a steady flow of products to consumers.

Competitors. Major Filipino industry players in each of Ambrosia's product categories were:

Company	Brand
Frozen Desserts and Snacks	
RFM	Selecta
Purefoods	Sorbetero
	Coney Island
CPC	Presto
	Tivoli
Ready-to-Drink Juice, Milk, and Chocolate	
SEMEXCO	Zest-O
	Sun-Glo
General Milling	Granny Goose
	Alaska
Nestlé	Bear Brand
Cream	
Nestlé	

EXHIBIT 8   Noncarbonated Beverages Product Lines

Ambrosia Fresh Cow's Milk (pasteurized)
Ambrosia Low-Fat Milk (pasteurized)
Ambrosia Flavored Milk (pasteurized)
   Chocolait
   Melon Milk
Ambrosia Fruit Juice (pasteurized)
   Orange
   Mango
Ambrosia Fresh n' Lite (pasteurized, sugar-free)
   Orange
   Mango
Ambrosia Fresh Milk (UHT)*
Ambrosia Full Cream (UHT)
Ambrosia Flavored Milk (UHT)
   Chocolait
   Strawberry
Ambrosia Sweet Dairy Milk (UHT sweetened full cream)
Ambrosia Fruit Drinks (UHT)
   Orange
   Mango
   Guyabano (soursap)
   Calamansi (Philippine lemon)
   Buco (young coconut water)
   Hi-C Fruit Drinks (UHT)
   Nestee
   Milo
Ambrosia Fruit Juice Concentrate

* UHT refers to ultra high temperature and is a form of cooking juice to preserve taste, flavor, and odor during processing.

EXHIBIT 9   Food Preparation and Supplements Product Lines

Creams
Ambrosia Dip n' Dressing
Ambrosia All Purpose Cream (UHT)
Ambrosia Whipping Cream (pasteurized)
Ambrosia Fresh Whipping Cream
Ambrosia Sour Cream

Fermented Products
Ambrosia Cottage Cheese
   Plain
   Fruited
Ambrosia Bulgarian Yogurt
   Plain
   Flavored
   Fruited
Ambrosia Lite n' Rite (sugar-free yogurt)
   Flavored
   Fruited

Frozen Desserts and Snacks

Industry volume in the frozen desserts and snacks category was expected to double by 1998, with the future belonging to single-serves and the targeting of provincial areas.[3] In the first half of 1992, Ambrosia's market share in the ice cream marketplace was about 75 percent, compared to 77.3 percent in 1991. The corporation's objective was to strengthen its market dominance and translate this into higher profits for the corporation. Strategies for achieving this objective were (1) a focus on the consumers' driving force (impulse buying), (2) expansion of capacity to meet market demand, and (3) attaining international quality standards.

Consumer Buying Behavior.   Ambrosia's market research found that 86 percent of Filipino consumers bought ice cream on impulse. The major reasons for eating ice cream were specific occasion/purpose, taste/flavor, fondness, and refreshment. Ninety-eight percent of consumers ate ice cream at home, with 73 percent of consumers eating ice cream as an afternoon snack.

The research also suggested that while consumers bought on impulse, brand and flavor were determined prior to purchase. This implied to Ambrosia that product availability, visibility, and desirability (key success factors in the industry) needed to be ensured and that there was a need to strengthen top-of-mind awareness and brand image. Distribution was such that about 60 percent of Ambrosia's frozen dessert and snack products were sold through retail stores (e.g., supermarkets, convenience stores), and about 30 percent through prepared food outlets (e.g., bakeshops, restaurants, ice cream shops). Communication activities included trade promotions (e.g., raffles with prizes such as generators), consumer promotions (e.g., "buy one, get one free," free gift items with minimum purchase), and advertising (e.g., media and free signage).

Since taste and quality were major motivations for eating ice cream (i.e., desirability), Ambrosia managers felt that the corporation needed to continually work on improving product quality and product formulation. As market leader in the industry, Ambrosia felt that it must dictate the tempo of development in the areas of new product introduction, flavors, and packaging to create excitement in the marketplace.

Competition.   Philippine consumption of ice cream was well behind that of other nations. The United States was the leader in 1989 with per capita consumption of 5.95 gallons. New Zealand was next with 5.05, followed by Australia (4.70), Canada (3.83), Japan (2.00), and South Korea (1.14). Per capita consumption in 1989 in the Philippines was 0.24 gallon, which was expected to be the same in 1992.

Including Ambrosia, four major competitors existed in 1992 to capture this untapped marketplace in the Philippines.

Selecta.   With market share in the ice cream industry of 15 percent for the first half of 1992 (7.3 percent in 1991), Selecta's overall strategy seemed to be a frontal attack on Ambrosia. Elements of this strategy appeared to be a parity of product offerings along with parity pricing, and premium positioning of its products. Selecta was focusing on major retail outlets in key provincial urban centers.

Recent developments within Selecta included (1) a doubling of capacity (an increase from 4,000 to 8,000 gallons per day, equivalent to 2.1 million gallons per year),

---

[3] A province is a geographic region in the Philippines.

(2) the purchase of a new single-serve machine capable of producing 3,000 gallons per day (equivalent to 0.8 million gallons per year), and (3) the purchase of 22 new refrigerated route trucks. Along with these internal operational developments, Selecta had started negotiations with Cadburry IC Bar for their single-serves.

Coney Island/Sorbetero.   Purefoods was also posing a frontal attack on Ambrosia through a multibrand strategy. Coney Island (2.4 percent market share in 1991) was using an "All American" positioning in the premium segment; Sorbetero (3.1 percent market share in 1991) was using its Filipino ice cream to attack Ambrosia's Flavor of the Month, Special, Regular, and Sorbetes directly.

Purefoods' attack against Ambrosia included (1) taking a census of Ambrosia carrito vendors[4] to attract them to carry Purefoods' products instead of Ambrosia's and (2) parity pricing with Ambrosia as of February 1992. Additionally, Purefoods had acquired an APV Glacier brand machine to produce single-serves, expanded distribution using Smokey's/Scoops n' Steaks outlets, launched three new flavors for Sorbetero Ice Sarap, and started offering a 10 percent rebate to selective retail outlets.

Presto.   Presto's overall strategy was to focus on single-serve novelty items and lower pricing. Market share in the total ice cream marketplace in 1991 for Presto was 10 percent. However, Presto's 1991 market share for single-serve ice cream was almost 30 percent (compared to Ambrosia's 69 percent). In bulk ice cream, Presto was only averaging around a 5 percent share.

Presto followed the launch of Ambrosia Sundae with Tivoli Sundae and Funwich. Presto's new entries in the candy bar segment in 1992 had been the Big Bang and Cloud Nine. Additionally, Presto planned to introduce two new variants of the Tivoli Bar (Ube-Nangka and Strawberry).

Exhibits 10 through 12 provide capacity information for all three of Ambrosia's major competitors in the frozen desserts and snacks category.

Foreign Investors

Corporate management knew of three foreign companies with interests similar to Ambrosia Corporation: Nestlé, Häagen-Dazs, and Mars.

Nestlé.   Nestlé S.A. (Switzerland) was a holding company in the food processing industry. Its principle products were drinks (coffees, chocolate drinks, tea, mineral water, fruit juices), dairy products (milk, cream, cheese, butter, breakfast cereals), infant and dietetic products (formula, baby foods), culinary products (soups, condiments, sauces), frozen foods and ice cream (entrees, pizza, Lean Cuisine), refrigerated products (yogurt, cold meat products, fresh pasta), chocolate and confectionery (Kit Kat, Nestlé Crunch), pet foods (cat and dog foods), restaurants and hotels (through Stouffer Corporation), pharmaceutical products, and cosmetics. Nestlé S.A. had 423 factories spread across 61 countries. Exhibit 13 analyzes Nestlé's sales by product groups.

Acquisitions and joint ventures had been important to Nestlé's growth since its incorporation in 1866. For example, Nestlé had acquired (and in some cases later sold off) such companies as Stouffer Corporation (which operated a chain of restaurants and a frozen food division) in 1973, Alcon Laboratories (ophthalmic products) in 1977, Beech-Nut Corporation (baby foods and dietetic specialty products) in 1979, and Hills Brothers Coffee, in 1985. Coca-Cola and Nestlé S.A. had formed a joint

---

[4] A carrito vendor is a vendor selling items from a pushcart.

EXHIBIT 10
Selecta Capacity

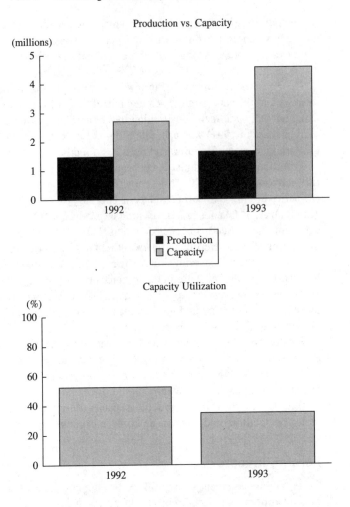

Production vs. Capacity

Capacity Utilization

venture to manufacture and market concentrates and beverage bases for the production of ready-to-drink coffee and tea beverages under the Nescafé and Nestea brand names.

Nestlé Philippines, Inc., was an affiliate company of the San August Group (51 percent of Nestlé Philippines being owned by San August and 49 percent by Nestlé). The affiliate produced and marketed instant drinks, full cream and filled milk, soya-based products, infant foods, and culinary products in the food and agribusiness market segment. There were four manufacturing plants.

Häagen-Dazs. Häagen-Dazs, a private subsidiary of Grand Metropolitan PLC (incorporated in England), made superpremium ice cream and frozen yogurt products. The company operated in the United States, Japan, Canada, and Europe. Headquartered in Teaneck, New Jersey, the company had 1,100 employees, with an estimated annual revenue of $340 million. Häagen-Dazs was committed to building its business worldwide and invested heavily in advertising, consumer promotions, manufacturing facilities, and research and development.

Häagen-Dazs accounted for approximately 60 percent of the superpremium ice cream (butterfat content between 14 and 18 percent) market in the United States. Its major U.S. competitors were Ben and Jerry's, Mars, and Breyers. Major European

EXHIBIT 11
Coney Island/Sorbetero
Capacity

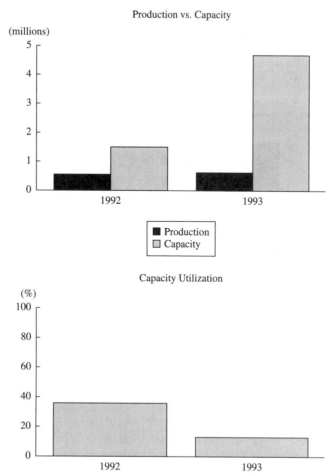

Production vs. Capacity

(millions)

■ Production
□ Capacity

Capacity Utilization

(%)

competitors included Carte d'Or, Movenpick, and Loseley. In Japan, competitors included Meiji, AYA, and Lady Borden. Häagen-Dazs anticipated a significant portion of its growth to come from Europe (the largest frozen dessert market outside North America). The company was making major inroads into the Far East through joint ventures in Japan and Korea.

Grand Metropolitan PLC conducted operations through three groups: Food (35 percent of turnover and 28 percent of trading profit in fiscal 1991), Drinks (28 percent of turnover and 42 percent of trading profit in fiscal 1991), and Retailing (23 percent of turnover and 22 percent of trading profit in fiscal 1991). Discontinued operations accounted for 14 percent of turnover and 8 percent of trading profit in 1990.[5]

The food group consisted of several well-known companies: Pillsbury Company for bakery, pizza, vegetable, dough, frozen, and canned products (brands included Pillsbury, Green Giant, Totino's, Jeno's, and Hungry Jack); Häagen-Dazs; Alpo Petfoods with its cat and puppy food and dog treats (Alpo brand name); Grand Metropolitan Foodservice USA, which made and supplied bakery and frozen foods at the

---

[5] Standard & Poor's, *Standard Corporate Descriptions* (New York: McGraw-Hill, 1992).

EXHIBIT 12
Presto Capacity

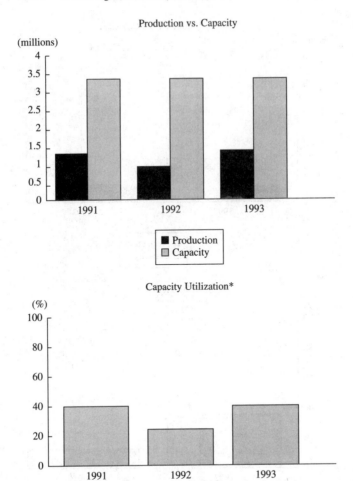

Production vs. Capacity

Capacity Utilization*

*Reflects single-serve capacity only

EXHIBIT 13   Nestlé S.A. Sales by Product Groups

	1990	1989	1988
Drinks	23.6%	24.7%	27.4%
Cereals, milks, and dietetic	20.1	20.0	20.3
Chocolate and confectionery	16.0	15.3	12.4
Culinary products	12.7	12.4	12.2
Frozen foods and ice cream	10.1	10.8	10.5
Refrigerated products	8.9	8.5	8.7
Pet foods	4.5	4.4	4.2
Pharmaceuticals and cosmetics	3.0	2.8	2.2
Other products and activities	1.1	1.1	2.1
	100.0	100.0	100.0

Source: *Moody's International Manual,* 1991, Vol. 2 (New York: Moody's Investors Service), pp. 3705–9.

EXHIBIT 14   Wholly Owned Principal Subsidiaries of Grand Metropolitan PLC

Pillsbury Co.
Burger King Corp.
Pillsbury Danada Ltd.
Pillsbury GmbH
Häagen-Dazs Co. Inc.
Pilstral SA
S&E&A Metaxa Distilleries SA
Paddington Corp.
Belin Surgeles SA
Conservas Chistu, SA
Express Foods Group (International) Ltd.
Express Foods Group Ireland Ltd.
Alpo Petfoods Inc.
International Distillers and Vintners Ltd.
R&A Bailey & Co. Ltd.
Carillon Importers Ltd.
Gilbey Canada Inc.
International Distillers and Vintners (UK) Ltd.
Justerini & Brooks Ltd.
Heublein Inc.
Driehock Beheer, BV
AED SA
Croft & Ca Lda
Croft Jerez SA
Pearle Inc.
Chef & Brewer Group Ltd.
Grand Metropolitan Estates Ltd.
Grand Metropolitan Finance PLC
Wyvern International Ltd.
(Cinzano International SA is an affiliate of Grand
   Metropolitan PLC with the corporation having 25 percent
   ownership.)

Source: Standard & Poor's, Standard Corporate Descriptions (New York: McGraw-Hill, 1992), p. 5279.

foodservice, bakery, and deli level (Green Giant and Pillsbury brands); Express Foods Group, which produced cheese, butter, and milk-based products in the UK and Ireland; and European Baked Goods and Prepared Foods (brands included Brossard, Erasco, and Peter's). Exhibit 14 lists principal wholly owned subsidiaries of the corporation.

Mars.   A privately held company headquartered in McLean, Virginia, M&M/Mars Inc. was number two to Hershey Foods Corporation in the $8.7 billion (wholesale) U.S. confectionery business. As of May 1991, Mars had a 38 percent share of chocolate product sales through wholesalers, a 2.5 share point gain over the same period a year earlier.[6] Four major divisions comprised Mars Incorporated: M&M/Mars (candy bars), Kal Kan Foods (pet foods), Uncle Ben's Inc. (rices and sauces), and Dove International (ice cream bars and snacks). Total worldwide sales in 1989 and 1990 were $8

---

[6] "P&G Spends $2.28 Billion, Surges to Head of Top 100," *Advertising Age,* September 25, 1991, pp. 47–48.

billion. Advertising spending for the corporation totaled $272.4 million for the 1990-91 fiscal year.

As of 1992, Dove International had introduced three ice cream bars: Snickers, Three Musketeers, and Milky Way. According to Nielsen Marketing Research, the Snickers bar had become a top 10 seller in the frozen novelties market. Other products produced by this division included Dove ice cream bars and Rondos bite-size ice cream snacks.

The Strategic Issue

The entry of foreign brands was expected to generate greater competitive activities in the global ice cream industry. More innovative new products, flavors, and packages were expected. As such, the industry would probably see an intense battle for shelf space, with heavy advertising and promotion activities and a greater deployment of trade assets. All in all, the industry expected to see the production of world-class and state-of-the-art products.

The strategic question facing Ambrosia Corporation was how best to maintain its competitive dominance in this rapidly changing industry where barriers to entry included strong brand loyalty, large capital requirements in manufacturing, selling, and distribution, and strong economies of scale. What should Bratten recommend to San August corporate? Was some kind of foreign partnership the way—maybe even the only way—to proceed as number one?

CASE 5–3
ELECTRO-PRODUCTS LIMITED

Mr. Josef Novak,[1] recently appointed manager of marketing and marketing analysis at Electro-Products Limited (EPL), is faced with a dilemma. A number of marketing issues important to his firm have surfaced suddenly. Some of these issues relate directly to the role marketing needs to play in the future operations of the firm; others relate to the strategic question of survival. The issue that is most troublesome is EPL's relationship with a large European client.

EPL, located in a semirural area of Czechoslovakia, is a manufacturer of small home appliances. Currently, a significant portion of EPL's production is being exported under an exclusive agreement with a large European-based international electronics manufacturing and marketing firm (LIEM). Under this agreement, EPL is responsible for manufacturing hand-held vacuum cleaners for LIEM. LIEM markets these products under its own brand name in Western markets. EPL has exclusive rights to market the products domestically under its own brand name ZETA.

The Czechoslovak economy is going through a major transition. A competitive domestic market is emerging. Domestic and foreign competitors are entering the market. Both EPL and LIEM have realized that the Czechoslovak market needs to be systematically reexamined in light of all the changes taking place. Not only is EPL looking for market opportunities in its own domestic market, but it is also concerned with survival in a rapidly changing economy—dealing with privatization, foreign ownership, and new consumer demand among other strategic uncertainties.

Prior to the changes in Czechoslovakia that began in late 1989, LIEM had no interest in its internal market. Since the changes, however, LIEM is actively looking for market opportunities in EPL's domestic market. EPL's small marketing group is faced with several issues that may potentially evolve into major confrontations with LIEM.

EPL realizes that its agreement with LIEM helps EPL understand product development efforts in the context of a large firm. It also helps EPL engineers comprehend the quality control requirements of Western markets. And, to a certain degree, the agreement assures EPL of future revenue. However, LIEM is a large international firm that views EPL as a captive supplier of a product whose attributes are set by LIEM's marketing personnel.

Mr. Novak would like to develop a cooperative relationship with LIEM. He is interested in working closely with LIEM's marketing personnel so that he and his staff can learn more about marketing practices in Western Europe. Mr. Novak is particularly curious about the entire product development process used by LIEM. He would like to know more about it. LIEM's management is not interested and is ignoring any such overtures from EPL.

This case was prepared by George Tesar, visiting professor, Uméa Business School, Uméa University, Uméa, Sweden, and Marie Pribova, Czechoslovak Management Center, Celakovice, Czechoslovakia. At the time this case was written, Professor Tesar was on sabbatical leave from the University of Wisconsin, Whitewater.

[1] All names of individuals and firms, domestic or foreign, have been changed.

EPL organized a small marketing group over two years ago. Until recently, this group did not play a significant role in EPL's strategic management. Under the current leadership of Mr. Novak, marketing concepts are slowly being recognized and accepted in the strategic development and growth of the firm. The marketing group is being asked to generate new opportunities for the entire firm. Plans and strategies are being developed as part of this new marketing effort.

The latest plans developed by the marketing group have three important objectives: (1) developing an effective and efficient domestic distribution and sales network for its products, (2) broadening its cooperation with foreign firms in areas of product development and cross-marketing arrangements, and (3) improving the overall image of its brand name ZETA in Western European markets.

According to Mr. Novak, these are realistic and strategically implementable objectives under normally operating market conditions. However, given the nature of the transitionary economy in Czechoslovakia today, these objectives present a complex combination of challenges not only to the small marketing group, but also the entire firm.

Background Information

EPL has been manufacturing and exporting small home appliances since 1943. After the general nationalization in the late 1940s, it became the sole producer of small home appliances in Czechoslovakia, and since late 1989 it has been trying to become an important competitor in the international small home appliance industry.[2]

In the past, EPL produced a wide range of small home appliances and heating elements. Its current catalog lists the range of products available for domestic and export sales (Exhibit 1). However, before late 1989, approximately 43 percent of its total production was vacuum cleaners and 13 percent was steam and dry irons. These two product lines accounted for a total of 56 percent of EPL's production.

EPL exported about one-quarter of its products to Eastern and Western European markets. Western European markets demanded higher quality and better-designed products from EPL. Quality was not an issue in Eastern Europe due to general shortages of consumer products in these markets. Vacuum cleaners accounted for 68 percent of exports and dry irons for 24 percent; all remaining products produced by EPL accounted for only 8 percent (Exhibit 2).

The primary activity of EPL has been manufacturing vacuum cleaners. According to the marketing group, hand-held vacuum cleaners represent the most lucrative and the most advanced product in EPL's product line. They believe that these products exemplify the level of quality found in most Western European products intended for the demanding Western consumer.

From the overall perspective of EPL's management, the contract with LIEM enabled the technical and administrative staff of EPL to understand the dynamics of Western markets. It enabled EPL to raise its manufacturing standards to world-class production, and, consequently, EPL is in a better position to market its own products in world markets.

---

[2] EPL has a relatively long history among manufacturers in Czechoslovakia. Over the past 50 or more years its ownership has been in question. Between the late 1940s and November 1989 it held a monopoly on the manufacture of small home appliances and a variety of home and industrial electrical heating elements. EPL still makes most of these products although the overall contribution of these products to its operations and profits is not known.

**EXHIBIT 1   Small Appliances Currently
Produced by EPL**

Blenders
Coffee grinders
Coffeemakers
Dry flat irons
Electric countertop units
Electric frying pans
Electric pans
Food mixers
Food processors
Hand-held food mixers
Heating elements (domestic use)
Heating elements (industrial use)
Plastic welding units
Portable electric plates
Portable grills
Portable space heaters
Roasting ovens
Steam irons
Vacuum cleaners
Warm air ventilators

The marketing group, now under the leadership of Mr. Novak, was formed at the end of 1990. It is positioned too low in the organization to make any significant impact on top management's decision-making performance. Mr. Novak came to the group from engineering; he was in charge of product design and development. Currently he and his group are developing promotional, retailing, and distribution strategies for EPL products in the domestic market.

Working with a Trading Company

In the past, EPL was represented exclusively by Alfa, a state-owned export trading company located in Prague. Alfa was responsible for all of EPL's exporting activities, including initiation of contacts, negotiations of sales agreements, and delivery of

**EXHIBIT 2   Production of Small Home Appliances, and Domestic and Foreign
Sales before 1989**

		Sales		
Product Line	Production	Domestic	Foreign	Total
Vacuum cleaners	43%	32%	68%	100%
Steam and dry irons	13	76	24	100
Other	44	92	8	100
Total	100%			

Note: The above percentages are estimates only. Actual production figures are not available.

finished products. EPL's marketing personnel, or in the past the individuals responsible for product development and sales, had little or no direct contact with customers. Alfa was also responsible for all communications between EPL and its customers abroad.

This was not unusual prior to late 1989. State-owned export trading companies represented all Czechoslovak manufacturing firms and state-owned enterprises abroad. Management of many firms and enterprises had no direct contact with foreign customers or consumers. It was only in early 1990 that Czechoslovak firms and enterprises were free to conduct business abroad without the state-owned export trading companies. But even after these changes were made, the state-owned export trading companies retained important information about foreign contacts, clients, customers, and consumers. In other words, they withheld the export technology from the firms they had represented.

In some cases, the client firms were completely dependent on individuals within the export trading companies and could not operate without them. This dependency resulted from the structural inability to communicate with the outside world, lack of foreign language competency, and even the inability to travel to foreign markets.[3]

Consequently, EPL's top management, and the entire engineering, manufacturing, and purchasing staffs had little or no direct contact with their clients such as LIEM. They did not understand LIEM's consumers. Alfa served as a filter for all marketing and competitive information.

The Agreement with LIEM

An agreement between EPL and LIEM to produce a new hand-held vacuum cleaner was negotiated by Alfa during 1987. Before the November 1989 political changes in Czechoslovakia, LIEM had insisted that the agreement be kept secret. The agreement clearly defines the roles and responsibilities of each party. LIEM is responsible for the development of product specifications based on marketing information. The overall product specifications can be classified into several categories as shown in Exhibit 3.

These product specifications not only represent engineering specifications, but they also provide clear cost and expense guidelines. In other words, under this contract EPL became a captive fabricator and supplier of hand-held vacuum cleaners to LIEM.

It was also agreed that during the engineering process, testing would be conducted by both parties separately. This included testing, verification, and documentation of each step in the engineering process. Any tooling, dies, or fixtures were subject to inspection and testing. The prototypes and products produced during pilot production runs would be subject to testing by both parties.

EPL was able to calculate the cost of engineering and manufacturing at the end of the pilot production of all models specified under the contract. It became apparent that EPL could not deliver any of the three models at the price specified by LIEM. After a series of negotiations, LIEM agreed to a price increase of 18 percent. At the same time the projected mix of models based on the original set of specifications was also changed as indicated in Exhibit 4.

An important factor in the arrangement between the two firms was the way in which the representatives of the two firms met to discuss important points during the engineering of the hand-held vacuum cleaner. All meetings were scheduled by Alfa and were held five times during the product engineering process as shown in Exhibit 5.

---

[3] Many of these situations were created by direct government policies. Individual manufacturing firms had no input into the creation or implementation of such policies.

EXHIBIT 3   Product Specifications for a Hand-Held Vacuum Cleaner

Dimensions and technical parameters
Physical design and color specifications
Number and type of models (economy, standard, and deluxe)
Purchase price of each model
Annual purchase schedule of each model for the next four years

Notes were taken during each meeting; the main points on which both sides agreed were recorded; new deadlines were set; and managers responsible for specific tasks were appointed.

EPL's representatives included the chief design engineer, the engineer directly responsible for the product, and the manager responsible for the pricing and delivery of the product. From the LIEM side the meetings were attended by the product manager, product designer, technical specialist, quality control specialist, and sales manager. Top management of EPL did not routinely meet with the product manager from LIEM, but held only informal discussions during trade fairs or industrial exhibitions.

Once the product engineering process had been completed for the hand-held vacuum cleaner, all the decisions regarding the production machinery, sourcing of raw material and components, and sourcing of packaging material were the responsibility of EPL. Product modifications during manufacturing were not allowed under the agreement. Only minor production changes, or changes that did not alter the cosmetic or functional characteristics of the product could be made without LIEM's approval.

Additional factors such as cosmetic modifications, including color changes, were incorporated into the engineering process as necessary. Color specifications were changed four times during the engineering process. Final performance and quality testing before commercialization was completed by LIEM. The final product was shown at two major exhibitions. Two months after the presentation of the product, the product was available for sale in retail outlets.

From the perspective of Mr. Novak, the agreement between EPL and LIEM has several problems:

1. EPL is not part of the marketing process managed by LIEM.
2. LIEM ignores requests by EPL for one or more of its managers to visit LIEM's operations.
3. EPL cannot communicate directly with LIEM due to the lack of language capabilities.

EXHIBIT 4   The Original Purchase Schedule by LIEM Compared to the Final Purchase Schedule for 1991

	Model		
Purchase Schedule	*Economy*	*Standard*	*DeLuxe*
Original	25%	55%	20%
Final	35	45	20

EXHIBIT 5   Hand-Held Vacuum Cleaner: List of Individual Steps from the Time of Negotiations to Product Completion

Beginning of 1987	Negotiations between EPL and LIEM begin
January 21, 1988	Product developed by LIEM.
March 15, 1988 Meeting	Product designed and engineering specifications completed by LIEM.
May 1, 1988 Meeting	Mutual agreement between EPL and LIEM on the final product design, engineering specifications, and cost structure.
August 1, 1988	Production of the first functional prototype by EPL.
November 1, 1988	Production of the final prototype by EPL.
December 1, 1988 Meeting	Testing and verification of the final prototype by LIEM.
February 1, 1989 Meeting	Product changes and modifications by EPL resulting from final prototype testing by LIEM.
February 1, 1990	Technical development and manufacturing engineering for mass production of the final product by EPL.
March 1, 1990	Delivery of manufactured products by EPL to LIEM for final testing and verifications. End of pilot production run for EPL.
May 1, 1990 Meeting	Testing completed by LIEM. Calculation of final costs by EPL completed.
July 1, 1990	Final product modifications completed by EPL.
October 1, 1990	LIEM's purchasing process begins.
December 1, 1990	Mass production begins by EPL.
January 15, 1991	First shipment left EPL's production facility.

The language barrier presents the most important problem for EPL. Representatives from Alfa sit in on all meetings, including meetings that are strictly technical in nature, and serve as translators and interpreters. Recently, LIEM offered to work directly with EPL without involving Alfa, but EPL does not have marketing personnel with the language capabilities needed to conduct negotiations.

EPL's Marketing Perspective

The situation at EPL has been changing rapidly since late 1989. The marketing department wants to play a greater role in strategic management of the firm. According to Mr. Novak, EPL as a manufacturer has learned a great deal from cooperation with LIEM. EPL learned how to enter highly competitive foreign markets at the same time that its own domestic market is going through a major transition.

Cooperation with a large international firm that is consistently concerned about product quality in highly competitive markets offers an opportunity for EPL to learn what these markets demand so that in the future EPL can enter these markets on its own. From a marketing perspective, this cooperation enables EPL, to a degree, to develop a fundamental understanding of the role marketing plays in the development and engineering of consumer products, and at the same time, realize how important quality standards are in competitive markets abroad.

EPL's management offered to cooperate with LIEM as part of the new marketing perspective. LIEM appears uninterested. The relationship with Alfa changed significantly after late 1989. Alfa's management established a new unit concerned only with export of EPL's products. Mr. Novak sees a strong potential for cooperation with this unit. EPL, with Alfa's assistance, also exports some of its vacuum cleaners to Western Europe under brand names owned by various retail store chains.

LIEM is interested in entering the Czechoslovak market with its own brand name, even with products manufactured by EPL. The same products manufactured under LIEM's label and under EPL's label would compete side by side. EPL offered to represent LIEM in the Czechoslovak market, but LIEM declined the offer and opened offices for all its products in Prague and Bratislava. Recently, LIEM's unit dealing with small home appliances offered EPL the possibility to negotiate representation in the future.

As part of the new marketing effort at EPL, some of the marketing specialists suggest that perhaps EPL should improve the image of its own brand name ZETA and concentrate on sales and distribution of its own products in Western Europe.

EPL is at a crossroads for its manufacturing and marketing operations. It wants to become better known in its own domestic market. It also realizes that it needs to enter foreign markets to generate foreign capital for its operations. The agreement with LIEM is bothersome for EPL's marketing group. And, most significantly, EPL's business climate and the domestic market are progressing through rapid changes.

CASE 5–4
SOUTHERN HOME DEVELOPERS

Initial sales inquiries had been high during the opening days of Southern Home Developers, a module home construction/sales company. Prospects were interested and excited at the possibility of having a new home in a matter of weeks at only a fraction of the cost of a site-built home. However, Bill Thompson, owner of Southern Home Developers, was concerned about the negative comments he had been receiving from his small construction crew. Additionally, Bill had begun to see an increase in construction costs (which ultimately increased the house price to the consumer) and construction time. Bill knew that his competitive advantages were low price and short cycle times. Loss of either of these held dire consequences for the small company that had been in business less than a year.

The Housing Market

Richard Gentry, president of the National Association of Housing and Redevelopment Officials (NAHRO), reported in 1996 that the housing industry was in the beginning stages of a "lean cycle where spending limits and money-saving program changes will dominate."[1] The housing industry was comprised of existing homes and new home starts. In the late 1980s and into the 1990s, national sales for both existing and new homes were low. However, the United States experienced a turnaround in home sales by the mid-1990s. "From the ashes of the late 1980s and early 1990s, the nation's residential real estate market is rising again . . . sales of both new and existing houses hit all-time highs nationally and in most regions in 1996."[2] (See Exhibit 1 for an historical look at existing home and new home starts in the United States.)

The demand for existing and new homes was thought to be influenced by several factors: (1) personal disposable income, (2) economic events, (3) demographic trends, (4) social attitudes toward home ownership, (5) affordability, and (6) work-related events.

The unemployment rate in the United States was holding nationally at around $5^1/2$ percent during the mid-1990s. Exhibit 2 shows unemployment rates by state for 1995 and 1996. The U.S. Bureau of Labor Statistics predicted that the labor force would increase from 131 million to 147 million in the 1994–2005 period. Compositionally, the 55-years-and-older segment of the labor force was expected to grow faster than younger segments reflecting the aging of the baby boomers. The 25–34-year-old segment was expected to decrease by 4,000,000 in this 10-year period. As well, profes-

This case was prepared by Victoria L. Crittenden, associate professor of marketing, Boston College, and William F. Crittenden, associate professor of management, Northeastern University. Research assistance was provided by David Angus, Boston College/Andersen Consulting Fund. The case is designed as a basis for class discussion and not intended to portray correct or incorrect administrative styles or processes.

[1] "Richard C. Gentry: New NAHRO President." *Journal of Housing and Community Development* (November/December 1995): 43.

[2] Ravo, Nick. "Housing Sales Show New Life with Good Year." *The New York Times* (December 25, 1996): sec. D, p. 1, col. 5.

EXHIBIT 1	**Existing Home Sales and New Home Starts in the United States**

Year	Units
Existing Home Sales	
1990	3,211,000
1991	3,220,000
1992	3,520,000
1993	3,802,000
1994	3,946,000
1995	3,802,000
Housing Starts	
1987	1,620,000
1988	1,488,000
1989	1,376,000
1990	1,193,000
1991	1,014,000
1992	1,200,000
1993	1,288,000
1994	1,457,000
1995	1,354,000

Source: *Real Estate Outlook: Market Trends & Insights* (Washington, DC: National Association of Realtors); U.S. Bureau of the Census, *Current Construction Reports,* 1996.

sional and managerial occupations were expected to show the fastest growth with around 5,000,000 new workers entering this sector. These labor force statistics were combined with relatively low inflation rates.

The Dow Jones was up nearly 40 percent during late 1995 and early 1996. This added around $1 trillion to American's net worth. This gain, however, had not affected the home building market. During the same period, there was no significant increase in the number of housing units sold. The home building industry had a 2.8 percent net after-tax profit during 1995, which was 50 percent below the average for all industries in the United States.[3] This came at the same time that interest rates fluctuated around 7 to 9 percent (compared to double-digit rates in the late 1980s). "Bullish" builders at the beginning of 1996 had started scaling back their expectations early in that year (which was particularly evident in single-family detached homes), as foot traffic declined throughout the year.

There were around 100 million households in the United States. The number of one-person households was increasing at a faster rate than the number of households in general. Work-related events such as working at home and four-day work weeks were expected to impact the number of purchased homes. However, household incomes were not keeping pace with housing prices. Housing costs were around 1/5 of personal consumption expenditures. Furthermore, the U.S. population was expected to grow at a decreasing rate. Throughout the 1950–80 time period, average population

---

[3] *The Corporate Growth Weekly Report* (August 26, 1996).

EXHIBIT 2   **State Unemployment Rates, June 1995 and June 1996**

State	June 1995	June 1996
East North Central		
Illinois	4.5%	5.5%
Indiana	4.9	5.1
Michigan	6.3	4.9
Ohio	4.6	5.0
Wisconsin	3.7	3.7
East South Central		
Alabama	5.1	3.5
Kentucky	5.0	5.3
Mississippi	7.5	7.1
Tennessee	5.5	5.3
Middle Atlantic		
New Jersey	6.7	6.2
New York	6.0	6.1
Pennsylvania	6.0	5.2
Mountain		
Arizona	5.5	5.7
Colorado	4.4	4.5
Idaho	4.2	4.6
Montana	5.4	5.2
Nevada	6.3	5.3
New Mexico	6.8	8.0
Utah	3.8	3.7
Wyoming	4.1	3.8
New England		
Connecticut	5.5	5.0
Maine	5.8	5.1
Massachusetts	5.6	4.9
New Hampshire	3.5	4.0
Rhode Island	6.2	4.3
Vermont	3.9	3.9
Pacific		
Alaska	6.5	7.2
California	7.7	7.2
Hawaii	5.6	6.8
Oregon	5.2	5.2
Washington	5.8	5.7
South Atlantic		
Delaware	4.2	4.7
District of Columbia	9.8	9.1
Florida	5.8	5.3
Georgia	5.5	5.0
Maryland	5.5	5.1
North Carolina	4.7	4.5
South Carolina	4.9	6.2
Virginia	4.8	4.8
West Virginia	7.5	7.2

EXHIBIT 2   (Continued)

State	June 1995	June 1996
West North Central		
Iowa	3.3	3.1
Kansas	4.8	4.2
Minnesota	4.2	3.9
Missouri	5.0	4.4
Nebraska	2.7	3.2
North Dakota	3.4	3.3
South Dakota	2.6	2.8
West South Central		
Arkansas	4.4	5.1
Louisiana	8.0	7.6
Oklahoma	4.7	4.2
Texas	6.8	6.6

Source: Dean Crist, "Housing Activity." *Housing Economics* (August 1996): 14–23.

Note: Data are not seasonally adjusted.

growth was around 2.5 million per year. This number was expected to drop to around 1.6 million by the year 2000. However, the 1990s experienced the largest wave of immigration in U.S. history. While a large majority of immigrants lived in rental housing, home ownership increased rapidly with the length of time in the United States. In 1990, 23 percent of the 1.8 million households headed by immigrants owned their home.

Based on results from the annual Project Outlook survey,[4] forecasts were for a very different housing market in the future. Pivotal to the industry was the forecast that houses manufactured off-site (prefabricated housing sections) would be used extensively and that the number of on-site construction hours would be reduced by at least 50 percent.

Manufactured Housing

Constructed in a factory, there were two main types of manufactured houses: mobile homes and modular homes.[5] There were 188,000 manufactured homes shipped in 1990. However, by 1995 the number of manufactured homes had increased to 340,000 (12 percent more than 1994), with 1997 expected shipments of around 375,000. Approximately one in three single-family homes sold in America in 1996 was factory-built (compared to one in four in 1990).

---

[4] The annual Project Outlook survey brought together corporate planners, consultants, and futurists to forecast events over a 20-year period.

[5] A third type of manufactured housing exists—prefab. With prefab, components of the house (such as walls, floors, stairs, and ceilings) are manufactured in the factory. The components are then assembled at the construction site. However, prefab houses are not making as large inroads into the housing industry as are modular and mobile homes.

Mobile Homes.   Section 603 of the Manufactured Home Construction and Safety Standards Act of 1974 defined a mobile home as

> a structure, transportable in one or more sections, which is eight body feet or more in width and is thirty-two body feet or more in length, and which is built on a permanent chassis and designed to be used as a dwelling unit with or without a permanent foundation when connected to the required utilities, and includes the plumbing, heating, air-conditioning, and electric systems contained within.

However by 1980, the U.S. Congress had recognized that calling a mobile home "mobile" was really a misnomer. In reality, few mobile homes ever left the initial home site once placed there. As such, legislation began referring to mobile homes as manufactured homes in all federal law publications. Mobile homes were constructed to comply with the American National Standards Institute's A119.1 Standards for Mobile Homes.

In 1993 *American Demographics* profiled the mobile home consumer as

- More likely than average[6] to be a two-member household.
- Less likely than average to have a college education.
- Having a household median income of $20,026.
- More likely than average to be headed by young adult (18 to 34 years old).
- Believing affordability was the dominant reason for purchase.

Mobile home residency increased from 4.6 million in 1980 to 13 million in the early 1990s. Exhibit 3 provides an overview of the number of mobile homes by state, based on the 1990 U.S. census.

Production of mobile homes declined from 240,000 units in 1981 to 170,000 units in 1991. The industry average for daily production was 10 home sections a day, with the top 25 manufacturers accounting for around 75 percent of the production output. Mobile home prices ranged from $10,000 to $20,000 for a single-wide unit (approximately 14 feet by 70), with double-wide unit prices as high as $50,000. Manufacturers' operating margins ranged from around 5 to 7 percent.

Modular Homes.   The similarity between mobile homes and modular homes stopped with the fact that both were built in a factory. Whereas mobile homes had wheels and essentially rolled to their destination (and other destinations thereafter), a modular home arrived at its destination in complete sections. These sections were assembled on the construction site. Once assembled, the home did not move again. Additionally, modular homes were built to the same building codes as conventional site-built homes (these codes being governed by the state in which the construction/manufacturing took place), while mobile homes met national HUD (U.S. Department of Housing and Urban Development) code, which might not be the same as the local state building code. Ultimately, this led to no visible differences in the appearance of modular and site-built homes. As with the construction of any home, the modular home had to meet zoning codes. City zoning codes generally specified a 1,800–2,000-square-foot minimum area in the house.

By 1996, modular homes had a 2 percent share of the nationwide housing market and 50 percent of the manufactured housing market. This market share was expected to double by the year 2001. Such growth would turn modular housing into a $2.5 billion industry. Major markets were New England (6 percent of the overall market),

---

[6] Average is the comparison to householders in other types of home structures.

EXHIBIT 3 Number of Mobile Homes per State per the 1990 Census
States Ranked by Percentage of Housing Units That Are Mobile Homes

Rank	State	Percent	Number
1	South Carolina	16.9%	240,525
2	Wyoming	16.5	33,474
3	New Mexico	16.3	102,948
4	North Carolina	15.3	430,440
5	West Virginia	15.2	118,733
6	Arizona	15.1	250,597
7	Montana	15.0	54,021
8	Idaho	13.7	56,529
9	Mississippi	13.6	136,948
10	Alabama	13.4	224,307
11	Nevada	13.4	69,655
12	Arkansas	13.1	131,542
13	Florida	12.5	762,855
14	Kentucky	12.3	185,336
15	Delaware	12.1	34,944
16	Georgia	11.6	305,055
17	Louisiana	11.4	196,236
18	Oregon	11.3	134,325
19	South Dakota	10.7	31,357
20	North Dakota	9.8	27,055
21	Tennessee	9.3	188,517
22	Maine	9.3	54,532
23	Oklahoma	9.2	129,850
24	Washington	9.2	187,533
25	Alaska	8.7	20,280
26	Vermont	8.4	22,702
27	Texas	7.8	547,911
28	Missouri	7.5	164,021
29	New Hampshire	7.0	35,334
30	Indiana	7.0	156,821
31	Kansas	6.8	71,195
32	Michigan	6.4	246,365
33	Virginia	6.4	159,352
34	Colorado	6.0	88,683
35	Utah	5.8	34,986
36	Nebraska	5.6	37,046
37	Pennsylvania	5.2	254,920
38	Iowa	5.0	56,857
39	California	5.0	555,307
40	Wisconsin	4.9	101,149
41	Minnesota	4.9	90,864
42	Ohio	4.7	205,595
43	Illinois	3.3	150,733
44	New York	2.7	194,934
45	Maryland	2.3	42,729
46	Rhode Island	1.1	4,689
47	New Jersey	1.1	33,551
48	Massachusetts	1.0	23,928
49	Connecticut	0.9	12,118
50	Hawaii	0.1	389

Source: William O'Hare and Barbara Clark O'Hare. "Upward Mobility." *American Demographics* (January 1993): 26–32.

Mid-Atlantic (7 percent), and East North Central (4 percent). With service to the final buyer becoming foremost in the mind of large modular home builders, growth was expected in the Midwestern and Southern states.

Modular home builders were able to build, deliver, and install a single-family dwelling for about half the cost of a site-constructed house. In 1994, the typical retail price of a modular home was $50,000. (The price range was reported to be from $45,000 to $350,000, with at least one builder selling land plus home at $550,000.) The average cost per square foot for a multisection house was $27.41. This compared to an average cost of $54.65 per square foot for a site-built house.[7] Since modular homes were delivered 85–95 percent finished, completion of the house, once at the site, could take as little as four days but typically three to four weeks. (Modules arrived at the site with bathroom fixtures, cabinetry, and flooring in place.) There were three major members in the channel for modular homes: the manufacturer of the modular home, the dealer (if different from the manufacturer), and the local builder. The local builder was estimated to save 10 to 20 percent in construction costs when compared to site-built homes of the same quality.

There were about 500 modular housing factories in the United States. Most of these companies employed fewer than 100 employees. The target region for each of these companies was limited, generally, to a 350-mile radius of the manufacturing facility due to shipping-related costs in moving the home's sections to the construction site. (Shipping accounted for 2 to 5 percent of total cost.) There were, however, larger players in the market: All American Homes (based in Elkhart, Indiana), Cardinal Industries (Columbus, Ohio), Chadwick International Inc. (Fairfax, Virginia), Ryland Group Inc. (Columbia, Maryland), and Westchester Modular Homes, Inc. (Wingdale, New York). Chadwick was able to capitalize on the housing shortage in various countries by manufacturing modular homes for shipment to the Ivory Coast, Benin, and Algeria.

Manufacturing Process.   The modules (sections) of a modular home were designed and constructed inside the factory. By the mid-1990s, most modular manufacturers utilized state-of-the-art CAD systems in the design process. The number of modules per house ranged all the way from 2 to 22, depending on the home's style and size. Workstations in the assembly line production process generally included framing, drywall, electrical, plumbing, cabinetry, molding, and window installation. Other workstations were dependent upon the level of customization provided by the manufacturer (e.g., fireplaces, dormers). Modulars contained 25 to 30 percent more lumber than site-built homes in order to withstand the transportation process of up to 350 miles. Upon completion of the modules (which had to pass stringent inspections by local building officials), they were trucked to the construction site. Each module had a shipping weight of around 18,000 pounds.

While there was no legal restriction to the number of modules contained in a home, highway regulations governed the size of each module. To adhere to these regulations, modules could generally be no more than 16 by 60 feet. However, most builders produced 12- or 14-foot-wide modules. Upon arrival at the home site, the modules were set upon the foundation with a crane and then bolted together. Builders could expect to have an airtight house on the same day.

After setting, the local builder took over the final stages of the construction process. This included utility connections, adding porches or decks, and landscaping. These fi-

---

[7] A. Gary Shilling, "Home Sweet Factory-Built Home." *Forbes* (February 12, 1996): 181.

nal stages could take anywhere from one to four weeks, depending upon the level of custom amenities desired by the prospective homeowner.

Southern Home Developers

Located in a rural town in central Arkansas, Southern Home Developers opened in the Spring of 1997. Bill Thompson served as owner, salesperson, and plant manager. Bill's career in manufactured housing started in the late 1960s when he and a friend opened a small mobile home factory and sales office, Urbane Homes, in Missouri. Within a five-year period, Urbane Homes had opened factory/sales offices in Arkansas and Texas. Fifteen years after opening the first facility, Bill and his partner sold the business for $10 million. Before starting Southern Home Developers, Bill had dabbled in oil and gas wells in Oklahoma and coal mines in Kentucky. Finally, Bill had returned to his first love of manufactured home production. After receipt of a small business grant from the state government, Bill opened Southern Home Developers.

Southern Home Developers operated out of an 80-by-200–foot corrugated metal production facility. A crew of five men built the modules in the facility. Once the modules were built, the same crew located the house at the site and finished the on-site construction process. Bill's wife Liz did all on-site interior finishing (e.g., wallpapering, cleaning). The entire crew could take a house from module construction to move-in capability in four weeks.

Initially Bill had purchased land on which to set his modular houses. Then the houses were listed with a local real estate firm and sold via that channel for around $27,500. Until sold, these houses also served as model homes. The typical design was a house built in three modules (module 1: two bedrooms and bath; module 2: family room; module 3: kitchen, master bedroom, and bath). The three modules, when combined, resulted in a house with about 1,500 to 1,700 square feet. Exhibits 4 and 5 show the two basic floor plans built by Southern Home Developers.

Current Situation

Recently, Bill had begun taking orders for customized homes. Bill's initial idea regarding customization options was to allow the buyer to have some flexibility with the two standard designs. While highway regulations limited the size of the modules to about 16 by 60 feet, there were no restrictions on the number of modules that comprised a house. Therefore, an easy route to customization was increasing the size of the house.

EXHIBIT 4
Ranch Design

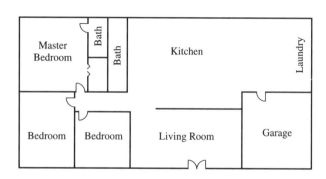

EXHIBIT 5
Split Design

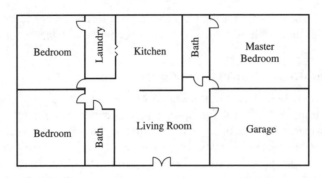

Randall Nyman worked for Southern Home Developers and was de facto in charge of on-site setting and completion of a home. Randall was not too pleased with Bill's customization commitments. The first "customized" house that Randall and the rest of the crew setup was basically an add-on module allowing the customer to have five bedrooms instead of three. While setup was uncomplicated, Randall and Bill had exchanged a few words over the setup time. Basically, Bill thought that it had taken too long to set the house. Randall's response was that he was adding on almost half of a house and that Bill should expect it to take 50 percent longer to set. Additionally, Randall reminded Bill that since the crew of five did both construction and setup, that setup was delayed due to having to build an additional module before moving to the site.

Just the previous day, Bill had overheard one of his crew, Wayne, commenting on Bill's apparent lack of understanding of manufacturing. Bill was shocked at the comment since he had always prided himself on the building of manufactured homes. Bill's shock quickly moved to outrage, and Bill had confronted Wayne about the comment. While Wayne clearly had not expected Bill to overhear him, he wasted no time in letting Bill know about what he thought were unreasonable construction expectations. Basically, Wayne told Bill that if he wanted to stay in business for a while, then Bill should stick to standardized homes. Wayne felt that there was a market for low-priced, standardized homes and predicted that customization would put Southern Home Developers out of business in less than a year.

Bill had found sleep to be somewhat elusive last night and had arrived at work very early this morning. Before others had arrived at the plant, Bill had already gone over the cost overruns and longer setup times for the past two houses. He was just starting to look over the specifications for a new modular home he had committed to earlier in the week when he heard Randall and Wayne arrive at the office. The house would involve more than just adding another module for enlargement purposes. This design had some new innovations, which included a second floor on half of the house. The second floor would have front dormers and a rear Dutch dormer. The dormers would give the house a Cape Cod look, but would also cause a new pitch to the roof. While the Cape Cod was an unusual style for the South, it was what the customer had wanted. (Exhibit 6 diagrams the roof.) The modules and dormers would be finished when delivered, but would require a significant amount of on-site detail due to the addition of the second level and the roof pitch. Now Bill was concerned that Southern Home Developers would not meet the completion deadline he had agreed upon with the customer (or would not be able to make the house in a profitable fashion).

Bill wondered if his crew's inability to deliver on-time and within budget was really due to unreasonable expectations on his part or if possibly the crew did not have the

Exhibit 6
Side View of Cape
Cod Roof

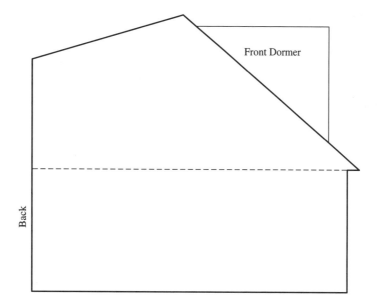

Front Dormer

Back

manufacturing expertise to mass customize his houses. What if Wayne was right? Bill's intuition told him that Wayne was wrong, but what market factors should guide Bill's decision? If Bill decided that Wayne was wrong, how could Bill convince his crew that mass customization was the way to build the business?

Bill could foresee a major conflict brewing between customer expectations and the operational side of his business. He wondered how best to address the issue.

Sources

"And Now for the Homeburger." *Economist* (August 10, 1996): 19–20.

The Corporate Growth Annual Report (August 26, 1996).

Bady, Susan. "Builders Grow Business the Modular Way." *Professional Builder* (August 1996): 62.

Crist, Dean. "Housing Activity." *Housing Economics* (August 1996): 14–23.

DiGeronimo, Richard J. "A Solution to Affordable Housing: Manufactured Homes." *The Real Estate Appraiser & Analyst* (Winter 1989): 18–25.

Enzer, Selwyn. "Project Outlook, Housing in America: Long-Term Trends." *New Management* (Winter 1987): 60–62.

Epstein, Joseph. "Home Cheap Home." *Financial World* (February 26, 1996): 48–50.

Gordon, Mitchell. "The Right Turf: Manufactured Homes Expand Hold in the Southeast." *Barron's/Investment News & Views* (June 9, 1986): 54–55.

"High Returns on Low-Income Housing." *Success* (November 1996): 30.

Kennedy, Kim. "Economic Trends Boost Manufactured Housing." *Professional Builder* (September 1996): 154.

Kroll, Luisa. "We Aim to Please." *Forbes* (November 4, 1996): 169–70.

Lahey, Karen. "Manufactured Housing: An Alternative to Site-Built Homes." *The Real Estate Appraiser & Analyst* (Winter 1989): 26–36.

Maddock, David T. "Meeting the Market with Manufactured Housing." *The Journal of Real Estate Development* (Summer 1989): 34–37.

McIntyre, Maureen. "Make Room for Modular." *Builder* (January 1996): 368.

Nolan, William T. "Modular Housing Can Help Alleviate the Nation's Housing Crunch." *The Real Estate Finance Journal* (Summer 1988): 87–89.

O'Hare, William and Barbara Clark O'Hare. "Upward Mobility." *American Demographics* (January 1993): 26–32.

Ravo, Nick. "Housing Sales Show New Life with Good Year'" *New York Times* (December 25, 1996): sec. D, p. 1, col. 5.

Real Estate Outlook: Market Trends & Insights. Washington, DC: National Association of Realtors.

"Richard C. Gentry: New NAHRO President." *Journal of Housing and Community Development* (November-December 1995): 43.

Rohan, Thomas M. "Affordable Homes from a Factory." *Industry Week* (January 16, 1989): 36–38.

Shilling, A. Gary. "Home Sweet Factory-Built Home." *Forbes* (February 12, 1996): 181.

Statistical Abstract of the United States, 1996.

U.S. Bureau of the Census, *Current Construction Reports.*

Wilson, Rand, and Mark Sommer. "Better Homes for Less." *Technology Review* (May-June 1990): 16–17.

CASE 5–5
KONARK TELEVISION INDIA

On 1 December, 1990, Mr. Ashok Bhalla began to prepare for a meeting scheduled for the next week with his boss, Mr. Atul Singh. The meeting would focus on distribution strategy for Konark Television Ltd., a medium-sized manufacturer of television sets in India. At issue was the nature of immediate actions to be taken as well as long-range planning. Mr. Bhalla was Managing Director of Konark, responsible for a variety of activities, including marketing. Mr. Singh was President.

TV Industry in India

The television industry in India started in late 1959 with the Indian government using a UNESCO grant to build a small transmitter in New Delhi. The station soon began to broadcast short programs promoting education, health, and family planning. Daily transmissions were limited to 20 minutes. In 1965, the station began broadcasting variety and entertainment programs and expanded its programming to one hour per day. Programming increased to three hours per day in 1970 and to four hours per day by 1976, when commercials were first permitted. The number of transmission centers in the country grew slowly but steadily during this period as well.

In July 1982, the Indian government announced a special expansion plan, providing 680 million rupees (Rs) for extending its television network to cover about 70 percent of India's population. By early 1988, the 245 TV transmitters in operation were estimated to have met this goal. The government then authorized construction of 417 new transmitters which would raise network coverage to over 80 percent of India's population. By late 1990, daily programming averaged almost 11 hours per day, making television the most popular medium of information, entertainment, and education in India. The network itself consisted of one channel except in large metropolitan areas where a second channel was also available. Both television channels were owned and operated by the government.

Despite the huge increase in network coverage, many in the TV industry would still describe the Indian government's attitude toward television as conservative. In fact, some would say that it was only the pressure of TV broadcasts from neighboring Sri Lanka and Pakistan that forced India's rapid expansion. Current policy was to view the industry as a luxury industry capable of bearing heavy taxes. Thus, the government charged Indian manufacturers high import duties on foreign manufactured components that they purchased plus heavy excise duties on sets that they assembled; in addition, state governments charged consumers sales taxes that ranged from 1 to 17 percent. The result was that duties and taxes accounted for almost one-half of the retail price of a color TV set and about one-third of the retail price of a black and white set.

This case was written by Fulbright Lecturer and Associate Professor James E. Nelson, University of Colorado at Boulder, and Dr. Piyush K. Sinha, associate professor, Xavier Institute of Management, Bhubaneswar, India. The authors thank Professor Roger A. Kerin, Southern Methodist University, for his helpful comments in writing this case. The case is intended for educational purposes rather than to illustrate either effective or ineffective decision making. Some data in the case are disguised. © 1991 by James E. Nelson.

**EXHIBIT 1   Production of TV Sets in India
(00,000 omitted)**

Year	Black & White 36 cm*	51 cm*	Color	Total
1980	—	3.1	—	3.1
1981	—	3.7	—	3.7
1982	—	4.4	—	4.4
1983	—	5.7	0.7	6.4
1984	1.8	6.6	2.8	11.2
1985	4.4	13.6	6.9	24.9
1986	8.2	13.3	9.0	30.5
1987	17.0	14.0	12.0	43.0
1988	28.0	16.0	13.0	57.0
1989	32.0**	18.0**	13.0**	63.0**

* Diagonal screen measurement.
** Estimated.

Retail prices of TV sets in India were estimated at almost double the prevalent world prices.

Such high prices limited demand. The number of sets in use in 1990 was estimated at about only 25 million. This number provided coverage to about 15 percent of the country's population, assuming five viewers per set. To increase coverage to 80 percent of the population would require over 100 million additional TV sets, again assuming five viewers per set. This figure represented a huge latent demand, almost 16 years of production at 1989 levels (see Exhibit 1). Many in the industry expected production and sales of TV sets would grow rapidly, if only prices were reduced.

Indian Consumers

The population of India was estimated at approximately 850 million people. The majority lived in rural areas and small villages. The gross domestic product per capita was estimated at only $450 for 1990.

In sharp contrast to the masses, however, the television market concentrated among the affluent middle and upper social classes, variously estimated at some 12 percent to 25 percent of the total population. Members of this segment exhibited a distinctly urban lifestyle. They owned video-cassette recorders, portable radio-cassette players, motor scooters, and compact cars. They earned MBA degrees, exercised in health spas, and traveled abroad. They lived in dual-income households, sent their children to private schools, and practiced family planning. In short, members of the segment exhibited tastes and purchase behaviors much like their middle-class, professional counterparts in the U.S. and Europe.

While there was no formal marketing research available, Mr. Bhalla thought he knew the consumer fairly well. "The typical purchase probably represents a joint decision by the husband and wife to buy. After all, they will be spending over one month's salary for our most popular color model." That model was now priced at retail at Rs 11,300, slightly less than retail prices of many national brands. However, a majority in the target segment probably did not perceive a price advantage for Konark. Indeed, the segment seemed somewhat insensitive to differentials in the range of Rs 10,000 to Rs 14,000, considering their TV sets to be valued possessions that added to the furnishing of their drawing rooms. Rather than price, most consumers seemed more influenced by promotion and by dealer activities.

TV Manufacturers in India

Approximately 140 different companies manufactured TV sets in India in 1989. However, many produced fewer than 1,000 sets per year and could not be considered major competitors. Further, Mr. Bhalla expected that many would not survive 1990—the trend definitely was toward a competition between 20 or 30 large firms. Most manufacturers sold in India only, although a few had begun the export of sets (mostly black and white) to nearby countries.

Most competitors were private companies whose actions ultimately were evaluated by a board of directors and shareholders. Typical of this group was Videocon. The company was formed in 1983, yet it was thought to be India's largest producer of color sets. A recent trade journal article had attributed Videocon's success to a strategy that combined higher dealer margins (2 percent higher than industry norms), attractive dealer incentives (Singapore trips, etc.), a reasonably good dealer network (about 200 dealers in 18 of India's 25 states), an excellent price range (from Rs 7,000 to Rs 18,000), and an advertising campaign that featured Indian film star Sridevi dressed in a Japanese kimono. Onida, the other leader in color, took a different approach. Its margins were slightly below industry standards; its prices were higher (Rs 13,000 to Rs 15,000); its advertising strategy was the most aggressive in the industry. Many consumers seemed sold on Onida before they ever visited a retailer.

Major competitors in the black and white market were considered by Mr. Bhalla to be Crown, Salora, Bush, and Dyanora. These four companies distributed black and white sets to most major markets in the country. (Crown and Bush manufactured color sets as well.) Strengths of these competitors were considered to be high brand recognition and strong dealer networks. In addition, several Indian states had one or two brands such as Konark or Uptron whose local success depended greatly on tax shelters provided by state governments.

All TV sets produced by the different manufacturers could be classified into two basic sizes: 51 centimeters and 36 centimeters. The larger size was a console model while the smaller was designed as a portable. Black and white sets differed little in styling. Differences in picture quality and chassis reliability were present; however, these differences tended to be difficult for most consumers to distinguish and evaluate. In contrast, differences in product features were more noticeable. Black and white sets came with and without handles, built-in voltage regulators, built-in antennas, electronic tuners, audio and video tape sockets, and on-screen displays. Warranties differed in terms of coverages and time periods. Retail prices for black and white sets across India ranged from about Rs 2,000 to Rs 3,500, with the average thought by Mr. Bhalla to be around Rs 2,600.

Differences between competing color sets seemed more pronounced. Styling was more distinctive, with manufacturers supplying a variety of cabinet designs, cabinet finishes, and control arrangements. Konark and a few other manufacturers had recently introduced a portable color set in hopes of stimulating demand. Quality and performance variations were again difficult for most consumers to recognize. Differences in features were substantial. Some color sets featured automatic contrast and brightness controls, on-screen displays of channel tuning and time, sockets for video recorders and external computers, remote control devices, high-fidelity speakers, cable TV capabilities, and flat-screen picture tubes. Retail prices were estimated to range from about Rs 7,000 (for a small-screen portable) to Rs 19,000 (large-screen console), with an average around Rs 12,000.

Advertising practices varied considerably among manufacturers. Many smaller manufacturers used only newspaper advertisements that tended to be small in size. Larger manufacturers, including Konark, advertised also in newspapers, but used quarter-page or larger advertisements. Larger manufacturers also spent substantial amounts on magazine, outdoor, and television advertising. Videocon, for example, was thought to have spent about Rs 25 million or about 4 percent of its sales revenue on advertising in 1989. Onida's percentage might be as much as twice this amount. Most advertisements for TV sets tended to stress product features and product quality although a few were based primarily on whimsy and fantasy. Most ads would not mention price. Perhaps 10 percent of the newspaper advertising appeared in the form of cooperative advertising, featuring the product prominently in the ad and listing local dealers. Manufacturers would design and place cooperative ads and pay upwards of 80 percent of media costs.

Konark Television Ltd.

Konark Television Ltd. began operations in 1973 with the objective of manufacturing and marketing small black and white TV sets to the Orissa state market. Orissa is located on the east coast of India, directly below the state of West Bengal and Calcutta. Early years of operation found production leveling at about 5,000 sets per year. However, in 1982 the company adopted a more aggressive strategy when it became clear that the national market for TV sets was going to grow rapidly. At the same time, the state government invested Rs 1.5 million in Konark in order to produce color sets. Konark also began expanding its dealer network to nearby Indian states and to more distant, large metropolitan areas. Sales revenues in 1982 were approximately Rs 80 million.

The number of Konark models produced grew rapidly to 10, evenly divided between color and black and white sets. (Exhibit 2 presents a sales brochure describing Konark's top-of-the-line color model.) Sales revenues increased as well, to Rs 640 million for 1989, based on sales of 290,000 units. For 1990, sales revenues and unit volume were expected to increase by 25 percent and 15 percent, respectively, while gross margin was expected to remain at 20 percent of revenues. In early 1990, the state government added another Rs 2.5 million to strengthen Konark's equity base, despite an expectation that the company would barely break even for 1990. Employment in late 1990 was almost 700 people. Company headquarters remained in Bhubaneswar, the state capital.

Manufacturing facilities were located also in Bhubaneswar except for some assembly performed by three independent distributors. Assembly activity was done to save state sales taxes and to lower the prices paid by consumers; that is, many Indian states charged two levels of sales taxes depending upon whether or not the set was produced within the state. The state of Maharashtra (containing Bombay), for example, charged a sales tax of 4 percent for TV sets produced within the state and 16.5 percent for sets produced outside the state. Sales taxes for West Bengal (Calcutta) were 6 percent and 16.5 percent while rates for Uttar Pradesh (New Delhi) were 0 percent and 12.5 percent. State governments were indifferent as to whether assembly was performed by an independent distributor or by Konark, as long as the activity took place inside state

EXHIBIT 2   Konark Sales Brochure

Presenting the amazing new colour TV 'Galaxy Plus'

EXHIBIT 2 **Konark Sales Brochure (continued)**

The New Colour TV from Konark. 'Galaxy Plus'.
Incorporating all the sophisticated features likely to be introduced in the next few years.

Superior German technology. That's what sets the new 'Galaxy Plus' apart from all other colour TVS.

One of the latest models of GRUNDIG (W. Germany), world leaders in entertainment electronics. Brought to you by Konark Television Limited.

A symbol of German perfection

The Galaxy Plus combines the best of everything: World-famous German circuitry and components. The latest international TV technology. And the most demanding standards of picture and sound quality.

All of which make it more sophisticated. More dependable.

Features that are a connoisseur's delight.

The Galaxy Plus has several advanced features which offer you an extraordinary audio-visual experience, the like of which you will probably not feel with any other make.

What the Galaxy Plus offers you that other TVs don't

Never-before picture quality

Through the world's latest Colour Transient Improvement (CTI) technology. Which reduces picture distortion. And improves colour sharpness. Giving you a crystal-clear picture and more natural colours.

Programmes from all over the world

The Galaxy Plus is capable of bringing you the best of international TV networks. Thanks to satellite dish antenna, a unique 7-system versatility, and 99 channels with memory.

These features of the Galaxy Plus also help it play all types of Video Cassettes. Without any picture or sound distortion.

Simultaneous connection with external devices

An exclusive 20 pin Euro AV socket helps you connect the Galaxy Plus simultaneously with all external audio/video devices: Computers, VCRs, Video games. And cable TV.

While its automatic colour and brightness tuning save you the bother of frequent knob-fiddling.

Catch all your favourite programmes. Always.

You can preset the Galaxy Plus to switch itself on and off for your favourite programmes. Or, for worry-free operation by your children, in your absence.

Your own musical alarm clock

An on-screen time display reminds you of an important programme or appointment. While a built-in chimer wakes you up every day. Pleasantly.

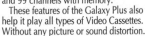

Automatic pre-selection and operation

Select specific stations or external functions, code them in the 39+AV programme memory of the Galaxy Plus. And then, get them at the touch of a button. On the full-function Remote Control.

Handles wide voltage fluctuation

From a heart-stopping low of 140V. To a shocking high of 260V. The Galaxy Plus performs merrily through such a large range.

Richer, better TV sound

A higher audio output (8W) brings you all the beauty and power of full-bodied sound and clarity.

Saves power and money

Unlike other TVs, the Galaxy Plus uses only 60W. Besides, it also switches to the stand-by-mode automatically, when there is no TV signal for over 10 minutes.

Both features help you save precious electricity and money.

From Konark Television Limited

The futuristic Galaxy Plus is brought to you by Konark Television Limited. Through its nationwide network of over 500 sales outlets. Each of which also provide you prompt after-sales service. Should you ever need it.

The revolutionary new Galaxy Plus.

See it in action at your nearest dealer.

Compare it with every other make available in the local market.

And see how, feature by advanced feature, the Galaxy Plus is truly years ahead of its time. And the competition.

A marvel of German Technology

Konark Television Limited
(A Government of Orissa Enterprise)
Electronic Bhawan, Bhubaneswar 751 010. Phone: 53441 Telex: 0675-271

borders. Present manufacturing capacity at Konark was around 400,000 units per year. Capacity could easily be expanded by 80 percent with the addition of a second shift.

The Konark line of TV sets was designed by engineers at Grundig, Gmbh., a German manufacturer known for quality electronic products. This technical collaboration saved Konark a great deal of effort each year in designing and developing new products. And the resulting product line was considered by many in the industry to be of higher quality than the lines of many competitors. Circuitry was well designed and production engineers at the factory paid close attention to quality control. In addition, each Konark set was operated for 24 hours as a test of reliability before being shipped. The entire line reflected Konark's strategy of attempting to provide the market with a quality product at prices below the competition. In retail stores in Orissa, the lowest priced black and white model marketed by Konark sold to consumers for about Rs 2,200 while its most expensive color set sold for about Rs 15,000. Sales of the latter model had been disappointing to date. The premium market for color sets was quite small and seemed dominated by three national manufacturers.

Konark had a well-established network of more than 500 dealers located in 12 Indian states. In eight states, Konark sold its products directly to dealers through branch offices (Exhibit 3) operated by a Konark Area Manager. Each branch office also contained two or three salesmen who were assigned specific sales territories. Together, branch offices were expected to account for about 30 percent of Konark's sales revenues and cost Konark about Rs 10 million in fixed and variable expenses for 1990. In three states, Konark used instead the services of independent distributors to sell to dealers. The three distributors carried only Konark TV sets and earned a margin of 3 percent (based on cost) for all their activities, including assembly. All dealers and distributors were authorized to service Konark sets. The branch offices monitored all service activities.

In the state of Orissa, Konark used a large branch office to sell to approximately 250 dealers. In addition, Konark used company-owned showrooms as a second channel of distribution. Konark would lease space for showrooms at one or two locations in larger cities and display the complete line. The total cost of operating a showroom was estimated at about Rs 100,000 per year. Prospective customers often preferred to visit a showroom because they could easily compare different models and talk directly to a Konark employee. However, they seldom purchased—only about 5 percent of Orissa's unit sales came from the 10 showrooms in the state. Buyers preferred instead to purchase from dealers because dealers were known to bargain and sell at a discount from the list price. In contrast, Konark showrooms were under strict orders to sell all units at list price. About half of Konark's 1990 revenues would come from Orissa.

The appointment of dealers either by Konark or its distributors was made under certain conditions (Exhibit 4). Essential among them was the dealer's possession of a suitable showroom for the display and sale of TV sets. Dealers were also expected to sell Konark TV sets to the best of their ability, at fixed prices, and in specified market areas. Dealers were not permitted to sell sets made by other manufacturers. Dealers earned a margin ranging from Rs 100 (small black and white model) to Rs 900 (large color model) for every TV set they sold. Mr. Bhalla estimated that the average margin for 1990 would be about Rs 320 per set.

The Crisis

The year 1990 seemed to represent a turning point in the Indian TV industry. Unit demand for TV sets was expected to grow at only 10 percent, compared to almost 40

EXHIBIT 3   **Branch Offices and Distributors for Konark Television India**

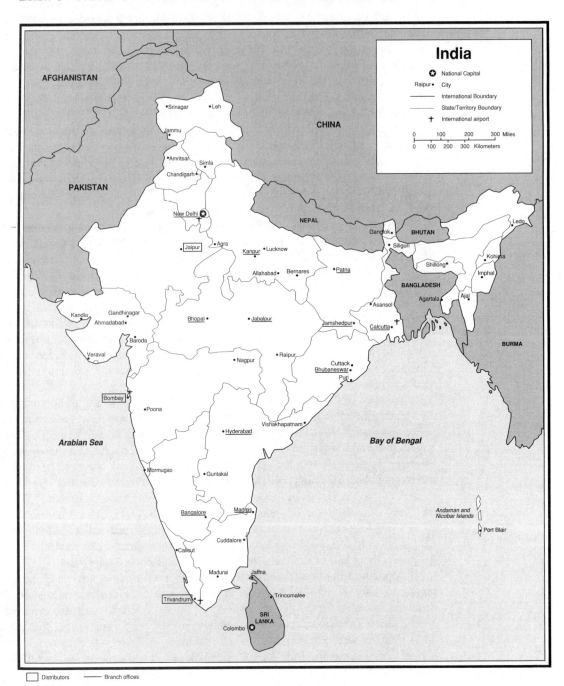

EXHIBIT 4   Terms and Conditions for Dealers of Konark TV Products

1. The Dealer shall canvass for, secure orders, and affect sales of Konark Televison sets to the best of his ability and experience and he will guarantee sale of minimum of sets during a calendar month.

2. The Company shall arrange for proper advertisement in the said area and shall give publicity of their product through newspapers, magazines, cinema slides, or by any other media and shall indicate, wherever feasible, the Dealer's name as their Selling Agents. The cost of such advertisements may be shared by the Company and the Dealer as may be mutually agreed to.

3. The appointment shall be confirmed after 3 months and initially be in force for a period of one year and can be renewed every year by mutual consent.

4. The Company reserves the right to evaluate the performance of a Dealer.

5. This appointment may be terminated with a notice of one month on either side.

6. The Company shall deliver the Konark Television sets to the Dealer at the price agreed upon on cash payment at the factory at Bhubaneswar. On such delivery, the title to the goods would pass on to the Dealer and it will be the responsibility of the Dealer for the transportation of the sets to their place at their cost and expenses.

7. The Company may, however, at their discretion allow a credit of 30 (thirty) days subject to furnishing a Bank Guarantee or letter of credit or security deposits toward the price of Konark Television sets to be lifted by the Dealer at any time.

8. The Company shall not be responsible for any damage or defect occurring to the sets after delivery of the same to the Dealer or during transit.

9. The Dealer shall undertake to sell the sets to customers at prices fixed by the Company for different models. Dealer margins will be added to wholesale prices while fixing the customer's price of the television sets.

10. The Dealer will not act and deal with similar products of any other company so long as his appointment with Konark Television continues.

11. The Dealer shall not encroach into areas allotted to any other Dealer.

12. Any dispute or difference arising from or related to the appointment of the Dealership shall be settled mutually and, failing amicable settlement, shall be settled by an Arbitrator to be appointed by the Chairman of the Company whose decision shall be final and binding upon the parties. The place of arbitration shall be within the State of Orissa and the Court in Bhubaneswar (Orissa) only shall have jurisdiction to entertain any application, suit, or claim arising out of the appointment. All disputes shall be deemed to have arisen within the jurisdiction of the Court of Bhubaneswar.

13. Essential requirements to be fulfilled before getting Dealership:
    a. The Dealer must have a good showroom for display and sale of Television sets.
    b. The Dealer should have sufficient experience in dealing with Electronics Products (Consumer Goods).

percent for 1989 and 1988. Industry experts attributed the slowing growth rate to a substantial hike in consumer prices. The blame was laid almost entirely on increases in import duties, excise taxes, and sales taxes, plus devaluation of the rupee—despite election year promises by government officials to offer TV sets at affordable prices! In addition, Konark was about to be affected by the Orissa government's decision to revoke the company's sales tax exemption beginning 1 January, 1991. "Right now we are the clear choice, as Konark is the cheapest brand with a superior quality. But with the withdrawal of the exemption, we will be in the same price range as the 'big boys' and it will be a real run for the money to sell our brand," remarked Mr. Bhalla.

Mr. Bhalla was also concerned about some dealer activities that he thought were damaging to Konark. He knew that many dealers would play with the assigned margin and offer the same Konark product at differing prices to different customers. Or, equally damaging, different dealers might quote different prices for the same product to a single customer. Some dealers recently had gone so far as to buy large quantities of TV sets from Konark and sell them to unauthorized dealers in Bhubaneswar or in neighboring districts. This problem was particularly vexing because the offending dealers—while small in number—often were quite large and important to Konark's overall performance. Perhaps as much as 40 percent of Konark's sales revenues came from "problem" dealers.

Early in 1990, Mr. Bhalla thought that an increase in margins that Konark allowed its dealers was all that was needed to solve the problem. However, a modest change in dealer compensation had resulted in several national competitors raising their dealer margins even higher—without an increase in their retail prices. The result was that prices of Konark's models became even closer to those of national competitors and Konark's decline in market share had actually steepened. By late 1990, Konark's unit share of the Orissa market had fallen from 80 percent to just over 60 percent. "Unless something is done soon," Mr. Bhalla thought, "we'll soon be below 50 percent."

The Decision

Some immediate actions were needed to improve dealer relations and stimulate greater sales activity. An example was Konark's quarterly "Incentive Scheme" which had begun in April 1989. The program was a rebate arrangement based on points earned for a dealer's purchases of Konark TV sets. Reaction was lukewarm when the program was first announced. However, a revision in August 1989 greatly increased participation. Other actions yet to be formulated could be announced at a dealers' conference that Mr. Bhalla had scheduled for next month.

All such actions would have to be consistent with Konark's long-term distribution strategy. The problem was that this strategy had not yet been formulated. Mr. Bhalla saw this void as his most pressing responsibility, as well as a topic of great interest to Mr. Singh. Mr. Bhalla hoped to have major aspects of a distribution strategy ready for discussion for next week's meeting. Elements of the strategy would include recommendations on channel structure—branch offices or independent distributors, company showrooms or independent dealers—in existing markets as well as in markets identified for expansion. The latter markets included Bombay, Jaipur, and Trivandrum, areas that contained some 2 million consumers in the target segment. Most importantly, the strategy would have to address actions to combat the loss of the sales tax exemption in Orissa.

In mid-January 1998, senior management at Powrtron Corporation was grappling with an unprecedented problem of constrained capacity. Allyson Shelton (chief operating officer), Bryce Thomason (sales and marketing manager), and Jason Stewart (manufacturing manager) were meeting to discuss the capacity situation and its snowball effect on late deliveries and customer dissatisfaction.

Tension was high at the start of the meeting, and Shelton feared the air would only become thicker when she delivered the message from Bradley Keith, the company's principal owner and CEO. Senior management had expected Keith to announce that the company would move to a larger location within the next year. However, on the previous day, Keith informed Shelton that such a move would definitely not take place within the next 12 months. Recognizing that some type of prioritizing would have to take place, he had advised Shelton to work out the capacity, delivery, and customer problems at her meeting with Thomason and Stewart on the next day.

A bottom-line person, Shelton knew that Powrtron management had to quickly devise a way to determine the appropriate mix of product development, existing product management, customer prioritization, and customer service.

The Company

Located in Newton, Massachusetts, Powrtron was a private, predominately family-held company with sales of around $8.4 million. Founded in 1965 by three brothers, the company still operated out of its original building (with some modest additions) on land owned by the founding families.[1] From its inception and into the late 1970s, the company exclusively manufactured products in the analog integrated circuit business using designs principally developed by the youngest of the brothers (then chief engineer), Bradley Keith.[2] Most Powrtron products were designed into customers' new applications. In the late 1970s, Bradley Keith developed a unique, slim design for power converters, which soon became a major part of the company's business. By the beginning of 1998, Powrtron engaged in the manufacture and sale of electronic analog circuit modules, isolation amplifiers, and power converters.

This case was prepared by Victoria L. Crittenden of Boston College and William F. Crittenden of Northeastern University as the basis for class discussion rather than to illustrate effective or ineffective handling of a managerial situation. Powrtron is a pseudonym and some data have been disguised. All relevant relationships remain constant.

---

[1] Increased real estate prices for industrial property in Newton (an immediate suburb of Boston) made the land worth many times its original cost. Estimated value exceeded $9 million.

[2] Unlike his older brothers, who were trained as financial economists at local Ivy League colleges, Bradley Keith received two math degrees from Boston College (BC). Then, over a seven-year span, while working on various defense-related projects at a local multinational electronics firm, Keith earned an engineering degree from Northeastern University (NU) in Boston. He had received four patents. He also had a number of other process and product inventions that likely were patentable if he took the time and effort to apply. Over the years, Keith also completed various graduate business courses at BC and NU, but he had not completed a business degree program.

EXHIBIT 1
Organization Structure

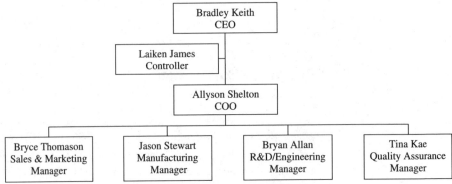

Exhibit 1 provides the firm's organizational structure. Three of the functional managers, including the heads of manufacturing and sales & marketing, had been with the firm less than two and a half years. Top management viewed manufacturing as the strongest functional area, with marketing seen as the weakest. The company's manufacturing capacity was physically constrained by the company's current location and a tight local labor market which made it difficult to find qualified new people at wages that would keep Powrtron's labor costs competitive. Exhibits 2 and 3 provide recent financial information.

Powrtron produced seven major products in-house. Powrtron's perceived competitive strength was providing customized, advanced technology products to quality-conscious customers. Quality was designed into the product and a rigorous quality assurance program kept returns to a level well below industry averages. A key accounts policy was viewed as the most effective way to take advantage of Powrtron's strengths, with a standard line of products being the means to initially generate accounts. Man-

EXHIBIT 2   Income Statement

	1997	1996	1995
Sales	$8,415,393	$7,781,933	$7,548,474
Cost of sales	5,380,077	4,702,145	4,462,281
Gross margin	3,035,316	3,079,788	3,086,193
Operating costs			
Research & Development	668,136	529,180	515,973
Sales & Marketing	659,393	786,827	761,452
General & Admin.	1,067,474	1,062,321	1,028,858
OC subtotal	2,395,003	2,378,328	2,306,283
Operating income	640,313	701,460	779,910
Other income	0	0	38,900
Interest expenses			
Shareholders	264,000	264,000	264,000
Bank	118,397	121,878	128,843
Other expenses	218,837	274,584	298,821
Income before taxes	$39,079	$40,998	$127,146

EXHIBIT 3 Balance Sheet

	Dec 31, 1997	Dec 31, 1996	Dec 31, 1995
Current assets			
Cash	$123,812	$98,634	$93,523
Accounts receivables	803,732	784,991	787,524
Less: Allowance for bad debts	(31,000)	(31,000)	(31,000)
Inventory	318,453	321,964	326,047
Less: Allowance for obsolescence	(50,000)	(50,000)	(50,000)
Prepaid expenses	16,026	9,877	7,794
Total current assets	1,181,023	1,134,466	1,133,888
Fixed assets			
Machinery & equipment	1,457,023	1,457,023	1,457,023
Furniture & fixtures	253,685	253,685	253,685
Leasehold improvements	0	0	0
Automobile	38,979	38,979	38,979
Less: Accumulated depreciation	(1,529,223)	(1,502,623)	(1,476,023)
Net fixed assets	220,464	247,064	273,664
Total assets	1,401,487	1,381,530	1,407,552
Current liabilities			
Demand note payable	1,392,902	1,392,902	1,392,902
Current maturities of lease	0	0	0
Accounts payable	266,538	253,048	274,736
Payroll taxes payable	34,923	33,876	$35,023
Accrued payroll	235,039	243,024	293,024
Accrued interest	280,000	300,085	323,054
Other	103,726	111,234	109,067
Total current liabilities	2,313,128	2,334,169	2,427,806
Long-term liabilities			
Notes payable to shareholders	1,750,000	1,750,000	1,750,000
Shareholders' equity			
Common stock	920,000	920,000	920,000
Retained earnings	(3,581,641)	(3,622,639)	(3,690,254)
Total liabilities & equity	$1,401,487	$1,381,530	$1,407,552

agement believed the key to implementing this strategy was to provide a balance of standard and custom products to its customers.

Products. Two analog business products—the pincushion integrated circuit module (PIN) and the isolation amplifier/analog multiplier (IAAM)—generally provided Powrtron with its best gross margins. The pincushion correction device corrected for geometric or focus distortion for CRT displays. Typical applications included airborne displays, air traffic control systems, medical monitors, and CAD displays. Two distinct lines of the PIN product existed. Powrtron manufactured PIN100s, with PIN300s being a buy/resale product. Isolation amplifiers could be used in a variety of situations, including industrial process control, instrumentation (data acquisition), and medical (ECG, EEG, ENG, and other medical monitoring). Worldwide sales of analog circuit devices were estimated at around US$12 billion, with the consumer market (video and portable phones) accounting for approximately 40 percent of demand.

With the increased use of sophisticated analog and digital devices in many types of electronic systems, DC/DC power converters were necessary products for design engineers. The converter provided the electronic system with the regulated voltage required through local transformation of power supply voltages. Applications included telecommunications, robotics, remote systems, battery-operated systems, uninterruptable power systems, test instrumentation, and ground support equipment. Five products comprised Powrtron's major lines of DC/DC converters: DCD, DCT, DCJ, DCX, and DCZ. The depths of these product lines varied and depended upon such issues as power range, input voltage, output voltage, and whether output was regulated. Problems had occurred in the DC/DC converter business, however, in that Powrtron had not been able to successfully produce large quantities of low-cost standardized products.

The worldwide power converter market was estimated around US$10 billion. These sales experienced less volatility than the more complex integrated circuits. However, there were industrywide concerns that this market had reached maturity, leading to long-term concerns about the overall health of the marketplace. At the same time, there was surprise that the market had proven to be as resilient as it was to market encroachment by analog devices.

Stewart and Thomason provided numerous personal insights and concerns about each of Powrtron's seven products. The PIN and DCT offerings were thought to be good, stable products with continued market potential. Although the IAAM was an important contributor to company margins, each manager independently expressed some concern as to whether Powrtron could compete long-term with this product. Stewart had determined that the DCD market was not growing and had plans to phase out the line. However, Powrtron had experienced recent interest in the product. Thomason was attempting to determine if this was just a short-term blip on the screen or if the market was beginning to resurrect. The DCJ was a small-volume business and had extremely volatile margins. However, the firm continued to make the product and had seen sales increase in 1996 and again in 1997. Stewart viewed the DCX product line as the big loser in the firm. Thomason acknowledged that the DCX was in a decline, but did not agree that it was a big loser. Both Stewart and Thomason agreed that the DCZ line of products was the future of power converters at Powrtron. However, although demand had jumped 600 percent, current sales were not meeting expectations and the company was having trouble perfecting the product for the marketplace.

Additionally, Powrtron made variations of the seven products ("specials") that did not fit solely within any of the product lines. Powrtron also would purchase products for resale if its customers needed products not available from Powrtron and did not want to shop around for the product themselves.

Customers.   Powrtron had three tiers of accounts. The first tier consisted of three major customers for which Powrtron made unique, specialized products. Close business relationships existed between Powrtron and these three accounts. CEO Bradley Keith had, himself, made the original contact and sale with these long-time customers. Allyson Shelton, COO, now personally oversaw individual account sales of around $850,000 annually to each of these accounts. Powrtron management considered the first tier of accounts as a "separate business." The margins on business from these accounts approximated Powrtron's average, and these customers kept their promises and paid in a timely fashion.

Second-tier accounts consisted of 10 major customers and seven minor customers, with total sales of around $4,000,000 annually. The 10 major second-tier accounts were labeled HF, TI, RO, GE, AT, GN, NA, AC, SA, and WC. Seven of the major ac-

EXHIBIT 4   Product/Account Purchases

	Products							
Accounts	*PIN*	*IAAM*	*DCD*	*DCT*	*DCJ*	*DCX*	*DCZ*	*Specials*
HF				x		x		x
TI			x	x	x	x		
RO	x	x	x	x		x		x
GE	x	x						x
AT				x	x	x		x
GN	x						x	
NA			x				x	
AC								x
SA							x	

counts provided between $400,000 and $580,000 each in yearly sales. Thomason indicated that the remaining three major accounts had strong potential for growth. Nine of the 10 major accounts purchased Powrtron-manufactured products. Purchases from the tenth account (WC) consisted of the company's buy/resale product offering only. Shelton, Thomason, and Stewart agreed that the seven minor accounts were important to Powrtron because of their market potential or the combination of products purchased.

Powrtron attempted to develop second-tier accounts into key accounts (tier 1 accounts) through individual service provided by sales and marketing. However, actual purchases were made through the local sales representative and not directly to Powrtron. Sales representative commissions were 7 percent for sales made to three of the accounts (TI, NA, AC) and 6 percent for sales made to the remaining accounts. Exhibit 4 provides an overview of Powrtron-manufactured products purchased by the nine major accounts. Exhibit 5 shows total 1993–97 second-tier account sales for each of the seven products manufactured by Powrtron.

The third tier of accounts consisted of around $1,900,000 in sales of Powrtron-manufactured standard products to many different customers. Individual sales to each of these customers did not amount to a large enough dollar total to warrant separate consideration of each account. These customers did not receive special sales attention from a Powrtron manager and they made purchases exclusively through the local manufacturer's representative organization. The rep organization's role was simply that of order taker.

Competition

Japanese manufacturers held the leading share (35%) in the $12 billion analog circuit business. This was followed by the United States (25%), Europe (20%), and then the rest of the world. Leading worldwide competitors and their estimated market shares included National Semiconductor (7%), Texas Instruments (6%), Philips/Signetics (5.7%), Toshiba (5.6%), Sanyo (5.5%), Matsushita (5.1%), SGS/Thomson (4.7%), Motorola Inc. (4.4%), NEC Corp. (4.3%), Hitachi (4.1%), and Mitsubishi (4.1%). These large firms had significant scale advantages throughout the value chain and tended to exclusively produce highly standardized products. The battle for market share among these firms was fiercely competitive as even a fraction of a percentage

EXHIBIT 5   Product Sales and Average Price
              for Second-Tier Accounts

	Unit Volume	Total Sales	Average Price
PIN			
1993	309	$117,487	$380
1994	310	123,054	397
1995	341	141,731	416
1996	1890	718,281	380
1997	2701	1,059,091	392
IAAM			
1993	17	1,683	99
1994	158	13,866	88
1995	1558	133,987	86
1996	5039	428,355	85
1997	5543	509,956	92
DCD			
1993	0	0	0
1994	66	10,248	155
1995	199	32,452	163
1996	66	11,838	179
1997	398	66,466	167
DCT			
1993	627	206,910	330
1994	1739	554,741	319
1995	1927	447,064	232
1996	1884	465,348	247
1997	1841	489,706	266
DCJ			
1993	1254	109,098	87
1994	1326	125,970	95
1995	838	71,896	86
1996	818	80,981	99
1997	917	80,696	88
DCX			
1993	1686	153,246	91
1994	2806	238,510	85
1995	123	14,637	119
1996	345	36,915	107
1997	80	9,280	116
DCZ			
1993	0	0	0
1994	0	0	0
1995	0	0	0
1996	2085	223,095	107
1997	13694	1,410,482	103

point meant millions of dollars in sales. Midsized firms (those with less than 2 percent market share) tended to come under close competitive scrutiny whenever they appeared to encroach on the high-volume, standardized portion of this business. The most profitable midsized firms tended to be subsidiaries of much larger, vertically integrated firms. Smaller firms tended to be highly focused around a single core technology that was used as the basis for quickly producing highly customized product.

Competition in the $10 billion power converter business was enormous, with thousands of worldwide competitors. The most successful competitors appeared to be able to blend high-margin customized production with high-volume, good-margin, standardized manufacturing. There were successful small firms that focused exclusively on customized production. However, these firms often incurred substantial problems in an economic downturn. Companies operating in this industry included Vicor Corp., Theta-J, Unitech P.L.C., Rifa, Astec, and Lambda Electronics. Competitors seemed keenly aware whenever Powrtron captured significant business beyond its first-tier accounts. Thus, bids for repeat business, which would allow Powrtron to obtain some learning curve advantages, were always highly competitive.

Operations at Powrtron

The manufacturing facility was located in the same building as management offices in Newton, Massachusetts. The manufacturing area totaled 14,500 square feet; the engineering area was 5,000 square feet; and the quality control area was 1,500 square feet. The engineering group (not including CEO Keith) encompassed over 40 years of experience in the power design field. A computer-aided design (CAD) system was used for schematic design, layout, and documentation processes utilized by the engineering group. The CAD system had a direct parts-list link to the materials requirements planning (MRP II) system utilized by the manufacturing group. The MRP II system continually monitored order status, inventory, and customer inquiries.

Although much of the manufacturing equipment was of an older vintage, every piece of equipment was kept in perfect operating condition. In addition, the shop floor was kept well organized and immaculate, and the equipment layout maximized the use of available space.

Powrtron employed 60 direct labor personnel and 10 indirect labor personnel in the manufacturing process. The manufacturing work force was unionized. Yet, CEO Keith had a strong affinity with his production people and labor issues were few and infrequent. Over 70 percent of the production work force had been with Powrtron for at least 20 years, and a number of workers had been with the company since its beginning. The company's location was near many long-time employees' homes and was convenient to mass transit systems. Keith knew all of his employees and a fair amount about their families as well. During the recession of the late 1980s/early 1990s, no one was ever laid off. Instead, workers were asked to take one day a month of unpaid time off.

Now that the economy was again strong and the firm was showing profitability, Stewart had suggested that a new office location/production facility be acquired to enhance the firm's capacity and production capabilities. With an order backlog of around 20 percent for tier 2 and tier 3 accounts (tier 1 account orders were prioritized and moved near the top of the queue) and sales projecting a 10 percent increase for 1998, Stewart looked toward moving to a larger facility with modern equipment and increased hiring to relieve capacity pressures.

While CEO Keith had established connections for off-shore manufacturing capabilities in the Caribbean and the Far East, the company had never augmented its

EXHIBIT 6   Expected Allocation of Available Production Hours (Quarterly)

Product	Hours
PIN	1,300
IAAM	1,300
DCD	350
DCT	1,000
DCJ	400
DCX	350
DCZ	5,800

production volume through any of these sources. Engineering head Bryan Allan and Quality Assurance Manager Tina Kae each expressed concerns regarding the sharing of proprietary information with firms in less developed countries (LDCs).

Every Powrtron product was subjected to a six-step quality inspection process as well as two electrical/functional tests. CEO Keith was proud that quality was designed into each of Powrtron's products and that the quality assurance program, although time consuming, ensured that Powrtron maintained a lower failure rate than most of its direct competitors.

Stewart allocated around 10,500 hours each quarter to producing the seven products for second- and third-tier accounts (approximately one-third of production time was allotted to servicing tier 1 accounts and remaining time was used for setup, maintenance and repair, and producing "specials" for second- and third-tier accounts). Overtime was very expensive and most of the current work force preferred to not work extra hours. Stewart's expected allocated hourly product capacity utilization during 1998 for each product is shown in Exhibit 6. However, since the major factor was total production hour availability, Stewart only used this as a general guide to allocation. Exhibits 7 and 8 provide cost information (variable and setup) and production time for each of the major product lines.

Although Powrtron's manufacturing group had not previously dealt with constrained capacity, Stewart and the production people were at no loss for ideas on how to approach the problem. Some people believed they should fill orders relative to the

EXHIBIT 7   Variable Cost per Unit and Setup Cost per Run

Product	Variable Cost/Unit	Setup Cost/Run
PIN	$75.00	$5.20
IAAM	35.00	4.15
DCD	65.00	4.15
DCT	75.00	7.25
DCJ	65.00	4.15
DCX	45.00	6.25
DCZ	55.00	6.25

Exhibit 8   **Production Time per Unit and Setup Time per Run**

Product	Production Time/ Unit (hours)	Setup Time/ Run (hours)
PIN	1.00	0.25
IAAM	0.60	0.20
DCD	1.00	0.20
DCT	1.50	0.35
DCJ	1.00	0.20
DCX	1.05	0.30
DCZ	1.33	0.30

desired amount. (Some thought this meant the largest orders should be filled first, while others believed this meant the accounts with smaller orders should be filled first.) Others thought the marketing group should be forced to rank orders by account priority. Some felt they should focus on producing the most standardized requests (those requiring the least customization of the core product), while others believed they should fill a certain minimum amount for each account. Other ideas generated throughout the organization included fill best prices first, fill orders by account profitability, and fill orders based on product profitability.

Current Problem

Basically, Shelton, Thomason, and Stewart were meeting to discuss how Powrtron could better balance supply and demand. But Shelton knew that the issue involved more than economics. Thomason and Stewart had literally been at each other's necks over the past couple of months. Not only did the company have irate customers due to slow or ever late deliveries, Powrtron's senior management was barely speaking to each other.

Not wasting any time on social interaction at the start of the meeting, Bryce Thomason told Shelton that Stewart's group was responsible for the problems he was having with his second-tier accounts. Thomason said that Powrtron's competitors were promising (and delivering) in a maximum of six weeks from the sale. Therefore, he felt that he had to make the same commitment if Powrtron's second-tier accounts were to continue doing business with the company. Unfortunately, while Thomason indicated Powrtron's competition was satisfying its delivery commitments, Shelton knew Powrtron had not delivered on time in the past four months. Thomason thought that Stewart was not dedicated to the firm's key account strategy. He felt that without this commitment, Powrtron might as well provide standard, off-the-shelf products and forget the key account focus.

Angrily, Jason Stewart told Thomason that Sales & Marketing were making unreasonable promises by pushing ahead their delivery date commitments. Stewart said that Thomason and his sales staff were being unrealistic by ignoring the firm's capacity limits, particularly with respect to backlog, run cycles, and downtime. With the current capacity situation, Stewart felt that the delivery cycle should be twice the time Thomason was telling customers. Stewart said that the only relief in sight was the upcoming move to a larger production facility. He said, "Powrtron will be able to expand its production capabilities once we are able to add equipment and laborers. Until then, the company will not be able to make and deliver products any faster."

Things were heating up much more quickly than Shelton had anticipated. The meeting had not gotten off to a good start. Unfortunately, Shelton knew that her announcement about the delay in company relocation was going to make an already bad situation even worse.

CASE 5–7
TAURUS HUNGARIAN RUBBER WORKS

Although Taurus had adjourned the three-day top management planning session conducted at its Lake Balaton retreat less than two years ago, many major company decisions had been made since that time. Still the basic implementation of the company's diversification strategy had not been accomplished. As director of the company's Corporate Development Strategic Planning Department, Gyula Bosnyak recognized both the timing and the enormity of the events and issues involved. In early 1988, the Hungarian government had passed its Corporation Law, which put all state-owned firms on notice to reprivatize and recapitalize themselves. Not only did the firm have to deal with the mechanics of going public, it had to obtain the ideal mix of debt and equity capital to ensure solid growth for a company that was operating in a stagnant economy and a low-growth industry. Top management was also concerned about the route they should follow in their attempts to invigorate the company. It was an accepted fact that Taurus had to maintain or even improve its international competitiveness, and that it had to diversify away from its traditional dependence on the manufacturing of truck and farm tires.

Rather than viewing this situation as a bothersome threat, Gyula had seen this as an opportunity for Taurus to deal with its working capital problem as well as to begin serious diversification efforts away from its basically noncompetitive and highly threatened commercial tire manufacturing operation. Now, in spring 1990, he was beginning to sort out his company's options before making his recommendations to both Laszlo Geza, vice president of Taurus's Technical Rubber Products Division, and Laszlo Palotas, the company's newly elected president.

Rubber and Rubber Production

Christopher Columbus was probably the first European to handle rubber. Haitian natives had used it for centuries as a football-sized sphere that they threw into a hole in the wall of a playing field. These balls were derived from a dried milky liquid obtained by cutting the bark of a "weeping wood" or cauchuc tree. While the natives also used this substance to make shoes, bottles, and waterproof cloth, the Western world's commercial use of the product was limited until two discoveries greatly expanded rubber's usefulness and properties. In 1819, Thomas Hancock discovered latex rubber could be masticated, which allowed it to be converted into products of different shapes by the use of pressure and the addition of other materials. Unfortunately, mastication deprived rubber of its elastic qualities.

The discovery of vulcanization by Charles Goodyear in 1839 solved this problem

This case was prepared by Joseph Wolfe, University of Tulsa; Gyala Bosnyak, Taurus Hungarian Rubber Works; and Janos Vecsenyi, International Management Center, Budapest. © 1990 University of Tulsa, Tulsa, Oklahoma, USA. Distributed by the European Case Clearing House Ltd, Cranfield Institute of Technology, Cranfield, Bedford MK43 OAL, England. This publication may not be reproduced, stored, transmitted or altered in any way without the written consent of the copyright owner, except as permitted under the Copyright, Designs and Patents Act 1988.

This case is intended for classroom discussion only, not to depict effective or ineffective handling of administrative situations. All rights reserved to the authors.

and also kept rubber products from becoming tacky. Goodyear found the addition of sulphur to crude rubber at a temperature above its melting point improved its mechanical properties and its resistance to temperature changes. After these twin discoveries, the commercial uses of rubber multiplied greatly with the greatest impetus coming from J. B. Dunlop's rediscovery of the pneumatic tire which he applied to his son's bicycle in 1888. Shortly thereafter, the rise of the automobile industry at the century's turn resulted in a tremendous increase in the demand for rubber and its principal application in the manufacture of automobile and truck tires. The world's long ton consumption of rubber prior to World War II in approximate 30-year periods was as follows:

1840–1872	150,000
1873–1905	1,000,000
1906–1940	18,850,000

The production of natural rubber entails collecting the juice of the 60-to-80–foot-high *Hevea brasiliensis* tree, which is now plantation-grown in such tropical countries as Brazil, Malaysia, and Indonesia. The trees are tapped by cutting through the tree's bark, which contains latex tubes. A flow of liquid amounting to about five pounds per year can be obtained from each tree. The milky substance is dehydrated for shipment by spraying and drying, by acidification, coagulation, washing and rolling, or by drying it with smoke. Natural rubber is usually transformed into sheet or crepe. Sheet rubber is smoke-dried and obtains a dark brown color while crepe is air-dried, is much lighter in color, and is passed through heavy rollers at the beginning of the drying process.

As shown in Exhibit 1, a wide range of rubber applications can be obtained through the addition of various ingredients to latex rubber during its masticating or compounding manufacturing stages. Carbon black is added for high abrasion resistance, oils for making the material more workable, and paraffin for better light resistance. Other ingredients, such as antioxidants, activators, and various organic and inorganic coloring substances, are also employed and various accelerators are used to (1) hasten the vulcanization process, (2) allow it to occur at room temperatures, and (3) improve the product's ultimate quality.

Because of the tremendous increase in the need for natural rubber in the early 1920s, and the realization of its strategic importance by both Germany and Russia from their World War I experiences, vigorous research into the creation of a synthetic

EXHIBIT 1   Major Nontire Rubber Uses

Mechanical goods	Hard rubber products
Latex foam products	Flooring
Shoe products	Cements
Athletic goods	Drug sundries
Toys	Pulley belts
Sponge rubber	Waterproof insulation
Insulated wire and cable	Conveyor belts
Footwear	Shock absorbers and vibration dampeners
Waterproofed fabrics	

EXHIBIT 2   **Predicted Demand for Synthetic Rubbers in 1992 (nonsocialist countries, in thousands of metric tons)**

Synthetic Rubber	Forecast
Styrene-butadiene*	2,819
Carboxylated styrene-butadiene	1,015
Polybutadiene	1,142
Ethylene-propylene diene	556
Polychloroprene	268
Nitrile	238
All others†	1,025
Total	7,063

Source: Adapted from International Institute of Synthetic Rubber Producers; Bruce F. Greek, "Modest Growth Ahead for Rubber," *Chemical & Engineering News* 66, no. 12 (March 21, 1988), p. 26.

*In both liquid and solid forms.

†Includes polyisoprene and butyl.

rubber was conducted in the 1930s. The first butadiene-styrene copolymer from an emulsion system (Buna S) was prepared at the research laboratories of I.G. Farbenindustrie, followed shortly thereafter by the analogous butadiene-acrylonitrile copolymer (Buna N). By 1936, Germany was able to produce 100 to 200 tons of synthetic rubber a month; by 1939, the factories at Schkopau and Hüls could produce 50,000 tons per year.

The family of "Buna" rubbers are produced by polymerizing butadiene, with sodium (natrium) acting as a catalyst. This process was originally conducted at a temperature of about 50° centigrade, but the copolymerization of butadiene and styrenes is now usually done in aqueous phase.[1] In an emulsion copolymerization process carried out at 50° centigrade, so-called *cold rubber,* the hydrocarbons to be polymerized are in emulsion and contain a constituent of the activator system dissolved in them. The second part of the activator system is present in the watery medium of the emulsion. The combined activator system initiates the process of polymerization and the polymer's molecule size is regulated by adding various substances. The entire process is stopped after about 60 percent of these substances have reacted. The resulting product is very much like latex rubber and from this phase on can be treated like the natural substance. A large variety of other synthetic rubbers can be produced in addition to the Buna rubbers. Exhibit 2 presents a forecast of the demand for these rubbers for the year 1992.

Combining both natural and synthetic rubbers, it has been estimated that world consumption of these substances will be about 15.9 million metric tons in 1992. According to William E. Tessmer, managing director of the International Institute of Synthetic Rubber Producers, this is an 11 percent increase from the 14.4 million tons estimated for 1987. As shown in Exhibit 3, about 70 percent of the world's rubber consumption is in the form of synthetic rubber. Exhibits 4 and 5 show the predicted geographic distribution of rubber demand for the year 1992.

---

[1] *Polymerization* is a reaction involving the successive addition of a large number of relatively small molecules (monomers) to form a final compound or polymer. A *polymer* is a giant molecule formed when thousands of molecules have been linked together end to end. A *copolymer* is a giant molecule formed when two or more unlike monomers are polymerized together.

EXHIBIT 3 **Predicted World Consumption of Rubber (in millions of metric tons)**

Type	1986	1987	1988	1989	1990	1991	1992
Synthetic	9.5	9.8	9.8	9.9	9.9	10.0	10.0
Natural	4.5	4.6	4.9	5.1	5.4	5.7	5.9
Total	14.0	14.4	14.7	15.0	15.3	15.7	15.9

Source: Based on Bruce F. Greek, "Modest Growth Ahead for Rubber," *Chemical & Engineering News* 66, no. 12 (March 21, 1988), pp. 25–26.
Note: One metric ton equals 2,204.6 pounds.

EXHIBIT 4 **Predicted Changes in Rubber Demand by Geographic Area (in thousands of metric tons)**

Geographic Area	1987	1992	Change
North America	3,395	3,432	1.09%
Latin America	788	944	19.80
Western Europe	2,460	2,953	20.04
Africa & Middle East	259	324	25.10
Asia & Oceania	3,060	3,541	15.72
Socialist countries	4,057	4,706	16.00
Total	14,019	15,900	13.42%

Source: Based on Bruce F. Greek, "Modest Growth Ahead for Rubber," *Chemical & Engineering News* 66, no. 12 (March 21, 1988), p. 26.

EXHIBIT 5 **Predicted Demand for Rubber in Socialist Countries (in millions of metric tons)**

Socialist Group	1987	1992
Eastern European		
Synthetic	2.90	3.30
Natural	0.40	0.37
Total	3.30	3.67
Asian Socialist		
Synthetic	0.30	0.43
Natural	0.47	0.61
Total	0.76	1.04

Source: Based on Bruce F. Greek, "Modest Growth Ahead for Rubber,"
Chemical & Engineering News 66, no. 12 (March 21, 1988), pp. 25-26.

Worldwide Rubber Company Competition

Rubber firms now compete on the international level because of a number of driving forces. Automobiles and trucks, which are the major users of tire and rubber products, are ubiquitous; the high operating scales required for efficient plant operations compel manufacturers to find markets that can support them; and growth opportunities no longer exist in many of the manufacturers' home countries. As has been the case within its domestic automobile industry, the United States has been invaded by a number of very competitive and efficient foreign tire and rubber manufacturers. Those foreign competitors in turn have acquired firms or have entered into joint ventures on a global scale, thereby increasing their penetration into a number of countries. Exhibit 6 displays the financial results that have been obtained by the major world rubber manufacturers for 1984 and 1988; Exhibit 7 reviews the alternative strategies and recent actions taken by the industry's principal actors. As best as can be determined, Exhibit 8 demonstrates that Michelin has recently become the world's largest tire manufacturing firm with a worldwide market share of 21.3 percent, with Goodyear and Bridgestone basically tied for second place in world sales.

Taurus Hungarian Rubber Works

Today's Taurus Hungarian Rubber Works has an ancestry dating back more than a century. From its earliest days with the founding of the factory by Erno Schottola, it has been Hungary's most important rubber producer. In growing to its current size, Taurus has both grown internally and has acquired several smaller manufacturers.

The first Hungarian rubber factory was established in 1882, and in 1890, it became a public company under the name Magyar Ruggyantaarugyar Rt. Because Hungary lacked a domestic producer of automobiles at the century's turn, the company supported the creation of an automobile plant, which was ultimately located in Arad, and the formation of the Autotaxi company in Budapest. During the period before World War I, Magyar Ruggyantaarugyar grew rapidly and was soon exporting between 30 percent and 35 percent of its products outside Hungary. Its rubber balls, toys, asbestos-rubber seals, and Palma heels gained a worldwide reputation for quality.

During the interwar period, the Hungarian rubber sector declined dramatically with its export sales dropping to 15 to 18 percent of total production. Its factory equipment deteriorated, and only its lines of rubber yarns and latex products could remain internationally competitive. Pre-World War I global market shares of 0.6 percent fell to 0.3 percent and its annual sales growth rates dropped to 1.5 to 2.0 percent per year.

EXHIBIT 6   **Selected Company Sales and Profits (in U.S. dollars)**

Company	1984		1988	
	Sales (billion)	Profits (million)	Sales (billion)	Profits (million)
B.F. Goodrich (U.S.)	$ 3.40	$ 60.6	NA*	NA
Bridgestone (Japan)	3.38	65.1	$ 9.30	$ 310.2
Cooper (U.S.)	0.56	23.9	0.73	35.0
Firestone (U.S.)	4.16	102.0	NA†	NA
GenCorp (U.S.)	2.73	7.2	0.50	NA‡
Goodyear (U.S.)	10.24	391.7	10.90	330.0
Michelin (France)	5.08	(256.5)	8.70	397.4
Pirelli (Italy)	3.50	72.0	7.01	172.1
Taurus (Hungary)	0.26	11.5	0.38	9.0
Uniroyal (U.S.)	2.10	77.1	2.19	11.8

Sources: *Akron Beacon Journal,* January 13, 1986, p. B8; "Powerful Profits around the World," *Fortune* 120, no. 3 (July 31, 1989), pp. 292, 294; Gary Levin, "Tire Makers Take Opposite Routes," *Advertising Age* 60, no. 6 (February 6, 1989), p. 34.

*Merged with Uniroyal in 1987.

†Acquired by Bridgestone in 1988.

‡Acquired by Continental in 1987.

Exhibit 7   Recent Activities of Various Tire and Rubber Companies

Bridgestone Corporation: Bridgestone's acquisition of the Firestone Tire & Rubber Company in 1988 for $2.6 billion vaulted it into a virtual tie with Goodyear as the world's second largest tire company. The acquisition has been a troublesome one for Bridgestone, with Firestone losing about $100 million in 1989, causing the parent company's 1989 profits to fall to about $250 million on sales of $10.7 billion. Bridgestone has already invested $1.5 billion in upgrading Firestone's deteriorated plants and an additional $2.5 billion will be needed to bring all operations up to Bridgestone's quality standards. Last year's North American sales were $3.5 billion, and the firm plans to quadruple the output of its La Vergne, Tennessee, plant. Currently, Bridgestone is attempting to increase its share of the American tire market while slowly increasing its share of the European market as Japanese cars increase their sales in that area. In mid-1989, nine top executives were forced to resign or accept reassignment over disputes about the wisdom of the company's aggressive growth goals. Bridgestone is a major factor in Asia, the Pacific, and South America, where Japanese cars and trucks are heavily marketed.

Continental Gummi–Werke AG: Continental is West Germany's largest tire manufacturer and is number two in European sales. It purchased General Tire from Gencorp in June 1987 for $625 million and is basically known as a premium quality tire manufacturer. Continental entered a $200 million joint radial tire venture in December 1987 with the Toyo Tire & Rubber Company and Yokohama Rubber Company for the manufacture of tires installed on Japanese cars being shipped to the American market. Another part of the venture entails manufacturing radial truck and bus tires in the United States.

Cooper Tire and Rubber Company: This relatively small American firm has been very successful by specializing in the replacement tire market. This segment accounts for about 80 percent of its sales and nearly half of its output is sold as private-labeled merchandise. Cooper has recently expanded its capacity by 12 percent with about 10 percent more capacity scheduled for completion in late 1990. About 60 percent of its sales are for passenger tires while the remainder are for buses and heavy trucks. The company is currently attempting to acquire a medium truck tire plant in Natchez, Mississippi, to enable it to cover the tire spectrum more completely.

Goodyear Tire and Rubber Co.: The last of two major rubber companies left in the United States, Goodyear has diversified itself into chemicals and plastics, a California-to-Texas oil pipeline, as well as into the aerospace industry. Automotive products, which include tires, account for 86 percent of sales and 76 percent of operating profits. Its recent sales growth has come from African and Latin American tire sales where the company has a dominant market share. Additional plant expansions have been started in Canada and South Korea (12,000 tires daily per plant) and will be available in 1991 although they should not produce significant revenues until 1992. Goodyear is attempting to sell off its All America pipeline for about $1.4 billion to reduce its $275 million per year interest charges on $3.5 billion worth of debt.

Michelin et Cie: Although it lost $1.5 billion between 1980 and 1984, Michelin has become profitable again. In late 1988, the company acquired Uniroyal/Goodrich for $690.0 million, which made it the world's largest tire company. Uniroyal had merged in August 1986 with the B.F. Goodrich Co., creating a company where 29 percent of its output was in private brands. Passenger and light truck tires were sold in both the United States and overseas, and sales grew 44.5 percent although profits fell 11.1 percent. Michelin has entered a joint venture with Okamoto of Japan to double that company's capacity to 24,000 tires a day. While a large company, Michelin is much stronger in the truck tire segment than it is in the passenger tire segment.

Pirelli: After having been frustrated in its attempts to acquire Firestone, Pirelli purchased the Armstrong Tire Company for $190 million in 1988 to gain a foothold in the North American market. Armstrong, under the guise of Armtek Corporation, was attempting to diversify out of the tire industry by selling off its industrial tire plant in March 1987. Pirelli, which is strong in the premium tire market, obtained a company whose sales are equally divided between the original equipment and replacement markets and one that has over 500 retail dealers. In the acquisition process Pirelli obtained a headquarters building in Connecticut, three tire plants, one tire textile plant, and one truck-tire factory. Armstrong's 1988 sales were $500 million.

Upon the nationalization of all rubber firms after World War II, the Hungarian government pursued a policy of extensive growth for a number of years. From 1950 to 1970, annual production increases of 12.5 percent a year were common while the rubber sector's employment and gross fixed asset value increased a respective average of approximately 6.2 percent and 15.7 percent per year. Although growth was rapid, great inefficiencies were incurred. Plant utilization rates were low and productivity ratios lagged by about 1.5 to 3.0 times that obtained by comparable socialist and advanced capitalist countries. Little attention was paid to rationalizing either production or the product line as sales to the Hungarian and Eastern bloc countries appeared to support the sector's activities. At various times, the nationalized firm produced condoms, bicycle and automobile tires, rubber toys, boots, and raincoats.

During this period, the government also restructured its rubber industry. In 1963,

EXHIBIT 8   Top Market Shares in World Tire Market

Company	1985	1990
Goodyear	20.0%	17.2%
Michelin	13.0	21.3
Bridgestone	8.0	17.2

Source: Adapted from Stuart J. Benway, "Tire & Rubber Industry," *The Value Line Investment Survey,* December 22, 1989, p. 127.

Budapest's five rubber manufacturers—PALMA, Heureka, Tauril, Emerge, and Cordatic—were merged into one company called the National Rubber Company, and new locations in Vac, Nyiregyhaza, and Szeged were created. Purchasing, cash management, and investment were centralized, and a central trade and research and development apparatus was created. Contrary to the normal way of conducting its affairs, however, the company pioneered the use of strategic planning when the classic type of centralized planning was still the country's ruling mechanism.

In 1973, the company changed its name to the Taurus Hungarian Rubber Works, and it currently operates rubber processing plants in Budapest, Nyiregyhaza, Szeged, Vac, and Mugi as well as a machine and mold factory in Budapest.

As shown in Exhibits 9 through 12, Taurus operates four separate divisions while engaging in a number of joint ventures. Sales have increased annually to the 20.7 billion Forint mark with an increasing emphasis on international business.

Tire Division. The tire division manufactures tires for commercial, nonpassenger vehicles after having phased out its production of automobile tires in the mid-1970s. Truck tires, as either bias-ply or all-steel radials, account for about 34 percent of the division's sales. Farm tires are its other major product category as either textile radials or bias-ply tires. Farm tires were about 20 percent of the division's sales in 1988. A smaller product category includes tire retreading, inner tubes, and fork lift truck tires. About 58 percent of the division's volume is export sales, of which the following countries constituted the greatest amounts (in millions of Forints):

United States	351.7
Algeria	298.2
Czechoslovakia	187.3
West Germany	183.5
Yugoslavia	172.0

The division has recently finished a World Bank-financed capacity expansion in the all-steel radial truck tire operation. This project was begun in December 1986. Eleven new tires within the Taurus Top Tire brand have been scheduled for the market of which two were completed in 1988 and another three in early 1990. The division is also developing a new supersingle tire under a licensing agreement with an American tire manufacturer.

Technical Rubber Division. This division manufactures and markets an assortment of rubber hoses, air-springs for trucks and buses, conveyor belts, waterproof sheeting, and the PALMA line of camping gear. The PALMA camping gear line has a

EXHIBIT 9   Taurus Hungarian Rubber Works Organization Structure

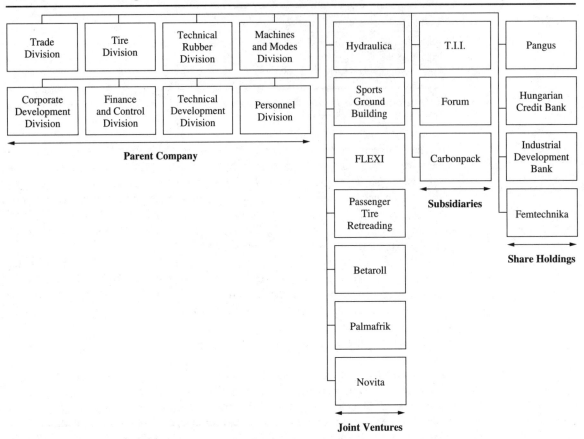

Source: *1988 Annual Report,* p. 17.

EXHIBIT 10   Total Company Sales (selected years; in millions of Forints)

Market	1981	1983	1985	1986	1987	1988	1989	1990
Export	2,560	2,588	3,704	4,055	4,517	5,349	6,843	7,950
Domestic	7,890	9,024	9,381	9,979	11,174	12,255	12,056	12,716
Total	10,450	11,612	13,085	14,034	15,691	17,604	18,899	20,666

Source: *1988 Annual Report* and internal company data.

15 percent world market share while the company's rotary hose business is a world leader with 40 percent of all international sales. The demand for high-pressure and large-bore hoses is closely related to offshore drilling activity while the sale of air-springs for commercial vehicles is expected to increase as this technology gains increasing acceptance with vehicle manufacturers. The former Soviet Union is this division's largest customer with 1989 sales of 380 thousand Forints. In recent years, sales within the division have been distributed in the following fashion:

EXHIBIT 11   Selected 1988 Division Performance Information (in millions of Forints)

	Division			
Item	*Tires*	*Technical Rubber*	*Machines and Molds*	*Trade*
Revenues	6,591	6,484	212	5,612
Assets				
Gross fixed assets	5,201	2,756	268	—
Net fixed assets	2,934	1,199	123	—
Inventories	1,024	601	100	—
Employees	3,987	3,912	557	208

Note: Machine and mold sales include output used in-house.

EXHIBIT 12   Selected 1989 Division Performance Information (in millions of Forints)

	Division			
Item	*Tires*	*Technical Rubber*	*Machines and Molds*	*Trade*
Revenues	8,547	7,183	242	4,694
Assets				
Gross fixed assets	5,519	2,787	292	—
Net fixed assets	3,016	1,120	135	—
Inventories	1,126	545	104	—
Employees	4,021	3,851	552	198

Note: Machine and mold sales include output used in-house.

Large-bore high-pressure hoses	6.7%
Rotary hoses	27.1
Hydraulic hoses	14.7
Camping goods	18.0
Waterproof sheeting	13.9
Air-springs	5.3
Conveyor belts	14.3

Machine and Molds Division.   This division manufactures products that are used in-house as part of Taurus's manufacturing process as well as products used by others. About 70 percent of its sales are for export, and its overall sales were distributed as follows in 1988:

Technical rubber molds	24%
Polyurethane molds	17
Machines and components	25
Tire-curing molds	34

Trade Division.   The Trade Division conducts Eastern European purchases and sales for Taurus as well as performs autonomous distribution functions for other firms. Its activities serve both Taurus's other divisions as well as those outside the company. It is expected that this division will continue to function as Taurus's purchasing agent while increasing its outside trading activities; its status with regard to trading in the former Eastern bloc is in a state of flux.

Implementing Taurus's Strategy of Strategic Alliances

Immediately after returning from his company's top management conference, Gyula began collecting materials to confirm the tentative decisions that had been made at Lake Balaton. Based on secondary data collected and assembled into Exhibits 13 and 14 he could see the general rubber industry had fallen from a better than average industry growth performance in the 1960–1970 period to one that was far inferior to the industrial average during the 1980–1990 period. He also saw that other industries, such as data processing, aircraft, medical equipment, and telecommunication equipment, had obtained sizeable growth rates from 1977 to 1988. Moreover, he was ex-

EXHIBIT 13   Comparative Average Annual Growth Rates

Period	Rubber Sector	All Industry
1960–1970	8.3%	6.8%
1970–1980	4.0	4.1
1980–1990	1.7	4.3
Average	4.7%	5.1%

Source: Internal company report.

EXHIBIT 14   Ten-Year Growth Rates for Selected Industries (1977 to 1988)

Sector	Annual Growth Rate
Data processing equipment	21.0%
Transistors	17.0
Aircraft	16.0
Medical equipment	15.0
Measuring and control equipment	13.5
Electronic games	13.2
Telecommunication equipment	12.9
Metal processing equipment	10.4
Synthetic fibers	7.8
Steel	7.4
Building materials	7.3
Fertilizers	7.0
Agricultural equipment	4.5
Coal	3.2
Passenger cars	2.5
Crude oil	0.5

Source: Internal report.

tremely aware of the increasing concentration occurring in the tire industry through the formation of joint ventures, mergers, cooperative arrangements, and acquisitions. It was obvious that at least the rubber industry's tire segment had passed into its mature stage. In response to this, most major rubber companies had obtained diversifications away from the heavy competition within the industry itself, as well as attempted to find growth markets for their rubber production capacity. For the year 1988 alone, Gyula listed the various strategic alliances shown in Exhibit 15, while Exhibit 16 reviews the diversification activities of Taurus's major tire competitors in 1990.

Within the domestic market, various other Hungarian rubber manufacturers had surpassed Taurus in their growth rates as they jettisoned their low profit lines and adopted newer ones possessing greater growth rates. Taurus's market share of the Hungarian rubber goods industry had slowly eroded since 1970, and this erosion increased greatly in the decade of the 1980s due to the creation of a number of smaller start-up rubber

EXHIBIT 15   Strategic Alliances in 1988

Goodrich (USA) and Uniroyal (Great Britain) operate as a joint venture.

Pirelli (Italy) acquired Armstrong (USA).

Firestone (USA) acquired by Bridgestone (Japan), which has another type of alliance with Trells Nord (Sweden).

General Tire (USA) acquired by Continental Tire (West Germany), which, in turn, operates in cooperation with Yokohama Tire (Japan). Continental also owns Uniroyal Englebert Tire.

Toyo (Japan) operates in cooperation with Continental Tire (West Germany), while also operating a joint venture in Nippon Tire (Japan) with Goodyear (USA).

Michelin (France) operates in cooperation with Michelin Okamoto (Japan).

Sumitoma (Japan) operates in cooperation with Nokia (Finland), Trells Nord (Sweden), and BTR Dunlop (Great Britain).

Source: Corporate annual reports.

EXHIBIT 16   Rubber Company Diversifications

Rubber Company	Nontire Sales (%)	Major Diversification Efforts
Goodyear	27%	Packing materials
		Chemicals
Firestone	30	Vehicle service
Cooper	20	Laser technology
Armstrong	NA	Heat transmission equipment
General Tire	68	Electronics
		Sporting goods
Carlisle	88	Computer technology
		Roofing materials
Bridgestone	30	Chemicals
		Sporting goods
Yokohama	26	Sporting goods
		Aluminum products
Trelleborg	97	Mining
		Ore processing
Aritmos	NA	Food processing
Nokia	98	Electronics
		Inorganic chemicals

Note: Major diversifications as of 1990.

companies encouraged by Hungary's new private laws. While the company's market share stood at about 68 percent in 1986, Gyula estimated Taurus's market share would fall another 3 percent by 1992. Exhibit 17 displays the figures and estimates he created for his analysis.

With the aid of a major consulting firm, Taurus had recently conducted the in-depth analysis of its business portfolio shown in Exhibit 18. It was concluded that the company operated in a number of highly attractive markets, but that the firm's competitive position needed to be improved for most product lines. Accordingly, the firm's emphasis was to be placed on improving the competitiveness of the company's current product lines and businesses. In 1991 Taurus was to implement two types of projects—software projects dealing with quality assurance programs, management development, staff training efforts, and the implementation of a management information system and hardware projects dealing with upgrading the agricultural tire compounding process as well as upgrades in the infrastructures of various plants.

Fundamental to Taurus's desire to be more growth oriented was its newly enunciated strategy shown in Exhibit 19. As formally stated, the company was seeking strategic alliances for certain business lines rather than growth through internal development which had been its previous growth strategy. While it was felt that internal development possessed lower risks, as it basically extended the company's current areas of expertise, benefited the various product lines already in existence, and better served its present customer base while simultaneously using the company's store of management knowledge and wisdom, internal development possessed a number of impediments to Taurus's current desires for accelerated growth. Paramount was its belief that management was too preoccupied with its current activities to pay attention to new areas outside its specific areas of expertise.

Now ranked at thirtieth in size in the rubber industry, Taurus found it was facing newly formed international combinations with enormous financial strength, strong market positions, and diverse managerial assets. Given the high degrees of concentration manifesting themselves in the rubber industry, and that even the largest firms have had to accomplish international cooperative relationships, Taurus determined that it too should seek cooperative, strategic alliances. In seeking these affiliations, the company would be very open and responsive to any type of reasonable alternative or combination that might be offered. These alliances could include participating with companies currently in operation or the creation of new, jointly held companies, whether they are related or unrelated to the rubber industry. The only real criteria for accepting an alliance would be its profitability and growth potential.

In pursuing strategic alliances, Gyula notes that Taurus's bargaining position differs greatly between the various business lines in its portfolio. As an aid to understanding

---

EXHIBIT 17   Distribution of Rubber Goods Production between Taurus and All Other Hungarian Rubber Manufacturers

	Percent of Market			
Manufacturer	*1970*	*1980*	*1986*	*1992*
Taurus	95%	80%	68%	65%
All others	5	20	32	35

Source: Internal company data for years 1970 to 1986 and personal estimate for 1992.

EXHIBIT 18   The Taurus Portfolio

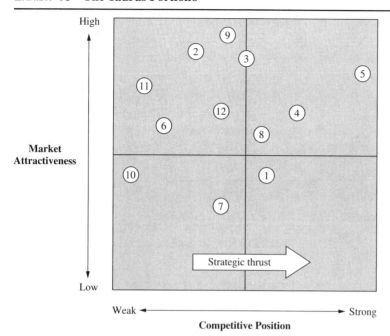

1. Bias tires
2. Steel radial truck tires
3. Agricultural tires
4. Rotary hoses
5. Special hoses
6. Conveyor belts
7. Camping mattresses
8. Rubber sheets
9. Air springs
10. V-belts
11. Precision technical rubber
12. Machines and molds

Source: Company documents and consulting group's final report.

EXHIBIT 19   Taurus's Strategy for the 90s

The decade of 1990 is predicted to be a busy stage of the rubber sector worldwide.

There are strong factors of concentration in traditional manufacturing business(es) and particularly in tire operations. The role of substitute products is growing in several areas. On the other hand, the fast end-of-century growth of industrial sectors is expected to stimulate the development of sophisticated special rubber products. In the face of these challenges, Taurus bases its competitive strategy on the following:

A continuous structural development program has been started aimed at *increasing the company's competitive advantage,* with scope to cover a range from manufacturing processes, through quality assurance, to the reinforcement of strengths and elimination of weaknesses.

Efficiency is a prerequisite of any business activity. The company portfolio must be kept in good balance.

Associated with profitability, the company keeps developing its sphere of operations, determining the direction of diversification according to the criteria of potential growth and returns.

Our pursuit of competitive advantages and diversification must be supported by a powerfully expanding *system of strategic alliance and cooperation.*

Source: Taurus's *Annual Report.*

its bargaining strategy with potential allies, Taurus's businesses are placed into one of three categories as shown in Exhibit 20. Category I types are those where Taurus's bargaining position is relatively weak as it feels it has little to offer a potential suitor. Category II types are those where Taurus can contribute a sizable "dowry" and has much to offer the potential ally, while Category III types are those businesses with mixed or balanced strengths and weaknesses.

EXHIBIT 20   Cooperation Potentials by Product Line

Product Lines	Cooperation Category		
	I	II	III
Truck tires	•		
Farm tires			•
Rotary hoses		•	
Specialty hoses			•
Hydraulic hoses	•		
Waterproofing sheets		•	
Belting	•		
Camping goods			•
Air-springs			•
Machines and molds		•	
Precision goods			•

Source: Internal company report.

The problem now comes to the restructuring of the company's current divisions to make them into rational and identifiable business units to outside investors, as well as serving Taurus's own needs for internal logic and market focus. Which product lines should be grouped together and what should be the basis for their grouping? Gyula saw several different ways to do this. Products can be grouped based on a common production process or technology. They can be based on their capital requirements, markets served, or trade relations that have already been established by Taurus. Depending on how he defines the company's new strategic business units (SBUs), he knows he will be making some major decisions about the attractiveness of the company's assets as well as defining the number and the nature of Taurus's potential strategic alliances. As he explained,

> If I create an SBU that manufactures hoses, a good joint venture partner might be someone who manufactures couplings for hoses—this would be a match that would be good for both of us and it would be a relatively safe investment. If, on the other hand, I create a business that can use the same hoses in the offshore mining and drilling business, and this is a business that is really risky but one that could really develop in the future, what do I look for in partners? I need to find an engineering company that's creating large mining exploration projects. For every type of combination like this I can create, I have to ask myself each time, "What are the driving questions?"

In reviewing the company's portfolio, he immediately saw three new SBUs he could propose to Laszlo Geza, vice president of the Technical Rubber Division. One SBU will serve the automobile industry through the manufacture of rubber profiles (rubber seals and grommets) that provide watertight fits for car windows, V-belts for engines and engine components such as their air conditioning, power steering, and electrical units, and special engine seals. Another unit would serve the truck and bus industry by manufacturing the bellows for articulated buses, and air-springs for buses, heavy-duty trucks, and long-haul trailers. The last newly created SBU will target the firm's adhesives and rubber sheeting at the construction and building industry where the products can be used to waterproof flatroofs as well as serve as chemical-proof and watertight liners in irrigation projects and hazardous waste landfill sites.

Although top management knows "the house is not on fire" and that a careful and deliberate pace can be taken regarding the company's restructuring, Gyula wants to make sure the proposals he is about to make are sound and reasonable. Moreover the success or failure of this restructuring will set the tone for Taurus's future diversification efforts.

Sources

Benway, S.J. "Tire & Rubber Industry." *The Value Line Investment Survey,* December 22, 1989, p. 127.

Garvey, B.S., Jr. "History and Summary of Rubber Technology." In *Introduction to Rubber Technology,* ed. M. Morton. New York: Reinhold, 1959, pp. 1–43.

Greek, B.F. "Modest Growth Ahead for Rubber." *Chemical & Engineering News* 66, no. 12 (March 21, 1988), pp. 25–29.

Thompson, A.A., Jr. "Competition in the World Tire Industry." In *Strategic Management: Concepts and Cases,* A.A. Thompson, Jr., and A.J. Strickland. Homewood, Ill.: Richard D. Irwin, 1990, pp. 518–48.

MARKETING PROGRAM DEVELOPMENT

Marketing strategy entails selecting target markets, setting marketing objectives, and developing, implementing, and managing marketing program positioning strategies. Marketing strategy builds competitive advantage by combining the customer-influencing strategies of the firm or business unit into an array of market-focused actions.

We examined market target strategy in Part IV. Part VI focuses on setting objectives and designing marketing program positioning strategies. Later Part VII will address planning, organizing, and implementing marketing plans as well as assessing the performance of marketing programs.

Setting Objectives

A marketing objective is a statement of what is to be accomplished through marketing activities, such as getting 150 people to test drive a new car during the month of January 1999, or obtaining customer satisfaction ratings of at least 90 percent on the 1999 annual customer satisfaction survey. Each objective should be clear, specific, and realistic; in addition, it should indicate a desired level of performance, how it will be measured, and who will be responsible for meeting it. Each marketing objective should also be relevant to overall results desired and should be consistent with other marketing and nonmarketing objectives. Well-stated objectives also include benchmarks such as a product's current sales volume per period or the current level of product awareness or preference in the target market.

When objectives meet these criteria, they motivate those charged with achieving the objectives. They also can serve as standards by which both the organization and employees charged with achieving the objectives can gauge their performance.

The process of developing objectives can also force executives to sharpen and clarify their thinking. Written objectives enable efforts in developing, implementing, and evaluating a marketing plan to be pointed in a consistent direction.

Among the troublesome problems encountered in setting objectives are the interrelationships among objectives and the shared responsibility for achieving them. Each objective does not fit neatly into an isolated task. Thus, considerable skill is required in determining a balanced set of objectives for different organizational levels and across different functional areas (e.g., advertising and personal selling).

Marketing objectives are normally set at the following levels:

1. The entire marketing organization within a particular company or business unit in a diversified firm.
2. Each target market served by the company or business unit.
3. The major marketing functional areas such as product planning, distribution, pricing, and promotion.
4. Subunits within particular functional areas (for example, objectives for individual salespeople).

The extent to which various levels of objective setting are relevant in a particular firm will depend on the size and complexity of the organization.

Marketing Program Positioning Strategy

The term *positioning* refers to developing a specific marketing mix to influence potential customers' overall perceptions of a brand, product line, or organization in general. *Position* is the place a product item, line, brand, or organization occupies in potential customers' minds relative to competing offerings. For example, Procter & Gamble markets 11 different laundry detergents, each with a unique position. Tide is positioned as a tough, powerful cleaner, Bold as a detergent with fabric softener, Dash as a value brand, Oxydol as a bleach-enhanced detergent for whitening, and so forth.[1]

Positioning assumes that potential customers compare products on the basis of important features. Choosing the positioning concept for a product item, line, brand, or business unit is an important first step in developing a marketing program positioning strategy. Effective positioning requires assessing the positions occupied by competitors, determining the important dimensions of these positions, and choosing a position where the organization's marketing efforts will have the greatest impact.

Once a position is selected, product, distribution, pricing, and promotion strategies are designed to communicate and reinforce the sought position. These so-called marketing mix elements represent a bundle of actions designed to (1) produce mutually satisfying exchanges with target markets and (2) achieve marketing objectives. Exhibit 1 illustrates the major decisions involved in marketing program positioning strategy development. The remainder of Part VI's introduction provides an overview of these decisions.

Product Strategies

The heart of a marketing program positioning strategy is a firm's product offerings. It is hard to develop a promotion program or distribution strategy, or to set prices without knowing the product to be marketed. Product strategy includes

- Deciding how to position a firm or business unit's product items, lines, and/or mixes.
- Setting strategic objectives for each product item and product line.
- Selecting a branding strategy.
- Developing and implementing strategies for managing products.

Product Positioning and Objectives.   Product positioning consists of deciding how to compete with a product or line of products against key competitors in the target

EXHIBIT 1   Major Decisions in Marketing Program Positioning Strategy Development

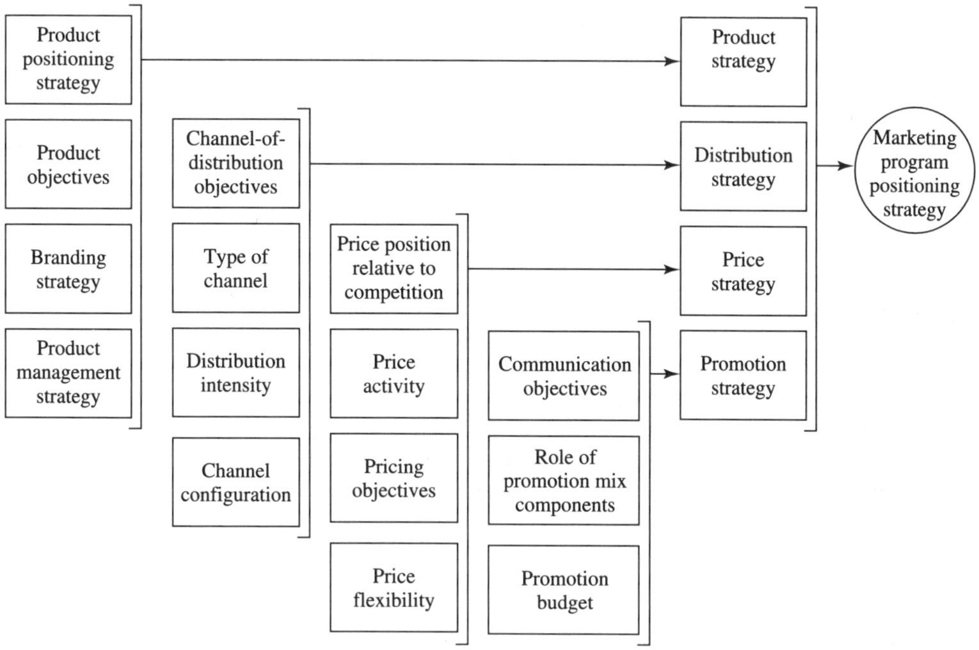

Source: Adapted from David W. Cravens, *Strategic Marketing,* 5th ed. (Burr Ridge, IL: Irwin, 1997), p. 207.

markets selected by management. Key decisions about quality, price, and features establish guidelines for product development and improvement. Closely associated with positioning decisions are the strategic objectives for the product strategy. Examples of objectives are market penetration, profit contribution, and establishing a reputation for quality.

Branding Strategy.   The major alternatives in the branding decision by a manufacturer are

- Make no attempt to establish brand identity, but instead offer a generic (no brand name) product.
- Produce products for private labeling by distributors—for example, True Value (hardware) or Janet Lee (Albertson's grocery stores).
- Establish brand names for lines of products, such as Sears' Craftsman tools.
- Build a strong brand identification for individual products, as in the case of Procter & Gamble.
- Use a combination of the above strategies.

Product Management.   Organizations with multiple products often use product managers to direct the marketing programs of one or more products within a product line or product mix. The primary responsibilities of product managers are to

- Create strategies for improving and marketing assigned product lines or brands.
- Make financial and operating plans for those products.

- Monitor the results of those plans and revise tactics to meet changing conditions.

Some firms that market similar products to diverse target markets assign market managers to coordinate marketing efforts designed to reach a particular group of customers rather than guiding a particular group of products. For example, personal computers are used by households, educational institutions, small businesses, government institutions, and large businesses. Apple Computer has a market manager to design and direct the program positioning strategy for each market segment. A variety of other organization designs are also used for managing new and existing products.[2]

Distribution Strategies

The channel of distribution connects suppliers and producers with end users of goods and services. An effective, efficient distribution channel provides the member organizations with an important strategic edge over competing channels. Distribution strategies focus on getting a firm's products to its target markets. While some producers market their products directly to end users, many others utilize various types of wholesalers and retailers to perform distribution functions and activities. A good distribution strategy requires a penetrating analysis of the available alternatives to select the most appropriate channel network.

Channel Objectives.   Management may seek to achieve one or more objectives using channel strategies. While the primary objective is gaining access to end users, other objectives—such as gaining promotional support, providing customer service, or obtaining market information—may also be important.

Type of Channel.   The major types of channels are conventional channels and vertical marketing systems (VMSs). A conventional channel of distribution is a group of loosely aligned manufacturers, wholesalers, and retailers that bargain with each other at arm's length, negotiate aggressively over terms of sale, and otherwise behave independently.

In contrast, a VMS consists of producers and intermediaries working together to achieve operating economies and maximum market impact. Three common types of vertical marketing systems are corporate, contractual, and administered.

- A *corporate* VMS exists when one firm owns successive stages in a channel of distribution, such as Sherwin-Williams, which operates over 2,000 paint stores.
- A *contractual* VMS exists when independent firms at different channel levels coordinate their distribution activities by contractual agreement. Franchises such as McDonald's and Holiday Inn illustrate this type of VMS.
- An *administered* VMS exists when a strong organization (usually a manufacturer or retailer) assumes a leadership position. The leader of an administered system influences or controls the policies of other channel members so that the channel works as a team to achieve efficiencies and market impact. Companies like Procter & Gamble and Wal-Mart are widely recognized as leaders of administrative channels.

Distribution Intensity.   Distribution intensity concerns how many outlets carry a product. Choosing the right distribution intensity depends on management's targeting and positioning strategies plus product and market characteristics. Low-cost convenience products are typically available in a large number of outlets in any area. *Intensive* distribution is aimed at maximum market coverage. *Selective* distribution is achieved by only using a few distributors within a geographic area. Maytag uses selective distribution for its household appliances. The most restrictive intensity of distribution is *exclusive* distribution, which entails one or a few distributors within an area. Rolls-Royce automobiles and Chris-Craft power boats are distributed exclusively.

Channel Configuration.   Channel configuration refers to the number of levels and the specific kinds of intermediaries used at each level. The type (conventional versus VMS) of channel and the distribution intensity selected help in deciding how many channel levels to use and the kinds to use at each level. Other factors include where end users expect to buy the product and whether the producer wishes to control pricing, positioning, and brand image. Products that are more complex, customized, or expensive tend to be marketed through shorter, more direct channels than simpler, standardized, inexpensive ones. Sometimes, however, the types of intermediaries, experience, skill level, or motivation desired are not available. Some channels are difficult to break into because of existing exclusive relationships.

Price Strategies

Pricing strategies are largely determined by three interrelated decisions: (1) the decision on price position relative to competition, (2) the decision on how active price will be in the marketing program, and (3) pricing objectives. The extent of price flexibility also influences price decisions. Price position is closely linked to several other aspects of the positioning strategy such as product quality, distribution strategy, and advertising and personal selling programs. Price position establishes, for example, how price will be used in advertising and personal selling efforts.

Price Activity   Exhibit 2 illustrates the options when deciding how active price will be in the marketing program. A high–active strategy is sometimes used for prestige brands seeking an affluent image. When the buyer cannot easily evaluate the quality of a product, price may serve as a signal of value. A high–passive strategy entails marketing high-priced items by featuring nonprice factors such as product characteristics and performance. A low–active strategy is often used when price is an important factor in buyers' decisions. It is most effective for firms that have cost advantages. A low–passive strategy entails selling at a relatively low price but not featuring the low price for fear of creating or reinforcing low-quality perceptions. So-called off brands with less expensive features targeting price-sensitive market segments often feature their value or economy rather than low prices. Once decisions have been made regarding price position relative to competition and how active price will be, guidelines can be established for price objectives.

Pricing Objectives.   To survive in today's highly competitive market environment, firms need pricing objectives that are specific, attainable, and measurable. Realistic pricing objectives then require periodic monitoring to determine the effectiveness of the firm's pricing strategies. Three general categories of pricing objectives are profit-oriented, sales-oriented, and status quo. Examples of profit-oriented objectives are profit maximization, satisfactory profits, and target return on investment. Sales-

EXHIBIT 2   Pricing Options

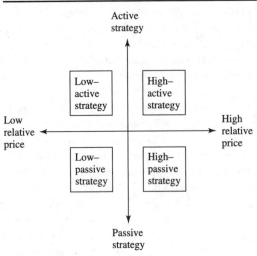

Source: David W. Cravens, *Strategic Marketing,* 5th ed. (Burr Ridge, Ill: Irwin, 1997), p. 360.

oriented pricing objectives include market share and sales maximization goals. Status quo objectives entail maintaining existing prices or meeting competitors' prices.

Price Flexibility.   Demand and cost factors determine the extent of pricing flexibility. Within these upper and lower boundaries, competition as well as legal and ethical considerations also influence pricing decisions. Management must determine where to price within the gap. In competitive markets, the feasibility range may be very narrow. New markets or emerging market segments may allow a firm more flexibility in strategy selection.

Promotion Strategies

Promotion is communication by marketers that attempts to inform, persuade, or remind present or potential customers or other selected audiences to influence their opinion or elicit a response. The promotion mix includes advertising, personal selling, sales promotion, direct marketing, and public relations. Target markets and product, distribution, and price decisions influence (1) the role of promotion strategies in the total marketing program and (2) the specific communications tasks of the promotion mix.

Major components of promotion strategy are (1) setting communication objectives, (2) deciding the role of promotion mix components in the overall promotion strategy, and (3) determining the promotion budget.

Communication Objectives.   Objectives need to be selected for the entire promotional program and for each promotion component. Certain objectives, such as sales and market share targets, are shared with other marketing program components. Illustrative promotion objectives include

- Creating or increasing buyers' awareness of a product item, line, or brand.
- Influencing buyers' attitudes toward a company, product item, line, or brand.
- Increasing the level of brand preference of the buyers in a targeted segment.
- Boosting sales and market share for specific customer or prospect targets.
- Generating repeat purchases of a brand.
- Encouraging trial of a new product.
- Attracting new customers.

Deciding the Role of Promotion Mix Components.   Promotion objectives can be linked to the specific role of each component in the promotion mix. For example, the role of the sales force may be to obtain sales or, instead, to inform the channel of distribution organizations about product features and applications. Advertising may play a major or minor role in the promotion strategy. Sales promotion (e.g., trade shows) may be used to achieve various objectives in the promotion mix.

Early in developing the promotion strategy, it is useful to set some guidelines for the promotion mix components. These guidelines help determine the strategy for each promotion component. It is necessary to decide which communications objective(s) will be the responsibility of each component. For example, advertising may be responsible for creating awareness of a new product. Sales promotion (e.g., coupons, samples) may encourage trial of the new product. Personal selling may be assigned responsibility for getting retailers to stock the new product. It is also important to decide how large each promotion component's contribution will be. Indicating the relative contribution of each component will help to determine the promotion budget.

Promotion Budget.   Theoretically, the promotion budget should be set at a level that maximizes profitability. This theory is not easy to apply, however, because it requires knowledge of the actual monetary benefits resulting from the promotion effort.[3] Factors other than promotion, such as competitors' efforts, influence sales.

The most popular and most scientific approach to setting a promotion budget is the objective and task approach. First, management sets objectives. Second, it defines the communication tools required to achieve those objectives. Then a budget is built by adding up the costs of the planned promotion activities. This approach requires that management understand the effectiveness of various promotion tools. It also assumes that achieving the objectives will be worth the costs. The major advantage of the objective and task method is that it explicitly incorporates planning into the budgeting process: Objectives are defined, alternatives are analyzed, and the costs of each element in the promotion plan are determined.

End Notes

1. Jennifer Lawrence, "Don't Look for P&G to Pare Detergents," *Advertising Age,* May 3, 1993, p. 2.
2. See, for example, David W. Cravens, *Strategic Marketing,* 5th ed., (Burr Ridge, Ill: Irwin, 1997), pp. 431–52.
3. Peter J. Danaher and Roland T. Rust, "Determining the Optimal Level of Media Spending," *Journal of Advertising Research,* January–February 1994, pp. 28–34.

CASES FOR PART VI

The seven cases in this part focus on the development of marketing programs in various types of organizations. The companies operate in the United States as well as countries such as The Netherlands, Zimbabwe, and France.

In **Dunkin' Donuts (Case 6–1),** a video case, we see an attempt to transform a firm's image from quality donut seller to bagel expert. The bagel introduction was Dunkin' Donuts' largest initiative ever and a host of problems erupted, mostly in supply and distribution. With two weeks left before the largest advertising campaign the bagel industry had ever experienced, the supply chain dried up. The purchasing director responsible for coordinating supply had to make an immediate recommendation about the continued rollout of the new product line.

The video case, **Rollerblade, Inc. (Case 6–2),** examines the company's concerns regarding brand recognition. Rollerblade's success is due to both the introduction of a new product and to the simultaneous creation of a sport. However, competition has increased dramatically and market saturation points to the need for a broader product line.

L'Oréal Nederland B.V. (Case 6–3) is the Netherlands subsidiary of the L'Oréal Group. Headquartered in Paris, L'Oréal was the largest cosmetics manufacturer in the world. The subsidiary must decide whether to introduce a facial skin care line, a hair colorant, or both. If a decision is made to market one or both of the product lines, then appropriate marketing programs must be developed.

Case 6–4, Apache Power, Inc., focuses on the introduction of a new gasoline engine. The introduction takes API into a new market of large engines, and the company has invested a substantial amount of money in the development of the engine. The product manager needs a marketing program.

Case 6–5, Capital, describes a decision facing Prisma Presse, the French subsidiary of the German publishing company Gruner+Jahr, itself a subsidiary of the giant multimedia Bertelsmann Group. Prisma Presse is considering the launch of a new business magazine tentatively called *Capital.* Should *Capital* be launched? If so, when and how?

The sole manufacturer of clear beer in Zimbabwe, **National Breweries (Case 6–6)** faces the entrance of two competitors at the same time as it is experiencing price increases, declining sales volume, and a negative perception by consumers. The marketing and public affairs director is reevaluating the company's marketing program in light of all these events.

Case 6–7, Chemical Additives Corporation–Specialty Products Group, focuses upon the company's strategy of moving away from large-volume commodity markets to niche markets. Critical to this move's success is the positioning and pricing of three corrosion inhibitors used during the transport and storage of liquid fertilizer. Market segmentation appears to be a major issue to be addressed.

CASE 6–1
DUNKIN' DONUTS

It was a hot Massachusetts day in late August 1996, and Chris Booras, the Dunkin' Donuts purchasing director responsible for coordinating supply, was feeling the heat. It was a trying time for Dunkin' Donuts as it tried to transform its image from quality donut seller to bagel expert. The bagel introduction was the largest initiative ever for Dunkin' Donuts, and a host of problems had erupted, mostly in supply and distribution. With two weeks left before the largest advertising campaign the bagel industry had ever experienced, the supply chain had dried up.

Chris Booras stared forlornly out the window. A lot was at stake here. The pressure was definitely on. Jack Shafer, the COO overseeing Dunkin' Donuts, had recently commented,

> The combination of the new Dunkin' Donuts freshly baked bagels and our legendary coffee is the key to our future growth. We have invested a year and a half developing the perfect bagel. When paired with the magic of the Dunkin' Donuts name, the equity in our coffee business, our advertising strength and our far reaching network of shops, we become uniquely positioned to lead the bagel category.[1]

Dunkin' always moved fast to stay ahead. Chris hoped he could get the supplier problems straightened out and keep pace with the expectations of Dunkin' Donuts top management.

The Backgroud

> Dunkin' Donuts will strive to be the dominant retailer of high quality donuts, bakery products and beverages in each metropolitan market in which we choose to compete.
>
> company mission statement

In 1948, Bill Rosenberg had a dream. He envisioned a morning destination shop centered around quality donuts and the freshest coffee. He opened his first donut shop, the Open Kettle, on the Southern Artery in Quincy, Massachusetts. The popularity of this shop convinced Rosenberg of his concept's potential and for the next five years, he opened one shop per year. In 1950, with a six-store operation, Rosenberg opened the first Dunkin' Donuts.

Rosenberg quickly realized that to maximize his organization's growth potential, he would have to franchise. In 1955 he signed the company's first franchise agreement, and he went to work aligning himself with business partners willing to take on the risks of the franchise system. These risks included paying Rosenberg a percentage of sales, paying a fee for the franchise name, and paying large up-front costs for land and

---

[1] Editor. *Milling and Baking News* (June 25, 1996): 1.

This case was prepared by Eric Nyman, Boston College, under the supervision of Victoria L. Crittenden, associate professor of marketing, Boston College, as the basis for class discussion rather than to illustrate either effective or ineffective handling of a managerial situation.

construction. This strategy allowed Rosenberg to grow Dunkin' Donuts to a 24-shop chain in New England with annual sales of US$3,000,000 by 1960.[2]

Astronomical growth continued into the next decade. In 1963, the 100th shop opened and the company attained revenues of US$10,000,000. In 1968, with Rosenberg at the helm as president and CEO, Dunkin' Donuts went public. Operating with the pledge to make donuts fresh every four hours and to brew fresh coffee every 14 minutes, Dunkin' Donuts reached US$44,000,000 in sales by 1969.

The 1970s was a big decade for the company. During this period, the company expanded internationally and developed new products. In 1974 the Dunkin' Munchkin was released and became one of the food service industry's most successful product spin-offs ever. The Munchkin, a donut hole, was offered in a variety of flavors and was considered to "truly be a bite-sized treat." Sales were strong, with the product remaining a mainstream product into the 1990s.

As the chain entered into the 1980s, sales reached US$300,000,000 in 1,000 shops. Plans were formulated to accelerate expansion. The strategy for growth and profits centered around distribution, advertising, new products, remodeling, and standards improvement. To implement, Dunkin' Donuts developed what would become known as the gold standard in franchise distribution when it created the first of six regional distribution centers. These regional distribution centers allowed for quick delivery to individual stores along with good pricing for all outlets in a given region. This period also marked the national advertising debut of "Fred the Baker." Fred was a hero to working class America as he rose at all hours of the night as a franchise owner to ensure that his customers were always given fresh products and a smile. Fred popularized the saying "It's time to make the donuts." Dunkin' began to remodel stores during this period as well. Brightly lit, colorful, nonsmoking stores were created to replace the dimly lit, smoky coffee shops consumers had been accustomed to. Standards were also improved to ensure freshness across all product lines.

In 1990 Dunkin' Donuts, with a firm balance sheet and strong brand equity in the morning food retail business, became an attractive takeover target. After trying unsuccessfully to ward off a hostile takeover, Dunkin' Donuts was acquired under friendly terms by Allied Domecq, a world leader in spirits and retailing. Its international spirits brands included Ballantines, Beefeater, and Kahlua. Allied was the world's leading brandy company and second largest distributor of Scotch whiskey, tequila, and liqueurs. The company had over 13,800 retail outlets comprising 4,100 pubs and 8,200 franchised stores, including the popular California-based Baskin Robbins ice cream chain. After the takeover, Dunkin' Donuts, acting as a wholly owned subsidiary of Allied Domecq, operated over 3,200 shops with total sales in excess of US$1 billion.[3]

By the mid-1990s, Dunkin' Donuts franchise stores were seeing sales of between US$20,000 and US$50,000 a month. Dunkin' Donuts reported sales of US$1.4 billion around the globe in 1995. Entering the mid-1990s, however, Dunkin' Donuts was experiencing organizational turbulence. Both of Allied Domecq's American concerns, Baskin-Robbins (based in California) and Dunkin' Donuts (headquartered in Massachusetts), were attempting to merge cultures, which was causing some discomfort on both sides. Baskin-Robbins had been experiencing flat growth for several years, and it was thought that the merge with Dunkin' Donuts would instill some life into the brand.

---

[2] The New England states include Connecticut, Maine, Massachusetts, New Hampshire, Rhode Island, and Vermont.

[3] Twenty-seven hundred of these shops were owned by Dunkin' Donuts; the rest were acquired when Dunkin' bought Mister Donuts.

Initial problems included simple logistics, resentment from the Baskin-Robbins organization over placement of Dunkin' Donuts people in high-level Baskin positions, and
general fear by all parties as to whether their jobs would continue to exist. To further
complicate matters, Dunkin' Donuts was restructuring along the lines of category management. That meant that individuals in a given department (e.g., marketing, purchasing, quality assurance) would be given a product category to manage. These categories
included bakery, beverages, and the product expected to redefine Dunkin' donuts—
bagels.

The Bagel Market

Once an ethnic specialty food, bagels had gained acceptance as an American breakfast
and lunch item. Bagels were a low-fat, boiled bread product. A study of national eating
trends conducted by the NPD Group Inc., a Chicago-area research firm, found that per
capita bagel consumption soared 65 percent between 1990 and 1995. Market reports
revealed that the bagel business was a US$2.5 billion industry by the mid-1990s.[4]

By 1995, there were over 700 bagel retail outlets and wholesale bakeries in the
United States, with annual sales of over US$1 billion. The market's growth rate was
estimated at over 30 percent.[5] Analysts projected growth to remain steady throughout
the decade. The major players in this primarily breakfast food segment were Brueg-
ger's, Manhattan Bagel, and Einstein Brothers. The rest of the market was dominated
by small chains and mom-and-pop operations. No dominant national market presence
by any one company had yet been established.

Most retailers agreed that bagels' popularity was a long-term trend. However, food
retail analysts expected shakeout as the marketplace became increasingly crowded.
Nancy Krause, V.P. of Technomic, Inc., thought that success in this industry was related to the rate of increase of bagel shops and the extent to which they cluster in the
same markets.[6]

The bagel marketplace was divided among various types of outlets. Approximately
44 percent of all bagels were sold in retail shops and bakeries, 26 percent sold at in-
store bakeries, 20 percent sold by foodservices, and 10 percent sold frozen by wholesale bakeries. At the beginning of 1995, only 15 percent of these sales were by multi-
unit chains. Furthermore, 70 percent of the bagel stores were concentrated in New
York, New Jersey, Florida, and California. This alluded to a positive growth situation
as bagel stores spread across America.[7]

The chains competed on quality of product, physical appearance of their facilities,
flavor variety of both bagels and cream cheese, and the bagel "experience" (a hard-to-
quantify atmosphere that bespoke of freshness and a homemade feel). These bagel
shops were beginning to grab market share from the dominant player in the breakfast
food category, Dunkin' Donuts, as more and more health-minded Americans jumped
on the bagel bandwagon. The product fit the perfect nutrition profile, as a plain 2.5-
ounce bagel had approximately one gram of fat. As a spokesperson from Lender's
Bagels said, "Bagels are the food of the nineties."[8]

---

[4] Brown, Jennifer. *Bagel Boom* (July 1996): 62.

[5] Malovany, Dan. *Bakery Production and Marketing* (May 24, 1995): 12.

[6] Brown, Jennifer. "Bagel Boom," *Baking & Snack,* Kanses City, Missouri: Sosland Publishing
Company, July 1996.

[7] Ibid.

[8] Malovany, Dan. "Don't Change that Dial; Wholesale Bakery Industry Trends," *Bakery Production and
Marketing,* Chicago, Illinois: Delta Communications, May 24, 1995.

The outlook for the bagel chains' future appeared to include rapid expansion through franchising and acquisition. Consolidation was predicted, so speed to market was essential. Already, Einstein Bros. had acquired Noah's Bagel, and Manhattan Bagel had joined forces with Specialty Bakeries, a franchiser of the Bagel Builders chain. The top two or three dominant players in this industry were expected to be the last ones standing. As stated by Ms. Krause, "Only those who really have established their brand image and dominance within their trade areas will survive."[9]

Dunkin' Donuts' Market Entry

In 1995 it was becoming quite clear to Dunkin' Donuts President Will Kussell and many members of senior management that the bagel industry, while hurting Dunkin' sales at that point, held a great deal of potential for the company. The Dunkin' Donuts sales mix at that time was

Coffee	65%
Donuts	25
Muffins and cookies	10

Kussell envisioned the company's sales mix changing dramatically and foresaw Dunkin' Donuts becoming the biggest and dominant player in the bagel industry. Simple math revealed that if Dunkin' Donuts jumped into the bagel business with its 2,700 North American outlets, it would more than triple the entire retail industry's 700 outlets. Furthermore, the sales opportunity that bagels could inspire in this growing billion-dollar U.S. retail market was staggering. After some initial research of the industry and a search for a high-quality supplier, Dunkin' Donuts made the decision to compete in the bagel business.

The company's goal was to have the best product in the market and to be the largest bagel retailer in the United States of America. Several research and development tests were conducted to discover the attributes that customers found most appealing in a bagel. Results of these tests showed that consumers desired a large bagel in a variety of flavors and insisted on the complementary product of cream cheese. Dunkin' Donuts then designed a bagel around these considerations and created a new cream cheese line to go with it.

The Search for Supply.   Dunkin' Donuts felt that it had developed the perfect bagel. Consistent with its outsourcing strategies for muffins and cookies, it needed someone to produce the bagel in large enough quantities to supply its geographically dispersed retail outlets.

Many suppliers wanted to get into the bagel business with Dunkin' Donuts. Manufacturing giants like Harold's Bakery Products,[10] Sara Lee, and Brooklyn Bagel Boys bid on the business. Criteria for supplier selection included a proven track record, a sizable cash flow to enter into a new business, and, most importantly, the speed to act quickly in building new lines for bagel production. No company had the existing capacity for a project of this scope. Therefore, when Harold's promised a nine-month delivery time on new bagel production lines with the ability to sign co-packer relationships in the interim, a deal was consummated. Harold's was chosen as the vendor that would supply Dunkin' Donuts with its fresh bagels.

---

[9] Brown, Jennifer. *Bagel Boom:* 62.

[10] A pseudonym is used to protect the Dunkin' Donuts supplier relationship.

Harold's gave Dunkin' Donuts a standard volume guarantee, including a nine-month construction promise for new lines. The $8 million cost of the new lines would be paid for by Harold's. However, the costs were to be amortized on these lines—meaning that the finished cost to Dunkin' Donuts for these bagels would be lower over the long term. Dunkin' provided Harold's with a volume guarantee along with the promise that outside vendors would not be looked at unless Harold's violated the supply guarantee. The supply guarantee centered around production numbers at Harold's and at co-packers' plants. (Co-packers were short term, outside vendors that would assist Harold's in supplying the Dunkin' system with bagels while Harold's' lines were being built.)

Dunkin' Donuts' Planned Rollout

Using Harold's theoretical capacity numbers on lines that had not yet been built, along with the projected capacity of co-packers, the Dunkin' Donuts marketing team went to work. A national rollout plan was developed that called for 2,700 stores to be supplied with bagels in one year. Some objections were raised by both Purchasing and Quality Assurance, as both departments pointed out the risks of creating such an aggressive schedule. However, these concerns were overshadowed by senior management's drive to get fiscal year 1997 (which started in September 1996) off to a great start. The new budget was built around the bagel program being a rousing success, with franchisees targeted to achieve a 10 percent growth in sales with the $0.55 bagel, up from an average of 2 to 4 percent.[11] Cream cheese would sell for US$1.29 to US$1.99. Expected bagel-related sales per store were projected at over US$1,000 a week for many stores.

There were several steps to follow for a Dunkin' franchisee to get into the bagel program. The cost of construction (to the franchisee) was expected to be around $25,000, as all enrolling shops were required to remodel with new signs, bagel cases, and cream cheese merchandisers to give the look and feel of a bagel enterprise. The Marketing Department expected that 80 percent of all shops in a given market would enroll and used that number as a goal for franchisee sell-in. Importantly all shops did not have to sign up as bagel carriers. However, a franchisee that did not sign up initially would go to end of the line on the rollout schedule. This could mean that a shop in Boston that did not sign up on the first rollout opportunity could have to wait up to nine months while the rest of the country's 2,700 stores were remodeled before being allowed to sell bagels. Furthermore, all participating shops had to agree to carry all of Dunkin' Donuts' proprietary bagel products (including all flavor varieties of bagels and all cream cheese types created by the company).

Before attempting to sell the product to franchisees, Dunkin' Donuts selected 20 of the best stores (termed fast-track stores—traditionally high performers) in various markets to serve as model stores. Dunkin' Donuts then used the fast-track stores' impressive sales results with the new bagels to entice other franchisees to join the bagel program. The average fast-track store had a sales boost of 15 percent with the new bagel program.

The U.S. rollout was to start in the New England states, the company's strongest sales region. From there, the rollout would go on to the Mid-Atlantic (which included New York, Baltimore, and Washington D.C.), continue to the Midwest (where markets such as South Bend, Indiana, existed), and finish off in the Southeast (which included

---

[11] This would mean greater profits for Dunkin' Donuts, which received a percentage of sales from the franchisees both for marketing support and for the brand equity the Dunkin' Donuts name provided.

Atlanta, Georgia, and Orlando, Florida). Once this phase of the rollout was complete, Dunkin' Donuts then planned to head westward, where its presence was much smaller, and then into Canada. The plan was to supply 65 stores a week with bagels starting the second week of May 1996 and continue until all interested Dunkin' Donuts stores were selling bagels.

Sales Projections.   Taking an aggressive approach, the bagel marketing team used past and present data to determine how many bagels the average shop would use. A case contained 96 bagels. The highest performing fast-track store (in South Weymouth, Massachusetts) had sold 60 cases a week of the new bagels—amazingly, without any advertising support!

Bagel usage projections, therefore, built in this pre-advertising sales jump. The Marketing Department projected that the average store would sell 18 cases of the new bagels each week before advertising. Once advertising had begun, historical Dunkin' figures showed that a 100 percent sales jump usually occurred. With this prediction, a US$25 million advertising campaign was planned.

The Crisis

Dunkin' Donuts' bagel team projected that, with advertising, it would be selling almost 40 cases of bagels a week per store. Through the month of July 1996, with no advertising, the current system supply of 14,500 cases per week was being used up on a weekly basis. This presented both short- and long-term problems.

In the short term, volume promises from the supplier were not being met, which was hurting the rollout plan. The rollout had already been delayed for three weeks in July, as demand had exceeded capacity. It was costly to delay the rollout, as lost sales could never be recaptured.

Supplying the system long term had presented challenges as well. Harold's was already experiencing several problems with regard to constructing the new lines. Harold's was having difficulty locating the proper equipment as well as suffering product-related problems with one of its co-packers.

The Decision

At a supplier meeting, President Kussell had stated,

> Bagels are a tremendous opportunity for our company. It is once in a lifetime that an opportunity comes along in the food service industry with this kind of growth. The speed at which the bagel market is growing is the kind of growth that high technology companies in the Internet are seeing. We cannot afford not to be in this game. Another point, however, is a business decision. I want to be out ahead of the competition. I don't want to send the message that we are pulling back, only that we are plowing ahead.

Chris Booras had several decisions to make. Should the rollout be slowed? Could the shops delayed in July be added back into the rollout schedule? Should advertising be pushed back and, if so, to what date? Should the contract with Harold's be reevaluated? Should Dunkin' Donuts begin looking for a new supplier?

These decisions were the basis for three options under consideration by Booras and the Dunkin' Donuts bagel team:

1. They could continue the rollout, at the current pace, with a partial product line.

2. They could slow the rollout by limiting advertising or by limiting the pace of store expansion.

3. They could stop the rollout until there was some certainty of supply.

If the Dunkin' team decided to stop the rollout until supply was guaranteed, they would have to do one of two things: (1) work with Harold's to find more co-packers in the short term or (2) terminate the contract with Harold's, since Harold's had been unable to keep its short-term supply commitments, and begin the process of finding a new supplier. Before dissolving the contract with Harold's, however, the Dunkin' team had to keep in mind the rumor that all U.S. production facilities capable of making bagels were signing long-term supplier contracts with different firms, leaving very few opportunities for additional capacity to be obtained.

Chris Booras knew that his and his team's reputations were on the line with Allied Domecq and the franchise community. And, a recommendation had to be forthcoming immediately!

CASE 6–2
ROLLERBLADE, INC.

Mary Horwath, vice president of marketing services and international at Rollerblade, Inc., summarized Rollerblade's success as a function of introducing a product along with the simultaneous creation of a sport. As an official of the number one leader in in-line skate sales in the 1990s, however, Horwath cringed when she heard people say that they were going "Rollerblading" on non-Rollerblade skates.

With at least 30 competitors in the in-line skate market, Rollerblade had to begin focusing upon brand recognition for Rollerblade skates. One of Horwath's major objectives was to make the Rollerblade skate distinct from the competition's products, all the while keeping *Rollerblade* from becoming a generic household term as had happened to brands such as Aspirin, Thermos, Yo-Yo, Shredded Wheat, and Lanolin. Building brand recognition in a market that could reach $1 billion by the late 1990s was critical for Rollerblade, Inc.

The Company

As a 19-year-old goaltender for a minor league hockey team, Scott Olson divined a simple idea that soon led him to multimillionaire status. The simple idea was ice skates that worked without ice.

In 1979, Olson came across a pair of roller skates where the wheels were arranged in a single row rather than two by two. This "in-line" skate originated in the Netherlands in the 1700s and was said to be the first roller skate.[1] Although slow and clumsy, the skate provided the feel of skating on ice. As a hockey player himself, Olson knew the outstanding potential of a skate targeted toward hockey players that could simulate the feel of ice skating but allow the hockey player to perform off the ice and during the off-season.

After locating the manufacturer of the in-line skate and buying up back stock (the manufacturer had quit making the skate by then), Olson proceeded to refine the skate (via good skate boots and better wheels for a faster, smoother ride) and began building them in his basement. In 1983, Olson's company, Rollerblade, Inc., based in Minnesota, became the only manufacturer of in-line skates. Olson soon sold most of his holdings in Rollerblade, Inc., to Robert O. Naegele Jr. and, in 1985, Olson left Rollerblade after a business dispute.[2]

The success of the company continued through the late 1980s and into the 1990s with Rollerblade, Inc., maintaining its number one position in a growing market expe-

---

[1] In-line skating was a fad in the 1860s.

[2] Olson introduced Switch-It skates in 1985. These skates had interchangeable ice and in-line blades. Fifty percent of this business was sold in 1990 and Olson went on to start two more new businesses. Nuskate Inc. focused on a product that married in-line skates to a cross-country ski track exerciser. O.S. Designs sold other of Olson's sporting good designs, such as a lightweight golf bag with wheels and built-in pull handle.

This case was prepared by Victoria L. Crittenden, associate professor of marketing at Boston College, as the basis for class discussion rather than to illustrate either effective or ineffective handling of a managerial situation. Research assistance was provided by Jennifer Fraser and David Angus, Boston College. All material was from secondary sources. Revised 1997.

riencing increased competitive activity. In 1991, Rollerblade, Inc., embarked on a partnership with Nordica Sportsystem (Italy). Nordica, a division of Edizione Holding (controlled by the Benetton family) and the world's number one ski boot maker, purchased 50 percent of Rollerblade, Inc., for an undisclosed sum.[3] Edizione Holding's product lines, under the Benetton Sportsystem umbrella, also included Prince tennis rackets, Asolo mountain boots, and Kastle skis.

In-Line Skating

Around 5,000 new sports and recreation products entered the market annually. Annual sales in this market totaled around US$31 billion. The U.S. economy during the early 1990s was said to be the cause of a downturn in sales of high-cost sports equipment for skiing and boating. However, this same downturn led to fast growth in areas such as camping, tennis, and all types of personal fitness products.

A 1996 Sporting Goods Manufacturers Association recreational and athletic survey found in-line skating to be the number one "frequent pursuit" of youth. In-line skating had become prominent enough to have its own industry association, the International In-Line Skate Association. After in-line skating, the other top 10 recreational/athletic activities were (in descending order) basketball, touch football, slow-pitch softball, volleyball, running, baseball, freshwater fishing, tent camping, and soccer. In-line skating was also America's fastest growing youth sport, with a 275 percent increase in frequent skaters from 1992 to 1996.

By 1990, sales of in-line skates were around $120 million, with Rollerblade capturing approximately 70 percent of the market. By 1993, the in-line skate market had become a $300 million industry with Rollerblade still the leader, accounting for 60 percent of the market. However, by 1995, the U.S. market for in-line skates and related equipment topped $650 million. Worldwide, in-line skate sales were projected to peak around $1 billion by 1998.

Estimates were that in-line skates were used by over 19 million Americans in 1995. Approximately half of these users were youths (ages 6 to 17 years). Almost 15 percent of all American households reported owning/using in-line skates. In-line skaters were evenly divided between males and females. It was estimated that worldwide there were over 30 million in-line skating participants.

As the number of in-line skaters increased, so did the number of in-line skating injuries.[4] With an estimated 83,000 skating injuries in 1994, in-line skating had been deemed a health hazard by the U.S. government. However, a full set of safety gear (gloves, elbow pads, knee pads, helmet, wrist guards) could be purchased for around $100.

By the mid-1990s, there were an estimated 30 competitors in the in-line skate market. Rollerblade held about 60 percent of the market, with First Team Sports, Inc., ranking second with 20 percent of the market. While the remainder of the market was comprised of knock-off versions, Bauer Precision In-Line Skates was considered a possible number three in the market. Olson's Switch-It skate (owned by Innovative

---

[3] Nordica ski boots and Rollerblade in-line skates were made from the same basic plastic composite material. Machines at the Nordica production plant in Italy could switch easily between components for the ski boot and the Rollerblade skate shell. Plans were for up to 50 percent of Rollerblade production to take place at Nordica plants. In the United States, Rollerblade operated out of its Minnesota facility and Nordica out of its Vermont facility.

[4] In-line skaters could reach speeds as high as 30 miles per hour.

Sport Systems, Inc.) was a rival, as was Fisher-Price with its size-adjustable kids' skates. Taiwanese knock-offs were capturing a large percentage of the low end of the market. The basic in-line skate was not difficult to copy. Rollerskate, ice skate, and boot manufacturers generally possessed the capabilities to manufacture some form of in-line skate.

The marketing effort for many new sports and recreation products began, traditionally, in February of each year at the Super Show in Atlanta, Georgia—a convention of around 90,000 buyers and sellers of sports and recreation equipment. Held in a garage sale environment, the New Products Show took up an entire convention hall at the Super Show. In a typical year, around 2,000 new products were introduced at the New Products Show.

Rollerblade's Marketing Strategy

Mary Horwath joined Rollerblade, Inc., in 1987 as director of promotion. At that time, the company had 16 employees, annual sales of less than US$3 million, and hockey players as customers. Horwath's challenge was to grow the company. To do this, she had to reposition the skate to attract a wider range of customers—with a marketing plan budget of US$200,000.

Initial Marketing Strategy.   Horwath relied on guerrilla marketing tactics to reposition Rollerblade products. Horwath described these tactics as aggressive, unorthodox methods that were fairly cheap but attracted positive publicity quickly. She determined the primary U.S. market for Rollerblade skates to be 46 million active adults, primarily between ages 18 and 35.

To get people talking about Rollerblade skates, Horwath gave the product to high-profile people such as cyclists, skiers, runners, walkers, football players, surfers, ice skaters, journalists, and celebrities. The publicity generated by these giveaways was worth about US$250,000 in advertising. Many of the people were seen on television or in magazines wearing their Rollerblades.

The next step involved cross-promotional tie-ins with other companies targeting the same audience. A joint promotion sweepstakes in 1987 with General Mills' Golden Graham cereal resulted in Rollerblade giving away 1,000 pairs of skates in return for Rollerblade products being displayed on 6 million cereal boxes. Also in 1987, Rollerblade skates were included in a feature-length film on action sports sponsored by Swatch. The film appeared on 40 college campuses across the United States. Rollerblade had to pay for additional filming and sponsorship rights only. Free exposure also occurred when Procter & Gamble and Pepsi featured Rollerblade skates in commercials.

Horwath then redesigned Rollerblade's packages and displays to better depict the company's mission of "fun." Also, she created videos for in-store displays. Twelve demonstration vans were then sent to community events targeting sports-minded people (such as the Los Angeles Marathon) to let people try the skates for free.

Finally, Horwath created Team Rollerblade. Team Rollerblade was a group of elite demonstration skaters who traveled around the United States appearing at top sporting events. The team displayed the sporty, exciting, healthy, and fun components of in-line skating. Early on, the team performed at the Super Bowl halftime and the opening ceremonies of the Winter Olympics in France.

The guerrilla marketing strategy worked better than expected. Rollerblade's sales skyrocketed between 1989 and 1991 from less than US$20 million to just under

US$90 million, and the in-line skate market expanded dramatically. Additionally, Rollerblade skates received "product of the year" status from both *Time* and *Fortune* in 1990.

In sum, Horwath's "Cheap Skate Strategies" focused upon four points:[5]

1. Give your product away to celebrities and athletes who attract media attention.
2. Team up with other companies to promote your product, but make sure the product you're affiliated with is used by the people you want to reach.
3. Demonstrate the product in places or at events where your prime target audience gathers.
4. Create related projects such as teams, books, and videos—anything that will catch consumers' eyes.

Product Line.   Rollerblade's products were initially positioned in the higher-price segment of the market. Until 1992, Rollerbladers ranged from $100 to $400 in price and were not available through mass merchandising stores such as Woolworth's, Ames, Target, or Wal-Mart. Rollerblade's strategy was to distribute products through sports stores and in-line skating specialty stores. However, the BladeRunner line of affordable skates and gear was introduced in mass merchandise stores in 1992.

While Horwath described Rollerblade's target market as the 46 million active adults between 18 and 35 years of age, she recognized diversity in this large group. Different market segments were defined based upon use: street hockey, exercise, transportation, racing, complex acrobatics, and fun. Examples of in-line designs targeted toward specific use segments included the Metroblade for transportation, the Problade for racing, the Mondoblade for the first-time skater, and the Microblade for kids.

Rollerblade also offered in-line skate apparel called Bladegear and a complete line of skating accessories such as knee pads, wrist guards, and helmets. As well, Rollerblade spearheaded in-line skating safety campaigns, including the use of proper equipment.

Rollerblade's Marketing Strategy, 1991–95.   Rollerblade's guerrilla marketing strategy led it to success both in creating the in-line skate market and in attaining the number one spot in the market. After such a successful start, the company did not want to veer too far from the strategy. However, the rapid growth market of the 1990s was bringing in many new competitors. If and when there was an industry shakeout, Horwath wanted Rollerblade to come out on top. Therefore, Rollerblade's marketing plan maintained many of the guerrilla tactics that had helped Rollerblade get to its 1991 number one position, while adding tactics that could help the company battle competitors directly and create brand recognition for Rollerblade skates.

Partnering became a prominent theme of Rollerblade's marketing strategy during the 1990s. Rollerblade and Procter & Gamble's Sunny Delight juice drink joined together for a joint communications campaign. There were coupon tie-ins and television spot airings on MTV. Rollerblade teamed with Coca-Cola Foods' HI-C to co-sponsor a 10-city "Rollerblade America Tour," which featured in-line skating races and demonstrations. HI-C's input into the co-sponsorship included extensive on-site signage and sampling. Mattel launched a Rollerblade Barbie and Friends line. The Rollerblade trademark appeared on the box, with Rollerblade coupons inside. Tie-ins for 1993 and 1994 were with Northwest Airlines and Warner Brothers. Since safety was such an

---

[5] " 'How I Did It' Guerrilla Marketing 101," *Working Woman,* December 1991, pp. 23–24.

important issue with in-line skating, Rollerblade expected its long-term relationship with Benetton to prove beneficial in its expansion into accessories such as knee pads. In 1994, Rollerblade became the exclusive distributor of Black Hole wheels, bearings, and aftermarket accessories via a strategic partnership with Black Hole.

By 1991, Rollerblade had expanded into a little conventional print advertising. One ad featured a skater rolling down a mountain highway. The caption read, "It's kinda like running a marathon. It's kinda like eating a hot-fudge sundae. Rollerblade." In 1992, measured media spending was just under $1 million. By 1993, the company had its first-ever television commercial, which was provided to its distributors for use in local markets. The 30-second spot was filmed in New Zealand. It depicted an in-line skater passing a carriage transporting an Amish girl. The skater and the girl exchanged glances before a voice-over said, "There are but a few ways to separate yourself from this hectic world. Rollerblade—let yourself go."

Team Rollerblade, featuring 25 skaters in black-and-neon attire, was also an important element of the marketing strategy in the 1990s. The team traveled, annually, around the United States performing stunts and skate dancing at festivals, theme parks, fairs, college campuses, and playgrounds. The tours were called "Rock 'N' Rollerblade Tours."

Rollerblade's most popular skates retailed for US$139 to US$199. The BladeRunner skate, however, retailed for less than US$100, with the company's top of the line retailing for as high as US$500.

Trying to position Rollerblade as a lifestyle rather than just a product, Rollerblade offered its Bladegear line of sportswear. The line included bright-colored lycra and nylon ensembles and T-shirts. The T-shirts were emblazoned with helpful hints such as "Skate Smart" and "Don't Skate Naked." There were plans to open Rollerblade boutiques in some sporting goods stores around the United States. The company's products were distributed worldwide, including Europe, Asia, Israel, Australia, and New Zealand.

Competitors on the Move

In 1995, sneaker giant Nike Inc. purchased Canstar Sports Inc. Canstar owned the Bauer and Cooper brands of ice hockey and in-line skating products. Bauer marketed in-line skates under the name Rollerz. Sales in 1995 were expected to increase 67 percent over 1994 figures. Nike debuted with a "Nike Inflatable Roller Hockey Rink" in a 1995 trade show in Munich, Germany.

The U.S. headquarters for Roces of Italy expected 1995 sales to top US$20 million. Strong gains were expected from Japan and Germany as well.

Koho, a Canadian hockey equipment manufacturer, entered the in-line skate market in 1994. Recognizing that the company name was well known in the recreational market, Koho targeted the roller hockey market. The company's customers covered Japan, Hong Kong, and Brazil in addition to the United States.

Oxygen, a unit of Austrian-based Atomic Ski, focused on stunt skaters and roller hockey players in Austria, Japan, and other Asian countries. Oxygen's product was a space-age–style skate that displayed a noticeable style difference from the competitors.

The Future

With the in-line skate market expected to peak by 1998, Rollerblade, Inc., knew that it needed to (1) build brand recognition for the Rollerblade name and (2) continue expanding its product offerings. Horwath wondered too if now was the time for Rollerblade to begin a shift away from the company's traditional pull strategy to more of a push approach.

Random House's *Webster's College Dictionary* had plans to include Rollerblade as a word in its next edition. While the name would be recognized as a trademark with the first letter in upper case, there was still uncertainty as to whether the verb form (*rollerblading*) and the shorter form (*blading*) would be included and, if so, whether they would be listed as trademarks. Horwath knew that loss of the Rollerblade name to the dreaded "genericide" would be horrible for the company.

With concerns about market saturation, Rollerblade needed to expand its product offerings to encompass the total skater and to increase the number of new participants. The youth and roller hockey markets seemed to hold promise. The pending merger of the World Roller Hockey League and Roller Hockey International could help the sport increase its television coverage.

Yet another fear lodged itself in the back of Horwath's head. Rollerblade, Inc., and other in-line skate manufacturers had stolen the rollerskate cash cow. Was there a new technology that could preempt in-line skating? Horwath was familiar with a new sport called snow skating. In this sport, snow skaters could slide down a mountain slower than skiers, without ski poles, using a motion similar to in-line skating. The snow skate looked like ski boots with smooth soles. Horwath knew that Rollerblade could not sit back with the "We've got it made" attitude.

Sources

Beard, Betty, "Getting Rolling: Mastering In-Line Skates Is Tough, but It's Worth It (Well, Maybe)," *The Arizona Republic,* August 20, 1994, p. D1.

Brauer, David, "Enterprise: Tough Sledding for Snow Skates," *Corporate Report Minnesota,* March 1995, p. 12.

Bultmeyer, Suzanne, "Lining Up Skaters," *Sporting Goods Business,* January 1994, pp. 65–66.

Comte, Elizabeth, "Blade Runner," *Forbes,* October 12, 1992, pp. 114–17.

Fahey, Alison, and Scott Hume, "Marketers Team in Time of Trouble," *Advertising Age,* February 18, 1991, p. 36.

Goerne, Carrie, "Rollerblade Reminds Everyone That Its Success Is Not Generic," *Marketing News,* March 2, 1992, pp. 1–2.

Greising, David, "First Team Sports: A Fleet No. 2 in the Rollerblade Derby," *Business Week,* May 24, 1993, pp. 67–68.

" 'How I Did It' Guerrilla Marketing 101," *Working Woman,* December 1991, pp. 23–24.

Jensen, Jeff, "Rollerblade Teams with Hi-C, Warner in Summer Tie-Ins," *Advertising Age,* June 14, 1993.

Macnow, Glen, "New Ideas for a Sporting Chance," *Nation's Business,* December 1992, pp. 62–63.

Marcial, Gene, "The Picks of a Pro Whose List Gained 18% Last Year," *Business Week,* January 25, 1993, p. 82.

McCabe, Kathy, "In-Line Skating's Big Prize," *Boston Globe,* August 28, 1995, p. 17.

Janofsky, Michael, "In-Line Skating Injuries Are Soaring," *The Des Moines Register,* June 10, 1994.

"Outdoor Sports Score," *Marketing News,* January 6, 1997, p. 2.

"Synergy Standouts," *Sporting Goods Business,* February 1994, p. 74.

"The Future Is Already Here," *Across the Board,* January 1994, pp. 22–25.

Therrien, Lois, "Rollerblade Is Skating in Heavier Traffic," *Business Week,* June 24, 1991, pp. 114–15.

Waters, Jennifer, "Rollerblade Sales Rumors Gain Fuel," *Minneapolis–St. Paul City Business,* May 12, 1995, p. 1.

CASE 6–3
L'ORÉAL NEDERLAND B.V.

Yolanda van der Zande, director of the Netherlands L'Oréal subsidiary, faced two tough decisions and was discussing them with Mike Rourke, her market manager for cosmetics and toiletries. "We have to decide whether to introduce the Synergie skin care line and Belle Couleur permanent hair colorants." Synergie had recently been successfully introduced in France, the home country for L'Oréal. Belle Couleur had been successfully marketed in France for two decades. Mr. Rourke responded:

> Yes, and if we decide to go ahead with an introduction we'll also need to develop marketing programs for the product lines. Fortunately, we only need to think about marketing, since the products will still be manufactured in France.

Ms. van der Zande replied:

> Right, but remember the marketing decisions on these lines are critical. Both of these lines are part of the Garnier family brand name. Currently Ambre Solaire (a sun screen) is the only product we distribute with the Garnier name in the Netherlands. But headquarters would like us to introduce more Garnier product lines into our market over the next few years, and it's critical that our first product launches in this line be successful.

Mr. Rourke interjected, "But we already sell other brands of L'Oréal products in our market. If we introduce Garnier, what will happen to them?" After some more discussion, Ms. van der Zande suggested:

> Why don't you review what we know about the Dutch market. We've already done extensive marketing research on consumer reactions to Synergie and Belle Couleur. Why don't you look at it and get back to me with your recommendations in two weeks.

Background

In 1992 the L'Oréal Group was the largest cosmetics manufacturer in the world. Headquartered in Paris, it had subsidiaries in over 100 countries. In 1992 its sales were $6.8 billion (a 12 percent increase over 1991) and net profits were $417 million (a 14 percent increase). France contributed 24 percent of total worldwide sales, Europe (both western and eastern countries excluding France) provided 42 percent, and the United States and Canada together accounted for 20 percent; the rest of the world accounted for the remaining 14 percent. L'Oréal's European subsidiaries were in one of two groups: (1) major countries (England, France, Germany, and Italy) or (2) minor countries (the Netherlands and nine others).

The company believed that innovation was its critical success factor. It thus in-

This case was prepared by Frederick W. Langrehr, Valparaiso University, Lee Dahringer, Butler University, and Anne Stöcker. This case was written with the cooperation of management, solely for the purpose of stimulating student discussion. All events and individuals are real, but names have been disguised. We appreciate the help of J. B. Wilkinson and V. B. Langrehr on earlier drafts of this case.

vested heavily in research and development and recovered its investment through global introductions of its new products. All research was centered in France. As finished products were developed, they were offered to subsidiaries around the world. Because brand life cycles for cosmetics could be very short, L'Oréal tried to introduce one or two new products per year in each of its worldwide markets. International subsidiaries could make go/no go decisions on products, but they generally did not have direct input into the R&D process. In established markets, such as the Netherlands, any new product line introduction had to be financed by the current operations in that country.

L'Oréal marketed products under its own name as well as under a number of other individual and family brand names. For example, it marketed Anaïs Anaïs perfume, the high-end Lancôme line of cosmetics, and L'Oréal brand hair care products. In the 1970s it acquired Laboratoires Garnier, and this group was one of L'Oréal's largest divisions. In France, with a population of about 60 million people, Garnier was a completely separate division, and its sales force competed against the L'Oréal division. In the Netherlands, however, the market was much smaller (about 15 million people), and Garnier and L'Oréal products would be marketed by the same sales force.

Dutch consumers had little, if any, awareness or knowledge of Garnier and had not formed a brand image. The Garnier sunscreen was a new product and few Dutch women knew of the brand. It was, therefore, very important that any new Garnier products launched in the Netherlands have a strong concept and high market potential. To accomplish this, the products needed to offer unique, desired, and identifiable differential advantages to Dutch consumers. Products without such an edge were at a competitive disadvantage, and would be likely not only to fail but to create a negative association with the Garnier name, causing potential problems for future Garnier product introductions.

The Dutch Market

In the late 1980s, 40 percent of the Dutch population (about the same percentage as in France) was under 25 years old. Consumers in this age group were the heaviest users of cosmetics and toiletries. But, like the rest of Europe, the Dutch population was aging and the fastest-growing population segments were the 25-or-older groups.

Other demographic trends included the increasing number of Dutch women working outside of the home. The labor force participation rate of women in the Netherlands was 29 percent. This was much lower than the 50 percent or above in the United Kingdom or United States, but the number of women working outside the home was increasing faster in the Netherlands than it was in the United Kingdom or the United States. Dutch women were also delaying childbirth. As a result of these trends, women in the Netherlands were exhibiting greater self-confidence and independence; women had more disposable income and more of them were using it to buy cosmetics for use on a daily basis.

Despite their rising incomes, Dutch women still shopped for value, especially in cosmetics and toiletries. In the European Union (EU), the Netherlands ranked fourth in per capita income; but it was only sixth in per capita spending on cosmetics and toiletries. Thus the Dutch per capita spending on personal care products was only 60 percent of the amount spent per capita in France or Germany. As a result of both a small population (15 million Dutch to 350 million EU residents) and lower per capita consumption, the Dutch market accounted for only 4 percent of total EU sales of cosmetics and toiletries.

Synergie

Synergie was a line of facial skin care products consisting of moisturizing cream, anti-aging day cream, antiwrinkle cream, cleansing milk, mask, and cleansing gel. It was made with natural ingredients, and its advertising slogan in France was "The alliance of science and nature to prolong the youth of your skin."

Skin Care Market.   The skin care market was the second largest sector of the Dutch cosmetics and toiletries market. For the past five quarters unit volume had been growing at an annual rate of 12 percent and dollar sales at a rate of 16 percent. This category consisted of hand creams, body lotions, all-purpose creams, and facial products. Products within this category were classified by price and product type. Skin care products produced by institutes such as Shisedo or Estée Lauder were targeted at the high end of the market. These lines were expensive and sold through personal service perfumeries that specialized in custom sales of cosmetics and toiletries. At the other end of the price scale were mass market products like Ponds, which were sold in drugstores and supermarkets. In the last couple of years a number of companies, including L'Oréal, had begun to offer products in the midprice range. For example its Plénitude line was promoted as a high-quality, higher-priced—but still mass market—product.

Skin care products could also be divided into care and cleansing products. Care products consisted of day and night creams; cleansing products were milks and tonics. The current trend in the industry was to stretch the lines by adding specific products targeted at skin types such as sensitive, greasy, or dry. An especially fast-growing category consisted of antiaging and antiwrinkling creams. Complementing this trend was the emphasis on scientific development and natural ingredients.

Almost 50 percent of the 5 million Dutch women between the ages of 15 and 65 used traditional skin care products. The newer specialized products had a much lower penetration, as shown in Exhibit 1.

The sales breakdown by type of retailer for the mid- and lower-priced brands is shown in Exhibits 2 and 3.

EXHIBIT 1   Usage of Skin Care Products by Dutch Women

Product	Percentage of Women Using
Day cream	46%
Cleansers	40
Mask	30
Tonic	26
Antiaging cream	3

EXHIBIT 2   Sales Breakdown for Skin Care Products in Supermarkets and Drugstores

Type of Store	Unit Sales (%)	Dollar Sales (%)
Supermarkets	18%	11%
Drugstores	82	89
	100	100

EXHIBIT 3   Sales Breakdown for Skin Care Products by Type of Drugstore

Type of Drugstore	Unit Sales (%)	Dollar Sales (%)
Chains	57%	37%
Large independent	31	39
Small independent	12	24
	100	100

EXHIBIT 4   Competitive Product Lines of Cosmetics

	Price Range (Guilders)*	Positioning
Lower End	9.50–11.50	Mild, modest price, complete line
Nivea Visage†	5.95–12.95	Antiwrinkle
Ponds		
Middle		
Dr. vd Hoog	10–11.95	Sober, nonglamorous, no illusions, but real help, natural, efficient, relatively inexpensive
Oil of Olaz (Procter & Gamble)	12 (day cream only)	Moisturizing, antiaging
Plénitude (L'Oréal)	10.95–19.95	Delay the signs of aging
Synergie	11.95–21.95	The alliance of science and nature to prolong the youth of your skin
Upper End		
Yvs Rocher	10–26.95	Different products for different skins, natural ingredients
Ellen Betrix (Estée Lauder)	12.95–43.50	Institute line with reasonable prices, luxury products at nonluxury prices

* One dollar = 1.8 guilders; one British pound = 2.8 guilders; 1 deutschmark = 1.1 guilders.

† Although Nivea Visage had a similar price range to Dr. vd Hoog, consumers perceived Nivea as a lower-end product.

Competition.   There were numerous competitors. Some product lines, such as Oil of Olaz (Oil of Olay in the United States) by Procter & Gamble and Plénitude by L'Oréal, were offered by large multinational companies; other brands, for example, Dr. vd Hoog and Rocher, were offered by regional companies. Some companies offered a complete line, while others, like Oil of Olaz, offered one or two products. Exhibit 4 lists a few of the available lines along with the price ranges and positioning statements.

The Dutch market was especially competitive for new brands like Oil of Olaz and Plénitude. The rule of thumb in the industry was that share of voice for a brand (the percent of total industry advertising spent by the company) should be about the same as its market share. Thus a company with 10 percent market share should have had advertising expenditures around 10 percent of total industry advertising expenditures. But there were deviations from this rule. Ponds, an established and well-known company with loyal customers, had about 9 percent share of the market (units) but only accounted for about 2.5 percent of total industry ad expenditures. Alternatively, new brands like Oil of Olaz (10 percent market share, 26 percent share of voice) and Plénitude (5 percent market share, 13 percent share of voice), spent much more. The higher ad spending for these brands was necessary to develop brand awareness and, ideally, brand preference.

Any innovative products or new product variations in a line could be quickly copied. Retailers could develop and introduce their own private labels in four months; manufacturers could develop a competing product and advertising campaign in six months. Manufacturers looked for new product ideas in other countries and then transferred the product concept or positioning strategy across national borders. They also monitored competitors' test markets. Since a test market typically lasted nine months, a competitor could introduce a product before a test market was completed.

Consumer Behavior.   Consumers tended to be loyal to their current brands. This loyalty resulted from the possible allergic reaction to a new product. Also, facial care products were heavily advertised and sold on the basis of brand image. Thus users linked self-concept with a brand image, and this increased the resistance to switching. While all consumers had some loyalty, the strength of this attachment to a brand increased with the age of the user. Finally, establishing a new brand was especially difficult since Dutch women typically purchased facial creams only once or twice a year. Dutch women were showing an increasing interest in products with "natural" ingredients, but they were not as familiar as the French with technical product descriptions and terms.

Market Research Information.   Earlier, Mike Rourke had directed his internal research department to conduct some concept and use tests for the synergie products. The researchers had sampled 200 women between the ages of 18 and 55 who used skin care products three or more times per week. They sampled 55 Plénitude users, 65 Dr. vd Hoog users, and 80 users of other brands.

The participants reacted positively to synergie concept boards containing the positioning statement and the terminology associated with the total product line. On a seven-point scale with 7 being the most positive, the mean score for the Synergie line for all the women in the sample was 4.94. The evaluations of the women who used the competing brands, Plénitude and Dr. vd Hoog, were similar, at 4.97 and 4.88, respectively.

EXHIBIT 5   **Buying Intentions for Synergie Products**

	All Participants	*Plénitude Users*	*Dr. vd Hoog Users*	*Other Brand Users*
Price Not Known				
Antiaging daycream				
After trial	5.37*	5.63	5.00	5.42
After use	5.26	5.55	5.08	5.17
Moisturizing cream				
After trail	5.34	5.60	5.38	5.11
After use	5.51	5.74	5.56	5.22
Price Known				
Antiaging daycream				
After trial	3.75	4.13	3.82	3.44
After use	3.60	3.76	3.54	3.54
Certainly buy†	24%	21%	23%	27%
Moisturizing cream				
After trial	4.08	4.36	4.17	3.77
After use	4.06	4.26	4.13	3.78
Certainly buy	39%	52%	38%	30%

* Seven-point scale with 7 being most likely to buy.
† Response to a separate question asking certainty of buying with "certainly buy" as the highest choice.

EXHIBIT 6   **Major Brands of Hair Colorant**

Market Shares of	1987	1988	1989
Upper end (14.95 guilders)			
Recital (L'Oréal brand)	35%	34%	33%
Guhl	9	12	14
Belle Couleur (12.95 guilders)	—	—	—
Lower-priced (9.95 guilders)			
Andrelon	12	14	17
Poly Couleur	24	23	21
Others	20	17	15
Total	100	100	100

The researchers then conducted an in-depth analysis of two major products in the line, antiaging day cream and the moisturizing cream. Participants reported their buying intentions after they tried the Synergie product once and again after they used it for a week. Some participants were told the price and others did not know the price. The results of this analysis are shown in Exhibit 5, on page 428.

Belle Couleur

Belle Couleur was a line of permanent hair coloring products. It had been sold in France for about two decades and was the market leader. In France the line had 22 shades comprising mostly natural shades and a few strong red or very bright, light shades. It was positioned as reliably providing natural colors with the advertising line "natural colors, covers all gray."

Hair Coloring Market.   There were two types of hair coloring: semipermanent and permanent. Semipermanent colors washed out after five or six shampooings. Permanent colors only disappeared as the hair grew out from the roots. Nearly three-quarters (73 percent) of Dutch women who colored their hair used a permanent colorant. Over the past four years, however, the trend had been to semipermanent colorants, with an increase from 12 percent to 27 percent of the market. Growth in unit volume during those years for both types of colorant had been about 15 percent per annum. The majority of unit sales in the category were in chain drugstores (57 percent) with 40 percent equally split between large and small independent drugstores. Food retailers accounted for the remaining 3 percent.

Competition.   In the Netherlands four out of 10 total brands accounted for 80 percent of the sales of permanent hair colorants, compared to two brands in France. Exhibit 6 gives the market share of the leading permanent color brands in the period 1987–1989. Interestingly, none of them had a clear advertising positioning statement describing customer benefits. By default, then, Belle Couleur could be positioned as "covering gray with natural colors."

Hair salons were indirect competitors in the hair coloring market. The percentage of women who had a hair stylist color their hair was not known, nor were the trends in usage of this method known. It was projected that as more women worked outside the home, home coloring would probably increase because it was more convenient.

Exhibit 7   Hair Coloring by Age (%)

	1986	1989
Less than 25 years	35%	50%
25–34	24	54
35–49	32	55
50–64	24	33
65 and over	15	19

L'Oréal's current market entry (Recital) was the leading seller, although its share was declining. Guhl's and Andrelon's increases in shares between 1986 and 1989 reflected the general trend to using warmer shades, and these two brands were perceived as giving quality red tones. In the late 1980s, Guhl had changed its distribution strategy and started selling the brand through drug chains. In 1987 less than 1 percent of sales were through drug outlets; in the first quarter of 1990 drug-outlet sales had reached nearly 12 percent. Guhl had also become more aggressive in its marketing through large independents, with its share in these outlets climbing from 16 to 24 percent over the same period. Both the interesting shares of the smaller brands and the decreasing shares of the leaders sparked a 60 percent increase in advertising in 1989 for all brands of hair coloring.

Consumer Behavior.   Consumers perceived permanent hair color as a technical product and believed its use was very risky. As a result users had a strong brand loyalty and avoided impulse purchasing. When considering a new brand, both first-time users and current users carefully read package information and asked store personnel for advice.

Traditionally, hair colorants had been used primarily to cover gray hair. Recently, however, coloring hair had become more of a fashion statement. This partially accounted for the increased popularity of semipermanent hair coloring. In one study the most frequently cited reason (33 percent) for coloring hair was to achieve warm/red tones; another 17 percent reported wanting to lighten their hair color, and covering gray was cited by 29 percent. It was likely that the trend to use colorants more for fashion and less for covering gray reflected the increase in hair coloring by consumers less than 35 years old. In 1989, 46 percent of Dutch women (up from 27 percent in 1986) colored their hair with either semipermanent or permanent hair colorants. Exhibit 7 contains a breakdown of usage by age of user.

Hair coloring was almost exclusively purchased in drugstores; only 3 percent of sales were through supermarkets. The percentage of sales for drug outlets was chains, 58 percent; large independents, 22 percent; and small independents, 20 percent.

Market Research.   As with Synergie Mr. Rourke also had the L'Oréal market researchers contact consumers about their reactions to Belle Couleur. Four hundred and twelve Dutch women between the ages of 25 and 64 who had used hair colorant in the past four months were part of a concept test, and 265 of these women participated in a use test. A little over 25 percent of the participants colored their hair every six weeks or more often while another 47 percent did it every two to three months. (The average French user colored her hair every three weeks.) Nearly 60 percent used hair color to cover gray, while the remainder did it for other reasons.

EXHIBIT 8   Buying Intentions

	Price Unaware	Price Aware	After Use
Certainly buy (5)	18%	26%	29%
Probably buy (4)	60	57	30
Don't know (3)	12	5	9
Probably not (2)	7	7	11
Certainly not (1)	3	6	21
Total	100%	100%	100%
Mean score	3.85	3.92	3.35

After being introduced to the concept and shown some sample ads, participants were asked their buying intentions. The question was asked three times—before and after the price was given and after Belle Couleur was used. The results are shown in Exhibit 8.

In most product concept tests (as with the Synergie line) buying intentions *declined* once the price was revealed. For Belle Couleur, buying intentions increased after the price was given, but decreased after actual use. As the exhibit shows, the percentage of participants who would probably or certainty *not* buy the product after using it increased from 13 to 32 percent. In Exhibit 9 only participants who gave negative after-use evaluations of Belle Couleur are included, and they are grouped according to the brands they were using at the time.

To try to determine why some users didn't like the product, the dissatisfied women were asked to state why they disliked Belle Couleur. The results are shown in Exhibit 10.

Many of the women thought that their hair was too dark after using Belle Couleur, and said it "didn't cover gray." Those who thought the Couleur was different from expected were primarily using the blond and chestnut brown shades of colorant. This was expected, since in France Belle Couleur was formulated to give a classical, conservative dark blond color without extra reflections or lightening effects and the product had not been modified for the Dutch test. The competing Dutch-manufactured hair colorant competitors, on the other hand, were formulated to give stronger lightening effects. Thus some of the negative evaluations of Belle Couleur were due to the fact that Dutch women tended toward naturally lighter hair colors and the French toward darker shades.

Role of Distributors

Distributors' acceptance of the two product lines was critical for L'Oréal's successful launch of both Synergie and Belle Couleur. At one time, manufacturers had more control in the channel of distribution than retailers. Retailers, however, had been gaining power as a result of the increasing size of retailers, the development of chains with their central buying offices, and the proliferation of new brands with little differentiation from brands currently on the market. Retailers had also increasingly been offering their own private-label products, since they earned a higher percentage profit margin on their own brands.

Following are the criteria, listed in order of importance (3 being "most important"), that retailers used to evaluate new products:

EXHIBIT 9   Purchase Intentions and Evaluation of Belle Couleur by Brand Currently Used

	Brand Currently Used				
	Total Sample	*Andrelon*	*Poly Couleur*	*Guhl*	*Recital (L'Oréal)*
After-Use Purchase Intentions of Belle Couleur					
Probably not (2)	11%	12%	12%	14%	5%
Certainly not (1)	21	24	29	20	5
	32%	36%	41%	34%	10%
Overall mean score	3.35	3.4	3.1	3.4	3.95
Evaluation of Final Color of Belle Couleur					
Very good (1)	25%	24%	31%	22%	35%
Good (2)	43	40	31	44	49
Neither good or bad (3)	10	10	14	6	8
Bad (4)	12	14	5	18	8
Very bad (5)	9	12	19	10	. . .
Mean	2.37	2.5	2.5	2.5	1.89
Comparison to Expectations					
Much better (1)	11%	12%	14%	14%	14%
Better (2)	26	12	21	24	38
The same (3)	29	38	26	28	32
Worse (4)	19	24	19	18	11
Much worse (5)	15	14	19	16	5
Mean	3.0	3.17	3.07	2.98	2.57
Compared with Own Brand					
Much better (1)		17%	17%	24%	14%
Better (2)		21	19	24	32
The same (3)		21	31	14	30
Worse (4)		21	12	16	16
Much worse (5)		19	21	22	8
Mean		3.05	3.02	2.88	2.73

*Data for total sample not available.

1. Evidence of consumer acceptance	2.5
2. Manufacturer advertising and promotion	2.2
3. Introductory monetary allowances	2.0
4. Rationale for product development	1.9
5. Merchandising recommendations	1.8

L'Oréal's own goal for developing new products was to introduce only those products that had a differential advantage with evidence of consumer acceptance. It did not want to gain distribution with excessive reliance on trade deals or higher than normal retail gross margins. L'Oréal also wanted to have its Garnier product lines extensively distributed in as many different types of retailers and outlets as possible. This approach to new product introduction had been effective for L'Oréal, and it currently had a positive image with Dutch retailers. L'Oréal was perceived as offering high-quality, innovative products supported with good in-store merchandising.

For L'Oréal's current products, 35 percent of sales came from independent drugstores, 40 percent from drug chains, and 25 percent from food stores. For all manufacturers, drug chains and supermarkets were increasing in importance. These stores required a brand with high customer awareness and some brand preference. The brands needed to be presold since, unlike independent drugstores, there was no sales assistance.

EXHIBIT 10   Reasons for Negative Evaluations of Belle Couleur by Brand Currently Used

	Brand Currently Used				
	Total Sample	*Andrelon*	*Poly Couleur*	*Guhl*	*Recital (L'Oréal)*
Hair got dark/darker instead of lighter	13%	14%	17%	14%	5%
Irritates skin	8	10	7	2	11
Ammonia smell	5	7	—	2	—
Didn't cover gray	5	12	2	4	3
Color not beautiful	5	7	5	6	3
Color different from expected	5	5	10	4	3

Note: Some of the cell sizes are very small and caution should be used when comparing entries of less than 10 percent.

Introducing a line of products rather than just a product or two resulted in a greater need for retail shelf space. Although the number of new products and brands competing for retail shelf space frequently appeared unlimited, the space itself was limited resource. With Belle Couleur, L'Oréal had already addressed this issue by reducing the number of Belle Couleur colorants it planned to offer in the Netherlands. Although 22 shades were available in France, L'Oréal had reduced the line to 15 variations for the Netherlands. As a result 1.5 meters (about 5 linear feet) of retail shelf space were needed to display the 15 shades of Belle Couleur. Synergie required about half of this shelf space.

Decision Time

After reviewing the information on the market research of the two product lines, Ms. van der Zande summarized the situation. L'Oréal Netherlands could leverage its advertising of the Garnier name by promoting two lines at once. Consumers would hear and see the Garnier name twice, and not just once. As a result Dutch consumers might see Garnier as a major supplier of cosmetics and toiletries. But she was concerned about the selling effort that would be needed to sell the L'Oréal brands that were already in the Dutch market and at the same time introduce not just one, but two, new brand name product *lines*. The Dutch L'Oréal sales force would have to handle both family brands, since the much lower market potential of the Netherlands market could not support a separate Garnier sales force, as in France. She was also concerned about retailer reaction to a sales pitch for two product lines.

Ms. van der Zande reflected that she was facing three decision areas. First, she had to decide if she should introduce one or both product lines, and she had to make this decision knowing that L'Oréal would not reformulate the products just for the Dutch market. Second, if she decided to introduce either one or both of the product lines, she needed to develop a marketing program. This meant she had to make decisions on the promotion of the product line(s) to both retailers and consumers, as well as the pricing and distribution of the line(s). Third, given that the Garnier product introductions might negatively impact the sales of her current product lines, she needed tactical marketing plans for those products.

CASE 6–4
APACHE POWER, INC.

It was February 1991. Kristy Furnas, product manager for gasoline engines at Apache Power, Inc. (API), was contemplating how to introduce and price a new gasoline engine, the FE21, for large outdoor power equipment. The FE21 was the first engine API had produced for use in large outdoor power equipment.

Background

API was principally a manufacturer of gasoline engines used in small outdoor power equipment (OPE), such as lawn mowers, rotary tillers, and snow throwers. API did not manufacture the completed piece of outdoor power equipment. Rather, API focused on designing and manufacturing engines and then selling them to outdoor power equipment manufacturers. In 1990, API's sales of small engines was about 85 percent of total sales. The other 15 percent came from parts and services. Exhibit 1 presents operating figures for the past five years. Exhibit 2 provides balance sheet information for three years. Apache manufactured exclusively in the United States, and virtually all sales were domestic.

API had an excellent reputation for the quality and dependability of its products in the small engine market. It was known for providing fast and reliable service. The company had been in business for over 90 years and had developed an established customer base. Its customers included Deere & Co., Toro, and Snapper. Additionally, it sold engines for use in private label brands, such as the Sears Craftsman line. Some of API's current customers also manufactured large outdoor power equipment. API's "newest" customer began buying from the company 15 years before.

API used its own sales force to sell engines to small outdoor power equipment manufacturers. It employed 14 salespeople responsible for selling engines and parts. The salespeople were paid a base salary plus a commission on sales. The salespeople were technically knowledgeable about the engines and spoke with and understood what the manufacturer wanted or needed from API. Unfortunately, it had become difficult finding qualified people to sell the engines in recent years.

The FE21 was a larger engine than API had ever produced. With the addition of the FE21, API was hoping to successfully expand into the large outdoor power equipment market. In 1989 and 1990, API experienced successive sales declines from previous years. However, this decline was experienced by the U.S. market overall. The economic downturn and unusually dry weather were generally attributed as causes for the decline in the demand for OPE, and with slight regional variations this was expected to continue throughout 1991. API was hoping its new engine and a turnaround in the economy would boost sales for 1992. Exhibit 3 provides actual and projected unit sales of small and large outdoor power equipment in the United States.

This case was prepared by Associate Professor William F. Crittenden and MBA candidate Sharon M. Doherty of Northeastern University as the basis for class discussion. The case situation is hypothetical and is not intended as an accurate portrayal of the outdoor power equipment engine industry nor of any of the participating companies. Rev. 12/03/91. Copyright 1991.

EXHIBIT 1   Income Statement—Apache Power, Inc.
(in thousands of dollars)

	1990	1989	1988	1987	1986
Gross sales	$12,556	$12,984	$13,095	$13,016	$12,938
Sales discounts	1,249	1,272	1,310	1,302	1,294
Net sales	$11,307	$11,712	$11,786	$11,714	$11,644
Cost of goods sold					
Raw materials	4,862	5,036	5,044	5,014	4,984
Direct labor	2,256	2,331	2,334	2,296	2,282
Variable overhead	678	679	684	691	675
Shipping	192	199	199	198	198
Gross margin	3,319	3,467	3,525	3,515	3,505
Selling costs					
Advertising	9	9	9	9	9
Salaries	554	539	530	515	501
Commissions	226	234	236	234	233
Promotional materials	226	234	224	224	245
Other costs					
Administrative	348	342	332	330	326
Depreciation	97	94	92	91	87
Research and development	1,583	1,523	1,090	351	349
Supplies	113	105	100	94	82
Insurance	187	184	180	179	175
Interest	167	166	165	164	163
Operating income	($192)	$36	$567	$1,324	$1,336
Taxes	(80)	15	238	556	561
Income after taxes	($111)	$21	$329	$768	$775

Industry and Economic Information

Over the last 10 years, fluctuations in the U.S. dollar had given API and most other U.S. manufacturers products a higher price compared to international competition. Although competition came from around the globe, small engine manufacturers from the Far East had especially taken advantage of this trend and gained significant market share. Japanese manufacturers, in particular, provided technologically advanced products. Their products were generally viewed as more reliable and fuel efficient than the American manufacturers' engines. OEMs continued to seek improvements from their engine suppliers in fuel efficiency, noise and air pollution abatement, and safety.

There had also been a trend in the buying behavior of the end user, the consumer. Over the past few years, consumers had been buying more powerful OPE that could do a variety of tasks, such as garden tractors, instead of buying a few smaller OPE for individual tasks.

Small OPE Engines.   The average market price to an original equipment manufacturer (OEM) for a small outdoor power equipment gasoline engine was $45 in 1990. The typical range was from $35 to $100. After adjusting for trade/sales discounts, the industry had seen no price increase the past two years. Total market in sales to OEMs of small engines was estimated at $256,500,000 in 1990. Finished small OPE products

**EXHIBIT 2   Balance Sheet—Apache Power, Inc.
(in thousands of dollars)**

	1990	1989	1988
Current assets			
Cash	$ 628	$ 854	$ 925
Accounts receivable	6,455	5,890	6,103
Inventory	3,329	3,146	3,719
Prepaid expense	1,340	1,174	1,023
Total current assets	$11,752	$11,064	$11,770
Fixed assets			
Land	2,500	2,500	2,500
Building, net	16,348	16,170	16,200
Machinery, net	37,418	32,715	31,002
Total fixed assets	$56,266	$51,385	$49,702
Total assets	$68,018	$62,449	$61,472
Current liabilities			
Accounts payable	$ 2,488	$ 2,122	$ 2,497
Notes payable	1,634	1,987	3,057
Accrued liabilities	3,551	3,454	3,872
Total current liabilities	$ 7,673	$ 7,563	$ 9,426
Long-term liabilities			
Notes payable	$14,634	$ 9,049	$ 6,215
Total liabilities	$22,307	$16,612	$15,641
Equity			
Common stock	9,000	9,000	9,000
Retained earnings	36,711	36,837	36,831
Total equity	$45,711	$45,837	$45,831
Total liabilities and equity	$68,018	$62,449	$61,472

**EXHIBIT 3   Actual and Forecasted Unit Sales
of Outdoor Power Equipment
(in thousands of units)**

Year	OPE Using Small Engines	OPE Using Large Engines
1986	5750	565
1987	5785	875
1988	5820	950
1989	5850	1050
1990	5700	1020
1991	5500	1025
1992	5700	1070
1993	5900	1100

typically listed at retail from $130 to $600, although discounters might have offered specials up to 25 percent off in highly competitive markets.

API's main competitor in the small engine market was Brighams, a U.S. manufacturer of engines for OPE. Although not a finished goods manufacturer, Brighams had exceptionally strong name recognition among males 35 years and older. It had been in the business for a long time and had an established customer base. No longer considered the industry's technological leader, Brighams still maintained an excellent reputation for the dependability of its products, and its parts and service network was second to none. Brighams currently was the small engine market leader with a 30 percent market share.

Hachi, a Japanese manufacturer of engines that manufactured its own OPE, was also a formidable, yet indirect competitor. Vertically integrated, with 98 percent captive sales, Hachi was second in small engine sales with approximately 13 percent of the market.

Brighams and Hachi were the only small engine manufacturers perceived as national in sales and distribution. The rest of the U.S. small engine market was fragmented, on a regional basis, among 25 U.S. and international manufacturers, including API. Three U.S. manufacturers had recently left the industry, citing decreasing margins and increased capitalization needs. Increased competition in the small engine market and changing consumer behaviors prompted API to expand its product line into larger engines.

Large OPE Engines.   Principal competitors in the large engine market were Brighams, Hachi, two other U.S. manufacturers, and a few companies that manufactured engines for their own large outdoor power equipment. Hachi's strengths in the market were its exceptional performance record, superior technology, and lower price. Hachi had been written up as the best engine in many trade journals. Its weaknesses included its distribution network for large finished outdoor power equipment and the availability of parts since all parts were manufactured in Japan.

Brighams virtually created the large engine market, working closely with an OEM that recognized the need for outdoor power equipment products that were smaller and lower priced than those needed on a farm, but larger than those available for the consumer market. With its established name recognition, reputation, and parts and service network, Brighams was the natural source for those OEM not seeking vertical integration. In the large engine market, Brighams was again the leader with a 42 percent market share. Exhibit 4 provides *estimated* costs for Brighams Large Engine Division.

Captive manufacturing comprised approximately 33 percent of the large engine market. Based on retail sales, Hachi appeared to have an 8 percent market share, all of it captive. Two other U.S. manufacturers held 6 percent and 7 percent, respectfully, of the market. These firms sold exclusively to the OEM market. Remaining market share for large engine sales was fragmented among a few smaller U.S. and international manufacturers, all supplying the small engine market as well. The market price to an OEM averaged $350, with a typical range of $300 to $500. Exhibit 5 shows financial ratios for the gasoline engine market.

New Product Information

API had invested a lot of time and money designing its large engine. The increased investment appeared to be paying off. API had developed a large gasoline engine for garden tractors that was even more fuel efficient, emitted lower noise levels, and included

Exhibit 4

FINANCIAL DATA—BRIGHAMS:
Large Engine Division*
(in thousands of dollars)

Net sales	$149,940
Cost of goods sold	104,209
Raw materials	$ 60,576
Direct labor	33,437
Variable overhead	8,397
Shipping	1,799
Gross margin	$ 45,731
General, sales & administration expenses	$ 39,690
Advertising	$ 1,649
Commissions	6,747
Promotional materials	3,374
Depreciation	2,999
Interest	3,749
R&D	5,623
Supplies	1,005
Insurance	2,249
Salaries	12,295
Operating income	$ 6,041

*Note: These approximations were made using Brighams' consolidated financial
statements and suggestions made by industry experts.

Exhibit 5   **Select Financial Ratios for U.S. Publicly Held Gasoline Engine Manufacturers, 1990**

Current	1.85
Quick	0.98
Net profit margin	2.4%
Gross profit margin	35.6%
Return on investment	4.1%
Inventory turnover	6.4
Collection period	98 days
Payables period	52 days
Days of inventory	178 days
Debt to asset	54.2%
Debt to equity	70.1%
Long-term debt to equity	51.0%
Times interest earned	1.17

Note: All gasoline engine manufacturers do not supply the outdoor
power equipment industry, although the majority do. Furthermore,
these ratios do not include data from captive manufacturers or those
divisions and subsidiaries where information is only reported in
consolidated statements.

more safety features than any other large engine on the market. For example, API's new large gasoline engine, the FE21, was 7 percent more fuel efficient than any other engine in its class currently on the market. In addition, the noise level was much softer and the cutting blade would stop within one second of when the tractor had been turned off (or turned over).

To design this new engine, API invested $3 million toward engineering costs and an additional $6 million was spent modifying and buying new equipment in order to manufacture the engine. It was estimated that an additional $1.5 million in expenses would be needed for the engine to be completely ready for release to the market by midyear, when OEMs finalized product decisions for the upcoming model year. API's total production capacity was 350,000 engines. The plant and equipment modifications allowed API to produce 50,000 large engines a year.

Product Introduction Alternatives

In the past, API had not spent much on promotion of its engines. Usually, API just put together sales materials that included product brochures, gave moderate trade discounts, and had a few ads in trade journals. Since it had held a solid market position for so long and had many of the same customers year after year, they had seen no reason to push its name and products aggressively. With the development of the large engine, API was contemplating increasing its promotional activity in order to compete in the market.

Furnas was investigating various promotion program alternatives. One alternative was to increase the number of ads in trade journals. It was estimated that Brighams spent about $2 million a year on trade journal advertising. Another alternative was to give more generous trade discounts. API's current trade discount was 10 percent, about the industry average. Furnas wondered if increasing the trade discount would increase sales. The final alternative being considered was using TV advertising to increase customer awareness. It was thought that if end consumers knew more about API, they would buy OPE made with API's engines. Hachi currently spent $6 million on TV advertising, while Brighams spent about $2.5 million.

Furnas had to decide what marketing program or combination of marketing programs would be most beneficial to the sale of API's new engine and overall sales, while considering what the company could afford to do and the price of the new engine.

CASE 6–5
CAPITAL

It is the end of July 1991 and most Parisians are preparing to leave on holiday. But not Dr. Andreas Wiele. He, as project and executive manager, and the other members of the Prisma Presse team developing a new business magazine called *Capital* have other things on their minds. The zero issue of *Capital* went down well with the focus group they have just been watching over closed-circuit TV. The problem is the market itself. The economic situation is bad—advertising in business magazines has dropped by about 20 percent since the beginning of the year and circulation is still stagnant. Should they go ahead with the planned launch in September or postpone until the economic situation improves? If they do launch, key marketing decisions still remain to be taken: the magazine's price, its distribution, and communication policies.

Prisma Presse: Gruner+Jahr's French Subsidiary

Prisma Presse, with offices in the center of Paris close to the Champs-Elysées, was founded in 1978 by the then 41-year-old Axel Ganz as the French subsidiary of Gruner+Jahr (Exhibit 1), the German publishing company headquartered in Hamburg, itself a subsidiary of the multimedia Bertelsmann group. Trained as a journalist, Axel Ganz had already held various senior positions with leading magazine publishing companies.

During its 13 years, Prisma Presse has launched six magazines and acquired two more, increasing the circulation of the latter by a factor of three since taking them over in 1989. All Prisma Presse magazines are among the leaders in their segments (Exhibit 2). This compares favorably with the industry average. Of a total 173 new consumer magazines launched between 1987 and 1990 in France, only 119 (69 percent) were still going at the end of 1990. This enviable track record has earned Axel Ganz such sobriquets as "magazine alchemist" and "man with the Midas touch."

With a 1990–91 turnover of F2 billion (Exhibit 3), Prisma Presse has become the second biggest magazine publisher in France. It concentrates effort on text and layout in its magazines, and outsources such activities as documentation, photography, printing, and distribution. Prisma Presse is structured around the individual magazine (Exhibit 4, page 444). Each is headed by a duo consisting of an executive editor and an editor-in-chief, jointly responsible for editorial policies, staffing, circulation, and revenues of the magazine. The executive editor, often working on two magazines, is specifically responsible for financial results, while the editor-in-chief, usually assigned to one magazine only, is specifically responsible for execution of editorial policy. Each magazine has its own staff of journalists, art team, and advertising department. The advertising departments of the different magazines compete vigorously for business,

This case was written by Reinhard Angelmar, professor of marketing, INSEAD, with the assistance of Wolfgang Munk and Thierry Azalbert. It is intended to be used as a basis for class discussion rather than to illustrate either effective or ineffective handling of an administrative situation. Copyright © 1994 INSEAD, Fontainebleau, France.

**EXHIBIT 1
Gruner+Jahr
Publications outside
France**

GERMANY

Magazines: *Art, Brigitte, Capital, Decoration, Elterns, Essen&Trinken, FF, Flora, Frau im Spiegel, Frau im Spiegel Rätsel, Geo, Geo Special, Geo Wissen, Häuser, Impulse, Marie-Claire*, Max*, Mein Kind und ich, Neues Wohnen, PM. Magazin, P.M. Logik Trainer, Schöner Wohnen, Prima, Saison, Sandra, Schöner Essen, Sonntagspost, Sports, Stern, Wochenpost, Yps.*

Newspapers: *Berliner Kurier, Berliner Zeitung, Dresdner Morgenpost, Chemnitzer Morgenpost, Hamburger Morgenpost, Mecklenburger Morgenpost, Leipziger Morgenpost, Sächsische Zeitung.*

SPAIN

Dunia, Geo, Mia, Mux Interessante, Natura, Ser Padres Hoy, Estar Viva, Cosmopolitan*

UNITED KINGDOM

Best, Prima, Focus

UNITED STATES

Parents, YM.

ITALY

Vera,* Focus*.

* Joint venture.

sometimes against other Prisma Presse magazines. Coordination of advertising policy is one of the tasks of the corporate advertising business manager.

The staff of a successful magazine is regarded by management as a pool of talent from which inside members of future magazines are recruited. For example, *Prima* was the breeding ground for subsequent women's magazines. These insiders usually account for about half of the staff of a new magazine. They are used especially on the

EXHIBIT 2 **Prisma Presses: Product Portfolio, 1991**

GEO
Travel/Discovery of the Beauty
of Nature and Civilization
upper middle class
Monthly circulation: 580,000
Nr. 1 travel magazine
Launch: 1979

ÇA M'INTÉRESSE
Scientific Popularization
adolescents/young adults
Monthly circulation: 350,000
Nr. 1 in segment
Launch: 1981

PRIMA
Women's Magazine
good housekeepers and wives
Monthly circulation: 1,220,000
Nr. 1 women's monthly
Launch: 1982

FEMME ACTUELLE
Women's Magazine
Weekly circulation: 1,800,000
Nr. 1 women's weekly
Launch: 1984

TÉLÉ LOISIRS
TV Magazine
Weekly circulation: 1,220,000
Nr. 4 TV Magazine
Launch: 1986

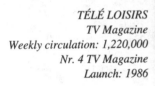

VOICI
The Celebrities' Private Lives
Weekly circulation: 600,000
Nr. 1 women's picture magazine
Launch: 1987

CUISINE ACTUELLE
Gourmet Magazine
Monthly circulation: 350,000
Nr. 1 food magazine
Acquired in 1989

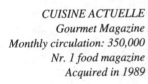

GUIDE CUISINE
Family food magazine
Monthly circulation: 230,000
Nr. 2 food magazine
Acquired in 1989

CAPITAL
Monthly Business Magazine

Planned launch date:
September 1991

art team, because the visual concept across the range is basically the same. Outside recruitment brings in journalists with knowledge in content areas like economics, business, fashion, cooking, and travel.

Market research, production and distribution management, and some other functions are taken care of by specialized departments covering all Prisma Presse magazines. Tight cost controls create a sense of leanness throughout the organization.

EXHIBIT 3   Key Data: Prisma Presse. Gruner+Jahr, Bertelsmann

	1987–88	*1988–89*	*1989–90*	*1990–91*
Prisma Presse (in Million FF)				
Total revenues	1,621	1,762	1,865	2,057
Growth		9%	6%	10%
Circulation revenues	1,253	1,335	1,433	1,606
Advertising revenues	347	401	405	424
Profits	83	104	119	159
% of revenues	5%	6%	6%	8%
Nr. of employees	414	448	481	527
Revenues/employee	4	4	4	4
Gruner+Jahr (in Million DM)				
Total revenues	2,773	2,987	3,099	3,284
Growth		8%	4%	6%
Profits	223	255	272	200
% of revenues	8%	9%	9%	6%
Nr. of employees	8,745	9,170	9,286	9,613
Bertelsmann Group (in Million DM)				
Total revenues	11,299	12,483	13,313	14,483
Growth		10%	7%	9%
Profits	362	402	510	540
% of revenues	3%	3%	4%	4%

Average 1991 exchange rates were: 3.3FF for 1DM, 5.6FF for 1$, 1.7DM for 1$. The financial year ends on June 30.

Editorial Principles at Prisma Presse

Axel Ganz has strong convictions regarding the basic editorial principles that he imprints on all Prisma Presse magazines, regardless of their content area.

Reader/Circulation Focus.   Magazines derive revenue both from readers (circulation) and advertising. In contrast to some publishers who are more advertiser- than reader-oriented, Axel Ganz's priority is clearly the reader: "Circulation is where the business is. You can act on it—and we must do everything we can to maximize it—whereas advertising also depends on factors beyond our control, like the overall economic situation." A Prisma Presse executive confirms: "Ganz is obsessed with circulation; when a magazine's circulation starts declining, he sounds the alarm." Circulation determines the major part of bonus payments, which range from 60 percent of the annual salary for the managing duo to two months' additional salary for some of the regular staff. "When circulation objectives are not met, Axel Ganz puts on enormous pressure," comments one editor-in-chief. Managers who repeatedly fail to achieve objectives are asked to leave. "In this company, we get rid of teams that don't win," explains one executive.

Because the bulk of Prisma Presse circulation comes from volatile newsstand sales rather than from more stable subscriptions, reader appeal shows up quickly in circulation figures. Days when circulation figures come out have everyone in a state of feverish excitement. Outstanding results are celebrated, whereas disappointing circulation

**EXHIBIT 4
Prisma Presse:
Simplified
Organization Chart,
1991**

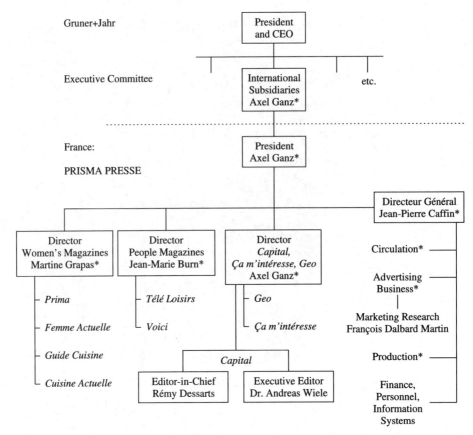

* Members of Prisma Presse's Executive Committee.

calls for quick remedial action, which may escalate from minor changes to a major overhaul. For example, *Voici*'s circulation increased from 240,000 at launch to 600,000 three years later, thanks to a series of changes resulting in the complete repositioning of *Voici* from a family magazine to one concentrating on the "celebrities' private lives."

A constant stream of market research data provides each magazine with information about its readers, and many team members are usually present to watch the focus groups which are organized regularly throughout France. This close attention to the reader is rather unusual in the French press. According to one Prisma Presse executive, "Competitors are managed by Parisian journalists who only think of their egos and their connections, and who impose the dictate of their good taste. This is intellectual terrorism. As for us, we can put ourselves in the shoes of the reader from the Creuse [a backward rural area in France]." One observer put it like this: "Prisma is to the French press what Disney is to the French cinema."

A Clear Concept and Consistent Implementation.   Each magazine must have a clear concept (for example, "to discover and show the beautiful things on earth, which need to be preserved," *Geo*), and every aspect of the magazine (topics, style of presentation, visuals, layout, cover, etc.) must be consistent with this concept. To Axel Ganz, a successful magazine is like any other successful brand that acquires a distinctive identity: "Why does a reader prefer one magazine to another, although often both cover the same subjects? Because each title projects a specific image and creates a special kind of relationship with the reader." The managing team must ensure that every issue fits the concept: "There may be doubts and discussions, but the managing team must identify enough with the concept of their magazine to sense immediately, nine times out of 10, whether a topic is right or not," Axel Ganz comments.

Precise, Well-Researched Information. Prisma Presse has a strict policy of not allowing advertisers to interfere in editorial content, unlike some other publishers, where advertisers sometimes influence articles that they judge detrimental to their own interests, or where journalists use company press releases as main sources for their articles.

Attractive Presentation. Presentation in all Prisma Presse magazines is geared for maximum readability: short articles ("right length for a ride in the Metro"), short words ("no more than three syllables"), short sentences, and comprehensible titles. "You have to understand the conditions in which people read—poor lighting, ill-fitting glasses, etc—it's these kinds of details that make the difference," explains one executive. The marrying of text and visuals is vital. The editorial policy of most Prisma Presse magazines stipulates that "topics are chosen only if it is possible to produce a matching visual representation."

The art directors are the guardians of the Prisma Presse formula for attractive presentation. They train the journalists in the magic formula, follow each issue through until the final check, and are always on the lookout for changes that would enhance appeal. Together with the editors-in-chief they comprise the main bottleneck and constraint for the launch of new magazines by Prisma Presse.

Searching for a New Idea

To sustain Prisma Presse's growth, Axel Ganz has set as an objective the launching of a new magazine every 18 months. The new products should have high circulation potential, be innovative rather than imitative, and use primarily newsstand distribution, Prisma Presse's main channel. The only segments specifically excluded are newspapers and news magazines. "There are sensibilities that should not be hurt," Axel Ganz explains. "Newspapers and news magazines deal with politics, and even if we took an objective stand on an issue, we would probably be accused of taking a German view. The time isn't right. In two generations, possibly . . ."

Axel Ganz, together with Martine Grapas and Jean-Marie Burn, directors for the women's and people magazines respectively, are responsible formally for coming up with ideas for magazines. Ideas may float around for many years, and only a few ever make it into development. In his own search for new product ideas, Axel Ganz monitors market trends in all segments and different countries, until "one day, out of this observation emerges a hunch that a particular area might be promising." Axel Ganz may see promise where others see only desolation. For example, he launched *Prima* and *Femme Actuelle* in a segment that, despite being crowded with 15 magazines, had been declining for 10 years. He reasoned that the decline was due not to a lack of demand, but because the offering was unsatisfactory.

Axel Ganz had a hunch that the business magazine market in France might be promising. Business magazines provide readers with business and economic news and analyses across all industries. The leading title in France was *L'Expansion* (a biweekly), which created the market in 1967, followed in 1975 by *Le Nouvel*

Economiste (a weekly). In 1984, the Mitterrand presidency's sudden shift from anti- to probusiness gave rise to an increased interest in business information and triggered a rash of product launches, not all of which survived.

Fortune France, the most recent business magazine launched in February 1988, was an intriguing case. The intention was clear: Take advantage of *Fortune*'s awareness and image among international advertisers and top executives, while overcoming the language barrier which resulted, for the English-language edition, in a circulation of a mere 5,000 in France. *Fortune France* was published by a 50–50 joint venture between *Fortune*'s U.S. publisher Time–Warner and its French partner Hachette, the leading publisher in France. They shared the launch investment of F40 million and expected to reach payback within three years. The circulation goal was 50,000 initially, rising to 80,000 after three to four years.

Fortune France's editorial team consisted of eight full-time French journalists plus a network of correspondents. Changes in content, layout, and paper quality resulted in a glamorous, lifestyle-oriented magazine which had little in common with its American counterpart. "This magazine does not appear to be willing to upset the business establishment. One finds in it neither the bite nor the impertinence which account for the appeal of the U.S. magazine," commented one observer. *Fortune France* cost F30, sold mainly through newsstands, and was launched with a F2.5 million advertising campaign on radio and in the national press as well as by a direct mail campaign. Advertising business took off briskly despite high rates, but circulation remained low. Paid circulation reached 37,000 when *Fortune France* was eventually discontinued in June 1990.

Axel Ganz felt that the French business magazines suffered from two weaknesses. First, the older magazines had not changed much and looked somewhat old-fashioned. Second, all titles appeared light on editorial quality, and most seemed to believe more in attracting subscribers through expensive direct mail campaigns than through a high-quality product.

Recruitment of a Management Team to Fill a Blank Sheet of Paper

In Fall 1989 Axel Ganz transformed his hunch into a formal development project codenamed *Hermès,* due for launch in 1991. Funds for development were budgeted in the three-year 1990–93 plan approved by Gruner+Jahr.

Gruner+Jahr was already familiar with the business magazine market as the publisher of *Capital,* the leading business magazine in Germany. But Axel Ganz decided to start from a blank sheet of paper, without any *a priori* ideas about the concept or name. "I don't believe in a Euro-magazine which would be completely identical in all countries. You can't simply export and translate magazines, which are cultural products. You can transpose to another country a concept which has proven its worth elsewhere, but you have to reshape and modify it to adapt it to the local context. Up-market magazines like *Geo* can be internationalized more easily, because these consumers become more similar, whereas mass market magazines like *Prima* address a more popular audience, for which local peculiarities—eating and leisure habits, for example—are very important."

In Spring 1990, Axel Ganz set out to recruit the management team for the new magazine. He found a project and executive manager in 28-year-old Dr. Andreas Wiele, an assistant to the president and CEO of Gruner+Jahr in Hamburg, who had previously worked for one year as a journalist for a Hamburg newspaper after studying law. Dr. Wiele joined Prisma Presse in Paris in July 1990.

Finding an appropriate editor-in-chief took much longer, despite the large number of candidates attracted by Prisma Presse's reputation. Ganz was looking for somebody with experience in the French business press, not a star journalist, but someone willing to apply Prisma Presse's editorial principles to business magazines. The choice finally went to 36-year-old Rémy Dessarts, a graduate of a Paris business school who had spent eight years at *L'Expansion* before becoming associate editor of the business magazine *A pour Affaires*. Rémy Dessarts joined in September.

Forty-eight–year-old Thierry Rouxel, assigned as art director for *Hermès,* was the third key member of the team. An old hand with Prisma Presse, Thierry Rouxel brought with him the all-important Prisma Presse presentation know-how to the project.

Through the recruitment process, word got out about Prisma Presse's intentions. But competitors did not take the project seriously, doubting that a company publishing mainly for women could successfully enter the business magazine market.

Analyzing the Market for Business Magazines

Dr. Wiele's major task during the initial months consisted of gathering and analyzing information on business magazines and other relevant publications (Exhibit 5, page 448). He found that circulation stagnation was hitting not only business magazines (Exhibit 6, page 449), but all segments of the economic press, with the exception of personal finance magazines like *Le Revenu Français* (170,000 circulation) and *Mieux Vivre* (139,000 circulation), which had enjoyed a compound annual growth of 8 percent over the last 10 years. The number of advertising pages in business magazines had been declining since 1988, with advertising revenues dipping slightly for the first time during 1990 (Exhibit 7, page 450).

Dr. Wiele noticed some striking differences between the French and German business magazine markets:

- Total circulation was higher in France, yet supply was much more fragmented. France had many more titles, each with a relatively small circulation; e.g., *L'Expansion,* with 150,000 was the leading title in France, compared to 250,000 for *Capital,* the leader in Germany.

- French magazines invested less in editorial content. They employed fewer journalists, everyone of whom had to produce more editorial pages than their counterparts in Germany.

- Subscription discounts and sales were both much higher in France than in Germany; e.g., 84 percent of *L'Expansion*'s circulation came from subscriptions (see Exhibit 8, page 451) compared to 59 percent for *Capital.*

- German business magazines featured many more "personal service" topics (e.g., how to reduce taxes, manage one's career, invest money) than French business magazines, which left these subjects to specialized magazines such as *Le Revenu Français* and *Mieux Vivre.*

To obtain a broader perspective on the topics that could be covered by *Hermès,* Dr. Wiele analyzed the leading business magazines in Europe and the U.S. This survey provided the basis for a detailed content analysis of the French business magazines (see Exhibit 9, page 452).

The total reader potential for business magazines in France was estimated at 4.8 million, comprising 1.5 million senior and middle managers in business firms *(chefs d'entreprise et cadres supérieurs en entreprise),* 1.2 million top nonbusiness

EXHIBIT 5
Main Economic
Magazines in
France, 1991

L'EXPANSION
general business magazine
twice a month
circulation: 149,000
Launch: 1967

LE NOUVEL ECONOMISTE
general business magazine
weekly
circulation: 89,000
Launch: 1975

SCIENCE & VIE ECONOMIE
general business magazine
monthly
circulation: 106,000
Launch: 1984

DYNASTEURS
general business magazine
monthly
circulation: 95,000
Launch: 1985

L'ENTREPRISE
business magazine for owners
of small businesses
monthly
circulation: 64,000
Launch: 1985

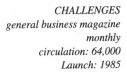

A POUR AFFAIRES
general business magazine
monthly
circulation: 42,000
Launch: 1985

CHALLENGES
general business magazine
monthly
circulation: 64,000
Launch: 1985

LE REVENU FRANÇAIS
personal finance magazine
monthly
circulation: 170,000
Launch: 1968

MIEUX VIVRE
personal finance magazine
monthly
circulation: 138,000
Launch: 1979

Note: All circulation figures refer to the average 1990 paid domestic circulation per issue.

professionals such as lawyers, doctors, and senior civil servants, and 2.1 million entry-level managers *(cadres moyens)*. François Dalbard-Martin, Prisma Presse's market research specialist, pointed out that only 45 percent of the 4.8 million potential readers had actually read a business magazine during the preceding 12 months. The main reader target for *Hermès* would be the 1.5 million senior and middle managers in business firms. Only 59 percent of these were readers of business magazines.

Advertisers in French business magazines were also interested in reaching the top nonbusiness professionals, in addition to senior and middle managers in business. The combined 2.7 million person advertising target group was called the executives *(affaires et cadres supérieurs)*. The price which a business magazine could charge for

EXHIBIT 6   Circulation of Main Business Magazines in France

	Launch Year	Frequency	Paid Domestic Circulation per Issue (in thousand copies)				Circulation Growth, 1987–90	Share of Monthly Paid Circulation, 1990	Gross Annual Circulation Revenue*** in million F (Estimate), 1990	Share of Annual Gross Circulation Revenue (Estimate), 1990
			1987	1988	1989	1990				
L'Expansion	1967	Biweekly	160	175	159	150	–6%	29%	74	31%
Le Nouvel Economiste	1975	Weekly	93	80	84	90	–3	34	56	24
Science & Vie Economie	1984	Monthly	111	116	117	107	–4	10	25	10
Dynasteurs*	1985	Monthly	100	100	100	95	–5	9	31	13
L'Entreprise	1985	Monthly	61	62	65	65	7	6	20	8
Tertiel/A pour Affaires**	1985	Monthly	33	34	35	47	42	4	11	5
Challenges	1986	Monthly	45	67	73	74	64	7	22	9
Total monthly paid domestic circulation (thousand copies)			1,042	1,049	1,044	1,048	1	100	239	100
Gross annual circulation revenue (millions of F)			217	233	240	239	10			

* Circulation as indicated by publisher. Circulation data of all other magazines are audited.

** *Tertiel* relaunched as *A pour Affaires* in September 1989.

*** Gross circulation revenue = Average price per copy (= Retail price – Subscription discount) × Total paid circulation (domestic and export).

449

EXHIBIT 7   **Advertising in Main Business Magazines in France**

	Number of Advertising Pages per Year				Growth in Net Rev., Adv. Pages 1987–90	Share of Adv. Pages, 1990	Gross Advertising Revenue,** 1990 (million F)	Share of Gross Adv. Revenue, 1990
	1987	*1988*	*1989*	*1990*				
L'Expansion	2,875	2,845	2,575	2,366	–18%	31%	274	42%
Le Nouvel Economiste	2,940	3,047	2,770	2,259	–23	30	184	28
Science & Vie Economie	242	231	225	224	–7	3	17	3
Dynasteurs	341	623	649	627	84	8	52	8
L'Entreprise	954	1,257	1,225	1,082	13	14	72	11
*Tertiel/A pour Affaires**	451	550	706	703	56	9	40	6
Challenges	222	223	352	343	55	5	19	3
Number of adv. pages per year	8,025	8,776	8,502	7,604	–5	100		
Gross advertising revenue per year (millions of F)	516	652	668	659	28		659	100

* *Tertiel* relaunched as *A pour Affaires* in September 1989.

** Gross advertising revenue: List price per advertising page × number of advertising pages.

   The net revenue amounts to approximately 60 percent of the gross revenue, with the difference including the commission for media wholesalers and the advertising agency.

advertising space depended mainly on (1) its absolute number (or, equivalently, its penetration) of "executive" readers, (2) the share of "executives" among its readers, and (3) the total number of buyers (paid circulation). Exhibit 10, page 453, shows the readership profile of the main competitors and the desired profile of *Hermès* readers.

Two focus groups were held with members from the *Hermès* target group in Fall 1990 to understand their perceptions and attitudes toward existing magazines, as well as their expectations. Exhibit 11, page 454, summarizes the results.

The Decisive Weekend: A New Concept Is Conceived

At the end of October 1990, Axel Ganz, Dr. Andreas Wiele, Rémy Dessarts, Thierry Rouxel, and François Dalbard-Martin met for a weekend to decide on the future course of the project. Most importantly, they decided to develop a prototype of *Hermès*. Prisma Presse develops products one at a time and, until now, every Prisma Presse project ever prototyped was subsequently launched.

The next major decision concerned the concept of the magazine. They decided that, compared to its competitors, the new magazine should be

- *Broader in scope.* In addition to the classic business coverage provided by French magazines, the new magazine should cover new trends, management techniques, and business philosophies (similar to the German *Manager Magazin*).
- *More entertaining.* The crucial role of individuals, with all their strengths and weaknesses, should be brought out more strongly; this required well-researched, thrilling success and failure stories, the description of interesting personalities, including those working outside Paris, an understanding of how they operated, and a coverage of lifestyle/leisure trends relevant to managers (similar to what the U.S. magazine *Forbes* offered).

EXHIBIT 8 Marketing Mix and Revenue Structure of Business Magazines in France, 1990

	L'Expansion	Le Nouvel Economiste	Science & Vie Economie	Dynasteurs	L'Enterprise	A pour Affaires Economiques	Challenges
Marketing Mix: Circulation Market							
Product							
Avg. nr. pages/issue	189	112	107	140	190	162	109
Editorial/total nr. of pages	46%	60%	81%	59%	52%	57%	74%
Nr. issues/year	23	50	11	11	12	10	12
Total nr. of editorial pages/year	1,998	3,349	956	906	1,200	923	963
Avg. nr. of staff members	38	40	12	15	21	19	13
Nr. edit. pages/staff member/year	53	84	80	60	57	49	74
Price							
Newsstand price per copy	25F	15F	22F	30F	30F	27F	25F
Subscription discount*	48%	24%	18%	33%	41%	20%	23%
Distribution: newsstand unit sales							
% of total domestic paid circ.	16%	23%	34%	16%	32%	35%	22%
1990 media adv. (million F)	F8.8	F5.9	F2.8	N.A.	F2.5	F5.4	2.4
Per paid domestic copy (in F)	2.60F	1.30F	2.40F	N.A.	3.20F	11.40F	2.70F
% of gross newsstand revenue	68%	38%	31%	N.A.	33%	131%	55%
Marketing Mix: Advertising Market							
Price							
List price per 4-color page (in F)	117,600F	70,000F	65,000F	80,900F	61,900F	59,000F	59,500F
Cost per 1,000 paid domestic circul.	784F	778F	607F	852F	952F	1,255F	804F
Cost per 1,000 dom. exec. readers	162F	232F	230F	234F	141F	N.A.	342F
Advertising department (nr. persons)	7	8	4	4	7	4	5
Revenue Structure							
1990 gross revenue (estimate)							
Gross circulation revenue	74	56	25	31	20	11	22
Gross advertising revenue	274	184	17	52	72	40	19
Total gross revenue	348	240	42	83	92	51	41
Adv. rev. as a % of total gross rev.	79%	77%	40%	63%	79%	78%	47%
% of publisher's total revenue	35%	2%	N.A.	15%	9%	2.5%	10%
Name of publisher	L'Expansion	Hachette/Filipacchi	Excelsior	Pearson France	L'Expansion	C.E.P.	Le Nouvel Observateur

*In calculating the subscription discount, the retail price of special issues (e.g., travel guides) made available free of charge to subscribers is included.

EXHIBIT 9 CONTENT ANALYSIS OF BUSINESS MAGAZINES IN FRANCE, 1990–91

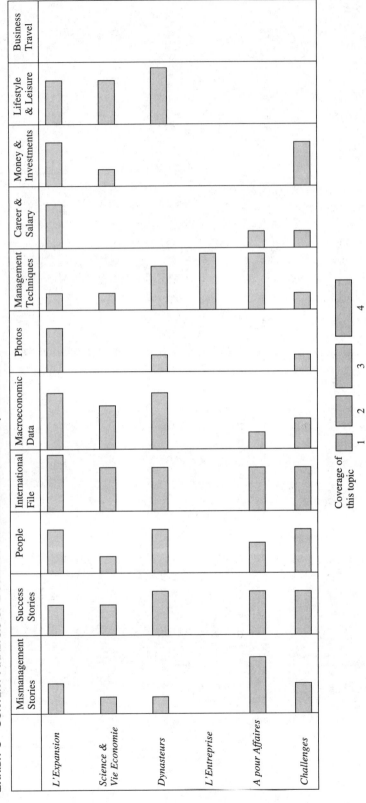

452

EXHIBIT 10   1991 Readership Profile of Business Magazines in France

	L'Expansion	Le Nouvel Economiste	Science & Vie Economie	Dynasteurs	L'Enterprise	A pour Affaires Economiques	Challenges	Total (in million)	Hermès Target Profile
All Target Groups: Magazine Penetration (in %)									
a. Senior and middle managers in business firms	21%*	10%	6%	14%	16%	7%	5%	1,5	
b. Highly educated professionals	8	4	5	2	3	0	2	1,2	
c. Entry-level managers	12	7	4	6	9	2	3	2,1	
Total (a+b+c)	14	7	5	7	10	3	4	4,8	
Advertising Target Group: "Executives" (a+b)									
Magazine penetration (in %)	15	7	5	8	10	4	4		
Share of "executives" among readers (in %)	62	56	60	63	57	66	58	2,7	
Hermès Reader Target Group									
Number of readers: senior & middle mgrs. in bus. firms	300,068	136,466	79,535	202,546	231,562	96,924	73,080	1,5	
Reader profile: senior & middle mgrs. in bus. firms									
Sex (in %)								(in %)	(in %)
Male	80	89	85	83	77	69	79	82	80
Female	20	12	15	17	23	31	21	18	20
Region (in %)									
Paris metropolitan region	42	47	39	50	39	42	46	45	40
Rest of France	58	53	61	50	61	58	54	55	60
Age (in %)									
<35	23	20	29	21	22	23	24	24	35
35–45	34	37	41	38	39	40	42	38	45
>45	42	44	30	41	39	37	34	38	20
Annual Income (1,000 F) (in %)									
<180	15	11	16	7	10	15	12	16	17
180–240	23	19	24	17	20	12	20	23	22
240–360	37	37	32	38	38	44	35	34	39
>360	19	27	21	31	25	23	27	20	22
Firm size (nr. employed) (in %)									
<10	22	17	18	18	18	21	18	21	15
10–50	20	17	20	16	26	27	20	18	15
50–200	14	16	22	20	17	18	11	18	20
200–500	13	14	11	10	11	8	13	8	20
>500	31	37	29	36	29	27	37	35	30
Type of business (in %)									
Manufacturing	32	41	31	36	45	41	40	41	40
Trade	17	17	12	21	14	12	10	14	15
Services	51	42	57	44	42	47	50	45	45

* Percentage of all French senior and middle managers in business firms who read the magazine during the week (*Nouvel Economiste*) or month (all other magazines) preceding the interview.
Source: IPSOS Cadres Actifs 1991.

EXHIBIT 11   **Perceptions, Attitudes, and Expectations Concerning Business Magazines**

---

1. The Existing Magazines
- Repetitive in content and style, from one issue to another, between one magazine and the others.
- No title with a clear profile; no originality.
- The journalists are not credible. They are either too ideologically dogmatic or mere spokesmen for the firms, or they provide inaccurate information.
- The readers feel trapped:
    They are obliged to read this press to be informed.
    The magazines make no effort to seduce them; reading is a real chore.
- Readers notice a timid change, but this more concerns the presentation (more color, more illustrations) than the content and basic philosophy of the magazines.

2. Readers' Expectations
- Useful information, instead of nebulous and pedantic discourse.
- Articles should be credible:
    The author's point of view should be clear.
    The article should be rigorous, well written, and well summarized.
    The issues should be put in perspective (comparisons over time, etc.).
- More controversy:
    Stop bootlicking well-known business figures and companies.
    Present conflicting theories and points of view.
    Show some detachment through humor and irony.
    Put issues in historical and geopolitical context.
- A wider angle:
    Greater international perspective, less French-oriented.
    Coverage of cultural topics.
    One or two humorous pages.
- A more attractive presentation:
    Clear table of contents.
    Facilitate reading through titles, subtitles, a clear visual code.
    Many illustrations and schemas.
    The articles should be more "airy."
    One or two very incisive and conclusive articles on specific topics (a double-page maximum).

Source: Report on two focus groups with senior and middle managers. Eliane Mikowski, Paris, Fall 1990.

- *More useful.* More coverage of personal interest topics like career management, continuing education, salaries, insurance, personal investments, etc. (similar to what the German magazines *Capital* and *DM* as well as *Le Revenu Français* and *Mieux Vivre* covered).
- *More informative.* All articles should be well researched and objective.
- *More international.* International aspects should be covered systematically and be based on facts rather than national stereotypes.
- *More visual.* The layout should be more attractive, reading should be facilitated, and the photographic material should be original, rather than relying on easily available photos of a small number of business celebrities.

This concept was immediately translated into a "flat plan." Such a plan allocates pages to the various content areas, defines specific articles in each content area, and, finally, describes the order of appearance of the articles. Development of the flat plan drew on everybody's industry knowledge, and many features were inspired by other magazines, both French and foreign. Two questions were asked throughout: (1) are the choices consistent with the product concept? and (2) do they lead to a clear competitive advantage?

The next immediate step was to produce a first prototype of the magazine by January 1991 and to test it with a group of potential readers. A second, revised prototype would be produced by April 1991 and a third by July 1991. The market launch was scheduled for September 1991.

Prototyping the New Concept

As Prisma Presse had no previous experience in the business market, five external journalists were recruited to work exclusively on the *Hermès* project. Some had extensive experience in the French business press, others were younger journalists. Just as for the editor-in-chief, it turned out to be difficult to find journalists having excellent business/economic knowledge, and willing to adapt to the editorial principles and culture of Prisma Presse. Recruitment remained a problem throughout, and several journalists were eventually asked to leave.

The team was given a separate, closed-off open-plan office in the Prisma Presse building. Access was highly restricted and, apart from the management duo, the art group, and Prisma Presse's senior management, the team had no contact with any other Prisma Presse staff, nor with other parts of the Gruner+Jahr organization, including the journalists working for Gruner+Jahr's *Capital* in Germany.

Organized around the main content areas of the magazine, the journalists immediately started to implement the flat plan. The important role of initiating them in the "Prisma Presse formula" fell to art director Thierry Rouxel, who discussed with each journalist at the outset the concept of the projected article, as well as the number and types of illustrations, and the layout on the page. Constant attention was paid to the integration of text, visuals, and layout as the articles progressed. At other magazines, the journalists' role was usually limited to writing articles, with editorial secretaries and visual staff adding their contributions afterwards. The tight schedule led to a very heavy workload, sometimes forcing journalists to work around the clock.

The first prototype was ready in January 1991. Kept under tight security control, the 50-page dummy had no cover page and no name. The articles chosen were deliberately sensational to find out how far one could go in the direction of entertainment and still be considered a serious business magazine. Many focused on power struggles (e.g., "1 seat for 3 pretenders," "The barons' conspiracy") or demolished well-known business figures (e.g., "Tapie doesn't have what it takes"). The dummy also included a psychological test ("Are you a real boss?"), an analysis of managers' difficulties with their children ("Daddy, I never see you!"), and a map of a fashionable Champs-Elysées restaurant indicating celebrities' preferred tables.

The dummy was immediately tested with two focus groups composed of target group members. After a first quick flick through they expressed pleasant surprise with the numerous photos, the big headlines, and the clear layout, which made for easy reading. But as they read the articles in greater depth, their mood turned negative and even angry. The magazine was too sensational, too negative ("vitriolic"), and too superficial for them—it was only good "to be read at the hairdresser's."

Undaunted, the team proceeded to produce a second prototype. They made small modifications in layout, headlines, and subheadings of articles already tested (see Exhibit 12), and concentrated on producing other articles that would demonstrate the seriousness of the magazine. A 16-page article on the battle between European and

EXHIBIT 12
The Evolution of
Capital

January '91

April '91

July '91

Japanese automobile manufacturers was the longest and most intensively researched article.

The second, 100-page prototype, still without cover page or name, was tested with two focus groups in April 1991. The magazine's presentation was again very well received. But this time, the content was also praised for its diversity, factual grounding, and good summarizing of important information. The managers liked the editorial style, which was "the opposite of the bland, insipid style" of the habitual business journalism and reflected a desire to "see things the way they really are." Most of them felt like buying the magazine, reading it from cover to cover, and keeping it for future reference.

As always, Axel Ganz was watching the focus groups over closed-circuit TV. Before the second group drew to an end, he fetched some champagne, popped the corks, and declared "we will launch this magazine!"

Up to this point, the project had cost about F6 million. Funding for further development including a test launch was available through the development budget already approved by Gruner+Jahr. A test launch would require some more recruitment, but the team of journalists would receive no guarantee of continuing beyond the test phase. A full-blown launch like the one Axel Ganz had in mind, however, involved a more massive and longer-term commitment and required the formal approval of Gruner+Jahr and Bertelsmann. Dr. Wiele prepared a 10-page (plus exhibits) report, which summarized the market situation, explained the product and marketing concept for *Hermès,* and specified the main assumptions underlying the eight-year projected income. If circulation after six months failed to exceed 50,000, the magazine would be discontinued. It was estimated that cumulative investment would have reached F60 million at this point. As expected, the Gruner+Jahr and Bertelsmann boards gave the green light in May and June, respectively.

The Zero Issue: *Hermès* Becomes *Capital*

The third prototype was the magazine's "zero" issue. Identical to a real magazine in presentation and editorial content, its main purposes were to test readers' response to the real product, to scale up and test the production process, and, last but not least, to draw advertising.

To produce the zero issue, the magazine's staff was increased to 32, mostly by hiring from the outside. Almost all articles were new. The main editorial response to April's market research results was yet another increase in the number of pages devoted to "service" topics (management techniques, career and salary, personal finance) to 26 out of 110 editorial pages in total (see Exhibit 13). A separate macroeconomic section printed on pink paper (the same color as the *Financial Times* and the economic supplement of a leading French newspaper) was added in the center of the magazine, and a tongue-in-cheek page appeared at the end.

What should the magazine be called? Because it was originally thought that the name *Capital* had negative connotations in France, other names had been considered, including the once more available *Fortune,* which might open doors with advertisers and information sources. Negotiations failed, however, and in the end the name *Capital* was chosen, with the subtitle "The Essence of the Economy."

Capital was the first Prisma Presse magazine created with a completely integrated PC-based publishing system. This permitted several iterations before the final version was transmitted electronically to the Bertelsmann printing plant in Gütersloh, Germany.

EXHIBIT 13   Number of Editorial Pages per Content Category

Content Categories	Capital		L'Expansion
	Flat Plan January 1991	Zero Issue July 1991	July 4–17 1991
People	14	12	3
Business	16	16	14
Success stories			
Mismanagement stories			
International file and macroeconomy	21	22	21
The economy in pictures and special topics	21	18	18
Service topics	15	26	1
Management techniques			
Career & salary			
Money & investments			
Lifestyle, leisure, business travel	21	16	5
Total number of editorial pages	108	110	62

Virtually everybody participated in the discussions of each version, including Axel Ganz. "He intervenes less in the content of articles than in the presentation, and occasionally shows a layouter how to solve a problem," commented Rémy Dessarts. In the end, all remaining issues were solved by hierarchy and, as always, Axel Ganz gave the green light after having gone through the final version page by page, line by line.

To Launch or Not to Launch . . .

Hot off the press, the zero issue of *Capital* was tested with two focus groups on July 23 and 24, with positive results (see Exhibit 14). Normally, this would be a good basis for drawing advertising, for which Constance Benqué, former head of *L'Expansion*'s advertising department, has just been recruited.

But is this the right time to launch a new business magazine? Since the beginning of the year, advertising volume in business magazines has declined by about 20 percent, and there are no signs of recovery, despite the end of the Gulf war. The entire economic press is suffering. The L'Expansion group, all of whose titles are in the economic press, is rumored to be in the red and reducing staff. *A pour Affaires* merged with *L'Entreprise* in June. *Science & Vie Economie* cut short its relaunch advertising campaign prematurely. The Reader's Digest group has just withdrawn its new personal finance magazine *Budgets famille* only six months after launch.

Dr. Wiele is wondering whether he should recommend that the planned September launch of *Capital* be postponed. If they do go ahead with the launch, they have to decide on its price, distribution, and communication policies. Dr. Wiele sees two main alternatives: a "subscription" strategy and a "newsstand" strategy.

The subscription strategy would be in line with the other business magazines: a high newsstand price (e.g., F25) combined with a high subscription discount and a massive direct mail investments, resulting in subscription sales mainly.

The newsstand strategy would be a new approach for the business magazine market: a F15 newsstand price, identical to that of the weekly news magazines, combined with a low subscription discount and high mass media advertising. If *Capital* were

EXHIBIT 14   Zero Number of *Capital:* Perceptions and Attitudes

The main attitude is one of surprise in front of an object that is new in the context of the economic press. This is backed up by the following perceptions:

- Great richness and variety:
   "This is life, this is the world."
- Great density and true information.
- Great ease of reading:
   "Freedom of reading, depending on the circumstances, how much time I have, and how I feel."
   "One can read over lightly, for entertainment, or go for a detailed reading."
- A style:
   "Sharp." "The journalists take position," "interrogative"
- Professional:
   "Well researched," "The journalists have good access," "The magazine is pleasant . . . good pictures . . . attractive colors."

Overall, *Capital* will create an event in the market. It has great competitive potential both in the business magazine market and in the news magazine market. But readers hesitate regarding the magazine's identity and personality:

- A business or a news magazine?
- A "people" or a business information magazine?
- Superficial or dense?
- Structured or muddled?
- Judicious advice or consumerism?
- Specialization or popularization?

Source: Report on two focus groups with senior and middle managers. Eliane Mikowski, Paris, July 23–24, 1991.

published on the same day as these news magazines (Thursday or Friday) and displayed prominently, a significant share of the 600,000 buyers of weekly news magazines at the newsstands might pick up *Capital* once a month in addition to, or instead of, a news magazine. About 20 percent of news magazine readers fall into *Capital's* reader target group.

Exhibits 15 and 16 summarize the key assumptions necessary to evaluate these alternative strategies. At Gruner+Jahr, magazines are expected to reach break-even within three to four years, pay back within five to eight years, and return 15 percent on investment in the long term.

Exhibit 15   **Key Economic Assumptions for *Capital***

	1991–92	1998–99
Product		
Number of editorial pages/issue	110	120
Number of issues/year	10 (Oct. –July)	12 (August–July)
Editorial costs/editorial page	20,000 F	Increase: 3% p.a.
Mechanical costs/printed page	0.05 F	Increase: 3% p.a.
Department costs (management, advertising department)/year	6 F million	Increase: 5% p.a.
Newsstand Distribution		
Distribution margin (% of newsstand price)	55%	55%
% unsold rate (% of copies delivered to newsstands that are not sold)	50%	30%
Subscription Distribution		
Avg. cost of a new subscriber		
Via direct mail (mailing list purchase, direct mail)	300 F–1,000 F per subscription*	300 F–1,000 F per subscription*
Via self-promotion (subscription appeals included in *Capital*)	20 F per subscription	Increase: 3%
Self-promotion yield (share of newsstand copies for which subscription forms are sent)	1%	1%
Subscription renewal rate (%)	50–60%*	50–60%*
Avg. cost of renewing a subscription	20 F–80 F*	20 F–80 F*
Cost of serving a subscription (administration, postage, etc.)	4 F per copy	Increase: 3% p.a.
Advertising Market		
4-color ad page cost/1,000 circulation	755 F	Increase: 4% p.a.
Avg. net adv. revenue/adv. page	57%	57%
Advertising promotion/adv. page	3,200 F	Increase: 4% p.a.

* The greater the number of subscriptions, the higher the average cost of acquiring and renewing a subscription, and the lower the subscription renewal rate.

Exhibit 16   **Circulation Market Mix**

	"Subscription" Strategy			"Newsstand" Strategy		
Year	Newsstand Price (Subscr. Disct: 30%)	Media Adv. per Copy	Subscription Share (% of Total Circul.)	Newsstand Price (Subscr. Disc: 17.5%)	Media Adv. per Copy	Subscription Share (% of Total Circul.)
1991–92	25F	11F	70%	15F	21F	9%
1992–93	28F	5F	70	18F	10F	17
1993–94	30F	3F	70	20F	5F	24
1994–95	33F	3F	70	22F	5F	30
1995–96	35F	3F	70	22F	5F	34
1996–97	38F	3F	70	25F	5F	36
1997–98	40F	3F	70	25F	5F	37
1998–99	43F	3F	70	25F	5F	38

While attending sessions during a four-week marketing program at the International Marketing Institute in Boston in July 1991, Herb Maridadi's thoughts were divided between what the speakers were saying and what was transpiring at National Breweries. Maridadi, marketing and public affairs director for National Breweries (NatBrew), would have to "hit the ground running" when his plane touched down in Zimbabwe the first week of August.

Since its inception in 1876, NatBrew had been the sole manufacturer of beer in Zimbabwe. However, two competitors were poised to enter the Zimbabwe market—one through a wholly owned South African subsidiary funded primarily by an American company and the other through a Zimbabwean conglomerate in a joint venture with a German brewery. The issue was magnified by escalating price increases, declining volume in sales, and a generally negative perception of NatBrew by its consumers.

Zimbabwe[1]

Zimbabwe, a land-locked country in southern Africa of about 151,000 square miles, is surrounded by Zambia, Mozambique, South Africa, Botswana, and Namibia (see Exhibit 1). The capital of Zimbabwe is Harare. In 1990, the population was around 9 million, comprised of 30 percent urban residents and 70 percent rural, with English as the official language. The labor force comprised a little over 25 percent of the population, with a civilian labor force of about 2 million and armed forces of 38,000.

Historically, political stability in Zimbabwe had been poor. From 1889 to 1922, Zimbabwe was administered by the British South Africa Company. In 1923, it became a self-governing colony renamed Southern Rhodesia. When Britain refused to grant independence to Zimbabwe, due to its proposed undemocratic style of government, a Unilateral Declaration of Independence was made in 1963. Following that, the United Nations imposed economic sanctions against Zimbabwe, and nationalist guerrilla warfare ensued throughout the 1970s. Independence and majority rule was finally accepted in 1979, with the new majority government formed in 1980. Since then, socialist policies have existed for Zimbabwe, yet some suggest only modest implementation of such policies. Military aid and training were received from the United Kingdom and the Democratic People's Republic of Korea.

Economically, an IMF World Bank package was adopted by the government in 1990, where prices and labor were decontrolled and government spending cut. In the short term, this led to high inflation, high unemployment, stronger growth in gross domestic product (GDP), reduction in balance of payments (BOP) deficit, and a

This case was prepared by Victoria L. Crittenden, associate professor of marketing at Boston College, and William F. Crittenden, associate professor of management at Northeastern University. The case is designed as the basis for class discussion. All material was obtained from secondary sources.

[1] Sources: *The Economics of Africa,* 1991, and *The Europe World Year Book,* 1990.

EXHIBIT 1   Map of Africa

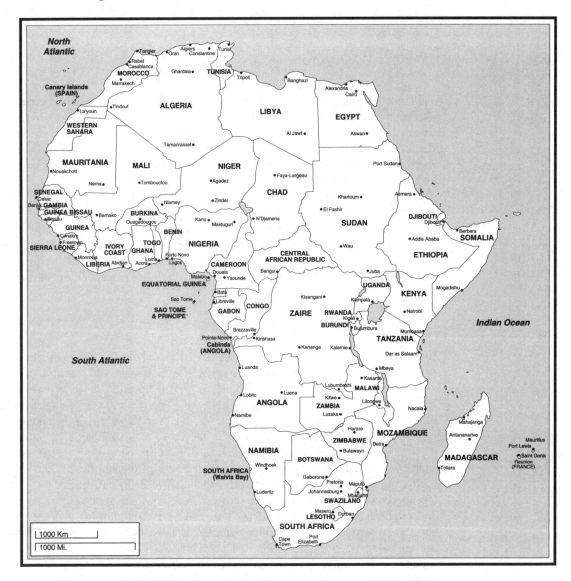

budget deficit. GDP growth was approximately 4.5 percent, with 17 percent inflation expected to continue to rise. There was growth in the private sector, with the government having a policy of purchasing shares in private sector enterprises. Zimbabwe exports (around US$1,690 million) included gold, tobacco, metals, and cotton to such destinations as the United Kingdom, Germany, South Africa, and the United States. The country imported around US$1,260 million such items as machinery, chemicals, and energy from these same countries. Per capita income was around Z$1,930 (approximately US$850) in 1990.

Beer Industry

Manufacturing.   The production of clear beer[2] consists of eight basic steps:

1. Malting—soaking the barley to start germination to unbind amylase enzyme (turns starch into sugar when heated).
2. Mashing—adding heated water to convert starches to sugar and filtering out liquid, making "wort."
3. Brewing—boiling the wort with hops to stop the conversion to sugar, adding a bitter flavor to the wort.
4. Fermenting—filtering and cooling wort, adding yeast to convert wort into beer.
5. Lagering—storing beer at freezing, with yeast settling out and beer becoming clearer and tastier.
6. Carbonating—adding purified water to rid beer of oxygen, which destroys flavor.
7. Pasteurizing—boiling at 142 to 145 degrees Fahrenheit to stop fermentation.
8. Packaging—bottling or canning of the beer.

In order to diversify products, brewers altered and manipulated the basic brewing process by, for example, adding stirring mechanisms or raising the temperature in the fermenting stage to speed the process or adding chemicals such as tannin to speed the lagering process. However, product differentiation was very difficult among competitive breweries because very few changes could be made in the manufacturing process to alter the product. Thus, much emphasis was on the marketing of the beer product to enhance perceptual differences among products.[3]

Worldwide Market.   Beer brewing was a worldwide industry with sales in 1989 totaling US$200 billion. The brewing industry was highly concentrated with seven countries dominating the market: United States (23 percent of the world market), Germany (12 percent), England (6 percent), Russia (5 percent), Japan (5 percent), Brazil (4 percent), and China (4 percent). (See Exhibit 2.) Beer production and sales increased yearly as countries became more and more sophisticated in their marketing and operations.

The largest exporters of beer, ranked by volume, were The Netherlands, Germany, Czechoslovakia, Belgium, and Canada. The largest importers of beer by volume were the United States, the United Kingdom, France, Italy, and Germany.

The internationalization of the beer brewing industry occurred by three major means: (1) cross-border buying and selling, (2) licensing agreements, and (3) foreign direct investment.[4] As such, there was heavy concentration in the beer industry.

In volume, world trade in beer tripled from 1965 to 1990, with an average annual growth rate of 6.5 percent. Such factors as lower trade barriers, more efficient communication and transportation technology, and growth in real personal income contributed greatly to this cross-border trade expansion.

---

[2] "Clear" beer was produced from ingredients such as water, barley malt, rice, yeast, hops, and tannin. Another type of beer, "opaque," was made from beans, maize, and sorghum. Nutritionists considered the opaque beer much healthier than clear beer. Opaque beer was also cheaper to produce than clear beer, resulting in a lower retail price.

[3] Anheuser-Busch, for example, marketed its "beech wood aging process" which meant that wood chips, washed in baking soda, were added to the beer during storage.

[4] Much of this information was obtained from Karrenbrock, 1990.

EXHIBIT 2
Brewing Industry Worldwide Market Shares

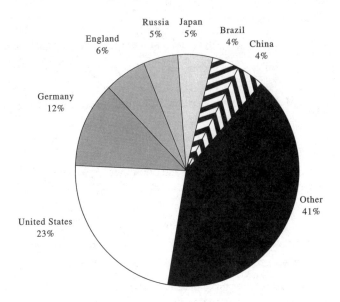

Russia 5%
Japan 5%
England 6%
Brazil 4%
China 4%
Germany 12%
Other 41%
United States 23%

Licensing agreements made it possible for brewers to make their products available to the foreign consumer by allowing a brewer in one country to brew and market the beer of a foreign company. Positive components of such arrangements included the circumventing of trade barriers, decreased transportation costs (beer is about 90 percent water, so a foreign brewer shipping complete product was paying for shipping a lot of water), and decreased cycle time from production to consumer (shipment could take almost a month).

Regarding foreign direct investment, a brewer might invest in a new or existing brewery in a foreign country. In addition to circumventing trade barriers and decreasing transportation costs and cycle time, the foreign brewer was encouraged by lower labor and energy costs and less government regulation in the foreign investment. For example, Lonrho, the sixth largest alcohol transnational company in 1986, operated 19 breweries in joint ventures with the African Governments and Municipalities and several wineries in France, as well as operating one of Scotland's major whiskey distilleries. Investments such as this allowed Lonrho to have a presence in over 80 countries.

African Breweries.   There were 36 clear beer breweries in all of Africa. Nine of these were found in Zimbabwe and its neighboring countries. There were three breweries in Mozambique. Fabrica de Cerveja da Beera, LDA, was located in Beira. The company was not involved in any exporting of its annual capacity of 240,000 hectoliters. Brands distributed by this company were Manica Clara, Monica Preta, and Impala. Cia. de Cerbesjas Erefrigerantes Mac-Mahon in Maputo had an annual capacity of 100,000 hectoliters. Fabricas de Cervesja Reunidas de Mocambique, Lda., with annual capacity of 230,000 hectoliters, was in Maputo also.

Zambia was home to one brewery, located in Lusaka. Annual capacity in Zambia Breweries Ltd. was 400,000 hectoliters, with brands Castle Lager and Lion Lager.

The Republic of South Africa had three breweries. Alrode Brewery in Alrode (Transvaal) employed 1,000 workers and had annual capacity of 4,300,000 hectoliters. Brands included Castle Lager, Lion Lager, Castle Milk Stout, Hansa Pilsener, Amstel

Lager, and Ohlsson's Lager. Ohlsson's Brewery in Claremont (Cape Town) was home to brands such as Castle Lager, Lion Lager, Amstel, Black Label, Hansa Pilsener, Castle Milk Stout, and Ohlsson's. Ohlsson's had 711 employees and an annual capacity of 2.2 million hectoliters, with an export volume of 5,000 hectoliters. The South African Breweries in Port Elizabeth (C.P.) had an annual capacity of 950,000 hectoliters for its brands of Castle Lager, Lion Lager, Black Label, Hansa Pilsener, Castle Milk Stout, Ohlsson's, and Amstel. The brewery had 633 employees. All three of these South Africa breweries were subsidiaries of The South African Breweries Beer Division with its central office in Johannesburg (Transvaal).

The other two breweries, owned by National Breweries, were in Zimbabwe. Located in Southerton and Harare, the two breweries employed 2,000 workers. Brands provided by National Breweries included Castle Lager, Lion Lager, Carling Black Label, Castle Pilsener, and Zambezi Lager. National Breweries exported the Zambezi brand to several countries, including Britain, United States, and the Nordic nations.

Zimbabwean Beer Market. The alcoholic beverages industry represented approximately 7 percent of Zimbabwe's gross output of manufacturing of Z\$4,196,267,000. Major players in the industry included National Breweries, Chibuku Breweries (an opaque beer brewer), African Distillers, and Cairns Wineries. Beverages and tobacco accounted for almost 25 percent of Zimbabwe's exports and less than 1 percent of imports.

Two types of beer were popular in Zimbabwe. "Clear" beer was an alcoholic beverage brewed from malts and hops. "Opaque" beer was made from beans, maize, and sorghum. Opaque beer was cheaper and healthier than clear beer. National Breweries was the sole clear beer manufacturer in Zimbabwe. The main opaque brew was "Chibuku."

Economic difficulties limited the local intake of clear beer in the early 1990s. The effects of the World Bank and International Monetary Fund austerity measures introduced in 1990 were expected to double the already high inflation rate of 25 percent. As well, drought conditions caused carbon dioxide, a key ingredient in beer, to be in short supply. (Carbon dioxide is a product of cane.) Additionally, unemployment was expected to be around 75 percent during the early 1990s. (Agriculture and manufacturing were the biggest contributors of employment in Zimbabwe.) Total employment was slightly over 1 million in 1990, with very little increase predicted.

All in all, such economic difficulties were expected to place stress on the highly price-sensitive brewing industry. The price of a pint of beer was expected to double from 1990 to 1992.

National Breweries

A private company founded in 1876 as a wholly owned South African subsidiary, NatBrew gained autonomy in 1980 with an equity structure of

South African Breweries (S.A.)	45%
Delta Corporation (Zim./U.K.)	40
Employees	10
Others	5

With expected 1991 sales of Z\$750 million, the company's principal mission was to manufacture, distribute, and market clear beer and malt for both the domestic and export markets. NatBrew operated one malting plant and two breweries. The Maltings Division, located in Kwekwe, had an annual capacity of 45,000 tons and exported about 18,500 tons of this. This division employed 90 individuals. The two breweries were located in Southerton and Harare, employing 2,000 workers.

Product. NatBrew maintained five or six brands in the marketplace at any point in time. The major market shareholder was the Castle Lager brand with 80 percent of the market. The brand was positioned as the mainstream, heritage brand in South Africa with the slogan "The taste that has stood the test of time." The beer was medium alcohol that was considered neither bitter or sweet. Lion Lager had 12 percent market share. The brand was targeted at the upper mainstream and masculine markets. "Go all the way with Lion Lager" was the advertising theme. Carling Black Label was NatBrew's third runner in the market, with 6 percent share. The target consumer for Carling Black Label was the manual worker. The beer, which was strong alcohol with a slightly sweet taste, was positioned as "America's lively, lusty beer."

The remaining 2 percent of the market went to what NatBrew referred to as niche brands. These included Amstel (Lager), Castle Pilsener, Castle Milk Stout, Bohlingers Export Premium Lager, and Zambezi Premium Lager.

Price. NatBrew followed a differentiated pricing structure for each of its brands. Lion Lager, targeted to the upper mainstream, was its premium-priced beer, followed by Castle Lager and Carling Black Lager. The average wholesale price of a NatBrew beer was Z$1.35 per 375 ml unit. The export wholesale price was about 20 percent lower than local market wholesale prices.

NatBrew did not have any control over retail price setting. A wide range of prices was reported, basically dependent upon retail outlet and packaging (e.g., draft/bottle, one bottle/six-pack). By 1991, retail outlets had taken price increases ranging from 20 percent ("off" consumption) to 80 percent ("on" consumption).

The price of beer was expected to double by 1993 with the structural adjustment program introduced by the World Bank and International Monetary Fund. This would be reflected in both wholesale and retail prices. Naturally, the removal of price controls would affect raw materials used to produce beer, with cost of goods sold increasing at a rate comparable to wholesale and retail prices.

There was concern that combined factors such as price deregulation, the drought, a drop in disposable consumer income, and a 41 percent excise duty on wholesale draught beer would push clear beer to luxury item status.

Communications. NatBrew's 1990 communications budget was approximately Z$4 million, allocated across all of its brands. The media advertising budget was comprised of television (two channels), radio (four channels), press, and magazines. Promotional components of the budget went to support sporting events and point-of-purchase displays.

NatBrew's three major brands and its niche brands were represented by different advertising agencies. The Castle Lager account was with Lintas; Barker McCormack was in charge of Lion Lager; Matthewman, Banks & Associates handled the Carling Black Label business; and Young and Rubicam serviced the niche brands.

The sales force at NatBrew was broken down into three levels. Two general sales managers worked with six sales managers, who in turn managed 18 sales representatives. The sales force compensation system was two-thirds salary and one-third commission.

Distribution.   NatBrew's brands of beer could be found in approximately 4,400 retail outlets, including supermarkets, bottle stores, restaurants, beer gardens, and hotels. The company operated 23 distribution depots throughout Zimbabwe. Accounts were serviced via 340 NatBrew trucks.

Sales Volume.   Sales volume had more than doubled from 1980 to 1990, with a moving average growth of around 13 percent. While increases were budgeted for both 1991 and 1992, there was doubt among management that such increases would be imminent in the local market. One local bottle store had reported a 50 percent drop in weekly clear beer sales. Additionally, nightclubs were unusually quiet during the week.

NatBrew hoped to cover at least some part of the expected drop in domestic market sales with its export business. The company exported to South Africa, Zambia, Mozambique, Tanzania, Australia, and Great Britain. Reportedly, however, exports accounted for only 1 percent of NatBrew sales.

Competition.   Since 1876, NatBrew was the sole manufacturer of clear beer in Zimbabwe. However, this was expected to change as two new players entered the Zimbabwean marketplace. Little competitive information was available to NatBrew regarding the marketing plan of the two breweries.

Nisbitt Breweries had plans to launch one draft and one bottled beer brand into the Zimbabwean market by September 1991. Nisbitt was a wholly owned South African subsidiary funded primarily from the American brewing company. The American company held around 5 percent of U.S. market share. The Zimbabwean partner in this arrangement was a former NatBrew employee who was considered to be very bright and self-made.

A major Zimbabwean conglomerate, T.A. Holdings, specialized in hotels, restaurants, and engineering industries. The conglomerate had just begun building a brewery in a joint venture with a German brewery. Rumor was that a well-known German beer brand would be launched from the new Zimbabwe brewery. T.A. Holdings was a rich, aggressive company with substantial financial and skills backup.

The Situation

Herb Maridadi's departure date was approaching rapidly. He had enjoyed the marketing program and felt that he had learned a lot about marketing. But, would he be able to apply this knowledge at his own company, National Breweries?

Herb knew that NatBrew was headed for difficult times. After 20 years of a "command economy," the government had lifted price and wage controls. As a result, retail outlets had taken tremendous price increases. Consequently, sales volume had dropped, as had consumer disposable income. In addition, two competitor breweries were expected to be commissioned within 1991. As Zimbabwe's sole clear beer manufacturer since 1876, NatBrew had never experienced direct competition. To add injury, recent market research had shown that consumers perceived NatBrew to be a "fat cat" (rich, monopolistic, arrogant, extravagant, uncaring) and would welcome competition.

Maridadi had to decide where to begin. He had to have concrete, implementable ideas immediately upon his return to Zimbabwe.

Sources

"Bitter Experience for Zimbabwe." *The Daily Telegraph,* September 15, 1992.

Clairmonte, Frederick F., and John H. Cavanagh. "TNCs and the Global Beverage Industry." *The CTC Reporter,* Autumn 1990.

Echeverria, Alfredo, Frank Keane, David Kerr, Jim LeGates, and Peter J. Moran. "Adolph Coors and the Brewing Industry." Classroom Report, Northeastern University, June 5, 1990.

Karrenbrock, Jeffrey D. "The Internationalization of the Beer Brewing Industry." *Federal Reserve Bank of St. Louis,* November-December 1990.

"Liquor Industry Hit by Drought, Inflation, Excise Duties." *Agence France Presse,* September 12, 1992.

MBA Blue Book '91.

Mackenzie, Ian. "Job Creation Critical for Zimbabwean Economy." *The Reuter Library Report,* May 7, 1992.

Olekanya, Paul. "Zimbabwe: Breweries Business on the Skids." *Inter Press Service,* November 3, 1992.

"Zimbabwe Alcohol Breweries Impressed with Turnover." *Reuters, Limited,* November 7, 1993.

Case 6–7
Chemical Additives Corporation–Specialty Products Group

Nick Williamson, general manager, Specialty Products Group (SPG), gazed out his window and sighed. It was August 1990 and the atmosphere inside his office was as unpleasant as the 100-degree weather of the Fort Smith, Arkansas, headquarters of SPG. He swiveled back to face his management team, and said, "OK, I've heard your arguments about positioning and pricing 'R&D 601, 602, and 603.' I wish there were some way to get a consensus from you guys. I'll consider our options over the weekend."

The decisions facing Williamson would have substantial impact on the future of SPG. A strategy of moving away from large-volume commodity wax markets toward becoming a premier supplier of specialty chemical additives to niche markets was not going as smoothly as anticipated. Three newly developed products might well be the catalyst to hasten that shift. These new products, known by their experimental designations R&D 601, 602, and 603, were corrosion inhibitors used during the transport and storage of liquid urea ammonium nitrate (UAN) fertilizer.

Liquid Fertilizers

Liquid fertilizers had numerous advantages over the traditional solid fertilizers principally used in U.S. agriculture: (1) excellent performance under a variety of weather conditions, (2) reduced toxicity, (3) ability to be easily blended with other nutrients, insecticides, and herbicides, and (4) milder environmental impact (but not benign; a spill or leak of undiluted UAN could still kill wildlife and vegetation).

Unfortunately, UAN liquids corroded the steel tanks, pipelines, railcars, and barges used for storage and transport, resulting in repair costs that could exceed $1 million per incident for the typical UAN producer. The industry had tried a variety of corrosion inhibitors (chemicals that were added in small dosages to UAN after production) to reduce the rate at which the UAN ate away a metal surface. Inhibitors did not prevent corrosion; they slowed the chemical reaction of metal dissolving into UAN. An excellent inhibitor might increase the average life of a typical $20 million storage system from as little as three years to longer than 20 years.

Leaks and spills also created liabilities for EPA fines. If a tank failure resulted in massive environmental damage, federal lawsuits could potentially bankrupt a producer. Corrosion inhibitor suppliers might also be liable for leaks and environmental damages.

Manufacturers produced UAN fertilizer in continuous-process facilities with typical minimum capacities of 10,000 tons a year. They then added corrosion inhibitors and stored the inhibited UAN in tanks to await shipment. Producers shipped UAN through a distributor/dealer network that delivered the product to the right farmer, at the right

The case was prepared by Charles Hoffheiser and Lester A. Neidell, University of Tulsa. Permission to reprint granted by the authors and the North American Case Research Association.

time, and with appropriate other agricultural chemicals added as necessary. Some larger dealers provided custom-application services to apply UAN blends to fields and crops. The same distribution system also handled the solid fertilizers UAN was slowly replacing.

SPG designed these experimental products to replace SPG's earlier entries into this market, as well as to regain business previously lost to a widely used, foreign-sourced material, Corblok 105-B. The sales and marketing managers each strongly argued contrary marketing tactics. Vice President of Sales Ron White reasoned that despite any performance advantages of the new SPG products, market conditions in the U.S. fertilizer industry required that SPG price the new products as low as possible using only the mandatory minimum corporate markup over standard cost. White had always operated with the objective of keeping company plants operating close to capacity to minimize standard costs. Price leadership and volume were, in his eyes, the key to SPG's success.

Jim Walker, newly hired as director of marketing (a new position at SPG), vehemently favored a value-based pricing approach, recognizing both product performance and competitive conditions. The technical director regularly reminded these two managers that the three products performed differently in different producers' UANs and added, "You guys better start selling some of this stuff soon to pay off our investment of over four years of technical effort!"

Chemical Additives Corporation

SPG was one of four divisions of the Chemical Additives Corporation (CAC), a multinational company providing solutions to production problems in oil fields, refineries, chemical plants, and other industrial applications. The corporate mission statement was

> to produce and market specialty chemical products and the technical service and equipment necessary to utilize CAC's products effectively.

CAC pursued a strategy of developing customized equipment and chemical treatment programs to add value to customers' operations through optimization of operating efficiency or increased reliability. CAC's strengths included expertise in organic phosphate ester chemistry (the key to advanced technology corrosion inhibitors) and in the mixing of incompatible fluids (e.g., oil and water). It considered itself to be the worldwide leader in oil industry corrosion control and had developed and patented much of the technology historically used in these applications. However, over the past 10 years, competitors found it increasingly easy to design products outside patent coverages, particularly as R&D departments began to use advanced computer modeling techniques. Computer modeling made it much easier to design new families of chemical products.

CAC organized its operations into four operating groups—Oil Field Chemicals, Refinery Chemicals, Instrument Group, and Specialty Products. Each group maintained its own sales, marketing, and product development functions. A central research department conducted long-range, basic chemical research for all divisions.

The Oil Field Chemicals Group was the world's largest supplier of oil field production chemicals, including corrosion inhibitors and drilling aids. Since its products went "down the hole," appearance, odor, and handling characteristics, such as foaming, were often not of concern to customers. The sales force's requests for customer-specific products drove product development. This division had over 4,000 products in its line. The group justified this product line breadth in two ways: (1) no two oil deposits were identical in chemical makeup, and (2) as wells aged, increasing amounts of exotic chemicals were needed to enhance oil production.

Refinery Chemicals marketed process efficiency aids for the production side of refineries. It also sold fuel additives such as fuel-injector cleaners to refiners and to wholesalers of gasoline and truck diesel fuel.

The Instrument Group designed and marketed filtration and purification systems that solved a variety of water and oil-related process problems in refineries. Customers often used this equipment in conjunction with CAC's chemical treatment programs. This group also sold a complete line of premium-quality corrosion monitoring instruments.

Specialty Products Group had two major product groups: (1) about 100 types of commodity petroleum waxes (similar but not identical to the types used in candles) that were separated from crude oil and (2) synthetic polymers based on a chemical called propylene. Common examples of polymers are plastic food wrap and vinyl siding for houses. SPG's synthetics, however, were not the type used in plastic film, cups, or containers. Customers often called them synthetic waxes because they had properties similar to commodity petroleum waxes. Nick Williamson tried to alter this perception by extensive trade advertising and by instructing division personnel to refer to all division products as "specialty polymers." SPG's products had hundreds of applications, ranging from shoe polish to chewing gum to cardboard box sealing adhesives. Various SPG products had also found modest use as antidust and anticaking additives for solid fertilizers, and as a result, SPG conducted all of CAC's business in the worldwide fertilizer industry.

Exhibit 1 contains selected CAC and divisional financial data; Exhibit 2 shows the distribution of SPG revenue and profit by end-use market and the allocation of salespeople.

SPG's Competitors

Each division had its own set of specialized competitors as well as competition from various divisions of large chemical companies such as DuPont, Dow, Witco, and Shell. The 1980s ushered in a new era in the chemical industry—worldwide competition. (Corblok, principal competitor to SPG's UAN anticorrosion additives, was an example of this.) Foreign suppliers also directly affected other SPG markets. These included Mitsui, BASF, Hoechst, and Dead Sea Works, an Israeli-government–owned coal gasification plant that produced waxes as by-products of gasoline production. Except for Dead Sea, all competitors were much larger than SPG (and CAC) and were reputed to be among the most efficient chemical companies in the world.

SPG found itself with a key disadvantage versus major chemical firms because its synthetic process required liquid polypropylene, a product form supplied by only one company. The majors often had captive suppliers and used much larger volumes of less expensive gaseous polypropylene, available from many suppliers.

SPG's Marketing.   Before 1980, SPG sold its products only through distributors. Galaxy Wax and Schmidt Associates, both of which maintained regional warehouses, served the U.S. market for SPG. The Leveque Group, headquartered in Brussels, Belgium, was responsible for sales to Europe, Africa, and the Middle East. Leveque also served as principal distributor of wax products manufactured by BASF and Hoechst, both headquartered in West Germany. A joint venture between CAC and Nissan Trading Company (Japan) sold into the Far East.

**EXHIBIT 1   Chemical Additives Corporation Financial Data, 1985–89
(in thousands of dollars)**

	1985	1986	1987	1988	1989
Income Statement Data					
Net sales	$253,841	$297,208	$302,567	$287,931	$294,068
COGS	160,268	189,498	181,531	174,919	171,769
Gross profit	93,573	107,710	121,036	113,012	122,299
Selling expense	33,623	41,532	49,746	53,235	56,292
R&D expense	6,370	7,520	9,487	11,537	12,065
G&A expense	10,860	12,470	14,107	14,614	15,455
Operating profit	42,720	46,188	47,696	33,626	38,487
Investment income	774	2,500	2,139	2,533	3,722
Interest expense	(2,089)	(1,893)	(1,552)	(1,384)	(1,191)
Other net	623	1,136	203	585	1,782
EBIT	42,028	47,931	48,486	35,360	42,800
Income tax	17,143	20,174	19,190	13,310	17,000
Net earnings	$ 24,885	$ 27,757	$ 29,296	$ 22,050	$ 25,800
Balance Sheet Data					
Cash	$ 16,581	$ 12,478	$ 3,018	$ 37,201	$ 43,461
Accounts receivable	45,127	61,981	55,836	51,055	56,896
Inventory	39,639	43,751	39,785	38,976	41,296
Other current assets	64,466	77,768	77,711	91,869	104,175
Total current assets	175,544	197,782	200,318	209,105	221,514
Current liabilities	44,468	48,579	39,957	39,808	45,675
Long-term debt	12,500	11,250	10,000	8,750	7,500
Stockholders' equity	112,999	132,989	145,159	153,042	164,148
Other Financial Information					
Shares (000)	5,972	11,864	11,864	11,865	11,715
Dividends per share	$1.20	$0.76	$0.95	$1.00	$1.03
CAC Revenue by Division					
Oil Field Chemicals	$158,048	$181,614	$201,378	$199,498	$211,804
Refinery Chemicals	33,069	32,524	32,117	30,342	32,499
Specialty Products	41,554	46,410	41,483	36,969	40,041
Instruments	21,170	36,660	27,589	21,122	9,724

In 1979, in an attempt to capture the distributor margin for SPG, Williamson hired Ron White to establish a direct sales force. By 1990, SPG had two regional managers and nine salespeople in the United States (Exhibit 2). After 11 years of direct selling, there were still situations in which SPG lost business to wax distributors on price, delivery, and, in some cases, technical service.

Annual salary and benefit costs for each sales representative were about $80,000, while the two regional managers were paid about 20 percent more. These figures included a company car, but not travel and other sales expenses, which averaged an additional 10 percent of sales revenue. These numbers did not include a profit bonus plan, which typically added 2 percent of sales revenue to selling costs. An annual "salesperson of the year" award, usually based on exceeding forecast poundage figures, provided a further bonus of 5 percent of the $50,000 base to one salesperson. Salespeople developed

EXHIBIT 2   SPG End Use Segments in 1989

End Use Market	Percent of Total SPG Sales in Dollars	Percent of Total Pretax Profits	Product Life Cycle
Plastics	5%	12%	Late growth, maturity
Coatings	10	18	Late growth, maturity
Sealants	25	25	Mature
Food additives	5	3	Mature
Laminating wax	25	15	Decline
Others	30	27	Mostly mature

Philadelphia	East regional sales office, 1 sales representative
Atlanta	1 sales representative
Boston	1 sales representative
Cleveland	1 sales representative
Chicago	2 sales representatives
Fort Smith	1 sales representative
Houston	1 sales representative
Los Angeles	West regional sales office, 1 sales representative

an annual territorial sales forecast to help plan production runs and order raw materials. The sales force devoted little effort to prospecting because White kept a "sales efficiency" log for each representative that did not adjust for this sales task. Sales efficiency was calculated by dividing sales calls that yielded an order by total sales calls.

The UAN Corrosion Inhibitor Opportunity

In February 1985, the general manager of the Refinery Chemicals Group (RCG) sent Nick Williamson a memo suggesting that certain CAC products might be useful in solving corrosion problems encountered by the Jackson Pipeline Company (JPL) of Fort Smith, Arkansas. One of the refinery group's (and CAC's) largest customers, JPL was a major U.S. pipeline company, active in the transport of crude oil, gasoline, diesel and jet fuels, chemicals, and natural gas. The memo noted that, as a result of the oil bust of 1980-83, JPL attempted to build its transportation volume of other products and began shipping UAN produced by JPL's wholly owned fertilizer company, Fertex Chemicals (also with its main plant in Fort Smith). Additional UAN shipments were procured from Farm Products (Kansas City, Missouri) and Agriproducts (Sioux Falls, South Dakota). JPL's pipeline system extended to Texas, Arkansas, Oklahoma, Missouri, Kansas, Iowa, the Dakotas, Illinois, and Indiana.

Historically, UAN was shipped by (in order of increasing cost) barge, rail tank cars, and tank trucks. To use JPL's pipeline system, UAN producers were required to incorporate a corrosion inhibitor approved by JPL. However, unexpected corrosion problems with UAN severely hurt profitability of JPL's fertilizer shipping business.

The RCG memo was timely; SPG, too, had suffered from the petrochemical industry recession of 1981–83. Also, Williamson was being pushed by CAC's executive committee to move away from commodity wax products into chemical specialties that could provide protection against the price wars affecting chemical commodity markets.

Initial Entry into the UAN Corrosion Control Market.   In late 1986, SPG introduced Stealth 3660, an oil field corrosion inhibitor, for use in transporting liquid UAN. SPG's choice of Stealth 3660 was based on its proven success in the oil field and the assumption that corrosion control was a similar phenomenon regardless of end use environment. After testing, JPL recommended 3660 to its Fertex subsidiary and to its two other customers: Farm Products and Agriproducts. SPG priced 3660 at its standard markup, 100 percent above its standard cost. At this price, 3660 cost fertilizer producers 50 percent less than the previously approved Corblok 105-B inhibitor. All three UAN manufacturers soon switched to 3660.

However, Fertex detected toxic fumes exceeding Occupational Safety and Health Administration (OSHA) defined lethal concentrations at the top hatch of trucks used to deliver the product from CAC's Chicago plant. In 1987, Fertex reverted to using Corblok.

Unwilling to lose this market, Williamson instructed R&D to select another product from the oil field corrosion inhibitor line. In mid-1987, SPG introduced Stealth 3662 to JPL and its three customers. The toxicity problem appeared to be solved, while the usage cost was the same as 3660. By late 1987, all three fertilizer companies were buying 3662 in tank-truck quantities. As mid-1988 approached, word of mouth in the fertilizer industry persuaded firms such as Iowa Fertilizer, Ferticon, Nitrogen Industries, Marathon Chemical, and others to use 3662.

Like Stealth 3660, SPG priced 3662 at 100 percent markup over standard cost. Tank-truck (40,000 pounds) quantities sold for $0.80 per pound, and 55-gallon drums for $0.83 per pound, with costs of $0.40 per pound and $0.415 per pound, respectively. According to CAC policy, if a product was not priced at least 100 percent above cost, it was not defined as a "specialty chemical" and did not qualify for recognition as supporting the corporate mission of becoming a specialty chemical firm. SPG's goal was to derive at least 30 percent of its gross sales revenue from specialties by 1990.

In late 1988, Fertex reported to SPG that its UAN was causing severe foaming problems when mixed with other fertilizer components such as pesticides and herbicides, a practice that was typical at the fertilizer dealer level. By spring 1989, Fertex switched back to Corblok. As a result of the foaming incidents, SPG became aware that UAN passed through a dealer/distributor network before farmers applied it to fields and crops. SPG salespeople had typically called on fertilizer producers and not on other channel members.

Worried about SPG's ability to compete effectively in the UAN corrosion control market, Williamson directed Ron White to hire a sales engineer or product manager to get the UAN corrosion inhibitor program on track. In August 1989, Bob Brown joined SPG in this capacity. Williamson also hired a director of marketing, Jim Walker, in October 1989 and charged him with changing the culture of SPG from a sales/manufacturing/technology-driven business to a market-driven business.

SPG's 1989 organizational chart is shown in Exhibit 3; Exhibit 4 contains background information on SPG's key personnel.

Corrosion Inhibitor Technology.   Corrosion results from a complex chemical reaction that changes steel to useless iron oxide. UAN producers used two basic types of corrosion inhibitors: passivators and film-formers. Passivators formed a protective coating by chemically reacting with the steel surfaces they were supposed to protect.

EXHIBIT 3 **SPG's Organization Chart**

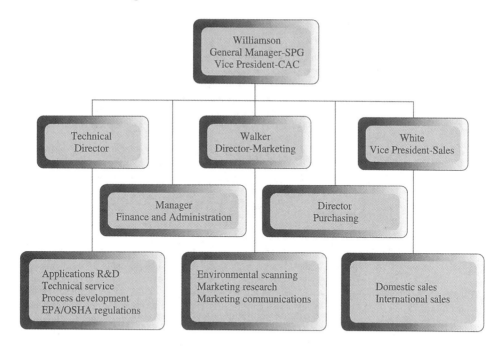

Although some people believed them to be effective, researchers found that corrosive materials could penetrate the coating, resulting in rapid formation of deep pits. Typical repair cost for a storage tank exceeded $1 million, and customers had even reported one or two complete tank failures.

Film-formers left a microscopic layer of inhibitor on the steel surface by incompletely dissolving in the corrosive liquid UAN. This new technology was considered by the National Association of Corrosion Engineers (NACE) to be a sound alternative to designing tanks and piping using expensive, exotic steel alloys or plastics.

All SPG's UAN products were of the film-forming variety. This technology and the related one of solubility control were basic and very strong technologies for CAC and were the source of numerous patents.

Corrosion Inhibitor Use in the U.S. Market. The 1980s were traumatic for U.S. farmers and the industries that supplied them. By 1988, the fertilizer industry (including UAN producers) experienced a shakeout that reduced industry capacity by 20 percent. One UAN plant with book assets of over $40 million netted just $3.5 million at auction. Although U.S. farmers detected improved prospects by the end of 1988, fertilizer producers faced stiff, low-cost foreign competition on their largest-volume solid products, sometimes losing money on every ton sold. The cost of liquid UAN ocean shipment kept imports from attacking the North American market, but domestic producers, in a competitive frenzy, cut UAN prices such that they sometimes made only $1 per ton pretax. The shakeout led many to believe the situation would soon return to a more "normal" $30 per ton.

Corrosion control was necessary once UAN entered the distribution system. A number of different products were used over the years to reduce corrosion. Some UAN producers tried unsuccessfully to differentiate their product based on the presence of a

EXHIBIT 4 **Key SPG Personnel**

Nick Williamson—Executive Vice President and General Manager

With a degree in chemical engineering, Williamson joined SPG in 1966 as a process engineer and worked his way through the production and process engineering ranks to his current position in 1982. He had no sales, marketing, or finance experience. Along the way, he completed his master's degree in chemical engineering and developed a process to make synthetic wax. He persuaded corporate management to invest $10 million in 1975 to build a plant for these products, and it came on stream in 1976. First commercial sale of any significance occurred in 1979 to a hot melt adhesive manufacturer, a mature industry at the time. His management philosophy was to be involved in every detail of the SPG operation.

Ron White—Vice President of Sales

A personal friend of Williamson's, he was hired in 1980. A former Air Force KC-135 tanker pilot, he had for years been a member of the leading country club in Fort Smith and was a 3 handicap golfer. Before his employment at SPG, he was the sole U.S. distributor of potassium permanganate, a commodity reagent widely used as a catalyst and in research laboratories. His college degree was in chemistry.

Jim Walker—Director of Marketing

With a chemical engineering degree, he joined American Cyanamid in 1970 as a process engineer. He moved to sales and marketing in 1974, responsible for contract sales of sulfuric acid and alum and became marketing manager for specialty urethane catalysts at Dow in 1978. By this time, he had earned his MBA in chemical marketing from Fairleigh Dickinson. He was appointed director of marketing for Corn Products Corp. in 1984.

Bob Brown—Sales Engineer

He graduated from Carnegie Mellon University with a chemistry degree in 1978 and was first employed by Firestone's chemical division concentrating in specialty urethane adhesives sales. Three years later, he became a water management chemicals and services specialist at Western Corporation. He was a highly successful salesman, with specific training in consultative needs satisfaction selling and technical service.

corrosion inhibitor. Dealers and farmers were more concerned with the cost per acre of fertilized land and on-time, fast delivery, especially during the hectic spring planting and fall harvest. Processing problems, such as incompatibility with other agricultural chemicals and foaming, were not tolerated. There was little dealer loyalty among farmers when they needed to plant or harvest.

Manufacturers produced UAN liquids as 28 percent and 32 percent blends in water. Dealers diluted UAN with additional water before it was suitable for crop application. As a rule, the more dilute the UAN, the more corrosive it was to steel. Once a fertilizer manufacturer added a corrosion inhibitor such as Corblok 105-B or Stealth 3662 at the proper dosage at the plant, corrosion control was effective through the entire distribution network.

Competitive Products.   The following inhibitors were in use in January 1989 as SPG began its program to develop a replacement for Stealth 3662. Except for borax, all were liquid materials (also see Exhibit 5).

Ammonia.   A toxic gas used as a fertilizer, ammonia was the cheapest source of nitrogen, the same nutrient provided by UAN. Some producers believed corrosion could be eliminated simply by neutralizing acids from the production process by adding am-

EXHIBIT 5   **Competitive Inhibitors, 1990**

Product	Supplier	Type*	Price ($/lb.)	Treat Cost ($/ton)†
Ammonia	Many	P	0	0
Borax	Many	P	0.14–0.17	0.28–0.35
Chromate	Many	F	0.47	0.28
Corblok	IWC	F	1.87	0.47
DAP	Many	P	0.082	0.20–0.25
Stealth 3662	SPG	F	0.80	0.24
RG 2064	Western	F	1.90	0.19–0.38
OA-5	Tennessee	F	0.375	0.30

* P = passivating; F = film-former.

† Treatment cost is per ton of UAN.

monia. It was one of the raw materials in the manufacture of UAN. Instances of rapid pitting corrosion in 1970 led many producers to try other inhibitors. The principal advantage was that it was virtually free.

Borax.   Classified as "acceptable" by the Tennessee Valley Authority (TVA), borax was used by only one manufacturer. Several other UAN manufacturers had found it to be unacceptable.

Sodium Chromate.   Why a material considered by the Environmental Protection Agency (EPA) to be a primary pollutant was allowed in fertilizer points out the strange regulatory environment typically faced by the chemical industry. This product was an excellent corrosion inhibitor but was also toxic to fish and wildlife. Only one plant used it. It was a film-former.

Corblok.   This phosphate ester film-former was produced in Germany by Servo, a well-respected chemical firm; supplied to North American markets by IWC, a Dutch company; and sold through M. Joseph & Co. of Philadelphia. Corblok was shipped to Houston via ocean freight. Storage facilities were leased at the port of Houston. This product did not foam, was difficult to dissolve in UAN, but provided excellent corrosion protection. Technical service was the responsibility of a corrosion engineer based in Holland. The Leveque Group confirmed claims of many European customers regarding the effectiveness of this product.

DAP.   Also a fertilizer (only at 100 percent strength), DAP was made by several UAN producers and tested "effective" by TVA. Jackson Pipeline had tried it, finding that it left deposits that interfered with pipeline pumps and that there was pitting corrosion beneath the deposits. Still, DAP enjoyed a 30 percent market share and was sold by direct sales reps or distributors, depending on location. The nutrient content that it imparted to UAN was negligible, but it enjoyed a psychological benefit of "providing crop nutrients."

Stealth 3662.   Similar in chemistry to Corblok but easily soluble in UAN, Stealth 3662 was an excellent inhibitor but, as noted previously, created foaming problems. It was produced in Chicago and Galveston, Texas, using the same process equipment as many other CAC products.

OA-5.   Tennessee Chemical produced this material in Knoxville. SPG's own tests proved it to be effective. But it was extremely difficult to dissolve in UAN, sometimes merely floating to the surface of the UAN storage tank, even after plant operators were sure they had mixed it properly. Several plants also reported foaming problems when attempting to mix OA-5 with their UAN. This foaming was of a different type than that reported for Stealth 3662. Sold by a direct sales force, this film-former was different in composition from Corblok or Stealth 3662.

RG-2064 and Equivalents.   Although neither Consolidated nor Western had promoted any products specifically for UAN transport and storage, both were strong in organic phosphate ester chemistry; but they had applied it to water treatment applications, a market much larger than UAN. Both companies employed many more sales reps than SPG and CAC and were already selling water treatment chemicals to UAN plants for boiler, cooling, and waste-water treatment applications. These operations were run by the same people that ran the UAN process equipment. These companies also were attacking CAC's oil field business and achieving significant success, even though their products were more expensive to use than CAC's. Consolidated's revenue was equal to CAC's, but its profit rate was 20 percent higher than CAC's. Western had sales and profits double those of CAC.

Exhibit 6 contains the 1989 capacities of all North American UAN producers and indicates the brand(s) of inhibitor used in mid-1988 and mid-1989.

Product Development.   In 1988, after the foaming problems with Stealth 3662, SPG initiated an R&D program to develop a product specifically designed for UAN corrosion control. SPG's technical director estimated four labor years of technical effort over two years was required. The typical cost per labor year was $100,000, including salary and benefits, the use of all group and corporate laboratory facilities, and the cost to build corrosion test apparatus. Jim Walker believed a one–labor-year marketing effort at $80,000 per year was needed to understand market needs adequately and to develop literature and marketing communications programs. Hosting a hospitality suite at the Ammonium Nitrate Producers Study Group (ANPSG) meeting held each fall would increase annual marketing expenses by $5,000.

White felt confident that his department could sell any product, given a good price; the technical director was confident in the success of the development effort. Two sales efforts were possible: (1) 100 percent of Brown's time at $80,000 per year (salary, benefits, car) plus 2 percent of revenue for travel and entertainment costs (T&E) or (2) 5 percent of the entire sales force's time (including regional managers') plus the same T&E.

Williamson considered these costs and alternative sales efforts and reviewed the following data:

- Tax rate 33 percent.
- Corporate cost of capital 8 percent.
- Corporate mandate for 30 percent present value after tax ROI.
- SPG requirement that new businesses generate $2 million in sales and/or $800,000 gross profit within three years of market entry.

He then instructed his technical director to develop a direct replacement for Corblok.

Early in 1989, Brown arranged a trip with a Fertex sales representative to several fertilizer dealers. His objective was to obtain extensive information about how UAN

EXHIBIT 6 UAN Corrosion Inhibitor Market, 1989 Capacities (0.25 lb./ton dosage)

Company*	City*	Capacity (000 Tons)	Potential SPG Volume (000 lbs.)	Mid-1988 Inhibitors	Mid-1989 Inhibitors	Needs Easy Mix Product	SPG Advantage
Farm Products	Kansas City, Kan.	250	63	3662	3662	No	—
Nitron, Inc.	St. Petersburg, Fla.	10	3	3662	3662	Yes	—
Can-Am Corp.	Edmonton, Alberta	15	4	3662	3662	Yes	—
Can-Am Corp.	Lincoln, Neb.	80	20	3662	3662	Yes	—
Agriproducts	Sioux Falls, S.D.	238	60	3662	3662	No	—
Iowa Fertilizer	Dubuque, Iowa	230	58	3662	Corblok	No	Service/cost
Marathon	Toledo, Ohio	180	45	3662	Corblok	No	Service/cost
Ferticon	New Orleans	510	128	3662	Corblok	No	Service/cost
Iowa Fertilizer	Santa Fe	10	3	3662	Corblok	Yes	—
Fertex	Fort Smith, Ark.	1,400	350	3662	Corblok	No	Service/cost
Nitrogen Inds.	Spokane, Wash.	160	40	3662	Corblok	No	Service/cost
Iowa Fertilizer	Miami	51	13	3662	RG-2064	Yes	?
Nitro Products	Pensacola, Fla.	65	16	Ammonia	Ammonia	No	Performance
RJS Inc.	Idaho Falls, Idaho	230	58	Ammonia	Ammonia	No	Performance
Georgia Chemical	Savannah, Ga.	680	170	Ammonia	Ammonia	No	Performance
Jackson Chemical	Jackson, Miss.	500	125	Ammonia	Ammonia	No	Performance
Illini Fertilizer	Marietta, Ga.	329	82	Ammonia	Ammonia	No	Performance
NC Fertilizer	Jacksonville, N.C.	230	58	Borax	Borax	No	Service/pits
RJS Inc.	Fresno, Calif.	129	32	Chromate	Chromate	No	Cost/safe
Novatec	Windsor, Ontario	175	44	Corblok	Corblok	No	Service/cost
Eagle Industries	Bettendorf, Ia.	175	44	Corblok	Corblok	No	Service/cost
RJS Inc.	Winnipeg, Manitoba	210	53	Corblok	Corblok	No	Service/cost
Edsel Chemical	Sacramento	90	23	Corblok	Corblok	No	Service/cost
Edsel Chemical	Portland, Ore.	55	14	Corblok	Corblok	Yes	Service/cost
Edsel Chemical	Spokane, Wash.	200	50	Corblok	Corblok	No	Service/cost
Comanche Powder	Tucson, Ariz.	20	5	Corblok	Corblok	No	Service/cost
Illini Fertilizer	Cincinnati	150	38	DAP	DAP	No	Service/pits
Nutricorp	Council Bluffs, Iowa	500	125	DAP	DAP	No	Service/pits
Ferticon	Evansville, Ind.	80	20	DAP	DAP	No	Service/pits
US Industries	Cherokee, Ala.	65	16	DAP	DAP	No	Service/pits
Illini Fertilizer	Dalton, Ga.	100	25	DAP	DAP	Yes	Service/pits
Illini Fertilizer	La Salle, Ill.	300	75	DAP	DAP	No	Service/pits
Farm Products	Hays, Kan.	250	63	DAP	DAP	No	Service/pits
Nitrotech	Kingston, Ontario	25	6	DAP	DAP	Yes	Service/pits
Cherokee Nitrogen	Enid, Okla.	270	68	DAP	DAP	No	Service/pits
Nutricorp	Baton Rouge, La.	1,000	250	DAP	DAP	No	Service/pits
Nitrogen Inds.	Lincoln, Neb.	158	40	DAP	DAP	Yes	Service/pits
Canadian Nitrogen	Niagara Falls, Ontario	120	30	OA-5	OA-5	No	Service/foam
Fertilex	Stockton, Calif.	200	50	OA-5	OA-5	No	Service/foam
Fertilex	Compton, Calif.	100	25	OA-5	OA-5	No	Service/foam
Edsel Chemical	Burlington, Iowa	200	50	OA-5	OA-5	No	Service/foam
Total		9,740	2,435				

* Names and locations changed to protect confidentiality.

was used at the dealer level—other nutrients added, mixing techniques, blending with pesticides and herbicides, and so on. Of particular interest to Brown was the extent to which dealers were affected by the foaming problem that had precipitated SPG's new R&D efforts. He was surprised when dealers responded negatively to his questions about foaming. Despite using Fertex UAN containing Stealth 3662, they had not experienced this condition. Brown began to wonder if only certain blends and ingredients foamed, and if these blends were used only in certain regions of the country.

He also learned that a considerable amount of UAN "trading" occurred in the industry. For example, if Fertex had a customer in North Dakota, it would receive the sales revenue, but Agriproducts' Sioux Falls plant would actually supply the UAN. Fertex would return the favor if Agriproducts had a customer in Arkansas. Computerized accounting systems kept track of the trades, and the companies settled accounts quarterly.

In addition to these market factors, the technical director's staff, after running hundreds of corrosion and foaming tests with several producers' UANs, discovered three factors that influenced the interaction between UAN and steel surfaces: (1) higher temperature, (2) higher UAN velocity, especially in a pipeline environment, and (3) presence of impurities. The technical department also found that different producers' UANs, though identical in nutrient content, required different dosages of *any* corrosion inhibitor for effective corrosion control. Other inhibitor suppliers (including IWC/Corblok) recommended the same dosage throughout the industry. SPG's technical director suggested using an industrywide inhibitor dosage rate of 1.5 to 2.0 pounds per ton of UAN so even the most drastic conditions would not cause corrosion problems.

While the three newly developed products were similar, each had slightly different performance characteristics. 601 worked well in Fertex UAN but would not function in several others; 601 was easier to disperse than 602, while the latter was effective in all UAN brands. Most UAN plants used high-speed pumps to move the UAN through their systems. For this reason, it was believed there would be few problems dispersing SPG's R&D 601 and 602 products into the UAN. Once dispersed, no separation occurred; 603 was easiest to disperse (though not quite as easy as the existing 3662 product), but it exhibited a slight foaming tendency (which was not believed to be as severe as that of 3662). Also, 603 was effective in all UANs.

All three products were deliverable in tank-truck (40,000-pound) quantities. Also, in response to increased state and local regulations on the disposal of empty drums, SPG planned to offer all three products in 300-gallon returnable and reusable tote tanks, each costing $1,200. Between 30 and 40 round-trips were obtainable before the tanks had to be refurbished at a cost of $300 each. Exhibit 7 shows the cost structure of SPG's products.

Sales (White) and marketing (Walker) continually debated the UAN corrosion inhibitor marketing program as fall 1990 approached. The planned October 1990 rollout would give SPG a strategic window of approximately three months as UAN producers went to high production rates to prepare for spring fertilizer consumption. Failure to obtain business by February would effectively close the window until July, when another production push would occur for fall fertilizer consumption.

Market Segmentation Possibilities.   Jim Walker and Bob Brown debated the possibility that different customers had different needs. It might be advantageous to offer multiple products, each with a distinct communication and pricing program. Superior performance characteristics, such as foaming control and ease of dispersion, could command a premium price from certain customers. Other customers and potential cus-

EXHIBIT 7 SPG Inhibitor Costs per Pound, Tank-Car Lots (October 1989)

Product	Fixed	Variable[4]	Total
Stealth 3662	$0.100	$0.300	$0.400
R&D 601[1]	0.160	0.480	0.640
R&D 602[2]	0.160	0.480	0.640
R&D 603[3]	0.160	0.480	0.640

Note: Billing terms net 30, freight collect, FOB CAC plant.
[1] R&D 601 for "easy-to-treat" UAN such as Fertex.
[2] R&D 602 for "hard-to-treat" UAN such as Agriproducts.
[3] R&D 603 for easy dispersion, all UAN's, but very slight foam.
[4] Add $0.015 to variable costs for 55-gallon drums, net weight 473 lbs.
(215 Kg). Add $0.06 to variable costs for 300-gallon returnable tote tanks,
net weight 2,580 lbs. (1173 Kg).

tomers were less concerned with performance (as their use of low-corrosion performance inhibitors indicated) than with price.

Walker and Brown identified three possible performance segments: (1) premium—requiring extensive corrosion control, (2) average—requiring moderate corrosion control, and (3) low—requiring minimal corrosion control. In addition, corrosion-oriented segments might be further stratified by dispersion needs and/or price. Segmentation strategies were among the issues raised at an earlier management meeting.

Decisions, Decisions, Decisions

As Nick Williamson shuffled the papers on his desk, he listed the decisions he had to make. The discussion earlier in the afternoon focused on pricing of the new products, but he realized pricing was only one of the factors that had to be resolved.

 VII

PLANNING, ORGANIZING, AND IMPLEMENTING MARKETING PLANS AND ASSESSING PERFORMANCE

The final decade of the 20th century has been an unprecedented period of organizational change. Companies have realigned their organizations to establish closer contact with customers, improve customer service, reduce layers of management, decrease the time between decisions and results, and improve organizational effectiveness in other ways. Organizational changes include the use of information systems to reduce organization layers and response time, use of multifunctional teams to design and produce new products, and creation of flexible organization units to compete in turbulent business environments.

This part begins with a brief review of the marketing plan. We next examine organization design because a sound organizational scheme must correspond to the marketing plan. For example, if the plan is structured around markets or products, then the marketing organizational structure should reflect this same emphasis. The third and fourth sections in this part opener examine marketing strategy implementation and performance assessment. The marketing plan guides implementation and performance assessment, indicating marketing objectives and strategies as well as tactics for accomplishing the objectives.

The Marketing Plan

Preparation of the strategic marketing plan is one of the chief marketing executive's most demanding management responsibilities. It requires folding together many different information-gathering and analysis activities into a comprehensive, integrated plan of action. As noted in Part I, following a step-by-step approach in building the strategic plan will ensure that all components of the plan are covered and that their important interrelationships are recognized.

Four important considerations should be part of the planning process. First, a logical process needs to be followed in developing the plan. Second, when the planning process raises relevant questions, management must supply the answers; decision makers develop strategic plans. Third, strategic marketing planning is a continuing activity that is adjusted and revised to take advantage of opportunities and avoid threats. Finally, marketing planning forms the leading edge of planning for the entire business unit or organization. Marketing plans must be closely coordinated with research and development, operations, financial, and other business functions.

Organizing for the 21st Century

Organizations today have fewer levels than traditional organizations and are beginning to be organized around processes such as order processing, new-product planning, and customer services. One estimate is that the typical large business in 2010 will have fewer than half the levels of management and no more than one-third the managers of its counterpart in the late 1980s.[1] These flat organizations will be information-based. Information storage, processing, and decision-support technology will move information swiftly up and down and across the organization. Levels of management can be eliminated since people at those levels function primarily as information relays rather than as decision makers and leaders.

A major motivation for reorganizing relationships is improving relationships with customers in the field. Many companies have restructured their sales and marketing organizations to move closer to their customers. For example, an electrical products manufacturer, previously organized on a functional basis, has set up four separate operating divisions, each with its own sales and engineering units. A packaging company, following the successful revamping of its sales force along industry lines, is now reorganizing its warehouse and customer service activities on a geographic basis, so as to ensure more familiarity with customers by area.[2]

These actions indicate marketing executives' continuing concern about organizational effectiveness. Organizational change will occur more frequently in the future as businesses respond to market turbulence and competitive pressures.

Multifunctional teamwork is critical to improving product and supporting-service quality. Union Pacific Railroad (UP) found that nearly one-fifth of its invoices contained errors.[3] Management formed a special team to analyze the problem. Statistical analysis identified 20 specific causes of the billing errors originating from several departments. A quality-improvement team was formed with the objective of reducing the errors to one-half the current level within a year for each of the 20 causes.

Selecting an Organization Design

The design of the marketing organization is influenced by market and environmental factors, the characteristics of the organization, and the marketing strategy followed by the firm. The organization should be structured so that responsibility for results corresponds to each manager's influence on results. While this objective is often difficult to fully achieve, it is an important consideration in designing the marketing organization.

The design of an organization also affects its ability (and willingness) to respond quickly. The advantage of doing things faster than the competition is clearly important. For example, The Limited's skill in moving women's apparel from design to the store in weeks instead of months enables the retailer to market new designs ahead of its competition. Organizations that can do things faster are more competitive.

Finally, a real danger in a highly structured and complex organization is the loss of flexibility. The organization should be adaptable to changing conditions.

Implementing Marketing Plans

Marketing plans are often ineffective unless they include detailed implementation plans. An implementation plan should specify what activities are to be implemented, who will be responsible for implementation, and the time and location of implementation.

Managers are important facilitators in the implementation process, and some are more effective than others. To be effective implementers, managers need

- The ability to understand how others feel.
- Good bargaining skills.
- The strength to be tough and fair in putting people and resources where they will be most effective.
- Effectiveness in focusing on the critical aspects of performance in managing marketing activities.
- The ability to create a necessary informal organization or network to match each problem that arises.[4]

The implementation of marketing strategy may partially depend on external organizations such as marketing research firms, marketing consultants, advertising and public relations firms, channel members, and other organizations participating in the marketing effort. These outside organizations present a major coordination challenge when they actively participate in marketing activities. Their efforts should be programmed into the marketing plan and their roles and responsibilities clearly established and communicated. There is a potential danger in not informing outside groups of planned actions, deadlines, and other implementation requirements. For example, the advertising agency account executive and other agency staff members should be familiar with all aspects of the promotion strategy as well as the major dimensions of the marketing strategy. Restricting information from participating firms can adversely affect their contributions to strategy planning and implementation.

Implementation/Execution Problems

Marketing managers frequently encounter problems when plans reach the implementation/execution stage. A four-year study of top marketing and general managers' key marketing concerns identified five specific problems: management by assumption, global mediocrity, empty-promises marketing, program ambiguity, and ritualization, politicization, and unavailability.[5]

Management by Assumption. Management assumes that someone, somewhere in the organization will do the analysis necessary for making knowledgeable pricing, sales promotion, or distribution decisions. Unfortunately, the function in question is often ignored until a crisis occurs.

Global Mediocrity. Management tries to excel at all of its marketing activities, rather than picking one or a few for special concentration. The firm does many things adequately, but is not outstanding at anything. Ultimately, it finds itself without a competitive advantage.

Empty-Promises Marketing.   Management creates programs it does not have the subfunctional capability to execute. Declaring that a program exists and appointing a competent individual to manage it is usually not enough for subfunctional success. The existence of too many programs generally means that none is pursued with a vengeance.

Program Ambiguity.   Lack of clear identity and direction results in a multitude of programs and no unifying theme. Clever programs fail because of an absence of shared understanding about identity (i.e., theme) and strong leadership.

Ritualization, Politicization, and Unavailability.   Errors of ritual arise when the firm's systems mandate a particular course of action because "things have always been done that way." Even if good judgment dictates a different course, habitual pathways may be chosen.

Management intelligence is often undermined by the politicization of data and information. Often, daily records are not prepared until the end of the month (when much may already be forgotten) or not turned in until inflammatory data are removed.

Systems installed to make managers' lives easier may quickly become unsuitable for current environmental conditions, or place the data in the hands of those completely removed from its significance. Many marketing managers do not have the data necessary to analyze profitability by segment, product, account, or order. These problems indicate that it is not enough to have a science of making plans. It is also necessary to understand how the plans are translated into actions and into marketplace results.

Performance Assessment

Performance assessment consumes a high proportion of marketing executives' time and energy. Management must establish performance criteria and measures so that information can be obtained for use in tracking performance. The purpose of evaluation may be to (1) find new opportunities or avoid threats, (2) keep performance in line with management's expectations, and/or (3) solve specific problems.

The starting point in performance assessment is a *strategic marketing audit*. The audit is a comprehensive review and assessment of marketing operations. It includes a careful examination of

1. Corporate mission and objectives.
2. Business composition and strategy.
3. Buyer analysis.
4. Competitor analysis.
5. Market target strategy and objectives.
6. Marketing program positioning strategy.
7. Marketing program activities.
8. Marketing planning.
9. Implementation and management.

There are other reasons for conducting a strategic marketing audit than its use in guiding the installation of a formal strategic marketing planning and performance assessment program:

1. Organizational changes may bring about a complete review of marketing operations.
2. Major shifts in business involvement such as entry into new product and market areas, acquisitions, and other alterations in the composition of the business may require strategic audits.

Although there is no norm as to how often a strategic audit should be conducted, the nature of the audit and costs involved suggest that the time span between audits should be at least three years and perhaps more, depending on the market and company situation.

Selecting Performance Criteria and Measures.   As marketing plans are developed, performance criteria need to be selected to monitor performance. Specifying the information needed for marketing decision making is important and requires management's concentrated attention. In the past, marketing executives could develop and manage successful marketing strategies by relying on intuition, judgment, and experience. Successful executives now combine judgment and experience with information and decision support systems. These information systems are becoming increasingly important in gaining strategic advantages.

Illustrative criteria for total performance include sales, market share, profit, expense, and customer satisfaction targets. Brand positioning analyses may also be useful in tracking position relative to key competitors. These measures can be used to gauge overall performance and for specific target markets. Performance criteria are also needed for the marketing mix components. For example, new-customer and lost-customer tracking is often included in sales force performance monitoring. Pricing performance monitoring may include comparisons of actual to list prices, extent of discounting, and profit contribution. Many possible performance criteria can be selected. Management must identify the key measures that will show how the firm's marketing strategy is performing in its competitive environment and where changes are needed.

Acquiring, Processing, and Analyzing Information.   The costs of acquiring, processing, and analyzing information are high, so the potential benefits of needed information must be compared to costs. Normally, information falls into two categories: (1) information regularly supplied to marketing management from internal and external sources and (2) information obtained as needed for a particular problem or situation. Examples of the former are sales and cost analyses, market share measurements, and customer satisfaction surveys. Information from the latter category includes new-product concept tests, brand-preference studies, and studies of advertising effectiveness.

Deciding What Actions to Take.   Many actions are possible, depending on the situation. Management's actions may include exiting from a product market, changing the target market strategy, revising objectives, adjusting marketing strategy components, improving efficiency, or extending the existing plan into the future. Keeping track of current performance and anticipating change are the essence of performance assessment.

End Notes

1. Peter F. Drucker, "The Coming of the New Organization," *Harvard Business Review,* January–February 1988, pp. 45–53.

2. Earl L. Bailey, *Getting Closer to the Customer,* Research Bulletin no. 229 (New York: The Conference Board, Inc., 1989), p. 5.

3. Brian Dumaine, "What the Leaders of Tomorrow See," *Fortune,* July 3, 1989, p. 51.

4. Thomas V. Bonoma, "Making Your Marketing Strategy Work," *Harvard Business Review,* March–April 1984, p. 75.

5. Thomas V. Bonoma and Victoria L. Crittenden, "Managing Marketing Implementation," *Sloan Management Review*, Winter 1988, pp. 7–14.

CASES FOR PART VII

The seven cases in this part address various concerns surrounding organization, implementation, and performance assessment issues. The cases involve consumer and business-to-business products.

Case 7–1, Cutco International, a video case, describes the only U.S. cutlery manufacturer to focus exclusively on worldwide direct selling. While the company's international sales are growing, international operations have yet to be profitable. The company operates offices in Korea, the United Kingdom, Australia, Germany, and Costa Rica. Top management must decide among several diverse countries for future expansion and needs to develop a sequence of countries for marketing entry.

Case 7–2, Yoplait USA, a video case, focuses on the yogurt's marketplace performance. The product has failed to meet company targets for two straight years. A situation analysis reveals that the product's marketing strategy has not changed since its introductory days.

Cima Mountaineering, Inc. (Case 7–3), a manufacturer of mountaineering and hiking boots, is trying to determine the best strategy for future growth. Margaret Simon, president of Cima Mountaineering, favors one approach, while her brother Anthony, executive vice president of the company, favors another.

Longevity Healthcare Systems, Inc., (Case 7–4) was beginning to experience increased competition and the uncertainty of health care reform. Kathryn Hamilton, president, is concerned that the company has neither developed a formal plan for future growth nor prepared a written marketing strategy.

In **Case 7–5, La-Z-Boy Chair Company** is experiencing growth rates four times that of the furniture industry. With a widely recognized brand name in the United States, the company should be content to continue with its current strategy. However, industry concentration and an aging population are pushing the company to examine its programs for continued growth and profitability.

Performance is not quite up to par at the **Bear Creek Golf Range (Case 7–6).** Beginning its second year of operations, the golf range has not come close to meeting its first-year objectives. The future survival and success of the business depend on the implementation of a sound marketing program.

Wentworth Industrial Cleaning Supplies (Case 7–7), located in Lincoln, Nebraska, is currently experiencing a slowdown in growth. Sales of all its products are below the projected volume. Total sales for the industry have increased, but Wentworth has not benefited as much from this growth as its competitors. Randall Griffith, vice president of marketing, has been directed to determine what factors are stunting growth and to institute a program that will facilitate further expansion.

CASE 7–1
CUTCO INTERNATIONAL

It was CUTCO Cutlery's 1997 midyear companywide meeting in Olean, New York. Record sales and profits had been achieved for the first six months. CUTCO had seen record weekly shipments in June. Over 27,000 packages had gone out just the week before. Unlike some recent years, needed inventory was in place to meet seasonal demand. Further, record sales and profits were projected for the entire year. CUTCO employees could look forward to significant year-end profit-sharing bonuses.

The management team was proud of these achievements. However, Erick Laine (CEO/president, ALCAS Corporation), Fran Weinaug (president/CEO, CUTCO International), Bob Haig (president/COO, Vector Marketing Corporation), Mike Lancellot (president, Vector East), Don Muelrath (president, Vector West), and Jim Stitt (president/CEO, CUTCO Cutlery corporation) were not satisfied. Growth was at record levels but not at plan.

According to Erick Laine, "Sales are up 11 percent over 1996, not the 20–25 percent we looked for. International sales in particular have been way off projections (15 percent growth versus the expected 75 percent). Although we've made some important adjustments, the second half of the year is unlikely to compensate."

He continued, "Other direct sales firms have had enormous success in the international arena. International markets are attractive to direct sellers. Direct selling allows market entry without fighting the battles of brand identity and entrenched distribution systems. With limited brick and mortar requirements, direct selling allows one to grow rapidly. We know it's [the market] there to be gotten."

CUTCO's corporate vision statement (see Exhibit 1) to be the world's "largest, most respected and widely recognized" cutlery firm required substantial growth. Although product development and company acquisitions might be part of the strategic mix, management clearly viewed the international market as a critical element to growth. Yet, decisions regarding which markets to enter, which approach to use, and sequencing and timing of entry still needed to be made.

The ALCAS Corporation (the Parent)

In 1949, Alcoa and CASE Cutlery formed a joint venture, ALCAS Cutlery Corporation, to produce kitchen cutlery known as CUTCO. The product was exclusively marketed via in-home demonstrations by WearEver, Inc. (However, CUTCO and WearEver products were treated as separate entities and were not sold together.) In 1972, Alcoa bought out CASE and ALCAS became wholly owned by Alcoa. In 1982, local management of ALCAS, headed by Erick Laine, a longtime Alcoa employee, purchased the company from Alcoa. Management converted ALCAS into a privately held corporation with headquarters in Olean, New York. Ownership remains closely held by five of the top managers. In 1996, the company acquired KA-BAR Knives, an

This case was prepared by William F. Crittenden at Northeastern University and Victoria L. Crittenden at Boston College as the basis for class discussion rather than to illustrate effective or ineffective handling of a managerial situation. The Direct Selling Education Foundation provided partial funding for the development of this case.

EXHIBIT 1

> # CORPORATE VISION
>
> **To become the largest, most respected and widely recognized cutlery company in the world while maintaining an equal commitment to these core values:**
>
> - Honesty, integrity and ethics in all aspects of business – founded on our respect for people.
>
> - Recognizing and rewarding our people for dedication and high levels of achievement.
>
> - Product pre-eminence, quality and reputation.
>
> - First-class customer service and customer satisfaction.
>
> - Strong consolidated corporate profitability and the strength and financial success of our field sales organization.
>
> - Creating opportunities for our people to grow and share in the success of the enterprise.

established sporting knife company. Exhibit 2 outlines the corporate structure. Worldwide revenues from direct marketing and direct sales operations exceeded $100 million in 1996. (Sales just exceeded $20 million in 1987.) All corporations within ALCAS operate as profit centers.

CUTCO Cutlery covers a broad range of food preparation knives as well as scissors and hunting, fishing and utility knives. (Exhibits 3–10 provide examples of CUTCO products.) The product line is identified as "CUTCO—*The World's Finest Cutlery.*" Product pricing is consistent with this positioning at the high end of the spectrum. The product is sold as individual open stock, in wood block sets, or in a variety of gift boxed sets. According to Mark George (now international sales director and a former CUTCO sales representative), numerous features make CUTCO the world's finest cutlery: "the ergonomically designed handle, the thermo-resin handle material, the full tang triple rivet construction, the high-carbon, stain-resistant steel, and the exclusive Double-D® edge. All products are backed by the CUTCO 'Forever Guarantee.'"

Recognizing the importance of satisfied customers, CUTCO devoted considerable space in its Olean headquarters to its service department. The company has a goal of two to three days turnaround on knives returned for free sharpening or guarantee issues.

CUTCO cutlery is marketed in North America by Vector Marketing Corporation. During peak selling periods, Vector Marketing operates around 400 offices in Canada and the United States. CUTCO is sold primarily by college students who are recruited

(continued on page 497)

EXHIBIT 2

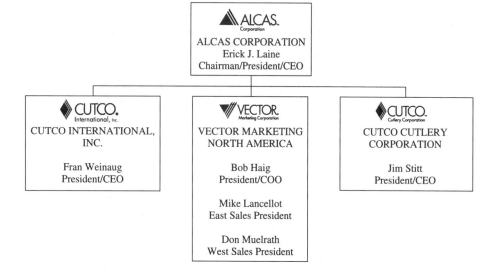

EXHIBIT 3

EXHIBIT 4

EXHIBIT 5

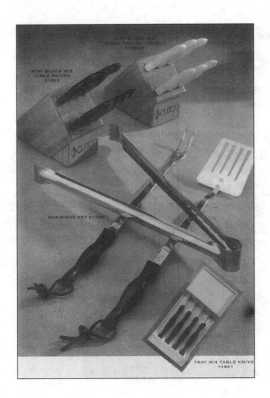

EXHIBIT **6**

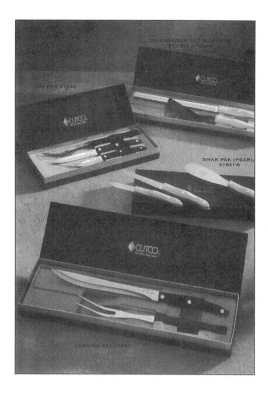

EXHIBIT **7**

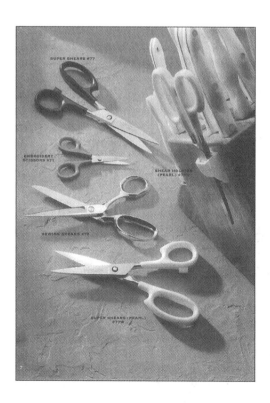

EXHIBIT 8

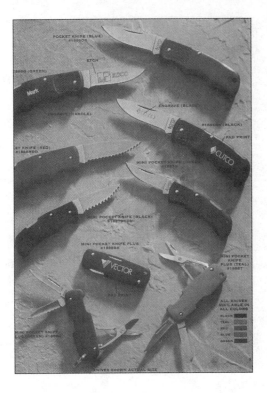

EXHIBIT 9

EXHIBIT 10
Fisherman's Solution

A total fillet knife system. Designed for lake, coastal or stream fishing.

The high-carbon, stain-resistant steel blade adjusts and locks from 6" to 9" to fillet any size fish. A patented Cam-Lock secures the blade tightly at any length. The Zytel® inner track system assures the blade's smooth adjustment. The sheath pivots open to become a gripper to help clean, skin and fillet or remove a hook. Notched line cutter and a built-in sharpening stone with a groove for fish hooks complete the sheath.

to work during vacations as sales representatives. (Exhibit 11 shows typical seasonal percentage of sales for CUTCO products.) Some students continue to sell during the school year. Recruiting, training, and ongoing management of the sales force is done utilizing over 200 district offices. Over 200 temporary branch offices are opened during the summer months and staffed by college students with prior selling and management experience. All sales representatives are independent contractors. Sales training is completed over a three-day period. Vector has experimented with some catalog sales and has special policies in place demonstrating a sensitivity to its sales representatives. The typical CUTCO customer has household income of approximately $60,000, is well educated (with most holding a bachelor's degree and some with postgraduate degrees), is married with older children, holds a professional or managerial position, is approximately 40 to 54 years old, is a homeowner, and enjoys cooking, gardening, reading, and traveling.

CUTCO Cutlery Corporation manufactures CUTCO products in Olean, New York, and sells at wholesale to Vector and CUTCO International. Unlike many manufacturers, CUTCO has reduced outsourcing in recent years and backward integrated into plastic molding (e.g., knife handles and cutting boards) and wood blocks. Jim Stitt, CUTCO Cutlery Corporation president and CEO, attributed the company's ability to stay competitive to its skilled work force and considerable investment in high technology equipment. Additionally, the company processes its product very differently from competitors to provide a high level of product distinction (e.g., its unique recessed edge grind, freezing the blades, applying a mirror polish finish to the blades).

EXHIBIT 11   Seasonal Sales

January–April	17%
May–August	67
September–December	16

Cutlery

Cutlery is a term applied collectively to all types of cutting instruments. More specifically, in the United States it refers to knives employed in the preparation of food and for sporting and utility use. The first U.S. cutlery factory was established in Worchester, Massachusetts, in 1829. As American steel improved in quality and decreased in price, the industry developed steadily, particularly in the Northeastern states. (Exhibit 12 provides cutlery sales by retail outlet for 1996.)

Cutting instruments are clearly of worldwide importance—numerous international manufacturing sites have gained some renown. Sheffield in the United Kingdom and Soligen in Germany are especially well known for cutlery. However, substantial innovation at the high end and inexpensive imports at the other have hurt some of those sectors that are long known for expertise and quality. For example, the cutlery industry in Sheffield has been reduced from over 300 firms to around 12 in the past 35 years. Several cutlery manufacturers have recently expanded into other product lines including kitchen tools, pantryware, and garden implements.

While the number of successful cutlery firms was declining, cutlery sales increased throughout the 1990s. Sales were especially strong in specialty product segments (e.g., multitool, pizza cutters, potato peelers, nonstick cheese slicers, under-the-counter knife blocks), with new product innovations initially targeting upscale channels. In 1995 and 1996, U.S. consumers demonstrated renewed interest in known brands of cutlery rather than private-label goods and were buying more expensive brands.

In addition to specialty product segments, many cutlery vendors had begun focusing upon niche markets such as bridal registries and Internet shopping. Regarding registries, Howard Ammerman, vice president of sales for J.A. Henckels (USA), stated, "Catching consumers early helps to avoid the looming issue of affordability. [Bridal] Registries are our opportunity to gain the next generation of Henckels' cutlery customers. They need to know why they're spending the money for high-end cutlery, and that it's a lifetime investment."[1]

EXHIBIT 12   Cutlery Sales by Retail Outlet, 1996

Mass merchants	33%
Department stores	20
Specialty stores	15
Warehouse clubs	13
Catalog showrooms	5
Other[1]	14

Note: Mass merchants, specialty stores, and warehouse clubs have gained in the past 10 years with the "Other" category seeing the greatest decline as a percentage of the total.

[1] Includes hardware stores, home centers, supermarkets, drug stores, and direct mail.

By 1996, some knife manufacturers and retailers also were testing the Internet as a medium for promoting and selling cutlery products. According to Brice Hereford, national sales manager at Lamson & Goodnow, "We were most intrigued by the demographics. The demographics of an Internet browser—typically a college-educated person with above-average income—fits well with the profile of most consumers of high-end cutlery. This type of person is much more likely to buy an $80 chef's knife."[2]

Direct Selling

Direct selling is a method of marketing and retailing consumer goods directly to the consumer without reliance on direct mail, product advertising, or fixed retail outlets. Most direct selling employs independent salespeople to call on consumers, mainly in their homes, to show and demonstrate products and to obtain orders. The goods are then supplied by the company, either directly to the consumer or through the salesperson who obtained the order. The direct sales industry exceeds US$80 billion in annual worldwide sales. The United States represented less than 25 percent of total sales. Leading international direct sales firms include Avon, Tupperware, Shaklee, Stanhome, Amway, and Mary Kay Cosmetics. The Direct Selling Association, a worldwide trade association, represented most leading direct sales firms.

Generically, direct selling is a push marketing strategy. Direct selling is an especially effective strategy for products and services with a high personal selling elasticity, where procrastination in purchasing is easy, and when the product is a household item that benefits from demonstration in that environment. Push marketing strategies have been effectively realized by direct selling firms entering newly emerging economies where distribution systems, supporting infrastructure, and capital access are limited. Further, direct selling jobs are often attractive to citizens in such economies. Direct selling is often seen as the ultimate in equal-income-earning opportunity with no artificial barriers based on age, race, sex, or education. Independent contractors have flexible hours and can pursue earnings fulltime or while pursuing additional education, raising a family, or holding down another job.

Two general forms of direct selling exist: party plan and one-on-one. With the party plan method, a salesperson presents and sells products to a group of customers attending a party in one of the customer's homes. The intention is to demonstrate the quality and value of a product to a group of people, many of whom would then purchase the product. The party, however, is more than just a sales presentation and is often viewed as a socializing opportunity for busy people. The party host/hostess is principally responsible for identifying, qualifying, and inviting attendees. Tupperware and Mary Kay Cosmetics principally utilize the party plan approach. The one-on-one approach is more personalized and requires the salesperson to focus on the needs and economic demand of each potential customer. This approach is especially useful when customers may require detailed instruction regarding product quality differences or appropriate use of the product.

CUTCO's Major Competitors

Henckels. J.A. Henckels Zwillingswerk Inc., a 266-year-old German manufacturer, is a dominant player in the upscale cutlery market and enjoys a global presence in over 100 countries with long-established subsidiaries in Canada, China, Denmark, Japan, the Netherlands, Spain, Switzerland, and the United States. Significant growth in sales over recent years has been attributable to increased accounts, the expansion of existing accounts, and a broadening of the company's customer base through development of non-German sources for production of moderately priced products for multiple channels under the Henckels International logo. Through non-German sources, Henckels has been able to offer additional price points: EverEdge, a never-needs-sharpening, Japanese-made brand has a suggested retail price of $29.99 for a seven-piece set; the Brazilian-made Classic and Traditional forged lines are considered a cost-efficient alternative at $149.99 to the German-made brands. Now offering over 10 brands in fine-edge and never-needs-sharpening cutlery, the company's products are available in virtually every high-profile retail account worldwide.

Further stimulating demand for Henckels Cutlery has been the development of specialty gift sets, providing a prestigious presentation of commonly grouped individual items. Henckels also has taken a strong stance on advertising to build brand awareness, substantially increasing its television, co-op, and bridal advertising budget in recent years. Henckels also has attempted to be innovative through new packaging (e.g., clam sets) and in working with retailers to develop appropriate displays. (A clam set is one or more product in thermoformed packaging allowing full view of product, shelf appeal, potential customer opportunity to grasp the handle, and blade protection. Clam sets can be pegged or self-supported on a shelf.) Numerous retailers and catalog firms have begun to advertise and sell their Henckel offerings through Internet Web sites. Henckel recently added new handles with an ergonomic "open-flow" design to comfortably accommodate each individual hand while maintaining safety.

In 1995, Henckels acquired German-based Wilkens tableware, moving the firm into the silverplate and stainless steel flatware business. In 1996, the U.S. subsidiary doubled its available warehouse space to improve delivery performance. Recent estimates suggest Henckels USA will have $70 million in 1997 trade sales. Karl Pfitzenreiter, president of J.A. Henckels, USA, explained, "We want to double our growth every five years, which we have so far been able to do by maintaining a 15 percent average annual growth rate in the U.S."[3]

Fiskars.   Fiskars, founded in 1649, is the oldest industrial company in Finland and one of the oldest in the western world. Over the years the company has solidified a reputation as a premier steel and ironworks company manufacturing a widening range of architectural, industrial, agricultural, and houseware-related products. Main market areas include North America and Europe, with 1997 estimated sales of US$550 million (of which over 90 percent was generated outside Finland). Headquartered in Helsinki, Fiskars has subsidiaries and/or manufacturing in Canada, the Czech Republic, Denmark, France, Germany, Hungary, India, Italy, Mexico, Norway, Poland, Russia, Sweden, the United Kingdom, and the United States. Markets targeted for further development or new expansion include Eastern Europe, Southeast Asia, Australia, and Latin America. The company is considered to be very strong financially and a major innovator in its many diverse product lines.

The Montana adjustable bread knife and the Raadvad cutter for bread, cabbage, and lettuce were examples of recent innovations. Fiskars cutlery features a full tang with synthetic handles, ergonomically designed and weighted and balanced to correspond to the blade length. Gift sets are housed in handcrafted, solid walnut boxes, lined with velveteen fabric and intended as heirlooms. Individual units may be purchased in clam shell packaging. Fiskars' worldwide sales of cutlery products are estimated to be US$70 million. Products in its homeware lines include scissors, knives, kitchen gadgets, and sharpeners. Trademarks include Alexander, Fiskars, Gerber, Montana, Raadvad, Knivman, Kitchen Devils, DuraSharp, and CutRite. The upscale Alexander line features such gift sets as a four-piece steak knife set retailing for US$197 and a two-piece carving set at US$260. Fiskars products are carried primarily in upscale channels, but the company continues to target mass merchants with select lines within its wide array of products. The Consumer Products Group generated 59 percent of its 1997 net sales in the United States. A 35 percent jump in U.S. sales was at least partly attributable to a strengthening U.S. dollar.

In late 1994, as part of its overall expansion strategy, Fiskars acquired Rolcut & Raadvad, a supplier of kitchen cutlery and garden tools. In July 1997, a greenfield start-up, A/O Baltic Tool, began production of garden tools. In August 1997, Fiskars agreed to acquire Italian knife manufacturer Kaimano S.p.A.

According to Stig Stendahl, Fiskars president, "Our goal is to generate one-fourth of sales from new products which have been in the market for less than three years. Fiskars has gained a lot of positive publicity thanks to innovative product development and design."[4]

CUTCO International

In 1990, Vector Canada was established as the company's first international marketing entity. Patterned after the U.S. sales model of utilizing college students as salespeople, the international entry is considered to be quite successful. (Sales should approximate US$7.5 million in 1997.) Fueled by the rather immediate success in Canada, the company entered into the Korean marketplace in 1992 as Vector Korea.

CUTCO Korea.   CUTCO entered into the Korean marketplace with the student salesperson model that had been successful in the United States and Canada. CUTCO's strategy for entering Korea was to utilize U.S.-trained, Korean-born managers to oversee administrative operations. CUTCO Korea operated in the student salesperson mode from May 1992 until early 1995. Sales were nowhere near company expectations during this 2$1/2$-year period. With the student program faltering, CUTCO Korean began entertaining, in early 1995, the group selling (party plan) approach to selling.

Tae S. Kim, former Korean manager in charge of administration and finance and current national administration manager for CUTCO Australia, identified two major reasons for the lack of success of CUTCO's original college program approach in Korea:

1. *Cultural.* Korean college students do not value earning income during their college days in the same manner as college students in the Western part of the world. Money is not a motivating factor for Korean students since their parents continue to provide total financial support. Mr. Kim described Korean students as less aggressive and uncertain about going into sales.

2. *Distribution.* Korean students do not generally own automobiles. The vast majority of Korean students utilize public transportation (subway or bus), which does not make it easy to make sales calls.

Once CUTCO Korea understood and accepted the fact that the student model could not work in Korea, a group selling approach, with a revised commission structure, was quickly implemented. This model started in March 1995 with five female-managed offices. At that point, Korean sales exploded. The typical Korean sales representative is now a married, middle-class female, age 20 to 50. The student program was abolished completely by the end of 1995. There were 21 female-managed offices by February 1996 and 1996 sales hit US$8.2 million. Unfortunately, due to the loss of sales offices, the temporary relocation of a key employee to head up a Philippine pilot office, and a very weak Korean economy, 1997 sales were likely to fall significantly below 1996 levels.

CUTCO United Kingdom.   In 1992, the company conducted a "college program" trial in the United Kingdom. An English-speaking country with a well-educated population exceeding 60 million, the UK seemed a promising market with approximately US$1.4 billion in direct sales. Although sales were reasonably successful, high expenses (e.g., office and warehousing rent, recruiting ads) led the company to delay entry. Instead, in 1995, the company made a trial entry using a group sales (party plan) approach. This approach was not successful and CUTCO's intention remains to reenter with the college program in 1999.

Distributorships.   The company has utilized one independent distributor in Mauritius. Sales there are small but growing. CUTCO has tried out two other distributorships, but neither succeeded. In the distributor agreement, CUTCO sells to the distributor on wholesale terms and the distributor organizes, develops, and manages its own sales force. Chris Panus (CUTCO international finance manager) indicated the company spent a lot of time selecting, training, and developing these distributors and wondered if the effort—versus opening up its own operation—was worth it.

CUTCO Australia.   In 1996, CUTCO entered Australia. The entry was modeled after Vector Marketing in the United States and Canada. Unlike the Korean entry, CUTCO Australia began with experienced CUTCO sales and administration people. Stephen McCarthy, national sales manager for CUTCO-Australia, has been with CUTCO since 1986. Steve had a reputation as a top CUTCO sales manager. Tae Kim was transferred from Korea and appointed national administration manager for CUTCO Australia. In addition to Steve and Tae, CUTCO moved five American managers to Australia. Each of these five had been with CUTCO between 7 and 13 years, and each manages his own sales office in Australia. (Three offices are in Sydney and two are in Melbourne.) Plans were to have a total of 21 sales offices by the end of 1998.

Australia appeared to offer significant opportunity. According to Mark George, "Australia is a territory with 19 million English-speaking, qualified-income people, and a university school break starting in November and ending in February. The culture is similar to that in the U.S."

With annual sales expected to be A$3.0 million by the end of 1997, CUTCO Australia had definitely beat the odds of the typical international startup. CUTCO products were virtually unheard of in Australia in 1996. McCarthy reported, "The Australians thought our method of marketing knives was crazy. Our solicitors, our accountants, our consultants . . . all said, 'Students? You have got to be crazy!' They could not have been more wrong! Australian students like being entrepreneurial and goal-oriented. The student model is working wonderfully in Australia."

McCarthy's goal is to make Australia the CUTCO hub for the Asia–Pacific. He envisions an all-Asian office to manage Singapore, Thailand, and Hong Kong as well as a proposed development into New Zealand by 1999. As with Canada and other countries entered, he says that the long-term plan is to turn management of CUTCO Australia over to the Australians.

CUTCO Germany.   In 1996, CUTCO began sales in Germany. Direct sales are extremely popular in Germany (almost US$5 billion) and other U.S. direct sales firms had garnered great success there. However, Germany appeared to be another country where recruiting college students would be difficult. Therefore, based on its Korean experience, CUTCO pursued a party plan format in Germany. The profile of sales representatives was similar to that found in Korea. Unfortunately, a sales director heading up the German expansion left the company and sales had not achieved the hoped-for level of success, with 1997 sales around US$400,000 (approximately two-thirds of goal).

CUTCO Costa Rica.   A launch in Costa Rica was made in June 1997. Two managers, from inside CUTCO, were available for transfer. One manager, a Spanish speaker with a Hispanic background, was from New York; the other was from Puerto Rico.

According to Mark George, "We picked Costa Rica because it was a small market with a nice middle- and upper-class structure. It is a safe place to do business and, although it's a small country, we believe we can develop Spanish-speaking managers that can help establish markets for CUTCO in the rest of Latin America. People are well educated and the literacy rate is around 97 percent. We utilize the university student model, which helps us qualify the recruit to be able to get into the market that can afford our product."

International Market Expansion.   CUTCO International was established in 1994 as a wholly owned subsidiary of ALCAS Corporation to manage the marketing and distribution of CUTCO products on an international basis. According to Fran Weinaug: "International operations are currently in the developmental stage." The management team had initially set a goal of wanting to open two countries each year for the foreseeable future.

Weinaug, George, and Panus all understood that a multitude of diverse issues could spring up in international markets. They had already experienced currency fluctuations, nontariff barriers, import duties, and language and gender considerations in recruiting sales representatives, plus variability in country laws for direct selling. Further, opening a market required a major outlay of capital. There are considerable cost-of-living considerations for expats (e.g., housing, cars, start-up funds). To facilitate market entry where language is a barrier, management has used an in-country sales manager and in-country financial officer. Selling a high-end set of cutlery isn't the same as selling plasticware or cosmetics, and using in-country managers requires a lengthy training process.

To ensure timely international delivery, CUTCO ships and warehouses product at each international site. Freight, warehousing, and insurance add approximately 10 percent to total costs. On a country-by-country basis, the company goal was to be at breakeven, covering annual costs, by its third year.

By mid-1997, international operations had yet to be profitable. Noting this lack of international profitability, Erick Laine commented, "Developing international markets is a very costly process, but we're convinced it's worth it for the long term—and we're grateful we have the financial resources to wait it out."

For the near term (in addition to a 1997 pilot test in the Philippines), Laine, Weinaug, and their management team are deciding among such diverse countries as Argentina, Austria, Brazil, Ireland, Italy, Japan, Mexico, Poland, Taiwan, and the United Kingdom. Longer-term markets under consideration include China, Hong Kong, India, and South Africa. (Exhibit 13 provides worldwide direct sales data. Country-specific information is provided in the Appendix.)

EXHIBIT 13 **Worldwide Direct Sales Data**

	Year	Retail Sales (U.S.$)	Number of Salespeople
Argentina	1996	1.004 billion	410,000
Australia	1996	2.02 billion	615,000
Austria	1996	340 million	40,000
Belgium	1996	111 million	13,500
Brazil	1996	3.5 billion	887,000
Canada	1996	1.825 billion	875,000
Chile	1996	180 million	160,000
Colombia	1996	400 million	200,000
Czech Republic	1996	75 million	70,000
Denmark	1996	50 million	5,000
Finland	1995	120 million	20,000
France	1995	2.1 billion	300,000
Germany	1995	4.67 billion	191,000
Greece	1996	41 million	25,000
Hong Kong	1995	78 million	98,000
Hungary	1996	53 million	110,000
India	1995	70 million	12,000
Indonesia	1995	192 million	750,000
Ireland	1995	19 million	5,000
Israel	1996	80 million	14,000
Italy	1996	2.12 billion	375,000
Japan	1996	30.2 billion	2,500,000
Korea	1995	1.68 billion	475,988
Malaysia	1995	640 million	1,000,000
Mexico	1996	1.3 billion	1,060,000
Netherlands	1993	130 million	33,750
New Zealand	1996	126.5 million	76,000
Norway	1996	90 million	9,000
Peru	1996	295 million	177,000
Philippines	1996	320 million	630,000
Poland	1996	155 million	220,000
Portugal	1995	60 million	23,000
Russia	1995	300 million	250,000
Singapore	1996	96 million	34,500
Slovenia	1994	58 million	15,500
South Africa	1994	330 million	100,000
Spain	1995	652 million	123,656
Sweden	1996	90 million	50,000
Switzerland	1996	245 million	5,700
Taiwan	1995	1.92 billion	2,000,000
Thailand	1996	800 million	500,000
Turkey	1996	98 million	212,000
United Kingdom	1996	1.396 billion	400,000
United States	1995	19.50 billion	7,200,000
Uruguay	1995	42 million	19,500
Total		79.5715 billion	22,291,094

Source: World Federation of Direct Selling Associations.

Weinaug, George, and Panus know that CUTCO management expects to move quickly into several of these new markets. During strategy meetings they have been fielding a laundry list of questions from the rest of the CUTCO management team. In developing a recommended sequence of countries for market entry (along with an overall entry timetable), the management team needs immediate answers regarding

1. What criteria should CUTCO use to select countries for market entry?
2. Which countries offer the best market opportunities for CUTCO products?
3. What should be the composition of the new country's management team?
4. Should CUTCO continue to develop countries using both the party plan/hostess program approach and the college program approach?

End Notes

1. *The Weekly Newspaper for the Home Furnishing Network,* April 14, 1997.

2. *The Weekly Newspaper for the Home Furnishing Network,* Feb. 26, 1996.

3. *The Weekly Newspaper for the Home Furnishing Network,* Oct. 7, 1996.

4. President's Message on Fiskars Web page, 1997.

Appendix A–1
Country Data

Argentina

The Argentine Republic has a population of some 34 million and a work force of almost 11 million. About 14 percent of the population lives in rural areas. The land area covers more than 2.7 million square kilometers (1 million square miles), making Argentina second in area only to Brazil within Latin America. The country is bounded by Chile on the west and south, Bolivia and Paraguay on the north, and Brazil, Uruguay, and the Atlantic Ocean on the east. The official language of Argentina is Spanish, but English, German, and Italian also are spoken by significant parts of the population. Although the country was settled by colonists from Spain, emigrants from many European countries settled in the central plains and south during the 19th century.

Major cities include the capital Buenos Aires (city, 2,960,976 people; metropolitan area, 9,967,826), Cordoba (1,179,067), and two industrial towns: Rosario (1,078,374) and La Plata (542,567). The country has a mostly temperate climate although great variation exists because of latitudinal extension and varying altitudes. The seasons are the reverse of those in the Northern Hemisphere. Argentina has one of the highest literacy rates in South America (approximately 95 percent). Primary education is compulsory and free, but further training is expensive. Leading universities include the University of Buenos Aires and national universities at Bahia Blanca, Cordoba, Corrientes, La Plata, Mendoza, Santa Fe, Santa Rosa, and San Miguel de Tucuman.

Argentina has traditionally been one of the more prosperous Latin American countries. Unlike many of its neighbors, the country has developed a strong manufacturing industry and has become less dependent on agriculture. Today the country is largely self-sufficient in consumer goods. Expenditures on household goods and services consume about 5.1 percent of the consumers total expenses, ranking behind food, housing, clothing, leisure, and education. There are approximately 790,000 retail outlets. Chief manufactured products include automobiles, beer, cattle and buffalo hides, cement, commercial vehicles, cotton yarn, crude steel, lumber, man-made fibers, merchant vessels, paper, petroleum products, plastics and resins, refined sugar, steel tubes, sulfuric acid, synthetic rubber, textiles, wine, wheat flour, and wood pulp. Unemployment is around 7 percent. The gross domestic product approximates $55 million (U.S. dollars). The country regularly runs a trade surplus. The largest quantity of imports (approximately 22 percent of total imports) comes from the United States, with whom Argentina regularly runs a trade deficit. Germany, the United Kingdom, Venezuela, and Brazil are other major suppliers. Chief imports are iron and steel products, fuels, chemicals, nonferrous metal products, lumber, and paper.

Argentina's airlines, railways, and bus and ship lines constitute the most extensive transportation system in Latin America. The rail network is the most complete on the continent, fanning out from Buenos Aires in all directions. Rail lines are government-

Information in this appendix was obtained from *Compton's Reference Collection 1996* (Compton's NewMedia Inc); Encarta 1994 (Microsoft); *International Marketing Data & Statistics 1996 Statistical Abstract of the World 1996*

owned. Roads are extensive and link all parts of the nation with the capital. Telephone and telegraph networks are mainly government-owned and considered modern.

Austria

The Republic of Austria has a population of almost 8 million in a land area of 82,730 square kilometers. Approximately 65 percent of the people live in urban area. Since the 1970s the population growth rate has decreased to zero due to a balancing out of the birth and the death rates. German is the official language, Roman Catholicism is the principal religion, and the population is nearly 100 percent literate. Major cities include the capital Vienna (population 1.5 million), Graz (237,810), Linz (203,044), Salzburg (143,978), and Innsbruck (118,112). The Austrian educational system is based on compulsory, free education for all children between ages 6 and 15 in a variety of primary and secondary schools. Leading universities and colleges include University of Vienna, University of Graz, University of Innsbruck, University of Technology (Vienna), and University of Salzburg. They are particularly noted for their technical and medical schools and clinics.

Austria is located at the meeting place of several important transportation routes. In the west is the Brenner Pass to Italy, and in the east is the Danube River, which flows through southeastern Europe. Austria also lies on the land route between the head of the Adriatic Sea and the Danube Plain. Differences between summer and winter temperatures are greater in the east than in the west. Interior valleys and the eastern lowlands have the warmest summer temperatures. In the latter area summers have average temperatures of about 68°F (20°C) and winter temperatures of about 29°F (–2°C). Austria has a good railroad network, half of which is electrified. Several four-lane highways are connected to the German and Italian road networks. Austria has a well-organized, efficient communications infrastructure.

Gross domestic product is almost $96 million (U.S. dollars). Austrian industry is characterized by a number of small specialized enterprises, many of them state-owned. Unemployment is approximately 6.5 percent. Chief manufactured products include machinery and equipment, ferrous and nonferrous base metals, food products, transport equipment, cement, bricks, and tiles. Chief exports are machinery, transport equipment, chemicals and related products, paper and paper products, iron, and steel. The country has regularly run a trade deficit. The United States is the source of approximately 4 percent of total imports. Chief imports include machinery, transport equipment, chemicals and related products, clothing, food products, crude petroleum, and petroleum products. The country requires a high withholding tax on direct sellers' representatives.

Brazil

The Federal Republic of Brazil, covering 8,456,510 square kilometers, is the world's largest tropical country. The only larger nations are the Temperate Zone lands of Russia, Canada, China, and the United States. Brazil has more than 160 million people spread unevenly over its huge land area, making it the sixth most populous country in the world. More than three-fourths of Brazil's people live in cities and towns, and more than 29 percent of them are in its 10 cities with more than a million inhabitants. These include the metropolitan areas of Sao Paulo with more than 10 million people and Rio de Janeiro with more than 5 million people. Other major cities are Belo Horizonte and Salvador. The work force numbers 60 million. Unemployment hovers around 6 percent. Around half of all Brazilians are under 20 years old.

Until about 1960 the Brazilian education system was deficient at every level, from primary school through university. Higher education was available only to upper–income-level families. About half of the population was illiterate; today this rate is about 19 percent. Branch university campuses have been built in a number of communities and today's Brazilian university graduates are especially well trained in scientific and technical skills, and for the first time many of these graduates come from families with lesser incomes. Portuguese is the official language of Brazil.

Some of Brazil's industries are well established. These include iron mills, textiles and clothing manufacture, food processing, furniture making, tanning, and leather goods. Two of Brazil's most successful industries, motor vehicles and petrochemicals, were established relatively recently. Brazil is unevenly served by land transportation. Because of the vast distances to be covered, excellent air services are maintained to all parts of the country. The railroads at one time were the chief means of transportation. However, they had a number of disadvantages. First, they were built to move agricultural and mining products to the seaports and not for connecting different parts of the country. Also they could not be linked because they had been built by private companies using different track gauges. This is slowly being changed. The country regularly runs a trade surplus, the United States being a principal trading partner. Gross domestic product is $280 billion. Expenses for household goods and services total around 4.9 percent of consumer expenditures, ranking behind food and housing (almost 60 percent), and leisure, education, and health. Brazil has around 810,000 retail establishments and annual sales in these outlets exceed $110 billion (U.S. dollars). Direct sales appear to be around $3.5 billion (U.S. dollars).

Ireland

The Republic of Ireland occupies about five-sixths of the island of Ireland. (Northern Ireland occupies the rest of the island and is part of the United Kingdom.) The Republic of Ireland covers 68,890 square kilometers. The population numbers about 3.5 million with 1.4 million in the work force. The unemployment rate generally exceeds 20 percent. About 60 percent of Ireland's people live in urban areas. Major cities are Dublin, Cork, Limerick, Galway, and Waterford. English (the dominant language in the educational system) is spoken throughout Ireland except in certain areas of the west coast. Government documents are printed in both Gaelic and English.

Ireland's maritime climate is moderated by prevailing southwesterly winds. Rain is frequent and relatively abundant. The highest peaks in the western mountains receive about 100 inches (250 centimeters) of rain annually. The driest areas, around Dublin in the east, have about 30 inches (75 centimeters). Temperatures average about 42°F (5°C) during the coolest month, February, and about 60°F (15°C) in the warmest month, August.

Ireland's economy has been changing from an agricultural to an industrial base. In the 1990s over 25 percent of the work force was employed in manufacturing, mining, and construction, and about a third in agriculture. The shift from agriculture to industry has been greater in Dublin (the capital and largest city) and in the eastern and southern sections of the country than in the west. The value of manufactured goods exported in 1991 was worth 40 percent of the gross domestic national product. GDP is approximately $27 billion (U.S. dollars).

Ireland's entry into the European Communities was a great boon to the nation's economy. Irish exports gained duty-free access to the European Communities' population market of 270 million people. Foreign companies, especially from the United

States, established businesses or branch firms in Ireland to gain tax advantages in exporting to the European market. By 1990 about 850 foreign firms, 300 from the United States, owned operations in Ireland, resulting not only in new products and jobs, but also in additional skills, markets, and technology. The United Kingdom is Ireland's principal trading partner. Others include the United States, Germany, France, and the Benelux countries.

Ireland is well served by highways, railways, airlines, and water transportation. The network of Irish roads, almost all of which are paved, totals more than 54,000 miles (86,900 kilometers). Regular rural bus routes extend to many small, isolated communities. Aer Lingus, the Irish international airline, has flights to and from European and transatlantic airports. Dublin, Limerick, and Cork have international airports, and Shannon Airport, near Limerick, was the world's first duty-free airport.

Irish children from 6 to 15 years old are required by law to go to school. The elementary schools are free. The literacy rate is virtually 100 percent. Secondary schools are private institutions, and most are operated by religious orders of the Roman Catholic Church. Nevertheless, Irish secondary schools receive substantial government aid and are subject to inspection by the Department of Education. The administration of the nation's vocational schools resembles that of the secondary schools. The University of Dublin, or Trinity College, was founded in 1592, and the National University was established in Dublin in 1908. The National University also has branches in Galway and Cork. In addition, Ireland has 10 regional technical colleges in the provincial centers of Athlone, Carlow, Cork, Dundalk, Galway, Letterkenny, Limerick, Sligo, Tralee, and Waterford. St. Patrick's College in Maynooth trains Roman Catholic priests but also admits other students. The National Institute for Higher Education, which offers mainly technological courses, has campuses in Dublin and Limerick. All universities and colleges receive financial support from the government.

Italy

The Italian Republic is dominated by two large mountain systems: the Alps in the north and the Apennines throughout the peninsula. The only two active volcanoes on the European continent are Mount Vesuvius near Naples and Mount Etna in Sicily. From northwest to southeast, Italy is a little more than 1,080 kilometers (670 miles) long. The widest part, in the north, measures about 560 kilometers from west to east. The rest of the peninsula varies in width from 160 to 240 kilometers. Italy has a total area of about 300,400 square kilometers (116,000 square miles). Italians divide their country into four main parts: northern Italy, central Italy, southern Italy, and the islands. Major cities of Italy are outlined in Appendix Exhibit 1. Maniago is the cutlery capital of Italy. Hundreds of artisans and companies have been manufacturing knives, scissors, and other cutting tools using a mixture of high technology and ancient traditions dating over 400 years.

Most of Italy has a Mediterranean type of climate of cool, rainy winters and hot, dry summers. Winter temperatures along and near the coasts of southern Italy seldom drop to freezing in winter, and summer temperatures often reach 90°F (32°C) or higher. The climate of northern Italy differs greatly from that of the south. Winters tend to be cold, with heavy snowfall in the Alps, much rain, and fog. Summers are not as hot.

Italy has a population of around 58 million, with a work force close to 24 million. Italy's population is around 65 percent urban. Rome, the largest city, had nearly 3 million people in 1990; Milan had about 1,500,000, and Naples, about 1,200,000. The Italian people are known to be among the most homogeneous, in language and

---

EXHIBIT 1   Major Cities of the Italian Republic (1990 estimate, city proper)

- *Rome* (2,803,931 people). Capital of Italy; cultural, commercial, religious, and political center; Roman Forum; Colosseum; Pantheon; Villa Borghese; Trevi Fountain; Vatican City.
- *Milan* (1,449,403). Leading financial, commercial, and industrial city; the Duomo; Pinacoteca di Brera; Brera Palace; La Scala; National Museum of Science and Technology.
- *Naples* (1,204,149). Leading port; educational and financial center; Villa Nazionale; National Museum; National Gallery; Castel Nuovo; Conservatory of Music.
- *Turin* (1,002,180). Industrial and commercial city; road and rail junction; notable architecture; Egyptian Museum; Sabauda Gallery; Fiat automobile plant.
- *Palermo* (731,418). Capital of Sicily; port; industrial, educational, and cultural city; Archaeological Museum; Teatro (Theater) Massimo; National Gallery; Norman Palace; Royal Palace; Quattro Canti (Four Corners); churches of La Mortorana and San Giovanni degli Eremiti.
- *Genoa* (706,754). Leading port and industrial city; Royal Palace, Doges' Palace; cathedral of San Lorenzo.
- *Bologna* (417,410). Transportation, industrial, and agricultural center; University of Bologna; Bevilacqua Palace; Pinacoteca Nazionale (National Picture Gallery); church of San Petronio.
- *Florence* (413,069). Commercial, educational, cultural, and traditional handicraft center; Ponte Vecchio; Pitti Palace; National Museum; National Central Library; Galleria degli Uffizi Palace; Santa Maria del Fiore Cathedral; Medici Chapels; Boboli Gardens.
- *Catania* (366,226). Industrial center and port; Mount Etna; Ursino Castle; Duomo; Church of San Nicolo; elephant fountain.
- *Bari* (355,352). Port and agricultural center; Basilica of San Nicolo; Norman castle; archeological museum; cathedral.
- *Venice* (320,990). Port; commercial and cultural city; Grand Canal; St. Mark's Square; St. Mark's Church; Doges' Palace; island of San Giorgio Maggiore; Bridge of Sighs.

---

religion, of all the European populations. The only significant minority group consists of several hundred thousand German-speaking people who live in the Alpine valleys in the north. About 95 percent of the Italian people speak Italian. For more than seven centuries the standard form of the language has been the one spoken in Tuscany, the region of central Italy centered around Florence. However, there are many dialects, some of which are difficult for non-Italians to understand, even if they have a good command of the language. At least two of the principal dialects, those of Sicily and Sardinia, may even be difficult for other Italians to comprehend.

Italy has 27 state and private universities. The private universities are supported by the Roman Catholic church. The University of Bologna, founded about 1200, is Italy's oldest university and one of the oldest in the world. The largest is the University of Rome, with more than 140,000 students. Other leading universities are located in Cagliari, Catania, Ferrara, Florence, Genoa, Lecce, Macerata, Messina, Milan, Modena, Naples, Padua, Palermo, Parma, Pavia, Perugia, Pisa, Salerno, Sassari, Siena, Trieste, Turin, Udine, and Venice. The national literacy rate is about 95 percent.

Measured in terms of overall production, Italy ranks fourth among the industrial nations of Western Europe after Germany, France, and Great Britain. Italy's gross domestic product is approximately $565 billion (U.S. dollars). Foreign trade has increased greatly as a result of Italy's industrial growth and its membership in the EC. Imports exceed exports in most years. However, that trade deficit is more than balanced by income from tourists. Italy carries on about half of its foreign trade, both imports and exports, with the other EC members. The United States contributes about 5.5 percent to Italy's imports and absorbs around 7 percent of Italy's exports. Unemployment runs about 11 percent and Italy offers a relatively generous unemployment benefit. In addition, a black market is generally believed to absorb more than 5 million people. Direct sales in Italy appear to be around $2.1 billion (U.S. dollars) and employ some 375,000 people. Italy is a service economy and appears open-minded to diverse selling methods.

The Italian railroad system, which is owned by the government, provides convenient transportation throughout the country. Ferries link the principal islands with the mainland, and those that travel between southernmost Italy and Sicily carry trains as well as cars, trucks, and people. The railroad system is most extensive in the north, but main lines run along both coasts, and other routes cross the peninsula in several places. The Simplon Tunnel, one of the world's longest railroad tunnels, connects Italy and Switzerland.

Italy and Germany have the most extensive networks of fast, limited-access highways in Europe. Motorists can drive without encountering traffic lights or crossroads, stopping only for border crossings, rest, or fuel, from Belgium, The Netherlands, France, or Germany across the Alps all the way to Sicily. Two highway tunnels through the Alps (under the Great St. Bernard Pass and through Mont Blanc) enable motor vehicles to travel between Italy and the rest of Europe regardless of weather. The expressways, called *autostradas,* are superhighways and toll roads. They connect all major Italian cities and have contributed to the tremendous increase in tourist travel.

Japan

Japan (in Japanese, Nippon) is the world's seventh most populous nation with 125 million people. Average life expectancy in Japan exceeds 75 years for men and 80 years for women. Average family size has been shrinking to about three members per family. The proportion of young people in Japan also has been decreasing. The work force numbers some 63 million. Unemployment hovers around 2.3 percent.

With an area of only 374,744 square kilometers, Japan is also one of the world's most thickly populated nations. Further, more than three out of every four Japanese live in cities. Thus, if only the urban land area is considered, the density becomes several times greater than it is for the entire land area. Japanese homes are rather small by Western standards. They generally have a kitchen and three or four rooms that serve as living and sleeping quarters. Japan's greatest concentration of population is in a 350-mile belt that extends from Tokyo and the Kanto Plain westward along the Pacific coast through Nagoya and Kyoto to Osaka and Kobe on the eastern edge of the Inland Sea. Within this belt, called the Tokaido Megalopolis, live about 42 percent of Japan's people. The belt comprises the six largest cities and a large percentage of the 180-odd cities with more than 100,000 population. Exhibit 2 covers major cities of Japan.

Rice, the mainstay of the Japanese diet for centuries, is eaten at almost every meal. At breakfast it is usually supplemented by misoshiru (a bean-paste soup) and tsukemono (pickled vegetables). In the cities, some Japanese have replaced these dishes with bread, butter, and eggs. Lunch—a light meal—may consist of salted fish, tsukemono, and tsukudani (seafood or vegetables cooked and preserved in soy sauce) in addition to rice or noodles. Supper—the most important meal of the day—in most homes includes fish, beef, pork, or chicken with vegetables and rice. Meat is usually cut into thin strips and fried. It is not as important in the Japanese diet as in that of Western nations.

EXHIBIT 2   Major Cities of Japan (1990 census)

Tokyo (8,163,127 people). Capital city of Japan; center of international commerce, manufacturing, culture, and military affairs; large harbor and shipyards; steel mills; petroleum refineries; petrochemical complexes; electronics; printing; fishing industry; Ginza shopping district; Tokyo Tower, Kabuki Theater; Metropolitan Museum of Art.

Yokohama (3,220,350). Capital of Kanagawa Prefecture; international port city; center of foreign trade; steel; electronic equipment; ships; automobiles; chemicals; Bank of Tokyo; Yokohama Archives of History; Sojiji Temple; Yokohama National University.

Osaka (2,623,831). Capital of Osaka Prefecture; industrial and transport center; textiles; chemicals; electrical machinery; food processing; printing; publishing; Bunraku puppet theater; Umeda shopping center; Osaka Castle; Kansai University; Shitennoji Temple.

Nagoya (2,154,664). Capital of Aichi Prefecture; industrial center; cotton weaving; clock- and watchmaking; cloisonné; bicycles; pottery; porcelain; lacquerware; embroidery; textiles; electrical machinery; seaport; international airport; Nagoya Institute of Technology; Higashiyama Park; Grand Shrine of Ise.

Sapporo (1,671,765). Capital of Hokkaido Prefecture; economic and commercial center; foodstuffs; chemicals; agricultural machinery; ceramics; hemp cloth; rubber goods; sawmilling; dairy products; handicrafts; winter sports center; Sapporo Beer's German-style beer hall; Ainu Museum.

Kobe (1,477,423). Capital of Hyogo Prefecture; domestic and international port city; shipbuilding; steel production; chemicals; machinery; paper; textiles; international airport; Motomachi shopping center; Hakutsuru Fine Art Museum.

Kyoto (1,461,140). Capital of Kyoto Urban Prefecture; former capital city of Japan; silk weaving; embroidery; porcelain; copper products; heavy machinery; chemicals; sake industry; Kyoto Imperial Palace; Nijo Castle; Toji Temple; Kyoto City University of Arts.

Fukuoka (1,237,107). Capital of Fukuoka Prefecture on Kyushu; center for industry, culture, education; fishing industry; merchant shipping; Sumiyoshi-jinja shrine.

Kawasaki (1,173,606). Center of Keihin Industrial Zone; large shipping port; petrochemicals; electrical machinery and appliances; automobiles; steel; New Year Festival; Kawasaki Daishi temple.

Hiroshima (1,085,677). Capital of Hiroshima Prefecture on Honshu; target of first atomic bomb during World War II; shipping center; military center; ships; automobiles; machinery; Peace Memorial Park; Shukkei-en miniature landscape garden.

Kitakyushu (1,026,467). Formed in 1963 when the cities of Kokura, Moji, Tobata, Wakamatsu, and Yawata were merged; coal mining; iron- and steelworks; chemicals; ceramics; machinery; electrical appliances; food processing; major airport.

Nearly all of Japan's school-age children attend school regularly. Attendance is compulsory through the lower level of secondary school. The adult literacy rate is virtually 100 percent. Further, the Japanese are among the world's most ardent newspaper readers. The Japanese upper-secondary school is comparable to the U.S. high school. It offers either a technical or a college preparatory course of instruction. Japanese students, especially those who plan to attend college, strongly compete with each other for grades and honors. To go beyond high school, Japanese boys and girls must pass difficult college entrance examinations. There are junior colleges, four-year universities, and graduate schools. Leading universities include Tokyo University; Kyoto University; Tohoku University, Sendai; Kyushu University, Fukuoka; Hokkaido University, Sapporo; Osaka University; and Nagoya University.

More than one-fourth of Japan's labor force is employed in manufacturing. Most Japanese manufacturing units are small workshops employing only up to three workers. These enterprises tend to be inefficient, to pay low wages, and to turn out goods of uncertain quality. But factories employing more than 300 workers, less than 1 percent of the total number, account for about 50 percent of Japan's industrial production. Manufacturing is heavily concentrated in the Tokaido Megalopolis, the heavily populated urban-industrial belt. Sakai is considered the cutlery center for Japan. About one-fourth of all Japanese workers (16.6 million) are union members. Most unions are organized by single enterprises rather than by industry or craft. However, local unions have combined to form nationwide federations. Unionized or not, average hourly compensation in Japan exceeds $16 (U.S. dollars).

Japan has one of the world's most advanced mass communications systems. Modern transportation facilities link all parts of Japan and facilitate the swift, efficient movement of people and goods. Railways are the main form of land transportation. Railway stations are the hubs of mass transportation systems, which also include buses, taxis, subways, and the vanishing trolleys. Modern highway construction has lagged badly behind the needs of automobile and truck traffic. Only one-tenth of the total mileage of national and local roads is paved. The government's road building program has been relying upon expressways to ease intercity traffic.

About four-fifths of Japan's 1.8 million retail stores have fewer than four employees. These small stores, many of which have a small stock and make little profit, are usually operated by an owner and members of his family. They generally live in quarters behind or over the store. In good weather, storefronts are open and goods are within easy reach from the street. Merchandise is also sold by peddlers who circulate in residential neighborhoods. Western-style stores with plate-glass windows and window displays are becoming common in the cities. Supermarkets based on American models have also sprung up. Japanese department stores are among the largest in the world. They have prime locations in the downtown areas and near key railway terminals. The typical department store has a wide selection of goods and offers many services, including a children's playground on the roof, cultural events, beauty parlors, dining facilities, and delivery services. Direct retail sales in Japan exceed $30 billion (U.S. dollars), yet this is dwarfed by the $1 trillion (U.S. dollars) in annual retail sales. Today's affluent Japanese spend more on household goods and services (6.2 percent) than on clothing or housing. Food, health, and education are the principal recipients of the Japanese consumer's expenditures.

Japan is one of the world's leading trading nations. The value of its annual exports and imports significantly exceeds the GDP for many other countries. Japan imports a huge volume of fuels and raw materials, upon which its manufacturing industries are greatly dependent. It exports great quantities of manufactured goods. Japan's domestic market is too small to absorb its entire output of manufactured goods. Total gross domestic product exceeds $1.6 trillion (U.S. dollars).

Manufactured items account for more than 95 percent of Japan's exports. Machinery, transportation equipment, and metals (especially steel) now make up about four-fifths of Japan's exports. Raw materials such as iron ore, coking coal, and scrap metal account for about half the value of Japanese imports; foodstuffs, such as wheat and meat, for about 15 percent; manufactured goods, including textiles, machinery, metals, and chemicals, for about 20 percent. Japan has had a favorable trade balance since 1964, exports having consistently exceeded imports.

Japan's principal trading partner is the United States, the supplier of about 22 percent of its imports and the market for about 29 percent of its exports. In this exchange, Japan's most important imports include foodstuffs, machinery, and coal; its most important exports are steel, metal products, and machinery. Nearly 30 percent of Japan's exports, largely machinery, iron and steel, chemicals, and textiles, go to southern and eastern Asia. Petroleum and petroleum products, foodstuffs, sawlogs, and other products and raw materials from this region constitute about 20 percent of its imports. Japan's trade with Western Europe is also strong and includes the export of ships and the import of machinery. The Middle East is a major source of oil. Most of Japan's foreign trade is handled by large firms that are part of the *zaibatsu*. Shipping is channeled through seven main international ports: Chiba, Yokohama, Nagoya, Kobe, Kawasaki, Osaka, and Tokyo. The deepwater ports of Chiba, Yokohama, Nagoya, Kobe, and Kawasaki handle four-fifths of Japan's exports and one-third of its imports. Japan's trade surplus with the United States remained a source of friction between the two countries during the Bush and Clinton presidencies. Visits to Japan by Bush in 1992 and Clinton in 1993 failed to make substantial progress in opening Japan's markets to more imports.

The language of Japan has many dialects, and speakers of different dialects do not always understand each other. But almost everyone in Japan uses standard Japanese as well as the dialect of her home area. Standard Japanese, originally the dialect spoken by the educated people of Tokyo, is now taught and understood throughout the country.

The islands of Japan are geologically young and unstable. They have been subjected to considerable folding, faulting, and volcanic activity. As a result, the land surface of the Japanese islands is dominated by mountains and hills. Undersea earthquakes in the northern Pacific basin stir up unusually large tidal waves, which are very destructive when they reach the Japanese coast. Severe earthquakes damage small areas every five or six years. For a small nation, Japan has a great variety of climatic conditions. This is because its islands have a long latitudinal spread and are in the zone where the conflicting air masses of the Asian continent and of the Pacific Ocean meet and interact. The nation is temperate with warm, humid summers and relatively mild winters except on Hokkaido, where snow falls an average of 130 days a year. June and September are rainy seasons. The whole country averages more than 40 inches (100 centimeters) of rain a year.

The major change in Japan during the early 1990s was the apparent end of the economic miracle that had dazzled the world for more than 30 years. By 1993, the Japanese stock market had lost more than half its value. Land prices plummeted, and many banks were caught with nonperforming loans worth hundreds of billions of dollars. Growth in productivity declined from 5.1 percent to less than 2 percent a year by 1993. Surveys of younger Japanese adults indicate dissatisfaction with hours worked, job value, and compensation. Japanese women are especially interested in jobs that are flexible and enjoyable. Meanwhile, Japan had ceased to be the lone economic giant of Asia. Japan faced fast-growing competition from Asian neighbors, notably South Korea, Taiwan, Hong Kong, Singapore, and Thailand. China, the world's largest nation, had emerged by the end of 1993 as the world's third largest economy.

Mexico

A country with slightly more than 1,940,000 square kilometers (750,000 square miles) in area, the United Mexican States (in Spanish, Estados Unidos Mexicanos) has a vast array of mineral resources, limited agricultural land, and a rapidly growing population. At present the nation's population is growing at a rate of 2.6 percent annually. This is about 50 percent higher than the world average and almost four times the rate of the United States. The country has a population of approximately 93 million with 75 percent living in urban settings. More than half of its inhabitants live in the country's central core (Mesa Central), while the arid north and the tropical south are sparsely set-

EXHIBIT 3   Major Cities of Mexico (1990 census)

Mexico City (8,236,960 people). Federal capital; economic, social, educational, and industrial center; Plaza Mayor; Chapultepec Park; Metropolitan Cathedral; National Palace.

Guadalajara (1,628,617). State capital of Jalisco; industrial and agricultural center; Plaza de Armas; Regional Museum of Guadalajara; Teatro Degollado, one of Latin America's finest theaters.

Netzahualcoyotl (1,259,543). In northeastern Mexico state; headquarters of municipality of Netzahualcoyotl; economy heavily dependent on Mexico City; Xochiaca Dam; Lake Texcoco.

Monterrey (1,064,197). State capital of Nuevo Leon; industrial center; Spanish atmosphere and architecture; Gran Plaza; Government Palace.

Puebla (1,054,921). Capital of Puebla state; military key to Mexico because of strategic location; Spanish architecture; agricultural and industrial region; church of Santo Domingo.

Leon (872,453). In northwestern Guanajuato; industrial and commercial center; surrounded by rich cereal-producing area.

Juarez (797,679). Opposite El Paso, Tex.; marketing center for cotton-growing area; Guadalupe mission.

Tijuana (742,686). In northwestern Baja California Norte; major tourist center; Avenida Revolucion; jai alai games at Palacio de Fronton; bullfights at Plaza de Toros Monumental.

Merida (557,340). Capital of Yucatan state; center for manufacture of henequen (Sisal hemp), fiber; tourist center; House of Montejo; cathedral; archaeological museum; Yucatan University.

Chihuahua (530,487). Capital of Chihuahua state; cattle-raising center; Church of San Francisco; monument to Miguel Hidalgo y Costilla; Autonomous University of Chihuahua.

tled. It was estimated that in 1993 the nation's active labor force was roughly 30 million people.

Within the hierarchy of Mexican urban places, Mexico City is the political, economic, social, educational, and industrial capital of the nation. The metropolis covers a solidly built-up urbanized area of some 24 by 32 kilometers. Mexico City's urban area has about 18 percent of the population. With some 2½ million people, Guadalajara is the nation's second largest urban center, and Monterrey, Mexico's iron and steel center has grown to more than 2 million. (Exhibit 3 gives additional information regarding major Mexican cities.)

Because of its topographic diversity and large range in latitude, Mexico has a wide array of climatic conditions, often occurring in very short distances. More than half of Mexico lies south of the Tropic of Cancer. Within the tropics, temperature variations from season to season are small, often less than 10°F (5°C) between the warmest and coldest months of the year. In these areas winter is defined as the rainiest rather than coldest months. The climate also changes significantly with increases in elevation. Geologically, Mexico is located in one of the Earth's most dynamic areas. It is part of the Ring of Fire, a region around the Pacific Ocean highlighted by active volcanism and frequent seismic activity.

Of the fewer than 50 universities in the country, 20 percent are located in Mexico City. A staggeringly high percentage of university students—perhaps more than 80 percent—are in the city. As with primary education, private secondary schools are normally vastly superior to public ones. This helps to maintain a socioeconomic imbalance in educational levels that greatly favors the middle and upper classes. A college degree is very much a passport to social mobility in Mexico. Leading universities include National Autonomous University of Mexico, Metropolitan Autonomous University, Women's University of Mexico, Spanish-American University, and National Polytechnic Institute, (all in Mexico City), University of Monterrey and Institute of Technology and Higher Education (both in Monterrey), University of Guadalajara, and

Veracruz University. Mexico's illiteracy rate is thought to be approximately 10 to 13 percent, down from nearly 25 percent in 1970.

Mexico is the most industrialized country in Latin America after Brazil, yet the nation is struggling to modernize its economy. Overall gross domestic product approximates $230 billion (U.S. dollars). Mexico has some 825,000 retail outlets. Annual consumer expenditures exceed $80 billion (U.S. dollars) in these establishments. Direct sales in Mexico appear to be $1.3 billion. Mexican families spend approximately 8.2 percent of their consumption on household goods and services.

A disproportionate share of manufacturing is located in the Mexico City metropolitan area, largely because of its huge market and superior infrastructure. Because of its physical diversity and economic status, Mexico has had a difficult time creating an integrated transportation network. Although it was one of the first in Latin America to develop railway lines, the nation is joined together by an extensive but inefficient railway system. Major rail routes extend outward from the Mexico City hub along the west coast to Mexicali, through the Central Plateau to El Paso and Laredo, via the Gulf Coastal Plain to the Yucatan peninsula, and south to Oaxaca. Rail traffic, both for passengers and freight, is slow and unreliable. Highways are the major mode for transporting goods. Cross-country trucking accounts for a high percentage of freight movement within the nation. Unfortunately, Mexico's highways are barely adequate to serve the national needs. As with rails, all roads focus on Mexico City. Five major two-lane highways link northern border cities to the capital. Similar roads connect the Yucatan peninsula and the Guatemalan border with the Mesa Central. Several parts of the country are lacking in rail and road connections, especially from east to west across northern Mexico. The country is well connected with an extensive cellular phone system.

Mexico's chief trading partners are the United States, Japan, Germany, France, Brazil, Canada, Italy, and the United Kingdom. Its major imports are industrial supplies, machinery, transportation equipment, foods and beverages, books, and chemicals. Mexico requires that each individual imported product must be labeled, which creates a nontarriff barrier. Major exports are crude and processed petroleum, natural gas, silver, vanilla, foods and beverages, hemp, and transportation equipment. The country has been running a trade deficit.

Poland

The Republic of Poland has an area of about 312,684 square kilometers (120,728 square miles). It is bordered on the east by Russia, Lithuania, Belarus, and the Ukraine, on the west by Germany, on the south by the Czech Republic and Slovakia, and on the north by the Baltic Sea. The population totals about 38 million and the work force is approximately 16 million. Currently, more than 98 percent of the people are Poles, with small groups of Ukrainians, Belorussians, Germans, Slovaks, and Lithuanians. The Poles speak a Slavic language and belong to the western branch of the Slavic peoples. The literacy rate is approximately 99 percent. Religion plays a major role in Polish life, and the Poles have remained faithful followers of the Roman Catholic church.

About 60 percent of the population lives in a number of large cities. Five have populations of more than 500,000. The largest is Warsaw, the capital, with about 1.7 million inhabitants. Lodz has approximately 850,000 people. Other large cities are Krakow (Cracow), 750,000; Wroclaw, 645,000; Poznan, 590,000; Gdansk, 470,000; and Szczecin, 415,000. (A smaller city, Bialystok, is the cutlery capital of Poland.) The oldest university in Poland is in Krakow, with others in Warsaw, Poznan, Lublin,

Gdansk, Wroclaw, Torun, Lodz, and Katowice. There is also a Roman Catholic university in Lublin. There are colleges of engineering, agriculture, and economics.

Unemployment is around 14 percent and the infrastructure is generally severely outmoded. Gross domestic product is around $53 billion (U.S. dollars). Chief trading partners are Germany and Russia with the country's trade balance regularly fluctuating from surplus to deficit. Major manufactured products are iron and steel, chemicals, sulfuric acid, salts, fertilizers, plastics, artificial fibers, ships, transportation equipment, agricultural machinery, and machine tools. The country's chief imports are crude petroleum, petroleum products, natural gas, iron ores, hot-rolled products, metalworking machines, cold-rolled sheets and other metallurgical products, steel pipes, agricultural equipment and tools, buses, and passenger cars.

Taiwan

Taiwan (officially the Republic of China) is now one of the wealthiest and most industrialized nations in Asia. With a population of approximately 22 million and less than 32,260 square kilometers of land, it also has one of the highest population densities in the world. There is concern that Taiwan will not be able to maintain its high standard of living if the birthrate does not decline. Taiwan is situated in the South China Sea, about 100 miles (160 kilometers) off the southeast coast of mainland China. More than two-thirds of the country consists of rugged mountains.

Major cities include the capital Taipei (2,724,800), Kaohsiung (1,398,700), Taichung (764,700), Tainan (685,400), and Keelung (353,600). With a labor force of approximately 8 million, unemployment is about 1.5 percent. Gross domestic product exceeds $90 billion (U.S. dollars). Taiwan has the fourth highest per capita income in East Asia after Japan, Singapore, and Hong Kong. Its average income is 20 times that of mainland China.

Improvements in education have been a major factor in Taiwan's economic success. Mandarin Chinese is the official language, but much of the population can converse in more than one language. The educational system is among the best in the world in terms of numbers served, levels of literacy, and the number of people who go to college. Leading universities and colleges include Fujen Catholic University, National Taiwan University, Tamkang University, all in Taipei; National Cheng Kung University, Tainan; and National Chunghsing University, Taichung.

The main markets for Taiwan's products are the United States, the nations of the European Union, and Japan. Exports account for more than half of Taiwan's gross national product. Chief exports include electrical machinery and apparatus, metal products, plastic products, plywood, wood products, furniture, textile products, and transportation equipment. Approximately $1/3$ of imports come from Japan and roughly 20 percent from the United States Chief imports are basic metals, chemicals, crude petroleum, electrical machinery and apparatus, food, logs, machinery tools, raw cotton, and transportation equipment.

United Kingdom

The United Kingdom of Great Britain and Northern Ireland is the political union of England, Scotland, Wales, and Northern Ireland. It is not a federation but a unitary state, and its inhabitants elect members to represent them in a parliament that meets in London. Scotland, Wales, and Northern Ireland retain a degree of autonomy in running their own affairs. Total land area is 241,590 square kilometers. The highly urban (91.5

EXHIBIT 4   Major Cities of the United Kingdom

London, England (5,100,000; Greater London, 6,767,500). Capital of the United Kingdom; international financial center; huge port.

Birmingham, England (1,008,000). Industrial center; metal manufacturing; machinery; engines; iron roofs; girders; railway cars; automobiles; University of Birmingham.

Glasgow, Scotland (773,800). Largest city in Scotland; center for commerce and industry; chief port city of western Scotland; textiles; food and beverages; tobacco; chemicals; engineering; printing; Kelvingrove Art Galleries and Museum; Hunterian Museum; Glasgow School of Art; University of Glasgow.

Leeds, England (710,000). Wool cloth; iron; boots; shoes; felt; ready-made clothing; stock and corn exchanges; music festivals; Civic Theater; City Museum; City Art Gallery; University of Leeds.

Sheffield, England (539,000). Fine steel cutlery; steel; plated ware; iron and brass goods; clothing; canned foods; paint and varnish; chemicals; shopping and cultural center; Sheffield University.

Liverpool, England (492,000). Large port in industrial region; textiles; machinery; chemicals; flour milling; agriculture; shipbuilding and repair; engineering works; Walker Art Gallery; University of Liverpool.

Bradford, England (464,400). Textile and clothing industries; Cartwright Memorial Hall; University of Bradford; Bolling Hall.

Manchester, England (451,100). A leading seaport and industrial area of England; engineering; printing; electrical products; machine tools; chemicals; financial and banking center; railway hub; Manchester University.

Edinburgh, Scotland (439,700). Capital of Scotland; center of medicine, law, banking, insurance, tourism; Edinburgh Castle; National Gallery; Royal Scottish Academy; University of Edinburgh.

Belfast, Northern Ireland (407,000). Capital of Northern Ireland; a seaport on the east coast; has large shipbuilding, aircraft and aerospace, and automobile industries. It also makes textile, marine, and mining machinery; rope and twine; and cotton textiles.

Bristol, England (394,000). Port city; industrial and educational center; sugar refining; tobacco processing; cocoa and chocolate making; wine bottling; glass, porcelain, and pottery making; aircraft design and construction; University of Bristol.

percent) population exceeds 60 million with approximately 625 persons per square mile (233.0 persons per square kilometer). Exhibit 4 identifies some of the major cities in the UK. Virtually 100 percent of the population is literate. The workforce numbers around 28 million and unemployment hovers around 10 percent. Estimated gross domestic product is $697,358 million (U.S. dollars). Germany is a chief source of imports followed closely by the United States. The UK regularly runs a trade deficit with the United States.

Major products manufactured in the UK include aircraft, automobiles, beer, chemicals, china, engines, helicopters, hovercraft, iron and steel, machinery, missiles, nonferrous metals, paper, refined petroleum, rope and twine, ships, space-exploration equipment, and textiles. Chief exports include china, automobiles and other vehicles, woolen goods, steel, electrical and mechanical machinery, tractors, scientific instruments, chemicals, and petroleum.

Leading universities include Cambridge University, Open University, Oxford University, University of Birmingham, University of Edinburgh, University of Glasgow, University of Leeds, University of Liverpool, University of London, and Victoria University of Manchester.

England's total area is about 130,000 square kilometers (50,000 square miles), or 53 percent of the total area of the United Kingdom. It is bounded by Scotland on the north and Wales on the west. From the Scottish border to the south coast is about 360 miles (580 kilometers), and from the western tip of Land's End to North Foreland on the east coast is about 330 miles (530 kilometers). The climate is dominated by the influence of the sea. England's location on the western edge of the European continent and within the westerly wind belt ensures that its climate is rainy and temperate. Winters are mild, summers cool, and rain falls in all seasons. Winter temperatures are modified by the warm current of the north Atlantic Drift, which moves along the west coast of the British Isles. Summer temperatures are influenced by the country's location in northern latitudes. Most of England has summer temperatures of 60 to 62°F (16 to 17°C) and winter temperatures of 40 to 42°F (4 to 6°C), with somewhat warmer temperatures in the southwest.

There are nearly 50 million people living in England, of which almost 80 percent live in cities. The density of population is 929 persons per square mile (359 persons per square kilometer), one of the highest in Western Europe. The greatest concentrations of population are in the London area, the Midlands area around Birmingham, West Yorkshire, and Lancashire including Manchester, and the northeast around Newcastle. There are also many people living along the southern coast. Greater London has a population of nearly 7 million. Birmingham has more than 1 million. Leeds, Sheffield, and Liverpool each have populations of more than 500,000. Birmingham has grown the most rapidly of all cities since 1900 apart from London and has overtaken Manchester and Liverpool to become England's second largest city.

The existence of several minority groups adds to the mixed racial composition. The Irish are the largest group, but there are also communities of such European peoples as Italians, Poles, and Greek and Turkish Cypriots. The most recent addition to the population has been the immigrants from the ex-colonies of the British Empire including blacks (mainly West Indians), Pakistanis, and Indians, who now total some 2.2 million—about 4 percent of the total British population. About 40 percent of these were born in Great Britain. The majority of the nonwhite population lives in London and the industrial cities of the Midlands such as Birmingham, Liverpool, and Manchester. The majority of the people of England belong to the Church of England, sometimes known as the Anglican church. The Jewish community is one of the largest in Europe. The biggest non-Christian group, however, is the Muslims, who number about 1.5 million. Most are Pakistani in origin, but there is also a sizable Arab community in London. There are also many Hindus and Sikhs living in London and the industrial cities of the Midlands.

The northern part of the island of Great Britain is Scotland. Rugged uplands separate it from England to the south. The land may be divided into three regions: the Highlands in the north, the central Lowlands, and the southern Uplands. The average temperature in January is about 40°F (4.4°C); in July it is about 58°F (14.4°C). The mountainous west coast has the most rainfall. The east is drier and sunnier. The wettest seasons are autumn and winter. The Scots have a reputation for being thrifty, cautious, careful of detail, and respectful of learning. Their history is full of people of humble birth who acquired university education. Education was made easier for poor students by the Scottish-born American industrialist, Andrew Carnegie. He set up the Carnegie Trust Fund in 1901 to help needy students and to foster research. At about 12 years of age all students are tested to determine entrance to a junior secondary school (for 12- to 15-year-olds) or to a senior secondary school (for 12- to 18-year-olds). The senior schools lead to the professional schools and the universities. Scotland has eight universities, the oldest being St. Andrews, founded in 1410. Edinburgh is known for its school of medicine. The University of Glasgow emphasizes science and engineering.

Wales (population about 2.7 million), located west of England, is 150 miles (240 kilometers) from north to south and 115 miles (185 kilometers) from east to west at its widest part. Its area is 8,017 square miles (20,764 square kilometers). Most of Wales consists of mountains and hills. The capital city is Cardiff, with 280,000 inhabitants. Other large cities are Swansea and Newport. The University of Wales has colleges in five cities. Welsh industry is based on the coalfields of the south. The coal is largely used in the iron and steel industry of southern Wales. A drop in demand for steel and coal in the late 1980s and early 1990s, however, resulted in the closing of numerous plants and coal mines and the reorganization of others. Unemployment is high and attempts to introduce new light industries have met with limited success. The mountainous nature of the country makes access to some areas difficult.

The northeastern part of the island of Ireland is occupied by Northern Ireland (population 1,570,000; 1991 estimate). It covers only one-sixth of the total area of the island but has about one-third of the population. About two-thirds of the people of Northern Ireland are descended from Scottish and English settlers who came to Ulster (mainly in the 17th century), and most of them are Protestants. The remainder of the population are Irish in origin and are mainly Roman Catholics. Temperatures in Northern Ireland range from an average daily maximum 65°F (18°C) in July to an average daily minimum of 34°F (1°C) in January. About one-quarter of the people live in Belfast, the capital. The second city in size is Londonderry, also called Derry, in the north on the River Foyle. It has a large clothing and footwear industry.

CASE 7–2
YOPLAIT USA

Chap Colucci, vice president of marketing and sales at Yoplait USA, was concerned about Yoplait's performance at the start of the 1990s. For two consecutive years, Yoplait had failed to meet targets set by top management at General Mills. Yoplait's share of market was declining and profitability was unacceptable by General Mills' standards. Yoplait USA was part of the Consumer Foods Group subsidiary of General Mills, Inc.

Colucci felt certain that a new marketing strategy was needed for Yoplait USA. A situation analysis had identified some very serious concerns surrounding Yoplait's marketing mix components and had pinpointed the fact that Yoplait's current strategy was a holdover from the product's introductory days.

The Company

Incorporated in 1928 in Delaware, General Mills, Inc., became the world's largest grain processor when James Ford Bell, president of Washburn Crosby Company, brought together several flour millers. General Mills' original product, Gold Medal Flour, was still popular in the 1990s.

Two very successful food-type groups were owned by General Mills. The Consumer Foods Group was comprised of products such as Big G cereals (e.g., Cheerios, Lucky Charms, Wheaties, Kix, Basic 4), Betty Crocker desserts, main meals, popcorn, and snacks (e.g., SuperMoist cake mixes, Creamy Deluxe frosting, Supreme brownie mixes, Hamburger Helper, Recipe Sauces, Pop Secret, FundaMiddles, Fruit Roll-Ups, Squeezits), flour and baking mixes (e.g., Gold Medal, Bisquick, Robin Hood), Gorton's (seafood), and Yoplait yogurt. Also included in the Consumer Foods Group were the foodservice division[1] and the international foods operations (in Canada and Latin America and in joint ventures with Nestlé and PepsiCo Foods International).

The Restaurants Group managed three casual-dining operations. The Red Lobster was a full-service seafood restaurant with 581 units in 47 states in the United States and 57 units in Canada; 50 more restaurants in the Tokyo market were a partnership venture with JUSCO, a leading Japanese retailer. The Olive Garden offered more than 110 different versions of its menu across the United States in 379 restaurants in 42 states, with 21 more units in Canada. The China Coast restaurant, a new business venture for General Mills, provided Mandarin, Cantonese, and Szechuan dishes. Plans were to open around 30 China Coast units in the United States by the mid-1990s.

---

[1] In addition to the grocery store channel, which sold to individual end consumers, many food manufacturers sold their products through foodservice channels to commercial (e.g., restaurants, cafeterias) and noncommercial (e.g., airlines, schools, hospitals) operations.

This case was prepared by Victoria L. Crittenden, associate professor of marketing at Boston College, as the basis for class discussion rather than to illustrate either effective or ineffective handling of a managerial situation. Research assistance was provided by Jennifer Fraser and Stephanie Hillstrom, Boston College. All material was from secondary sources. Revised 1997.

Consumer Foods Group was the larger of the two groups.[2] It accounted for approximately two-thirds of the company's total sales revenue from the food and restaurant groups. The consumer foods business contributed slightly over $640 million in operating income (on sales of almost $5 billion) in 1990. This was more than twice the level in 1985.

In the 1980s and 1990s, the U.S. food industry grew about 1 percent yearly. General Mills sales volume in the United States increased 6 percent in 1990. Net earnings at General Mills increased 20 percent annually from 1985 to 1990.

Dairy Products

A number of socio-economic and demographic factors contributed to consumers' tastes and preferences for dairy products.[3] These factors included

- Size and composition of the household consuming unit.
- Age distribution of the population.
- Degree of urbanization and regionality.
- Employment status of household members.
- Degree of nutritional education and lifestyle.

Just as important, however, was that by the late 1980s American consumers had become very concerned with their dietary intake. Emphasis was on the need to reduce total fat while increasing complex carbohydrates. Americans wanted the nourishment of dairy products without the potential hazards of cholesterol, calories, fat, and sodium. Additionally, convenience, variety, and premium choices had begun to dominate the American consumer's buying habits. As such, category sales rose 5 percent from 1988 to 1989, with a 58 percent increase in dairy product introductions.

The Yogurt Marketplace.   The dairy product benefiting the most from the beginning of the health craze was yogurt. Yogurt was produced by adding bacteria to milk. The bacteria then multiplied in the milk, consuming the milk's sugar lactose and replacing it with acids. These acids then curdled the milk and gave the yogurt its tart flavor and thick consistency. There were three general types of yogurt: (1) whole milk yogurt, which contained at least 3.25 percent milkfat, (2) low-fat yogurt, which contained between 0.5 and 2 percent milkfat, and (3) nonfat yogurt, which contained less than 0.5 percent milkfat.

Yogurt was touted as the fat-free alternative to cream cheese and salad dressings, as well as a convenient breakfast and snack food. Low-fat and nonfat yogurt was recommended as a substitute for the mayonnaise, sour cream, or cream cheese called for in many recipes. In addition to complying with the needs of the health food craze of the late 1980s, research had shown that yogurt had biological benefits. It was thought that yogurt could strengthen the immune system and help prevent recurring yeast infections. However, "heat-treated" yogurt (heat treating being done to maintain shelf life in some yogurt brands) lost the health benefit from the live cultures thought necessary for the medicinal benefits of yogurt. This often confused consumers when selecting a yogurt.

---

[2] The Consumer Foods Group and the Restaurant Groups comprised General Mills' business. A third group, New Business Ventures, covered General Mills' development of new businesses. However, each of the new businesses in this third group fit nicely within one of the two food groups. For example, China Coast was technically still a new business venture.

[3] These were reported in published research by Al-Zand and Andriamanjay.

Exhibit 1   Brand Rankings and Market Shares, 1991

Rank	Brand	Market Share
1	Dannon	32.8%
2	Yoplait	17.7
3	Private label	13.3
4	Light n' Lively six-pack	4.3
5	Breyers	4.3

Source: Julie Liesse, "Yogurt Grows as a Staple of U.S. Culture." *Advertising Age* (January 18, 1993): 18.

For years, yogurt had been popular in France. Yet, only 55 percent of Americans had tried yogurt by the beginning of the 1980s, which amounted to around 90 million cases consumed annually.[4] Annual per capita consumption was 1.1 pounds in 1971, 2.5 pounds in 1981, and 4.4 pounds in 1991.[5] However, Europeans reportedly consumed as much as 17 pounds per person annually. By the early 1990s, at least one member of a household ate yogurt once a month in almost 60 percent of U.S. homes. It was predicted that U.S consumption of yogurt products would increase to 10 pounds per capita by the year 2000.

Supermarket sales of yogurt were nearly $1.2 billion by the early 1990s. Sales of low-fat yogurt accounted for around 11 percent of yogurt sales. Gary Rodkin, president of Yoplait USA, cited four reasons for yogurt's popularity: image as a healthy product, price/value relationship, portability and convenience, and taste.[6]

It was reported that there were 45 brands of cup yogurt in the market, with more than 30 producers. The top five yogurt products in 1991, along with their market shares, are shown in Exhibit 1. Dannon was owned by a French company, BSN-Gervais Danone; Light n' Lively and Breyers were owned by Kraft, Inc.

Beatrice Foods was one of the leading food corporations in the United States. In 1982, Beatrice Foods sold Dannon yogurt to BSN-Gervais Danone, for $84 million. A Beatrice spokesperson later said that the company, believing yogurt to be a mature product, unfortunately sold a money machine.

Dannon yogurt was positioned as a nutritional product that offered value. Dannon attempted to transform yogurt's image from a health food to a healthy snack. Advertising portrayed nontraditional yogurt eaters and placed yogurt as a competitive item against fast foods. Dannon used both TV and print advertising from Grey Advertising in New York. Unlike other yogurt producers that shipped to chain warehouses, Dannon distributed its products via store door delivery.[7]

Kraft, Inc., was a multibillion-dollar franchise owned by Philip Morris Companies, Inc. In addition to Breyers and Light n' Lively yogurt products, Kraft produced cheese products, spoonable dressings, dry dinners, ketchup, and peanut butter. Kraft focused on value for consumers, high quality and visibility, efficient manufacturing, and focused marketing. It had won worldwide consumer loyalty across different food categories and markets.

---

[4] There were 12 eight-ounce cups per case, with an average retail price per cup of 40 cents.

[5] Patti Stang and Elys A. McLean, "USA Snapshots: A Look at Statistics That Shape our Lives." *USA Today* (November 8, 1993).

[6] Julie Liesse, "Yogurt Grows as a Staple of U.S. Culture." *Advertising Age* (January 18, 1993): 18.

[7] With store door delivery, the yogurt was delivered direct to the supermarket, where delivery truck drivers actually stocked the shelves.

The strategy for Breyers was to focus on its superior taste as a natural yogurt. Light n' Lively was targeted toward light users and nonusers of yogurt. Emphasis was upon its superior, natural taste. Media expenditures were almost equally divided between the two yogurt products. Model celebrity Cheryl Tiegs was the spokesperson for Kraft's yogurt, sour cream, and cottage cheese products. Combined spending on media was greater than Yoplait's expenditures, but not as large as Dannon's media expenditures.

Yoplait USA

Yoplait was the leading yogurt in the French market in the 1970s. Sodima, a French dairy cooperative, sold the rights to market Yoplait products in the United States to General Mills in October 1977.[8] Yogurt was not a standard product for General Mills. Products such as flour, breakfast cereals, and cake mixes had long shelf lives, while yogurt had to be refrigerated and had a 30-day shelf life. The nontraditional status of yogurt prompted General Mills to integrate the Yoplait acquisition into the company by forming the Yoplait USA subsidiary of the Consumer Foods Group and recruiting the marketing director of General Mills' New Business Division, Steven M. Rothschild, as president of Yoplait USA.

Rothschild (age 33 years) formed an entrepreneurial management team to lead Yoplait USA and General Mills into the yogurt market. Early market research conducted by the team found that around 95 percent of yogurt consumed by Americans was flavored and/or mixed with fruit. Yogurt came in one of four styles: sundae (fruit on the bottom), swiss (fruit blended into the yogurt), western (fruit on the bottom with flavored syrup on top), and frozen. Product research also found that the typical container for yogurt was an eight-ounce cup.

Yoplait was introduced in Southern California in April 1978. Amid bicycle races, hot-air balloons, and prime-time TV advertising, Yoplait outsold Cheerios in terms of unit sales. Yoplait's advertising campaign focused on the idea that Yoplait was the yogurt of France. Ads featured Loretta Swit and Tommy Lasorda speaking French while devouring and adoring Yoplait yogurt.[9] Yoplait was offered in six-ounce cups rather than the traditional eight-ounce cups. It was thought that a six-ounce serving was the serving size consumers wanted and that an eight-ounce serving was a little more than consumers really wanted to eat at one time.

The early yogurt market was regional and fragmented. This regional focus led Yoplait USA to a geographic marketing organization, with three regions: Eastern, Central, and Western. By 1988, the most established markets were in the Northeast, the West, and Florida. The best opportunities for yogurt growth existed in the Southwest and Midwest.

Current Situation.   While Yoplait had quickly become a national brand preferred by many Americans and had gained the number two market position, Yoplait's performance, at the beginning of the 1990s, was not at the level hoped for by General Mills management.

---

[8] Sodima had been licensing the rights to sell Yoplait Yogurt in the United States to Michigan Brand Cottage Cheese. Bill Bennett, owner of this regional dairy company, had not been as successful as General Mills thought possible. A major problem was that the package Bennett used was faulty and leaked on the store shelf.

[9] Swit was a well-known actress from the television series "M*A*S*H." Lasorda was manager for the Los Angeles Dodgers baseball club.

Chap Colucci conducted a situation analysis as a starting point in revamping the product's marketing strategy. Colucci found

- Yoplait's pricing was not in tune with the market. Its retail price for a six-ounce cup was, at times, higher than competitors' prices for eight-ounce cups. For example, Yoplait's four-pack cups were priced 20 percent higher per cup than Dannon's and Kraft's six-pack cups.

- Yoplait's communication strategy was out of line with the market. Yoplait was still using the advertising campaign of its introductory days. No follow-up campaign had been developed. Competitors were focusing heavily on couponing. Yoplait was not. Yoplait was spending a disproportionate amount relative to the competition on trade promotions, with very little directed toward the end consumer.

- Yoplait's product strategy was not keeping up with (1) changes in consumers' tastes and demands or (2) offerings by direct competitors. The only product line extension was Yoplait's Lite products. Competitors had begun to target product extensions to new markets (e.g., yogurt targeted toward children,[10] yogurt drinks).

- Yoplait USA's geographic marketing organization had caused management to focus on geographic issues such as increased sales to a particular account in a particular region rather than focusing on increasing sales of Yoplait as a whole.

- The product was bringing in below-standard gross margins. Production and overhead costs were escalating, causing the product to experience margin problems.

Colucci needed to use these findings, along with his understanding of the dairy and yogurt markets and the company's competitors, to formulate a new marketing strategy for Yoplait yogurt. What did all of this suggest for Yoplait? Colucci wondered if he needed more information. He did not have a lot of time, but a hurried mistake could mean serious problems for his subsidiary. General Mills top management wanted to see a strategy that would move Yoplait out of its doldrums. As stated by General Mills President Mark Willes, "We can introduce new product after new product, but we'll never succeed with Yoplait, or with any other business, unless we fix the core product."[11]

Sources

Al-Zand, Osama A., and Andriamanjay, Eric. "Consumer Demand for Dairy Products in Canada." *Agribusiness,* May 1988, pp. 233–44.

Cohn, Fred. "Consumer Expenditures Study: Dairy." *Supermarket Business,* September 1988, pp. 139, 210.

Dagnoli, Judann, and Erickson, Julie Liesse. "Yogurt Breaks Out of Chilled Section." *Advertising Age,* October 3, 1988, p. S6.

Edwards, Brian. "Consumer Expenditures Study: Dairy." *Supermarket Business,* September 1990, pp. 149–50.

"Factoids." *Research Alert,* January 21, 1994.

Gershman, Michael. "Packaging's Role in Remarketing." *Management Review,* May 1987, pp. 41–45.

Hammel, Frank. "Dairy." *Supermarket Business,* September 1992, pp. 111–12.

Lazarus, George. "Even More Visibility Krafted for Tiegs." *Chicago Tribune,* July 11, 1991, section 3, p. 4.

---

[10] Children, ages 6 to 14, spent an estimated $7 million annually. They were thought to influence another $120 million annually in family spending.

[11] Patricia Sellers and Sally Solo. "A Boring Brand Can Be Beautiful." *Fortune* (November 18, 1991): 169.

Leber, Co. "This Culture Promotes Health." *Rockford Register Star,* Gannett News Service, August 4, 1992.

Liesse, Julie. "Brand Extensions Take Center Stage." *Advertising Age,* March 8, 1993, p. 12.

Liesse, Julie. "Fat-Free: Fad or Food of the Future?" *Advertising Age,* September 10, 1990, p. 6.

Liesse, Julie. "Yogurt Drinks Have Juicy Future." *Advertising Age,* May 3, 1993, p. 17.

Liesse, Julie. "Yogurt Grows as Staple of U.S. Culture." *Advertising Age,* January 18, 1993, p. 18.

Liesse, Julie. "Yogurts Sprinkle in Fun to Stir Kids." *Advertising Age,* February 8, 1993, p. 17.

McMath, Robert. "Hot Ice Cream, Frozen Yogurt Market Is More than Seasonal." *Brandweek,* September 20, 1993, pp. 66–67.

Miller, Alan B., Jr. "SAMI Charts Slight Food-Store Gains in '86." *Advertising Age,* December 29, 1986, pp. 4, 6.

Perlis, Paula. "Dairy." *Supermarket Business,* September 1989, pp. 173–74, 210.

Petreycik, Richard M. "Perishables; 1990 Supermarket Sales Manual." *Progressive Grocer,* July 1990.

Sellers, Patricia, and Solo, Sally. "A Boring Brand Can Be Beautiful." *Fortune,* November 18, 1991, pp. 169–79.

Smith, Katherine. "It's Much Easier to Cheat a Lot of Customers out of 10 Cents than to Cheat One Person out of a Million Dollars." *Supermarket Business,* September 1993, pp. 43–44.

"Sports Drink, Yogurt Marketers Try to Mine Gold in Kids' Market." *Marketing News,* April 26, 1993, p. 2.

Williams, Rebecca D. "Yogurt: The Curds and Whey to Health?" *FDA Consumer,* June 1992.

CASE 7–3
CIMA MOUNTAINEERING, INC.

"What a great hike," exclaimed Anthony Simon as he tossed his Summit HX 350 hiking boots into his car. He had just finished hiking the challenging Cascade Canyon Trail in the Tetons north of Jackson, Wyoming. Anthony hiked often because it was a great way to test the hiking boots made by Cima Mountaineering, Inc., the business he inherited from his parents and owned with his sister, Margaret. As he drove back to Jackson, he began thinking about next week's meeting with Margaret, the president of Cima. During the past month they had been discussing marketing strategies for increasing the sales and profits of the company. No decisions had been made, but the preferences of each owner were becoming clear.

As illustrated in Exhibit 1, sales and profits had grown steadily for Cima and by most measures the company was successful. However, growth was beginning to slow as a result of foreign competition and a changing market. Margaret observed that the market had shifted to a more casual, stylish hiking boot that appealed to hikers interested in a boot for a variety of uses. She favored a strategy of diversifying the company by marketing a new line of boots for the less experienced, weekend hiker. Anthony also recognized that the market had changed, but he supported expanding the existing lines of boots for mountaineers and hikers. The company had been successful with these boots, and Anthony had some ideas about how to extend the lines and expand distribution. "This is a better way to grow," he thought. "I'm concerned about the risk in Margaret's recommendation. If we move to a more casual boot, then we have to resolve a new set of marketing and competitive issues and finance a new line. I'm not sure we can do it."

When he returned to Jackson that evening, Anthony stopped by his office to check his messages. The financial statements shown in Exhibits 2 and 3 were on his desk along with a marketing study from a Denver consulting firm. Harris Fleming, Vice President of Marketing, had commissioned a study of the hiking boot market several months earlier to help the company plan for the future. As Anthony paged through the

EXHIBIT 1 Cima Mountaineering, Inc. Revenues and Net Income, 1990–95

Year	Revenues	Net Income	Profit Margin (%)
1995	$20,091,450	$857,134	4.27
1994	18,738,529	809,505	4.32
1993	17,281,683	838,162	4.85
1992	15,614,803	776,056	4.97
1991	14,221,132	602,976	4.24
1990	13,034,562	522,606	4.01

Lawrence M. Lamont is Professor of Management at Washington and Lee University. Eva Cid and Wade Drew Hammond are seniors in the class of 1995 at Washington and Lee, majoring in Management and Accounting, respectively. Case material is prepared as a basis for class discussion, and not designed to present illustrations of either effective or ineffective handling of administrative problems. Some names, locations, and financial information have been disguised. Copyright © 1995, Washington and Lee University.

EXHIBIT 2   Cima Mountaineering, Inc., Income Statement (Years Ended December 31, 1995, and December 31, 1994)

	1995	1994
Net sales	$ 20,091,450	$ 18,738,529
Cost of goods sold	14,381,460	13,426,156
Gross margin	5,709,990	5,312,373
Selling and admin. expenses	4,285,730	3,973,419
Operating income	1,424,260	1,338,954
Other income (expenses)		
Interest expense	(160,733)	(131,170)
Interest income	35,161	18,739
Total other income (net)	(125,572)	(112,431)
Earnings before income taxes	1,298,688	1,226,523
Income taxes	441,554	417,018
Net income	$ 857,134	$ 809,505

report, two figures caught his eye. One was a segmentation of the hiking boot market (see Exhibit 4) and the other was a summary of market competition (see Exhibit 5). "This is interesting," he mused. "I hope Margaret reads it before our meeting."

History of Cima Mountaineering

As children, Anthony and Margaret Simon watched their parents make western boots at the Hoback Boot Company, a small business they owned in Jackson, Wyoming. They learned the craft as they grew up and joined the company after college.

In the late 1960s the demand for western boots began to decline and the Hoback Boot Company struggled to survive. By 1975, the parents were close to retirement and they seemed content to close the business, but Margaret and Anthony decided to try to salvage the company. Margaret, the older, became president and Anthony became the executive vice president. By the end of 1976, sales had declined to $1.5 million and the company earned profits of only $45,000. It became clear that to survive, the business would have to be refocused on products with a more promising future.

Refocusing the Business.   As a college student, Anthony attended a mountaineering school north of Jackson in Teton National Park. As he learned to climb and hike, he became aware of the growing popularity of the sport and the boots being used. Because of his experience with western boots, he also noticed their limitations. Although the boots had good traction, they were heavy and uncomfortable, and had little resistance to the snow and water always present in the mountains. He convinced Margaret that Hoback should explore the possibility of developing boots for mountaineering and hiking.

In 1977, Anthony and Margaret began 12 months of marketing research. They investigated the market, the competition, and the extent to which Hoback's existing equipment could be used to produce the new boots. By the summer of 1978, Hoback had developed a mountaineering boot and a hiking boot that were ready for testing. Several instructors from the mountaineering school tested the boots and gave them excellent reviews.

EXHIBIT 3 **Cima Mountaineering, Inc., Balance Sheet (Years Ending December 31, 1995, and December 31, 1994)**

	1995	1994
Assets		
Current assets		
Cash and equivalents	$ 1,571,441	$ 1,228,296
Accounts receivable	4,696,260	3,976,608
Inventory	6,195,450	5,327,733
Other	270,938	276,367
Total	12,734,089	10,809,004
Fixed assets		
Property, plant, and equipment	3,899,568	2,961,667
Less: accumulated depreciation	(1,117,937)	(858,210)
Total fixed assets (net)	2,781,631	2,103,457
Other assets		
Intangibles	379,313	568,087
Other long-term assets	2,167,504	1,873,151
Total fixed assets (net)	$ 18,062,537	$ 15,353,699
Liabilities and shareholder equity		
Current liabilities:		
Accounts payable	$ 4,280,821	$ 4,097,595
Notes payable	1,083,752	951,929
Current maturities of long-term debt	496,720	303,236
Accrued liabilities		
Expenses	2,754,537	2,360,631
Salaries and wages	1,408,878	1,259,003
Other	1,137,940	991,235
Total current liabilities	11,162,648	9,963,629
Long-term liabilities		
Long-term debt	3,070,631	2,303,055
Lease obligations	90,313	31,629
Total long-term liabilities	3,702,820	2,334,684
Other liabilities		
Deferred taxes	36,125	92,122
Other noncurrent liabilities	312,326	429,904
Total liabilities	14,672,043	12,820,339
Owner's equity		
Retained earnings	3,390,494	2,533,360
Total liabilities and owner's equity	$ 18,062,537	$ 15,353,699

The Transition. By 1981, Hoback was ready to enter the market with two styles of boots: one for the mountaineer who wanted a boot for all-weather climbing, and the other for men and women who were advanced hikers. Both styles were made of water-repellent leather uppers and cleated soles for superior traction. Distribution was secured through mountaineering shops in Wyoming and Colorado.

Hoback continued to manufacture western boots for its loyal customers, but Margaret planned to phase them out as the hiking boot business developed. However, because they did not completely understand the needs of the market, they hired Harris Fleming, a mountaineering instructor, to help them with product design and marketing.

EXHIBIT 4 Segmentation of the Hiking Boot Market

	Mountaineers	Serious Hikers	Weekenders	Practical Users	Children	Fashion Seekers
Benefits	Durability/ruggedness, Stability/support, Dryness/warmth, Grip/traction	Stability, Durability, Traction, Comfort/protection	Lightweight, Comfort, Durability, Versatility	Lightweight, Durability, Good value, Versatility	Durability, Protection, Lightweight, Traction	Fashion/style, Appearance, Lightweight, Inexpensive
Demographics	Young, Primarily male, Shops in specialty stores and specialized catalogs	Young, middle-aged, Male and female, Shops in specialty stores and outdoor catalogs	Young, middle-aged, Male and female, Shops in shoe retailers, sporting goods stores, and mail order catalogs	Young, middle-aged, Primarily male, Shops in shoe retailers and department stores	Young marrieds, Male and female, Shops in department stores and outdoor catalogs	Young, Male and female, Shops in shoe retailers, department stores and catalogs
Lifestyle	Adventuresome, Independent, Risk taker, Enjoys challenge	Nature lover, Outdoorsman, Sportsman, Backpacker	Recreational hiker, Social, spends time with family and friends, Enjoys the outdoors	Practical, Sociable, Outdoors for work and recreation	Enjoys family activities, Enjoys outdoors and hiking, Children are active and play outdoors, Parents are value-conscious	Materialistic, Trendy, Socially conscious, Nonhikers, Brand name shoppers, Price-conscious
Examples of brands	Asolo Cliff, Raichle Mt. Blanc, Salomon Adventure 9	Raichle Explorer, Vasque Clarion, Tecnica Pegasus Dry, Hi-Tec Piramide	Reebok R-Evolution, Timberland Topozoic, Merrell Acadia, Nike Air Mada, Zion, Vasque Alpha	Merrell Eagle, Nike Air Khyber, Tecnica Volcano	Vasque Kids Klimber, Nike, Merrell Caribou	Nike Espirit, Reebok Telos, Hi-Tec Magnum
Estimated market share	5%, Slow growth	17%, Moderate growth	25%, High growth	20%, Stable growth	5%, Slow growth	28%, At peak of rapid growth cycle
Price range	$210–$450	$120–$215	$70–$125	$40–$80	Up to $40	$65–$100

EXHIBIT 5   Summary of Competitors

Company	Location	Mountaineering (Styles)	Hiking (Styles)	Men's	Women's	Children's	Price Range
Raichle	Switzerland	Yes (7)	Yes (16)	Yes	Yes	Yes	High
Salomon	France	Yes (1)	Yes (9)	Yes	Yes	No	Mid
Asolo	Italy	Yes (4)	Yes (26)	Yes	Yes	No	High
Tecnica	Italy	Yes (3)	Yes (9)	Yes	Yes	No	Mid/high
Hi-Tec	UK	Yes (2)	Yes (29)	Yes	Yes	Yes	Mid/low
Vasque	Minnesota	Yes (4)	Yes (18)	Yes	Yes	Yes	Mid/high
Merrell	Vermont	Yes (5)	Yes (31)	Yes	Yes	Yes	Mid
Timberland	New Hampshire	No	Yes (4)	Yes	No	No	Mid
Nike	Oregon	No	Yes (5)	Yes	Yes	Yes	Low
Reebok	Massachusetts	No	Yes (3)	Yes	Yes	Yes	Low
Cima	Wyoming	Yes (3)	Yes (5)	Yes	Yes	No	High

Source: Published literature and company product brochures, 1995.

A New Company.   During the 1980s, Hoback prospered as the market expanded along with the popularity of outdoor recreation. The company slowly increased its product line and achieved success by focusing on classic boots that were relatively insensitive to fashion trends. By 1986, sales of Hoback Boots had reached $3.5 million.

Over the next several years, distribution was steadily expanded. In 1987, Hoback employed independent sales representatives to handle the sales and service. Before long, Hoback boots were sold throughout Wyoming, Colorado, and Montana by retailers specializing in mountaineering and hiking equipment. Margaret decided to discontinue western boots to make room for the growing hiking boot business. To reflect the new direction of the company, the name was changed to Cima Mountaineering, Inc.

Cima Boots Take Off.   The late 1980s were a period of exceptional growth. Demand for Cima boots grew quickly as consumers caught the trend toward healthy, active lifestyles. The company expanded its line for advanced hikers and improved the performance of its boots. By 1990, sales had reached $13 million and the company earned profits of $522,606. Margaret was satisfied with the growth, but she was concerned about low profitability as a result of foreign competition. She challenged the company to find new ways to design and manufacture boots at lower cost.

Growth and Innovation.   The next five years were marked by growth, innovation, and increasing foreign and domestic competition. Market growth continued as hiking boots became popular for casual wear in addition to hiking in mountains and on trails. Cima and its competitors began to make boots with molded footbeds and utilize materials that reduced weight.[1] Fashion also became a factor, and companies like Nike and Reebok marketed lightweight boots in a variety of materials and colors to meet the demand for styling in addition to performance. Cima implemented a computer-aided

---

[1] Two processes are used to attach the uppers to the soles of boots. In classic welt construction, the uppers and soles are stitched. In the more contemporary method, a molded polyurethane footbed (including a one-piece heel and sole) is cemented to the upper with a waterproof adhesive. Many mountaineering boots use classic welt construction because it provides outstanding stability, while the contemporary method is often used with hiking boots to achieve lightweight construction. Cima used the classic method of construction for mountaineering boots and the contemporary method for hiking boots.

design (CAD) system in 1993 to shorten product development and devote more attention to design. Late in 1994, Cima restructured its facilities and implemented a modular approach to manufacturing. The company switched from a production line to a system in which a work team applied multiple processes to each pair of boots. Significant cost savings were achieved as the new approach improved the profit and quality of the company's boots.

The Situation in 1995.   As the company ended 1995, sales had grown to $20.0 million, up 7.2 percent from the previous year. Employment was at 425, and the facility was operating at 85 percent of capacity, producing several styles of mountaineering and hiking boots. Time-saving innovations and cost reduction had also worked, and profits reached an all-time high. Margaret, now 57, was still president, and Anthony remained executive vice president.

Cima Marketing Strategy

According to estimates, 1994 was a record year for sales of hiking and mountaineering boots in the United States. Retail sales exceeded $600 million, and about 15 million pairs of boots were sold. Consumers wore the boots for activities ranging from mountaineering to casual social events. In recent years, changes were beginning to occur in the market. Inexpensive, lightweight hiking boots were becoming increasingly popular for day hikes and trail walking, and a new category of comfortable, light "trekking" shoes were being marketed by the manufacturers of athletic shoes.

Only a part of the market was targeted by Cima. Most of its customers were serious outdoor enthusiasts. They included mountaineers who climbed in rugged terrain and advanced hikers who used the boots on challenging trails and extended backpacking trips. The demand for Cima boots was seasonal, and most of the purchases were made during the summer months when the mountains and trails were most accessible.

Positioning.   Cima boots were positioned as the best available for their intended purpose. Consumers saw them as durable and comfortable with exceptional performance. Retailers viewed the company as quick to adopt innovative construction techniques but conservative in styling. Cima intentionally used traditional styling to avoid fashion obsolescence and the need for frequent design changes. Some of the most popular styles had been in the market for several years without any significant modifications. The Glacier MX 350 shown in Exhibit 6 and the Summit HX 350 boot shown in Exhibit 7 are good examples. The MX 350, priced at $219.00, was positioned as a classic boot for men with a unique tread design for beginning mountaineers. The Summit HX 350 was priced at $159.00 and was a boot for men and women hiking rough trails. Exhibit 8 describes the items in the mountaineering and hiking boot lines, and Exhibit 9 provides a sales history for Cima boots.

Product Lines.   Corporate branding was used and "Cima" was embossed into the leather on the side of the boot to enhance consumer recognition. Product lines were also branded, and alphabetic letters and numbers were used to differentiate items in the line. Each line had different styles and features to cover many of the important uses in the market. However, all boots had features that the company believed were essential to positioning. Standard features included water-repellent leather uppers and high-traction soles and heels. The hardware for the boots was plated steel, and the laces were tough, durable nylon. Quality was emphasized throughout the product lines.

EXHIBIT 6   **The Glacier MX 350 Mountaineering Boot**

EXHIBIT 7   **The Summit HX 350 Hiking Boot**

Glacier Boots for Mountaineering.   The Glacier line featured three boots for men. The MX 550 was designed for expert all-weather climbers looking for the ultimate in traction, protection, and warmth. The MX 450 was for experienced climbers taking extended excursions, while the MX 350 met the needs of less-skilled individuals beginning climbing in moderate terrain and climates.

Exhibit 8   Cima Mountaineering, Inc., Mountaineering and Hiking Boot Lines

Product Line	Description
Glacier	
MX 550	For expert mountaineers climbing challenging mountains. Made for use on rocks, ice, and snow. Features welt construction, superior stability and support, reinforced heel and toe, padded ankle and tongue, step-in crampon insert, thermal insulation, and waterproof inner liner. Retails for $299.
MX 450	For proficient mountaineers engaging in rigorous, high-altitude hiking. Offers long-term comfort and stability on rough terrain. Features welt construction, deep cleated soles and heels, reinforced heel and toe, padded ankle and tongue, step-in crampon insert, and waterproof inner liner. Retails for $249.
MX 350	For beginning mountaineers climbing in moderate terrain and temperate climates. Features welt construction, unique tread design for traction, padded ankle and tongue, good stability and support, and a quick-dry lining. Retails for $219.
Summit	
HX 550	For experienced hikers who require uncompromising performance. Features nylon shank for stability and rigidity, waterproof inner liner, cushioned midsole, high-traction outsole, and padded ankle and tongue. Retails for $197.
HX 450	For backpackers who carry heavy loads on extended trips. Features thermal insulation, cushioned midsole, waterproof inner liner, excellent foot protection, and high-traction outsole. Retails for $179.
HX 350	For hikers who travel rough trails and a variety of backcountry terrain. Features extra cushioning, good stability and support, waterproof inner liner, and high-traction outsole for good grip in muddy and sloping surfaces. Retails for $159.
HX 250	For hikers who hike developed trails. Made with only the necessary technical features, including cushioning, foot and ankle support, waterproof inner liner, and high-traction outsole. Retails for $139.
HX 150	For individuals taking more than day and weekend hikes. Versatile boot for all kinds of excursions. Features cushioning, good support, waterproof inner liner, and high-traction outsoles for use on a variety of surfaces. Retails for $129.

Exhibit 9   Cima Mountaineering, Inc., Product Line Sales

	Unit Sales (%)		Sales Revenue (%)	
Year	Mountaineering	Hiking	Mountaineering	Hiking
1995	15.00%	85.00%	21.74%	78.26%
1994	15.90	84.10	22.93	77.07
1993	17.20	82.80	24.64	75.36
1992	18.00	82.00	25.68	74.32
1991	18.80	81.20	26.71	73.29
1990	19.70	80.30	27.86	72.14

Summit Boots for Hiking.   The Summit line featured five styles for men and women. The HX 550 was preferred by experienced hikers who demanded the best possible performance. The boot featured water-repellent leather uppers, a waterproof inner liner, a cushioned midsole, a nylon shank for rigidity, and a sole designed for high traction. It was available in gray and brown with different types of leather.[2] The Summit HX 150 was the least expensive boot in the line, designed for individuals who were beginning to hike more than the occasional "weekend hike." It was a versatile boot for all kinds of excursions and featured a water-repellent leather upper, a cushioned midsole, and excellent traction. The HX 150 was popular as an entry-level boot for outdoor enthusiasts.

Distribution.   Cima boots were distributed in Arizona, California, Colorado, Idaho, Montana, Nevada, New Mexico, Oregon, Washington, Wyoming, and western Canada through specialty retailers selling mountaineering, backpacking, and hiking equipment. Occasionally, Cima was approached by mail order catalog companies and chain sporting goods stores offering to sell their boots. The company considered the proposals, but had not used these channels.

Promotion.   The Cima sales and marketing office was located in Jackson. It was managed by Harris Fleming and staffed with several marketing personnel. Promotion was an important aspect of the marketing strategy, and advertising, personal selling, and sales promotion were used to gain exposure for Cima branded boots. Promotion was directed to consumers and to the retailers that stocked Cima mountaineering and hiking boots.

Personal Selling.   Cima used 10 independent sales representatives to sell its boots in the western states and Canada. Representatives did not sell competing boots, but they sold complementary products such as outdoor apparel and equipment for mountaineering, hiking, and backpacking. They were paid a commission and handled customer service in addition to sales. Management was also involved in personal selling. Harris Fleming trained the independent sales representatives and often accompanied them on sales calls.

Advertising and Sales Promotion.   Advertising and sales promotion were also important promotional methods. Print advertising was used to increase brand awareness and assist retailers with promotion. Advertising was placed in leading magazines such as *Summit, Outside,* and *Backpacker* to reach mountaineers and hikers with the message that Cima boots were functional and durable with classic styling. In addition, cooperative advertising was offered to encourage retailers to advertise Cima boots and identify their locations.

Sales promotion was an important part of the promotion program. Along with the focus on brand name recognition, Cima provided product literature and point-of-sale display materials to assist retailers in promoting the boots. In addition, the company regularly exhibited at industry trade shows. The exhibits, staffed by marketing

---

[2] Different types of leather are used to make hiking boots. *Full Grain:* High-quality, durable, upper layer of the hide. It has a natural finish, and is strong and breathable. *Split Grain:* Underside of the hide after the full-grain leather has been removed from the top. Light weight and comfort are the primary characteristics. *Suede:* A very fine split-grain leather. *Nubuk:* Brushed full-grain leather. *Waxed:* A process in which leather is coated with wax to help shed water. Most Cima boots were available in two or more types of leather.

Mountaineering and hiking boots are made water-repellent by treating the uppers with wax or chemical coatings. To make the boots waterproof, a fabric inner liner is built into the boot to provide waterproof protection and breathability. All Cima boots were water-repellent, but only those styles with an inner liner were waterproof.

personnel and the company's independent sales representatives, were effective for maintaining relationships with retailers and presenting the company's products.

Pricing.   Cima selling prices to retailers ranged from $64.50 to $149.50 a pair depending on the style. Mountaineering boots were more expensive because of their construction and features, while hiking boots were priced lower. Retailers were encouraged to take a 50 percent margin on the retail selling price, so retail prices shown in Exhibit 8 should be divided by two to get the Cima selling price. Cima priced its boots higher than competitors, supporting the positioning of the boots as the top-quality product at each price point. Payment terms were net 30 days (similar to competitors), and boots were shipped to retailers from a warehouse located in Jackson, Wyoming.

Segmentation of the Hiking Boot Market

As Anthony reviewed the marketing study commissioned by Harris Fleming, his attention focused on the market segmentation shown in Exhibit 4. It was interesting, because management had never seriously thought about the segmentation in the market. Of course, Anthony was aware that not everyone was a potential customer for Cima boots, but he was surprised to see how well the product lines met the needs of mountaineers and serious hikers. As he reviewed the market segmentation, he read the descriptions for mountaineers, serious hikers, and weekenders carefully because Cima was trying to decide which of these segments to target for expansion.

Mountaineers.   Mountain climbers and high-altitude hikers are in this segment. They are serious about climbing and enjoy risk and adventure. Because mountaineers' safety may often depend on their boots, they need maximum stability and support, traction for a variety of climbing conditions, and protection from wet and cold weather.

Serious Hikers.   Outdoorsmen, who love nature and have a strong interest in health and fitness, comprise the serious hikers. They hike rough trails and take extended backpacking or hiking excursions. Serious hikers are brand-conscious and look for durable, high-performance boots with good support, comfortable fit, and good traction.

Weekenders.   Consumers in this segment are recreational hikers who enjoy casual weekend and day hikes with family and friends. They are interested in light, comfortable boots that provide good fit, protection, and traction on a variety of surfaces. Weekenders prefer versatile boots that can be worn for a variety of activities.

Foreign and Domestic Competition

The second part of the marketing study that caught Anthony's attention was the analysis of competition. Although Anthony and Margaret were aware that competition had increased, they had overlooked the extent to which foreign bootmakers had entered the market. Apparently, foreign competitors had noticed the market growth and they were aggressively exporting their boots into the United States. They had established sales offices and independent sales agents to compete for the customers served by Cima. The leading foreign brands such as Asolo, Hi-Tec, Salomon, and Raichle were marketed on performance and reputation, usually to the mountaineering, serious hiker, and weekender segments of the market.

The study also summarized the most important domestic competitors. Vasque and Merrell marketed boots that competed with Cima, but others were offering products for segments of the market where the prospects for growth were better. As Anthony examined Exhibit 5, he realized that the entry of Reebok and Nike into the hiking boot market was quite logical. They had entered the market as consumer preference shifted from wearing athletic shoes for casual outdoor activities to a more rugged shoe. Each was marketing footwear that combined the appearance and durability of hiking boots with the lightness and fit of athletic shoes. The result was a line of fashionable hiking boots that appealed to brand- and style-conscious teens and young adults. Both firms were expanding their product lines and moving into segments of the market that demanded lower levels of performance.

Margaret and Anthony Discuss Marketing Strategy

A few days after hiking in Cascade Canyon, Anthony met with Margaret and Harris Fleming to discuss marketing strategy. Each had read the consultant's report and studied the market segmentation and competitive summary. As the meeting opened, the conversation developed as follows:

Margaret: It looks like we will have another record year. The economy is growing, and consumers seem confident and eager to buy. Yet, I'm concerned about the future. The foreign bootmakers are providing some stiff competition. Their boots have outstanding performance and attractive prices. The improvements we made in manufacturing helped to control costs and maintain margins, but it looks like the competition and slow growth in our markets will make it difficult to improve profits. We need to be thinking about new opportunities.

Harris: I agree, Margaret. Just this past week we lost Rocky Mountain Sports in Boulder, Colorado. John Kline, the sales manager, decided to drop us and pick up Asolo. We were doing $70,000 a year with them and they carried our entire line. We also lost Great Western Outfitters in Colorado Springs. They replaced us with Merrell. The sales manager said that the college students there had been asking for the lower-priced Merrell boots. They bought $60,000 last year.

Anthony: Rocky Mountain and Great Western were good customers. I guess I'm not surprised though. Our Glacier line needs another boot, and the Summit line is just not deep enough to cover the price points. We need to have some styles at lower prices to compete with Merrell and Asolo. I'm in favor of extending our existing lines to broaden their market appeal. It seems to me that the best way to compete is to stick with what we do best, making boots for mountaineers and serious hikers.

Margaret: Not so fast, Anthony. The problem is that our markets are small and not growing fast enough to support the foreign competitors who have entered with excellent products. We can probably hold our own, but I doubt if we can do much better. I think the future of this company is to move with the market. Consumers are demanding more style, lower prices, and a lightweight hiking boot that can be worn for a variety of uses. Look at the segmentation again. The "Weekender" segment is large and it's growing. That's where we need to go with some stylish new boots that depart from our classic leather lines.

Anthony: Maybe so, but we don't have much experience working with the leather and nylon combinations that are being used in these lighter boots. Besides, I'm not sure we can finance the product development and marketing for a new market that already has plenty of competition. And I'm concerned about the brand image that we have worked so hard to establish over the past 20 years. A line of inexpensive, casual boots just doesn't seem to fit with the perception consumers have of our products.

Harris: I can see advantages to each strategy. I do know that we don't have the time and resources to do both, so we had better make a thoughtful choice. Also, I think we should reconsider selling to the mail order catalog companies that specialize in mountaineering and hiking equipment. Last week, I received another call from REI requesting us to sell them some of the boots in our Summit line for the 1997 season. This might be a good source of revenue and a way of expanding our geographic market.

Margaret: You're right, Harris. We need to rethink our position on the mail order companies. Most of them have good market penetration in the East where we don't have distribution. I noticed that Gander Mountain is carrying some of the Timberland line and that L.L. Bean is carrying some Vasque styles along with its own line of branded boots.

Anthony: I agree. Why don't we each put together a proposal that summarizes our recommendations and then we can get back together to continue the discussion.

Harris: Good idea. Eventually we will need a sales forecast and some cost data. Send me your proposals and I'll call the consulting firm and have them prepare some forecasts. I think we already have some cost information. Give me a few days and then we can get together again.

The Meeting to Review the Proposals

The following week, the discussion continued. Margaret presented her proposal, which is summarized in Exhibit 10. She proposed moving Cima into the "Weekender" segment by marketing two new hiking boots. Anthony countered with the proposal summarized in Exhibit 11. He favored extending the existing lines by adding a new mountaineering boot and two new Summit hiking boots at lower price points. Harris presented sales forecasts for each proposal and after some discussion and modification, they were finalized as shown in Exhibit 12. Cost information was gathered by Harris from the vice president of manufacturing and is presented in Exhibit 13. Following a lengthy discussion, in which Margaret and Anthony were unable to agree on a course of action, Harris Fleming suggested that each proposal be explored further by conducting marketing research. He proposed the formation of teams from the Cima marketing staff to research each proposal and present it to Margaret and Anthony at a later date. Harris presented his directions to the teams in the memorandum shown in Exhibit 14. The discussion between Margaret and Anthony continued as follows:

Margaret: Once the marketing research is completed and we can read the reports and listen to the presentations, we should have a better idea of which strategy makes the best sense. Hopefully, a clear direction will emerge and we can move ahead with one of the proposals. In either case, I'm still intrigued with the possibility of moving into the mail order catalogs, since we really haven't developed these companies as customers. I just wish we knew how much business we could expect from them.

Anthony: We should seriously consider them, Margaret. Companies like L.L. Bean, Gander Mountain, and REI have been carrying a selection of hiking boots for several years. However, there may be a problem for us. Eventually the catalog

EXHIBIT 10   Margaret's Marketing Proposal

MEMORANDUM

TO: Anthony Simon, Executive Vice President
           Harris Fleming, Vice President of Marketing
FROM: Margaret Simon, President
RE: Marketing Proposal

I believe we have an excellent opportunity to expand the sales and profits of Cima by entering the "Weekender" segment of the hiking boot market. The segment's estimated share of the market is 25 percent and according to the consultant's report it is growing quite rapidly. I propose that we begin immediately to develop two new products and prepare a marketing strategy as discussed below.

Target Market and Positioning
Male and female recreational hikers looking for a comfortable, lightweight boot that is attractively priced and acceptable for short hikes and casual wear. Weekenders enjoy the outdoors and a day or weekend hike with family and friends.

    The new boots would be positioned with magazine advertising as hiking boots that deliver performance and style for the demands of light hiking and casual outdoor wear.

Product
Two boots in men's and women's sizes. The boots would be constructed of leather and nylon uppers with a molded rubber outsole. A new branded line would be created to meet the needs of the market segment. The boots (designated WX 550 and WX 450) would have the following features:

	WX 550	WX 450
Leather and nylon uppers	X	X
Molded rubber outsole	X	X
Cushioned midsole	X	X
Padded collar and tongue	X	X
Durable hardware and laces	X	X
Waterproof inner liner	X	

Uppers: To be designed. Options include brown full-grain, split-grain, or suede leather combined with durable nylon in two of the following colors: beige, black, blue, gray, green, and slate.
Boot design and brand name: To be decided.

Retail Outlets
Specialty shoe retailers carrying hiking boots and casual shoes and sporting goods stores. Eventually mail order catalogs carrying outdoor apparel and hiking, backpacking, and camping equipment.

Promotion

Independent sales representatives	Point-of-sale display materials
Magazine advertising	Product brochures
Co-op advertising	Trade shows

Suggested Retail Pricing
WX 550: $89.00
WX 450: $69.00

Competitors
Timberland, Hi-Tec, Vasque, Merrell, Asolo, Nike, and Reebok.

Product Development and Required Investment
We should allow about one year for the necessary product development and testing. I estimate these costs to be $350,000. Additionally, we will need to make a capital expenditure of $150,000 for new equipment.

EXHIBIT 11 **Anthony's Marketing Proposal**

MEMORANDUM

TO: Margaret Simon, President
          Harris Fleming, Vice President of Marketing
FROM: Anthony Simon, Executive Vice President
RE: Marketing Proposal

We have been successful with boots for mountaineers and serious hikers for years, and this is where our strengths seem to be. I recommend extending our Glacier and Summit lines instead of venturing into a new, unfamiliar market. My recommendations are summarized below:

Product Development
Introduce two new boots in the Summit line (designated HX 100 and HX 50) and market the Glacier MX 350 in a style for women with the same features as the boot for men. The new women's Glacier boot would have a suggested retail price of $219.99, while the suggested retail prices for the HX 100 and the HX 50 would be $119.00 and $89.00 respectively to provide price points at the low end of the line. The new Summit boots for men and women would be the first in the line to have leather and nylon uppers as well as the following features:

	HX 100	HX 50
Leather and nylon uppers	X	X
Molded rubber outsole	X	X
Cushioned midsole	X	X
Padded collar and tongue	X	X
Quick-dry lining	X	X
Waterproof inner liner	X	

The leather used in the uppers will have to be determined. We should consider full-grain, suede, and nubuck since they are all popular with users in this segment. We need to select one for the initial introduction. The nylon fabric for the uppers should be available in two colors, selected from among the following: beige, brown, green, slate, maroon, and navy blue. Additional colors can be offered as sales develop and we gain a better understanding of consumer preferences.

Product Development and Required Investment
Product design and development costs of $400,000 for the MX 350, HX 100, and HX 50 styles and a capital investment of $150,000 to acquire equipment to cut and stitch the nylon/leather uppers. One year will be needed for product development and testing.

Positioning
The additions to the Summit line will be positioned as boots for serious hikers who want a quality hiking boot at a reasonable price. The boots will also be attractive to casual hikers who are looking to move up to a better boot as they gain experience in hiking and outdoor activity.

Retail Outlets
We can use our existing retail outlets. Additionally, the lower price points on the new styles will make these boots attractive to catalog shoppers. I recommend that we consider making the Summit boots available to consumers through mail order catalog companies.

Promotion
We will need to revise our product brochures and develop new advertising for the additions to the Summit line. The balance of the promotion program should remain as it exists since it is working quite well. I believe the sales representatives and retailers selling our lines will welcome the new boots since they broaden the consumer appeal of our lines.

Suggested Retail Pricing
MX 350 for women: $219.00
HX 100: $119.00
HX 50: $89.00

Competitors
Asolo, Hi-Tec, Merrell, Raichle, Salomon, Tecnica, and Vasque.

Exhibit 12   Cima Mountaineering, Inc., Sales Forecasts for Proposed New Products (Pairs of Boots)

	Project 1		Project 2		
Year	*WX 550*	*WX 450*	*MX 350*	*HX 100*	*HX 50*
2001–02	16,420	24,590	2,249	15,420	12,897
2000–01	14,104	21,115	1,778	13,285	11,733
1999–2000	8,420	12,605	897	10,078	9,169
1998–99	5,590	8,430	538	5,470	5,049
1997–98	4,050	6,160	414	4,049	3,813

Note: Sales forecasts are expected values derived from minimum and maximum estimates.

Some cannibalization of existing boots will occur when the new styles are introduced. The sales forecasts provided above have taken into account the impact of sales losses on existing boots. No additional adjustments need to be made.

Forecasts for WX 550, WX 450, HX 100, and HX 50 include sales of both men's and women's boots.

Exhibit 13   Cima Mountaineering, Inc., Cost Information for Mountaineering and Hiking Boots

	Inner Liner	*No Inner Liner*
Retail margin	50%	50%
Marketing and Manufacturing Costs		
Sales commissions	10	10
Advertising and sales promotion	5	5
Materials	42	35
Labor, overhead, and transportation	28	35

Cost information for 1997–98 only. Sales commissions, advertising and sales promotion, materials, labor, overhead, and transportation costs are based on Cima selling prices. After 1997–98, annual increases of 3.0 percent apply to marketing and manufacturing costs and 4.0 percent apply to Cima selling prices.

companies expect their boot suppliers to make them a private brand. I'm not sure this is something we want to do since we built the company on a strategy of marketing our own brands that are made in the U.S.A. Also, I'm concerned about the reaction of our retailers when they discover we are selling to the catalog companies. It could create some problems.

Harris: That is a strategy issue we will have to address. However, I'm not even sure what percentage of sales the typical footwear company makes through the mail order catalogs. If we were to solicit the catalog business, we would need an answer to this question to avoid exceeding our capacity. In the proposals, I asked each of the teams to provide an estimate for us. I have to catch an early flight to Denver in the morning. It's 6:30; why don't we call it a day.

The meeting was adjourned at 6:35 PM. Soon thereafter, the marketing teams were formed with a leader assigned to each team.

EXHIBIT 14   **Harris Fleming's Memorandum to the Marketing Staff**

MEMORANDUM

TO:	Marketing Staff
CC:	Margaret Simon, President
	Anthony Simon, Executive Vice President
FROM:	Harris Fleming, Vice President of Marketing
SUBJECT:	Marketing Research Projects

Attached to this memorandum are two marketing proposals (see case Exhibits 10 and 11) under consideration by our company. Each proposal is a guide for additional marketing research. You have been selected to serve on a project team to investigate one of the proposals and report your conclusions and recommendations to management. At your earliest convenience, please complete the following.

Project Team 1: Proposal to enter the "Weekender" segment of the hiking boot market.
Review the market segmentation and summary of competition in Exhibits 4 and 5. Identify consumers that would match the profile described in the market segment and conduct field research using a focus group, a survey, or both. You may also visit retailers carrying hiking boots to examine displays and product brochures. Using the information in the proposal, supplemented with your research, prepare the following:

1. A design for the hiking boots (WX 550 and WX 450). Please prepare a sketch that shows the styling for the uppers. We propose to use the same design for each boot, the only difference being the waterproof inner liner on the WX 550 boot. On your design, list the features that your proposed boot would have, considering additions or deletions to those listed in the proposal.

2. Recommend a type of leather (from among those proposed) and two colors for the nylon to be used in the panels of the uppers. We plan to make two styles, one in each color for each boot.

3. Recommend a brand name for the product line. Include a rationale for your choice.

4. Verify the acceptability of the suggested retail pricing.

5. Prepare a magazine advertisement for the hiking boot. Provide a rationale for the advertisement in the report.

6. Convert the suggested retail prices *in the proposal* to the Cima selling price and use the sales forecasts and costs (shown in Exhibits 12 and 13) to prepare an estimate of before-tax profits for the new product line covering a five-year period starting in 1997–98. Assume annual cost increases of 3.0 percent and price increases of 4.0 percent beginning in 1998–99. Discount the future profits to present value using a cost of capital of 15.0 percent. Use 1996–97 as the base year for all discounting.

7. Determine the payback period for the proposal. Assume product development and investment occurs in 1996–97.

8. Provide your conclusions on the attractiveness of these styles to mail order catalog companies and their customers. You may wish to review current mail order catalogs to observe the hiking boots featured. Assuming Cima is successful selling to mail order catalog companies, estimate the percentage of our sales that could be expected from these customers.

9. Prepare a report that summarizes the recommendations of your project team, including the advantages and disadvantages of the proposal. Be prepared to present your product design, branding, pro-forma projections, payback period, and recommendations to management shortly after completion of this assignment.

10. Summarize your research and list the sources of information used to prepare the report.

Project Team 2: Proposal to extend the existing lines of boots for mountaineers and hikers.
Review the market segmentation and summary of competition in Exhibits 4 and 5. Identify consumers that match the profile described in the market segment and conduct field research using a focus group, a survey, or both. You may also visit retailers carrying hiking boots to examine displays and product brochures. Using the information in the proposal, supplemented with your research, prepare the following.

1. Designs for the hiking boots (HX 100 and HX 50). Please prepare sketches showing the styling for the uppers. We propose to use a different design for each boot, so you should provide a sketch for each. On each sketch, list the features that your proposed boots would have, considering additions or deletions to those listed in the proposal. No sketch is necessary for the mountaineering boot, MX 350, since we will use the same design as the men's boot and build it on a women's last.

2. Recommend one type of leather (from among those proposed) and two colors for the nylon to be used in the panels of the uppers. We plan to make two styles, one in each color for each boot.

3. Verify the market acceptability of the suggested retail pricing.

4. Prepare a magazine advertisement for your hiking boots. Include a rationale for the advertisement in the report.

EXHIBIT 14   **(concluded)**

5. Using the suggested retail prices *in the proposal,* convert them to the Cima selling prices and use the sales forecasts and costs (shown in Exhibits 12 and 13) to prepare an estimate of before-tax profits for the new products covering a five-year period starting in 1997–98. Assume annual cost increases of 3.0 percent and price increases of 4.0 percent beginning in 1998–99. Discount the profits to present value using a cost of capital of 15.0 percent. Use 1996–97 as the base year for all discounting.

6. Determine the payback period for the proposal. Assume product development and investment occurs in 1996–97.

7. Provide your conclusions on the attractiveness of these styles to mail order catalog companies and their customers. You may wish to review current mail order catalogs to observe the hiking boots featured. Assuming Cima is successful selling to mail order catalog companies, estimate the percentage of our sales that could be expected from these customers.

8. Prepare a report that summarizes the recommendations of your project team, including the advantages and disadvantages of the proposal. Be prepared to present your product design, pro-forma projections, payback period, and recommendations to management shortly after completion of this assignment.

9. Summarize your research and list the sources of information used to prepare the report.

CASE 7–4
LONGEVITY HEALTHCARE SYSTEMS, INC.

Kathryn Hamilton, president of Longevity Healthcare Systems, Inc., located in Grand Rapids, Michigan, was reviewing the 1993 annual statements. "We concluded another terrific year," she commented. "Our sales and earnings exceeded expectations, but I'm concerned about the next few years." Although Longevity was successful, it was beginning to experience competition and the uncertainty of health care reform. In February 1994, a large hospital in Grand Rapids, Michigan, had converted an entire wing to a long-term care facility. The hospital also initiated an aggressive sales and advertising campaign and was competing with Longevity for new nursing home residents.

Longevity's recent acquisition of seven nursing homes in Toledo, Ohio, was also proving to be an unprofitable venture. Many of the residents were on Medicare and Medicaid, and these health insurance programs generally did not reimburse the full costs of care. Additionally, the families of the Toledo residents were becoming value-conscious and they frequently commented about the quality and cost of nursing care. Kathryn realized that, to improve the profitability, attention would have to be given to customer satisfaction and attracting more profitable private-pay residents. Health care reform was also a source of concern. It was her belief that reform of the health care industry would be comprehensive, with increased emphasis on cost control, competitive pricing, and quality of care. She wondered what effect reform would have on Longevity and what the timetable for legislative action would be.

While increased competition and health care reform seemed certain, the most profitable path for future growth was not clear because several marketing opportunities existed. An aging population had created a strong demand for long-term care in nursing homes. Alzheimer's disease was also becoming more common. Longevity had recently lost some nursing home residents to Alzheimer's treatment centers because the company did not offer a specialized facility. Kathryn had to decide whether offering Alzheimer's treatment would be desirable.

Opportunities to expand existing businesses were also an option. The Grand Rapids pharmacy acquired in 1992 had been successfully phased in Longevity, and Kathryn was wondering if a similar acquisition would work in Toledo. However, she was concerned about the impact of reform on the pricing of prescription drugs and medical supplies. To date, the pharmacy had been very profitable, but what would the future hold?

Geographic expansion of the firm's nursing and subacute care facilities might also be a profitable avenue for growth. Industry consolidation was making it possible to acquire nursing homes and unprofitable hospitals that could be converted to health care facilities. However, Kathryn envisioned that a future industry trend might be toward vertical integration of health care services. If so, it might make sense to further integrate Longevity's business in the Grand Rapids and Toledo markets before committing to additional geographic expansion.

This case was written by Professor Lawrence M. Lamont and Elizabeth W. Storey, Washington and Lee University. Case material is prepared as a basis for class discussion, and not designed to present illustrations of either effective or ineffective handling of administrative problems. The names of the firms and individuals, locations, and/or financial information have been disguised to preserve anonymity. Copyright © 1994, Lawrence M. Lamont. Used with permission.

Beyond decisions on the future direction of Longevity, Kathryn wondered if it was time to begin thinking about a more formal approach to marketing. "I really need to get some ideas about marketing in our different businesses down on paper so I can see how they fit with my views on an overall corporate marketing strategy," she remarked.

History of Longevity Healthcare Systems, Inc.

In 1972, Kathryn Hamilton, R.N., was searching for a nursing home for her mother in Grand Rapids, Michigan. Discouraged by a six-month wait for admission, she decided to move her into the home she occupied with her husband Richard. Dr. Hamilton, M.D., enjoyed a medical practice in Grand Rapids specializing in care for older adults.

A Nursing Home Business.   In 1974, Richard's mother and father joined the household and Kathryn and Richard continued to learn how to care for older adults. In 1976, the Hamiltons leased a small, outdated, 40-bed hospital in a nearby suburb and converted it into a long-term care facility. Following certification, the facility was opened in 1977 as the Longevity Nursing Home. In addition to their parents, 10 other adults over 65 entered the home during the year. All were "private-pay," meaning they paid directly for services with personal assets, but without government assistance. By 1979, the nursing facility was fully occupied with private-pay residents. Longevity was incorporated, and Kathryn Hamilton became the president and its director of nursing, while her husband, Richard, provided medical services and continued his practice. The leased facility was purchased in 1979.

New Nursing Services.   By 1980, Longevity found it necessary to add additional nursing services for aging residents. Two levels of care were added, and professional nurses were hired to provide the services. The new services were favorably received, and the referrals from residents and physicians kept the facility filled.

Expansion by Acquisition, 1980–85.   The demand for nursing care was strong in the early 1980s, and Longevity expanded. Eight unprofitable nursing homes with a total of 480 beds were acquired in Grand Rapids and nearby communities. All of the homes were licensed, certified by Medicare and Medicaid, and occupied by residents requiring a variety of nursing services. Shortly after the acquisition, Dr. Hamilton left his medical practice to join Longevity full-time as its medical director. He added skilled nursing care for residents requiring 24-hour-a-day care, and rehabilitation services for those needing physical, speech, and occupational therapy.

Nursing Home Construction.   From 1986 to 1988, Longevity expanded by constructing three 70-bed nursing homes in nearby communities. Each provided the full range of nursing and rehabilitation services and was licensed for Medicare and Medicaid-patients.[1] The homes were quickly filled, and by the end of 1988 Longevity operated 12 nursing homes with a total of 730 beds. Employment had grown to 1,200 full-time and part-time employees.

---

[1] By 1988, all Longevity nursing homes were certified to receive Medicare and Medicaid patients. Medicare is a federally funded and administered health insurance program that reimburses health care facilities for nursing and medical services. Medicaid is a state-administered reimbursement program that covers skilled and intermediate long-term care for the medically indigent. The benefits paid by Medicaid programs vary from state to state.

EXHIBIT 1 **Longevity Healthcare Systems, Inc., Historical Development, 1972–93**

Date	Activity
1972–75	Nursing care for parents.
1976–77	Leased a 40-bed hospital and converted it to a nursing home.
1979	Business incorporated as Longevity Nursing Home.
1979	Corporation purchased leased nursing home.
1980–85	Acquired eight nursing homes in Grand Rapids area, 480 beds.
1986–88	Constructed three nursing homes in Grand Rapids area, 210 beds.
1990–91	Converted a 30-bed wing of Grand Rapids nursing home into subacute care.
1992–93	Constructed a 50-bed subacute care facility in Grand Rapids area.
1992	Acquired a retail pharmacy in Grand Rapids.
1992–93	Acquired seven nursing homes in Toledo area, 280 beds.
1993	Corporation name changed to Longevity Healthcare Systems, Inc.

New Business Opportunities. During a medical convention in 1990, Kathryn Hamilton noted a growing concern over the escalating costs of hospital care and the desire of insurance providers to shorten the hospitalization of patients requiring medical supervision, but not the other services traditionally provided by hospitals. Sensing an opportunity, the Hamiltons converted a 30-bed wing of one of the Grand Rapids nursing homes to a subacute care facility for patients that did not need the full services of a licensed acute care hospital.[2] For patients moved from a hospital to the Longevity facility, the needed care was provided for about half the cost. The subacute care facility was licensed in 1991 and it quickly filled with referrals from hospitals, physicians, and health care insurers.

The growing recognition that treating patients requiring subacute care in low-overhead nursing facilities was a cost-effective alternative, substantially increased the demand for Longevity's subacute care. In 1992, following marketing research, Longevity constructed a 50-bed subacute care facility near one of its nursing homes. It was completed in 1993 and, within a few months, operated at capacity with patients referred from insurance companies, physicians, and Longevity nursing homes.

As the demand for specialized nursing and medical care expanded, it became apparent that profitability could be improved by operating a pharmacy. In 1992, Longevity acquired a retail pharmacy in Grand Rapids from a retiring pharmacist. It was converted into an institutional pharmacy to provide prescriptions, medical equipment and supplies, and consulting services to Longevity facilities.

Geographic Expansion. Late in 1992, what appeared to be an exceptional business opportunity came to the attention of Kathryn and Richard Hamilton. A few hundred miles away, in Toledo, Ohio, a large health care company was selling seven unprofitable nursing homes with a total of 280 beds for $12,000,000. The homes were occupied primarily by Medicare and Medicaid patients and operated at 70 percent of

---

[2] Medical services fall along a continuum from intensive care, acute care, subacute care, nursing care, and home health care. Hospitals offer intensive and acute care for patients with complex medical conditions. They have fully equipped operating and recovery rooms, radiology services, intensive and coronary care units, pharmacies, clinical laboratories, therapy services, and emergency services. Subacute care facilities owned by nursing homes serve the needs of patients who require nursing and medical care but not many of the specialized services and equipment provided by an acute care hospital.

EXHIBIT 2   **Longevity Healthcare Systems, Inc., Geographic Location of Facilities**

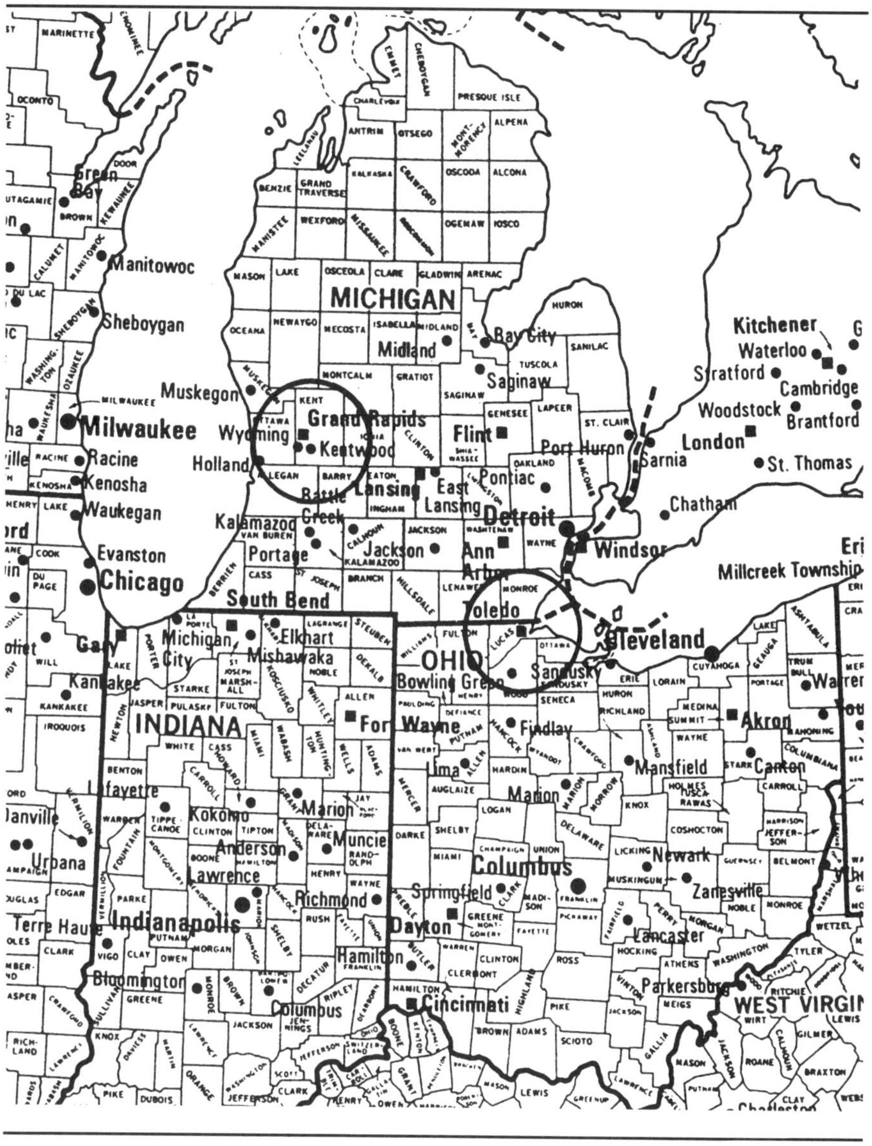

capacity. The Hamiltons decided to take a one-year option on the facilities while they raised the money to complete the purchase. Eventually, 40 percent of Longevity's common stock was sold to a large insurance company, and some of the proceeds were used to exercise the purchase option. Kathryn Hamilton hired an experienced administrator and assigned him the task of returning the nursing homes to profitability. To reflect its broadening scope in the health care industry, the Hamiltons decided to change the company name to Longevity Healthcare Systems, Inc. As shown in Exhibits 1 and 2, Longevity ended 1993 with 12 nursing homes, two subacute care facilities, and a pharmacy located in Michigan, and seven nursing homes located in Ohio. Exhibits 3 and 4 contain the financial statements for the year ending December 31, 1993.

EXHIBIT 3 Longevity Healthcare Systems, Inc., Income
Statement (Year Ending 12-31-93)

Net revenues	
Basic LTC services	$ 45,500,000
Subacute medical services	9,000,000
Pharmacy services	3,000,000
Total revenues	$ 57,500,000
Operating expenses	
Salaries, wages, and benefits	$ 20,125,000
Patient services	21,275,000
Administrative and general	3,450,000
Depreciation and amortization	575,000
Total costs and expenses	$ 45,425,000
Income from operations	$ 12,075,000
Interest expense	1,726,111
Earnings before taxes	$ 10,348,889
Income taxes	4,139,555
Net income	$ 6,209,334
Net income per share	$ 0.78

EXHIBIT 4 Longevity Healthcare Systems, Inc., Balance Sheet
(Years Ending 12-31-93 and 12-31-92)

Assets	1993	1992
Current assets		
Cash and equivalents	$ 841,770	$ 501,120
Accounts receivable	3,265,584	2,702,552
Inventory	2,262,816	1,624,399
Property, plant, and equipment		
Land	9,959,051	7,690,249
Buildings and improvements	27,002,416	13,622,079
Equipment	2,917,136	2,179,842
Accumulated depreciation	(4,028,149)	(2,464,535)
Other assets		
Goodwill	791,794	655,278
Other long-term assets	5,163,275	4,063,190
Total assets	$ 48,175,693	$ 30,574,174
Liabilities and Shareholders' Equity		
Current liabilities		
Accounts payable	$ 1,250,201	$ 1,043,648
Accrued expenses	708,447	586,301
Accrued compensation	416,734	344,883
Current portion of long-term debt	2,041,995	2,700,120
Accrued interest	196,694	203,954
Long-term debt (net)	10,506,622	12,871,452
Shareholders' equity		
Common stock, $.01 par value	50,000	50,000
Additional paid-in capital	17,870,666	3,848,816
Retained earnings	15,134,334	8,925,000
Total liabilities and shareholders' equity	$ 48,175,693	$ 30,574,174

EXHIBIT 5   Longevity Healthcare Systems, Inc., Historical Revenues and Net Income

Year	Revenues	Net Income
1993	$57,500,000	$6,209,334
1992	46,575,000	5,029,560
1991	37,260,000	3,017,736
1990	26,715,420	2,987,692
1989	21,799,783	1,334,147

EXHIBIT 6   Longevity Healthcare Systems, Inc., Selected Pharmacy Information (Year Ending 12-31-93)

Income Statement

Net revenue	$3,000,000
Operating expenses	2,430,000
Operating income	570,000
Net income	390,000

Financial Ratios

Current ratio	1.94
Inventory turnover	4.20
Profit margin (percent)	13.00%
Return on assets (percent)	9.29%

EXHIBIT 7   Longevity Healthcare Systems, Inc., Operating Information for Facilities (Year Ending 12-31-93)

	Grand Rapids	Toledo	Total
Payor mix			
Private and other	69.7%	18.7%	44.2%
Medicare	8.4	17.8	13.1
Medicaid	21.9	63.5	42.7
Occupancy	96.4%	81.2%	88.8%
No. of beds	780	280	1,060

Exhibit 5 presents a five-year sales and earnings history, while Exhibit 6 provides some financial information for the pharmacy.

Longevity Marketing

Marketing was used to promote high occupancy in Longevity facilities, expand the percentage of private-pay residents, and increase the profits of its institutional pharmacy. Operating information for the health care facilities is shown in Exhibit 7, and the products and services marketed by Longevity are summarized in Exhibit 8.

Nursing care was marketed locally. The administrator and admissions director of each facility designed a marketing strategy to increase awareness of the nursing home

**EXHIBIT 8   Longevity Healthcare Systems, Inc.,
Products and Services**

Business	*Products/services*
Nursing care	Custodial care Assisted living Intermediate nursing care Skilled nursing care
Subacute care for	Lung and heart disease Coma, pain, and wound care Spinal cord injuries Head injuries Intravenous therapy Joint replacements
Rehabilitation services	Occupational therapy Physical therapy Speech therapy
Institutional pharmacy	Prescription drugs Nonprescription drugs Medical supplies Medical equipment Consulting services

and its services in the market it served. Personal selling using telemarketing and direct contact was targeted to referral sources such as physicians, hospital administrators, home health agencies, community organizations and churches, senior citizens groups, retirement communities, and the families of prospective residents. Longevity also distributed promotional literature discussing its philosophy of care, services, and quality standards. Frequently the literature was provided to prospective residents and their families when they inquired about nursing or toured the facilities.

Marketing for subacute care was directed by Kathryn Hamilton, who contacted insurance companies, managed care organizations such as HMOs, hospital administrators, and other third-party payors to promote Longevity's services.[3] Kathryn also attended professional meetings where she maintained contact with the various referral sources.

The products and services of the institutional pharmacy were marketed by the pharmacy manager and his assistant by direct contact with Longevity facilities, other nursing homes, hospitals, clinics, and home health agencies. In addition to drugs and medical supplies, management also provided consulting services to help ensure quality patient care. These services were especially valuable because they enabled the nursing homes to admit patients that required more complex and profitable medical services.

---

[3] Managed care organizations provide health care products that integrate financing and management with the delivery of health care services through a network of providers (such as nursing homes and hospitals) who share financial risk or who have incentives to deliver cost-effective services. An HMO (health maintenance organization) provides prepaid health care services to its members through physicians employed by the HMO at facilities owned by the HMO or through a network of independent physicians and facilities. They actively manage patient care to maximize quality and cost-effectiveness.

EXHIBIT 9 **Longevity Healthcare Systems, Inc., Example Resident Statement for Nursing Care (per Month)***

Semiprivate room, $105.00 per day	$3,150.00
Basic telephone service	15.00
Rehabilitation therapy, 7.0 hours per month	840.00
Pharmacy and other specialized services	360.00
Miscellaneous personal expenses	50.00
Total	$4,415.00
Per day	147.17

*Based on private pay. Includes room and board, 24-hour professional nursing care, meals, housekeeping, and linen services. Social and recreational activity programs are also included.

Nursing Home Services. Longevity nursing homes provided room and board, dietary services, recreation and social activities, housekeeping and laundry services, four levels of nursing care, and numerous specialized services. Custodial care was provided to residents needing minimal care. Assisted living was used by persons needing some assistance with personal care such as bathing and eating. Intermediate care was provided to residents needing more nursing and attention, but not continual access to nurses. Finally, skilled nursing care was available to residents requiring the professional services of a nurse on a 24-hour-a-day basis. Rehabilitation therapy was also available for residents that had disabilities or were returning from hospitalization for surgery or illness. Rehabilitation was an important part of Longevity's care because it helped residents improve their quality of life.

Most of the residents in Longevity nursing homes were female and over 65. Although rates depended on accommodations and the services used, a typical nursing home bed generated monthly revenues of $4,415. It was common for a resident to initially enter the nursing home needing only custodial care or assisted living and to progress to higher levels of nursing care as they aged. Exhibit 9 provides a typical schedule of monthly charges for a resident in a semiprivate room with seven hours of therapy.

All of the Longevity nursing homes were licensed in their respective states. Generally, the licenses had to be renewed annually. For renewal, state health care agencies considered the physical condition of the facility, the qualifications of the administrative and medical staff, the quality of care, and the facility's compliance with the applicable laws and regulations.

Subacute Care. Longevity marketed subacute care for patients with more complex medical needs that required constant medical supervision, but not the expensive equipment and services of an acute care hospital. Subacute care generated higher profit margins than nursing care, although patient stays in the facility were usually shorter.[4] Daily patient rates varied from $250.00 to $750.00, depending on the services and equipment required. Longevity's services included care for patients with lung and heart disease, spinal cord and head injuries, joint replacements, coma, pain and wound

---

[4] Longevity profit margins for subacute care facilities were about 25 percent higher than for nursing care facilities. The length of stay was usually 20 to 45 days versus eight months for private-pay nursing care and two years for Medicaid patients.

care, and intravenous therapy. Services at the subacute care facilities were not limited to the elderly. Younger patients discharged from hospitals were attractive because of their longer life expectancy and eventual need for nursing and rehabilitation. Based on an average rate of $1,000 per day charged by acute care hospitals. Longevity knew that its prices were substantially lower for comparable services. Like the nursing homes, the subacute care facilities were subject to licensing by the state health care agencies and certification by Medicare. All Longevity subacute care facilities were licensed and certified.

Pharmacy Products and Services.   Longevity provided pharmacy products and services to nursing homes, retirement communities, and other health care organizations. The pharmacy's products were frequently customized with special packaging and dispensing systems and delivered daily. The pharmacy also consulted on medications and long-term care regulations, and provided computerized tracking of medications, medical records processing, and 24-hour emergency services.

The Market for Long-Term Health Care

Long-term health care includes basic health care (such as that provided in nursing homes), rehabilitation therapy and Alzheimer's care, institutional pharmacy services, subacute care, and home health care. In recent years, spending for these and other health care services has increased significantly. For example, in 1993, one out of every seven dollars that Americans spent went to purchase health care. Total expenditures are projected to increase from $585.3 billion in 1990 to $3,457.7 billion in 2010, an annual growth rate of over 9 percent.

Nursing homes are important providers of long-term health care. Expenditures for nursing home care are expected to increase at a comparable rate, from $53.1 billion in 1990 to $310.1 billion in 2010. This industry consists of about 16,000 licensed facilities with a total of 1,700,000 beds. It includes a large number of small, locally owned nursing homes and a growing number of regional and national companies. The industry is undergoing restructuring in response to stricter regulation, increasing complexity of medical services, and competitive pressures. Smaller, local operators who lack sophisticated management and financial resources are being acquired by larger, more established companies. At present, the 20 largest firms operate about 18 percent of the nursing facilities. Consolidation is expected to continue, but the long-term outlook is extremely positive for the businesses that survive. Nursing home revenues increased by about 12 percent in 1993 and they are expected to experience similar gains in 1994. Several factors account for the optimistic outlook: favorable demographic trends, pressures to control costs, advances in medical technology, and limited supply of nursing beds.

Favorable Demographic Trends.   Demographic trends, namely growth in the elderly segment of the population, are increasing the demand for health care and the services of nursing homes. Most of the market for nursing care consists of men and women 65 years of age and older. Their number was approximately 25 million in 1980 and is projected to increase to 35 million by 2000 and to 40 million by the year 2010. The 65-and-over segment suffers from a greater incidence of chronic illnesses and disabilities and currently accounts for about two-thirds of the health care expenditures in the United States.

Pressures to Control Costs.   Government and private payers have adopted cost control measures to encourage reduced hospital stays. In addition, private insurers have begun to limit reimbursement to "reasonable" charges, while managed care organizations are limiting hospitalization costs by monitoring utilization and negotiating discounted rates. As a result, hospital stays have been shortened and many patients are discharged with a continuing need for care. Because nursing homes are able to provide services at lower prices, the cost pressures have increased the demand for nursing home services and subacute care following hospital discharge.

Advances in Medical Technology.   Advances in technology leading to improved medications and surgical procedures have increased life expectancies. Adults over age 85 are now the fastest-growing segment of the population, and their numbers are expected to double over the next 20 years. Many require skilled care and the medical equipment traditionally available only in hospitals. Nursing homes are acquiring some of the specialty medical equipment and providing skilled nursing care to older adults through subacute care facilities.

Limited Supply of Nursing Beds.   The supply of nursing home beds has been limited by the availability of financing and high construction and start-up expenses. Additionally, the supply has been constrained by legislation limiting licenses for new nursing beds in states that require a demonstration of need. The effect has been to create a barrier to market entry and conditions where demand for nursing home services exceeds the available supply in many states.

National Health Care Reform

The next decade will be a period of reform for the health care system. Although it is not clear how comprehensive the reform will be and how it will be financed, the focus will be to control costs and provide universal access to quality health care. The most likely plan will probably reform the health insurance industry, build on the current employer-financed approach, and call for market incentives to control costs. To ensure universal access, insurance and managed care companies will be prohibited from dropping, rejecting, or pricing out of the market anyone with an expensive medical condition.

Reform will affect long-term care providers, such as nursing homes, in several ways. It will regulate the insurance companies to make health insurance more price-competitive and affordable. This change will favorably impact long-term health care providers by increasing the number of residents paying with insurance benefits. Reform may also extend Medicare coverage for home health care. A change such as this would encourage more older adults to receive health care at home instead of at a nursing facility, resulting in an unfavorable impact.

Employers will also have incentives to control costs and deliver quality care. Increasingly they will rely on managed care organizations, such as HMOs, who are likely to contract lower-cost providers, such as nursing homes, for subacute care and other cost-effective services. Companies capable of providing a variety of health care services at attractive prices should see opportunities to expand demand.

Institutional pharmacies will also be impacted by health care reform. President Clinton's Health Security Act called for the addition of prescription drug coverage to the Medicare program. If adopted, this provision would probably decrease prices of prescription drugs by regulation of pharmaceutical manufacturers. Price decreases, either legislated or achieved through managed care and the market system, may allow institutional pharmacies to enjoy higher profit margins while still providing medications at affordable prices to patients.

Regulation and Competition

Health care providers are regulated at the state and federal levels. Regulation impacts financial management and the quality and safety of care. Ensuring that health care facilities are in compliance with regulatory standards is an important aspect of managing a health care business. In addition, management is increasingly confronted with competition. Nursing homes and subacute care facilities compete for patients who are able to select from a variety of alternatives to meet their needs. Managed care and insurance organizations also negotiate aggressively with health care providers to ensure quality care at attractive prices.

Financial Regulation.   The Health Care Financing Administration (HCFA) is the federal regulatory agency for Medicare and Medicaid. Both programs are cost-based and use a per diem payment schedule that reimburses the provider for a portion of the costs of care. Each facility must apply to participate in the Medicare and Medicaid programs and then have its beds certified to provide skilled nursing, intermediate, or other levels of care. A nursing home may have a mix of beds at any time, but it must match patient services to each bed. A facility cannot place a Medicare patient requiring skilled nursing care in a bed certified for intermediate care without recertifying the bed for skilled care. Recertification often required a month or more.

Quality and Safety of Care.   Much of the current regulation facing nursing homes was developed in the Omnibus Budget Reconciliation Act of 1987 (OBRA 87). Facilities that participate in Medicare and Medicaid must be regularly inspected by state survey teams under contract with HCFA to ensure safety and quality of care. OBRA 87 also established a resident "bill of rights" that essentially converted nursing homes from merely custodial facilities into centers for rehabilitation. Nursing homes are now required to establish a care plan for patients and conduct assessments to ensure that the facility achieves the highest practical well-being for each resident.

Competition.   Longevity competes with acute care and rehabilitation hospitals, other nursing and subacute care facilities, home health care agencies, and institutional pharmacies. Some offer services and prices that are comparable to those offered by Longevity.

Nursing homes compete on the basis of their reputation in the community, the ability to meet particular needs, the location and appearance of the facility, and the price of services. When a nursing facility is being selected, members of a prospective resident's family usually participate by visiting and evaluating nursing homes over a period of several weeks.

Some of the competing nursing homes in Grand Rapids and Toledo are operated by nonprofit organizations (churches and fraternal organizations) that can finance capital expenditures on a tax-exempt basis or receive charitable contributions to subsidize their operations. They compete with Longevity on the basis of price for private pay residents.

Longevity competes for subacute care patients with acute care and rehabilitation hospitals, nursing homes, and home health agencies. The competition is generally local or regional and the competitive factors are similar to those for nursing care, although more emphasis is placed on support services such as third-party reimbursement, information management, and patient record keeping. Insurance and managed care organizations exert considerable influence on the decision and increase the competition by negotiating with several health care providers.

The institutional pharmacy market has no dominant competitor in the markets served by Longevity. Twenty percent of the market is accounted for by the institutional pharmacies owned by nursing homes. Independent institutional pharmacies control about 35 percent of the market, and retail pharmacies supply the remainder. Retail pharmacies are steadily being acquired by nursing homes and independents to gain market share and achieve economies of scale in purchasing prescriptions and medical supplies. Institutional pharmacies compete on the basis of fast, customer-oriented service, price, and the ability to provide consulting and information management services to customers.

Marketing Issues and Opportunities

Kathryn Hamilton believed that Longevity could improve its marketing. She was concerned about the efforts of individual nursing homes and the need to improve the marketing of subacute care to managed care providers. Finally, she believed that customer satisfaction would become an important competitive factor and Longevity would need to assess the reactions of nursing home residents and their families to the quality of its services.

Continued growth was also on Kathryn's mind. Population demographics and health care reform would create outstanding opportunities for businesses that could design and implement successful marketing strategies. For some time, she had been thinking about expanding into Alzheimer's treatment because of the demographics and the growing need for facilities in the Grand Rapids area. Additionally, she saw an opportunity to further integrate Longevity by establishing a pharmacy in Toledo or by acquiring nursing homes in a new market such as South Bend, Indiana. Each marketing opportunity seemed to make sense, so the final choices would be difficult.

Local Marketing of Health Care Services.   Although local marketing had worked well, duplication of effort and overlapping market areas were becoming problems as the number of nursing homes in a market increased. Kathryn wondered what the marketing strategy for nursing home services should be and whether the marketing efforts of the Grand Rapids and Toledo nursing homes could be coordinated in each area to eliminate duplication and preserve local identity. One approach she was considering was to hire a marketing specialist to work with the nursing homes to attract more private-pay customers. Advertising was a related issue because it had not been used and Kathryn questioned whether it should be part of the marketing strategy. Should an advertising campaign be created for all of the nursing homes in a market, or should it be left to nursing home administrators to decide if advertising was appropriate in their strategy? If advertising were to be used, then a decision would have to be made on the type of advertising, the creative strategy, and the appropriate media.

Marketing Subacute Care.   Subacute care was viewed as an attractive marketing opportunity because of the profit margins. However, to further penetrate the market, a marketing strategy would have to be developed. Kathryn noted that managed care organizations and other referral sources were like organizational buyers as they made decisions on subacute care for the cases they managed. Instead of marketing the service to physicians and patient families, Longevity would negotiate directly with HMOs and insurance companies to determine services and a rate structure based on the patient's medical needs. Personal selling would be used to build a relationship with the case managers for both the insurance company and the hospital. The marketing objective was to convince the insurance companies that the subacute unit could achieve the same patient outcomes at a lower cost than a hospital. If a marketing strategy could be developed along with appropriate staffing, it might be desirable to expand this part of Longevity's business. Economics favored conversion of a wing of an existing nursing home into a subacute care facility at a cost of $25,000 per bed. One possibility existed in Toledo where an unprofitable 80-bed facility was operating at 60 percent of capacity. If part of the facility were upgraded to subacute care, she expected that, within a short time, it would operate at capacity.

Customer Satisfaction.   Occasional complaints from nursing home residents about the price and quality of care were of concern to management. Since Longevity depended on referrals, customer satisfaction was an important element of a successful marketing strategy. In thinking about the issue, Kathryn noted that the license renewal process generally assured the maintenance of high standards in each facility, but it focused heavily on the inputs necessary to provide quality nursing care and not on customer satisfaction. Kathryn needed to decide what should be done to monitor individual nursing homes to assure customer satisfaction with Longevity's services.

Acquisition of a Toledo Pharmacy.   One marketing opportunity being considered was the acquisition of a Toledo pharmacy. From management's perspective, an acquisition was interesting because it further integrated the existing health care operations and provided an incremental source of earnings from the Toledo market.

Management had identified an institutional pharmacy serving 15 nursing homes with 700 beds. It was offered at a cash price of $1,050,000 and generated annual revenues of approximately $1,450 per bed served. The pharmacy was quite profitable, with an average profit margin of 12.5 percent over the past five years. To consider the profitability of the acquisition, Kathryn believed it was reasonable to assume that the pharmacy would be able to serve the Longevity facilities in Toledo and retain 60 percent of the nursing home beds it presently served if it was staffed with appropriate marketing support.

One concern was the impact of health care reform. Most of the nursing homes served by the pharmacy had a high percentage of Medicare and Medicaid patients. If the reimbursement rates for prescription drugs and medical supplies were to decline, then what seemed to be an attractive opportunity could quickly change.

Alzheimer's Treatment.   Alzheimer's treatment was being considered because the demand for care was not being met and the development of a cure or drug therapy for the disease was progressing slowly. Kathryn believed that the demand for Alzheimer's treatment would grow at least as fast as the over-65 population. Projections from the U.S. Department of Health and Human Services indicated that, by the year 2000, the Alzheimer's care market would increase by 50 percent from the present base of 4,000,000 presently suffering from the disease.

Longevity was considering establishing an Alzheimer's wing in two of the Grand Rapids nursing homes that served areas near older community residents. Each unit would serve 30 patients and it would be self-contained and secured to protect residents against their wandering habits. The furniture and fixtures would also be renovated to meet the needs of the Alzheimer's patient, including softer colors, more subdued lighting, a separate nurses station, and a secured entrance. If an existing facility was converted, about six nursing rooms would have to be taken out of service to provide a separate activity and dining space. However, management reasoned that the revenue loss would be offset by average monthly revenues of $3,400 per patient and 15 percent lower costs than those for the average nursing home resident. Alzheimer's patients frequently required less costly care because of their younger age, better health, and a tendency to use fewer services. Longevity management had secured cost estimates that indicated the conversion costs would be $2,000 to $3,000 per bed.

In thinking about the opportunity, Kathryn also recalled that Alzheimer's units typically had occupancy levels above 95 percent. Patients averaged a three-year length of stay and were almost always private pay. The marketing for Alzheimer's units focused on Alzheimer's associations, Alzheimer support groups, and church groups. Kathryn would have to decide how to position and market the Alzheimer's units so they would not appear to conflict with or be confused with the nursing home services. This would be a difficult but important marketing challenge because nursing homes that were known to operate Alzheimer's units tended to have better relationships with referral sources. Apparently they were perceived as providing an important community service.

Toward a Comprehensive Marketing Strategy

As Kathryn Hamilton completed her review of the financial statements, she was reminded of the need to make improvements in Longevity's marketing strategies. "I wish I could just write a one-paragraph statement of the corporate marketing strategy for this company. Then I could address each of the marketing issues and opportunities using my corporate strategy as a guide," she remarked.

Certainly one issue was improving existing marketing efforts. Marketing of nursing care, subacute care, and the institutional pharmacy had been reasonably successful, but Kathryn felt uneasy about going another year without making needed changes. Since most of Kathryn's time was now needed to manage the business, additional marketing personnel would be necessary to develop and implement the marketing strategies for the various services. How many people would be needed and how the marketing effort would be organized also had to be decided.

Because Longevity was still evolving as a company with an uncertain marketing strategy, the most profitable direction for future growth was also important. Selecting attractive marketing opportunities was complicated because the choice depended on financial resources. Should Longevity expand the institutional pharmacy business or the subacute care business, or would resources be better utilized by offering Alzheimer's care? Each would bring Longevity closer to becoming an integrated health care provider.

Just as Kathryn moved to turn her personal computer off for the day, she noticed an electronic mail message from the administrator of the Toledo nursing homes. It said that, for the first quarter of 1994, the seven nursing homes were breaking even at 81 percent occupancy and 25 percent private-pay residents. When she arrived home that evening, she was greeted by her husband, Richard, who mentioned that she had received a telephone call from a commercial real estate broker in South Bend, Indiana. The broker had located five nursing homes with a total of 450 beds that were being sold in a bankruptcy proceeding for $5,000,000. During dinner that evening, Richard mentioned that they needed to discuss the South Bend opportunity because the homes were attractively priced in a desirable market. It was his belief that, in the future, the most profitable health care businesses would be vertically integrated and geographically diversified. Kathryn nodded in agreement as he handed her the summary information provided in Exhibit 10 and mentioned that a decision would have to be made in five days. She thought to herself, I wonder if it's financially possible?

EXHIBIT 10   Longevity Healthcare Systems, Inc., Selected Demographic Information

Category	Grand Rapids*		Toledo		South Bend†	
	Number	Percent of Adult Population by Category	Number	Percent of Adult Population by Category	Number	Percent of Adult Population by Category
Retired	235,513	18.9%	161,630	19.9%	119,401	20.0%
Age, household head						
55–64	77,383	12.4	54,421	13.2	40,661	13.4
65–74	71,142	11.4	52,772	12.8	39,448	13.0
75 and older	56,165	9.0	40,816	9.9	30,951	10.2
Median age	44.5		46.1		46.7	
Lifecycle stage						
Married, 45–64	87,992	14.1	58,544	14.2	44,910	14.8
Married, 65+	61,157	9.8	42,053	10.2	34,289	11.3
Single, 45–64	44,932	7.2	31,746	7.7	23,365	7.7
Single, 65+	56,789	9.1	43,702	10.6	30,951	10.2
Median income	$32,928		$32,194		$31,264	
Adult population	1,246,101		812,212		597,003	
Nursing facilities‡	439		988		590	
Total nursing beds	49,927		92,518		64,263	

Source: *The Lifestyle Market Analyst, 1993. Health Care Financing Administration, 1991.*

*Includes Kalamazoo and Battle Creek, Michigan.

†Includes Elkhart, Indiana.

‡Statewide statistics for certified Medicare and Medicaid facilities and beds.

CASE 7–5
LA-Z-BOY CHAIR COMPANY

One of the most widely recognized trademarks in the United States, La-Z-Boy seems to connote a relaxed, lazy atmosphere. Is the La-Z-Boy Chair Company (LZB) like the visions its trademark suggests? Hardly! Consider the percent increase in net sales and percent increase in net profit in the last six years. Exhibits 1 and 2 show the income statements and balance sheets for the years 1983 through 1988, respectively. This dramatic growth, which made LZB number three in the furniture industry and the largest producer of upholstered furniture, was achieved by acquiring four other companies as well as by internal growth. The four acquisitions are shown in Exhibit 3, with their annual sales in the year prior to acquisition.

While the furniture industry sales grew by 52 percent in the last 10 years from sales of $9.7 billion in 1978 to $14.8 billion in 1987, LZB sales grew at a much faster rate of 216 percent. During the 10-year period, the top 10 manufacturers moved from 20 percent to 33 percent of the total market, growing by 139 percent. During this same 10-year period, LZB moved from eighth to third place in the industry. Can this performance be continued? What can LZB do for encores?

Company Background

LZB was founded by Edward M. Knabusch and his cousin Edwin J. Shoemaker in 1927 as a partnership known as Kna-Shoe Manufacturing Company in Monroe, Michigan. In 1928, the first reclining chair was developed as a wooden-slat porch chair. Although the Lion Store in Toledo, Ohio, refused to handle it, the buyer suggested that if it were an upholstered chair it would have a much wider market year-round. The two partners followed the suggestion and produced and patented the first "La-Z-Boy Chair" in 1929. In that same year the company was incorporated as the Floral City Furniture Company, the name selected because Monroe was then known as the "Floral City" since it was the home of the world's two largest nurseries.

During the depression years of the 1930s, the chair was leased to established companies on a royalty basis, with Floral City retaining the rights for Monroe County. In 1938, a new mechanism was developed that was so revolutionary that new patents had to be secured. Floral City took back the patent in 1939 and continued to manufacture chairs through 1941. La-Z-Boy Chair Company was formed in 1941 to separate the production function from the merchandising activity. Beginning in 1942 and continuing through World War II, LZB produced seats for military vehicles and naval vessels.

In 1947, chair production began again and sales grew to $52.7 million by 1970. The first out-of-state plant was built in Newton, Mississippi, in 1961. Edward Knabusch, who died in 1988, continued as president of LZB until 1972, when he was succeeded by his son Charles. Edwin Shoemaker continues to be active in LZB as vice chairman of the board and executive vice president of engineering.

This case was prepared by Robert P. Crowner, associate professor of management of Eastern Michigan University, as a basis for class discussion. Copyright © 1988 by Robert P. Crowner. Distributed by the North American Case Research Association. All rights reserved to the author and the North American Case Research Association. Published with permission of the North American Case Research Association.

EXHIBIT 1

LA-Z-BOY CHAIR COMPANY
Income Statement
for Years Ending April 30
(in thousands of dollars)

	1983	1984	1985	1986	1987	1988
Net sales	$196,973	$254,865	$282,741	$341,656	$419,991	$486,793
Costs and expenses:						
Cost of sales	136,952	167,387	191,312	235,524	289,779	352,069
Selling, general, and administrative	38,595	45,962	54,713	65,610	85,469	91,354
Interest expense	1,031	963	1,146	1,570	1,877	4,008
Total	176,578	214,312	247,171	302,704	377,125	447,431
Operating income	20,395	40,553	35,570	38,952	42,866	39,362
Other income	2,062	3,037	3,117	2,807	2,081	2,662
Income before taxes	22,457	43,590	38,687	41,759	44,947	42,024
Income taxes:						
Federal:						
Current	237	14,790	9,201	14,797	19,558	17,931
Deferred	8,717	4,010	6,508	2,809	(1,175)	(4,832)
State	732	1,505	1,619	1,143	1,900	2,444
Total taxes	9,686	20,305	17,328	18,749	20,283	15,543
Net income	$ 12,771	$ 23,285	$ 21,359	$ 23,010	$ 24,664	$ 26,481
Net income per common share	0.69	1.16	1.17	1.26	1.34	1.45

Sales and Marketing

Sales and marketing are under the direction of Patrick H. Norton, senior vice president. Norton, who is 66 years old, joined LZB in September 1981, following a successful career with Ethan Allen, Inc. Exhibit 4 shows the organization chart for the upper management of LZB. In addition to the activities of advertising and sales communication, residential sales, contract sales, and sales for Burris Industries, the following activities also report to Norton: corporate interior design for Showcase Shoppes, national merchandising manager, sales and service administration, manufacturing services manager, sales and marketing research, product design, and store development for Showcase Shoppes. Norton's strategy is responsible for the dramatic expansion of LZB into the broader lines of furniture since he arrived. He believed that for LZB to continue to expand and be competitive it must offer a full line of furniture.

Sales.   Sales are divided into two broad categories. The Residential Division, which is by far the largest segment of the business, sells a complete line of reclining chairs and other upholstered chairs, sofas and sleep sofas, and modular seating groups. The Burris Division sells upscale upholstered furniture to the residential market, which is complemented by an extensive line of wooden occasional tables sold by the Hammary Division. Within these divisions traditional, transitional, and contemporary styles are sold.

The Contract Division sells desks, chairs, and credenzas to the general business market. The Rose Johnson Division complements the contract division by providing office panel walls, chairs, and work centers.

EXHIBIT 2

LA-Z-BOY CHAIR COMPANY
Balance Sheets
for Years Ending April 30
(in thousands of dollars)

	1983	1984	1985	1986	1987	1988
Current assets:						
Cash	$ 1,115	$ 3,220	$ 2,062	$ 2,419	$ 1,393	$ 2,207
Short-term investments	14,973	25,957	18,250	13,305	21,172	14,740
Receivables	70,762	79,557	92,167	106,638	116,952	135,560
Less allowances	2,140	2,300	2,445	2,814	3,118	4,976
Net receivables	68,622	77,257	89,722	103,824	113,834	130,584
Inventories						
Raw materials	11,463	11,992	12,209	15,305	19,541	24,522
Work in process	6,740	8,965	11,630	14,771	17,143	23,323
Finished goods	4,563	5,147	4,097	5,157	8,791	18,977
Total	22,766	26,104	27,936	35,233	45,475	66,822
Other current assets	452	585	2,985	3,229	5,037	5,085
Total current assets	107,928	133,123	140,955	158,010	186,911	219,438
Other assets	500	2,572	7,726	18,095	9,488	6,737
Fixed assets:						
Land	$ 1,954	$ 2,197	$ 2,344	$ 2,842	$ 3,586	$ 5,266
Buildings	28,853	31,316	37,314	44,088	52,782	64,637
Machinery	29,024	33,410	40,248	51,041	66,821	69,437
	59,831	66,923	79,906	97,971	123,189	139,340
Less depreciation	27,535	31,095	35,157	41,082	49,701	55,180
Net fixed assets	32,296	35,828	44,749	56,889	73,488	84,160
Goodwill						26,257
Total assets	$140,724	$171,523	$193,430	$232,994	$269,887	$336,592
Current liabilities:						
Notes payable			$ 1,077	$ 3,682	$ 6,099	$ 10,744
Current portion of long-term debt	$ 936	$ 1,098	1,087	1,717	979	7,039
Accounts payable	10,414	10,966	15,470	11,033	20,134	16,815
Payroll	6,173	7,987	8,265	13,144	15,941	16,046
Other liabilities	4,345	4,182	6,383	7,478	10,014	13,098
Income taxes	993	4,655	1,185	2,392	7,168	1,764
Deferred income taxes	6,649	9,321	12,016	12,196	11,241	6,868
Total cur. liab.	29,510	38,209	45,483	51,642	71,576	72,374
Long-term debt	11,763	13,222	11,165	24,463	23,270	76,215
Deferred income taxes	2,136	3,474	7,288	9,917	9,687	9,238
Equity:						
Common stock, $1 par value	18,641	18,641	18,641	18,641	18,641	18,641
Capital in excess of par value	5,168	5,540	5,514	5,783	6,054	6,493
Retained earnings	73,984	92,862	108,354	124,951	142,485	161,629
Currency adjustments	(131)	(271)	(654)	(659)	(449)	320
	97,662	116,772	131,855	148,716	166,731	187,083
Less treasury shares	347	154	2,361	1,744	1,387	8,318
Total equity	97,315	116,618	129,494	146,972	165,344	178,765
Total liabilities and equity	$140,724	$171,523	$193,430	$232,994	$269,877	$336,592

EXHIBIT 3   Acquisitions and Their Annual Sales

Burris Industries, Inc.—acquired July 1985	$10.6 million*
Rose Johnson, Inc.—acquired January 1986	$20.0 million
Hammary Furniture, Inc.—acquired September 1986	$22.0 million
Kincaid Furniture, Inc.—acquired January 1988	$85.0 million

*Sales in the year prior to acquisition.

Residential sales are carried out by 100 independent manufacturer's representatives who are under annual contract to sell the LZB line exclusively within their geographic area. These reps are paid by commission equivalent to 3 percent of direct shipments plus 2 percent from an incentive pool for performance against an order goal. The incentive begins when the rep reaches 70 percent of the goal and reaches the full 2 percent when 100 percent of the goal is attained. Sales in excess of the goal receive a commission of 7 percent. The established goal is based upon history and the corporate target regarding market share and growth. (The rep can protest the goal.) LZB's new sales strategy is to reduce the size of the exclusive territories, often limiting them to a county in populous areas. Therefore, over time, the number of reps has been increased. This is accomplished by only changing territories as existing reps retire or are dismissed.

The reps are managed by four regional managers—South Central, Eastern, Midwest, and Western. The regional managers spend two to three days per week on the road working with sales reps. The regional manager breaks the region's sales goal down into goals for individual sales reps. LZB has the right to interview and approve any "associates" whom the sales reps may hire to work with them.

The yearly sales goal is developed by using a demographic profile. Factors considered are age groups, racial groups (since minorities historically have purchased few chairs), home owner status (since the major market is home owners or those living in single-family dwellings), and furniture dollars spent within an area. The average customer is in the middle class, with chair customers being 35 and older as contrasted with sleeper customers being younger, newly married, and renters.

To determine each region's goal, a regional factor is applied. Marketing Statistics, a firm located in New York, is used to obtain a buying power index for each county as a percent of the total U.S. market. A separate index is used for recliners and for sleepers. The American Furniture Manufacturers Association collects and provides information about the industry. Industrial Marketing Research in Chicago provides quarterly and annual customer surveys which are useful. Sales for LZB are about equally divided between the first and second halves of its fiscal year.

Distribution for LZB is divided into three major categories. General furniture dealers account for about 50 percent of sales. The Gallery Program—which currently includes about 75 stores, 25 percent of the general furniture market, and is increasing—is featured with the general dealers. Under this program, the dealer must dedicate 3,500 square feet to LZB products, and LZB designs the area. The dealer is licensed on an open-end basis by location. Department stores, which do 20 percent of the total furniture business, have been a weak category for LZB. Department stores always want special pricing and LZB does not engage in discounting.

National accounts make up 10 percent of sales. The largest single account is Montgomery Ward, which is handled by the home office, but a 3 percent commission is paid the local sales rep for servicing the account. Most accounts are regional, such as Art Van in Detroit and Macy's.

EXHIBIT 4 Organization Chart, La-Z-Boy Chair Company

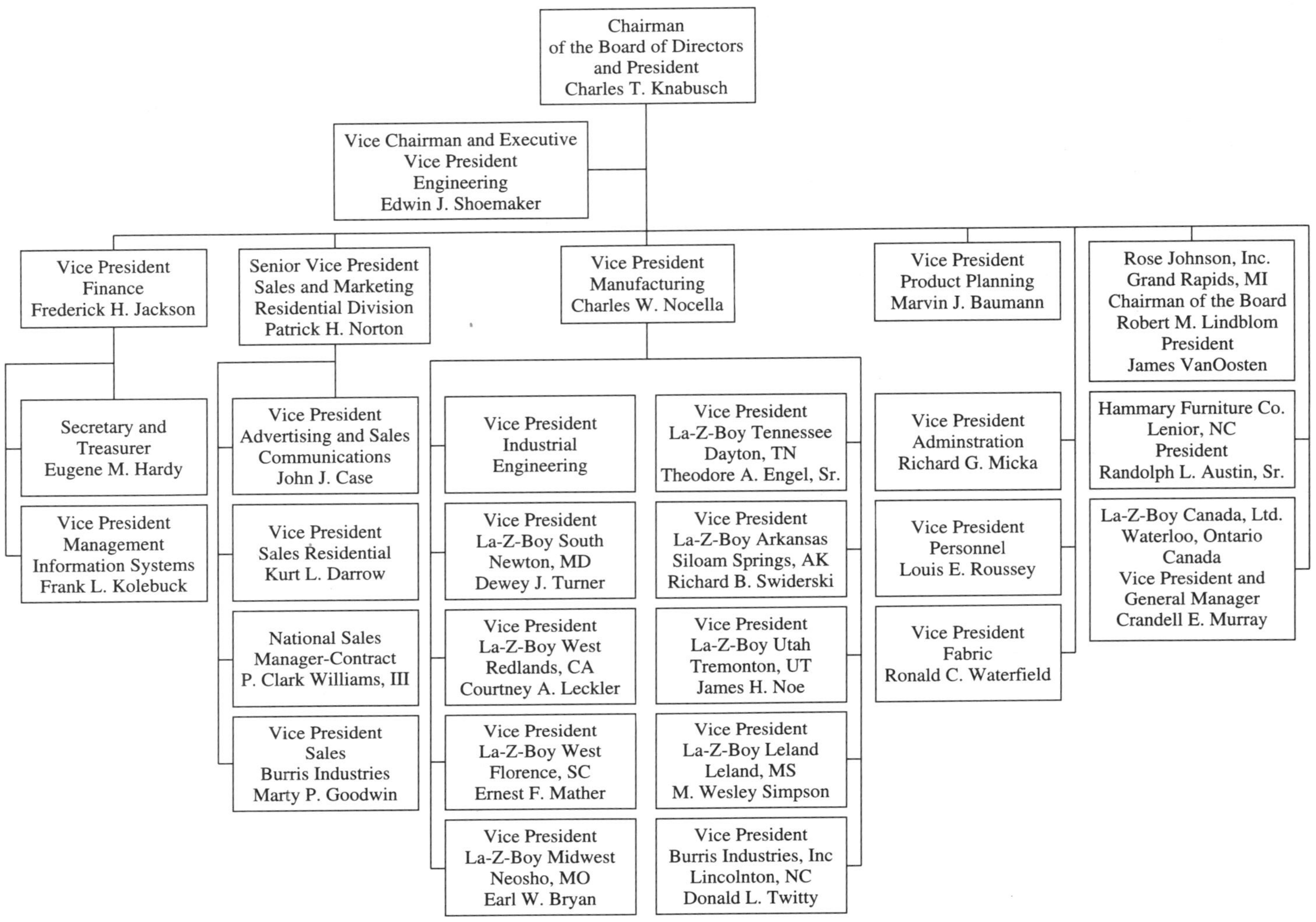

Chairman of the Board of Directors and President
Charles T. Knabusch

Vice Chairman and Executive Vice President Engineering
Edwin J. Shoemaker

Vice President Product Planning
Marvin J. Baumann

Vice President Adminstration
Richard G. Micka

Vice President Personnel
Louis E. Roussey

Vice President Fabric
Ronald C. Waterfield

Rose Johnson, Inc. Grand Rapids, MI
Chairman of the Board
Robert M. Lindblom
President
James VanOosten

Hammary Furniture Co. Lenior, NC
President
Randolph L. Austin, Sr.

La-Z-Boy Canada, Ltd. Waterloo, Ontario Canada
Vice President and General Manager
Crandell E. Murray

Vice President Manufacturing
Charles W. Nocella

Vice President La-Z-Boy Tennessee Dayton, TN
Theodore A. Engel, Sr.

Vice President La-Z-Boy Arkansas Siloam Springs, AK
Richard B. Swiderski

Vice President La-Z-Boy Utah Tremonton, UT
James H. Noe

Vice President La-Z-Boy Leland Leland, MS
M. Wesley Simpson

Vice President Burris Industries, Inc Lincolnton, NC
Donald L. Twitty

Vice President Industrial Engineering

Vice President La-Z-Boy South Newton, MD
Dewey J. Turner

Vice President La-Z-Boy West Redlands, CA
Courtney A. Leckler

Vice President La-Z-Boy West Florence, SC
Ernest F. Mather

Vice President La-Z-Boy Midwest Neosho, MO
Earl W. Bryan

Senior Vice President Sales and Marketing Residential Division
Patrick H. Norton

Vice President Advertising and Sales Communications
John J. Case

Vice President Sales Residential
Kurt L. Darrow

National Sales Manager-Contract
P. Clark Williams, III

Vice President Sales Burris Industries
Marty P. Goodwin

Vice President Finance
Frederick H. Jackson

Secretary and Treasurer
Eugene M. Hardy

Vice President Management Information Systems
Frank L. Kolebuck

563

LZB Showcase Shoppes, which number about 265, account for about 35 percent of sales. A Showcase Shoppe is licensed on an open-end basis by location. Location is everything—that is, the site should be located in an area where the city is growing, with a reasonable concentration of quality homes, apartments, or condominiums which are less than 15 years old within a seven-mile radius; the activity in the surrounding area should be conducive to retail activity; the street should be a heavily traveled major artery that is well known to everyone; the site should be readily visible and located near the street with maximum window frontage and should be easily accessible and convenient to shoppers; and the building should be free-standing. Small strip centers can be effective, but large strip centers or regional malls are ineffective. The minimum showroom size is 6,000 square feet, with the normal Shoppe expected to be 7,000 to 10,000, with an additional 1,500 to 2,400 square feet on-site area required for warehouse, office space, and so on. An initial investment of $132,000 is typical, of which $75,000 is required for working capital and the balance for capital improvements. LZB provides the Shoppe with an operating manual, which includes advice on advertising, personnel policies, freight, service, interior design, and signage.

Contract sales are handled through a different group of manufacturers's reps who do not handle LZB products exclusively. These reps typically have other employees working for them. Sales of subsidiaries are handled in a manner similar to the residential sales with their own reps.

Advertising.   John J. Case, vice president of advertising and sales communications, joined LZB in 1977 as assistant national accounts manager and progressed through several positions to his present one in 1985. He is responsible for all of LZB's national corporate advertising and public relations for the residential, office products, and Burris divisions, as well as the sales training program for dealer and sales representatives. He graduated from Michigan State University with a B.A. degree in telecommunications.

Prior to 1982, LZB spent money on corporate advertising and on retail advertising materials but had no control over its image in the local market-place. Its corporate image and its local image were not compatible. Retail outlets bought seasonally and promoted seasonally. As a result, manufacturing was adversely affected by the two peak sales periods in May and November.

Beginning in 1982, LZB began to regain control over its local image by combining "retail" and "corporate" budget strength, harnessing dealer advertising dollars, and maintaining the corporate message. To accomplish this, it was necessary to force advertising in March and September. This was done by creating four sales events a year, instead of the previous two for Father's Day and Christmas. A national LZB Recliner Sale in March and a Fall Sale in September were developed, which eventually smoothed out the manufacturing cycle.

Each sale was supported with national retail advertising that contained the dealer name and location in Sunday supplement magazines. These local supplements were supported by a heavy national television campaign. Alex Karras was used as an effective salesman in the ads. Not only did he have the obvious sports image for men but, even more important, he appealed to women who usually make the final decision when purchasing furniture. He seemed to have a friendly "teddy bear" image for women. In 1987, four 15-second TV spots, one for each sales event, were made by Alex, as well as the effective TV commercial called "Facts."

In addition to the national TV advertising and Sunday supplements, LZB provided dealers, who signed up for the sales event, with a Point-of-Sale Kit, including newspaper slicks, counter cards, hang tags, window banner, wall poster, and ceiling danglers. Colorful Hi-Fi preprints were available for each sale. A total of 16, 30-second radio spots which could be customized and the TV commercial "Facts" and the 15-second national TV spots could be ordered and tagged with the dealer's own message. LZB offered co-op advertising help for its participating dealers and offered four all-expenses–paid one-week trips for two to Hawaii to those who tied in with their local advertising and shared the results with LZB. In 1987, all of these plans were summarized in a 34-page, 11-inch by 14-inch colored Advertising Planning Calendar, which was sent to each of the 3,200 dealers. Co-op usage ran from 65 percent to 90 percent in recent years. Advertising expense for LZB runs about 3 percent of net sales.

In addition to these four major sales events, LZB promotes its full line of residential products in national home and family magazines. Ross Roy, Inc, located in Detroit, is the advertising agency used by LZB for its magazine and TV advertising.

Competition

There has been a consolidation going on within the furniture industry over the last few years, with the top 10 companies now controlling 33 percent of the market. Through a series of mergers many small and medium-sized companies have been absorbed into larger companies. Exhibit 5 shows statistics for the top 10 U.S. furniture manufacturers as of 1987, according to *Furniture/Today*, April 4, 1988. Exhibit 6 shows comparative ratios for LZB and the upholstered household furniture industry (SIC 2512) for the years 1984 through 1987.

The good results in 1987 are the result of several factors: a strong 1986 housing market, continued consumer confidence, the diversion of spending from a saturated automobile market, and an increase in furniture exports. The outlook for growth in the upholstered furniture business in 1988 and 1989 is about 3.2 percent annually, or about 1 percent in constant dollars, according to the American Furniture Manufacturers Association. The aging of the "baby boomers," which will be the fastest growing segment of the population between 1987 and 1992, should have a positive impact on consumer demand during those years. Further consolidation at the manufacturing level for furniture suppliers is expected in the future. These large firms are expected to use national multimedia advertising to create home-furnishing-company images in addition to individual brand-name identification.

Furniture exports increased 15 percent in 1987 after declining at a compound rate of 9 percent per year from 1981 to 1986. In contrast, furniture imports slowed for the third consecutive year. Taiwan, which is the largest foreign furniture supplier, experienced a competitive disadvantage when its currency appreciated against the dollar, causing a 24 percent decline in the value of the dollar. Even so, Taiwan was expected to increase its shipments to the United States to over the one billion mark in 1987. Strong furniture demand is being experienced in Canada, and the decline in the value of the dollar versus European and Japanese currencies has helped U.S. exports.

At the retail level, the major trend is clearly toward gallery programs, which were pioneered by Ethan Allen. Galleries are independent manufacturer-directed outlets or stand-alone displays in furniture or department stores. *Furniture/Today* estimated that there were 2,400 installed galleries by the end of 1986 and expected the number would increase to 5,700 by 1991. Shipments by manufacturers to galleries are expected to increase from 21 percent in 1986 to 43 percent in 1991. The increasing competition for retail floor space will require manufacturers to provide more support to the retailers.

According to a survey made in 1985 by *Better Homes & Gardens,* most customers

EXHIBIT 5   **Top 10 U.S. Furniture Manufacturers**

Rank*	Company	1987		1986	
		Revenues in $ Millions	*Market Share (%)*	*Revenues in $ Millions*	*Market Share (%)*
1	Interco St. Louis-based, publicly held conglomerate, powered by last April's acquisition of Lane (Action, Hickory Business Furniture, Hickory Chair, Hickory Tavern, HTB, Lane, Pearson, Royal Development, and Venture), became industry's first manufacturer to exceed $1 billion in furniture. Entered furniture arena in 1978–80 with purchase of Ethan Allen and Broyhill. Added Highland House in 1986.	$ 1,100	7.4%	$ 635	4.6%
2	Masco Since mid-1966 furniture entry, this publicly held, Detroit-based home products powerhouse has assembled, mainly through aggressive acquisition, an array of companies now including Baldwin Brass, Drexel Heritage, Frederick Edward, Henredon, Hickorycraft, La Barge Mirrors, Lexington (Dixie, Henry Link, Link-Taylor, and Young-Hinkle), Maitland-Smith, Marbro Lamp, Marge Carson, The Roberts Co., and Smith & Gaines.	600	4.0	335	2.4
3	La-Z-Boy Publicly held motion chair specialist, based in Monroe, MI, further broadened product reach with acquisition early this year of solid wood furniture maker Kincaid. Burris, Hammary, and Rose Johnson also acquired since mid-'80s. Revenues for 1987 include $85 million from Kincaid.	538	3.6	418	3.0
4	Mohasco Publicly held furniture/carpet company, relocated last year from Amsterdam, NY, to Fairfax, VA. Furniture operations are Chromcraft, Cort Furniture Rental, Mohasco Upholstered Furniture (Avon, Barcalounger, Stratford, Stratolounger, and Trendline), Monarch, Peters-Revington, and Super Sagless. Cort, a retail rental chain, accounts for about one-fifth of furniture revenues.	507	3.4	460	3.3
5	Bassett Broadly diversified, publicly held furniture company based in Bassett, VA. Divisions are Basset Bedding, Bassett Contract, Bassett Furniture, Commonwealth Contract, Impact, Montclair, MCI, National/Mt. Airy, and Weiman.	475	3.2	423	3.1

(continued)

(89.4 percent) shop at more than one store when buying furniture. The survey also showed that 58.2 percent of the customers took a month or more to make a purchase commitment. To get ideas before they bought, 75 percent said they shopped various stores. Decorating information was considered important to purchasers, although 90 percent said they did not hire an interior designer the last time they decorated their homes. About half admitted they needed advice. About 80 percent of married purchasers indicated that it was important for the spouse to be pleased and, therefore, they

EXHIBIT 5   (concluded)

Rank*	Company	1987		1986	
		Revenues in $ Millions	Market Share (%)	Revenues in $ Millions	Market Share (%)
6	Universal	399	2.7	191	1.4
	Publicly held wood furniture specialist, with Far East supply based and U.S. headquarters in High Point, NC, expanded into upholstery last year by acquiring Benchcraft and its casual dining unit, Cal-Style. Acquisition accounted for $162 million of 1987 sales.				
7	Ladd	387	2.6	379	2.7
	Publicly held, broadly diversified furniture company based in High Point, NC. Owns Lea, American Drew, Daystrom, American of Martinsville, Barclay, Clayton Marcus, Lea Lumber & Plywood, and Ladd Transportation.				
8	Armstrong	361	2.4	314	2.3
	Publicly held furniture/floorings/ceiling company based in Lancaster, PA. Furniture operations, based in Thomasville, NC, are Armstrong, Thomasville, Gilliam, and Westchester. Westchester, with about $12 million in annual sales, was acquired late last year.				
9	Chicago Pacific	245	1.7	111	0.8
	Publicly held, Chicago-based furniture/appliance company entered furniture in 1986 with purchase of Pennsylvania House, Kittinger, and McGuire. Last year, added over $100 million to volume with acquisition of contract specialist Gunlocke and summer-and-casual major Brown Jordan. Established Charter Group for hotel-motel market in January 1988.				
10	Sauder Woodworking	255	1.5	203	1.5
	Privately owned company based in Archbold, OH, specializes in ready-to-assemble furniture.				
	Top 10 total	$ 4,837	32.6%	$ 3,469	25.1%
	U.S. Industry total	$14,830	100%	$13,820	100%

*Ranked by total 1987 furniture revenues of companies or subsidiaries whose principal revenue source is household furniture manufacturing. Totals include all component, bedding, retail, or contract sales.

Notes:

Company revenue figures were compiled by *Furniture/Today* market research from financial statements of publicly held companies and other information supplied by authoritative industry sources. Totals reflect results of 1987 calendar year—except for Bassett (Nov. 30 fiscal year-end), La-Z-Boy (Jan. 23 trailing 12 months), and Interco (Feb. 29 fiscal year-end).

Totals for companies making acquisitions within past fiscal year are pro forma, including full 12-month revenues of companies acquired.

For market-share calculations, *F/T* used the recently revised estimates of U.S. Department of Commerce for shipments by producers of wood, upholstered, and metal household furniture, excluding bedding and contract furniture. The computations preceded any rounding of figures.

usually shopped together. Other data regarding furniture purchases are shown in Exhibits 7 and 8.

In a marketing research report in 1985 done by the Marketing Research Bureau, consumers raised ethical issues regarding in-store designers. They believed there was a potential conflict of interest in that the designer might be motivated by the desire to sell more furniture, rather than solving the customer's problems. The same survey indicated that the usual shopping procedure was for customers to visit their local home

EXHIBIT 6 Comparative Ratios: La-Z-Boy Chair Company versus Upholstered Household Furniture (SIC 2512) from Dun's Key Ratios

			1984	1985	1986	1987
NP / NW	%	Company	16.5	15.7	14.9	17.4
		Industry	14.3	13.3	16.1	14.3
NP / NS	%	Company	7.6	6.7	5.9	5.4
		Industry	2.8	2.4	3.1	3.0
NP / TA	%	Company	11.0	9.9	9.1	7.9
		Industry	7.7	6.3	7.9	7.1
CA / CD		Company	3.1	3.1	2.6	3.0
		Industry	2.1	2.2	2.3	2.1
Quick ratio		Company	2.5	2.4	2.0	2.1
		Industry	1.0	1.0	1.1	0.9
FA / NW	%	Company	34.6	38.7	44.4	55.2
		Industry	41.4	35.2	36.1	42.4
CD / INV	%	Company	162.8	146.6	157.4	108.3
		Industry	104.4	110.9	99.8	98.5
TD / NW	%	Company	49.4	58.5	63.2	97.4
		Industry	75.8	84.1	74.6	86.5
CD / NW	%	Company	35.1	35.1	43.3	47.4
		Industry	59.7	59.1	52.5	58.4
NS / NW		Company	2.2	2.3	2.5	3.2
		Industry	5.3	5.5	5.2	4.8
NS / NWC		Company	3.0	3.2	3.6	3.3
		Industry	8.5	8.1	8.2	8.8
NC / INV		Company	10.1	9.7	9.2	7.3
		Industry	9.6	10.1	10.3	10.5
TA / NS	%	Company	68.4	68.2	64.3	69.1
		Industry	33.1	34.5	31.6	30.5
C.P.	Days	Company	115.8	110.9	98.9	97.9
		Industry	27.7	30.3	29.0	27.2
AP / NS	%	Company	5.5	3.2	4.8	3.5
		Industry	4.6	46.3	4.0	4.3

Note: La-Z-Boy's fiscal year is changed to the previous calendar year above.

furnishing dealer, obtain numbers of the desired furniture, and then buy the furniture from discount outlets at a substantially lower price.

Unlike LZB, the competing brands of Action Chair, which is a division of Lane Chair, LZB's largest competitor, specialize in selling through department stores. Department stores like to have exclusives, which is one of the reasons LZB does not use them as dealers. Most of LZB's competitors are not fully integrated in manufacturing and typically buy their mechanisms from Leggett & Platt, Super Sagless, or Hoover.

Manufacturing

Charles W. Nocella, vice president of manufacturing, is responsible for the extensive manufacturing organization shown in Exhibit 4, which includes all plants except the Waterloo, Canada, plant and those for Rose Johnson, Kincaid, and Hammary. In addition to the activities shown, Nocella is responsible for purchasing, safety, and traffic. The plants operate quite autonomously under the direction of a vice president in each

EXHIBIT 7   Influences on Buying, La-Z-Boy Chair Company

Influences on Buying: Although consumers cite price as the "most difficult" factor about buying furniture, construction, comfort and durability are considered to be stronger influences in the furniture buying decision.

	Very Important	Somewhat Important
Construction	85.3%	14.7%
Comfort	93.8	6.0
Durability	87.3	12.3
Fabric	68.0	31.0
Finish on wooden parts	64.4	32.2
Styling/design	65.2	32.9
Soil- and stain-resistant fabrics	67.3	30.3
Material used	65.7	31.3
Guarantee/warranty	59.1	36.1
Retailer's reputation	39.5	46.9
Size	52.6	40.9
Manufacturer's reputation	45.9	42.8
Price	59.4	35.6
Brand name	26.0	56.5
Delivery time	21.9	44.4
Decorator/designer	7.5	29.6

Shopping Activities: Before making a furniture purchase, 75 percent of consumers visited home furnishings stores for ideas. It tops activities leading to a final selection.

Shopped stores to get ideas	75.0%
Watched local newspaper ads for furniture	59.6
Looked in a Sears, Penney, or Ward catalog to check prices	39.4
Looked in a manufacturer's catalog I have (such as one for Ethan Allen, Pennsylvania House, etc.)	37.0
Got suggestions from friends, relatives, etc.	27.6
Clipped manufacturers' ads and tried to locate a specific piece of furniture	16.3
Telephoned different local stores about prices and brands	15.9
Talked to a decorator from a local store	13.9
Sent for manufacturers' brochures featured in magazine ad	12.0
Talked to a decorator other than one in store	7.7
Called "800" toll-free number to see what local store carried a certain brand	2.6
Other	2.4
No answer	2.6

Quality Measures: Construction features are considered by consumers to be the best measure of quality of a piece of furniture.

Construction features (coil construction, joint construction, etc.)	87.3%
Brand name	68.5
Finish on wood surface	61.1
Price	28.4
Salesperson's recommendation	23.1
Friends' and relatives' recommendations	22.4
Just by looks	18.3
Other	2.6
No answer	0.2

*Source: *Better Homes & Gardens.*

plant. The 14 plants employ about 6,650 people, with a combined floor space of 4,536,000 square feet. Much of this floor space was constructed quite recently—527,800 in 1987, 74,000 in 1985, and 120,000 in 1984, plus the additions made through acquired companies. A listing of the plants is shown in Exhibit 9, with pertinent information as of April 25, 1987.

LZB manufacturing is characterized by backward integration. Lumber for the furniture framing is purchased from sawmills and kiln dried at the plants. LZB makes its own chair mechanisms and purchases its sleeper mechanisms from Leggett & Platt. Metal for the recliner mechanisms is purchased in coils, and the parts made at the plants. Fabric is purchased direct from the mills in large quantities to fulfill the needs of all plants. It is received, stored, and shipped from the Fabric Processing Center in Florence, South Carolina, to all plants for use in upholstering. The center has automated storage and is controlled by computer, so little manpower is required to operate this centralized facility.

EXHIBIT 8   **Information Sources for Furniture Purchases, La-Z-Boy Chair Company**

Information Sources: Consumers rate magazines (65.9 percent) as the most important source of information in planning home furnishings purchases. Magazines are closely followed by regular newspaper advertisements (65.7 percent).

	Very Important	Somewhat Important	Neither Important nor Unimportant	Somewhat Unimportant	Very Unimportant	No Answer
Advertisements or circulars that are delivered to your home	9.4%	45.0%	29.7%	6.0%	7.0%	2.9%
Advertisement supplements or circulars which are included in your Sunday newspaper	12.7	52.7	22.6	4.3	4.8	2.9
Regular newspaper advertisements in your Sunday newspaper	11.3	54.4	24.0	4.3	2.6	3.4
Regular newspaper advertisements in your daily newspaper	9.4	49.3	29.8	3.8	2.9	4.8
Magazine ads	14.9	51.0	26.2	3.1	4.8	2.9
Catalogs	14.2	49.8	23.6	4.3	3.1	5.0
Radio advertisements	2.2	23.3	43.3	14.9	9.1	7.2
TV advertisements	5.5	34.7	38.9	9.4	6.0	5.5
Friends' and neighbors' opinions	16.8	36.3	26.9	6.5	7.2	6.3

Buying Factors: Price is the "most difficult" factor about buying furniture for the home, according to a *BH&G* consumer panel.

Cost of furniture	52.9%
Determining quality	30.3
Choosing a style	21.9
Choosing a fabric	15.9
Choosing a color	11.8
Other	1.9
No answer	1.0

Source: *Better Homes & Gardens.*

EXHIBIT 9   **Manufacturing Plants, La-Z-Boy Chair Company**

Location	Floor Space (square feet)	Operations Conducted	Built	Employees
Monroe, MI	215,200	Home office, research, and development	1941	415
Newton, MS*	464,200	Recliners, rockers, and hospital seating	1961	678
Redlands, CA	179,900	Assembly of recliners and rockers	1967	289
Florence, SC*	407,900	Recliners and hospital seating	1969	801
Florence, SC	48,400	Fabric processing center and parts warehouse	1975	19
Neosho, MO*	473,400	Residential and contract furniture	1969	992
Dayton, TN	564,200	Recliners, sofas, sleepers, and modular seating	1973	1,076
Siloam Springs, AK	189,600	Recliners and sleepers	1943	246
Tremonton, UT*	402,400	Recliners and contract	1979	617
Leland, MS*	153,500	Desks and contract	1985†	130
Waterloo, OT	209,800	Recliners, rockers, sofas, and contract	1979†	412
Lincolnton, NC	379,000	Upholstered furniture	1986†	299
Grand Rapids, MI	428,000	Manufactures office furniture and panels	1986†	223
Lenoir, NC	420,800	Upholstered products, case goods, and hospitality furniture	1986†	453
Praire, MS	453,800	Distribution center and small parts warehouse	1986†	6
Hudson, NC	730,000	Solid wood bedroom and dining room furniture	1987*	1,427

*These plants and the Fabric Processing Center at Florence are leased on a long-term basis. All other plants are owned by LZB.
†Year acquired as a result of purchasing a company.

LZB's manufacturing philosophy could be characterized as rather conservative. LZB usually waits until a new technique is thoroughly perfected before beginning to use it. For instance, computerized cutting of fabric at the plants was only instituted within the last two years, even though the concept had been around for over 10 years. The punch presses and methods used in the pressrooms in the plants have not been updated in the last 20 years.

The manufacturing process is twofold, involving both wood and metal. The wooden parts are manufactured from kiln-dried hardwood lumber. The raw boards are brought into the wood room, where they go through the ripsaw operation. Here, the lumber is cut into predetermined lengths, with the knotholes and major blemishes being removed. Only the good portions of the lumber are used. An 80 percent yield is strived for, but 65 to 70 percent is normally attained.

Following cutting, the wood pieces go through a series of planing, squaring, and sizing operations. Then the pieces are measured and glued together, parallel to the long side to provide wood slabs, which are again trimmed and cut into the final subassembly sections. From here, the pieces go through a series of operations, which include drilling dowel holes, contouring specific shapes on band saws, and sanding. Wood assembly is the final operation, wherein the various pieces are doweled, glued, and pressed together into frames. These wooden frames are then ready for subassembly with metal parts.

The metal parts are produced in the punch press room, where coils and strips of unhardened steel are run through dies to produce engineered components. The metal parts are not heat-treated because hardness is not required, but some must be painted if they will be visible on the final product. The metal parts are then riveted together as required and go to the "metal-up" department, where they are assembled. The metal parts are then combined with the wooden parts to form a subassembly ready to be upholstered in the "frame-up" department. The marriage of metal and wood working together as one unit is what has provided LZB with its quality reputation.

None of the plants—except Monroe, Michigan; Florence, South Carolina; and Waterloo, Ontario—are unionized, which is unusual in the upholstered furniture industry. Factory workers have been paid on a piecework concept from the beginning. Typically, one employee upholsters the seat and back of a chair and a second employee does the body, since there are too many styles for one employee to do the whole chair. A base rate is paid based on local wage surveys, but each employee has the opportunity to make quite a bit more depending on the number of pieces produced.

Each plant employs two to four time-study engineers to keep the piece rates up to date. Normal time was changed to 150 percent to facilitate the 150 percent normal performance. The company's policy is never to retime a job just because people are making money on the standard rate. Rather, jobs are retimed when there has been a change in methods or design. A complaint procedure is in place, so anyone can grieve a rate he or she believes is unfair. One rule of thumb is that the rate is good if the standard for the day can be made in five hours. Employees are reluctant to change jobs, because it temporarily cuts into their incentive performance.

LZB is very committed to quality, which is made somewhat trickier to accomplish by the incentive program. Constant vigilance is required by supervision. Piece rates are only paid for producing the item once—employees must rework their defective production on their own time. Each part is distinctively marked by the employee, so it can be traced back to him if a quality problem develops. There is about one inspector for every 125 chairs produced per day. A typical plant produces 1,200 to 1,300 chairs per day and some produce 300 to 400 sleeper sofas per day. A rule of thumb for planning purposes is one and three-quarter chairs can be produced per man day. One employee can upholster about 10 chairs per day and another employee can frame 15 per day.

Products are basically produced to order, with only about 2.5 percent made for inventory. There is a 14-week window used for computer scheduling in Monroe by the manufacturing services manager. Two weeks before the product is to be in its shipping box, the fabric is shipped to the plant and subsequently cut. For actual plant scheduling, order tickets are used, which are accumulated for individual items in the same style. Fabrics are grouped by a lay (40 sheets of fabric) for cutting of a given pattern. Sometimes different fabrics can be combined, but stripes and plaids have to be cut separately. The optimum layout of pieces on a sheet of fabric is determined by the pattern layout department via computer transmission from Monroe. The material is actually cut by CNC (computer numerical control) equipment in the plant. Foremen meet informally each morning at each plant to develop a mutually beneficial daily schedule. The foremen of cutting and sewing work together to balance the load in sewing. Most dealers do not want to receive an early shipment, so the shipping schedule is the controlling element.

As stated before, each plant operates quite autonomously and often with a unique management style. LZB does not have a strong corporate policy regarding management, but in general it is loosely knit, and with a friendly small-town atmosphere. Edward Knabusch's philosophy was "to treat people like people." The style could be said to be somewhere between participative and authoritarian, although some of the most successful plants are more authoritarian.

Product Planning and Development

Marvin J. Baumann, vice president for product planning and development, is responsible for product development, product engineering, and the mechanical engineering and test laboratories, all of which employ 75 people. Development has been aided by product development's use of CAD/CAM. LZB is somewhat unique in its industry in that it extensively tests its products. Recently an independent testing lab (ETL) was added to test such products as the Lectra-Lounger and the Lectra-Lift Chair.

All product designs are developed internally. A natural process for design is utilized; an idea is developed, the parts are framed, an approval process is followed leading to final approval, and then the design is implemented at the plants with appropriate training. New versions of the reclining mechanism are being developed, since the patent has expired. New ideas for furniture design are often found through sales and marketing techniques like consumer demand surveys, furniture markets, and travel into Europe. In fact, the most popular current style of chair is the Eurostyle, the plush overstuffed look. Competitors have the impression that LZB overengineers its products, but LZB believes that good engineering can only result in good quality. An annual review of LZB's products with the vendors is made. Cost, styling, and convenient transportation are considered in developing a new style. The removable-back reclining chair is an example of convenient transportation, because the back can be separated from the rest of the frame, allowing more chairs to be loaded on a truck.

Once a style is approved, technicians use computerized pattern layout systems to generate the cutting patterns for upholstery fabrics. The objective is to minimize waste by maximizing the number of pattern pieces attainable from a given sheet of fabric. The resulting patterns become part of an electronic library store in the company's central computer. On demand, digitized cutting instructions are downloaded to fabric cutting machines at LZB's plants. Currently, some 700 patterns are available online. A subsequent step will be to upload data from the cutting machines to analyze actual efficiencies.

Fabric Department

LZB is unique in the industry in that it has a separate fabric department. This department has provided special attention to purchasing attractive, durable fabrics for upholstering. LZB uses about 11 million yards of fabric per year to produce 7,140 units per day. At any one time LZB has a fabric purchasing commitment of 6.4 million yards on hand or on order.

LZB has five committees to make fabric decisions. These committees are the following: chairs and sofas, office furniture for contract sales, Rose Johnson, Burris, and LZB Canada, which is separated because color trends and style are about 18 months behind the United States. While the look of the fabric is important, of even greater importance is the production practicality of the fabric. A fabric is tested for nominal wear and the minimum standards for a fabric must be surpassed after color or pattern have been determined. Fabric lines are reviewed twice a year for all product divisions except the Contract Division, which is reviewed annually.

Finance

Frederick H. Jackson, vice president of finance, who is 60 years old, has been a director of LZB since 1971 and was the treasurer prior to election to vice president in 1983. Reporting to Jackson are the secretary and treasurer, the vice president of management information systems, and the director of corporate taxes.

LZB has a very conservative financial philosophy. The balance sheet is stated conservatively (i.e., assets are written down rapidly). Contingency liabilities, such as warranties, are shown on the balance sheet. All cash discounts on accounts payable are taken but not paid earlier than necessary. The current ratio has historically been in the 3 to 4 range, with 2 as a minimum. The current debt-to-equity ratio target has been not to exceed 40 percent.

Cash management has become more important in recent years. Gene Hardy, the treasurer, believes cash management is an art and forecasts cash receipts by month for a year's period. He is shooting for a weekly forecast. Short-term investments are made in certificates of deposits and commercial paper, with the overriding concept being not to risk the principal. He deals with the banks with whom LZB has a working relationship—National Bank of Detroit, Manufacturers Bank, Monroe Bank and Trust, Mellon Bank of Pittsburgh, and First Union Bank of North Carolina. Working capital is forecasted on a corporate basis.

Normal terms of sale are 2 percent, 30 days, net 45 days, but only 15 percent of LZB's sales are made on this basis. The four sales events each year are billed with a 2 percent discount at 90 to 120 days as determined by the sales department. Nine people follow up on delinquent accounts after they are 15 days past due. At 30 days past due a letter is sent requesting payment within 10 days. Continuing problem accounts are put on a credit hold and eventually submitted to Dun & Bradstreet for collection and are written off the books at that time. In May of 1988 approximately 9.5 percent of the accounts were overdue, and the figure has been as high as 11 percent at Christmas. Accounts are noted by one of four different risk codes to facilitate credit management.

Capital expenditures are evaluated by using the payback method, with two to three years being considered an acceptable payback. The internal rate of return (IRR) is calculated, but LZB does not have a hurdle (minimum) rate that projects must meet. A Request for Authorization form is made out for each project, including a narrative with plants being able to approve up to $5,000, corporate officers approving up to $100,000, and the board of directors approving all expenditures over $100,000. Capital expenditures are projected for a three-year period by plant.

Budgets are made up for each plant by the treasurer, with input from the plants for the last eight years. The individual departments in the plants typically have only limited involvement in the budgeting process.

Inventory is stated on a LIFO basis. Semiannual physical inventories are taken. Cycle counts are taken of fabric at the Fabric Center. Inventory turns are measured for lumber and fabric, which are maintained on a perpetual inventory basis. LZB is moving in the direction of setting guidelines for inventory levels at the plants. Kincaid, which was acquired in January 1988, builds inventory to stock while most LZB divisions build to order.

The general, selling, and administrative expenses are running at 20 percent of sales, which is considered alarming by the treasurer. However, commissions are 5 percent or a quarter of the total. He would like to see the figure in the 15 percent to 16 percent range.

LZB paid $53 million to acquire the stock of Kincaid Furniture Company, Inc. The book value of Kincaid's assets at the time of purchase was $27 million. As a part of the net assets acquired, Kincaid had $12 million in debt.

Management

The chairman of the board and president is Charles Knabusch, who is the son of one of the founders of LZB and is 48 years old. He has been a director of the company since 1970. He literally grew up with LZB and has been a part of the growth and maturing of the company. He has been described as a "shirt-sleeves manager."

The board of directors is composed of six inside members and four outside members, as noted in Exhibit 10.

Approximately 30 percent of the common stock is controlled by the Monroe Bank & Trust, of which about half belongs to the founders. The Knabusch family owns about 13.4 percent of the common stock and Edwin Shoemaker owns about 6.6 percent. Other officers and directors own 0.7 percent.

EXHIBIT 10   LZB Board of Directors

Director	Position
Charles T. Knabusch	Chairman and president
Edwin J. Shoemaker	Executive vice president of engineering
Gene M. Hardy	Treasurer and secretary
Frederick H. Jackson	Vice president of finance
Patrick H. Norton	Senior vice president, sales and marketing
Lorne G. Stevens	Vice president of manufacturing, retired
Warren W. Gruber	Retail businessman
David K. Hehl	Public accountant
Rocque E. Lipford	Attorney
John F. Weaver	Executive vice president of Monroe Bank & Trust

LZB believes in treating each employee as an important person. The fact that LZB has labor unions at only 2 of its 11 plants attests that this policy works and is appreciated by the employees. LZB believes that the values of the manager make the company. Time is taken out of the busy schedules to make other people feel good. Programs to keep communication flowing between employees and management are stressed, such as "Lunch with the Boss." Vacant positions within the company are posted and employees may apply for the position. Most of management has been with the LZB for an extended time, having been promoted from within.

Supervisory, technical, and clerical employees are paid by rating jobs using a point factor method. Jobs are matched against common factors, such as education, related experience, mental skill, human relations responsibility, complexity and impact of work decisions, and necessity for accuracy. Employees are evaluated regularly on achievement of their department's mission statement and how the goals were achieved. To foster continued individual growth, required training is used to equip people to rotate into new positions.

LZB is committed to the concept of incentive pay. Factory workers are paid on a piece rate concept. Office workers are included in profit sharing and receive merit pay based on performance. Executives and middle managers receive bonuses for quality work. All employees have a comprehensive benefit plan, including paid vacations, health and dental insurance, prescription medicine program, term life insurance, and a defined benefit retirement plan.

The Future

Forbes magazine in its February 22, 1988, issue ran an article entitled "Takeover Bait?" in which it listed LZB as one of 22 likely prospects for a takeover. It fits the picture of high cash reserves, low debt, a low price/earnings ratio, and a strong cash flow from operating income. Is LZB worried? Gene Hardy says such defense measures as staggered three-year terms for directors and 67 percent stockholder vote required for approval of any merger are already in place. Perhaps most important is the distribution of stock among family and friends, although a leveraged buyout could occur under the right circumstances. The price range for LZB stock for recent years is shown in Exhibit 11.

As might be expected, Charles Knabusch does not wish LZB to be acquired. He said, "We are happy doing our thing, our way." His goals for the company are to continue growing while remaining profitable. But how is this to be accomplished in an industry that is becoming increasingly concentrated and with a stable but aging population?

EXHIBIT 11 Price Range of LZB Stock

Fiscal Year	*Price Range*
1983	2⅝–7⅞
1984	7⅞–12⅛
1985	6¾–10⅝
1986	10⅞–16⅞
1987	15⅝–20⅛
1988	13⅛–22⅝

On a clear but cool day in mid-January, Dan Shay, co-owner and manager of Bear Creek Golf Range, stood looking out over his golf range where two hearty golfers were taking their swings. Turning to his partner, George Patton, he observed,

> Well, George, at this time last year, we were on top of the world with our plans for the new golf range. Here we are a year later and things aren't nearly so rosy. We're starting our second year in the business and, let's face it, we didn't come close to meeting our objectives last year. In fact, if we don't do a lot better this year, we'll probably go under, which will cost us both a lot of money. However, I'm not ready to throw in the towel. We had some significant start-up problems in our first year, and we didn't do the business that we expected, but we're still here and I think we have a chance to turn things around. But we sure have to figure out how to attract a lot more customers in '94.

Background of the Golf Range

Bear Creek Golf Range, the newest range in the Dallas/Fort Worth area, opened for business the previous May. Dan Shay, the owner and manager, was a professional golfer who had recently retired from active tournament play. Dan graduated from Wake Forest University in 1973, where he was a member of the varsity golf team. Upon graduating, he decided to turn professional. He played on the tour for several years and his career earnings were quite respectable. When a wrist injury forced him to retire in 1990, he had saved enough money to invest in his own business venture. Many retired golf professionals chose to continue on as golf course pros at private courses, but Dan felt that he would have more independence and a higher income potential if he ran his own business. Reflecting on his career shortened by an injury, Dan observed, "If I can't make it as the best golf tour player, I will try to become the best golf teacher." Over the years, he had been quite successful as a golf instructor and had earned recognition as one of the most knowledgeable PGA Class A professionals in America. He had been actively involved with Junior Golf in the North Texas area and had received many awards for his efforts. Not surprisingly, Dan's business interests focused on utilizing his experience and abilities in the area of golf instruction.

Dan was approached in early 1991 by his long-time friend and fellow PGA professional, George Patton, about the possibility of jointly starting their own golf driving range in the Dallas/Fort Worth area. Dan felt that this was an ideal opportunity to combine his interest in golf and golf instruction with a promising business undertaking. Although Dan and George were to be equal investors and partners in the business, George was to continue to compete on the tour while Dan assumed responsibilities for managing the day-to-day operations of the business. As they considered the requirements for success in this business, they felt that they had the necessary qualifications.

This case has been prepared by Ray Keyes, associate professor of marketing, and Donna Moore, student, Boston College. The situation is based on an actual business experience.

c c   They had excellent golfing backgrounds, genuine knowledge of the game, and good
contacts in the golfing community to go along with their experience as golfing instructors. Also, they had between them adequate financial resources. They were confident
that they could even raise additional funds if necessary.

In discussing their ideas for the new driving range, the partners agreed that they
should focus on serious golfers who were interested in improving their golfing skills
Product   through practice and instruction. The range would cater to these serious golfers by pro-
Mix   viding first-class facilities (driving range and hitting areas), high-quality equipment
(clubs, balls, and merchandise), and professional services (lessons, club repair, advice,
and assistance). This driving range would establish an image as "the professional golfing center" run by professionals. The partners agreed that they were not interested in
attracting customers who enjoyed golf as a form of entertainment. They referred to
these golfers as "Yahoos." Their observations of other driving ranges led them to feel
that the Yahoos were more trouble than they were worth. They tended to be loud, dis-
ruptive, very hard on equipment, and often less concerned with developing skills than
with showing off. As Dan observed, "We can really do without the aggravations."

In weighing the driving range potential, the partners were aware of the growing interest in golf nationally and in the Dallas/Fort Worth area in particular. On the national
level, the $40 billion golf market (golf and related products and services) enjoyed an
estimated annual growth rate of 5 percent. The growth rate had been even higher in the
Dallas/Fort Worth area because of the availability of golf courses, practice facilities,
and the warm weather found there nine months of the year. The Dallas/Fort Worth
Metroplex was one of the fastest growing metropolitan areas in America. There were
86 private and municipal golf courses in the area, and several of these were new. All
courses had high memberships and many had long waiting lists. The increase in population of Dallas/Fort Worth, the increase in beginner golfers (up 15 percent since
1980), and the warm climate led the partners to conclude that this could be a very
healthy opportunity area for a golf-related business.

Dan and George decided to proceed with the driving range business. They were fortunate in identifying a 22-acre plot of land on an access road to Route 183, the connecting highway between Dallas and Fort Worth. They agreed that this would be a
good location because it was midway between the two cities and very close to the Dal-
las/Fort Worth International Airport. The people who used the highway were primarily
people living in the surrounding suburban townships of Irving, Bedford, Grapevine,
Euless, Arlington, Grand Prairie, Hurst, and Coppell. Many of these people worked in
either Dallas or Fort Worth and traveled regularly on Route 183. In addition, the Route
183 access road connected with the International Parkway leading to the International
Airport. The partners estimated that their golf range would draw people within a 10-
mile radius (population 777,082). There were 15 golf courses in this market area, public and private.

The Plan

After considering several locations, the partners decided to purchase the 22-acre piece
of property on Route 183 (with an option to purchase the adjacent 10-acre piece of
land). They secured a mortgage on the property and set about developing their plan.
First, they visited a number of driving ranges in the state to get ideas. Then they identified the facilities and services that they felt would be most appropriate for the kind of
professional range that they had in mind. The plan included the following facilities and
services.

Facilities and Equipment

- A first-class driving area with quality grass for the range, several target greens, distance flags, and a system of trees and fencing around the outer rim of the range. The back tree-lined boundary would be 300 yards from the driving tees.
- Thirty-five individual hitting areas (tees) with Astroturf mats. Six of these tees would be set aside as a teaching area. The teaching area was to include a sand trap.
- Video equipment for instructional purposes.
- An awning to cover 12 of the hitting areas for golfers to use in inclement weather.
- A top-quality putting green for lessons and practice.
- Hitting areas and range to be lit for night use.
- A permanent clubhouse-style building including

    customer service counter

    snack bar/restaurant with tables and chairs

    business office

    video game area

    bulletin boards

    sink and toilets (indoor plumbing)

    merchandise sales area (Pro Shop) where they would sell items (gloves, balls, spikes, golf shirts, sweatshirts, etc.) at lower prices than the typical golf course pro shop

    picture windows that look out over the tees and the driving range
    public telephones

- A paved parking area (for approximately 30 cars).
- A lighted sign visible from Route 183 (both lanes).
- Landscaping and decorative shrubbery.

Services

- PGA instruction (individual and group lessons).
- Custom club-fitting and repair.
- Advice and ordering of merchandise (clubs, bags, etc.).

Exhibit 1 provides a sketch of the facility as they planned it, and Exhibit 2 shows their financial development plan.

Competitive Situation.   The partners reviewed the competitive situation in their market area. There were two full-service golf ranges and two limited-service ranges within the 10-mile radius. The two full-sevice ranges were very different from one another and each offered a significant competitive threat to the Bear Creek Range. The largest of the two, Greenbrier Golf Range, was a full-service range with 40 hitting areas, a putting green, two golf instructors, a full-service snack bar (with hot dogs, hamburgers, sandwiches, cold drinks, etc.), and a retail golf equipment and supplies shop. Although the proprietors of the Greenbrier were not recognized PGA golfing pros, they were both experienced and knowledgeable golf enthusiasts known to be good instructors. The driving range and buildings were well constructed, and everything about

EXHIBIT 1   Bear Creek Golf Range

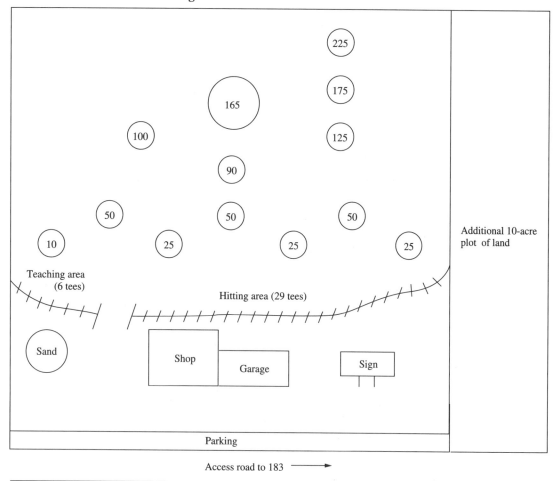

the operation was first class. It was not unusual to see long lines, especially on summer evenings and weekends when the waits could run as long as an hour. At these busy times, some golfers became impatient and went to one of the other golf ranges in the area where there were no waiting lines. Although there were no published figures on Greenbrier's profitability, it was generally believed that they were quite profitable.

The second successful driving range, the Golfarama Golfing Center, was located closer to Dallas, where it appealed to the less serious golfers with its entertainment-oriented facility. The facility included a driving range with 30 hitting areas, a pitch-and-putt area, and an 18-hole miniature golf course. Golfarama also attracted good crowds on summer evenings and weekends, but waiting was not as much of a problem because of the other activities to engage in while waiting for open tees. In fact, significant numbers of people came specifically to play miniature golf and the other games. Golfarama was located next to the Bowlarama Bowling Center (owned by the same company) which featured 10 bowling alleys, six pool tables, and a video game arcade. They had added an indoor/outdoor pitching machine and batting cage. The Golfarama/Bowlarama complex also featured a restaurant and a separate sports bar

EXHIBIT 2

FINANCIAL DEVELOPMENT PLAN
Bear Creek Golf Range
for Year Ending December 31, 1993

	Planned	Actual
Sources of Net Working Capital		
Net income	$ 50,000	($ 24,942)
Depreciation	500	500
Long-term debt	240,000	240,000
Owner/manager input (Shay)	100,000	100,000
Partner input (Patton)	100,000	100,000
Total sources	$ 490,500	$ 415,558
Applications of Net Working Capital		
Procurement of land	$ 180,000	$ 180,000
Land clearing	10,000	12,000
Installation of electricity	5,000	5,790
Installation of water main, pipes	4,000	4,200
Auto parking area (paved)	18,750	5,400
Construction of building	165,000	75,000
Fairway construction (grading, etc.)	30,000	40,000
Toilet and septic tank	9,500	2,000
Lights for night range play	8,000	8,450
Practice putting green	10,000	0
Equipment	20,000	22,000
Signs	12,800	4,250
Awning	3,000	0
Landscaping (trees, shrubs, fencing)	13,500	2,000
Drainage system (additional)	0	40,000
Total applications	$ 489,550	$ 401,090
Increase in net working capital	$ 950	$ 14,468

that was quite popular with the younger sports crowd. As the Golfarama Center was part of the overall entertainment complex, it was difficult to determine its profitability. However, the parent company for this national chain of franchise recreation centers was regularly reporting growth in units, sales, and profits.

The other two driving ranges, the Hit 'Em Out Range and the Discount Driving Range, were both minimum operations. They were cleared fields with some crude hitting areas, inexpensive balls and clubs, and low prices.

At various times during the summer and fall months, Dan Shay and/or one of his employees would scout the competition to observe their levels of business activity. On the basis of these observations, Dan was able to develop some estimates of the hitting area usage and the market shares for the five golf ranges in his market area. Exhibit 3 presents a summary of these business activity estimates and a review of the facilities and services offered by each of the driving ranges.

Pricing. Dan noted that price elasticity in the golf range business varied depending on the kind of golfing customer. Serious golfers tended to be less price-sensitive and more willing to pay a higher price if the facilities and instruction were superior. The

EXHIBIT 3 **Area Golf Ranges**

	Greenbrier	Golfarama	Bear Creek	Hit 'Em Out	Discount
Total number of tees	40	30	35	24	20
Tees available for lessons	6	—	6	—	—
Price per bucket balls	$7.50/100	$6.00/100	$6.50/90	$4/100	$4/100
Individual lessons* (3/4 hr.)	$25	—	$60	—	—
Group lessons† (3–6)	$15	—	$20	—	—
Paved parking	yes	yes	gravel	dirt	gravel
Putting green	yes	—	—	—	—
Covered hitting area	yes	yes	—	—	—
Pitch and putt	—	yes	—	—	—
Miniature golf	—	yes	—	—	—
Golf equipment and supplies	yes	yes	will order	—	—
Restaurant	—	yes	—	—	—
Snack bar	yes	yes	—	—	—
Vending machines	yes	yes	yes	yes	yes
Video games	—	yes	—	—	—
Club cleaning and repair	yes	—	yes	—	—
Usage rate‡	35%	33%	20%	25%	25%

*The cost of lessons includes balls and video analysis.

†The cost of lessons includes balls.

‡Usage rate was determined by noting the number of hitting areas in use at a given time as a percentage of the total number of hitting areas in the range. Hourly counts of golfers were recorded for days, evenings, and weekends to determine patterns of play and percentage of use.

frequent golfers were more price-conscious, yet they too were influenced by the quality of the facilities. Occasional golfers were unpredictable. Some were interested primarily in hitting as many balls as possible for the lowest price. They were not particularly concerned with the quality of the range, the equipment, or the balls themselves. Other recreational golfers were willing to pay higher prices if the surroundings provided a variety of entertainment opportunities.

Each of the driving ranges used different pricing approaches to differentiate one from another and to promote higher usage. They sold different sizes of buckets of balls at the following prices:

Bear Creek	$2.75 for 30	$4.50 for 60	$6.50 for 90	$10.50 for 150
Greenbrier	$4.50 for 50	$6.00 for 75	$7.50 for 100	
Golfarama	$4.00 for 50		$6.00 for 100	(2 for 1 specials)
Hit 'Em Out	$2.50 for 50		$4.00 for 100	
Discount	$2.50 for 50		$4.00 for 100	

All of the ranges provided golf clubs for their customers, and the quality of the clubs varied significantly. Bear Creek provided premium irons (3, 5, and 7 irons) for both men and women. They did not provide woods (drivers) because of the costly repairs when misused by inexperienced golfers. Most serious golfers brought their own clubs (irons and woods), so this was not much of a problem for Bear Creek. Greenbrier followed a similar policy, but they had a limited amount of woods available. The other ranges provided irons and woods that were of an inferior grade. These ranges reasoned that their customers were not as concerned with the quality of the clubs and balls as they were with the entertainment value of driving the balls as far as possible.

Both Bear Creek and Greenbrier used high-quality, durable (premium) golf balls. These balls were of higher quality and cost than those normally used on golf courses. The other ranges tended to use seconds and used balls, which were considerably less expensive.

The pricing of golfing instruction presented a different situation. Many serious golfers were inclined to shop around for an instructor whose style produced "winning golfers." The price for golfing lessons related directly to the reputation and success record of the instructor. Experienced teachers and golf course pros set their prices in line with the value of the service that they provided. A few highly respected pros charged as much as $100 to $200 per 3/4 hour instruction session. With Dan's background on the tour and his recognized teaching success, he felt comfortable in charging $60 per 3/4 hour. This was higher than the $30 to $40 charged by most of the golf course pros in the area and more than the $25 per 3/4 hour charged by the two instructors at the Greenbrier Range. The other three ranges did not have instructors on site but they could make arrangements to have an instructor available by appointment.

The First Year (1993)

By the end of October 1992, Dan and George completed the arrangements to purchase the property and were ready to proceed with their building plans. Their schedule called for them to complete the land preparations (clearing, grading, seeding, fencing, etc.) during November and December. The hitting areas, fairway, greens, clubhouse facilities, and parking area were to be completed during January and February. They hoped to have their work completed by the end of the off-season and the driving range ready to operate by March 1, the beginning of the busy golfing season. This would give them 10 business months to operate. They did not believe that the abbreviated year was a negative factor as most of the golf courses and driving ranges were inactive during the off-season months of November through February. Dan and George projected reasonable profits for the first year.

Full of optimism and naivete, the two partners set out on November 1 to launch the new business. Almost immediately, they ran into difficulty getting the necessary clearances from the local planning board. Complications in the application led to delays in processing the papers. However, a potential delay of two months was reduced to three weeks with a timely $500 contribution to the political campaign fund of one of the planning board members. However, just when they thought that they were ready to proceed, the Environmental Protection Agency raised questions concerning whether putting a building on this protected flood plain area was appropriate. After several hearings and three more weeks delay, the agency agreed that the driving range was an appropriate use of flood plain land and the clubhouse building could be built on higher ground beyond the boundaries of the flood plain area. In the middle of December, all of the necessary clearances were received and work was begun. Unfortunately, the delays put them into the worst part of the winter and weather conditions were unusually severe. As a result, land clearing was delayed and the costs of clearing and preparing the site ran almost 27 percent higher than they had originally projected. The whole project was threatened again in mid-February when it became apparent that the land preparations had disturbed an underground spring at the front of the property and water was seeping onto the access road leading to Route 183. Once again, local authorities objected and required that the owners install a culvert and drainage system to carry the water away. This unanticipated development cost them an additional $40,000.

By the targeted March 1 opening date, the golf range was only partially completed.

The range itself was in good shape but the building, the parking lot, and the landscaping were not yet started. At this point, it was painfully obvious to the owners that they were running out of money to complete their dream. They did not have adequate financial resources to complete the facility as planned. If they delayed much longer, they would be so late in opening that they would suffer significant revenue losses. Faced with the cash squeeze and the impact of further delays on their revenues, the owners decided to take some emergency steps to get the facility opened by May 1. They determined that they could not afford to build the permanent clubhouse that they had originally envisioned. However, they were fortunate in locating a portable classroom building which they were able to transport to the site and refurbish to meet their immediate needs (see Exhibit 4). This resulted in considerable savings. They also decided to go with a gravel parking area instead of the paved one, minimal exterior landscaping, and a more modest sign. The snack bar, the practice putting green, and the awning were put on hold, and they decided to have outdoor portable toilets for the immediate future. Although disappointed at not being able to start out with their dream facility, Dan believed that most of the necessary changes had been in areas that he considered "cosmetic." The range, the hitting areas, the equipment, and the services were all in place to meet the primary requirements of their prospective golfing customers.

On May 1, Bear Creek Driving Range finally opened for business. Dan assumed responsibilities as manager and instructor. He hired an assistant inside manager and three employees to work outside on maintenance tasks (ball collecting, lawn cutting, clean-up, etc.). In June, he hired a college student on a part-time basis to assist him

EXHIBIT 4   Bear Creek Shop Layout

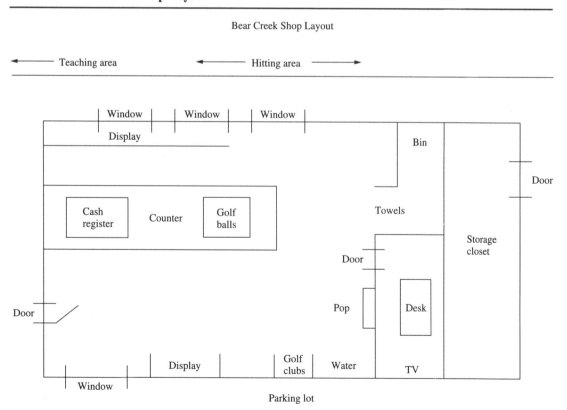

Bear Creek Shop Layout

with customer service, administrative details, and paperwork. Dan half-seriously introduced his new employee as "Martha Rawls, my new vice president of marketing."

By the first of September, Bear Creek was not doing the business that the partners had envisioned when they laid out their business plan for the year. Although a fair number of customers were finding the range, there were not enough of them to generate a positive cash flow. It was not unusual to see most of the 35 hitting areas unoccupied. According to Dan's calculations, the range needed a 33 percent usage rate during the summer months if they were to break even for the year. This 33 percent usage rate called for an average daily rate of 105 customers. (This assumes that the typical customer hits 90 balls and takes a little less than an hour to do so). Bear Creek's actual usage rate during the year was closer to 20 percent. What was most disturbing to Dan was the apparent disparity between his usage rate and that of his two major competitors. While there was no formal data available on the usage rates of the driving ranges, Dan had developed a way of monitoring his competition to observe their business activity. Using a system devised by his college student, Martha, the activity rates (percentage of hitting areas being used) were recorded for each of the competitors at various times during the week. On the basis of these observations, Dan could conclude that his range was capturing a significantly smaller share of the business than his competitors. According to these calculations, Dan's in-season usage rate was 20 percent compared to 35 percent for Greenbrier, 33 percent for Golfarama, and a surprising 25 percent for each of the other two discount ranges. Although the methodology was crude, the result was quite clear. Bear Creek Driving Range was not capturing its fair share of the business in spite of its new facilities and its professional orientation.

Dan began to think more about his customers. As he had anticipated, many of them were serious golfers who came because they knew about Dan and his golfing know-how. In discussions with these customers, several of them observed that they liked the easy, informal atmosphere of the place but they missed some of the amenities such as telephones, indoor plumbing, snacks, and a lounge area. Although most of these serious golfers were members of local golf courses, they chose to come to Bear Creek because of its convenient location, first-class hitting areas and fairway, excellent instruction, and privacy. Not surprisingly, a high proportion of these customers used their own clubs. In her scouting trips, Martha noted that the golfers at the other ranges were more apt to use clubs provided by the driving range.

As the summer progressed, Dan began to question one of his earlier decisions in relation to advertising and promotion expenditures. Caught up in the financial squeeze, the partners decided that they could not afford to allocate scarce dollars for advertisements in local papers or in the *Par Fore* or *North Texas Golfer* magazines. However, they did purchase a listing in the local *Yellow Pages*. Both of their competitors advertised in local papers and in the trade journals, offering coupons and specials (two-for-one offers). Dan was not convinced that aggressive advertising and couponing was the way to attract the kind of customers that they were seeking. Up until this time, he had felt that word-of-mouth advertising would be sufficient for attracting the serious golfers to Bear Creek. Now he wasn't so sure. He wondered if their emphasis and preoccupation with the serious golfer segment was too limiting.

The rest of the year showed no great improvement. Bear Creek plugged along with a modest business base, but the partners were forced to seek short-term financing to get them over the hump. The usage rate averaged out to be 20 percent for the first year instead of the desired 33 percent. No additional facilities improvements were accomplished, and this left the range without a permanent clubhouse, snack bar, pro shop, putting green, awning, or paved parking area. One bright spot had been the demand for golf lessons. Dan's excellent reputation did, in fact, attract customers for individual lessons and for his group clinics. Revenues from this source exceeded the forecasts by almost 16 percent. However, in spite of this hopeful sign, the end of the year results were discouraging with an operating loss as of December 31 of $25,000. The loss not only placed them in a difficult financial position, but it also deprived them of this important source of funds which they had included in their financial development plan. As they reviewed the financial returns for the first year (Exhibits 5 and 6), the partners were indeed anxious for ideas to improve their operations and their customer usage rate.

The Market Study

Dan referred to his part-time employee, Martha Rawls, as his "marketing vice president," and he was quite serious about calling on Martha to assist him in strengthening the marketing aspects of his business. As a marketing major and a member of the women's golf team at the University of Texas, Arlington, Martha was willing to help Dan gain a better understanding of the golf range market in the Dallas/Fort Worth area. Martha was even able to conduct a market study as part of a project in one of her marketing courses in the fall semester. Upon reviewing Martha's study, Dan noted the following relevant facts and figures concerning the golfing industry and the local market situation:

The Industry

- The golfing industry as a whole (including golf, golf equipment, instruction, club repair, soft goods merchandising, playing facilities, practice facilities, etc.) was a $42 billion business.
- There were 24.8 million golfers in this country, and the market was growing at a rate of approximately 3 percent per year.
- Women constituted the fastest-growing segment of the market and accounted for 5.4 million out of the 24.8 million total. Women made up 37 percent of beginner golfers, up from 23 percent in 1983. The female golfer spent about $1,789 per year on the sport, about $100 more than her male counterpart.

The Dallas/Fort Worth Area

- The total population of the Dallas/Fort Worth area was 3,855,415. The population in the 10-mile radius comprising the Bear Creek market area was 777,082. Seventy percent were adults (16 years old or over).
- There were eight private golf courses in the market area and an additional seven public courses.
- The average membership at a private club was approximately 1,500 with 80 percent of these being family memberships with an average of four golfers per family unit.
- The number of individual golfers using each of the public golf courses (at one time or another during the year) was estimated to be 13,500.
- Because of the excellent climate and the long season, golf was a very popular form of recreation in the Dallas/Fort Worth area. It was estimated that 25 percent of the adult population played golf with varying frequencies during the year. In addition, a sizable and growing number of nongolfers enjoyed the sport of hitting golf balls for recreation at local driving ranges.

EXHIBIT 5

INCOME STATEMENT
Bear Creek Golf Range
December 31, 1993

	Pro Forma	Actual
Income		
Range ball revenue	$ 190,000	$ 124,900
Lessons	47,280	54,660
Merchandise	24,000	17,609
Club repair	5,000	5,400
Food and beverage	35,000	3,705
Total income	$ 301,270	$ 206,274
Expense		
Cost of Sales		
Merchandise	10,000	16,750
Repair supplies	3,250	3,530
Food and beverage	16,000	1,950
Total cost of sales	$ 29,250	$ 22,230
Payroll		
Salaries	60,000	60,000
Hourly wages	52,000	49,144
Total payroll	$ 112,000	$ 109,144
Range Expenses		
Range balls	6,000	6,200
Equipment	2,500	2,350
Fertilizer, seed, chemicals	15,000	11,490
Total range expenses	$ 23,500	$ 20,040
Operating Expenses		
Office expenses and supplies	3,000	2,520
Utilities	3,000	2,412
Telephone	4,000	3,328
Auto and truck expense	7,000	7,275
Depreciation and amortization	5,050	5,050
Insurance and liability	7,500	6,012
Irrigation	0	1,350
Legal and accounting	3,500	3,875
Postage and freight	500	630
Sales taxes, other taxes	3,000	1,360
Advertising and promotion	5,000	800
Miscellaneous	1,400	1,430
Total operating expense	$ 42,950	$ 36,042
Professional Expenses		
Dues, education, fees	3,000	3,212
Travel, entertainment, lunches	4,000	4,237
Total professional expense	$ 7,000	$ 7,449
Interest	36,000	36,311
Total expense	$ 250,700	$ 231,216
Profit/Loss (before income tax)	$ 50,570	$ (24,942)

EXHIBIT 6

BALANCE SHEET
Bear Creek Golf Range
December 31, 1993

	Pro Forma	Actual
Assets		
Current Assets		
Cash	$ 4,000	$ 3,217
Accounts receivable	3,220	6,451
Prepaid interest	0	472
Total Current Assets	$ 7,200	$ 10,140
Fixed Assets		
Land	$ 180,000	$ 180,000
Improvements	57,000	70,440
Building	174,500	77,000
Parking area	18,750	5,400
Practice green	10,000	0
Equipment	20,000	22,000
Other fixed assets	29,300	46,250
Total Fixed Assets	$ 489,550	$ 401,090
Total Assets	$ 496,770	$ 411,230
Liabilities and Net Worth		
Liabilities		
Current liabilities		
Accounts payable	$ 4,000	$ 4,472
Accrued taxes	2,000	250
Expenses payable	0	1,000
Total Current Liabilities	$ 6,000	$ 5,722
Long-term liabilities		
Bank loans	$ 240,000	$ 230,450
Total long-term liabilities	$ 240,000	$ 230,450
Total Liabilities	$ 246,000	$ 236,172
Net Worth		
Shay, capital	$ 100,000	$ 100,000
Patton, capital	100,000	100,000
Retained earnings	50,770	(24,942)
Total Net Worth	$ 250,770	$ 175,058
Total Liabilities and Equity	$ 496,770	$ 411,230

- There was an increasing interest on the part of young adults (16–36) in sports-related recreational activities. This included attendance at sporting events (Dallas Cowboys, etc.), participation in sports activities (team sports, video games, baseball hitting machines, golf ranges, etc.), and socializing at sports bars and clubs featuring large-screen TVs and other sports-centered entertainment. This sports segment was spending significant dollars on various sports-related activities. However, problems sometimes developed with this younger group when alcohol and exuberance combined to produce unruly behavior.

Market Segments. In her study of the golf market, Martha identified and described the major segments as follows:

1. **Serious Golfers:** Serious golfers were those who played frequently (25 or more rounds per year), generally belonged to private clubs, had low handicaps, used premium equipment, and played to win. They enjoyed the game for its competitive aspects and enjoyed it more if there was money on the line ("$10 Nassau," "Skins," "Birdies," "Sandies," "Greenies," etc.). Serious golfers wanted to be the best. They practiced and took lessons if they thought it would help them improve their games. Money was not an obstacle. Serious golfers comprised approximately 9 percent of the total golfing population.

2. **Frequent Golfers:** Frequent golfers enjoyed the game, played when possible (between 7 and 24 times per year), had respectable handicaps, might have belonged to private clubs or played at public courses, and played to win. They would play more often if business and/or personal circumstances allowed it, and often combined business with golf. They enjoyed the camaraderie and worked to improve their games. They also took lessons. Frequent golfers accounted for 29 percent of the golfing population.

3. **Occasional Golfers:** Occasional golfers played when invited to do so (between 1 and 6 times per year). They enjoyed the game but were not usually skilled players. They would play more often if time and economic circumstances permitted it. Typically, occasional golfers played on public courses or as guests at private courses. They would have liked to be able to play more often and more skillfully, but were not likely to take lessons. They described themselves as recreational golfers rather than serious golfers. Occasional golfers made up 62 percent of the total golfing population.

Martha considered other ways to segment the market focusing on other characteristics than "frequency of play." She considered the "Women's Golf Segment," which was the fastest growing segment, at 5.4 million players. She learned that the profile of a woman golfer was age 43, four years of college, $60,000 annual earnings, and married with no children living at home. One-third were members of a golf facility. Private clubs were changing their rules to allow equal playing opportunities for women members.

Martha identified another significant segment that she identified as the "Learners Segment." Each year, a significant number of newcomers joined the golfing community. New golfers included young players, females, retired people, and midlifers who enjoyed exercising. Learners were often confronted with confidence problems as they struggled to master the game. They were good candidates for lessons in either group or individual instruction sessions. Many of them were interested in learning the rules of the game (golfing etiquette) as well as the skills.

Finally, Martha considered a less obvious segment comprised of "Wanabee Golfers" or "Entertainment Golfers." This growing segment included persons who did not have the skills or the economic circumstances to be golfing regulars. Nevertheless, they saw and heard about golf often, and they enjoyed an occasional opportunity to play the game. They played for fun. For this aspirational group, driving ranges, miniature golf games, pitch-and-putt facilities, and video games offered opportunities that were both economical and enjoyable.

Martha's research indicated that competitors were active in marketing their ranges to the various markets. Greenbrier advertised periodically in the *Par Fore* and the

North Texas Golfer publications, featuring their up-to-date facilities and excellent instructional services and equipment. Golfarama appeared regularly in the daily and weekly newspapers with their special promotions (two-for-one offerings). They aimed specifically at the recreational market, emphasizing in their ads the variety of entertainment opportunities at the Center, "The place to come for Sports Entertainment." The discount ranges mainly featured their low prices in their ads.

Martha learned that the costs for advertising in the local media were not unreasonable. A quarter-page ad in the *Yellow Pages* cost $110 per month. The local golf magazines charged $150 per weekly issue, and the daily newspapers ran between $50 to $100 per insertion, depending on ad size and frequency.

Business Operations.   In her review of the local golf range market, Martha noted that local weather conditions permitted outside activities for most of the year but, for all practical purposes, the driving range "season" ran from March 1 through October 31. Most area ranges closed during the four-month off-season. In this first year, however, Dan decided to remain open during the off-season to try to make up some of the business lost due to the delayed opening in the spring. Success in this business depended on making the numbers in the eight-month period. During the season, Bear Creek, like the other ranges in the area, was open 11 hours a day (10:00 AM to 9:00 PM). During the week, business was slow during the daytime hours and picked up after 5:00 PM. Saturdays and Sundays were the busiest for both range business and for lessons. It was not unusual during June and July to have all 35 hitting areas in use on evenings and on weekends. On good days, the range had 100 to 150 customers. However, according to Dan's daily records, the range averaged closer to 75 customers per day over the six-month period and 10 per day in the off-season.

Martha was concerned about the low customer traffic during the weekday daytime hours. Although this was understandable, she pointed out the importance of building more off-hour business. She suggested various ways that they might attract customers to the range during these daytime hours, including off-hour pricing, introductory offers, special group rates for high school and college golf teams, discount prices for learner clinics, coupons for visitors staying at local hotels and motels in the airport area, and other promotional devices designed to introduce customers to the range. Overall, Martha's report to the partners showed that the market was healthy and growing but that Bear Creek was not exploiting the opportunities that were there.

Reconsideration of Strategy

After reviewing Martha's data and the disappointing results from their first year's business, the Bear Creek partners met to discuss possible ways that they might increase the number of golfing customers to accomplish their targeted 33 percent usage rate.

Dan was experiencing some misgivings concerning the practice and instructional focus of the range. Although the majority of serious golfers were members of private golf courses that had their own practice ranges and professional instructors, Dan was convinced that many of these golfers would be attracted to a practice range that offered high-quality facilities, a convenient location, and a congenial golfing milieu. He believed that his own reputation as a top-flight teacher would attract people to the range for lessons and advice. He thought that would encourage these customers to use the range for their regular practice sessions. This idea was working to some extent, but it was not generating enough customers to accomplish Dan's objectives. Dan and George realized that the shortened six-month year accounted for some of their customer shortfall. They were confident that things would improve with a full year of operation and with further easing of the recession. They also felt that business would improve as their existing customers spread the word about their practice range.

In terms of their financial constraints, they were inclined to postpone further range improvements pending the results of the second year. However, they were concerned that customers were turned off by the unfinished facilities. They were further concerned that they might be overlooking the recreational golfers, a significant, high-spending segment of the market. Keeping in mind that this segment was attracted by such additional activities as miniature golf, pitch-and-putt, video games, and sports bars, the partners gave some thought to expanding their operation to include some of these attractions. The opportunity was available to them because the 10-acre adjoining piece of property was offered to them on a 10-year lease/buy arrangement. The partners believed that these additional facilities would bring in more customers, but they still wondered if this was the kind of customers that they wished to attract.

Time for Action.   It was now January 1994, and Martha Rawls knew that Dan and his partner were looking forward to her recommendations concerning the marketing strategy for the coming year and for the years ahead. As she reviewed her experience working at Bear Creek Golf Range and the information that she had collected, she felt that the future survival and success of the business depended largely on the implementation of a sound marketing program. This program would identify the appropriate market segments to explore, determine the needs and behavior of the golfing customers in these markets, and weigh various alternatives (product/service offerings, pricing tactics, and promotional programs) for responding to the needs of the target markets. As she learned in her marketing courses, Martha needed to provide a sound analysis of the situation as a basis for evaluating the options and supporting her recommendations. Her resulting recommended marketing strategy should include a full description of the marketing strategy, its objectives, necessary changes, and specific action steps for carrying it out.

CASE 7–7
WENTWORTH INDUSTRIAL CLEANING SUPPLIES

Wentworth Industrial Cleaning Supplies (WICS), located in Lincoln, Nebraska, is experiencing a slowdown in growth; sales of all WICS products have leveled off far below the volume expected by management. Although total sales volume has increased for the industry, WICS's share of this growth has not kept pace. J. Randall Griffith, vice president of marketing, has been directed to determine what factors are stunting growth and to institute a program that will facilitate further expansion.

Company and Industry Background

WICS is a division of Wentworth International, competing in the janitorial maintenance chemical market. According to trade association estimates, the total market is roughly $2.5 billion in 1992. Exhibit 1 shows the nature of this market. Four segments comprise the institutional maintenance chemical market, which consists of approximately 2,000 manufacturers providing both national and private labels.

EXHIBIT 1   Institutional Maintenance Chemical Market

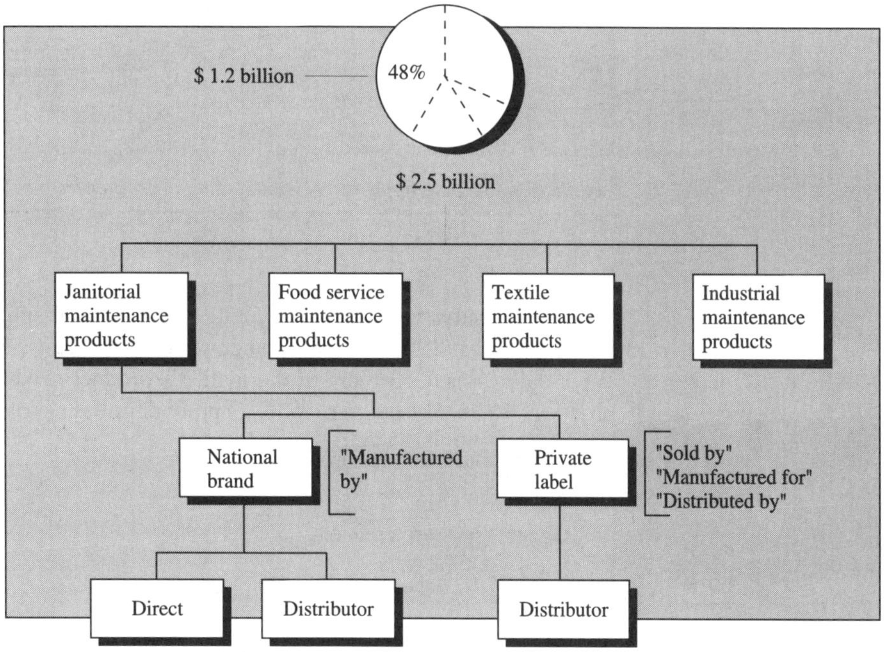

Reprinted by permission from Gilbert A. Churchill, Jr., Neil M. Ford, and Orville C. Walker, Jr., *Sales Force Management,* 4th ed. (Burr Ridge, IL: Richard D. Irwin, Inc., 1993), pp. 861–77.

EXHIBIT 2   **WICS "Served" Portion of the Janitorial Maintenance Chemical Market**

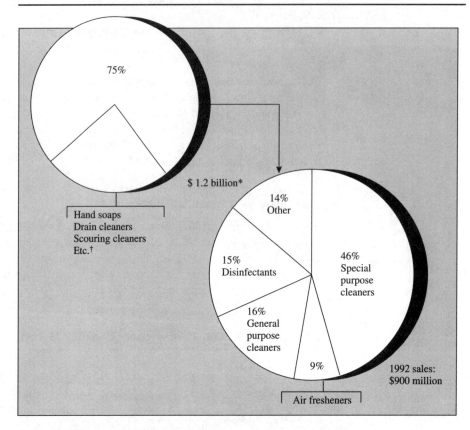

*End-user dollars.

†Includes some general purpose cleaners and air fresheners that WICS does not manufacture.

Total industry sales volume in dollars of janitorial supplies is approximately \$1.3 billion. Exhibit 2 shows the breakdown by product type for the janitorial market. WICS addresses 75 percent of the market's product needs with a line of high-quality products. The composition of WICS's product line is as follows:

Special purpose cleaners	46%
Air fresheners	9
General purpose cleaners	16
Disinfectants	15
Other	14

The janitorial maintenance chemical market is highly fragmented; no one firm, including WICS, has more than 10 percent market share. Agate and Marshfield Chemical sell directly to the end-user, while Lynx, Lexington Labs, and WICS utilize a distributor network. Most of WICS's competitors utilize only one channel of distribution; only Organic Labs and Swanson sell both ways. Most private-label products move

EXHIBIT 3   Janitorial Maintenance Chemical Market (End User Dollars)

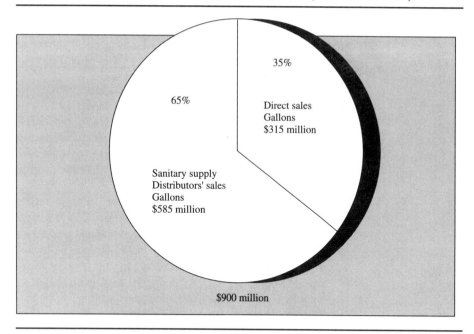

through distributors. Sanitary supply distributors (SSDs) deliver 65 percent of end-user dollars, while direct-to-end-user dollar sales are 35 percent (Exhibit 3).[1] The following shows the sales breakdown by target market, by type of distribution:

Distributor Sales	
Retail	20%
Industrial	18
Health care	18
Schools	11
Building supply contractors	10
Restaurants	3
Hotels	3
Other	17

Direct Sales	
Retail	47%
Building supply contractors	35
Health care	15
Hotels	2
Restaurants	1

Trade association data plus information from other sources estimate the number of SSDs to be between 5,000 and 6,000. The following shows the sales volume breakdown for the SSDs based on an average 5,500:

---

[1] Includes paper supply distributors that carry janitorial supplies.

Size in Sales Volume

Less than $100,000	1,210
$100,000–$500,000	2,475
$500,000–$1,000,000	1,375
More than $1,000,000	440
Total	5,500

According to a recent analysis of end-users, WICS provides cleaning supplies for approximately 20,000 customers. WICS's sales force is expected to call on these accounts as well as prospect for new business. These 20,000 end-users receive product from the SSDs who supply cleaning supplies manufactured by WICS and others as well. About one-third of the average SSD's total sales is accounted for by WICS's products. An exception is the paper supply distributor, where WICS's products account for an average of 10 percent of sales.

The typical SSD carries other related items. In fact, according to a survey conducted by an independent firm, SSDs almost always carry a private-label line of cleaning supplies plus one to two additional branded products besides the WICS line. This survey revealed that 60 percent of the SSDs carry a private-label line along with WICS and one other national brand. Forty percent carry two national labels and WICS and a private label. The private label may be a regional label or the SSD's own label.

WICS places almost total reliance on selling through the SSDs, although a small amount of sales (less than 10 percent) are made direct. WICS sells its janitorial maintenance products through roughly 400 distributors, who in turn "see" 65 percent of the end-user dollar market. Thus, 65 percent of sales in the total janitorial maintenance market are made through SSDs (35 percent are direct sales); and the 400 SSDs used by WICS provided 65 percent coverage. The market seen by each distributor, referred to as his or her *window* on the market, is a function of

Product lines carried (paper versus chemical).

Customer base (type and size).

Nature of business (specialization by market versus specialization by sales function).

The combination of these factors produces end-user market coverage of 42 percent (65 percent distributor sales × 65 percent coverage). WICS has very limited direct sales.

To reach its market, WICS uses a sales force of 135 area managers, 21 territory managers, and 4 regional managers (Exhibit 4). Regional managers are located in San Francisco, Denver, Chicago, and Boston. Although WICS is viewed as a giant in the industry, it does not produce a complete line of janitorial chemicals. Janitorial chemicals are rated based on their performance. WICS produces products that have average to premium performance ratings: WICS has no products in the economy class. Moreover, due to various factors, WICS's coverage in the average and premium classes is not complete. The emphasis on premium and average products results in providing only 75 percent of the market's product needs.

To provide high distributor margins and extensive sales support, WICS charges premium prices. Recent estimates reveal that only 40 percent of the served market is willing to pay these premium prices. The impact of WICS's limited product line coupled with its premium price is evident in Exhibit 5.

An overall description of WICS's marketing program shows that it has focused on market development. Distributors receive high margins (30 to 40 percent) and sales costs are high (10 to 15 percent) due to emphasis on selling technical benefits, demon-

EXHIBIT 4 **WICS's Access to the Market**

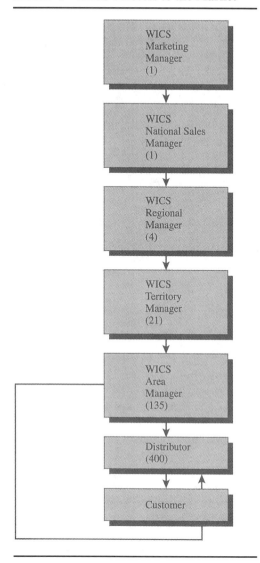

strations, and cold calls. Area managers call on prospective end-users to develop the market for the SSD. By comparison, WICS's competitors offer SSDs low margins (15 to 20 percent) and incur low sales costs (5 to 8 percent).

Griffith recently received a memo from Steve Shenken, WICS's national sales manager, reporting on a study of the effectiveness of SSDs. Territory managers evaluated each SSD in their respective regions on a basis of reach (advertising and promotional programs) and frequency of sales calls. The composite report indicated distributors as a whole were doing an excellent job servicing present accounts. In other words, 400 SSDs provide WICS with a sizable share of the market.

Area managers (AMs) represent WICS in distributor relations. The AMs' prime focus is to sell and service existing key end-user accounts and selected new target ac-

EXHIBIT 5   **End User Product Coverage**

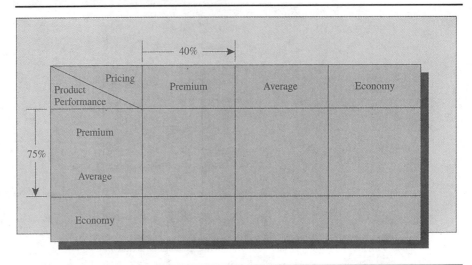

counts in their assigned territories. According to a recent study, maintenance of current accounts comprises approximately 80 percent of the AMs' time (Exhibit 6). In addition to handling old accounts, the AM makes cold calls on prospective distributors as directed by the territory manager. However, the number of cold calls made monthly has decreased substantially in the past year since the major SSDs now carry WICS products. A study of AM and SSD attitudes, conducted by MGH Associates, management consultants, is presented in Appendixes A and B. Some of the sales management staff question the use of AM time; however, there has been no indication that formal changes will be made in the future regarding sales force organization and directives. The AM job description has seen few revisions, if any, during the firm's past 10 years of rapid growth (Exhibit 7).

Area managers are compensated with a straight salary, enhanced periodically by various incentive programs and performance bonuses. Incentive programs generally require that AMs attain a certain sales level by a specified date. For example, the "Christmas Program" necessitated that AMs achieve fourth-quarter quotas by November 15; on completion of this objective, the AM received a gift of his or her choice, such as a color television. To date, management considers the Zone Glory Cup the most effective incentive program. The Glory Cup is an annual competition among areas within territories, which entails meeting or exceeding sales objectives by a specified date. An all-expense-paid vacation at a plush resort for area, territory, and regional managers and their "legal" spouses is the prize for the winning team. However, management at WICS believes that prestige is the prime motivator in this competition and the underlying reason for the program's success.

In a recent meeting, Terry Luther, executive vice president of the WICS division of Wentworth International, expressed his concern to Griffith about WICS's mediocre performance. Luther indicated corporate cash flow expectations from WICS were not being met and that a plan was needed from Griffith concerning how WICS could improve its overall operating performance. Griffith was quite aware that Wentworth International would make personnel changes to meet corporate objectives and that selling off divi-

EXHIBIT 6   **Allocation of Area Manager Duties***

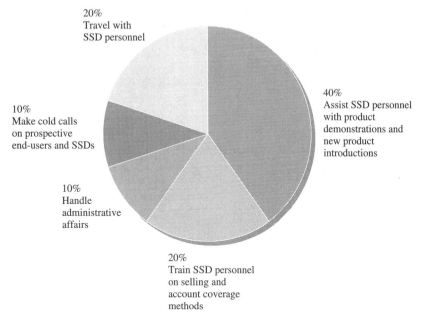

20%
Travel with
SSD personnel

10%
Make cold calls
on prospective
end-users and SSDs

40%
Assist SSD personnel
with product
demonstrations and
new product
introductions

10%
Handle
administrative
affairs

20%
Train SSD personnel
on selling and
account coverage
methods

*Based on an analysis of call reports.

sions not able to meet corporate expectations was not unlikely. Griffith informed Luther that an action plan would be developed and be on his desk within 30 days.

Griffith's first step was to approve an earlier request made by Mike Toner, sales and distributor relations manager, for a study of sales force and distributor attitudes and opinions (Appendixes A and B). Next, the following memo was sent, discussing Griffith's assignment from Luther:

Intra-Office Memorandum

To: Steve Shenken, National Sales Manager
       Caitlin Smith, Manager—Sales Analysis
       Ryan Michaels, Manager—Sales Training
       Calla Hart, Manager—Special Sales Program
       Charlotte Webber, Senior Product Manager
       Mike Toner, Sales and Distributor Relations Manager

From: Randall Griffith, Vice President—Marketing

Subject: WICS Performance Review

As you all know, our performance has not met corporate expectations. To rectify this situation, before we all lose our jobs, we need to meet to discuss ways for improving our market performance.

At our next meeting, I want each of you to develop proposals for your areas of responsibility. These proposals need not be detailed at this time. For the moment, I am seeking ideas, not final solutions.

Staff reaction to Griffith's memo was one of frustration and anger. Several managers thought they had already complied with Griffith's request. One person

EXHIBIT 7   Wentworth Industrial Cleaning Supplies Position Description

Date: January 1, 1983	Position:	Area Manager, Maint. Prods.
Approved by: (1) _____	Incumbent:	135 Positions Nationally
(2) _____		
(3) _____	Division:	Janitorial Maintenance Products Division
		Reports to: Territory Manager, Janitorial Maintenance Products Division

POSITION PURPOSE:

To sell and service user accounts and authorized distributors in an assigned territory to assure that territory sales objectives are attained or exceeded.

DIMENSIONS:

Annual sales:	$300 M	(average)
Number of distributors:	4	(average)
Number of distributor salesmen:	12	(average)
Annual expense budget:	$4.2 M	(average)
Company assets controlled or affected:	$8 M	(average)

NATURE AND SCOPE

This position reports to a territory manager, janitorial maintenance products. Each district is subdivided into sales territories that are either assigned to an individual member of the district or to a team effort, based on market and/or manpower requirements.

The janitorial maintenance products division is responsible for developing and marketing a broad line of chemical products for building maintenance purposes.

The incumbent's prime focus is to sell and service existing key user accounts and selected new target accounts in his assigned territory. He multiplies his personal sales results by spending a major portion of his time working with distributor sales personnel, selling WICS maintenance products and systems to key accounts such as commercial, industrial, institutional, and governmental accounts, and contract cleaners. When working alone, he sells key user accounts through an authorized distributor as specified by the user customer.

The incumbent plans, schedules, and manages his selling time for maximum sales productivity. He interviews decision makers and/or people who influence the buying decision. He identifies and evaluates customer needs through careful observation, listening and questioning techniques to assure proper recommendations. He plans sales strategy to include long-term/quick-sell objectives and develops personalized user presentations to meet individual sales situations, utilizing product literature, manuals, spot demonstrations, and sales aids to reinforce presentations. This position sells systems of maintenance to major volume user accounts through the use of surveys and proposals, test programs, and other advanced sales techniques. He develops effective closing techniques for maximum sales effectiveness. This position trains custodial personnel in product usage techniques through the use of product demonstrations and/or audiovisual training to assure customer satisfaction. He follows up through the use of product demonstrations and/or audiovisual training to assure customer satisfaction. He follows up promptly on customer leads and inquiries. He services customer

commented, "I've told Randy numerous times what we need to do to turn the division around, and all he does is nod his head. Why go through this 'wheel-spinning' exercise again?" Another said, "The only time old J. R. listens to us is when the top brass leans on him for results." Despite staff reaction, the meeting would be held, and everybody would have suggestions for consideration.

To provide adequate time, Griffith scheduled an all-day meeting to be held at Wentworth's nearby lodge, located on Lake Woebegone. Griffith started the meeting by reviewing past performance. Next, he asked each manager to outline his or her proposal. First to speak was Steve Shenken, who indicated that Mike Toner would present a proposal combining both of their ideas. Shenken also said he would listen to all sales force proposals and try to combine the best parts into an overall plan.

EXHIBIT 7   (concluded)

and distributor complaints or problems and provides technical support as required. On a predetermined frequency basis, he surveys and sells assigned local accounts currently being sold on national contract. He represents the division in local custodial clinics and trade shows as required. He maintains an adequate current supply of literature, forms, and samples and maintains assigned equipment and sales tools in a businesslike condition.

The incumbent is responsible for training, developing, and motivating distributor sales personnel. This is accomplished by frequent on-the-job training in areas of product knowledge, selling skills, and demonstration techniques. He sells distributor management and assists distributors to maintain an adequate and balanced inventory of the full product line. He introduces marketing plans and sells new products and sales promotions to distributor management. He participates in distributor sales meetings to launch new products or sales promotions, or for training and motivational purposes. He keeps abreast of pertinent competitive activities, product performance, new maintenance techniques, and other problems and opportunities in the territory. Periodically, he communicates Wentworth growth objectives versus distributor progress to distributor management (i.e., sales coverage, volume and product sales, etc.). He assists the distributor to maintain a current and adequate supply of product literature, price lists, and sales aids.

The incumbent prepares daily sales reports, weekly reports, travel schedules, weekly expense reports, and the like, and maintains territory and customer records. He maintains close communication with his immediate supervisor concerning products, sales, distributor and shipping problems.

He controls travel and business expenses with economy and sound judgment. He handles and maintains assigned company equipment and territory records in a businesslike manner.

Major challenges to this position include maintaining established major users, selling prospective new target accounts, and strengthening distribution and sales coverage to attain or exceed sales objectives.

The incumbent operates within divisional policies, procedures, and objectives. He consults with his immediate supervisor for recommendations and/or approval concerning distributor additions or terminations, exceptions to approved selling procedures, and selling the headquarter's level of national or regional accounts.

Internally, he consults with the editing office concerning distributor shipments, credit, and so forth. Externally, he works closely with distributor personnel to increase sales and sales coverage and with user accounts to sell new or additional products.

The effectiveness of this position is measured by the ability of the incumbent to attain or exceed territory sales objectives.

This position requires an incumbent with an in-depth and professional knowledge of user account selling techniques, product line, and janitorial maintenance products distributors, and a minimum of supervision.

PRINCIPAL ACCOUNTABILITIES

1. Sell and service key user accounts to assure attainment of territory sales objectives.
2. Sell, train, develop, and motivate assigned distributors to assure attainment of product sales, distribution, and sales coverage objectives.
3. Plan, schedule, and manage personal selling efforts to assure maximum sales productivity.
4. Plan and develop professional sales techniques to assure maximum effectiveness.
5. Train custodial personnel in the use of Wentworth products and systems to assure customer satisfaction.
6. Maintain a close awareness of territory and market activities to keep the immediate supervisor abreast of problems and opportunities.
7. Perform administrative responsibilities to conduct an efficient territory operation.
8. Control travel and selling expenses to contribute toward profitable territory operation.

Mike Toner's Proposal

Toner's proposal was rather basic. If improving market was WICS's objective, then more SSDs were needed in all territories. According to Toner,

> Each area manager serves, on the average, four SSDs. Since we can only get so much business out of an SSD, then to increase sales we need more SSDs. I suggest that each area manager add two more distributors. Of course, this move will require that either we add more area managers or we hire and train a special group to call on new end-users and new distributors. It's difficult to attract new SSDs unless we show them a group of prospective end-users who are ready to buy WICS's products. Now, I have not made any estimates of how many more people are needed, but we do know that present AMs do not have enough time to adequately seek new business.

After Toner presented this proposal, Griffith asked if the existing AMs could not be motivated to apply more effort toward securing new business. Calla Hart thought the AMs could do more and that her proposal, if adopted, would alleviate the need for expansion of the AMs and SSDs.

Calla Hart's Proposal

As expected, Hart's proposal revolved around her extensive experience with WICS's incentive programs. This satisfactory experience led Calla to suggest the following:

> If I thought that the AMs and the SSDs were working at full capacity, I would not propose more incentive programs. But they are not! We can motivate the AMs to secure more new business, and we can get more new business from our distributors. We all know that the SSDs are content to sit back and wait for the AMs to hand them new business. Well, let's make it worthwhile to the SSDs by including them in our incentive programs. For the AMs I suggest that we provide quarterly incentives much like our Christmas Program. AMs who achieve their quotas by the 15th of the second month of the quarter would receive a gift.
>
> In addition, we need to develop a program for recognizing new end-user sales. Paying bonuses for obtaining new end-user accounts would be one approach. For example, let's reward the AM from each territory who secures the highest percentage increase in new end-user accounts. At the same time, we need to reward the distributor from each territory who achieves the highest percentage increase in new end-user sales dollars. And let's recognize these top producers each quarter and at year-end as well. Our incentive programs work. We know that, so let's expand their application to new sales.
>
> Finally, on a different note, I support establishing quotas for our distributors. We have quotas for our sales force, and we enforce them. AMs who do not make quotas do not stay around very long. Why not the same procedures for some of our SSDs? We all know that there are some distributors who need to be replaced. Likewise, I have not made any cost estimates but feel that we are just searching for new ideas.

Griffith thanked Hart for her comments. He wondered whether applying more pressure to the distributors was the most suitable approach. He agreed with Hart that WICS's incentive programs seemed to be very popular but questioned if other techniques might not work. Griffith then asked Ryan Michaels for his comments.

Ryan Michaels's Proposal

During his short time with WICS, Michaels has gained respect as being very thorough and analytical. He is not willing to accept as evidence such comments as "We know it works" as a reason for doing something. Determining the value of sales training, Michaels's area of assignment, has caused him considerable concern. He knows it is useful, but how useful is the question he is trying to answer. According to Michaels, WICS needs to examine the basic selling duties of the area managers:

> Before we recruit more AMs and SSDs, or try to motivate them to obtain more new business with incentive programs, we need to examine their job activities. I favor doing a job analysis of the area manager. Some evidence that I have seen indicates that job descriptions are outmoded. AMs do not perform the activities detailed in the job descriptions. For example, most AMs spend very little time calling on prospective end-users. Accompanying distributor sales reps on daily calls does not lead to new end-user business. Possibly the AMs could better spend their time doing new account development work. But before we make any decisions concerning time allocation, we need to conduct a job analysis. And, while we are collecting data, let's ask the AMs what rewards are important to them. How do they value

promotions, pay increases, recognition, and so forth? Maybe the AMs do not want more contests.

Griffith agreed that the job descriptions were out of date. He also contended this is typical and nothing to be concerned about in the short run. The idea of finding out what rewards AMs value intrigued Griffith. Next, Griffith asked Charlotte Webber for her reactions to WICS's market share problem.

Charlotte Webber's Proposal

Webber's proposal was more strategic in nature than the previous suggestions. Her experience as a product manager led her to consider product-oriented solutions and to suggest the following:

> I think we can increase market share and sales volume through the expansion of current lines and the addition of a full line of economy-based products. We can expand our present premium and average lines to cover 100 percent of the product class by adding air fresheners and general purpose cleaners. In addition we must introduce the economy-based products to counter competition.
>
> The proposed plan would not be costly because we could use our existing distributor network. If additional SSDs are necessary, we can select those in the $500,000 to $1,000,000 sales volume range. I feel that through these extensions and an increased number of SSDs we can address 75 percent of the SSD end-user dollars.

Griffith agreed that line extensions were a viable means of achieving some corporate goals. He expressed concern over entry into the low-quality segment of the market due to WICS's present customer perceptions of the company as a high-quality producer. Griffith turned to Caitlin Smith for additional suggestions on how to increase market share.

Caitlin Smith's Proposal

Smith's proposal came as no surprise to those attending the meeting. Her position in sales analysis made her critically aware of WICS's high cost of sales. It was only recently, however, that she developed a plan incorporating market share and cost of sales. Her views were accurate, but often given little weight due to her inexperience. According to Smith,

> Our cost of sales are currently running at 10 to 15 percent, while our competitors' costs average 5 to 8 percent. As many of you know, I am in favor of changing the job description of the area manager and the sales presentation. These changes are necessary due to our products' stage in the life cycle and customer service level preferences. Recently I have become convinced that there is another means of reducing sales costs. By reducing prices we could increase sales volume and reduce the cost of sales. This strategy would also increase penetration and market share.

Griffith conceded that price reductions were a possibility but expressed concern over the possibility of weakening consumer perceptions of WICS as a high-quality manufacturer. He also questioned Smith's assumption that the industrial cleaning supplies industry was presently in the mature stage of the product life cycle.

Following these comments, Griffith thanked the participants for their input and adjourned the meeting. On retiring to his room, he reflected on the suggestions presented during the meeting and his own beliefs. He knew he must begin to formulate an action plan immediately since the 30-day deadline was drawing near.

Appendix A
Conclusions of Study of Area Manager Attitudes

MGH Associates, management consultants, was retained by WICS to investigate attitudes and opinions of field personnel and sanitary supply distributors. Initially, MGH conducted lengthy interviews with selected individuals, followed by the administration of a comprehensive questionnaire. The results below identify role expectations and attitudes toward their reasonableness.

Territory Manager's Role Expectations

MGH Associates's interviews included territory managers because the territory manager is really the only management level contact the distributor has.

The territory manager interprets his or her role to be that of an overseer, to assure that WICS objectives are achieved, and that quotas are met.

The territory manager interprets his or her role to include

- Training the area managers to
  Sell WICS products.
  Train and motivate the distributor sales force.
- Coordinating area manager activities with headquarters in Lincoln.
- Hiring and firing area managers.
- Striving for new product commitments from the distributors.
- Acting as "referee" for competition between distributors.
- "Building the book" for the adding or deleting of distributors.
- Submitting the "study" to the regional manager, who writes a proposal based on the territory manager's "study." It is submitted to corporate management where the final decision is made.

Area Manager's Role Expectations

The following is the area manager's view of the role he or she believes WICS management expects to be performed:

- Multiply sales effort through distributor's sales force (listed first because it was consistently mentioned first).
- Teach and motivate the distributor's sales force to sell WICS products.
- Introduce new products to the market through
  Direct calls on end users.
  Distributors.
- Keep margins high to keep distributors happy. If they are happy, they will push WICS.
- Follow through on direct sales responsibilities.
- Collect information for management.

- Fulfill responsibilities relating to incentives.
  New gallon sales.
  Repeat gallon sales.
  Demonstrations.
  30, 35, 40? calls/week.
  Major account calls.
  Cold calls—"to develop business the distributor is reluctant to go after."

Area Manager's Role Problems

The area manager's perception of what management expects does not imply that the area manager feels that management's approach is working. In general, the sales force appears frustrated by a sales role they see as ineffective:

- A sales role that stresses
  New gallon sales.
  Cold calls on end users.
  Product demonstrations.
  New product introduction.
- "Checking the boxes" rather than being "creatively productive."
  15 demos.
  10 cold calls.
  5 distributor training sessions.
- Incentives stress selling techniques that may not be the most productive ways to sell.

  Emphasis is on new gallon sales over repeat gallon sales. Incentives weigh new gallons over repeat gallons (two to one).

  Emphasis to "demonstrate as often as possible" for the points. Demonstrate to show you are a "regular guy" who gets his or her hands dirty, not necessarily to show product benefits.
- Bonus incentives appear to be a "carrot" only for those who don't regularly make bonus, that is, "hit 106 for maximum bonus and minimum quota increase."
- The sales role gives the area manager little ability to impact his or her own success to
  Change distribution.
  Move distributor outside his or her window.
- The area manager describes his or her role as
  A "lackey."
  A "chauffeur."
  A "caretaker of old business."

Area Manager's Role: Making Cold Calls

One of the causes of area manager frustration is the general ineffectiveness of their cold calls sales role:

- The area manager makes cold calls on end users not presently sold by the WICS distributor, with the difficult objective of moving these accounts to the WICS distributor.

- If the area manager succeeds in moving this account over to WICS products, chances are small that the distributor will keep the business. Without a major portion of the account's total purchases, the distributor cannot afford to continue to call on the account.

  Distributor sales rep is on commission.

  After five calls, will stop calling if purchases have not begun to increase.

- The distributor that lost the account will try extremely hard to get back the business. This may mean giving the product away to keep control of the account—maintain majority of the account's purchases. Past experience indicates it is very difficult to move distributors outside their "window."

APPENDIX B
CONCLUSIONS OF STUDY OF WICS SANITARY SUPPLY DISTRIBUTOR ATTITUDES

WICS Distributor's Role Expectations

The following is the WICS distributor's role as outlined by WICS management and sales force.

- Act as an extension of the WICS sales force.

- Push and promote WICS product line in a *specified area.*

  Sell WICS over other brands.

  Always sell the premium benefits of WICS products to the end user, instead of distributor's private label.

  Be aware that the WICS line could be lost if private-label sales grow too large.

- Actively market new WICS products.

Distributor's Role Problems.   Distributors have been angered by WICS's attempt to run their businesses ("WICS is trying to tell me what to do").

- WICS makes demands—"uses pressure tactics."

  Distributors say they are told "our way or no way."

  Distributors feel they are forced to carry products they don't want.

  High minimum buy-ins.

  "Won't see area manager if we don't carry the new product."

  Distributors say WICS management doesn't "realize we make our living selling all our products—not just WICS."

- Communication is poor with WICS management.

  One way—"Our opinions never reach Lincoln."

- "WICS uses the distributor as a testing ground for new products."

  Distributor is not told what to expect.

  After 14-week blitz, "You never hear about the product again."

  The distributor sales force is not trained to sell to, and cannot afford to call on, certain segments of the market.

- Growth takes the distributor into new geographical market areas, and WICS may elect not to go/grow with the distributor.

  New branch in different city.

Growth may take distributor sales personnel out of area manager's district.
Receives no support from WICS.
Worst case—distributor sales rep's territory is completely outside district.
No WICS representative at any accounts.
Prefer to sell other than WICS.

- WICS does not realize that a distributor's total business extends beyond "its own backyard" in many markets.

Distributor's Role Selling Costs.   Distributors have shown concern over the high cost of selling WICS products. Sales costs are approximately 45 percent of the total operating costs.

- "WICS products are basically no better than anyone else's."
- Yet WICS asks distributors to switch competitor's accounts over to WICS products.
  Price advantage is very rare.
  A problem must exist.
  A demonstration is required.
- All these make the "problem-solving" sale time-consuming and costly.
- Result: When WICS product is sold, it is easy for competitive WICS distributors to cut price to try to get the business.
  They have very low sales costs.
- Required action: Original distributor must cut margin to keep the business.
  This frustrates distributor salespeople.
  Causes them to sell private label.

APPENDIX A
MARKETING FINANCIAL ANALYSIS

Several kinds of financial analyses are needed for marketing analysis, planning, and control activities. Such analyses represent an important part of case preparation activities. In some instances it will be necessary to review and interpret financial information provided in the cases. In other instances, analyses may be prepared to support specific recommendations. The methods covered in this appendix represent a group of tools and techniques for use in marketing financial analysis. Throughout the discussion, it is assumed that accounting and finance fundamentals are understood.

Unit of Financial Analysis

Various units of analysis that can be used in marketing financial analysis are shown in Exhibit A–1. Two factors often influence the choice of a unit of analysis: (1) the purpose of the analysis and (2) the costs and availability of the information needed to perform the analysis.

Financial Situation Analysis

Financial measures can be used to help assess the present situation. One of the most common and best ways to quantify the financial situation of a firm is through ratio analysis. These ratios should be analyzed over a period of at least three years to discern trends.

Key Financial Ratios. Financial information will be more useful to management if it is prepared so that comparisons can be made. James Van Horne comments upon this need:

> To evaluate a firm's financial condition and performance, the financial analyst needs certain yardsticks. The yardstick frequently used is a ratio or index, relating two pieces of financial data to each other. Analysis and interpretation of various ratios should give an experienced and skilled analyst a better understanding of the financial condition and performance of the firm than he would obtain from analysis of the financial data alone.[1]

As we examine the financial analysis model in the next section, note how the ratio or index provides a useful frame of reference. Typically, ratios are used to compare historical and/or future trends within the firm, or to compare a firm or business unit with an industry or other firms.

Several financial ratios often used to measure business performance are shown in Exhibit A–2. Note that these ratios are primarily useful as a means of comparing

1. Ratio values for several time periods for a particular business.
2. A firm to its key competitors.
3. A firm to an industry or business standard.

There are several sources of ratio data.[2] These include data services such as Dun & Bradstreet, Robert Morris Associates' *Annual Statement Studies,* industry and trade associations, government agencies, and investment advisory services.

Other ways to gauge productivity of marketing activities include sales per square foot of retail floor space, occupancy rates of hotels and office buildings, and sales per salesperson.

Contribution Analysis. When the performance of products, market segments, and other marketing units is being analyzed, management should examine the unit's profit contribution. Contribution margin is equal to sales (revenue) less variable costs. Thus, contribution margin represents the amount of money available to cover fixed costs, and contribution margin less fixed costs is net income. An illustration of contribution margin analysis is given in Exhibit A–3. In this example, product X is generating positive contribution margin. If product X were eliminated, $50,000 of product net income would be lost, and the remaining products would have to cover fixed costs not directly traceable to them. If the product is retained, the $50,000 can be used to contribute to other fixed costs and/or net income.

Financial Analysis Model

The model shown in Exhibit A–4 provides a useful guide for examining financial performance and identifying possible problem areas. The model combines several important financial ratios into one equation. Let's examine the model, moving from left to right. Profit margin multiplied by asset turnover yields return on assets. Moreover, assuming that the performance target is return on net worth (or return on equity), the product of return on assets and financial leverage determines performance. Increasing either ratio will increase net

[1] James C. Van Horne, *Fundamentals of Financial Management,* 4th ed. (Englewood Cliffs, NJ: Prentice Hall, 1980), pp. 103–4.

[2] A useful guide to ratio analysis is provided in Richard Sanzo, *Ratio Analysis for Small Business* (Washington, DC: Small Business Administration, 1977).

EXHIBIT A–1   **Alternative Units for Financial Analysis**

Market	Product/Service	Organization
Market	Industry	Company
Total market	Product mix	Segment/division/unit
Market niche(s)	Product line	Marketing department
Geographic area(s)	Specific product	Sales unit
Customer groups	Brand	Region
Individual customers	Model	District branch
		Office/store
		Salesperson

worth. The values of these ratios will vary considerably from one industry to another. In grocery wholesaling, for example, profit margins are typically very low, whereas asset turnover is very high. Through efficient management and high turnover, a wholesaler can stack up impressive returns on net worth. Furthermore, space productivity measures are obtained for individual departments in retail stores that offer more than one line such as department stores. The measures selected depend on the particular characteristics of the business.

Evaluating Alternatives

As we move through the discussion of financial analysis, it is important to recognize the type of costs being used in the analysis. Using accounting terminology, costs can be designated as fixed or variable. A cost is *fixed* if it remains constant over the observation period, even though the volume of activity varies. In contrast, a *variable* cost is an expense that varies with sales over the observation period. Costs are designated as mixed or semivariable in instances when they contain both fixed and variable components.

Break-Even Analysis.[3]   This technique is used to examine the relationship between sales and costs. An illustration is given in Exhibit A–5. Using sales and cost information, it is easy to determine from a break-even analysis how many units of a product must be sold in order to break even, or cover total costs. In this example 65,000 units at sales of $120,000 are equal to total costs of $120,000. Any additional units sold will produce a profit. The break-even point can be calculated in this manner:

$$\text{Break-even units} = \frac{\text{Fixed costs}}{\text{Price per unit} - \text{Variable cost per unit}}$$

[3] This illustration is drawn from David W. Cravens, Gerald E. Hills, and Robert B. Woodruff, *Marketing Decision Making: Concepts and Strategy,* rev. ed. (Homewood, IL: Richard D. Irwin, 1980), pp. 335–36.

Price in the illustration shown in Exhibit A–5 is $1.846 per unit, and variable cost is $0.769 per unit. With fixed costs of $70,000, this results in the break-even calculation:

$$\text{BE units} = \frac{\$70,000}{\$1.846 - \$0.769} = 65,000 \text{ units}$$

This analysis is not a forecast. Rather it indicates how many units of a product at a given price and cost must be sold in order to break even. Some important assumptions that underlie the above break-even analysis include the use of constant fixed costs and one price.

In addition to break-even analysis, several other financial tools are used to evaluate alternatives. Net present value of cash flow analysis and return on investment are among the most useful. For example, assume there are two projects with the cash flows shown in Exhibit A–6.

Though return on investment is widely used, it is limited in its inability to consider the time value of money. This is pointed out in Exhibit A–7. Return on investment for *both* projects X and Y is 10 percent. However, a dollar today is worth more than a dollar given in three years. Therefore, when assessing cash flows of a project or investment, future cash flows must be discounted back to the present at a rate comparable to the risk of the project.

Discounting cash flows is a simple process. Assume the firm is considering projects X and Y, and its cost of capital is 12 percent. Additionally, assume that both projects carry risk comparable to the normal business risk. Under these circumstances, the analyst should discount the cash flows back to the present at the cost of capital, 12 percent. Present value factors can be looked up, or computed using the formula $1/(1 + i)n,$ where i equals our discounting rate per time period and n equals the number of compounding periods. In this example, the present value of cash flows is as shown in Exhibit A–7.

Because both projects have a positive net present value, both are good. However, if they are mutually exclusive, the project should be selected with the highest net present value.

Exhibit A–2   Summary of Key Financial Ratios

Ratio	How Calculated	What It Shows
Profitability Ratios		
1. Gross profit margin	$\dfrac{\text{Sales} - \text{Cost of good sold}}{\text{Sales}}$	An indication of the total margin available to cover operating expenses and yield a profit.
2. Operating profit margin	$\dfrac{\text{Profits before taxes and before interest}}{\text{Sales}}$	An indication of the firm's profitability from current operations without regard to the interest charges accruing from the capital structure.
3. Net profit margin (or return on sales)	$\dfrac{\text{Profits after taxes}}{\text{Sales}}$	Shows after-tax profits per dollar of sales. Subpar profit margins indicate that the firm's sales prices are relatively low or that its costs are relatively high or both.
4. Return on total assets	$\dfrac{\text{Profits after taxes}}{\text{Total assets}}$ or $\dfrac{\text{Profits after taxes} + \text{Interest}}{\text{Total assets}}$	A measure of the return on total investment in the enterprise. It is sometimes desirable to add interest to after-tax profits to form the numerator of the ratio, since total assets are financed by creditors as well as by stockholders; hence it is accurate to measure the productivity of assets by the returns provided to both classes of investors.
5. Return on stockholders' equity (or return on net worth)	$\dfrac{\text{Profits after taxes}}{\text{Total stockholders' equity}}$	A measure of the rate of return on stockholders' investment in the enterprise.
6. Return on common equity	$\dfrac{\text{Profits after taxes} - \text{Preferred stock dividends}}{\text{Total stockholders' equity} - \text{Par value of preferred stock}}$	A measure of the rate of return on the investment that the owners of common stock have made in the enterprise.
7. Earnings per share	$\dfrac{\text{Profits after taxes} - \text{Preferred stock dividends}}{\text{Number of shares of common stock outstanding}}$	Shows the earnings available to the owners of common stock.
Liquidity Ratios		
1. Current ratio	$\dfrac{\text{Current assets}}{\text{Current liabilities}}$	Indicates the extent to which the claims of short-term creditors are covered by assets that are expected to be converted to cash in a period roughly corresponding to the maturity of the liabilities.
2. Quick ratio (or acid-test ratio)	$\dfrac{\text{Current assets} - \text{Inventory}}{\text{Current liabilities}}$	A measure of the firm's ability to pay off short-term obligations without relying upon the sale of its inventories.
3. Cash ratio	$\dfrac{\text{Cash \& Marketable securities}}{\text{Current liabilities}}$	An indicator of how long the company can go without further inflow of funds.
4. Inventory to net working capital	$\dfrac{\text{Inventory}}{\text{Current assets} - \text{Current liabilities}}$	A measure of the extent to which the firm's working capital is tied up in inventory.
Leverage Ratios		
1. Debt to assets ratio	$\dfrac{\text{Total debt}}{\text{Total assets}}$	Measures the extent to which borrowed funds have been used to finance the firm's operations.
2. Debt to equity ratio	$\dfrac{\text{Total debt}}{\text{Total stockholders' equity}}$	Provides another measure of the funds provided the creditors versus the funds provided by owners.
3. Long-term debt to equity ratio	$\dfrac{\text{Long-term debt}}{\text{Total stockholders' equity}}$	A widely used measure of the balance between debt and equity in the firm's overall capital structure.
4. Times-interest-earned (or coverage ratios)	$\dfrac{\text{Profits before interest and taxes}}{\text{Total interest charges}}$	Measures the extent to which earnings can decline without the firm's becoming unable to meet its annual interest costs.
5. Fixed-charge coverage	$\dfrac{\text{Profits before taxes and interest} + \text{Lease obligations}}{\text{Total interest charges} + \text{Lease obligations}}$	A more inclusive indication of the firm's ability to meet all of its fixed-charge obligations.

Exhibit A–2 (concluded)

Ratio	How Calculated	What It Shows
Activity Ratios		
1. Inventory turnover	$\dfrac{\text{Cost of goods sold}}{\text{Inventory}}$	When compared to industry averages, it provides an indication of whether a company has excessive inventory or perhaps inadequate inventory.
2. Fixed-assets turnover*	$\dfrac{\text{Sales}}{\text{Fixed assets}}$	A measure of the sales productivity and utilization of plant and equipment.
3. Total-assets turnover	$\dfrac{\text{Sales}}{\text{Total assets}}$	A measure of the utilization of all the firm's assets; a ratio below the industry average indicates the company is not generating a sufficient volume of business given the size of its asset investment.
4. Accounts receivable turnover	$\dfrac{\text{Annual credit sales}}{\text{Accounts receivable}}$	A measure of the average length of time it takes the firm to collect the sales made on credit.
5. Average collection period	$\dfrac{\text{Accounts receivable}}{\text{Total sales} \div 365}$ or $\dfrac{\text{Accounts receivable}}{\text{Average daily sales}}$	Indicates the average length of time the firm must wait after making a sale before it receives payment.

*The manager should also keep in mind the fixed charges associated with noncapitalized lease obligations.

Source: Adapted from Arthur A. Thompson, Jr., and A. J. Strickland III, *Strategy and Policy,* 4th ed. (Homewood, IL: Richard D. Irwin, 1987), pp. 270-71.

Exhibit A–3 Illustrative Contribution Margin Analysis for Product X ($000)

Sales	$ 300
Less: Variable manufacturing costs	100
Other variable costs traceable to product X	50
Equals: Contribution margin	150
Less: Fixed costs directly traceable to product X	100
Equals: Product net income	$ 50

Exhibit A–4 Financial Analysis Model

Profit margin ↓	Asset turnover ↓		Return on assets ↓	Financial leverage ↓		Return on net worth ↓
$\dfrac{\text{Net profits (after taxes)}}{\text{Net sales}}$	×	$\dfrac{\text{Net sales}}{\text{Total assets}}$ →	$\dfrac{\text{Net profits (after taxes)}}{\text{Total assets}}$	×	$\dfrac{\text{Total assets}}{\text{Net worth}}$ =	$\dfrac{\text{Net profits (after taxes)}}{\text{Net worth}}$

Exhibit A–5
Illustrative Break-Even Analysis

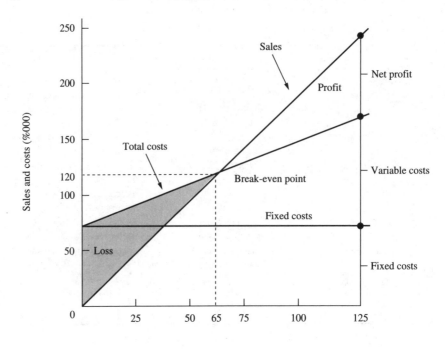

Number of units (000s)

Exhibit A–6   Cash Flow Comparison ($000s)

	Project X	Project Y
Start-up costs	$ ⟨1,000⟩	⟨1,000⟩
Year 1	500	300
Year 2	500	400
Year 3	200	600

Exhibit A–7   Present Value of Cash Flows

Time	Cash Flow	PV Factor	NPV of Cash Flow
Project X			
0	⟨1,000⟩	$1/(1 + 0.12)^0 = 1$	⟨1,000⟩
1	500	$1/(1 + 0.12)^1 = 0.8929$	= 446.45
2	500	$1/(1 + 0.12)^2 = 0.7972$	= 398.60
3	300	$1/(1 + 0.12)^3 = 0.7118$	= 213.54
		Present value	+ 58.59
Project Y			
0	⟨1,000⟩	$1/(1 + 0.12)^0 = 1$	⟨1,000⟩
1	300	$1/(1 + 0.12)^1 = 0.8929$	= 267.87
2	400	$1/(1 + 0.12)^2 = 0.7972$	= 318.88
3	600	$1/(1 + 0.12)^3 = 0.7118$	= 427.08
		Net present value	+ 13.83

Financial Planning

Financial planning involves two major activities: (1) forecasting revenues and (2) budgeting (estimating future expenses). The actual financial analyses and forecasts included in the strategic marketing plan vary considerably from firm to firm. In addition, internal financial reporting and budgeting procedures vary widely among companies. Therefore, consider this approach as one example rather than the norm.

The choice of the financial information to be used for marketing planning and control will depend on its relationship with the corporate or business unit strategic plan. Another important consideration is the selection of performance measures to be used in gauging marketing performance. Our objective is to indicate the range of possibilities and to suggest some of the more frequently used financial analyses.

Pro forma income statements can be very useful when projecting performance and budgeting. Usually, this is done on a spreadsheet so that assumptions can be altered rapidly. Usually, only a few assumptions need be made. For example, sales growth rates can be projected from past trends and adjusted for new information. From this starting point, cost of goods can be determined as a percent of sales. Operating expenses can also be determined as a percent of sales based on past relationships, and the effective tax rate as a percent of earnings before taxes. However, past relationships may not hold in the future. It may be necessary to analyze possible divergence from past relationships.

APPENDIX B
GUIDE TO CASE ANALYSIS

A case presents a situation involving a managerial problem or issue that requires a decision. Typically, cases describe a variety of conditions and circumstances facing an organization at a particular time. This description often includes information regarding the organization's goals and objectives, its financial condition, the attitudes and beliefs of managers and employees, market conditions, competitors' activities, and various environmental forces that may affect the organization's present or proposed marketing strategy. Your responsibility is to sift carefully through the information provided in order to identify the opportunity, problem, or decision facing the organization; to carefully identify and evaluate alternative courses of action; and to propose a solution or decision based on your analysis.

This appendix provides an overview of the case method. It begins with a discussion of the role that cases play in the teaching/learning process. This is followed by a series of guidelines for case analysis. After carefully reading this material, you should be prepared to tackle your first case analysis. Even if you have had previous experience with cases, the discussion will provide a useful review.

Why Cases?

The case method differs substantially from other teaching/learning approaches such as lecture and discussion. Lecture- and discussion-oriented classes provide students with information about concepts, practices, and theories. In contrast, cases provide an opportunity to use concepts, practices, and theories. The primary objective of the case method is to give you a hands-on opportunity to apply what you have learned in your course work.

Consider this analogy: Suppose that you want to learn to play a musical instrument. Your instruction might begin with several classes and reading assignments about your particular instrument. This could include information about the history of the instrument and descriptions of the various parts of the instrument and their functions. Sooner or later, however, you would actually have to play the instrument. Eventually you might become an accomplished musician.

Now suppose you want to become a marketing professional, instead of a musician. You started with classes or courses that introduced you to the foundations of marketing management. Your prior studies may have also included courses in areas of specialization such as marketing research, buyer behavior, and promotion, as well as other business dis-

ciplines such as management, finance, accounting, economics, and statistics. You need practice and experience to become a professional. This is precisely the purpose of the case method of instruction. The cases in this book will give you opportunities to apply your knowledge of marketing and other business subjects to actual marketing situations.

Case studies help to bridge the gap between classroom learnings and the practice of marketing management. They provide us with an opportunity to develop, sharpen, and test our analytical skills at

- Assessing situations.
- Sorting out and organizing key information.
- Asking the right questions.
- Defining opportunities and problems.
- Identifying and evaluating alternative courses of action.
- Interpreting data.
- Evaluating the results of past strategies.
- Developing and defending new strategies.
- Interacting with other managers.
- Making decisions under conditions of uncertainty.
- Critically evaluating the work of others.
- Responding to criticism.

In addition, cases provide exposure to a broad range of situations facing different types and sizes of organizations in a variety of industries. The decisions that you encounter in this book will range from fairly simple to quite complex. If you were the managers making these decisions, you would be risking anywhere from a few thousand to several million dollars of your firm's resources. And you could be risking your job and your career. Obviously the risk, or the cost of making mistakes, is much lower in the classroom environment.

A principal difference between our earlier example of learning to play a musical instrument and the practice of marketing lies in what might be called consequences. A musician's expertise is based on his or her ability to perform precisely the same series of actions time after time. The outcome of perfect execution of a predetermined series of actions is the sought consequence: a beautiful melody. Marketing, on the other hand, is often described as a skillful combination of art and science. No two situations ever require exactly the same actions. Although the same skills and knowledge may be required in different situations, marketing executives must analyze and diagnose each situation separately and conceive and initiate unique strategies to produce sought consequences. Judgment, as opposed to rote memory and repetition, is one key to marketing success. When judgment and a basic understanding of the variables and interrelationships in marketing situations are coupled, they form the core of an analysis and problem-solving approach that can be used in any marketing decision-making situation.

The Case Method of Instruction

The case method of instruction differs from the lecture/discussion method that you have grown accustomed to since you began your formal education 14 or more years ago. It is only natural that you are a bit anxious and apprehensive about it. The methods of study and class preparation are different, your roles and responsibilities are different, and the "right" answers are much less certain. The case method is neither better nor worse than alternative methods; it is just different.

The case method is participative. You will be expected to take a more active role in learning than you have taken in the past. The case method is based on a philosophy of learning by doing as opposed to learning by listening and absorbing information. Case analysis is an applied skill. As such it is something you learn through application, as opposed to something someone teaches you. The more you practice, the more proficient you will become. The benefit you receive from case analysis is directly proportional to the effort you put into it.

Your Responsibilities.   Your responsibilities as a case analyst include active participation, interaction, critical evaluation, and effective communication.

Active Participation.   We have already noted that the case method is participative. It requires a great deal of individual participation in class discussion. Effective participation requires thorough preparation. This entails more than casually reading each case before class. The guidelines in the next section of this appendix will assist you in preparing case analyses. Also, keep in mind that there is a difference between contributing to a class discussion and just talking.

Interaction.   Interaction among students plays an important role in the case method of instruction. Effective learning results from individual preparation and thinking combined with group discussion. Whether you are assigned to work independently or in groups or teams, most instructors encourage students to discuss cases with other students. This, of course, is common practice among managers facing important business decisions. Case discussions, in and out of class, are beneficial because they provide immediate feedback regarding individual perspectives and possible solutions. Other important benefits of case discussions are the synergism and new insights produced by group brainstorming and discussion.

Critical Evaluation.   One of the most difficult responsibilities of student case analysts is learning to critique their peers and to accept criticism from them. Typically, students are reluctant to question or challenge their classmates or to suggest alternatives to the perspectives proposed by others in the class. Students find this difficult because they are generally inexperienced at performing these functions and are also unaccustomed to being challenged by their peers in the classroom. However, the case method of instruction is most effective when all parties engage in an open exchange of ideas. Good cases do not have one clear-cut superior solution. Don't be shy about expressing and defending your views. Moreover, the reasoning process you use and the questions you raise are often more important than the specific solution that you recommend.

Effective Communication.   Each of the three responsibilities discussed above requires effective communication. It is important that you organize your thoughts before speaking. You will develop and refine your communication skills by making class presentations, participating in case discussions, and writing case analyses. Furthermore, the focus of the case method is the development and sharpening of quantitative and qualitative analytical skills. Your analytical skills will improve as you organize information, diagnose problems, identify and evaluate alternatives, and develop solutions and action plans.

Case analysis plays an important role in your overall education. What you learn in a course that uses the case method may be your best preparation for securing your first job and launching your career. If you ask a sample of recruiters to assess the students who are completing undergraduate and graduate programs in business administration today, you will probably hear that these students are extremely well-trained in concepts and quantitative skills but that they lack verbal and written communication skills and decision-making skills. The case method offers students an excellent opportunity to enhance and refine those skills.

A Guide to Case Analysis

There is no one best way to analyze a case. Most people develop their own method after gaining some experience. As with studying, everybody does it a little bit differently. The following suggestions are intended to give you some ideas of how others approach cases. Try these suggestions and make your own adjustments.

Begin by reading each case quickly. The purpose of the first reading should be to familiarize yourself with the organization, the problem, or the decision to be made, the types and amount of data provided, and in general to get a feel for the case. Your second reading of the case should be more careful and thorough. Many students find it helpful to underline, highlight, and make notes about symptoms, potential problems and issues, key facts, and other important information.

Now you should be in a position to investigate the tabular and numerical data included in the case. Ask yourself what each figure, table, or chart means, how it was derived, whether or not it is relevant, and whether further computations would be helpful. If calculations, comparisons, or consolidations of numerical data appear useful, take the necessary action at this time.

A large part of what you will learn from case analysis is how to define, structure, and analyze opportunities and problems. The following information is intended to provide you with a general framework for problem solving. In essence, it is the scientific method with some embellishment. If your instructor does not assign a preferred analytical framework, use the approach shown in Exhibit B–1. A discussion of each step follows, and a detailed outline of analytic issues and questions is provided in this appendix.

Step 1: Situation Audit.   The situation audit phase of the problem-solving process is basically a synopsis and evaluation of an organization's current situation, opportunities, and problems. This phase of case analysis is typically han-

dled in a worksheet form rather than as a formal part of the written case. The primary purpose of the audit is to help you prepare for problem definition and subsequent steps in the problem-solving process. The situation audit interprets and shows the relevance of important case information. Thus it is important that your situation audit be diagnostic rather than descriptive.

It is descriptive to recognize that, "Company A's current and quick ratios are 1.03 and 0.64, respectively." A diagnostic look at these figures indicates that Company A may not be able to meet maturing obligations. The poor quick ratio shows that without inventory, the company's least liquid asset, short-term obligations could not be met. In other words, Company A is insolvent. If you have information about a number of different problems or challenges facing Company A, knowing that the company is insolvent helps you to focus your attention on those that affect the firm's short-term survival needs.

The breadth and depth of an appropriate situation audit are determined by the nature and scope of the case situation, and your instructor's specific instructions. Each case will re-

EXHIBIT B–1
An Approach to Case Analysis

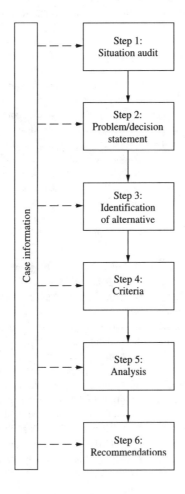

quire a situation audit that is a little different from any of the others because of the information available and the decision to be made.

There are at least two philosophies regarding the appropriate depth and scope of a situation audit. One philosophy holds that the situation audit should include a thorough and comprehensive assessment of the organization's mission and objectives; each business unit of interest; present and potential customers and competitors; the organization's market-target objectives and strategies; its marketing program positioning strategy; its product, distribution, pricing, and promotion strategies; current planning, implementation, and management activities; its financial condition; and an overall summary of the organization's situation. If your instructor favors a thorough and comprehensive situation audit, you will find the outline for case analysis in this appendix quite helpful in organizing your work.

Some instructors, however, feel that the situation audit need not be a thorough and comprehensive study, but rather a short, concise analysis of the organization's major strengths, weaknesses, opportunities, and threats—reserving the comprehensive effort for the analysis step. Some call this a SWOT analysis, and recommend including only information that is crucial in preparing to analyze the case. The emphasis here is on *analysis, diagnosis, synthesis, and interpretation* of the situation. In a written assignment you should be able to present this in less than two pages.

A Note on Gathering More Data and on Making Assumptions.   Students often feel that they need more information in order to make an intelligent decision. Decision makers rarely, if ever, have all the information they would like to have prior to making important decisions. The cost and time involved in collecting more data are often prohibitive. Decision makers, like you, therefore have to make some assumptions. There is nothing wrong with making assumptions as long as they are explicitly stated and reasonable. Be prepared to defend your assumptions as logical. Don't use lack of information as a crutch.

For example, an assumption that Company A, mentioned previously, cannot borrow large sums of money is both reasonable and defendable. To assume that it could borrow large sums of money would require a clear explanation of why some lender or investor would be willing to lend money to, or invest money in, a firm with a quick ratio of 0.64.

Step 2: Problem/Decision Statement.   Identification of the main problem, opportunity, or issue in a case is crucial. To paraphrase from *Alice in Wonderland,* if you don't know where you are going, any solution will take you there. If you don't properly identify the central problem or decision in a case, the remainder of your analysis is not likely to produce recommendations necessary to solve the organization's main problem.

You may become frustrated with your early attempts at problem/decision identification. Don't feel alone. Most students and many experienced managers have difficulty with this task. Your skill will improve with practice.

A major pitfall in defining problems/decisions occurs in confusing symptoms with problems. Such things as declining sales, low morale, high turnover, or increasing costs are symptoms that are often incorrectly identified as problems. You can frequently avoid incorrectly defining a symptom as a problem by thinking in terms of causes and effects. Problems are causes, and symptoms are effects. The examples cited above are the effects or manifestations of something wrong in the organization. Why are sales declining? Why is morale low? Why is turnover high? Why are costs increasing? The key question is *why.* What is the cause? Sales may be declining because morale is low and turnover is high. Why is morale low, and why is turnover high? These effects may be caused by an inadequate compensation plan, which in turn may be caused by inadequate profit margins. Profit margins may be low because products have been incorrectly priced or because the distribution system is outdated. As you can see, symptoms may appear in one part of the overall marketing program, and the true problem may lie elsewhere in the program. Keep asking why, until you are satisfied that you have identified the problem (cause) and not just another symptom (effect).

Think about this analogy. You are not feeling well, so you make an appointment to see your physician. The physician will ask you to describe what is bothering you. Suppose you say you have a headache, a sore throat, chills, and a fever. The physician will probably take your temperature, look in your throat, and perhaps examine you in other ways. The goal, of course, is to diagnose your problem so that a remedy can be prescribed.

How does this relate to case analysis? Your headache, sore throat, chills, and fever are symptoms of something wrong. They are signals to you to seek help. This information also assists your physician in making his or her diagnosis. These symptoms are similar to the declining sales, poor morale, high turnover, and increasing costs that we discussed earlier. They are the effects of some underlying cause. Your role in case study, like the role of your physician, is to analyze the combination of symptoms that can be identified, and then to determine the underlying problem.

Let's carry the analogy a bit farther. Suppose the physician's diagnosis is that you have a common cold. Since there is no cure for a cold, all he or she can do is prescribe medication to treat the symptoms. The cold will cure itself in a matter of days.

Now suppose the diagnosis of the cause is incorrect. Instead of just a common cold, you contracted malaria during a recent vacation in Southeast Asia. If the physician treats the symptoms or effects, they will be temporarily reduced or eliminated, but they will soon reappear. Each time they reappear they will be more severe, until the ailment is properly diagnosed or you die. This is precisely what will happen in an organization if a symptom is incorrectly identified as a problem. Treating the symptom will temporarily reduce its dysfunctional impact on the organization, but sooner or later it will reappear. When it reappears it will probably be more severe than it was previously. This is why carefully identifying the root problem, decision, or issue in your case analysis is so important.

When you identify more than one major problem or decision in a case, ask yourself whether or not the problems or decisions are related enough to be consolidated into one problem/decision statement. You may not yet have reached the central problem. If, however, you have identified two or more problems that are not directly associated with one another, we recommend that you rank them in the order of their importance and address them in that order. You may find that although the problems do not appear to be closely linked, the solutions are related. One solution may solve multiple problems.

A final suggestion regarding defining problems or decisions is to state them concisely and, if possible, in the form of a question. Try to write a one-sentence question that is specific enough to communicate the main concern. For example,

- Should Brand A be deleted from the product line?
- Should General Mills implement a cents-off campaign, or should it use coupons to stimulate trial of its new cereal Gold Rush?
- Which two of the five sales candidates should be hired?
- How should L.A. Gear define its marketing planning units?
- What is the best marketing program positioning strategy for Rollerblade?

In addition to your problem/decision statement, you may find it useful to provide a brief narrative describing the main parameters of the problem/decision. This is helpful when you have a compound problem/decision that can be subdivided into components or subproblems.

Step 3: Identification of Alternatives. Alternatives are the strategic options or actions that appear to be viable solutions to the problem or decision situation that you have determined. Often, more than two seemingly appropriate actions will be available. Sometimes these will be explicitly identified in the case, and sometimes they will not.

Prepare your list of alternatives in two stages. First, prepare an initial list of alternatives that includes all the actions that you feel might be appropriate. Group brainstorming is a useful technique for generating alternatives. Be creative, keep an open mind, and build upon the ideas of others. What may initially sound absurd could become an outstanding possibility.

After you have generated your initial list of alternatives,

begin refining your list and combining similar actions. Use the information that you organized in your situation audit regarding goals, objectives, and constraints, to help you identify which alternatives to keep and which to eliminate. Ask yourself whether an alternative is feasible given the existing financial, productive, managerial, marketing, and other constraints and whether it could produce the results sought. That is, does the alternative directly address the problem or decision you identified in Step 2? If your problem/decision statement and your alternatives are inconsistent, you have erred in one step or the other. To help avoid this mistake, be explicit in showing the connections between the situation audit, the problem/decision statement, and the final set of alternatives.

Doing nothing and collecting more data are two alternatives often suggested by students with limited case experience. These are rarely the best actions to take. If you have identified a problem or a decision that must be made, ignoring the situation probably will not help. Likewise, recommending a survey, hiring a consultant, or employing some other options associated with gathering more data is rarely a viable solution to the central problem or issue. In some cases, a solution may include further study, but this will normally be part of the implementation plan rather than part of the solution. Most cases, at least those included in this book, are based on real business situations. You have the same information that was available to the decision maker when the decision was made. The major difference is that your data are already compiled and organized. If complete information were available, decisions would be easy. This is not the case in business situations, so it may help you to become familiar with making decisions under conditions of uncertainty. Executives, like case analysts, must rely on assumptions and on less-than-perfect information.

Step 4: Criteria. Next you should develop a list of the main criteria that you will use to evaluate your strategic options. By expressly stating the criteria you intend to use in evaluating alternatives, you make clear the measures you plan to use in assessing and comparing the viability of your alternative courses of action.

Perhaps the best place to start in identifying criteria is to ask yourself what factors, in general, should be considered in making a strategic decision regarding this particular problem. For example, assume that your task is to identify the most attractive product-market niche. Your alternatives are niches X, Y, and Z. Your question then would be, What criteria should be employed in assessing the choices of product-market niches? An appropriate set of criteria might include (for each niche) potential sales volume, variable costs, contribution margins, market share, total niche sales, business strength, and niche attractiveness. This will provide an evaluation relative to the market and to competition.

The single most important factor in many decisions is

profitability. Since profits are a principal goal in all commercial organizations, nearly every marketing decision is influenced by monetary considerations that ultimately affect profits (or expected profits). Sometimes several profit-oriented criteria are involved. These may include future costs and revenues, break-even points, opportunity costs, contribution margins, taxes, turnover, sales, and market share, for example.

Many criteria are only indirectly linked to profits. Such things as the impact of a decision on employees, the local economy, the environment, suppliers, or even customer attitudes may not directly affect profits. Because profits are almost always the overriding criterion, all factors bearing on them, directly or indirectly, must be considered.

Step 5: Analysis. Analysis is the process of evaluating each alternative action against the issues that were identified in Step 4. Often, analysis includes assessment of advantages and limitations associated with each issue. A tendency exists when first starting a case analysis to identify important issues carefully and then to analyze each issue superficially. The consequence is a weak analysis. Your analysis will be much more penetrating and comprehensive if you use the same criteria in assessing each alternative.

One way of assuring that you assess each alternative in terms of each critical issue is to organize your analysis in outline form as follows.

Step 5 Analysis
  Alternative A: (Specify the alternative.)
    1. Identify the criterion and thoroughly discuss Alternative A in terms of criterion number 1.
    2. For the remaining criteria, follow the same procedure.
  Alternative B: (Specify the alternative.)
    1. Criterion 1. Thoroughly discuss Alternative B in terms of critical issue number 1.
    2. Criterion 2-*n*. Follow the same procedure.

Following is a brief, unedited example from a student paper. The problem/decision was whether Wyler Foods, a powdered soft-drink subsidiary of Borden, should introduce a new line of unsweetened powdered drink mixes to compete with the market leader, Kool-Aid. One alternative was to introduce the product and attempt to compete head-to-head with Kool-Aid. Criteria identified by the student were

1. Projected profit impact.
2. Long-term growth implications.
3. Competitor reactions.
4. Resource requirements.
5. Competitive advantages and/or disadvantages.

Analysis of the alternative in terms of each criterion follows. (*Note that exhibits identified in the analysis are not included.*)

Step 5   Analysis
Alternative A.   Head-to-head competition with Kool-Aid
1.1 *Projected profit impact.*   The profit potential for head-to-head competition with Kool-Aid does not seem promising. Assuming that the product will perform nationally as it did during test marketing, it should achieve a 4 percent share of the $143.51 million unsweetened powdered drink mix (UPDM) market (see Exhibit 1).

This represents sales of $5.74 million. Long-term share could be as low as 2.5 percent of the overall market. A retail price of 12 cents per packet, and cost of goods sold of 9.4 cents per packet will produce a contribution margin of approximately $1.24 million (see Exhibit 2). This level of contribution margin will not be sufficient to cover advertising and sales promotion expenditures, which will exceed $4 million, and could rise to $8-10 million.

Quantity allowances to stimulate grocer acceptance will have to be in the $800,000 area. Adopting this alternative would lead to substantial first-year losses, minimally in the $4-5 million range, and possibly much higher (see Exhibit 3).

1.2 *Long-term growth implications.*   Long-term corporate growth factors are dependent upon how deeply the new product can penetrate the Kool-Aid-dominated UPDM market. If the product performs no better than the test market results indicate, this strategy would be a long-term money loser. The product will have to capture roughly 15.4 percent of the UPDM market to break even (see Exhibit 4).

1.3 *Competitor reactions.*   Kool-Aid can be expected to spend $10–12 million more on advertising and sales promotion than is proposed for the new product in its first year. Kool-Aid can also be expected to emphasize its traditional position as the favored UPDM. The leading brand is able to exercise considerable influence in established distribution channels to keep the new product line off the grocers' shelves, necessitating huge quantity allowances to achieve penetration. Through 50 years of acclimation, the consumer is now at the point of utilizing the Kool-Aid product as the taste benchmark; this imperils the new product line even before the contest starts. Perhaps of greatest importance, Kool-Aid may opt for price competition. Because of sales volume considerations, Kool-Aid can cut prices and maintain profitability. Wyler simply could not afford to match Kool-Aid's potential price cuts. To do so would further darken its bleak profit outlook (see Exhibit 5).

1.4 *Resource requirements.*   Wyler seems to be short on financial resources necessary to implement this alternative (see Exhibit 5). Substantial cash infusions would be needed for some time before any cash outflows would be generated. Wyler's personnel seem to be capable of executing the strategy.

1.5 *Competition advantages and/or disadvantages.* Implementation of this alternative involves doing battle with Kool-Aid on Kool-Aid's home ground. Rather than exploiting a key Wyler strength, this alternative seems to favor Kool-Aid's strengths and Wyler's weaknesses. Wyler will be playing by Kool-Aid's rules, which isn't likely to produce a successful outcome.

Although this is a fairly simple example without any financial comparisons, it illustrates a useful approach for evaluating alternative actions. Note that each alternative should be evaluated in terms of each criterion. After the alternatives are analyzed against each criterion, you should complete your analysis with a summary assessment of each alternative. This summary will provide the basis for preparing your recommendations.

One approach that students sometimes find useful in preparing their summary analyses is illustrated in Exhibit B–2. Its preparation involves the following five steps:

Step 1:   List criteria on one axis and alternative actions on the other axis.

Step 2:   Assign a weight to each criterion reflecting its relative importance on the final decision. For convenience, assign weights that add up to one.

Step 3:   Review your analysis and rate each alternative on each criterion using a scale of one to five with one representing very poor and five representing very good.

Step 4:   Multiply the weight assigned to each criterion by the rating given to each alternative on each issue.

Step 5:   Add the results from Step 4 for each alternative.

It is important to understand that this type of analytical aid is *not* a substitute for thorough, rigorous analysis, clear thinking, and enlightened decision making. Its value is in encouraging you to assess the relative importance of alternatives and criteria, and helping you to organize your analysis.

Step 6: Recommendations.   If your analysis has been thorough, the actions you recommend should flow directly from it. The first part of your recommendations section addresses what specific actions should be taken and why. State the main reasons you believe your chosen course of action is best, but avoid rehashing the analysis section. It is important that your recommendations be specific and operational. The following example of a recommendation deals with whether a manufacturer of oil field equipment (OFE) should introduce a new product line.

> The key decision that management must make is whether viscosity-measurement instrumentation represents a business venture that fits into the overall mission of the firm. The preceding analysis clearly indicates that this would be a profitable endeavor. If OFE concentrates on the high-accuracy and top end of the intermediate-accuracy ranges of the market, sales of $500,000 appear feasible within two to four years, with an estimated contribution to overhead and profits in the $145,000 range. This is assuming that manufacturing costs can be reduced by 20 to 25 percent, that effective marketing approaches are developed, that further product development is not extensive, and that price reductions per unit do not exceed 10 percent.

The second part of your recommendations section addresses implementation. State clearly who should do what, when, and where. An implementation plan shows that your recommendations are both possible and practical. For example,

> OFE should initially offer two instruments. One should provide an accuracy of 0.25 percent or better; the second should be in the accuracy range of 0.1 to 0.5 percent. Top priority should be assigned to inland and offshore drilling companies. Next in priority

EXHIBIT B–2   ABC Company Summary Assessment

Criteria	Relative Weights	Alternatives (ratings)		
		(1)	*(2)*	*(3)*
Corporate mission and objectives	(.2)	(5)	(2)	(3)
Market opportunity	(.3)	(2)	(3)	(5)
Competitive strengths/weaknesses	(.2)	(2)	(3)	(2)
Financial considerations	(.3)	(1)	(1)	(4)
Index: Relative weight × Rating		2.3	2.2	3.7

should be R&D laboratories in industry, government, and universities, where accuracy needs exist in the range offered by OFE. Based on experience with these markets, other promising targets should be identified and evaluated.

OFE needs to move into the market rapidly, using the most cost-effective means of reaching end user markets. By developing an original-equipment-manufacturer (OEM) arrangement with General Supply to reach drilling companies and a tie-in arrangement with Newtec to reach R&D markets, immediate access to end user markets can be achieved. If successful, these actions will buy some time for OFE to develop marketing capabilities, and they should begin generating contributions from sales to cover the expenses of developing a marketing program. An essential element in the OFE marketing strategy is locating and hiring a person to manage the marketing effort. This person must have direct sales capabilities in addition to being able to perform market analysis and marketing program development, implementation, and management tasks.

The last part of your recommendations section should be a tentative budget. This is important because it illustrates that the solution is worth the cost and is within the financial capabilities of the organization. Too often, students develop grandiose plans that organizations couldn't possibly afford even if they were worth the money. Budgeting and forecasting are discussed in Appendix A.

Your instructor realizes that the numbers used in your tentative budget may not be as accurate as they would be if you had complete access to the records of the company. Make your best estimates and try to get as close to the actual figures as possible. The exercise is good experience, and it shows that you have considered the cost implications.

Students often ask how long the recommendations section should be and how much detail they should go into. This question is difficult to answer because each case is different and should be treated that way. In general it is advisable to go into as much detail as possible. You may be criticized for not being specific enough in your recommendations, but you are not likely to be criticized for being too specific.

An Outline for Case Analysis

The outline shown here is an expanded version of the approach to case analysis discussed in this appendix. Although reasonably comprehensive, the guide can be shortened, expanded, and/or adapted to meet your needs in various situations. For example, if you are analyzing a business unit that does not utilize channels of distribution, section VIIIB of the outline will require adjustment. Likewise, if the salesforce represents the major part of the marketing program, then section VIIIE should probably be expanded to include other aspects of salesforce strategy.

This guide is not intended to be a comprehensive checklist that can be applied in every case. Instead, it is illustrative of the broad range of issues and questions you will encounter

in analyzing the strategic decisions presented in this book and elsewhere. The key is to *adapt the outline to the case,* not the case to the outline.

Step 1. Situation Audit

I. Corporate mission and objectives.
   A. Does the mission statement offer a clear guide to the product markets of interest to the firm?
   B. Have objectives been established for the corporation?
   C. Is information available for the review of corporate progress toward objectives, and are the reviews conducted on a regular (quarterly, monthly, etc.) basis?
   D. Has corporate strategy been successful in meeting objectives?
   E. Are opportunities or problems pending that may require altering marketing strategy?
   F. What are the responsibilities of the chief marketing executive in corporate strategic planning?

II. Business unit analysis.
   A. What is the composition of the business (business segments, strategic planning units, and specific product markets)?
   B. Have business strength and product-market attractiveness analyses been conducted for each planning unit? What are the results of the analyses?
   C. What is the corporate strategy for each planning unit (e.g., growth, manage for cash)?
   D. Does each unit have a strategic plan?
   E. For each unit, what objectives and responsibilities have been assigned to marketing?

III. Buyer analysis.
   A. Are there niches within the product market? For each specific product market and niche of interest to the firm, answer items B through I.
   B. What are estimated annual purchases (units and dollars)?
   C. What is the projected annual growth rate (five years)?
   D. How many people/organizations are in the product market?
   E. What are the demographic and socioeconomic characteristics of customers?
   F. What is the extent of geographic concentration?
   G. How do people decide what to buy?
      1. Reason(s) for buying (What is the need/want?).
      2. What information is needed (e.g., how to use the product)?
      3. What are other important sources of information?
      4. What criteria are used to evaluate the product?

5. What are purchasing practices (quantity, frequency, location, time, etc.)?

H. What environmental factors should be monitored because of their influence on product purchases (e.g., interest rates)?

I. What key competitors serve each end user group?

IV. Key competitor analysis. For each specific product market and each niche of interest to the firm, determine

A. Estimated overall business strength.
B. Market share (percent, rank).
C. Market share trend (five years).
D. Financial strengths.
E. Profitability.
F. Management.
G. Technology position.
H. Other key nonmarketing strengths/limitations (e.g., production cost advantages).
I. Marketing strategy (description, assessment of key strengths and limitations).
   1. Market-target strategy.
   2. Program positioning strategy.
   3. Product strategy.
   4. Distribution strategy.
   5. Price strategy.
   6. Promotion strategy.

V. Market-target strategy.

A. Has each market target been clearly defined and its importance to the firm established?
B. Have demand and competition in each market target been analyzed, and key trends, opportunities, and threats identified?
C. Has the proper market-target strategy (mass, niche) been adopted?
D. Should repositioning or exit from any product market be considered?

VI. Market-target objectives.

A. Have objectives been established for each market target, and are these consistent with planning-unit objectives and the available resources? Are the objectives realistic?
B. Are sales, cost, and other performance information available for monitoring the progress of planned performance against actual results?
C. Are regular appraisals made of marketing performance?
D. Where do gaps exist between planned and actual results? What are the probable causes of the performance gaps?

VII. Marketing program positioning strategy.

A. Does the firm have an integrated positioning strategy made up of product, channel, price, advertising, and salesforce strategies? Is the role

selected for each mix element consistent with the overall program objectives, and does it properly complement other mix elements?

B. Are adequate resources available to carry out the marketing program? Are resources committed to market targets according to the importance of each?
C. Are allocations to the various marketing mix components too low, too high, or about right in terms of what each is expected to accomplish?
D. Is the effectiveness of the marketing program appraised on a regular basis?

VIII. Marketing program activities.

A. Product strategy.
   1. Is the product mix geared to the needs that the firm wants to meet in each product market?
   2. What branding strategy is being used?
   3. Are products properly positioned against competing brands?
   4. Does the firm have a sound approach to product planning and management, and is marketing involved in product decisions?
   5. Are additions to, modifications of, or deletions from the product mix needed to make the firm more competitive in the marketplace?
   6. Is the performance of each product evaluated on a regular basis?

B. Channels of distribution strategy.
   1. Has the firm selected the type (conventional or vertically coordinated) and intensity of distribution appropriate for each of its product markets?
   2. How well does each channel access its market target? Is an effective channel configuration used?
   3. Are channel organizations carrying out their assigned functions properly?
   4. How is the channel of distribution managed? What improvements are needed?
   5. Are desired customer service levels reached, and are the costs of doing this acceptable?

C. Price strategy.
   1. How responsive is each market target to price variation?
   2. What roles and objectives does price have in the marketing mix?
   3. Does price play an active or passive role in program positioning strategy?
   4. How do the firm's price strategy and tactics compare to those of competition?
   5. Is a logical approach used to establish prices?
   6. Are there indications that changes may be needed in price strategy or tactics?

D. Advertising and sales promotion strategies.

1. Are roles and objectives established for advertising and sales promotion in the marketing mix?
2. Is the creative strategy consistent with the positioning strategy that is used?
3. Is the budget adequate to carry out the objectives assigned to advertising and sales promotion?
4. Do the media and programming strategies represent the most cost-effective means of communicating with market targets?
5. Do advertising copy and content effectively communicate the intended messages?
6. How well does the advertising program meet its objectives?

E. Sales-force strategy.
1. Are the roles and objectives of personal selling in the marketing program positioning strategy clearly specified and understood by the sales organization?
2. Do the qualifications of salespeople correspond to their assigned roles?
3. Is the sales force the proper size to carry out its function, and is it efficiently deployed?
4. Are sales force results in line with management's expectations?
5. Is each salesperson assigned performance targets, and are incentives offered to reward performance?
6. Are compensation levels and ranges comparable to those of competitors?

IX. Marketing planning.
A. Strategic planning and marketing.
1. Is marketing's role and responsibility in corporate strategic planning clearly specified?
2. Are responsibility and authority for marketing strategy assigned to one executive?
3. How well is the firm's marketing strategy working?
4. Are changes likely to occur in the corporate/marketing environment that may affect the firm's marketing strategy?
5. Do major contingencies exist that should be included in the strategic marketing plan?

B. Marketing planning and organization structure.
1. Are annual and longer-range strategic marketing plans developed and used?
2. Are the responsibilities of the various units in the marketing organization clearly specified?
3. What are the strengths and limitations of the key members of the marketing organization? What is being done to develop employee skills? What gaps in experience and capability exist on the

marketing staff?
4. Is the organizational structure for marketing appropriate for implementing marketing plans?

X. Financial analysis.
A. Sales and cost analyses and forecasts.
B. Profit contribution and net profit analyses and projections.
C. Liquidity analyses.
D. Break-even analyses.
E. Return on investment.
F. Budget analyses.
G. Pro forma statements.

XI. Implementation and management.
A. Have the causes of all performance gaps been identified?
B. Is implementation of planned actions taking place as intended? Is implementation being hampered by marketing or other functional areas of the firm (e.g., operations, finance)?
C. Has the strategic audit revealed areas requiring additional study before action is taken?

XII. Summary of the situation.
Has the situation audit revealed opportunities that would enable the organization to gain a competitive advantage based upon its distinctive competencies?
A. What are the major opportunities available to the organization?
B. What are the major threats facing the organization?
C. What are the requirements for achieving success in selected product markets?
D. What are the organization's and the principal competitors' distinctive competencies regarding these requirements? Do these areas of strength complement a given opportunity, or do strategic gaps exist that serve as barriers to pursuing the opportunity?
E. What strategic gaps, problems, and/or constraints relative to competitors appear?
F. What time and resources are required to pursue an opportunity or close a strategic gap?
G. Does the organization's mission (or objectives) need to be redefined?

XIII. Opinions and assumptions.
A. Are opinions or assumptions provided by others? Are they reasonable, given the source?
B. Is it necessary to make assumptions about the organization's objectives, competition, the environment, or something else?

Step 2.   Problem/Decision Statement

A. What are the symptoms that suggest a problem exists?

B. What is the major problem or decision that must be addressed?

C. Are there secondary problems or decisions?

Step 3.   Identification of Alternatives

A. What actions might provide viable solutions to the problem or decision?

B. Can actions be combined?

C. Can actions be eliminated without further consideration?

Step 4.   Criteria

What criteria should be used to evaluate the strategic options? Any of the items listed in the situation audit may be relevant issues in analyzing the alternatives.

Step 5.   Analysis

A. Examine each alternative in terms of each criterion.

B. What are the relative advantages and disadvantages of each choice in terms of each of the criteria?

Step 6.   Recommendations

A. What specific actions, including the development of marketing or other plans, should be taken and why?

B. Who should do what, when, and where?

C. What are the expected costs and returns associated with your recommendations?

D. What contingencies may alter the attractiveness of your recommendations?

Index of Cases